*Assessment, Measurement,
and Prediction for Personnel Decisions*

Assessment, Measurement, and Prediction for Personnel Decisions

Robert M. Guion
Bowling Green State University

LEA LAWRENCE ERLBAUM ASSOCIATES, PUBLISHERS
1998   Mahwah, New Jersey   London

Lawrence Erlbaum Associates
10 Industrial Avenue
Mahwah, NJ 07430

Library of Congress Cataloging-in-Publication Data

Assessment, measurement, and prediction for personnel
decisions / Robert M. Guion
       p. cm.
   Includes bibliographic references and index.
   ISBN 0-8058-1577-5 (cloth : alk. paper).
   1. Personnel management—Decision making. 2.
Prediction of occupational success. 3. Employees—Rating of. 4. Employment tests. I. Title.
   HF5549.G794 1998
   658.3'125—dc20   96-36765
                                        CIP

Printed in the United States of America
10 9 8 7 6 5 4 3 2 1

Dedicated to C. H. LAWSHE
Teacher, Mentor, Colleague, and Friend

Contents

Part III: Methods of Assessment

Preface

In the early 1960s, I wrote a book *Personnel Testing* (Guion, 1965).[1] It focused on testing candidates for employment as a basis for predicting probable effectiveness; it was rather well received—well beyond my expectations. It has long been out of print—appropriately. It is now old and, in many respects, out of date. The manuscript was finished before the enactment of the Civil Rights Act of 1964, before the computer revolution made new measurement and data analysis methods practical, before the return of cognition as a dominant concept in psychology, before a major change in demographic trends, and, in fact, before an awful lot of other things that influence the way personnel decisions are or should be made.

That book did not have the impact I had hoped. When I sent the manuscript off for publication, I believed that the principles it contained, if applied by its readers, would result in higher productivity in American industry and fewer personnel decisions based on whim and prejudice. The decline in productivity is a frequent topic in the press and in politics. Fewer private organizations use tests or other systematic, validated assessment procedures. Of those that do, fewer seem to have good reasons for choosing the assessment methods they use. Choices are based on whim and a kind of prejudice—not social prejudice but a prejudice about procedures. To say, "we like our tests"—and to use them without regard for their validity—is an exercise of prejudice. Too many people use tests, interviews, assessment centers, or other assessment methods simply because they like them, or because they have always used them, not because they are demonstrably useful. Other people refuse to use them simply because they do *not* like them, regardless of evidence of their value.

Unwilling to consider the possibility that the book was poorly written, I attribute the decline in testing to two quite different influences. One was the passage of the Civil Rights Act of 1964. It was passed, I add hastily, after the manuscript had gone to the publisher for production, and it took effect after

---

[1] Guion, R. M. (1965). *Personnel testing.* New York: McGraw-Hill.

the book was published. Fear of litigation induced many company executives to drop testing programs because they seemed more vulnerable than less noticeable, less discussed alternatives.

The other influence was the emergence of a generation of people trained as industrial psychologists, preferring (circa 1965) to call themselves *organizational psychologists*, who looked on personnel selection as wholly atheoretical and uninteresting. This movement coincided with the move in personality theory toward the denial of relatively permanent and general traits. The whole idea of selection in the 1960s was anathema to a growing number of organizational psychologists—and remained so until fairly recent times. That is not so any longer; traits have returned, although sometimes disguised as "dispositional tendencies," and personnel selection has again achieved some prominence under the term "staffing." Schneider (1987), in his presidential address to the Society of Industrial and Organization Psychology, said, "My main thesis is that the attributes of people, not the nature of the external environment, or organizational technology, or organizational structure, are the fundamental determinants of organizational behavior" (p. 437).[2] Those who want their organizations to be effective, to prosper, to grow, to change with the times must fill them with competent, adaptable people. This book, although stubbornly persisting in some old-fashioned language, is written in the belief that the time is ripe for renewed interest in making wise and competent personnel decisions, and that some who might not be interested in testing might be ready to apply psychometric principles to other forms of assessment.

This is not a revision of *Personnel Testing*. The middle part of that book—more than one third of it—was devoted to specific assessment procedures, including detailed descriptions of specific tests. As nearly as I can tell, not much use was ever made of that section. A very small part of the book was devoted to psychometric theory, and even that was only rudimentary by today's standards. Latent trait theory, for example, had been invented but no one would have known it from reading *Personnel Testing*. In the meantime, much thought and attention has been given to expanded concepts of validity and reliability, modern measurement theory has emerged, the law has provided boundaries as well as influences on measurement practices for employment, meta-analysis has influenced much in measurement practice, and more and more the actual assessment instruments are home grown for specific local purposes. This book focuses more on general concepts and problems and less on descriptions. It is truly a new book.

Having said that, I think of a colleague who used to be a member of our department at Bowling Green. Each year a salary and promotion committee was charged with the responsibility of recommending salary levels for each faculty member and, in carrying out its deliberations, requested information

---

[2]Schneider, B. (1987). The people make the place. *Personnel Psychology, 40,* 437–453.

from faculty members about their activities during the preceding year. To the question about innovations in teaching, the remembered colleague invariably answered, "I used the tried-and-true methods that have served well for years." In trying to write a new, more up-to-date book, one that might show what I have learned in three intervening decades, I have often found that I, too, had to return to tried-and-true ideas and methods of testing and test evaluation that have served well. Indeed, much of the section on reliability was lifted verbatim from the old book, although it has suffered much cutting to make room for that advance on reliability known as generalizability theory.

There is a strong tendency, especially, I suppose, among those of us whose professional lives are centered in a university, to want to be new, up-to-date, "with-it," on the cutting edge, a leader of the field. Indeed, so many of us want so much to impress others with the innovativeness of our thinking that we do not follow the ideas of others very closely. The result is a fragmented, scattered research literature that rarely provides the kind of history of achievement that those tried-and-true but out-of-date methods have accumulated. This book, therefore, is in many respects less different from the earlier one than might be expected—certainly less different than I had expected at one time.

It is, nevertheless, different. My concept of validity is much larger, much more inclusive, and, I hope, much improved over the first tentative efforts to offer an integrated view of the topic in the light of the four aspects of validity offered in the 1954 Technical Recommendations (American Psychological Association, American Educational Research Association, & National Council on Measurements Used in Education [APA, AERA, & NCME], 1954).[3] I have come to recognize that factor analysis is a useful tool for exploring, confirming, or disconfirming ideas—not a grand scheme for organizing one's thought about the universe. But most of all, this book differs from the earlier one in that it considers human judgment, fallible as it may be, a central fact of personnel decision making. This change comes from several sources, the greatest of which is the realization that the circumstances in which a single, definitive criterion-related validation study can actually be carried out are far less likely to occur than any of us book writers of 30 years ago were aware. Along with that is the further realization that results of a single study, even if it is feasible, are untrustworthy without replication.

This book shows more interest in theories, albeit tentatively and with some trepidation. Jay Tolson (1994), editor of *The Wilson Quarterly*, wrote an editorial titled "By Theory Possessed."[4] Briefly, the theme of the piece was that, beginning about the middle of the 1960s (about the time my earlier book

---

[3]American Psychological Association, American Educational Research Association, and National Council on Measurements Used in Education. (1954). Technical recommendations for psychological tests and diagnostic techniques. *Psychological Bulletin, 51,* 201–238.
[4]Tolson, J. (1994). By theory possessed. *The Wilson Quarterly, 18*(3), 4–6.

appeared!) the elite universities of America began a revolution, moving away from factual substance to ideological theory. When facts intruded, they were handled as quickly as possible "to leave plenty of room for theory" (p. 4). The editorial acknowledged that theory is necessary; it is how we make sense and put order in the knowledge we have accumulated. But although theory is essential to knowledge, it is not identical to it. And neither scholars nor those who conduct the world's affairs dare to be possessed by their theories; theories are to be used, tested, discarded, and replaced with better ones.

This process is less painful if we are not excessively wrapped up in our theories, and if the theories themselves are not too grand. There are calls to theory in this book, but they are calls for quite limited theories, invoked for their practical value. Perhaps the dominant theory du jour in personnel selection circles is validity generalization, which may seem the antithesis of theory with its emphasis on the accumulation of empirical data. It is, nevertheless, a little theory with big assumptions, and someday, details of the theory will be challenged and changed. There are several allusions in the book to a theory of the attribute, in which I exhort readers who are responsible for assessment of either predictors or criteria to have some reasoning—some theory and articulation of understanding—about what it is that is to be assessed. I do not exhort people to have theories of attributes that get more and more generalized and placed in some conjunction with theories of other attributes in a grand theory of human functioning, nor do I expect theories of the attributes to be unchanging even within their limited spheres.

In short, I hope this book, like the earlier one, is practical in orientation and that it may increase awareness of the practicality of theory—that it will be perceived as helping people in employing organizations make better, more valid decisions about other people on the basis of better, more valid assessments of some of their characteristics.

I confess to inconsistency in thinking about the intended audience for this book. Mainly, it is intended to be a textbook, to be augmented by lectures and discussions by informed instructors as well as by readings in the source literature. I am fairly sure it can be used as a text for graduate students in industrial and organizational psychology or organizational behavior, and I hope it will be useful in some programs for advanced undergraduate students. But it is also intended to be a reference for professional psychologists doing consulting, serving as expert witnesses in litigation involving psychological assessment and measurement, or working as staff psychologists in consulting organizations. Too often these people are too busy to plow through the many articles appearing in a burgeoning number of journals, and the result is that too much work is done—and challenged in litigation—that might have been considered excellent 15 or 20 years ago but does not meet *contemporary* standards of excellence. I do not see this as a book for most managers except for some specialists in human resources management, but most human resources departments should have someone in them who can read it with comprehension. I think much this book should be treated as necessary reading for EEO attorneys, even if they find it hard going.

Many statistical as well as psychometric concepts are in it. I assume that most readers have had at least one course in statistics, like the one-semester course we teach at the sophomore level, followed perhaps by a course or two in mental measurement theory and practice. For that reason, I blithely use some basic concepts as if the reader knew all about them—and later, to prove my inconsistency, present them again as if the reader had no prior knowledge. A case in point is linear regression. In early chapters, someplace, I refer to the equation $Y = a + bX$ without explanation and then, in chapter 7, write as if readers had no idea what the a and b meant. This, and many other statistical equations, concepts, and issues are presented at a very elementary level for several reasons. One is the recognition that many readers will in fact have little background in statistics. (I hope that those with minimal statistical background will do the laborious reading that may be required rather than simply skip the statistical sections.) The major reason, however, for the elementary nature of many of the statistical presentations is that it enables me to make or clarify some points I think are important but often unrecognized or forgotten in the transition between a statistics classroom and practice in doing personnel research. By starting at the beginning, as it were, I meld what the more sophisticated reader may once have known about elementary points and what must be considered in using statistical reasoning as a foundation for actual personnel decisions. I also urge the more sophisticated reader to do what may be boringly easy reading in order to get the point being made. To be plain: Don't simply skip the easy statistical sections and don't skip them if they are not easy!

I have consistently given old-fashioned equations for computing statistics by desk or hand-held calculators—or even paper and pencil—despite full awareness that nearly every user will nearly every time turn to modern computers. I think it is important, however, for computer users to understand what ought to be happening when they turn to a computer package for statistical analyses. I have avoided mentioning specific packages; each computer center will have its own package, and the packages touted today may surely be mere history by tomorrow when a new, improved one comes along. The basic equations change in notation as styles of statistical communication change, but not in basic substance.

There are many references. They are given to be used, not simply as an indication that I have read them. A case in point involves setting cut scores. I have described two out of dozens of standard-setting procedures found in the educational measurement literature. That is enough for a flavor, but not enough for actually doing the work. References are given to more complete discussions of standard-setting procedures so that readers who need them can easily locate them.

No preface is complete without acknowledgments, and I have several to make. One is that many of the ideas in this book are actually the ideas of people who are not cited. In my "golden years," I find it hard to remember who I got an idea from or, if I do remember that, where I might find it to provide a reference.

A special acknowledgment must go to Frank Landy, who has been asked to review this entire manuscript. He must feel like the man in the commercial of some years ago who showed his gastric (ghastly?) misery by moaning, "I can't believe I ate the whole thing!" He did eat the whole thing, or at least read it, and it was much longer then than now!

A lot of other people have given me specific help by critically reading parts of that earlier version that fit their own special competencies. I tried to write words of appreciation, but they were so inadequate that I decided simply to say thank you to them and let you, the reader, know who they are—not to blame them, because I did not always take their advice, but so you too can say thank you to them: They include R. Lawrence Ashe, Walter Borman, Michael Doherty, Marvin Dunnette, Xiao Hong Gao, Milton Hakel, Richard Jeanneret, Ann Marie Ryan, Frank Schmidt, Patricia Smith, and Vicki Vandaveer. Thanks to all of you. Thanks also to my son David, a librarian and author, for his excellent advice on developing the subject index, and to my wife Emily for developing the author index.

It is neither superfluous nor pro forma to acknowledge the help and encouragement I have received throughout the ordeal of writing this book from Emily, my friend as well as my wife. She has not complained about the time taken away from the things we might have done had I not been reading in my office at home, going to the library, sitting at the computer, or reading the many papers people have sent me. She has done chores like proofreading, looking up publisher's addresses, and writing permission letters. Most important, she has supported this project by telling others that it has been an important one—a kind of encouragement I have often needed. For everything, deeply and sincerely, thanks Em.

Foreword

Frank Landy

A great deal can happen in 32 years. In 1964, I was a student in a graduate seminar being offered by Bob Guion on the topic of personnel testing. As a text, we were using the prepublication galley sheets of his forthcoming text to be published in the following year. It is now 1996, and I have had the privilege of reading and commenting on Bob's newest text. I have already blocked out a chunk of the year 2028—May and June to be exact—for reviewing his next effort. During the period between 1964 and 1996, I managed to extract a PhD from Bob, assume and retire from a University faculty position at Penn State University, and write several books on topics similar to those addressed in *Personnel Testing*.

Between 1964 and 1996, psychology, generally, and industrial and organizational psychology, specifically, have experienced more than a few "revolutions." In psychology, these revolutions would include the paradigm shifts from behaviorism to cognition and neuroscience, from trait theory to interactionism, and the analytic shift from noncausal to causal inference. In industrial and organizational psychology, the revolutions have included the appearance of new employment discrimination statutes (e.g., the Age Discrimination in Employment Act, the Americans with Disabilities Act, the Civil Rights Act of 1991) and the further codification (some might say calcification) of existing discrimination statutes through case law and administrative guidelines (e.g., the Uniform Guidelines on Employee Selection Procedures). From a more substantive direction, there has been a marked shift toward legitimizing personality testing, toward developing more detailed specifications of both predictor and criterion domains, and away from the "holy trinity" of validity models. Analytically, meta-analysis has turned lead into gold by extracting general conclusions from previously confounded and severely limited single studies. All in all, we are in much better shape now than we were in 1964. All of these evolutionary and revolutionary changes are captured in this volume.

In 1964, *Personnel Testing* was a hit because of the balance between research and practice. Like Kurt Lewin, Bob believed that the most practical thing was a good theory. As a result, he produced a theoretically grounded text that provided the platform for 32 years of practice. In the current text, he has once again, in his usual painstaking manner, provided theoretical and research support for his conclusions and recommendations. When such support is not available, he protects the consumer/reader by identifying his comments as speculation (and, in doing so, probably provides the raw material for theses and dissertations for the next decade).

As Bob indicates in the Preface, I have read every word of this text. As a result, I can say with confidence that this text will be another hit. The material is carefully integrated across chapters, is current, and directly addresses the most troublesome topics in research and practice. I consider myself very lucky to have had access to this material for more than a year before it was made available to the general scientist/practitioner community.

On a more personal note, I am grateful that Bob let me share in the development of this book. Everything that I may have been able to accomplish in my professional life has been due to Bob. He taught me to simplify apparently complex issues, to complicate apparently simple issues, and to show righteous indignation on occasion. I expect that my copy of *Assessment, Measurement, and Prediction for Personnel Decisions* will quickly become as tattered and dirty from extended use as my copy of *Personnel Testing*. From the publisher's perspective, this book will be a gem as well. There will be no used book market to worry about. Everyone who buys a copy of this book will keep it!

I

FOUNDATIONS FOR PERSONNEL DECISIONS

The four chapters in this first part of the book describe the context within which assessment-based personnel decisions are made. The first chapter is introductory and brief, identifying varieties of personnel decisions but treating personnel selection decisions as a prototype for other kinds of decisions (e.g., transfer, assigning people to special training, even termination decisions insofar as they are based on assessments of performance or predictions of future performance). The second chapter describes procedures to be followed in setting goals to be achieved through assessment and prediction. The third describes the goals and processes in terms of variables (i.e., constructs) to be predicted or to be used as predictors. Finally, the foundation includes a chapter on the legal context in the United States—requirements and constraints that govern what organizations can and cannot do in making assessment-based decisions about people.

1

Membership Decisions in Organizations

Organizations take many forms and serve many purposes. Some are business organizations intended to earn profit for owners and stockholders through production of specified goods and services. Some are governmental organizations designed to provide services to citizens or other arms of government. Some are recreational or social in nature, designed to provide fellowship, amusement, or exercise for their members. Some organizations pay their members, others rely on volunteers, still others confer special status on members. Some organizations are very large; others may be very small (e.g., a partnership or a family).

Organizations consist of members, investments for tools, equipment, supplies, and research, and specific environments, both social and physical. Organizations change. They grow or decay; they merge with others or divest themselves of functions; members die, retire, or change jobs and may be replaced; functions of some members disappear in organizational restructuring, and these members are not replaced. Member roles change as functions change in an evolving organization. Consider the automotive industry. At one point, groups of skilled craftsmen joined together to make automobiles, and the quality of the product depended mainly on the skills of individual workers. Then assembly lines were made possible by mechanical equipment; relatively unskilled workers on the lines could do much of what craftsmen had done before with precision permitting interchangeable parts. Much of automotive assembly has now become automated, with computerized robots doing many of the things unskilled workers did before; fewer workers are needed, and those who are left tend to be highly trained in the new electronic crafts. As work environments move from the social environment of the craftsmen, through the mechanical environment of machinery, to the electronic environment of automation, member roles change and so do the qualifications to fill these roles.

In any case, however, an organization still functions through its members. New members are chosen in the belief that they will benefit the organization. They do so mainly by accepting a fairly specific organizational role—a fairly specific set of functions, duties, and organizational responsibilities. I say "fairly specific" because organizational roles are often flexible and influenced by the people who have them. The role can be quite specific if someone else played it before and the new member is simply a replacement. It is less specific if the newcomer is assigned to share duties in an overgrown role or to take over functions that no one has formally or adequately handled before—or if the organization itself is informal and gives its members a lot of latitude. Organizational roles evolve over time, starting with some specified boundaries or goals, but shedding or adding some functions along the way.

Functions and purposes are defined more by organizational needs and technology than the needs and abilities of potential new members. It is best, of course, if the relationship of organization and member is mutually beneficial, but when existing members of an organization seek a new member for a designated role, the suitability of the new member for that role is the dominant consideration. Whether that role is narrow or broad, whether the organization is small or large, whether members are paid or donating their time, whether organizational purposes are humanitarian or commercial, whether the organization exists to provide services, to make products, or to have fun—whatever its nature, new members are expected to help achieve organizational purposes. This is true for informal organizations like a bridge club or for community organizations relying on unpaid volunteers; it is especially true for employing organizations whose members must competently and consistently do the things they are hired to do. Once hired, a person may stay in the original job, be transferred or promoted, get special training for a somewhat changed role, or be terminated. All of these are personnel decisions. All of them are based, if the organizational leaders are not too whimsical and impulsive, on some sort of assessment of the person. Decision makers hope to make wise decisions.

Results of wise decisions can range from the mere absence of problems to genuinely excellent outcomes promoting organizational purposes. Cumulative effects in hiring decisions can result in substantial increases in mean performance levels and productivity. Consequences of unwise decisions can range from inconvenience to disaster.

ANTECEDENTS OF PERSONNEL DECISIONS

Decisions, wise or otherwise, are usually based on some kind of information, whether good or bad. The best personnel decisions are based on information that permits the decision maker to make at least an implicit prediction that the person chosen will function satisfactorily, or perhaps do better than others, in the anticipated role. The prediction is based on known or assumed attributes (traits) of the potential new member. In initial selection, the decision is the end of a longer chain of events, and the sequence should be deliberate: (a) determination of the relevant traits, (b) assessment of candidates in terms of those traits, (c) prediction of probable performance or other outcomes of a decision to hire, and (d) the decision to hire or to reject (or, with more promising candidates than positions to fill, the decision to hire one in preference to others). The chain is longer for some kinds of jobs, or some organizations, than for others but if the decisions are not arbitrary and whimsical, this sequence is included.

One example of an employment process is shown in Fig. 1.1. It begins by identifying job candidates, those who have responded to recruiting efforts or have submitted applications in writing or in person. Sometimes a person may not be considered an applicant, even if applying, unless he or she meets certain minimum qualifications such as legal minimum age to drive a vehicle or possession of required documents.

Minimum qualifications, and desired further qualifications, must be established somehow. This requires some form of analysis of the job, its requirements, and of organizational needs (see chapter 2). Assessments of qualifications should have at least some demonstrable validity; the line from validation to preliminary assessments is dotted because often these assessments are not validated. Preliminary assessment looks primarily for major disqualifying information. Employment office staff may make a preliminary decision whether to send an applicant for more formal assessment (or the final decision in a highly centralized organization), but the manager or supervisor who has requested someone to fill an opening may make the final decision. Both preliminary and final decisions are based on the predictions made possible by the assessments. "Final" decisions are rarely final; there are often further steps that might result in the rejection of an otherwise desirable candidate. Certain diseases would preclude employment in a restaurant; a background investigation might unearth a felony making it illegal to hire the candidate as a law enforcement agent.

For the sequence to be effective, the assessments should be relevant and competently done. Characteristics important for one organization, or for one role, may not be highly valued or appropriate for another. Wisdom

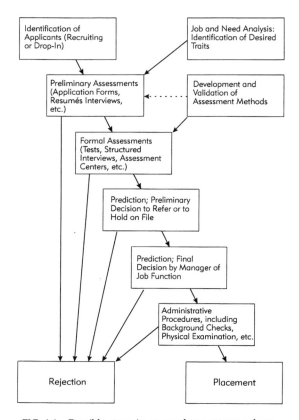

FIG. 1.1.   Possible steps in an employment procedure.

in selection decisions depends greatly on knowing the characteristics that are truly important in an anticipated role and on not being distracted by irrelevant characteristics.

Competence in assessing relevant characteristics may be no more than a matter of looking at a driver's license and being able to tell whether it is current, but most characteristics are more abstract. If it is inferred from job analysis that a qualified candidate is one with special skill in getting along with others, that characteristic *might* be assessed in an interview, or from personal history information, but special efforts are needed to be sure that these procedures provide valid information and that the assessments are in fact related to some subsequent behavior on the job. Qualifications may often be assessed by tests or by specially developed exercises. Kipnis (1994) suggested that success in technical training, not tests, is a better way to screen applicants in technologically highly advanced organizations.

A POINT OF VIEW

This book emphasizes employing organizations and how they may improve the chances that their personnel decisions will be wise ones. Wisdom in decision is elusive; there are opposing points of view about what is wise, desirable, and valued. I want to be explicit about mine.

Organizations exist when people join forces voluntarily to reach a common goal; they earn their existence by producing goods or services valued in at least a segment of the larger society. An organization, therefore, prospers according to its contribution to society (Eels & Walton, 1961), and individual members contribute by functioning well in their assigned roles. The interests of the consumers of the goods or services are compromised, no less than the personal interests of those in the organization, when a person who can function very well is denied a position given to one less qualified. Enough multiplication of such selection errors, and the organization fails—with resulting human and economic waste.

When there are more applicants than openings, some basis for choosing among them is necessary. Choices could be random, or quasi-random, like first come, first chosen. Choice might be based on social values, giving preference to veterans, women, or minorities. The choice might be based on nepotism, prejudice, or a similar-to-me bias. Or it can be based on valid prediction of future performance.

I believe the principal basis for personnel decisions should be merit, a concept that seems to be going out of style (Tenopyr, 1994). Some people think merit does not matter because they endorse a more egalitarian point of view. A few do not support profit-oriented concepts of merit, considering them inimical to the interests of a broader society. Some people dismiss the idea of merit in the belief that situational factors account for more in performance at work than do the personal characteristics people bring to the job. Most of these views challenge the basic idea of meritocracy.

If a merit principle is accepted, methods for establishing relative merit are needed. Some who accept meritocracy in principle reject typical psychometric assessment as its instrument (Tenopyr, 1994), but I prefer psychometric methods that give standardized, even-handed assessments of all candidates, similar results from one time or situation to another, and demonstrable relevance to performance.

It is wasteful to deny qualified people employment for invalid reasons, including whims known only as "company policy." Wasting human resources is at least as inexcusable as wasting physical resources; the call by Paterson (1957), echoed by Dunnette and Borman (1979), was a call for the "conservation of human talent" (p. 134). An organization has a responsibility to itself, to the society that supports it, and to the people who seek membership in it to be sure that it conserves and optimizes human talent.

Other points of view exist. Herriot (1993) suggested that two subcultures coexist in the psychology of assessment and that the assumptions in each are different. One he called the *psychometric subculture*. It assumes general stability in jobs and organizations, the predictability of human performance from human attributes, and selection by organizations for their own purposes. In contrast, he suggested and preferred a *social subculture* that assumes that change occurs constantly, that people and their self-perceptions are crucially important, that performance is a process of social interaction, and that selection is a mutually negotiated act. If these are mutually exclusive (I am not sure that they are), this book must be recognized as reflecting the psychometric subculture.

SCOPE OF MEMBERSHIP DECISIONS

I use the term, *selection*, in a generic sense. Although it is most commonly associated with hiring new people, and although the technology has developed largely from this common selection practice, I suggest a broader view. Certainly, hiring new people from outside is one kind of membership decision; candidates are recruited, their qualifications are assessed, and some of them are hired. This is not procedurally different from assessing people within the organization for an open position and then transferring one of them to fill the opening. Ordinarily, we use the term *transfer* rather than selection, but the decision process follows similar steps. A similar selection decision is made when one of several people already in the organization is promoted to a higher level position. In a sense, a termination decision is a selection decision. Perhaps an individual has been identified as unsatisfactory in some respect; before firing the individual, some form of assessment (prior and current performance evaluations, recommendations of supervisors or counselors, or whatever) is done, and a decision is made either to retain or fire the person. In a larger reduction in force, where certain people are to be terminated, the existing force is analogous to the body of recruits; people in it are somehow assesssed (e.g., performance, uniqueness of contribution, or simply seniority) and choices are made. Less common but procedurally similar *selection decisions* are made when people within an organization are to be chosen for special training, recognition, certification, or other opportunity. Different kinds of decisions may require very different kinds of assessments, but in all of them, the chance that the decisions will prove wise ones is enhanced if the assessments are valid and relevant to the new organizational role the person will play.

Organizational Settings

Different kinds of employing organizations have different kinds of personnel decision processes; there is no one typical way of doing things. The broad outlines of the process—recruiting, assessment, and decision—are common enough, but the differences can be profound. We can see some of the differences by looking at three different kinds of organizations.

Civil Service Organizations. Employment testing in America has its origins in hiring public employees. As early as 1814, the Army used tests to select surgeons, and tests were used in the selection of Navy midshipmen and Army cadets not long after (Hale, 1982). When Congress established the Civil Service Commission in 1883, it insisted that examinations be "practical in nature"—or, in more contemporary words, job-related. At first, it covered only about 10% of federal jobs, but a little more than 10 years later, 60% of federal positions, mainly in jobs employing large numbers of people, were filled by civil service examination.

Civil service procedures differ in different jurisdictions. In any of them, however, the heart of any civil service program is the examination. Examinations may be written tests, work samples, or "assembled"—an evaluation of documents. (The latter is used primarily when only one or a very few positions are to be filled.) The prototypical case tests for jobs in which large numbers of people are hired; for example, clerical workers, police in a large jurisdiction, and so on. For such cases, a date is picked for the examination and recruiting begins. Recruiting consists of posters, advertisements, or perhaps calls to prospective recruits in local schools, churches, or other promising sources of applicants. The new examination, even if an earlier one had been used, is developed during the recruiting period to reduce the chance that a security lapse gives some candidates prior knowledge of it; in any case, even a new exam must be carefully protected to assure even-handedness. In a truly large jurisdiction, the logistics of testing require extremely careful planning, both for test security and for the sheer mechanics of administration. Maybe many thousand candidates will all be tested at the same time; in New York City, tests for sanitation workers were once given to 80,000 in one day (Frank Landy, personal communication, October, 1995). In such circumstances, a standard testing situation for all test takers is hard to provide—but necessary.

An eligibility list is established on the basis of test scores, the highest scores at the top of the list. People will be hired from that list during a period of perhaps 2 years or more as openings occur. The person at the top of the list, the one with the best score, has preference over the next person; a person several places down the list will not be employed until all higher scoring people have been hired or have declined the opportunity and removed their names from the list. This is known as *top-down selection*. Statutes require modification of the top down procedure in some civil service jurisdictions. A common example is the "rule of three," which requires, when an opening occurs, that the three names at the top of the list be sent to the hiring manager for consideration. Until an eligibility list is "closed" and a new examination scheduled, hiring for the position continues from the top of the surviving members of the list. At some point, the qualifications of the highest scoring people remaining on the list, as indicated by test score, may be unsatisfactory, so most civil service eligibility lists specify a minimum qualifying score, below which the applicants tested will not be considered eligible. When top-down selection reaches people with scores below the minimum, the list is said to be "exhausted."

Private Business Organizations. Procedures are different in private business. Applicants, whether for specific jobs or more generally for employment in the organization, present themselves at any time, in person or by mail. They may come in response to specific recruiting activities, but they are as likely to come because they are seeking employment and, for whatever reason, consider the organization a good prospect. Assessment is likely to take place immediately. Applicants often specify the position or kind of position they seek, and they are rarely considered for other roles.

A first screening may be a preliminary interview, completion of an application form, or both. If an applicant is to be seriously considered after the preliminary screening, more rigorous assessment of applicant characteristics follows. This may begin with subjective assessments of behavior during interviews or of information on an application blank or résumé. In earlier times it included writing to or calling people listed as references; now, when organizations are so often sued, calling a previous employer will rarely elicit more than confirmation of the dates of prior employment. More formal assessment procedures used in some organizations include written tests, performance tests, structured and scored interviews, assessment centers, carefully developed personal history forms, and the like. These examples all provide numerical values to represent assessments, values that can be used in research to determine the value of the procedure for the selection enterprise.

Following assessment, a preliminary decision might be made. That decision might be to file the application in a list of potentially desirable applicants—particularly if there are no current openings for the job sought. It might be a rejection decision. It might be a decision to send the applicant to the supervisor who will make a final decision. Even if the personnel or human resources experts and the supervisor agree on a decision to hire, problems can still arise from medical examinations, security checks, or similar hurdles.

Military Organizations. Although military organizations are public, they are not (except for support staff) under civil service regulations. The hiring of sworn military personnel illustrates a still different form of employment practice.

The first difference is that people enter the organization in groups. Recruiting officers may work with individual candidates, but those brought into the service are sent to training centers in groups, and subsequently placed. The procedure is often to accept candidates in terms of general qualifications; it is more likely that a candidate will be rejected for physical, mental, or social problems than that a specific decision will be made to select the most wanted candidates. Those selected (or not rejected) and given basic training are then assessed for subsequent assignment. The emphasis is less on selection than on placement, that is, finding a job assignment that is optimal both for the organization and for the recruit.

In short, we have three patterns that may be followed in organizations. Although the differences across organizations and across jobs under any of these headings are so great that the foregoing descriptions are somewhat like caricatures, they do identify substantially different processes: (a) the eligibility list process in which an ordered list of potential employees is developed and is virtually the sole source of employees for a period of time, (b) the continuous consideration process, in which matches of position openings and applicants are made more or less serendipitously according to the timing of the opening and application, and (c) the placement process in which candidates are first declared acceptable for the organization and a later effort is made to find places for them, optimal or at least satisfactory to both candidate and organizational interests.

Using Assessments in Personnel Decisions

Practice varies in using assessments to reach personnel decisions; choices must be made. A basic policy choice is whether decisions should be based on meeting a designated standard of merit, or relative merit. A standard may be a minimum score in a distribution of relative scores (a *cut score*) or a standard level of performance (defined in chapter 11 as *domain-referenced assessment*). Cut scores present several psychometric problems that are discussed in chapter 7. They may also present practical policy problems. What is to be done when the number of passing applicants greatly exceeds the number of job openings? Clearly, decisions must be based on something other than the measured qualifications—first come, first chosen; random choice; interviewers' intuitions; different or unique qualifications; or (too often) unpredictable whim.

Rank ordering candidates (like a civil service eligibility list) is feasible even if there is no single day of mass testing. If many positions are likely to open at different but reasonably predictable times, the number of positions expected, say, over the next year can be predicted. As applicants appear and are assessed, they can be placed on a list in order of merit. The list can be revised every time there is a new name to put on it, and choices can be made from the list as openings develop. Although this idea was put forth long ago (Thorndike, 1949), it has never been widely used. More often, those who favor relative merit as a governing principle search applicant files when openings occur and contact those who appear to be among the best qualified of recent applicants.

A further option (explored in chapter 8) is a choice between a successive hurdles assessment procedure and simultaneous assessment. *Successive hurdles* starts with partial assessment of all candidates; those who pass the first cut are assessed further in one or more subsequent steps. Generally, the postponed assessments are the more expensive and time-consuming procedures. With *simultaneous assessment*, all assessment procedures are completed at roughly the same time and combined in some way; decisions are based on the combination.

Whatever pattern is used, these various approaches have in common the need for a sound appraisal of the relevant characteristics of the people being considered. Deciding what is relevant, and how to assess it, can be done more or less intuitively, by whim, or by arbitrary procedural rules, but it is far better to base them on competent research.

THE ROLE OF RESEARCH IN PERSONNEL DECISIONS

The purpose of personnel research is to evaluate the assessments and other procedures used for making personnel decisions; the research process is called *validation*. It is such a crucial, central process that this book gives more attention to questions of validity than to the various assessment procedures being evaluated.

The history of assessment for personnel selection is old, as shown in ancient Chinese civil service examinations (Bowman, 1989; DuBois, 1970) or in Greek philosophy; my favorite example is Biblical. Gideon faced an embarrassment of riches: he had far too many candidates for his army. On God's advice, he used a two-stage personnel testing procedure. The first was a single-item preliminary screening test ("Do you want to go home?"); on the basis of the answers, he cut 22,000 candidates down to 10,000. The remaining candidates were then put through an assessment center exercise—to observe candidates drinking from a stream—and 300 were chosen. No one has ever questioned the validities of these procedures for they were given by God. Unfortunately, many 20th-century testers have behaved as if they believed that they, too, had God-given tests and did not need to worry about their validities. Personnel researchers, however, recognize that tests and interpretations of test results are fallible and that the validity of any given procedure for assessing candidate characteristics needs to be questioned. Such questioning has led to fairly standard procedures for evaluating (validating) selection procedures.

The standard paradigm for personnel selection research has been described in most standard text books (Albright, Glennon, & Smith, 1963; Dunnette, 1966; Guion, 1965; Lawshe & Balma, 1966; Rose, 1993; Schneider & Schmitt, 1986; Thorndike, 1949), but the general pattern was described well long ago in a three-installment article by Freyd (1923).

Fundamental Assumptions

Freyd (1923) acknowledged five assumptions fundamental to his outline of the research process. I accept them as also fundamental to this book, at least as I have added to them.

1. People have abilities: mental abilities, psychomotor abilities, specifically learned skills (including social skills), and habitual ways of dealing with things and events in an environment (including temperament). It is *not* assumed that abilities are permanently fixed, either by heredity or early life experiences. It *is* assumed, however, that abilities are reasonably stable for most adults, stable enough that the level of ability observed in a candidate will stay pretty much the same for a useful period of time unless there has been some intervention.

2. People differ in any given ability. The fact of individual differences in levels of relevant abilities is the basis for decisions; those with higher levels of abilities relevant to the performance of a job are expected to perform better, other things being equal, than those with lower levels.

3. Relative differences in ability remain pretty much the same even after training or experience. People with higher levels of a required ability before exposure to a job will be the better performers on that job after training, whether formal or informal. Where an ability is used in the performance of the job, measures of the ability may be enhanced by that experience, but the relative rank orders of people in a group will not often be substantially changed.

4. Different jobs require different abilities. Although testing research in World War I had resulted in a rank order listing of occupations based

on mean intelligence test scores (Yoakum & Yerkes, 1920, pp. 196-200), it was generally believed by the 1920s (as forecast by Yoakum and Yerkes) that different occupations called for different patterns of more specific abilities and that effective selection must consist of matching the abilities demanded by the job with the abilities of the candidate—putting the round peg in the round hole, as it is said.

5. The required abilities can be measured. Cognitive abilities, for example, can be measured with many different kinds of tests; cognitive tests have been successful not only for employee selection but for many other purposes as well. The record in the measurement of psychomotor abilities is generally less favorable. The measurement of such traits as sense of responsibility, achievement motivation, and other motivational requisites of successful performance has been underresearched and has a less impressive record of success in employee selection. Perhaps the record will be more impressive when the level of research effort expended on their definition and measurement approaches that expended on cognitive abilities.

Steps in Personnel Research

Personnel research has traditionally concentrated on factory, sales, clerical, and supervisory jobs—jobs that employ relatively large numbers of people. For such jobs, the dominant pattern of personnel research and employment test validation follows steps like the ones described here.

Analyze Jobs and Organizational Needs. Procedures are sometimes casual, sometimes very systematic; usually, job analysis concentrates on one job (or job family) at a time, one where the need and opportunity for improvement seems greatest. Job and organizational need analysis should consider whether relatively poor performance on a job is a selection problem or is approached better by other organizational interventions. Need analysis asks whether the best approach is likely to be to redesign the job and immediate work environment, to change people already on the job through training or improved management, or to improve selection procedures. Clearly, no new selection procedure can solve a problem that springs primarily from inadequate equipment or inept management.

Job analysis asks what a worker does, how it is done, and the resources (personal and organizational) used in doing it. Contemporary debate about it centers on the amount of job information needed for competent selection research, the degree to which a target job must be clearly differentiated from similar jobs, and the level of sophistication and technical foundations needed for the job analysis procedures. Much of the debate seems unnecessary; the essential reason for analyzing the job is to get a reasonable understanding of the nature and purposes of the job so that one will know what it is one seeks to predict and also have a reasonably rational basis for specifying the applicant characteristics that will predict it. Jobs are not static. Job analysis also needs to provide information on any changes expected, how quickly they may occur, a job incumbent's responsibility for initiating change, and potential problems of adapting to change.

Choose a Criterion. The criterion in personnel research is that which is to be predicted. It is a measure of performance, or of some aspect of performance, or of some valued behavior associated with the assigned job role.[1] It might be a measure of trainability, production quality and quantity, or earnings. Criterion choice is a matter of organizational values and organizational needs. Some organizational needs and values may be more general, extending beyond performance on specific jobs. For example, if an organization maintains tight production schedules, punctuality, and regular attendance, workforce stability may be the most important criteria for production jobs generally. Adaptability to change may be valued above other criteria in some organizations.

Form Predictive Hypotheses. Criterion performance is often complex, attributable to multiple causes and to multiple characteristics of the workers; it is likely that more than one kind of ability must be measured if the criterion is to be predicted in all of its complexity. Each predictor constitutes a hypothesis to be tested by research. Most personnel research has evaluated mental abilities as predictors. From its beginning, employment psychology has been closely tied to psychological testing, so the predictors most commonly chosen have been those successfully measured by psychological tests and inventories, including work samples and job knowledge tests. Relatively little attention has been given to attributes not readily measured by conventional testing procedures. It is argued in chapter 3 that selection hypotheses should consider a broader array of traits.[2] Most employers, if not most psychologists, would consider traits

---

[1]It is unfortunate that such an ambiguous word has become the standard term to designate the behavior or evaluation of behavior to be predicted. In court cases, for example, the term *criterion* is often used by lawyers and judges to refer to the basis for selecting people, such as a cutting score on a test. Such a difference in the denotative meaning of the word has caused much confusion between attorneys and their expert witnesses.

[2]It is, I hope, clear that I use the terms *trait, attribute,* and *characteristic* interchangeably. The word *trait* seems to have fallen in some disrepute among some organizational psychologists, perhaps because of a fear that it is tainted somehow with genetic implications. The tendency to replace it with multisyllabic terms (e.g., "dispositional tendencies") seems too clumsy to me, and I shall use the shorter terms, without distinctions, to refer to any trait that is attributed to or deemed characteristic of people. On some days I write "trait." On others, I write "attribute" or "characteristic." The choice among these is as trivial as that!

like dependability, motivation level, work values, and other relatively amorphous constructs to be very important predictors of work performance in a wide variety of jobs. Such constructs are difficult to measure, but the list of potential predictors should not, at least initially, be constrained because of anticipated measurement problems.

Organizational variables may be considered in developing the list of predictors. Bray, Campbell, and Grant (1974) and Vicino and Bass (1978) offered evidence that the degree of challenge on an early job was an important determiner of managerial success; likewise, Kaufman (1974) demonstrated that early challenge reinforced professional contributions among engineers with high technical abilities. Such studies suggest that organizational variables, relevant to employee placement perhaps more than to employee selection, might predict important criteria, either by themselves or in combination or interaction with applicant traits.

A predictive hypothesis is sometimes a casual one, but it may nevertheless prove to be a good one. If done with great care and knowledge, however, a well-reasoned hypothesis will ordinarily have a better chance to be supported in research.

Select Methods of Measurement. Research should not be limited to any particular assessment method, but more research seems done for tests and questionnaires than for other methods. There are several reasons. Practical research follows success, and the predictive value of tests has been demonstrated more persuasively and more frequently than for competing approaches to assessment. Further, testing is easily standardized, enabling a fairer assessment than is possible where the method of assessment varies from one person to another. Test use is not, however, free from problems. One serious problem is the tendency to assess candidates on traits for which tests are available rather than to assess other candidate characteristics not easily assessed by testing procedures (Lawshe, 1959).

Design the Research. Good research tries to assure that findings from the research sample can generalize to the population of interest, job applicants. One aspect of research design is the choice of subjects; this is discussed later, but here it is enough to point out that inappropriate subjects may limit generalizability. Incumbents and applicants may differ in motivation to do well on a test, in means and variances of the measured predictors, or demographics. Research subjects may not match applicant populations because of rapid changes in work-force demographics (Greller & Nee, 1990; Offermann & Gowing, 1993). Entry-level positions are traditionally filled by students emerging from school, and there will not be enough of them. Older workers—not only retirees but people who are unemployed or underemployed—may increasingly define applicant populations for these jobs. Moreover, rapid increases in the workforce and in applicant populations are mainly expected from women, minorities, and immigrants. Demographic variables so far have shown little effect on the validities of assessments, but research attention should continue as applicant populations and associated variables become more diverse. If the potential problems are not obvious, consider the assessment problems associated with frequent characteristics of the minorities and immigrants whose principal (or only) language is Spanish and whose interest in mastering English is not strong. Demographic diversity has become a watchword in organizational staffing (Jackson & Associates, 1992). The research implications of tapping currently underused sources of job candidates in the search for diversity must be carefully monitored.

All too often, the procedures studied in the research differ from those actually in operation; research results in such cases may not necessarily apply. Examples include rigorous timing of tests in the research but careless timing in practice, using continuous score distributions for research but cut scores in practice, or allowing casual, conversational instructions to replace the formal, standard instructions given in the research setting. Good research anticipates the expected manner of use and is designed accordingly; good administrative practice makes sure that operational use of the predictors is consistent with evaluative research.

When the complexity of criterion performance calls for multiple predictors, some means of simultaneous or sequential consideration of predictors is needed. Usually that involves combining predictor data into some sort of composite, and it is the composite that is to be evaluated. Again, the composite or sequence anticipated in operational use should be the composite or sequence used in research.

Collect Data. Predictors must be administered with both standardization and tact. The first of these is technical; the second is both technical and civil. Tactless, uncaring treatment of those to be interviewed or tested undermines motivation to do well and, therefore, introduces an extraneous and uncontrolled variable into the research. Beyond that, however, it is simply uncivil to fail to appreciate the apprehension people have when being assessed, and an examiner who appreciates these feelings will approach the research task more humanely than one who does not (see several chapters in Schuler, Farr, & Smith, 1993). If nothing more, civility is good public relations. The need for civility is equally great for operational assessment.

Since the early days of testing, the concept of standardization of procedure has been accepted as a sine qua non of good practice; it has been virtually unquestioned throughout most of the history of personnel selection research. Everyone who is tested is given the same set of items, identically worded; if there are established time limits, they are rigidly adhered to whenever the test is given; instructions are verbatim, the same for everyone; if the test is printed, type size and style and paper quality always remain the same. Standardization in this sense is similar to the concept of the experimental control of variables not a part of the hypothesis to be tested; it is also an assurance of procedural fairness. Nevertheless, the concept of standardization is due for reappraisal. Recent advances in psychometric theories suggest that the ideals of standardization may be better realized by individually tailoring sets of items to each applicant, perhaps using different numbers of items as well as different items for the different applicants; new methods of administration by computer may call for varying de facto time limits by controlling response times for individual items.

Evaluate Results. Freyd (1923) referred to evaluating measurement; the idea subsequently became known as *validating* the predictor trait as measured. Whether called evaluation or validation (I prefer to call it evaluation), the traditional procedure has been to correlate scores or ratings on predictor variables with numerical values on criterion measures. If the correlation is high, the predictor is said to be a good one (i.e., a "valid" one), and if the correlation is low, the predictor is said to be poor. High and low are relative terms, often evaluated more against experience than against specified coefficients. Despite the vagueness of this approach, some empirical evaluation of predictors has traditionally been deemed essential: "A personnel selection program which does not involve empirical checks of the selection procedures against criteria of success is at best a static and untested one. At worst it may be outright charlatanism" (Thorndike, 1949, p. 119).

The quotation needs qualification in the light of views developed later in this book. These steps, as a group, constitute what has been known as validation, research explicitly testing hypotheses about the relationship of predictors to criteria, that is, about how well the criterion can be predicted by one or more predictors. There is, however, an even older tradition defining validation as finding out how well the predictor (in this case, usually a test) "measures what it purports to measure" (Drever, 1952, p. 304; Sutherland, 1996, p. 490). These views of validation are not the same. A test that purports to measure spelling ability may do so very well, but it is not likely to be very good at predicting how well mechanics repair faulty brakes. For this reason, I distinguish between the validity with which a trait or attribute is measured and the validity with which the measured trait predicts something else—between validity of measurement (psychometric validity) and validity as the job-relatedness of a predictor. Evidence for either concept of validity may be collected by several forms of empirical investigation (Landy, 1986).

Justify the Use of the Selection Procedure. Empirical research permits two kinds of justification. One is *incremental validity*, the degree to which a proposed selection procedure adds something to the procedures already in use. If the new procedure does not add very much, then even if its correlation with the criterion is high, its value to the organization is questionable. The second is "economic value," usefulness, or *utility*. The principal ingredients in computing utility are the correlation of predictor (or predictor composite) with the criterion, the proportion of employees hired by existing methods and showing satisfactory performance, the proportion of the applicants who will be hired, and the variability of performance expected in a selected and an unselected set of people. Modern utility research has demonstrated quite substantial savings possible, even with modest correlations between predictors and criteria.

Varieties of Research Designs

From the beginning of employment testing, tests have been evaluated by variants of one of two basic design choices: studying people already on the job, the *present employee* method, versus testing job applicants and getting criterion data later for those hired, the *follow-up* method of research (Lawshe, 1948; Lawshe & Balma, 1966; Tiffin, 1942, and later editions). The follow-up method, especially an idealized version of it, is widely, although not universally, considered the best design, in part because the research actually uses subjects from the applicant population.

In the idealized follow-up design, the research tests are given to all applicants but not scored until criterion data are available for those who are hired. (This is to assure that neither judgments of decision makers nor subsequent criteria are affected by knowledge of the test scores.) Hiring decisions are made as if these new tests were not available at all, using existing methods—application forms, interviews, references, tests, hunches, or whatever—whether previously validated or not. After a time, criterion data are collected for those actually hired; the tests are then scored and the scores are compared to criterion data.

In the early days of employment testing, such ideal data collection procedures were rare; now they are virtually nonexistent. Nevertheless, the ideal provides a standard against which other designs can be discussed. Traditionally, the only other option was the present employee method where employees are taken off the job, tested, and the test scores are correlated with existing or concurrently obtained criterion measures. It is a faster method, and practical considerations often seem to favor it.

These terms now seem archaic. Today's discussions are more likely to refer to *concurrent* and *predictive* research designs—terms introduced in the 1954 *Technical Recommendations* (American Psychological Association, American Educational Research Association, & National Council on Measurements Used in Education, 1954). They are similar but not identical to the ideas of present employee and follow-up research. The essential differences between these designs is the time span for data collection, not the employment status of the research subjects. Predictive designs include a substantial time interval between the availability of predictor data and collection of subsequent criterion data; concurrent designs do not. Thus, a predictive design may use existing employees if the data to be evaluated can be collected from them at one time and criterion data collected some weeks or months later.

Does it matter whether the research design is concurrent or predictive? Opinions differ. Barrett, Phillips, and Alexander (1981) argued that the importance of the issue has been exaggerated; they cited my earlier statement as an extreme, "The present-employee method is clearly a violation of scientific principles" (Guion, 1965, p. 20). Acknowledging that the design differences are potentially important, they presented arguments to show that the differences do not in fact have much impact on the results of studies. If anything, concurrent studies have generally given somewhat larger correlations; Schmitt, Gooding, Noe, and Kirsch (1984) found average validity coefficients of .341 among concurrent designs, .296 for predictive designs where the predictor was not used for selection decisions, and .259 for predictive designs where it was used for selection prior to the study. These results make sense. For one thing, the review covered a period starting in 1964, a period when nearly all reported validity studies were based on cognitive tests. (Noncognitive traits, especially personality traits, are more influenced by job experiences; there is no assurance that they would be similarly immune to design differences.) Moreover, abilities are enhanced through job training and experience (Alvares & Hulin, 1973). A further plausible assumption is that people who do well on the job develop their abilities more than do those whose performance is not as good.

One criticism of concurrent designs is that present employees lack those at the low end of the predictor distribution who were not hired or who have been lost through attrition and also lack those at the high end who have left because of disuse of ability or because of promotion out of the job. Barrett et al. (1981) correctly pointed out that this is a restriction of range problem. Restriction of range (see chapter 7) is a problem because it results in an understatement of the predictor–criterion relationship, but the understatement can be corrected statistically. Unfortunately, a closer look at the design options shows many more than two (at least 11; Guion

& Cranny, 1982; Sussman & Robertson, 1986), and not all designs permit the correction. Restriction of range does occur in concurrent designs, but as Barrett et al. (1981) pointed out, it also occurs in predictive designs (a) directly selecting on the basis of the predictor being validated, (b) using it indirectly by selecting on the basis of a correlated predictor, or (c) using a long enough time interval that high-scoring people have moved out of the job by the time criterion data are collected. The vital question is not which method restricts variance more; it is whether the study design provides information that permits the correction (Guion & Cranny, 1982).

Correlation, of course, does not say anything about direction of causality, even if a causal relationship exists. The act of prediction, however, says something about timing. Without a time interval, even the direction of permitted prediction is uncertain; it is as appropriate to predict the trait from the criterion as to go the other direction.

Practical constraints frequently require procedures lacking somewhat in scientific rigor, but the Guion and Cranny (1982) conclusion reiterated the idea that present employee, and some predictive designs violate scientific principles—that decision makers should "avoid relying on a presumed equivalence of the various predictive and concurrent designs for estimating the appropriate population parameters" (Guion & Cranny, 1982, p. 243). I conclude from the Sussman and Robertson (1986) discussion of problems associated with 11 designs that those using random selection (whether predictive or concurrent) are the most desirable, and that a predictive design where selection is based on the test itself is least desirable.

Concurrent and predictive designs are all variations on a single theme, the correlation between a predictor and a criterion. Validation research is not limited to that theme (Landy, 1986). Part II of this book considers other designs and considerations for assessing not only job-relatedness as an aspect of validity but also for assessing the meaning of scores on an assessment procedure. Because a predictor–criterion correlation is the traditional meaning of "validity coefficient," it serves as a way to introduce the problems and complexities of validation, but it is only an introduction. Even for introductory purposes, read on!

Problems With Conventional Research

This recital of traditional personnel research is quite conventional, but it describes a paradigm that needs to be re-examined. It is subject to several problems, and they are potentially serious ones.

Numbers of Cases. The conventional paradigm needs large numbers. It is designed for situations where large numbers of people have been or will be hired for a given job or job family. We used to think that large numbers meant 30 or more; considerations of power in evaluating statistical significance have shown that large numbers may mean hundreds of research subjects. Validation developed its tradition for factories that hire dozens or hundreds of assembly-line workers each year. However, a major change in the American workforce has occurred and seems likely to continue: most people do not work in large corporations on jobs also done by hundreds of other workers. Hodge and Lagerfeld (1987) reported that only about 10% of working Americans work in organizations employing more than 1,000 people. Moreover, there is more differentiation of jobs; technological growth has produced a wider variety of jobs. Many employment decisions must now be made where only a few people are to be hired (perhaps only one) from a relatively small group of candidates. Further, more hiring is being done in professional, semi-professional, and managerial occupations, where the costs of error in individual selection decisions may be much higher than for the mass-market decisions, but where one person must be chosen from perhaps not more than a half-dozen candidates. The numbers for many decisions are too small for reliable correlation coefficients. The traditional paradigm makes no provision for the small business, for the selection of the replacement for a retiring manager, or for hiring a unique specialist in even a large organization.

Consideration of Prior Research. Traditional validation ignores prior research. The tradition developed when it was thought that validities of selection procedures are specific to, even unique in, the situation in which they are established (see, e.g., Guion, 1976). One of the more influential changes in the thinking of personnel researchers in the late 1970s and 1980s was the development of techniques for studying validity generalization (e.g., Schmidt & Hunter, 1977), a quantitative analysis of the results of many independent studies of a given research hypothesis (e.g., performance of clerical workers is predictable from tests of general mental ability).

Need for Judgment. The traditional paradigm is purely statistical; it leaves no room for judgment. In some respects, that is good. The view held by some people that human judgment yields better predictions than can be had statistically is a myth (or a superstition based on hope); it persists in spite of overwhelming evidence to the contrary. Such evidence was presented long ago by Meehl (1954), who later updated it by citing a "box score" in which, of 35 studies comparing statistical and clinical predictions, the score was 35 to 0 in favor of statistical prediction (Meehl, 1967).

Nevertheless, statistical prediction is often impossible, infeasible, or insufficient. The circumstances for a candidate at hand may differ enough from the research circumstances so that generalizing from the research is questionable. The most obvious example lies in testing the skills of people with disabilities. One cannot intelligently (or legally in the United States) refuse to consider a blind applicant for a job in which visual acuity is not a genuine requirement simply because the applicant does not match the research sample of people with sight. One can, of course, make some modification of the selection procedure (such as reading items orally), but the research does not apply to these nonstandard modifications. The decision maker must therefore make a judgment based on the applicant's performance on a procedure of unknown validity, on interviewer judgments of unknown validity, prior work experience of unknown validity, or on some random basis known not to have any validity. To disqualify an applicant because the possible assessment procedures have not been validated is likely to be illegal. Moreover, from an organizational point of view, it is probably stupid as well; no other term adequately describes a practice that would deny an organization an employee who might be superior to others because of special motivation, unusual skills, or other unresearched attributes for no better reason than the applicant's failure to be ordinary.

Uniqueness and Prediction Error. Closely related is the more general fact that the traditional paradigm overlooks uniqueness or individuality, simply letting it slide into the category of prediction error. Prediction in traditional validation is based on a regression equation that considers everyone in a research sample alike in everything except the equation variables. A regression equation is a mathematical statement of averages; it says that, on the average, people with a given predictor score will have a given criterion score. In fact, almost no one precisely fits this average; for most people in a sample, criterion scores will be close to the average but miss it a little bit in either direction. Some people will be far from the average. There may be many reasons: pure chance, measurement error, influence of third variables such as motivational levels, or simply that people are unique. Let us not get carried away with this idea. Despite uniqueness, people are pretty much alike in many ways, and averages work. Traditional validation does not try to explain errors in prediction; it should. One such attempt has focused on moderator variables (see chapter 8).

A systems approach to research would be useful; it was called the "fifth discipline" (Senge, 1990, p. 12) in fostering a "learning organization" (p. 14), an organization that can adapt to change and know the many implications of that adaptation. From the individual point of view,

> Psychologists have been slow to recognize that the patterning of activity is the most individual thing about a person. The study of individual differences has been almost exclusively concerned with the amounts of various components that are present. . . . Organic chemists could never have dis-

tinguished between most of the complex substances that make up the biological world had they continued to do nothing except measure the amounts
of carbon, nitrogen, oxygen, and rarer elements in organic substances. . . .
It was the discovery of the structure or the organic molecule, of the way
atoms are linked to the hexagonal benzene ring, that constituted the real
breakthrough. (Tyler, 1978, p. 107)

I do not know whether a structure in human behavior, analogous to the
benzene ring, exists. If it does, however, the traditional validation research
paradigm will not find it.

There is a tension between the uniqueness of individual candidates
and the commonalities that define research populations. It is indeed
strange that the aspect of psychological research known as the study of
individual differences, from which principles of assessment are derived,
has become methodologically the study of averages. Only a few psychologists, at least in recent years, have examined human individuality, and
their work seems not to have influenced personnel assessment (e.g.,
Mumford, Stokes, & Owens, 1990; Snyder & Fromkin, 1980; Tyler, 1978).

I do not know if uniqueness is genuinely important for the practical
problems of making personnel decisions. Two people may have precisely
the same measured traits but have unmeasured differences that lead one
to success on the job and the other to failure or mediocrity on the same
job. Uniqueness offers no basis for statistical prediction, but it does, I
think, require us to be less than arrogant about our predictions of future
behavior.

Minimum Qualifications. The traditional paradigm does not face the
question of minimum standards. In general, it assumes that a valid
selection procedure is one in which, if some of the trait indicates good
performance and more of the trait indicates better performance, then still
more of it would indicate still better performance. This is generally a
good assumption, and it leads directly to top-down selection.

Suppose, however, that no applicant has scored very high. Will the
job be offered (other considerations identifying no problems) to the one
with the best score, or is the best score too low? But how does one decide
that a given score is too low? The determination of a qualifying standard,
such as a minimum cut score, is difficult, requiring serious thought and
research. In practice, minimum standards have been dictated largely by
supply and demand, but some procedures (e.g., certification of competence in the performance of specific skills) require a more rational basis.

Static Versus Dynamic Research Models. The changing importance
of change itself is not recognized in traditional research designs. By the
completion of a predictive validation study with a fairly long time interval,

the applicant population, the nature of the job responsibilities, and the definition of success on the job may all have changed; demographic, technological, and value changes are occurring at unprecedented rates. Yet the traditional design assumes that the conditions of the study will remain the conditions under which the results will be applied. As Gershwin's song says, "It ain't necessarily so." The assumption is neither inevitable nor uncorrectable. Of the many considerations in evaluating assessments, a validity coefficient is only one. Even within the traditional paradigm, however, contribution to change, or at least readiness for and adaptability to change, can be the criterion to be predicted.

Two figures provided by Howard (1991) indicate the scope of change in work environments and the variety of assessment options that can respond to expected change. Figure 1.2 shows the paths by which technological, economic, and demographic changes influence work environments and organizational responses. Figure 1.3 shows, for each broad category of organizational response, three areas of human resources management that must be part of the response; organizational changes and training are essential responses, but individual assessment remains necessary even—perhaps especially—during periods of rapid change. Her call is for a much broader approach to assessment and prediction than traditional thinking has recognized.

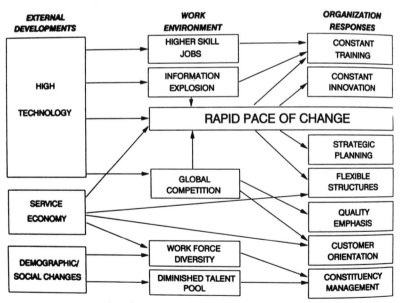

FIG. 1.2. Sources of change in the work environment. From Howard, A. (1991). New directions for human relations practice. In D. W. Bray & Associates, *Working with organizations and their people: A guide to human resources practice.* New York: Guilford Press. Reprinted with permission.

Human Resources Areas

ORGANIZATION RESPONSES	THEMES OF HR PRACTICE	ORGANIZATION DEVELOPMENT	TRAINING	INDIVIDUAL EVALUATION
CONSTANT TRAINING	Continuous learning	Link organization renewal to continuous learning	Training and re-training; support external development	Select for learning ability; appraise/reward development
CONSTANT INNOVATION	Generating change	Foster climate supporting new ideas; quality improvement programs	Re-train for new products/services; develop innovativeness	Select for creativity; appraise/reward risk-taking
RAPID PACE OF CHANGE	Responsiveness to change	Team building for responsiveness; intergroup problem solving; conflict resolution	Re-train for new products/services; develop adaptability; resistance to stress	Select and appraise for adaptability, coping
STRATEGIC PLANNING	Coordination of strategy	Team building for goal clarity and agreement	Gap analysis; help develop plans and tie training to them	Environmental scans & force analysis; tie selection to strategic plans
FLEXIBLE STRUCTURES	Participation	Survey feedback & employee input; autonomous work groups	Training for empowerment and leadership	Selection for participativeness and leadership
QUALITY EMPHASIS	Excellence	Quality improvement programs	Group problem-solving skills for quality improvement programs	Selection for high work standards
CUSTOMER ORIENTATION	Service	Team building to facilitate customer service	Training for customer service	Selection for interpersonal skills
CONSTITUENCY MANAGEMENT	Equitable treatment; flexible HR policies	Foster equitable climate via team building, survey feedback	Training to value diversity; basic skills training; gear training to diverse population	Fair selection practices; drug and honesty testing; wide recruiting

FIG. 1.3. Work environment changes and human resource practice. From Howard, A. (1991). New directions for human relations practice. In D. W. Bray & Associates, *Working with organizations and their people: A guide to human resources practice*. New York: Guilford Press. Reprinted with permission.

Global or Specific Assessments. How general, or how narrow, should predictor or criterion variables be? A multiple regression equation permits specificity in defining predictors but encourages generality in criterion measurement. Such an equation is sometimes criticized for being both too atomistic in its analysis of people and their traits and too general and nonspecific in its definition of criteria. Is either criticism justified? Should we seek global, general descriptions of traits or performance, or narrower, more specific ones?

Far too much energy has been wasted on this question. Smith (1985)

> pointed out that measurements can always be arranged along a specific-to-general continuum, that they can be constructed to fit different levels of generality of the same basic domain, and that measures at those different levels are not interchangeable but can be useful for different purposes. She argued for greater specificity of measurement if the criterion to be predicted is very specific and for generality in measurement if the criterion is very global in nature. *Somehow, that very sensible view seems lost in too many discussions.* (Guion & Gibson, 1988, p. 364, italics added)

There is another, quite different sense in which the global-specific difference is an issue. A guiding theme of this book is that a predictive hypothesis can be developed, that it can specify that people strong in a certain trait, or collection of traits, are likely to be strong in a certain aspect of performance or performance composite. An alternative point of view is the *whole person* view—the idea that people are more than bundles of independent traits, that assessments should be holistic, looking globally at "the whole person." Dachler (1989) suggested that selection be considered a part of personnel development, considering patterns of behavior rather than scorable dimensions, focusing more on probability of future growth and adaptability than on fitness for a particular job. There is much to recommend his position.

The two positions are not so far apart as they might seem. Two major reasons exist for their divergence. One is methodological; the traditional correlational method requires measurable dimensions. This does not preclude a more systemic approach; correlations between levels of fitting a pattern of characteristics and a criterion can be hypothesized and tested just as easily as are correlations between individual traits and criteria. The second reason is legalistic, at least in the United States; the *Uniform Guidelines* (Equal Employment Opportunity Commission, Civil Service Commission, Department of Labor, & Department of Justice, 1978, Section 5I, p. 38298) follow the traditional methods, and holistic evaluation of people and their likelihood of adapting to change are nowhere mentioned in them. I personally believe that the courts are not so rigid—that a well-reasoned, well-developed selection procedure that improves productivity without violating the values of the larger society will be permitted by courts. I think a third reason precluding a more holistic approach is that not enough people have thought about it often enough or deeply enough to develop a solid paradigm for its use.

A Special Problem: The Unit of Analysis

Traditional validation is done at an individual level of analysis, that is, with data collected from individuals and interpreted as predictions of individual criterion performance. As Schneider (1996) pointed out, research at the individual level does not show a clear link to organizational effectiveness. I describe two growing problems requiring research at group or organizational levels: selection for teams, and selection of people to fit in organizations or work groups.

Selection of Team Members. Current trends place less emphasis on individual, relatively permanent jobs and more on collaborative groups, or teams. Choosing people to form teams or to join existing teams pose special problems, and different kinds of teams pose different problems (Klimoski & Jones, 1995). A decision-making management team may be formed for a specific project, its members chosen for specific areas of expertise; it may be disbanded at the project's conclusion, its members reassigned to new teams with other projects where their expertise will be useful (Hollenbeck, LePine, & Ilgen, 1996); members are chosen for specialized knowledge or skill. Production teams might be long term, ask members to work collaboratively as needed, and require flexibility and cooperation; members are generalists, doing any of the various things that need to be done.

In a traditional work unit, the members work jointly to accomplish a specified aim, but with specialized division of labor. Responsibility for specific functions is assigned to some members of the group; other members have different responsibilities as defined by the boxes on an organization chart. Roles are intended to be equal, but work may pile up for one member of the unit while another has a temporary lull. If people in the unit form a reasonably cohesive and congenial group, a person with available time may help the overworked one, leaving his or her assigned box (from the chapter title, Mohrman & Cohen, 1995). Such help is common enough that the idea of a discrete, unchanging division of duties is fictional; people who get along with each other tend to work collaboratively. To do so, however, requires some competence in doing things ordinarily assigned to other boxes—it requires at least some versatility.

If a team is formed from available employees for a specific, temporary purpose, its members may already know each other and have shown an ability to work together. Team members might be picked by someone in authority, one member might be picked who then chooses the others, or they might choose each other by some process of common consent. If a team is formed from outside applicants, they may be assessed individually for competence and interpersonal skills, some of them may be selected and assigned to work groups. Traditional research can be expanded to include skills not ordinarily assessed, but turning individuals into a genuine team may rely more on training and development than on initial selection. A group may have functioned as a team for a long time. If one member departs, for whatever reason, someone must be selected who will fit in with the others and keep the team functioning. The replacement might be chosen by the remaining team members themselves or by some authority.

Klimoski and Jones (1995) identified various kinds of teams, each with its own implications for team formation. They noted that, for most teams, individual competencies are exceedingly important; two or three highly competent members are not likely to compensate for serious inadequacy in another (Tziner & Eden, 1985). Moreover, individual competencies among team members must be augmented by interpersonal skills.

Team formation is not always appropriate (Fisher, 1994), but the trend toward groups as performance units will probably continue. It poses new and as yet unmet challenges for assessment and personnel decisions. Although the formation and use of work groups has long been a fact of organizational life, the fact has been largely ignored by traditional approaches to individual assessment and decisions.

It may be less important to form teams by selection than to train the members to function as a team once they are chosen. There is little scientific evidence to draw on. Noting the problem, Cannon-Bowers, Tannenbaum, Salas, and Volpe (1995) offered a conceptual framework of 16 propositions to stimulate research on training. They saw the team as the unit of analysis, with some team competencies dependent on characteristics of the team and others on characteristics of the task; simple advice to develop teams through training seems excessively glib. Surely, training works better if those chosen for training have attributes useful to the development of group competencies; individual assessment and group training should complement each other. How should individual assessments be distributed? Is an effective group homogeneous or heterogeneous? The question is complicated by the trend toward more diversity in organizations. In some respects, diversity means heterogeneity. If diversity means no more than demographic diversity, however, it has little meaning; "demographic variables are simply boxcars carrying important differences in personality or values . . . and it is on these latter differences that we should focus our attention" (Landy, Shankster-Cawley, & Moran, 1995, p. 278).

Person–Organization Fit. Schneider (1987) argued that people who stay in an organization tend to have similar attitudes and values. When one applies for work in an organization, one seeks an opportunity to work with the people who are there. If a newcomer is not to remain an outsider long after joining an organization or group, he or she must somehow fit in.

The term *fit in* has a rather disreputable history. A group of White males seeking a replacement for a departed member may reject a woman or an ethnic minority on the grounds of not fitting in; the term is often a surrogate for a poorly disguised prejudice. Used in this way, it may also serve diagnostically to reveal a serious flaw of group identity. Like Mohrman and Cohen (1995), I consider a well-functioning team as one with a clear focus on the work goals of the group—on the tasks the group is supposed to accomplish. If "fitting in" is simply an expression of prejudice, it indicates a group more self-centered than work-centered, a group preserving its social identity rather than its functional identity. Fitting into a group commitment to its work implies merging with the others to facilitate the work, not camaraderie.

The issue of fit is placed in a broader and clearer perspective when the fit is between the person and the organization as a whole. At an organizational level, one useful definition says person–organization fit is the "congruence of the personality traits, beliefs, and values of the employee with the culture, strategic needs, norms, and values of the organization" (Adkins, Russell, & Werbel, 1994, pp. 605–606).

Assessment of fit is difficult. It is likely to consist of interviewer judgments. A more systematic procedure reported by Chatman (1991) measured fit as the congruence of the recruit's profile of values and an aggregated profile developed by managers for the organization. It may be premature to worry about measuring fit; a prior question is whether close fit is desirable. Hiring people who can meet organizational needs is desirable; hiring people who fit into an organization's normative values may not be. In fact, it may be necessary to hire an occasional misfit to turn around a complacent, drifting organization.

Schneider (1987) presented an *attraction-selection-attrition* cycle as a model for the relationships between individual people and the organizations that hire them. People look for employment in organizations that already exist; they are attracted to some organizations more than to others and apply to the most attractive ones. Whether the basis for attraction is factual or exists only in rumor, organizations can choose only among those who are attracted enough to apply to them.

If the basis for attraction was wrong, and people once in the organization find that the fit is poor, they leave. Schenider's contention is that the combination of initial attraction and subsequent attrition leads to greater organizational homogeneity; those who are attracted, hired, and stay tend to be alike. Such homogeneity can have a major impact on the organization's ability to survive and change in a rapidly changing world. Selection for fit may be not only counterproductive but hazardous.

Failure to consider fit can also be hazardous. Deliberately selecting people with wholly different values and beliefs can result in newcomers who cannot function well within the existing organizational culture, people who are neither accepted nor believed by the dominant and homogeneous core already there and with whom the newcomers cannot clearly communicate. "So, the motto from the model is to be sure that newcomers brought in to turn around an organization (i.e., to change the old-timers' inclinations) share some attributes with those they are expected to change" (Schneider, 1987, p. 446). Changing structures and organizational processes will not by themselves create necessary change and organizational adaptability; the people in them must change, and that change occurs slowly.

I am persuaded by Schneider's view. I am uncertain about ways for implementing it. In what attributes should newcomers be like most of those already in the organization? What newcomer attributes are most likely to increase organizational adaptability to external events and changes? Is the answer to this question dependent more on those external processes or internal needs? Having answered those questions, how can the relevant attributes be assessed? These are, of course, questions for scientific research, but when the consequences of error can be as great as an organization's failure to survive, the answers have enormous practical value.

The Research Implications. Research on team performance, including team formation, requires that the unit of analysis be the teams, not the individual members. Individual traits may be the focus in team formation or in replacing departed members, but an individual-level criterion may not be sensible. If a group is truly functioning collaboratively, it may be next to impossible, even if it were desirable, to identify and assess individual contributions to team performance.

I have given particular emphasis to the unit of analysis problem because the traditional validation paradigm does not address it. Perhaps the correlational paradigm could be used at work unit or total organizational levels if both predictors and criteria are measured at these levels, but it would not be likely to work well very often. Every predictor–criterion pair of scores is a data point in correlation analysis. It is hard to get enough data points at individual levels to provide reliable correlations; it is still harder if the data points describes work units or organizations. Quasi-experimental methods (see chapter 8) are needed to evaluate predictive hypotheses at the higher levels of analysis (Schneider, 1996).

THE ROLE OF POLICY IN PERSONNEL DECISIONS

Staffing decisions are usually made by managers, not by test developers, staff psychologists, or human resources specialists. Managers and testers occupy different worlds with different concerns. Managers, despite occasional talk about wanting the best people, are typically interested in making a decision to fill a vacancy with a satisfactory person as quickly as possible (Herriot, 1993); testers and other human resources people are concerned with technical matters like validity, reliability, and compliance with government regulation (Heneman, Huett, Lavigna, & Ogsten, 1995). Most managers have not had training in psychometrics or test theory, they may not understand the assessments, and they may hold unwarranted views about tests. Some managers distrust tests and rely very little on test scores. What is worse (from a tester's perspective) is a manager who believes tests are great, who defers to test scores even when evidence shows them invalid, and who simply does not hear warnings or qualifications about them. Such true believers are surprisingly common and harder to work with than the skeptics. To deal with both kinds of unwarranted views, some staff psychologists establish rules for using tests, and perhaps for using other assessment procedures, in making decisions, and these rules may have the weight of organizational policies. They might specify preferred score levels or patterns, circumstances that may justify overlooking poor scores, or further information to be considered along with scores on tests or other systematic assessment procedures. In some organizations individual managers are free to decide for themselves whether to use test information and, if so, how to use it. That seems an odd policy. If an investment has been made to develop and validate a systematic, standardized assessment program, it is strange to let unsystematic, individual whims determine how or whether the results of the investment will be used.

Strange it may be, but it is likely when managers are not satisfied with established staffing procedures (cf. Heneman et al., 1995). Those responsible for the assessment portions of staffing programs must expect resistance, at least passively, from managers who do not understand or appreciate the applicable scientific and legal principles.

Decisions are influenced by information, and personnel research should provide useful, understandable information. Decisions are also influenced by policies—policies of individual decision makers, of organizations, and of the society in which the organizations exist. Procedural justice requires that individual decision makers in an organization follow common information, policies, and principles.

Organizational Policies

Too often, organizational policies are not explicitly stated. As a result, bases for decision vary remarkably across time and across decision makers. Many kinds of policies might be developed, but here I concentrate on four that I consider especially important for personnel decisions.

Time Perspective. Usually, at least with cognitive predictors, performance is easier to predict for the immediate than for the remote future (e.g., Hulin, Henry, & Noon, 1990). Criteria collected 3 months after hire will ordinarily be predicted more successfully than criterion data collected after 3 years. Performance is ordinarily predicted better for the short run than for the long run and better for the immediate job than for one to which the person may later be promoted. Many organizations make initial selection decisions based on potential for growth into more responsible assignments. A time perspective measured in years rather than months may make more organizational sense. The alternative is a policy based on more accurate predictions, a shorter time perspective. The choice may not be organization-wide. For lower level jobs, promotion may be too unlikely to consider in decisions. For higher level positions, however, policy may favor a longer perspective.

A long-range policy makes several assumptions. First, it assumes organizational stability, that the skills needed for the immediate decision will remain relevant for a long time—even though the longer the interval between decision and outcome, the greater the opportunity for intervening events to reduce prediction accuracy. A further assumption is that decisions to hire, promote, or give special training are followed with appropriate developmental experiences. A genuinely long-term perspective is feasible only in an organization in which human resources functions are genuinely integrated in systems thinking (Schneider, 1996; Senge, 1990). In too many organizations, selection is left to one department, training to another, career development to yet another, and the systematic development of relevant managerial policies and practices to no one in particular. Such organizations would do well to choose shorter term objectives.

Governmental regulations in the United States favor short-term objectives. The *Uniform Guidelines* (EEOC et al., 1978) say that an employer may consider an applicant for a job at a level higher than the entry job if, "within a reasonable period of time and in a majority of cases," persons hired at the lower level will in fact reach the higher. An organization seeking a pool of qualified people from which to choose for a promotion-from-within policy, say 5 years from now, is not permitted under this rule to look beyond the job level attained by a *majority* of those remaining employed after 5 years. This provision should be reconsidered.

Decision Factors. On what basis will personnel decisions be made? A researcher is tempted to suggest that decisions (other than termination decisions) be based only on information shown by research to be useful predictors of future performance or behavior. If the suggestion were followed, how could decisions be made in situations where no such research finding is available? To make the same point somewhat differently: A tester would suggest that decisions be based on test scores validated for the decision at hand. But what is to be done in situations where there are no validated test data and not much hope of getting any?

Let us dispense quickly with various forms of favoritism. Jobs and other special opportunities often go to friends, friends of friends, family members, or other favorites. Where favoritism rules, there is little point in assessing potential contribution to the organizational enterprise. Bolda (1989) reported that a distribution of valid test scores of recommended favorites in one organization was essentially normal with a mean at about the 50th percentile on national norms; in short, he argued, selecting by favoritism is pretty much like random selection.

Cognitive tests are generally valid methods of assessment, and non-cognitive tests and inventories (personality measures, psychomotor skill tests, etc.) are often valid predictors of performance. A basic policy question is whether to use such tests. Obviously, I favor testing. In my view, the basic question is not whether to test but whether, for a given purpose, there are any better alternatives. In the face of public pressure, the United States government has at least twice abandoned certain tests (one a generalized test for civil service applicants and the other a test used by local employment services for referring candidates to local employers) without considering the relative merits of remaining alternatives. To be as mild about it as possible, such policy decisions are seriously flawed.

Testing has been perennially under criticism while simultaneously being touted as a magic solution to organizational (and social) problems. In education, for example, some critics have consistently sought to reduce or eliminate testing, whereas others have induced legislatures to mandate testing for competence of graduates or of teachers. In employment, critics have claimed variously that tests induce conformity, invade privacy, deceive applicants, or discriminate unfairly against minorities and women. Such criticisms, although often carried to extremes, have enough core truth in them that, if the policy is to use tests, organizational leaders must include safeguards against such problems in their policies. Fairness is difficult to define, let alone to determine, but many organizations have written policies declaring the intent to be fair in decision making; some also have written policies against invasion of privacy or deception. Whether such policies are really in effect depends less on memos than on the behavior of key organizational leaders.

Policy formation should consider the use of unvalidated assessments. Tests can be validated, but they are fallible, and the fallibility leads to calls for treating them as just one factor in decision (e.g., National Commission on Testing and Public Policy, 1990). Arguments can go both ways. The calls usually assume, without evidence, that decisions based on other factors are enriched by them.

Minimal Versus Maximum Qualifications. Simon (1979), discussing rational thought or decision, introduced the concept of *satisficing*. He argued that rational people, faced with a set of potential actions or decisions, each with its own outcome utility, will search until they find one with an outcome that is "good enough," or "satisficing." An older alternative model of thought suggested that people consider all options and choose one that will maximize payoff.

Under a satisficing suggestion, decision makers consider applicants serially until one is found who is expected to be good enough rather than choosing the very best among all applicants. The suggestion is attractive, but it has pitfalls, such as defining good enough qualifications. An alternative policy is to search for excellence persistently, seeking the best of the available candidates, operationalized by the top-down procedure. Even under an excellence policy, practical problems may lead to the use of something like a satisficing policy. For example, where hiring for a job is done almost daily, the best may differ from day to day. The result may be a fairness issue, in which a person rejected today actually has higher qualifications than one accepted yesterday.

Reporting Scores to Decision Makers. If tests are used, how should scores be reported to decision makers? Different options may have different implications for designing research to evaluate test use.

1. *Report actual scores.* It may be the policy to report raw scores (or perhaps percentile ranks or standard scores). Under this option, there is a technical and ethical obligation to train decision makers so that they become qualified to interpret scores and score differences.

2. *Report scores as passing or failing.* Many managers are more comfortable with the idea of a passing score. That preference, coupled with the belief of many staff psychologists that decision-making managers cannot be trained or trusted to interpret test scores, often leads to cut scores. Among candidates who have passed, the manager is free to choose at random or to base choices on any available information he or she thinks is valuable. This may help gain acceptance (although I do not know that it does), but it has a bizarre feature. Despite investment in testing and test validation (usually before setting a cut score), actual decisions are based on the chance availability of information that may be interpreted and valued differently by different managers.

3. *Report expectancies or predictions.* I know of no one who reports predicted criterion levels rather than test scores, but it might be a good idea. It is, however, common to report scores and concomitantly provide expectancy charts for their interpretation. An expectancy chart gives the probability of achieving a designated criterion level (e.g., a rating of satisfactory, or above average production level) for various score ranges.

Developing such charts and teaching managers how to use them can promote competent use of assessments. Responsibilities of an organization's staff psychologist, in my judgment, include assuring that decision makers are trained in (a) the nature of the genuine qualifications for jobs and how they are determined, (b) the fundamental principles for evaluating their assessment, (c) the defensible and indefensible inferences from scores, and (d) acceptable limits of individual judgments to override ordinarily defensible inferences. A further responsibility is to provide judgment aids to help managers use test data sensibly in making decisions. Expectancy charts can help with both responsibilities. They help teach their users that prediction of either success or failure is rarely certain but is instead probabilistic—perhaps the most difficult lesson to learn for people who tend to view choices as either right or wrong. They help teach the principle that the probability of success usually gets greater at higher score levels—and the fact that the rate of increase depends on the level of validity. It should be easy to add a further lesson that the probability within a score interval is better at the high end of the interval than at the low end. A good training program would also teach the limits of predictions based on an expectancy chart. It should be made clear that some limits are established by the limits of the criterion chosen; a chart showing the probability that a candidate will achieve a superior level of production gives no clue about that candidate's probable performance on a criterion the decision maker might have preferred, such as dependability or ingenuity.

4. *Report score bands.* "Banding" is somewhat controversial; it is discussed in chapter 10. For now it is sufficient to identify a *score band* as a set of scores in which score differences are deemed too trivial to consider. What is reported is not the score of an individual but the individuals who all have the same (or trivially different) scores. The logic of the procedure is that decision makers choose among these on some basis other than the test score.

5. *Report only interpretations.* For higher level or nonroutine jobs, expectancy charts and score bands may not be sensible. Test scores and assessment ratings may be reported as narrative, descriptive interpretations rather than as scores or score ranges. Such a report can be a judgment aid and also serve instructional functions; it can define the qualifications assessed, distinguish them from other traits with which they might be confused, and provide detailed descriptions of the inferences that can (and cannot) be drawn from their assessment.

Conflicting Information. Many managers are impatient with probabilities; they want definite answers from the assessment process. The impatience may be enhanced immeasurably if two or more predictions or probability statements are not compatible, as when the probability of being satisfactory on one criterion is high but is accompanied by a low probability of being satisfactory on another. An example might be a candidate for a job who is predicted to perform job tasks very well but also presents a strong risk of being counterproductive in other ways.

Training in assessment use should stress the reality that people do not necessarily function at the same level in all aspects of work-related performance. A nice, cooperative person is not necessarily a good performer; one who works carefully and does not make any errors may not get much done. Incompatible predictions require reconciling judgments, not denunciation of the assessments. Where the research program permits predictions of independent criteria, managers should be trained to expect some incompatibility and to use a predetermined policy to deal with it.

Monitoring Assessment Use.   Training wears off. Personnel decisions like selection, promotion, or transfer are not everyday events for individual managers, and the training may be old when assessment results are reported. Human resources specialists, if themselves competently trained, can work with the manager, refreshing principles of interpretation, as part of the decision process.

Public Policy

America can no longer rely on an abundant, largely unskilled labor supply. Instead the nation is facing a shrinking entry-level workforce increasingly composed of linguistic, racial, and ethnic minorities, whose talents are often underdeveloped and underutilized. Yet in a global economy that is becoming more competitive and interdependent, we need more than ever the talents of all our people. (National Commission on Testing and Public Policy, 1990, p. ix)

Several policy concerns are embedded in that statement. It includes concerns over national productivity, changing demography of the workforce, equal employment opportunity, and the need for individual personal development for those whose opportunities have been limited. Concern for equality of employment opportunity has been a dominant preoccupation in employment testing since the passage of the Civil Rights Act of 1964. Legal responsibilities will influence discussions of research design throughout this book, in detail in chapter 4, but they should not blot out attention to other relevant social issues. Debate over privacy as a constitutionally protected right is illustrated in concern over invasion of privacy in personality testing, expressed long ago in Congressional hearings (Amrine, 1965) and still a worry. There is no clear public consensus about testing; some people condemn nearly all testing, but others demand tests (e.g., to certify teachers or the worthiness of students for diplomas).

Is it in society's best interest that each organization look only for the very best applicants? In the interests of productivity, it probably is. However, if that were to become a nearly universal practice, it might create a chronically unemployed segment of society; people at the low ends of the distributions of qualifying characteristics would find jobs only in rare times of virtually full employment. Should criteria always be directly related to performance? Would it not serve the broader social interest to consider also predicting a criterion measure such as psychological well-being (Clegg & Wall, 1981)? Policy debates that focus on one pet concern and ignore others, without considering balances and trade-offs, are narrow, unintelligent, and in the final analysis counterproductive.

Policy on Testing. The National Commission on Testing and Public Policy (1990) made eight policy recommendations for testing in schools and the workplace. Their focus is on multiple-choice paper-and-pencil tests, but their recommendations provide food for thought concerning other methods of assessment as well. I comment on four of them that are explicitly related to workplace assessment:

"Testing programs should be redirected from overreliance on multiple-choice tests toward alternative forms of assessment" (p. 26). Suggested alternatives include trainability tests (e.g., presenting training materials and then testing to see what has been learned from them), work sample tests, biodata, and assessment centers. The list of alternatives could be extended—and is in subsequent chapters. Extending the list should carry the caveat, however, that multiple-choice tests currently have an edge over alternatives in demonstrated reliability and validity; the move to any alternative should be carefully evaluated.

"Test scores should be used only when they differentiate on the basis of characteristics relevant to the opportunities being allocated" (p. 27). This principle is well-established in employment testing, although far too many employers simply assume the relevance of tests on the basis of test names.

"Test scores are imperfect measures and should not be used alone to make important decisions about individuals . . . ; in the allocation of opportunities, individuals' past performance and relevant experience must be considered" (p. 30). I am bothered by this recommendation. The assessment of experience is usually not done very well. Where past performance— where past behavior more generally—is relevant to the decision at hand, I agree fully that it should be considered. The first part of the

recommendation is what makes me uneasy. True, test scores are imperfect measures and imperfect predictors. So also are other forms of assessment. To recommend that imperfect measures should not be used alone is to recommend that sets—sometimes unique sets—of imperfect measures be considered jointly. The unstated assumption is that the imperfections will cancel out, thereby improving the predictions made. I know of no evidence to support that assumption. Public policy is usually formalized in laws; I would hate to see laws requiring that decisions be based combining valid but imperfect test scores with other information that may be even more imperfect and have no known validity.

"Research and development programs must be expanded to create and use assessments that promote the development of the talents of all our peoples" (p. 32). In a sense, the research being recommended seems to be going on already. However, the Commission's interest is in research on test use as a tool for developing society's human resources to the fullest. It is a useful recommendation. Indeed, recommending research over rhetoric would be useful in an America of "discontents" (Handlin & Handlin, 1995, p. 15).

National Policies. Different nations have different employment policies, whether by law or by custom. Most Western countries have laws requiring nondiscrimination in employment, many modeled somewhat after Title VII of the 1964 Civil Rights Act in the United States. Public policy in many European countries includes the idea of full employment and a fundamental *right to work* (Shimmin, 1989). Such a policy discourages dismissal of employees even when old jobs disappear and the emerging new ones call for wholly different skills. The basic idea of a predictive hypothesis, postulating that a certain variable will predict performance on a specific job, does not fit such a policy. New models will be needed but are unlikely to be developed in the United States where statutes and governmental regulations, if not public opinion, have so far frozen the traditional orthodoxy of predicting performance on a specific job. A policy of long-term, stable employment could be served, of course, by a sequence of on-the-job hurdles, such as a meaningful and varied probationary period. That would require a level of psychometric integrity in evaluating probationary performance on the job that, so far, seems unlikely.

The prevailing habits in a society may be as influential as formal policy. Again referring to Europe, the tradition of individual assessment in hiring, a tradition similar to that of vocational counseling, is stronger than the American tradition of using tests as screening devices, predictors, and aids to decision. Perhaps this accounts for European calls for more democracy in selection: greater attention to a candidate's perspective, the inclusion of workers' representatives in determining selection procedures, more emphasis on self-selection, and a greater emphasis on social and developmental psychology than on the psychology of individual differences (Shimmin, 1989, p. 117).

THEORY AND PRACTICE IN PERSONNEL DECISIONS

Theories abound in law, in literature, in music, in philosophy, and in science. A scientific theory not supported by data is only a hunch—even if it is an internally consistent hunch, logically derived from sensible premises. A good scientific theory is, of course, internally consistent and derived from sensible premises, but is also derived from and supported by data. Scientific research is more often intended to find flaws in an existing theory than to find reasons for its expanded use. Scientific theory is meant to be treated with informed skepticism.

It is almost ritualistic to ask for more theory in industrial and organizational psychology. Good practice requires an understanding of what one is doing in developing, evaluating, or using assessment procedures and in making operational decisions based on them, and such understanding *is* theory. A previously developed, well-supported, relevant theory can promote understanding, but the mere existence of something called a theory does not assure it. I call for more attention to theory to promote understanding of what is done in practice. Too much of what we know about personnel assessment and decision making, and therefore too much of this book, is limited to techniques. Better theories of work and work effectiveness can sharpen, prune, and expand those techniques and improve decisions.

Unfortunately, many theories of work are irrelevant to making personnel decisions. Tenopyr (1981) pointed out that a theoretically oriented chapter on organizational behavior in the *Annual Review of Psychology* made only passing reference to the word *ability*; few theories include competence, skill, or ability as major components. It is as important for a theory to be informed by practice as for practice to be informed by theory.

An unfortunate but growing gap seems to separate academic science from organizational practice. Academics often seem interested only in building theories. Practitioners tend to decry the triviality and impracticality they perceive in academic theories, yet some of the theories they decry could inform many practical decisions in their organizations. There is, or should be, a symbiotic relationship between theory and practice and between basic and applied research (Leibowitz, 1996). The dictum attributed to Kurt Lewin, that nothing else is as practical as a good theory, holds true. To be practical, however, a theory has to be a good one, internally consistent, supported by solid data, and tested in practice to find out how well it works beyond the boundaries of an experimental situation.

A third member of this symbiotic partnership is society at large. Both science and practice must heed the social issues and problems they solve or exacerbate. Many scientific questions, especially in the behavioral sciences, stem from the concerns of that larger society. Practice within an organization is also practice within that larger society; for many practical decisions, both the relevant scientific foundations for decisions and their social effects must be considered.

Consider Fig. 1.4. Traditionally, personnel research was limited to the shaded area, and usually to a single outcome, perhaps with some attention also to organizational needs. Research was validation of assessment procedures, valid ones were used to make personnel decisions that had a predicted outcome. Science was limited to methods, judgment was not trusted, and if a broader community was considered, it was only as a source of external recruits.

The tradition needs the expansion implied in Fig. 1.4. I place organizational needs at the top to remind us of the purpose of assessment and decisionmaking; they are articulated as the judgments of organizational leaders, and they define outcomes that are wanted or perhaps those that are not. Research and development (R & D) must be informed by the needs and be consistent with them (Schneider, 1996). Research must also be evaluated in informed judgments before being used in decision making; if the evaluations are favorable, decisions should be based on the research. Research should not be limited to just one chosen criterion; decision outcomes are likely to be plural. They need to be understood. Understanding requires human resources research and development programs at least on par with product and market research, and these programs work best if informed by competent theory. Outcomes and reasons for unexpected ones can be clarified through research, providing further practical guidance for decision making. All of this occurs within a community (including the larger society) that experiences the effects of many of the outcomes and seeks to influence them. With a well-funded R & D program, unspecified and unintended outcomes, whether relevant to community concerns or to organizational needs, could be investigated much as medical research looks for side effects of medical interventions.

We must not, however, be so wrapped up in psychometric research, statistical analyses, and the contextual influences of the community that we forget that the purpose of all this is to optimize the process by which

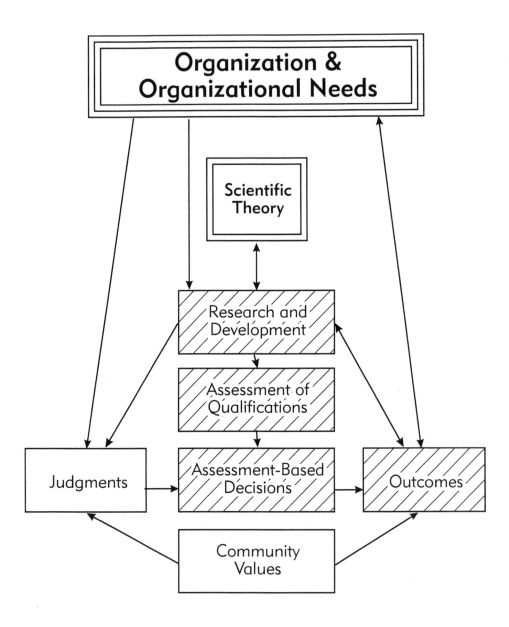

FIG. 1.4. Schematic representation of forces on personnel decisions and outcomes.

some people get rewards and opportunities and others do not. The central focus of this process—the one intended to reach the best possible outcomes—is a decision. Decisions are based on assessments; they also imply judgment, preferably informed judgment. Some of the information comes from research and theory; some of it comes from knowing the organization's needs; some of it comes from community influences.

Theory and practice both begin with a need to be filled, a question to be answered, or an observation to be explained and understood. In assessment, the explanation typically invokes a hypothesized scientific construct, stemming perhaps from prior theory, hunch, or experience. In psychology, a construct is an idea or concept constructed or invoked to explain relationships between observations. A hypothesis about a construct is to be tested, not merely swallowed; typically there are several plausible answers or explanations, so there can be several hypotheses. Theory development proceeds by eliminating some of these optional hypotheses by targeted research studies, perhaps until only one is left. If all are eliminated, new ones must be sought; if several survive, a full understanding may require their integration. Many ritual calls for theory ignore the symbiosis of theory and practice. Assessment practice should be guided by theory; it is a theoretical act, even if an unacknowledged one, to choose a variable to be evaluated as a predictor. The corollary, however, is that accumulated evidence of how well that variable actually predicts criteria of concern, and of possible influences on that prediction, should also inform, guide, and modify more formal theory development.

I hope that this book contributes to improved use of assessment practices, and to improved methods of assessment, by encouraging thinking about the development of such a theory.

REFERENCES

Adkins, C. L., Russell, C. J., & Werbel, J. D. (1994). Judgments of fit in the selection process: The role of work value congruence. *Personnel Psychology, 47*, 605–623.

Albright, L. E., Glennon, J. R., & Smith, W. J. (1963). *The use of psychological tests in industry.* Cleveland: Howard Allen.

Alvares, K. M., & Hulin, C. L. (1973). An experimental evaluation of temporal decay in the prediction of performance. *Organizational Behavior and Human Performance, 9*, 169–185.

American Psychological Association, American Educational Research Association, & National Council on Measurements Used in Education. (1954). Technical recommendations for psychological tests and diagnostic techniques. *Psychological Bulletin, 51*, 201–238.

Amrine, M. (1965). Special issue: Testing and public policy. *American Psychologist, 20*(11), 857–870.

Barrett, G. V., Phillips, J. S., & Alexander, R. A. (1981). Concurrent and predictive validity designs: A criticial reanalysis. *Journal of Applied Psychology, 66*, 1–6.

Bolda, R. A. (1989, May). *Favoritism in selection.* (Available from Robert A. Bolda, Ph.D., 11127 Erdman, Sterling Heights, MI, 48078.)

Bowman, M. L. (1989). Testing individual differences in ancient China. *American Psychologist, 44,* 576–578.

Bray, D. W., Campbell, R. J., & Grant, D. L. (1974). *Formative years in business: A long-term AT&T study of managerial lives.* New York: Wiley.

Cannon-Bowers, J. A., Tannenbaum, S. I., Salas, E., & Volpe, C. E. (1995). Defining competencies and establishing team training requirements. In R. A. Guzzo & E. Salas (Eds.), *Team effectiveness and decision making in organizations* (pp. 333–380). San Francisco: Jossey-Bass.

Chatman, J. A. (1991). Matching people and organizations: Selection and socializing in public accounting firms. *Administrative Science Quarterly, 36,* 459–484.

Clegg, C. W., & Wall, T. D. (1981). A note on some new scales for measuring aspects of psychological well-being at work. *Journal of Occupational Psychology, 54,* 221–225.

Dachler, H. P. (1989). Selection and the organizational context. In P. Herriot (Ed.), *Assessment and selection in organizations: Methods and practice for recruitment and appraisal* (pp. 45–69). Chichester, England: Wiley.

Drever, J. (1952). *A dictionary of psychology.* Baltimore: Penguin.

DuBois, P. H. (1970). *The history of psychological testing.* Boston: Allyn & Bacon.

Dunnette, M. D. (1966). *Personnel selection and placement.* Belmont, CA: Wadsworth.

Dunnette, M. D., & Borman, W. C. (1979). Personnel selection and classification systems. *Annual Review of Psychology, 30,* 477–525.

Eels, R., & Walton, C. (1961). *Conceptual foundations of business.* Homewood, IL: Irwin.

Equal Employment Opportunity Commission, Civil Service Commission, Department of Labor, & Department of Justice. (1978). Uniform guidelines on employee selection procedures. *Federal Register, 43*(166), 38290–38315.

Fisher, K. (1994). Diagnostic issues for work teams. In A. Howard (Ed.), *Diagnosis for organizational change: Methods and models* (pp. 239–264). New York: Guilford.

Freyd, M. (1923). Measurement in vocational selection: An outline of research procedure. *Journal of Personnel Research, 2,* 215–249, 268–284, 377–385.

Greller, M. M., & Nee, D. N. (1990). Human resource planning for the inevitable—The aging work force. In M. London, E. Bassman, & J. F. Fernandez (Eds.), *Human resource forecasting and strategy development: Guidelines for analyzing and fulfilling organizational needs* (pp. 181–193). Westport, CT: Quorum Books.

Guion, R. M. (1965). *Personnel testing.* New York: McGraw-Hill.

Guion, R. M. (1976). Recruiting, selection, and job placement. In M. D. Dunnette (Ed.), *Handbook of industrial and organizational psychology* (pp. 777–828). Chicago: Rand-McNally.

Guion, R. M., & Cranny, C. J. (1982). A note on concurrent and predictive validity designs: A critical reanalysis. *Journal of Applied Psychology, 67,* 239–244.

Guion, R. M., & Gibson, W. M. (1988). Personnel selection and placement. *Annual Review of Psychology, 39,* 349–374.

Hale, M. (1982). History of employment testing. In A. K. Wigdor & W. R. Garner (Eds.), *Ability testing: Uses, consequences, and controversies, Part II* (pp. 3–38). Washington, DC: National Academy Press.

Handlin, L., & Handlin, O. (1995). America and its discontents. *American Scholar, 64,* 15–37.

Heneman, H. G., III, Huett, D. L., Lavigna, R. J., & Ogsten, D. (1995). Assessing managers' satisfaction with staffing services. *Personnel Psychology, 48,* 163–172.

Herriot, P. (1993). Commentary: A pardigm bursting at the seams. *Journal of Organizational Behavior, 14,* 371–375.

Hodge, R. W., & Lagerfeld, S. (1987). The politics of opportunity. *Wilson Quarterly, 11*(5), 109–127.

Hollenbeck, J. R., LePine, J. A., & Ilgen, D. R. (1996). Adapting to roles in decision-making teams. In K. R. Murphy (Ed.), *Individual differences and behavior in organizations* (pp. 300–333). San Francisco: Jossey-Bass.

Howard, A. (1991). New directions for human resources practice. In D. W. Bray (Ed.), *Working with organizations and their people: A guide to human resources practice* (pp. 219–251). New York: Guilford.

Hulin, C. L., Henry, R. A., & Noon, S. L. (1990). Adding a dimension: Time as a factor in the generalizability of predictive relationships. *Psychological Bulletin, 107,* 328–340.

Jackson, S. E., & Associates. (1992). *Diversity in the workplace: Human resources initiatives.* New York: Guilford Press.

Kaufman, H. G. (1974). Relationship of early work challenge to job performance, professional contributions, and competence of engineers. *Journal of Applied Psychology, 59,* 377–379.

Kipnis, D. (1994). *Organizational psychology in the year 2000.* An address to the American Psychological Society, July, Washington, DC.

Klimoski, R., & Jones, R. G. (1995). Staffing for effective group decision making: Key issues in matching people and teams. In R. A. Guzzo & E. Salas (Eds.), *Team effectiveness and decision making in organizations* (pp. 291–332). San Francisco: Jossey-Bass.

Landy, F. J. (1986). Stamp collecting versus science: Validation as hypothesis testing. *American Psychologist, 41,* 1183–1192.

Landy, F. J., Shankster-Cawley, L., & Moran, S. K. (1995). Advancing personnel selection and placement methods. In A. Howard (Ed.), *The changing nature of work* (pp. 252–289). San Francisco: Jossey-Bass.

Lawshe, C. H. (1948). *Principles of personnel testing.* New York: McGraw-Hill.

Lawshe, C. H. (1959). Of management and measurement. *American Psychologist, 14,* 290–294.

Lawshe, C. H., & Balma, M. J. (1966). *Principles of personnel testing* (2nd ed.). New York: McGraw-Hill.

Leibowitz, H. W. (1996). The symbiosis between basic and applied research. *American Psychologist, 51,* 366–370.

Meehl, P. E. (1954). *Clinical versus statistical prediction.* Minneapolis: University of Minnesota Press.

Meehl, P. E. (1967). What can the clinician do well? In D. N. Jackson & S. Messick (Eds.), *Problems in human assessment* (pp. 594–599). New York: McGraw-Hill.

Mohrman, S. A., & Cohen, S. G. (1995). When people get out of the box. In A. Howard (Ed.), *The changing nature of work* (pp. 365–410). San Francisco: Jossey-Bass.

Mumford, M. D., Stokes, G. S., & Owens, W. A. (1990). *Patterns of life history: The ecology of human individuality.* Hillsdale, NJ: Lawrence Erlbaum Associates.

National Commission on Testing and Public Policy. (1990). *From gatekeeper to gateway: Transforming testing in America.* Chestnut Hill, MA: National Commission on Testing and Public Policy, Boston College.

Offermann, L. R., & Gowing, M. K. (1993). Personnel selection in the future: The impact of changing demographics and the nature of work. In N. Schmitt & W. C. Borman (Eds.), *Personnel selection in organizations* (pp. 385–417). San Francisco: Jossey-Bass.

Paterson, D. G. (1957). The conservation of human talent. *American Psychologist, 12,* 134–144.

Rose, R. G. (1993). *Practical issues in employment testing.* Odessa, FL: Psychological Assessment Resources.

Schmidt, F. L., & Hunter, J. E. (1977). Development of a general solution to the problem of validity generalization. *Journal of Applied Psychology, 62,* 529–540.

Schmitt, N., Gooding, R. Z., Noe, R. A., & Kirsch, M. (1984). Meta-analyses of validity studies published between 1964 and 1982 and the investigation of study characteristics. *Personnel Psychology, 37,* 407–422.

Schneider, B. (1987). The people make the place. *Personnel Psychology, 40,* 437–453.

Schneider, B. (1996). When individual differences aren't. In K. R. Murphy (Ed.), *Individual differences and behavior in organizations* (pp. 548–571). San Francisco: Jossey-Bass.

Schneider, B., & Schmitt, N. (1986). *Staffing organizations* (2nd ed.). Glenview, IL: Scott, Foresman.

Schuler, H., Farr, J. L., & Smith, M. (Eds.). (1993). *Personnel selection and assessment*. Hillsdale, NJ: Lawrence Erlbaum Associates.

Senge, P. M. (1990). *The fifth discipline: The art and practice of the learning organization*. New York: Doubleday.

Shimmin, S. (1989). Selection in a European context. In P. Herriot (Ed.), *Assessment and selection in organizations: Methods and practice for recruitment and appraisal* (pp. 109–118). Chichester, England: Wiley.

Simon, H. A. (1979). *Models of thought*. New Haven: Yale University Press.

Smith, P. C. (1985). *Global measures: Do we need them?* The Division 14 Scientific Contributions Award Address to the American Psychological Association, Los Angeles.

Snyder, C. R., & Fromkin, H. L. (1980). *Uniqueness: The human pursuit of difference*. New York: Plenum.

Sussman, M., & Robertson, D. U. (1986). The validity of validity: An analysis of validation study designs. *Journal of Applied Psychology, 71*, 461–468.

Sutherland, S. (1996). *The international dictionary of psychology* (2nd ed.). New York: Crossroad.

Tenopyr, M. L. (1981). Trifling he stands. *Personnel Psychology, 34*, 1–17.

Tenopyr, M. L. (1994). Science, measurement, and social problems. An address to the American Psychological Society, July, Washington, DC.

Thorndike, R. L. (1949). *Personnel selection: Test and measurement techniques*. New York: Wiley.

Tiffin, J. (1942). *Industrial psychology*. New York: Prentice-Hall.

Tyler, L. E. (1978). *Individuality: Human possibilities and personal choice in the psychological development of men and women*. San Francisco: Jossey-Bass.

Tziner, A., & Eden, D. (1985). Effects of crew composition on crew performance: Does the whole equal the sum of its parts? *Journal of Applied Psychology, 70*, 85–93.

Vicino, F. L., & Bass, B. M. (1978). Lifespace variables and managerial success. *Journal of Applied Psychology, 63*, 81–88.

Yoakum, C. S., & Yerkes, R. M. (1920). *Army mental tests*. New York: Holt.

2

Analysis of Selection Problems

Organizations face many challenges, only some of which are addressed best by improving assessment-based decisions about individual candidates or employees. Before deciding how to assess, what to assess, or even whether to assess, organizational challenges, needs, and problems—and appropriate courses of action—must be identified. The scope of organizational need analysis is broader than can be addressed fully or appropriately in this book; it is important, however, to consider need analysis as providing the context in which selection (in the broad sense of the term) and other interventions can be compared for appropriateness.

Need analysis may lead directly to a hypothesis about appropriate selection procedures; often, however, hypothesis development requires analysis of individual jobs (or job families). Traditionally, job analysis has been considered the first step in building a selection system; its use is strongly encouraged in equal employment opportunity (EEO) case law. It contributes to criterion development by identifying the most important or most critical aspects of performance, and it is a basis for choosing potential predictors.

ORGANIZATIONAL NEED ANALYSIS

Need analysis is typically precipitated by a problem or by change in organizational goals. It may be done to solve a problem or to achieve a new plan. Whatever the purpose, effective need analyses generate plausible hypotheses about potentially fruitful courses of action. Some actions may be more effective than others. For example, a specific human resources (HR) problem might be addressed, among other options, by improved selection, improved training, job redesign, or changes in organizational structure or policy; informed judgments of relative effectiveness (and relative costs) of the options determine the focus of further study and action.

Effective need analysis is organization-wide in scope. Organizations function as systems, and the needs and actions that appear to focus on only one aspect of the organization will also have implications for others (see, e.g., Schneider, 1996; Senge, 1990; Weisbord, 1991). In the HR problem, whichever action is chosen influences the other HR activities, and the influence extends beyond HR functions. Effective need analysis is also forward looking; it typically fosters useful organizational change. Indeed, titles of recent books emphasize change (Howard, 1994; Kanter, Stein, & Jick, 1992). Senge (1990) described healthy organizations as *learning organizations*—those that not only adapt to external change but continue to learn and change in response to external events and internal experience.

If organizational need analysis suggests improved selection (organization-wide or for a specific job or job family) as potentially useful, it also suggests criteria important enough to measure and predict. It may also identify personal characteristics needed. In these ways, organizational need analysis can be sufficient to identify a selection problem that cuts across organizational units.

Goals, Outcomes, and Organizational Needs

An admittedly cynical view of the financial world of corporate mergers and takeovers is that it denies or ignores the idea that organizations may have built-in purposes, that an organization exists to produce specific goods or services. Long-term objectives such as building brand loyalty, or a reputation for excellence, or long-term profitability, or even organizational survival seem to have been replaced by short-term objectives such as a good-looking financial report for the most recent quarter. Organizational leaders may go to great lengths to build long-term mission statements, but organizational rewards, perhaps driven by shareholder expectations, tend to focus on short-term objectives.

This apparent shortsightedness should be a matter of serious concern to the larger society. Productivity, especially long-range productivity, is essential to the economic growth and stability of a society or a nation, and all-encompassing concerns for the current quarter do little to enhance it. Maybe it is overly romantic to suggest that organizations should include the goal of contributing something of value to the communities and societies that support them—something more intrinsic than "community service" by managers—such as producing goods and services in the public interest. Nevertheless, I suggest that inclusion of such goals, over the long run, make the attainment of the less "romantic" goals possible.

Work and Organizational Outcomes

The many kinds of organizational outcomes on the road to lofty objectives need to be placed in a preferential hierarchy (Kahn, 1977). The hierarchy is not stable. In any given organization, at any given time, some outcomes pose greater threat or offer greater promise for goal achievement than do others; they should have top priority. Priorities cannot be set by consulting a handbook; they must be set after careful thinking by organizational leaders who keep the major, common objectives clearly in mind and (setting internal competition aside) consider critically the procedures and intermediate outcomes that may lead to (or thwart) their attainment.

Outcomes Wanted and Outcomes To Be Avoided

Economic outcomes at an overall organizational level include profit or loss, stability or fluctuation of stock value, market share, and so on, each of these somewhere on a short- to long-term continuum. Reasonable profit, stable or rising stock value, and growing market share please organizational leaders. Losses, fluctuations, and low market share are not pleasing; they are problems to be avoided or overcome. Overcoming them may call for new strategy, capital investment, high level personnel changes, changes in manufacturing processes or inventory controls, or human capital investments such as supervisory training or hiring more highly skilled employees.

People-oriented outcomes include performance (quality, quantity, and stability); workforce stability and dependability (exhibited in such statistics as turnover, absenteeism, or tardiness); workforce health and well-being (or, in the negative, worker stress and stress-related illness, or accidents); employee attitudes and motivation (job satisfaction, organizational commitment, willingness for or resistance to change, and other examples in an endless list); or responsible versus counterproductive or antisocial behavior (helping or mentoring others, acceptance of and commitment to organizational goals, or "self-starting" vs. undesirable actions such as excessive use of alcohol or drugs, pilfering, theft, or even sabotage). Some of these are pleasing; others are problems. Some are organization-wide; others may be concentrated in specific units.

Consider performance problems. An enormous number of variables may contribute to them; formal organizational variables, informal groups, physical conditions, a variety of individual needs and desires, technological factors influencing raw materials and processes may be as influential, or more so, than personal abilities, background, and motivation (Sutermeister, 1976). Most of them are fairly stable but modifiable through organizational initiatives. The problem is to decide which organizational initiatives are most likely to be effective. To do so, questions must be asked and answered. What, in detail, is the nature of the precipitating performance problem? What potential contributing factors can be identified, and which of them (if any) can clearly be ruled out? Answers must come from those most knowledgeable about the problem; they can include declining morale, worn equipment, lax selection, inadequate training, poor quality of tools and work aids, poor supervision—or failure to select people based on assessment of genuinely important qualifications. Each of these suggests its own corrective action, and several of them may be needed. New selection procedures may or may not be among them.

Most jobs will be done better if filled by people selected because of their relevant traits. Finding a relevant basis requires thought and work, but focusing on designing, developing, or using procedures for personnel decisions should not obscure the importance of other management tools. Too often, managers assume that better selection in the personnel office will fix whatever is wrong (see Howard, 1994, p. 3, for an example).

Workforce instability due to excessive turnover or absenteeism or tardiness is an outcome to be avoided—not necessarily through staffing. Instability on assembly lines or in customer contact jobs may create temporary but potentially devastating results. One may be that customers cannot be given firm promises about what will get done or by what date.

Instability may be due to a general "I don't care" organizational culture, or a widespread morale problem (Schneider, 1996). Those who quit may be the ones the organization will miss, or maybe those it can well do without. Absences may be attributed to a consistent few, or everyone may do it. If stability problems center in only some work units, the solution might be better selection—but better selection of unit managers who do not make showing up for work an unpleasant choice for employees.

Questions about accidents and health problems must also be asked and answered. Do such problems reside in individual temperaments or skills or in the work environment? A heavily stressful environment can cause illness; an unsafe environment can cause accidents. Choosing people with greater stress tolerance or less clumsiness may help if the stresses and hazards are inherent in the nature of the work, but changing the environment is likely to be more fruitful. Even so, individual differences in reactions to environmental factors should be considered. In one interesting and provocative article, Olian (1984) suggested that genetic screening may identify job candidates who are hypersensitive to toxins in the work environment at levels not troublesome to most people; such screening could be useful either for selection or for placement in less hazardous areas.

Counterproductive behavior is a catchall phrase including such undesirable behaviors as quitting before being fully trained, absence, tardiness, belligerence with customers or fellow employees, "bad-mouthing" the organization, sabotage of products or equipment, excessive drug or alcohol use, or the theft of goods or cash. Although integrity testing is becoming a major topic in employment testing, attempts to select people who are honest may be less fruitful than establishing better security systems, changing systems of reward and punishment (e.g., Greenberg, 1990), or other organizational changes—including a slow but valuable change in the general organizational climate (Schneider, 1996).

Some Approaches to Organizational Need Analysis

A systematic, effective approach to analyzing organizational needs is elusive, partly because of habitual ways of thinking and long-held values. Too often, people closely associated with social psychology emphasize the social aspects of organizational problems, human factors specialists emphasize equipment and process, and personnel selection researchers emphasize employment testing as solutions to organizational ills. And people in these groups emphasize people-oriented problems and solutions more than financial or engineering problems and solutions. Defining an organization's needs depends on one's habitual focus.

Social values also play a role. Identifying a hierarchy of desirability (or undesirability) of potential work or organizational outcomes is an exercise in values clarification. What are the relative values of quantity and quality of production? Of production and employee health and safety? Of organizational well-being and the well-being of the community in which the organization exists? Organizational needs cannot be defined solely in terms of organizational self-interest; they must also be defined in terms of the social zeitgeist which, at this time in history, includes great concern for the quality of life, the specific quality of work life, and the provision of opportunities for those whose opportunities have previously been limited.

Because people responsible for different functions, or who have developed different personal habits and values, are likely to view a precipitating issue or problem differently, organizational need analysis must attempt to gain expression of different views and, to the extent possible, reconcile them.

Conference Methods. Dialogue among people with different views is an essential condition for effective communication, which in turn is essential for clear identification and definition of problems—and their solutions (Schein, 1993). One approach to need analysis, then, gets knowledgeable people together to talk about an issue or problem. Talking may range from argumentative to inhibited; whether the talking is called discussion, dialogue, conferring, or argument, this approach generally is aided by an outside consultant who can facilitate the process and its focus. The first product of the discussion is clearer and more honest identification and communication of differences. Others may include agreement to disagree after the different perspectives are understood or, it is hoped, consensual definition of the problem and setting priorities in studying alternative courses of action.

A facilitator might try to assure that questions like these are asked and answered:[1]

1. What is the nature of the issue or problem at hand?
2. What is its history?
3. What are the perceived outcomes or consequences of the problem? What observations have led to these perceptions? How consistent or how variable are people's perceptions?
4. What is occurring system-wide that is or might be related, or that might have an impact on the investigation of the issue or problem?

The facilitator probes beyond these basic questions, the probes varying depending on the answers. Questions of structure, processes, key systems or subsystems, policies, and external forces might be explored. Systemic issues that are part of the overall problem are explored that they might be either identified or systematically ruled out. The approach is planned in advance only in a general way; it is not a standardized approach to be used consistently for all organizations, all issues, or all problems.

Organizational Assessment Surveys. On the other hand, survey methods are often proposed precisely because they are standardized. Questionnaires can be developed after interviews and conferences to be sure that major questions are asked. They do not, of course, shout out the optimal corrective actions; appropriate action is inferred by people making informed judgments. We cannot be sure of the validity of the inferences because they are influenced by the habits and values of those who draw them (Cooper & O'Connor, 1993; Peters & O'Connor, 1988). Their validity is not, however, the main issue; the main point is the kind and quality of thinking they promote—broad, comprehensive thinking that should take place before assuming that a favorite course of action, such as improving selection, is needed. Any need analysis is useful when it helps people in organizations overcome force of habit in studying organizational problems.

---

[1]I'm indebted to Vicki V. Vandaveer for these summarizing questions.

Those of us interested in employee selection habitually think good selection procedures are always needed. The alternative—either poor selection or some form of random selection—does not make much sense. However, our habit requires two qualifications. First, selection has only a chronological priority; it is the *first* organizational intervention influencing the achievement of organizational goals, but subsequent interventions can enhance or destroy the benefits of effective selection. Second, changes in selection or assessment practices may not be very effective; indeed, under some conditions (e.g., poor equipment), efforts to improve selection cannot work unless other problems are solved first.

Raising questions about unwanted outcomes should be systematic and ongoing (Beer & Spector, 1993). To some organizational experts, *systematic* requires careful measurement, and *ongoing* means periodic. Scheduled surveys can meet both requirements. Van de Ven and Ferry (1980) developed the Organizational Assessment Instruments (OAI) for survey research; it has five components, or modules:

1. A *performance module* for recording data on performance efficiency at an overall organizational level, at work unit levels, and for individual jobs also provides a process for clarifying and operationalizing values and goals of organizational policy.

2. A *macroorganizational module* for studying organizational structure provides a procedure for recording data about the organization as a whole (e.g., organization chart, span of control at specific position levels, etc.); these data permit a measure of perceived authority or influence for different kinds of decisions.

3. An *organizational unit module* guides the study of tasks, structures, or processes in work units using questionnaires and records.

4. A *job design module* is a set of questionnaires for analyzing jobs or positions, incumbents, job functions, and employee attitudes. It helps in developing a task list and in identifying areas of specialization. It is more than an extensive job analysis form, seeking data on satisfaction, motivation, and salary. It also asks about individual differences among incumbents, apparently limited to the usual demographic variables and one personality variable (growth need strength); the instrument seems remarkably unconcerned with job knowledge, mental ability, or psychomotor skills.

5. An *interunit module* with questionnaires to study the control and coordination within and between interdependent work units or positions; some sample items and instructions are shown in Fig. 2.1.

Organizational assessment is, like other forms of assessment, a measurement process, and validity concerns are relevant, but appropriate use of the OAI does not stop with simple scoring or tallying of responses.

IN A PREVIOUS SURVEY, THE CONTACT PERSONS FROM THE FOLLOWING UNIIT[S] IN XYZ FIRM REPORTED THAT THEY COORDINATED IN SOOME WAY WITH YOUR ORGANIZATIONAL UNIT DURING THE PAST SIX MONTHS

UNIT 1. Name _____ Contact person _____

UNIT 2. Name _____ Contact person _____

UNIT 3. Name _____ Contact person _____

UNIT 4. Name _____ Contact person _____

WE WOULD LIKE YOUR PERSPECTIVE ON THESE INTERUNIT RELATIONSHIPS. PLEASE ANSWER THE QUESTIONS FOR EACH OF THE DESIGNATED OTHER UNITS INDIVIDUALLY. WRITE IN THE APPROPRIATE COLUMNS THE NUMBER FROM THE ANSWER SCALE THAT REFLECTS YOUR MOST ACCURATE ANSWER TO EACH QUESTION FOR EACH OTHER UNIT. BE SURE TO USE THE COLUMN WITH THE SAME UNIT NUMBER AS THAT DESIGNATED ABOVE TO ANSWER THE QUESTIONS FOR EACH OF THE OTHER UNITS. IF NO NAMES ARE WRITTEN ABOVE FOR UNITS 2-4, THEN LEAVE THOSE COLUMNS BLANK.

	UNIT 1	UNIT 2	UNIT 3	UNIT 4

1. *How well* are you *personally acquainted* with the *contact person* in this other unit?

NO PERSONAL ACQUAINTANCE	NOT VERY WELL	SOMEWHAT WELL	QUITE WELL	VERY WELL
1	2	3	4	5

5. During the past six months, *how much* was your unit involved with this other unit for *each of* the following *reasons:*

   d. to receive or send *information* for purposes of coordination, control, planning, or evaluation?

NOT AT ALL	A LITTLE	SOME-WHAT	QUITE A BIT	VERY MUCH
1	2	3	4	5

13. During the past six months, *how frequently* have people in your unit *communicated or been in contact* with people in this other unit?

NOT ONCE	1-2 TIMES	ABOUT MONTHLY	ABOUT EVERY 2 WEEKS	ABOUT WEEKLY	ABOUT DAILY	MANY TIMES DAILY
0	1	2	3	4	5	6

17. To what extent did individuals in this other unit *hinder* your unit in performing its functions during the past six months?

DON'T KNOW	TO NO EXTENT	LITTLE EXTENT	SOME EXTENT	CONSID-ERABLE EXTENT	GREAT EXTENT
0	1	2	3	4	5

FIG. 2.1. Sample items from the interunit module of the Organizational Assessment Instruments. Adapted and abridged from Van de Ven and Ferry (1980, pp. 502–509). Used by permission of Andrew Van de Ven.

For example, if analysis indicated that one or more other units had "hindered" the work of the respondent's unit. Further inquiry would be needed to determine whether the hindrance should be attributed to interunit conflict or to perceived ineptness in the hindering unit. Perceived ineptness might suggest a need for improved selection or training, but perceived conflict probably does not.

Despite the potential usefulness of instruments such as the OAI, the organizational assessment research literature seems strangely sparse. The problem may lie in the reluctance of top executives to participate in such assessments. Beer and Spector (1993), after offering several euphemisms, finally referred to *executive blindness* to describe the defensive attitudes of executives. At the executive level, "resistance to change" takes on a new and daunting meaning. Nevertheless, given the uncertainty created by global competition and domestic deregulation, organizational analysis is necessary and executive participation in it is essential to its success. It "must do more than simply add new information to the organization; it must help organizational members acquire the willingness, skills, and ability to discuss the undiscussable" (Beer & Spector, 1993, p. 644). In the meantime, need analysis can focus on narrower, more specific categories.

Identification of Work Facilitators or Constraints. Moeller, Schneider, Schoorman, and Berney (1988) developed a *Work Facilitation Diagnostic* for diagnosing work unit problems. They reported its use in two kinds of organizations—university departments and sales units in a national tele-marketing firm. It called for job or work unit experts to identify and reach consensus on things facilitating or inhibiting effective work within the units. The method combined the discussion and questionnaire procedures, but the questionnaires were developed specifically for each organization.

Another procedure, reported by Peters and O'Connor (1988), used a questionnaire to identify situational constraints that interfered with getting work done and done well. Here the emphasis was on the work of the individual rather than of the unit. The procedure considered 11 kinds of constraints, including problems associated with job information, tools and equipment, materials and supplies, budgetary support, and so on.

Nothing in this list, of course, makes it possible to say whether a problem calls for better selection or something else; these categories can help identify criteria for evaluating whatever solutions are tried. The emphasis in this line of research is on factors in one's work environment that limit effectiveness in using one's abilities, whatever they are. Nevertheless, the kinds of questions that bother Peters and O'Connor should bother selection researchers. If people hired by old procedures or standards are thwarted in using their abilities, what gain can be expected from hiring people with even more ability to be thwarted?

Somewhat different principles and findings were reported by Olson and Borman (1989) in the development of a work environment questionnaire for the United States Army. Critical incidents were reported about especially effective or ineffective performance of Army jobs—incidents that could be attributed to situational factors not under the worker's control. Subsequent factor analysis[2] (at the item level) suggested five factors: (a)

---

[2]Factor analysis is described in chapter 6.

general situational constraints, including both lack of resources and lack of information, (b) supervisor support, (c) training or opportunity to use skills, (d) job or task importance, and (e) unit cohesion and peer support.

A General Approach to Need Analysis

Organizational need analysis is a managerial, not a research, function. Its immediate purpose is to generate hypotheses, not to test them. It must be done systematically, recognizing that the outcome of need analysis is a judgment (or a set of judgments) that can be framed in the language of hypotheses, and the quality of the judgment depends on the experience, knowledge, and wisdom of those who reach it. The best advice I can offer, whether the focus is on dialogue or on questionnaires, is to consider five general questions as carefully and with as much collaboration as possible:

1. What work outcomes are most in need of improvement? That is, what outcomes are most highly valued and not satisfactorily attained, and what ones are most deplored and too much in evidence? In either case, remedial action is needed; what priorities can be set for the importance of such remedies? Answers provide the criterion concepts for *any* hypotheses geared to improving the situation.

2. How widespread is the problem? Is it pervasive throughout an organization or organizational unit, or is it found in specific instances (i.e., specific people or specific units)?

3. At what level of analysis (organizational unit or individual) is the problem most accurately defined and approached? Consider, for example, a serious turnover problem. Should it be approached at the work unit level or the individual level or a broader organizational level?

4. What kinds of corrective actions are plausible? That is, what might reasonably, feasibly, be expected to help? What is the range or scope of sensible possibilities? Identifying a full range seems to call for the collective experience of people with a variety of backgrounds. Discussions with different people in the organization, and perhaps with outside consultants, can provide an initial list of plausible actions.

5. How effective have the various options been in prior use, in this organization or elsewhere? It is probably this question that gives some edge to attempts to improve individual selection decisions when the problem is one of improving performance levels; most other activities lack the strong research base, with the relatively substantial levels of predictive power and utility, that characterizes the testing literature.

Insiders—people who know the organization intimately—are necessary participants in seeking the answers; this is not something that a manager can delegate to an outside consultant and merely await the report—although an outsider can facilitate the discovery of answers and the reduction of internal barriers to their expression. Collectively, participants must have a wide range of knowledge, of interest, and of technical expertise—more than is likely to be found in any one person. The best procedure for organizational need analysis may be to form a task force of bright people who know the organization from a variety of perspectives, augment them as necessary with hired specialists in various problem solutions or in discussion processes, and let them study, question, argue, and arrive at their best collective judgments.

JOB ANALYSIS

When organizational needs require improved personnel decisions for people on specific positions, jobs, or groups of jobs, job analysis (or position analysis) is necessary. Jobs are analyzed to understand them clearly enough to know which variables or performance constructs should be predicted and to identify variables or constructs that might be effective predictors—that is, to develop predictive hypotheses.

Some Definitions

Following McCormick (1979), with some additions and liberties of my own, here are some more or less standard definitions:

Position: The duties and tasks carried out by one person. A position may exist even where no incumbent fills it; it may be an open position. There are at least as many positions in an organization as there are people.

Job: A group of positions with the same major duties or tasks; if the positions are not identical, the similarity is great enough to justify grouping them. A job is a set of tasks within a single organization or organizational unit. This definition does not preclude flexibility. Members of a self-contained work unit may, on any given day, be doing different tasks, but each member may also be expected to do on another day any task the group as a whole must do.

Occupation: An occupation is a class of roughly similar jobs, found in many organizations and even in different industries. Examples include attorney, computer programmer, mechanic, and gardener.

Job family: A group of jobs similar in specifiable ways, such as patterns of purposes, behaviors, or worker attributes. Pearlman (1980) applied the *family* concept to occupations, but the term is usually applied to sets of jobs within an organization.

Job analysis: Job analysis is a study of what a jobholder does on the job, what must be known in order to do it, what resources are used in doing it, and perhaps the conditions under which it is done. What the jobholder does may be defined in several ways: as tasks, classes of duties or responsibilities, broad activities, or general patterns of behavior. What must be known includes job knowledge and job skills. What resources are used may include those the person may bring to the job (relevant experiences, general abilities, or other personal characteristics), tools and materials used (e.g., manuals or handbooks, supplies, or equipment) or the work products of other jobs or work units.

Element: The smallest feasible part of an activity or broader category of behavior or work done. It might be an elemental motion, a part of a task, or a broader behavioral category; there is little consistency in meanings of this term.

Task: A step or component in the performance of a duty or activity. A task has a clear beginning and ending; it can usually be described with a brief statement consisting of an action verb and a further phrase.

Activity (or *responsibility* or *duty*): A relatively large part of the work done in a position or job. It consists of several tasks related in time, sequence, outcome, or objective. A clerical example might be "sorting correspondence" or "handling cash" or "preparing reports." All tasks grouped under these activities are done for a common end. One task in correspondence sorting might be "identify letters requiring imme-diate response." Putting together a report includes such tasks as laying out or formatting tables and charts, typing text, typing tables or charts, proofing for errors, and perhaps duplicating, collating, and binding copies of the reports. Activities and tasks are both components of jobs, but activities are usually considered more general, more encompassing.

Essential function: A term introduced in the *Americans With Disabilities Act (ADA)*, which defines a "qualified individual with a disability" in part as one who "can perform the essential functions of the employ-ment position that such an individual holds or desires" (Schneid, 1992, p. 28). The meaning of many terms in the ADA, including this one, waits on court decisions and developing case law. In the meantime, EEOC regulations identify three considerations: (a) whether the position exists for the purpose of carrying out the function, (b) whether the number of employees who can perform the function is limited, and (c) whether the function is highly specialized so that people are hired because of their special expertise or ability to carry out the function (Schneid, 1992, pp. 33–34).

Job description: A written report of the results of job analysis. A job description is usually narrative, sometimes given in a brief summarizing paragraph. It may be more detailed. Where job analysis was done by survey methods, the description may include listings of task statements found to define or characterize the job being studied, along with statistical data.[3]

Job specification: Required qualifications for the job (or position), as revealed in the job description. Depending on the job or job category, specifications can include legal requirements (age, licenses, residency, etc.), education, skills, or perhaps assessment standards (although the latter requires research beyond the job description).

Detail Versus Generality in Job Analysis

In job analysis, a job as a whole is analyzed into component parts; the level of detail can vary widely. Detailed statements may be best for developing training programs, but more general statements are more useful for identifying criteria and predictors for selection (Lawshe, 1987).

Clarity counts more than detail. Lawyers and courts want more detail than is useful. Too much detail can muddle matters; what is needed is a clear enough understanding of the job to move on to the next step, the development of one or more predictive hypotheses. These require the wisdom, insight, and even introspection of people who know and understand the job. Job analysis can tap the wisdom and knowledge of job experts. Highly detailed, cover-all-bases, formal job analysis may not be needed at all—except possibly for convincing others that the analysis was done well.

Information *needed* is not necessarily the information *desired*. In an age of litigation, actions are governed as much by what is prudently filed away as by what is actually needed. Fine details may not be needed for any purpose beyond a trial. Failure to convince a trial judge that the job analysis was "adequate"—lots of questions asked, results recorded in a lengthy job description along with lots of statistical analyses—may be the

---

[3]In a peculiar pair of definitions, the *Uniform Guidelines* defines job analysis as "a *detailed* statement of work behaviors. . . ." and job description as "a *general* statement of job duties. . . ." (Equal Employment Opportunity Commission, Civil Service Commission, Department of Labor, & Department of Justice, 1978, p. 38307, italics added). Obviously, these definitions were written without much regard for the meanings of the verbs *to analyze* or *to describe*. In my judgment, the failure to recognize a difference between the process of analyzing something and the description of the results has resulted in mischief in court cases.

basis for an adverse decision if a selection procedure is legally challenged (Kleiman & Faley, 1985).

Establishing Job Relatedness. Job relatedness of a predictor has historically been shown by a correlation between it and an important criterion measure—a criterion-related validity coefficient. It may also be shown by logical argument based in part on job analysis. Doing so requires a two-step argument. First, it must be demonstrated from job analysis that the hypothesis of a predictive relationship between the predictor construct and the criterion construct is a sensible, well-reasoned one. Then, it must be shown that the measures actually used as predictors are indeed valid measures of the predictor traits. This two-step argument needs more detailed job information than required for criterion-related validation. Thorough, detailed coverage of the job is best assured by asking many questions and getting answers from many people who know the job well—enough people to provide reliable responses. Where the evidence of job relatedness is to be based in substantial part on such consensus, descriptions of the job, the component tasks, and the possible predictors should be complete. Part of the argument of job relatedness is that nothing substantial has been overlooked.

New Jobs. Thoroughness is also needed when analyzing a job that does not yet exist. Jobs may be created because organizations are new or changed, or because of technological, environmental, or social change. The analysis of jobs merely anticipated is really planning, and careful planning is usually detailed.

Detail should not be confused with rigidity. When a new position is authorized within an organization, detailed statements of expected duties and responsibilities are needed to specify characteristics of people required to fulfill them. If the specifications are too detailed and rigid, it may be next to impossible to find someone to meet them. Moreover, an incumbent usually puts his or her own imprint on the position, capitalizing on personal strengths and minimizing personal weaknesses. The position itself undergoes some change as do the positions of those that interact with it. Rigid adherence to an initial plan can result in less than optimal performance for everyone.

METHODS OF JOB ANALYSIS

Fundamentally, all job analysis consists of observing what can be seen and asking questions about what cannot. A job analyst watches, questions, understands, and summarizes the information received in a job description. Some jobs can be adequately analyzed just by watching workers work; others require extensive questioning by interview or survey. Job incumbents can be observed or questioned in several ways; a job analysis that provides the best job understanding usually uses several of them.

Observation and Interviews

Direct observation consists of watching—and taking appropriate notes. It is the most obvious way to learn about a job; it makes minimal demand on, and causes minimal disruption for, the incumbent being observed. But it poses problems. The incumbent may work differently in the presence of an observer, perhaps going more by the book than is necessary, or perhaps puffing up the job by adding things not ordinarily done, or perhaps failing to do some things because of nervousness about being watched. It is time consuming and expensive. To observe a sample of several workers requires extensive observer time and skill. The biggest problem, however, is that much work is simply not observable. Questions must be asked and answered to augment and interpret what can be directly observed.

Direct observation can be supplemented in several ways. Videotapes help, particularly if observation of fine detail is needed; a tape can be studied over and over to be sure that everything done has been noted. One might listen in on telephone or computer activity. One might try doing the job oneself for a kind of introspective observation, although such amateur efforts are often misleading.

Introspective reports of incumbents may be useful, especially in the development of work diaries (Freda & Senkewicz, 1988). In this procedure, a job incumbent who does a variety of things during a work period identifies with a brief note what is being done at specific times during the day. The record allows the analyst not only to identify tasks and activities but sequences. Knowledge of sequences permit verifiable inferences about activities or tasks that are prerequisite to others and, in that sense, of major importance. Such inferences should be verified in a follow-up interview of the incumbent who filled out the diary.

Interviews are useful in other ways. An initial interview with an incumbent before work observations can clarify the nature and purpose of the observation and reassure the person being watched. It can also provide a broad view of the job being observed and help in planning the observations. Will the work be done all in one place, or will it be necessary to move around to see everything? Are certain crucial aspects of the work likely to be done so quickly that only an alert observer will see them? Such questions, answered during an initial interview, can guide the analysis. Verification interviews after observations can verify (or modify) other information, and the other information may stimulate incumbents to mention things otherwise overlooked (Gael, 1988a).

The advantage of interviewing as an adjunct to observation seems obvious. What may be less obvious is that questioning, as in an interview, may need to be augmented with observations. Landy (1989) pointed out several problems with interviewing alone. One is that interview results may describe what should be done ideally or in theory rather than the way the job is actually done. Another is that experienced incumbents often have forgotten just how they do a job; part of it becomes virtually automatic, done without thought and therefore not reported.

Most problems with observational methods can be softened by using multiple observations: observing several different incumbents, working in different locations or on different shifts, will increase the reliability of major observations and also produce information that might otherwise be lost. Observation alone is probably not a sufficient approach to job analysis, but it is at least a preliminary stage even if other approaches are anticipated.

United States Employment Service Methods. The most extensive job analysis program was that of the United States Employment Service (USES) in developing the *Dictionary of Occupational Titles* (DOT; United States Department of Labor [USDL], 1977). The brief DOT descriptions were backed by extensive descriptions based on combined methods of observation and interviewing. The procedures were described in the *Handbook for Analyzing Jobs* (United States Department of Labor [DOL], 1972) and in Droege (1988). The job analysis report form not only provided a record of information but served to structure the analysis itself. I am not going to describe the form or procedure because a new procedure is being developed for a revised DOT. However, the early USES form is helpful even for job analysis on a smaller scale; working loosely from it, I offer a 10-item list of information to seek from observations and questions:

1. *Establish a descriptive job or position title that will be locally meaningful and that will make sense to prospective candidates.* If the title seems too broad for local purposes, choose a subtitle or limiting phrase to clarify initial communication about the job.

2. *Identify and describe the major tasks and activities.* If solving problems is one task; describe the type and difficulty of problems to be solved and the incumbent's latitude for decision making (i.e., what decisions can the incumbent make and what requires approval). Order activities in importance; the order should be reached by a consensus of those participating in the analysis: incumbents, supervisor, HR staff person, and perhaps others who know the job well.

3. *Identify relationships to other jobs or positions* in the organization or externally. What jobs of other people depend on the work done by the incumbent, or what tasks of the incumbent depend on what is done on other jobs? To what job might an incumbent be promoted; from what background job might a qualified candidate be promoted to this one? What personal interactions are expected with people on other jobs? To whom (the role or position, not the person) is the incumbent to report? How closely supervised is work on this job likely to be? Does the incumbent supervise others; if so, does he or she make personnel decisions about those supervised or merely monitor the progress and quality of the work done?

4. *Identify and describe machines, tools, equipment, and work aids used on the job, and describe how they are used.* Identify also the specific tasks or activities for which they are used.

5. *Identify and describe materials, products, or resources used on the job, and describe how they are used.* Again, identify tasks, activities, or problems where these are used; if not obvious, the nature of their use should be clarified. Remember that other people may be resources providing information or service or material. Identify resources available for use when needed even if not routinely used.

6. *Identify and define specialized terms used in the job,* organization, or occupation that anyone claiming qualifications for the job should know.

7. *Describe the major characteristics of the work context,* the physical environment (particularly health or safety hazards), hours or shifts worked, social context, and any job-specific policy constraints.

8. *Identify any externally demanded qualifications* such as licenses or bonds.

9. *Identify specific educational and experience requirements.* Ordinarily, expressing these requirements in terms of diplomas or degrees received or number of years is inadequate. Express educational requirements in terms of courses or course content used on the job, ranging from basic literacy to specialized academic programs. Express experience requirements in terms of expected knowledge or skill levels learned through prior experience.

10. *Identify knowledge, skills, abilities, or other personal characteristics required to do this work.* Are some abilities—cognitive, physical, sensory, social, or perceptual—demonstrably essential? What would be desirable, if not so essential, and why? If the work environment includes hazards, would certain personal characteristics tend to reduce or to exacerbate these hazards? Answers to most of these questions should be clearly relevant to performance of one or more of the major job activities or tasks; glittering generalities have no place in a job description.

The last four items in the list, as a set, help establish *job specifications* (or *personnel specifications*). They identify charactistics of candidates, or of their backgrounds, to be assessed in determining candidate qualifications for the job. As *hypothesized* predictors, they may need research to establish validity and minimum qualifications, but some of them (such as the demand for a license) may be bases for selection—or rejection—for reasons other than validity.

Functional Job Analysis (FJA). A job analyst must distinguish what people do on the job from what gets done as a result; FJA provides a grammar for doing so. Things people do are called *worker functions* (Fine, 1955, 1988; Fine & Getkate, 1995); they are action verbs in task statements in which the subject is always understood to be the worker, statements fleshed out in subsequent phrases more fully describing the task, as in Fig. 2.2. Instructions for using the FJA approach to develop an inventory of task statements is available in Fine and Getkate (1995, pp. 29–41).

The system assumes that everything workers relate to in the course of their work can be subsumed under three headings: people, data, and things. These headings are even broader than they seem; interactions with *people* may include analogous interactions with animals; *data* includes a full spectrum of information, ideas, statistics, and so on; and *things* include virtually any tangible object touched or handled, such as complex machinery, books, or the top of the desk. A small set of verbs has been ordinally scaled for each of the three functional categories; the most recent of the evolving versions is shown in Fig. 2.3. There have been some

Sentence Element	Task Statement
Subject: Who?	(Always the worker; unstated)
Action verb: Perform what action?	Schedules
Object of verb: To whom or what?	Appointments, meetings, events
Phrase: Upon what instruction? Source? Specificity?	Supervisor, caller, or memo; usually a vague "set it up", perhaps with deadline
Phrase: Using what tools, equipment, work aids?	Calendar, appointment pad, telephone, or conference room schedule book as needed
In order to...: To produce or achieve what? (Expected outcome)	To assure presence of those expected to be present

Task Statement: Schedules appointments, meetings, or events according to instructions from supervisor or memo, or requests received from callers, using as needed appointment pads, calendars, telephone, or conference room schedule book in order to assure that all those expected to be present at the meeting or event will be able to do so.

FIG. 2.2. An example of a task statement developed by task sentence structure in functional job analysis.

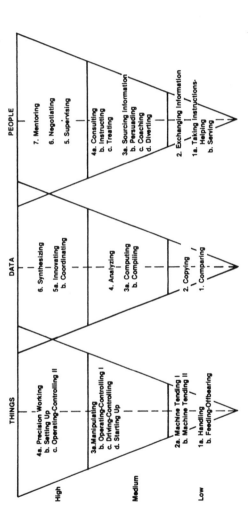

NOTES:

1. Each hierarchy is independent of the other. It would be incorrect to read the functions across the three hierarchies as related because they appear to be on the same level. The definitive relationship among functions is within each hierarchy, not across hierarchies. Some broad exceptions are made in the next note.

2. Data is central since a worker can be assigned even higher data functions although Things and People functions remain at the lowest level of their respective scales. This is not so for Things and People functions. When a Things function is at the third level (e.g., Precision Working), the Data function is likely to be at least Compiling or Computing. When a People function is at the fourth level (e.g., Consulting, the Data function is likely to be at least Analyzing and possibly Innovating or Coordinating. Similarly for Supervising and Negotiating. Mentoring in some instances can call for Synthesizing.

3. Each function in its hierarchy is defined to include the lower numbered functions. This is more or less the way it was found to occur in reality. It was most clear-cut for Things and Data and only a rough approximation in the case of People.

4. The lettered functions are separate functions on the same level, separately defined. The empirical evidence did not support a hierarchical distinction.

5. The hyphenated functions, Taking Instructions-Helping, Operating-Controlling, and so on, are single functions.

6. The Things hierarchy consists of two intertwined scales: Handling, Manipulating, Precision working is a scale for tasks involving hands and hand tools; the remainder of the functions apply to tasks involving machines, equipment, vehicles.

FIG. 2.3. The people-data-things hierarchies in functional job analysis. From Fine, S. A., & Getkate, M. (1995). *Benchmark tasks for job analysis: A guide for functional job analysis (FJA) scales.* Mahwah, NJ: Lawrence Erlbaum Associates. Reprinted with permission.

65

difficulties in ordinality. Only the numbers in the hierarchies identify ordinal levels; letters identify functions at about the same level.

Definitions of the functions have been given in several sources, but many job analysts need examples, or benchmarks, for the various levels. This need has been met in Fine and Getkate (1995), which also includes benchmarks for four other scales for rating (a) level of prescribed or discretionary instructions to the worker, (b) reasoning development, (c) mathematical development, and (d) language development.

Critical Incidents. In the critical incident method, developed by Flanagan (1954), the job analyst meets with a group of incumbents (or others with expert knowledge of the job) and draws from them their recollections things people have done that resulted in noteworthy consequences, good or bad. For each incident, the description is limited to facts, not inferences, but it is detailed, reporting environmental contributing factors (e.g., equipment problems) or antecedents that may have contributed to the incident. Extraordinary events are more likely than ordinary ones to have memorable consequences and to be recalled, so this is not a good technique for getting complete job descriptions. It is, however, an excellent way to gain insights into crucial aspects of performance. It seems more useful for criterion development than for designing or choosing predictors.

Job Analysis Surveys. Observational and interview methods are useful when studying a single job where adequate information can be obtained from a few experts. When simultaneously studying sets of related jobs, especially in multiple locations, survey research may be the preferred method of collecting observations. It has been used in consortium research projects within broad industries. The life insurance industry has long sponsored such research, and, for validation of selection procedures, similar large scale studies have been done for the electric power industry and the petroleum industry, among others. Job analysis in such research typically uses a job description checklist or inventory as a questionnaire.[4]

Surveys are useful where many people have jobs with the same or similar titles but do different things. Even where jobs seem standard, such as police patrol officers, work performed may vary widely. A survey of job incumbents permits study of virtually all positions to determine

---

[4]In a checklist, one simply checks the statements that describe the job and makes no response to others. In an inventory, a response is given to each statement along a scale; the scale includes an opportunity to say the statement is not part of the job. Although I acknowledge the distinction, I generally use these terms interchangeably.

whether there is enough uniformity among them to treat them as one job, or whether the positions should be grouped into different jobs with distinguishable patterns of duties.

Survey methods of job analysis are amenable to psychometric analysis. They call for the development of inventories of items of job information that can be combined into internally consistent, scorable job dimensions. Dimension scores can identify differences or similarities of positions within jobs, quantify aspects (e.g., importance) of major duty categories, or be used to infer predictor constructs of greatest potential job relevance.

Quantification helps even for analysis of a single job or position in a single location. Scores on major job dimensions clarify the degree to which one feature of a job is more important than another, and help in choosing criterion or predictor constructs.

Task Inventory Development

McCormick (1959) distinguished two types of inventories, *job-oriented* (or *task-oriented*) and *worker-oriented*. A job-oriented inventory is a set of brief task or activity statements (usually much briefer than the example in Fig. 2.2), each of which may describe what is done and what gets done as a result, for example, (a) "translates correspondence from French to English," (b) "coordinates departing, en route, arriving, and holding aircraft by monitoring radar and communicating with aircraft and other air traffic control personnel," or (c) "writes special reports." Each example includes an action verb saying what is done and a further phrase describing what is accomplished. Correspondence is changed into words English-only readers can comprehend, aircraft activities are the things coordinated, and reports are written.

In contrast, worker-oriented inventories describe work activities in terms that describe behavior, not accomplishments. McCormick's example, instead of describing a baker's job with the statement "bakes bread" (a job-oriented statement), described the activity with statements such as "manually pours ingredients into containers" and "observes condition of product in process" (McCormick, 1959, p. 411). These are worker-oriented in that they describe behaviors that might be required in a variety of jobs, for example, chemists, some quality-control inspectors, or candymakers.

The core of a job-oriented task inventory is a set of task statements, or items, each with its action verb, direct object, and necessary delimiting phrases. Developing the set of statements is usually an iterative process in which the preliminary statements are edited, perhaps several times, during the various phases of inventory development.

A first step in item writing is to consult available information such as training manuals, earlier job descriptions, organization charts, reference materials or manuals used in doing the work, or procedural guides and work aids. Such documents provide initial understanding of the job and may, perhaps, suggest some preliminary task statements. Information gleaned from documents can be augmented (or corrected) through on-the-job obervations and interviews with knowledgeable people; such information can add to the pool of preliminary task statements.

Using Job Experts. Job experts, meeting in groups, can add, delete, or edit statements. Job experts may be incumbents, supervisors, engineers, quality-control staff, trainers, occupational safety officers, job evaluation staff, or others who have relevant knowledge about the targeted jobs. Job experts are often known as subject matter experts (SMEs), but job expert is a better, more descriptive term.

Item Categories. Grouping inventory items into categories promotes clarity. Where the main purpose of an inventory, or a part of one, is to identify required traits or competencies to serve as predictors, items may be grouped into general kinds of requirements. The *Job Requirements Inventory* developed by Lawshe (1987) has 14 categories of items, grouped further under four more general categories, as shown in Table 2.1. The *Position Analysis Questionnaire* (PAQ) groups worker-oriented statements

TABLE 2.1
Outline of a Job Requirements Inventory

Performance Domain	Number of Items
Basic education proficiency requirements	
A. Understanding printed or written material	5
B. Performing calculations	9
Other proficiency requirements	
C. Understanding oral communication	4
D. Making oneself understood orally	4
E. Making oneself understood in writing	6
F. Understanding graphic information	3
Decision making and information processing requirements	
G. Exercising mechanical insight	7
H. Making estimates	5
I. Making choices and/or solving problems	5
Physical and sensory requirements	
J. Making visual or auditory discriminations	6
K. Using hands or fingers in work activity	4
L. Making gross body movements	4
M. Climbing or balancing	2
N. Exercising strength and/or endurance	12

Note. From Lawshe (1987). Reprinted with permission.

into information-processing categories. In multipurpose inventories, task items might be grouped under broader activities.

Writing Items. Inventory items must be descriptive but brief. They may be written by staff members or consultants, or in conference by groups of experts. They may be written at various levels of specificity. General statements are usually preferable to highly specific ones, but not always; what seems important is to keep the level at least somewhat similar across statements. Unfortunately, there seems to be no standard method for doing so. I offer a suggested, but untested, method:

1. Write preliminary items, each on a card, without concern for level of generality.
2. Have job experts sort them, independently, into sets with fairly consistent content.
3. Conduct a consensus meeting to reconcile differences in items placed in the different content sets.
4. Within each set, have each expert arrange the items in a hierarchy from most specific to most general, placing the most general at the top of the stack with more specific statements below to illustrate it.
5. Conduct a consensus meeting for a final arranging of statements and to judge the similarity of level among statements topping the sets. If the experts think those statements are comparable in generality, inventory development may be complete, but items judged too general or too specific probably need editing; if the top item in a hierarchy is excessively general, items lower in the arrangement may fit better.

Response Scales. Several options exist for the kinds of responses to be made. For a simple checklist, the response may be a check mark or the absence of one to show which tasks actually occur on the job. Even that simple response is ambiguous without clearer instruction. Does a checked statement describe something done occasionally if the person who usually does it is not available, something trivial that any available person would do, or critically important things?

A variety of scaled responses is possible, as shown in Fig. 2.4. In each case, the nature of the responses defines the measurement purpose of the scale; for example, a task difficulty scale asks how long it takes to learn to do the task, and an importance scale asks for responses ranging from unimportant to crucial. Ambiguity remains, whether responses are scaled or are dichotomous. Distinguishing between adjacent points in a scale may depend as much on a respondent's use of language as on the job.

Two or more response scales are typically used. Ratings of importance or criticality are almost always requested. Ratings of complexity or task

Relative Time Spent Compared to Other Tasks	Part of Job
0- Never do task	1- Definitely not
1- Very small amount	2- A minor part
2- Small amount	3- A moderately important part
3- Same amount	4- A major part
4- Large amount	5- A critical part
5- Very large amount	

Importance	Task Difficulty—Absolute Scale
1- Unimportant	1- Short demonstration only (less than 1 hour)
2- Minor importance	2- Over 1 hour up to and including 8 hours
3- Important	3- Over 1 day up to and including 1 week
4- Very important	4- Over 1 week up to and including 1 month
5- Critical	5- Over 1 month up to and including 3 months
	6- Over 3 months up to and including 6 months
	7- Over 6 months up to and including 1 year
	8- Over 1 year up to and including 2 years
	9- Over 2 years

Scales for Knowledge, Skill, and Ability Items

Relative Importance	Usefulness
0- Not important at all	1- Not useful
1- Much less important than others	2- Slightly useful
2- Less important than others	3- Moderately useful
3- About the same as most other	4- Very useful
4- More important than others	5- Extremely useful
5- Much more important than others	

Scales for Job Demand or Job Characteristics Items

Frequency of Occurrence	Characteristic of Position
5- Very often	1- Not characteristic
4- Often	2- Slightly characteristic
3- Sometimes	3- Moderately characteristic
2- Occasionally	4- Almost completely characteristic
1- Rarely	
0- Never	

Degree of Involvement

1- Assist	I aid or help someone else to perform the task, or I carry out the task under relatively close supervision. The other person(s) is primarily accountable for the action.
2- Do	I perform the task independently or with very minimal supervision; I am primarily accountable for action.
3- Do and Supervise	I perform the task and supervise others in the task performance.
4- Supervise only	I give orders/instruction, followed up by personal observation/monitoring. Do not take part in the action itself but am accountable for its overall accomplishment

FIG. 2.4. Some examples of task inventory response scales. From Drauden, G. M. (1988). Task inventory analysis in industry and the public sector. In S. Gael (Ed.), *The job analysis handbook for business, industry, and government* (Vol. 2, pp. 1050–1071). New York: Wiley. Reprinted by permission of John Wiley & Sons, Inc.

difficulty can help target levels of ability to be assessed. Frequency of task occurrence, or time spent on it, are commonly used scales. It is often important to ask whether the task can be performed as soon as one gets on the job or only after extended training or experience. Multiple scales are used because analysts want a variety of task information, but they may also increase reliability of ratings by forcing greater attention to them. A problem with multiple response scales, however, can be that the distinction seen by the investigator may not make much difference to respondents. Task inventories often call for ratings of both importance and frequency of performance; correlations between these scales often approach 1.0, suggesting that they mean the same thing to respondents. Nevertheless, both scales may be necessary. The correlations only approach unity; they are not perfect. There *are* tasks that take up a lot of time, or recur frequently, but are not very important; there *are* tasks that are rare but are immensely important when they need to be done.

The distinctive features of a job might define it and its critical components or its essential functions. A distinctive feature might be one that (a) takes up the bulk of the respondent's work time, (b) is crucial to some important work outcome (something would not result, or would not turn out well, if the task were not done effectively), or (c) no one else does it. Such tasks seem to me to define the job; to differentiate among somewhat similar jobs, I have come to use a response scale that combines all three. On a 4-point response scale, the responses may be:

0. I *do not do* the work described in this statement.
1. This statement describes something I may *occasionally* do, but it is neither an important nor a frequent part of my work.
2. This statement clearly *describes* my work; I do it, but it is not very time consuming, nor as important as other things I do, nor unique to my job.
3. This statement *defines* my job either because it is one of the most important things I do, or because it describes my work a great part of my time, or because no one else in my work unit is responsible for doing it.

Actual wording changes in different surveys because I prefer that the job experts choose wording they think communicates best for a given survey. Whatever the precise words, the scale is a composite of three scales and may therefore seem ambiguous. However, it has a unifying theme, job definition, and job experts seem not to have been bothered by the ambiguity.

A Comment. Surveys have largely replaced earlier forms of job analysis based on observation and interview. There are good reasons. Selection research has become less parochial, particularly in industry-wide consortia. Moreover, survey research helps identify differences in work done under a common title—differences that may affect the kinds of traits to be assessed. Nevertheless, mass survey techniques may be overdone; one unfortunate reason for survey use is the threat of litigation where quantity of data often seems rewarded more than quality.

Inventory Research and Data Analysis

Pilot Studies. Inventories should be pretested for clarity and content. Christal and Weissmuller (1988), writing with a lot of experience with job analytic surveys, said that not even changes should be made in established survey instruments or procedures "without extensive pretesting" (p. 1038). One kind of pretest asks a few people to read instructions and complete the inventory, "thinking aloud" throughout. As they verbalize their thoughts, ambiguities, unintended meanings, and other problems come to light. At some point, the draft inventory should be given to a sample of job incumbents. If possible, it should be completed in the presence of investigators so that problems with individual task statements or response scales can be observed and recorded. The task list for this preliminary study should include places for incumbents to identify tasks they perform that did not appear in the list.

Task Inventory Administration. If there are a great many potential respondents, or if they are widely scattered, a sampling plan is needed. In an industry-wide consortium, people in individual units are to be sampled, but a sampling plan is also needed for units to assure representation of various characteristics of the jobs being studied: organizations, organizational units, levels of responsibility, categories of job titles, or demographic groups. Experience levels should be proportionately sampled (Landy & Vasey, 1991). Proportional sampling is the usual rule, but proportionality gives way to reliability if the proportional number of cases for some characteristic is too small for reliable analysis.

The sample may include both incumbents and their supervisors. The two levels may not provide the same information. In comparisons of inventory data from supervisors and their own supervisors describing the lower level supervisory job, Meyer (1959) found substantial disagreement in the two levels, but Smith and Hakel (1979) found little difference between these two groups, professional job analysts, and a group of students. The 20-year period between the studies could account for the different findings if supervisory jobs became more crystalized in that interval. I suspect, however, that the difference is due more to differences in questionnaires. The Meyer questionnaire was an ad hoc one developed for the study; Smith and Hakel used the PAQ, an inventory form developed with extensive research.

Nevertheless, it is often desirable to gather data independently from incumbents and their supervisors. People who have held a job a long time, at least one permitting some autonomy, may come to do some things routinely without the supervisor's awareness; they may do some things so automatically that they are not aware of it themselves. Supervisors may expect some things to be done without checking to be sure they are or clearly communicating the expectation to the worker. An incumbent may inflate the nature of the job; a supervisor may disparage it. If the incumbent and supervisor both complete the survey questionnaire independently, the two versions of the job can be reconciled in meetings with job analysts. The resulting description can be more readily accepted as correct.

Sources of Unreliability and Other Error. If all job experts give identical responses to virtually all items, the job is the same for all incumbents, and the resulting job description can easily be accepted as correct. This rarely happens. One reason is statistical sampling error, inversely related to sample size. Another is that scaled responses are not perfectly reliable; there are always some sources of measurement error (see chapter 5 for a fuller treatment of reliability). Respondents bring with them their own sources of error—their values, their perspectives, the differences in their specific areas of expertise, their response styles; respondents differing in organizational status may differ systematically in all these respects. Different purposes of analysis (e.g., job evaluation versus job redesign) may induce different responses. Ambiguities in the items themselves, the kinds of responses required, the numbers of items for the different activities, and other questionnaire characteristics cause error. These things cannot be wholly avoided, but careful development and pretesting can limit their extent. A level of item generality that can be called "glittering" is too general for reliable responses. Response scales identifying whether tasks are done tend to be most reliable; task frequency responses are more reliable than time spent, and both seem more reliable than importance ratings; ratings of task difficulty are less likely to be reliable (Gael, 1983).

When expert responses to many items are less than identical, the experts may be describing different jobs or the differences may be due to error. Which interpretation is chosen requires informed judgment; there is no foolproof formula to be followed.

Data Analysis. Minimal analysis identifies means and standard deviations of responses to individual task statements. Statements with high means (or low, depending on the direction of the scale) and low standard deviations are the ones that describe the job or occupational group surveyed. However, more can be said with more analysis.

Response scales are typically short, rarely more than six levels. The proportion of responses at each level should be identified. If the distribution is bimodal, the statement may differentiate two classes of jobs among those studied, especially if there are several such statements and the differentiation is consistent across respondents.

Response scales sometimes have more categories than needed if pilot studies showed that respondents preferred extra options. A job analyst using importance ratings to learn whether a task occurs on the job, requires no distinction between responses of important, very important, or crucial. If so, the 5-point response scale may be dichotomized for that part of the analysis, putting the scale values of 1 or 2 (in Fig. 2.4) in one category and scale values of 3, 4, or 5 in another.[5]

Grouping Task Statements. Information obtained in a job analysis survey is generally used in making inferences of potentially useful (a) differentiation of jobs among those surveyed, (b) criterion variables, and (c) predictors. To facilitate these inferences, statements in a task inventory of 200–400 items—not uncommon—must somehow be grouped into reasonably independent, meaningful categories.

Two ways are used to group task statements: *rational* or *statistical* (Drauden, 1988). It can be done rationally by job experts who, independently, identify broad categories and assign the statements to them. More often cluster or factor analysis is used. The results may describe either functional dimensions of the job or specific skill requirements. A functional dimension may identify a broad task activity, performance of which might be a criterion. Skill factors, on the other hand, identify some potential predictors.

Factor analysis for job analysis inventories is widespread, but it has been criticized by Cranny and Doherty (1988). Factors, they said, are defined not by task properties but by patterns of response disagreement. Universal agreement in responses to each of two statements results in no correlation at all; where there is unanimity, no factor can emerge. Their illustrative table is reproduced in Table 2.2. The illustration assumes three dimensions of firefighter performance: protecting property, saving lives, and following rules. Different responses by different respondents, as in items 1 and 2, permit correlation (here, $r = 1.0$) and a common property-protection factor can be inferred. However, for just one job, different judges should not give different ratings; if ratings are uniform, as in the other two pairs, there is no variance, hence no correlation, hence no factor. If different respondents

---

[5]This may appear inconsistent with my position in later chapters, where I vigorously protest the dichotomization of variables in correlational analysis. I protest it in job analysis, too, if item responses are to be correlated with other variables or across items—or if factor analysis of the inventory is contemplated. However, where dichotomization leads to simplification or clarification of description, I am quite willing to advocate it.

TABLE 2.2
Hypothetical Ratings, Means, and Standard
Deviations of Six Job Behaviors by Ten Job Experts

	Item Content					
	Protecting property		Saving lives		Following rules	
Job expert	1	2	3	4	5	6
A	1	1	7	7	1	1
B	1	1	7	7	1	1
C	1	1	7	7	1	1
D	4	4	7	7	1	1
E	4	4	7	7	1	1
F	4	4	7	7	1	1
G	4	4	7	7	1	1
H	7	7	7	7	1	1
I	7	7	7	7	1	1
J	7	7	7	7	1	1
M	4	4	7	7	1	1
SD	2.45	2.45	0	0	0	0

Note. From Cranny, C. J., & Doherty, M. E. (1988). Importance ratings in job analysis: Note on the misinterpretation of factor analyses. *Journal of Applied Psychology, 73*, 320–322. Copyright by the American Psychological Association. Reprinted with permission.

do different things, or if things they do vary in importance for different jobs, a factor analysis of importance ratings *can* identify a substantive, distinguishing factor. However, spurious correlations can result from variance in respondent values and response styles. Factor analysis of importance ratings does not say whether factors reflect true position differences or spurious but correlated variance. Cranny and Doherty (1988) concluded that the procedure is "totally inappropriate" (p. 322).

I prefer rational grouping. Rational judgments may be informed by distributions of responses to task statements, but statistics are less salient than the informed inferences. It is useful to remember that task statements are grouped to assist in distinguishing jobs within a group of jobs, to define criterion measures for evaluating performance, and to infer predictors of those criteria. Any method of grouping that does not contribute to at least one of these purposes is simply not useful. I suggest the following steps (or some variant of them):

1. When the list of task statements is available, and the responses from the survey are at hand, identify the most critical or important or defining tasks from mean responses.
2. Have a panel of judges, meeting in concert, decide which two of these statements describe the most clearly different tasks.

3. Have them sort the remaining statements (from step 1) into one of three piles: like one, like the other, or like neither (presumably the "like neither" stack will be largest).

4. Repeat the process with the "like neither" pile until all of the most important or most critical task statements have been allocated.

5. Check for consistencies of responses across task statements within each group. Where inconsistencies are noted, either reassign the statement, or remove it from consideration.

Linkage of Required Worker Characteristics to Activities. Inventories typically include questions about the circumstances of job performance and about resources required for effective performance. By circumstances I mean the physical work environment, work schedule, safety or health hazards, or contact with other people. Resources may be physical resources (tools in a broad sense, materials, supplies and supply sources), financial resources (discretionary funds, noncash assets), people resources (people from whom information, advice, or help may be obtained), other informational resources (handbooks, technical manuals, job-related periodicals), feedback from work done (conformity to standards or specifications, results of inspections), or internal, personal resources (information known, cognitive skills, sensory or perceptual or motor skills, work habits, various personality or temperament traits). Personal resources include a lot, such as adaptability to circumstances and skill in the use of other resources. They include job knowledge such as that drawn from written material, tables or schematic diagrams, or accumulated experience. They include skills: how to operate a piece of equipment, how to perform a complex analysis, how to find needed information, how to use available resources—in short, how to do the tasks. An example of a questionnaire on job knowledge is shown in Fig. 2.5.

Personal resources have come to be known widely as KSAs, that is, the *Knowledges, Skills,* and *Abilities* required to do the work well. Sometimes the term is expanded to KSAPs or KSAOs, where the letter O or P stands for "other personal characteristics." (One colleague likes to refer to SKAPs, and Gael (1988b) refers to KASOs, both acronyms more easily pronounced but less often encountered.) I am not fond of these terms, in part because of problems distinguishing skills from abilities, or knowledge from skills, with reasonable satisfaction. Nevertheless, reference to KSAs or KSAPs has become so widespread, and is such a convenient shorthand, that I will use it rather than fight it. However, *when* I use it, a reader should see it as shorthand for a more inclusive term, *job requirements* (Lawshe, 1987).

Many job analysis inventories include items listing possible job requirements, and many of them ask respondents to link job requirements to

**KNOWLEDGE AND ABILITIES NEEDED
IN SOCIAL SERVICES OFFICE**

POSITION_____ DEPARTMENT_____

Check if Needed	KNOWLEDGE OR ABILITY CATEGORY	Importance: 1 - Not at all 2 3 - Important 4 - 5 - Essential	Experience Required: 1 - None 2 - Some 3 - Moderate 4 - Substantial 5 - Extensive
	Ability to take notes accurately in interviews, telephone messages, conferences, or similar settings		
	Ability to read, understand, and use complex written materials such as guidelines, rules, regulations, agency policy, etc.		
	Knowledge of and ability to use standard programs for word processing.		
	Ability to speak clearly and effectively in English		
	Ability to understand or empathize with people in stressful or emotional situations		
	Ability to understand, and to follow accurately and correctly, written and oral directions, instructions, and suggestions		
	Ability to choose, and use pertinent schedules, charts, tables, and other forms used in the agency		
	Ability to find pertinent information in forms and records		
	Knowledge of, and ability to check for, required and acceptable information from materials and to identify inconsistencies in the materials		
	Knowledge of, and ability to perform, the four basic arithmetic functions and work with decimals, fractions, and percentages		
	Ability to use standard office equipment such as word processors, copiers, fax machines, and similar equipment		
	Ability to establish and maintain files in chronological, alphabetical, or policy section order		
	Ability to compare, evaluate, or develop information relative to established criteria		
	Ability to recognize significant changes in client circumstances		

FIG. 2.5. Selected items of knowledge, skills, and abilities from a job analysis form used in a social services agency.

tasks or, more often, activities. One way to request linkage judgments is illustrated in Fig. 2.6. In the inventory from which it is drawn, general duties were listed and KSAs were restricted to ability factors. Each cell represents a potential predictive hypothesis. Job experts entered a 0, 1, 2, or 3 in each of the cells, and mean judgments of experts was computed. Arbitrarily, a prestated mean value (perhaps 1.5, 1.7, 2.0) may be interpreted as suggesting a useful hypothesis, and that value might change from one predictor construct to another.

A linkage matrix like Fig. 2.6 can be used to generate predictive hypotheses in several ways. If an overall performance criterion is to be used,

Linkage of KSA Categories to Major Job Duties

In the table below, the major job duties have been listed down the left hand side. The KSA categories agreed upon have been listed across the top. Each job duty is a row in the table; each KSA is a column. The place where a row and a column intersect is a cell. The definitions for the brief phrases here are given in the help sheets; please keep those definitions before you all the time you are going through this exercise.

Each cell calls for your judgment about the relevance of the ability listed in the column to performance of the duty listed in the row. You should record your judgment as a 0, 1, 2, or 3 according to this scale:

    0 - not at all relevant to the performance of this duty

    1 - relevant, but only slightly, to performance of this duty

    2 - relevant to an important degree to performance of this duty

    3- of the highest relevance to the performance of this duty

Job Duty	KSA				
	Verbal Comp	Clerical Sp & Acc	Interview Skill	Number Facility	General Reasoning
1. Questions clients					
2. Evaluates documentation					
3. Explains, answers questions					
4. Refers clients to resources					
5. Codes information					
6. Develops budget worksheet					
7. Calculates needs, allowances					

FIG. 2.6. Linkage of KSA categories to major job duties.

a summary statistic for each ability column may be used; it might be a simple average or an average weighted by ratings of the importance of the various duties. It might be simply the number of cells in the column with cell means exceeding the prestated value. The same options exist if duties are grouped for independent performance evalations.

If job relatedness is to be determined by criterion-related validation, errors in the linkages will be corrected by failure to find satisfactory correlations. If job relatedness is to be determined by expert judgments, however, the duty and KSA definitions must be tested in pilot studies to assure common interpretations, and the rules for inferring job relatedness must be carefully considered in advance; any subsequent deviations must be justified, if indeed they can be, with very great care.

Job Families

Job analysis surveys permit classifying jobs into broader groups, or job families. Job families serve several purposes, including the development of more widely useful assessment procedures. Developing an initial selection procedure for every identifiably different job in an organization may be prohibitively time consuming and expensive; time and other costs can be lower if common procedures can be developed for large groups of similar jobs.

Job families can be developed by a number of different rules, but methods using statistical data generally require survey data. A variety of statistical techniques have been proposed for such grouping, usually a form of hierarchical cluster analysis (Harvey, 1986). Some procedures use expert judgments. Sackett, Cornelius, and Carron (1981) had supervisors rate pairs of jobs for overall similarity or difference on a 7-point scale. Analysis of these ratings gave job clusters similar to those obtained by defining clusters by task statements. As many have suggested (e.g., Pearlman, 1980), the elegance of quantitative methods is not necessarily superior to purely rational methods used by genuine job experts. Statistical results are not invariant; they may depend on a variety of characteristics of the job analyses and of the dimensions used for clustering (e.g., abilities vs. tasks; Garwood, Anderson, & Greengart, 1991; Pearlman, 1980). If the family in which a job is placed depends on the method used, we cannot have much confidence that quantitative analysis has provided an optimal set of job families—or even a very good one. The problem might be because most analyses have used only a few highly similar jobs, so Hartman, Mumford, and Mueller (1992) developed a large database (more than 1,200 people, more than 150 jobs) with job descriptions containing both task statements and job requirements. They found strong convergence of job families based on the two kinds of content.

It appears that quantitatively determined job families, based on large scale survey responses, are likely to be stable, giving results that converge across different methods. That does not suggest that it makes no difference which quantitative method is chosen; Garwood et al. (1991) gave guidance on choosing clustering methods for different sets of job analysis characteristics. Nor does it suggest that quantitative methods should be used even when databases are small and homogeneous. In those cases, job families based on the judgments of genuine experts may be more useful.

An Inventory Based on Personality Linkages

In his presidential address to the Division on Measurement and Evaluation, American Psychological Association, Douglas Jackson said that job analysis techniques have largely overlooked personality predictors and that that is one reason for their poor history. So challenged, a Bowling

Green research group developed an inventory specifically intended to generate hypotheses about potential predictors among personality traits. It is based on a list of 12 personality dimensions, shown, with definitions and contrasts, in Table 2.3. A sample page is shown in Fig. 2.7.

We cannot yet say whether this instrument will provide more fruitful hypotheses about personality variables as predictors.[6] We can say, with some assurance, that a job analysis that ignores tasks potentially linked to predictor traits other than abilities and skills may overlook some different but useful predictors.

There are other efforts in this direction. Inwald (1992) developed an inventory geared to personality traits that has been used for occupations such as police, managers, and bus drivers. There are also two inventories linked to specific instruments or theories. Costa, McCrae, and Kay (1995) described the NEO Job Profiler, designed for use with the Revised NEO Personality Inventory, and Gottfredson and Holland (1994) developed the Position Classification Inventory to match the Holland RIASEC personality theory (for a summary, see Rounds, 1995).

Position Analysis Questionnaire (PAQ)

A job-oriented inventory must be explicitly developed for each job or occupational group studied. This fact reduces the generality of job dimensions identified and renders comparisons across jobs and occupations difficult. By definition, a worker-oriented approach is applicable across widely differing occupations. For this reason, many people prefer to use the latter approach to position, job, or occupational surveys.

The most widely used is the *Position Analysis Questionnaire* (PAQ) by McCormick, Jeanneret, and Mecham.[7] It is evolving document, it is in Form C as of 1989, but the evolution has had more steps than the letter C implies. Earlier forms over a research span of more than 30 years included questionnaires under other names as well as the two preceding forms of the PAQ. Changes have not been dramatic but have been more in the form of additions, deletions, or modifications based on ongoing research.

Form C has 187 job descriptive statements, each describing behavior. They are organized under six major divisions, outlined in Table 2.4, the first three of which follow an input-process-output model. Sources of information are inputs. Mental processes, physical activities (under work output in Table 2.4), interactions with other people, and adaptation to the job context are process components. The output component is work

---

[6]The project continues under the direction of Dr. Patrick Raymark, The Ohio State University, Newark Campus, 1177 University Drive, Newark, OH.

[7]The Position Analysis Questionnaire, copyrighted by the Purdue Research Foundation, is available from Consulting Psychologists Press.

TABLE 2.3
Twelve Personality Dimensions
Tentatively Considered Relevant to Work

Dimension	Definition
I. Surgency	
I–A: General leadership	A pattern of visibility and dominance relative to others; the tendency to initiate action, to take charge of situations or groups, to influence or motivate behavior or thinking of other persons or groups of people to bring about or maintain work effectiveness.
I–B: Interest in negotiation	An interest in bringing together contesting parties through mediation or arbitration of disputes or differences in view or, as a contesting party, deal or bargain with others to reach agreement, synthesis, or compromise; a style of leadership characterized by an ability and willingness to see and understand differing points of view, and an interest in making peace and achieving workable levels of harmony.
I–C: Achievement striving	A strong ambition and desire to achieve; in competition with others, a desire to win and a continuing tendency to exert effort and energy to win or to do better than others; in competition with one's self, a desire to exert effort to advance, to do better than one's own prior achievement in specific activities; a tendency to excel relative to others or to a personal standard; to go beyond what is expected and required in an attempt to become the best; not to accept satisfactory or good enough but to strive for excellent.
II. Agreeableness	
II–A: Friendly disposition	A tendency to be outgoing in association with other people, to seek and enjoy the company of others; to be gregarious, to interact easily and well with others, to be likable and warmly approachable.
II–B: Sensitivity to interests of others	A tendency to be a caring person in relation to other people, to be considerate, understanding, and even empathic and to have genuine concern for others and their well-being.
II–C: Cooperative or collaborative work tendency	A desire or willingness to work with others to achieve a common purpose and to be part of a group; a willingness and interest in assisting clients and customers as a regular function of the person's work, or assisting coworkers as needed to meet deadlines or achieve work goals.
III. Conscientiousness	
III–A: General trustworthiness	A pattern of behavior that leads one to be trusted by other people with property, money, or confidential information; a pattern of honoring the property rights of others and general concepts of honesty, truthfulness, and fairness; a deserved reputation for following through on promises, commitments, or other agreements—in short, a pattern of behavior that leads people to say approvingly, "This person can be counted on."

(Continued)

TABLE 2.3
(Continued)

Dimension	Definition
III–B: Adherence to a work ethic	A generalized tendency to work hard and to be loyal; to give a full day's work each day and to do one's best to perform well—following instructions and accepting company goals, policies, and rules—even with little or no supervision; an approach to work characterized by industriousness, purposiveness, persistence, consistency, and punctuality.
III–C: Thoroughness and attentiveness to details	A tendency to carry out tasks with attention to every aspect, including attention to details that others might overlook or perform perfunctorily; a meticulous approach to one's own task performance or the work of others, including careful inspection or analysis of objects, printed material, proposals, or plans.

IV. Emotional Stability

IV: Emotional stability	A calm, relaxed approach to situations, events, or people; emotionally controlled responses to changes in the work environment or to emergency situations; an emotionally mature approach to potentially stressful situations with tolerance, optimism, and a general sense of challenge rather than of crisis; maturity in considering advice or criticism from others.

V. Intellectance

V–A: Desire to generate ideas	A preference for situations in which one can develop new things, ideas, or solutions to problems through creativity or insight, or try new or innovative approaches to tasks or situations; to prefer original or unique ways of thinking about things.
V–B: Tendency to think things through	A habit of thinking, of mentally going through procedures or a sequence of probable events before actually taking actions; a tendency to seek information, to evaluate it, and to consider the consequences or effects of alternative courses of action.

accomplished, the subject of task oriented inventories and therefore not part of the PAQ. A sixth division is for characteristics that do not obviously fit the other five. Figure 2.8 shows a set of the individual items and some of the kinds of rating scales used.

Several differences distinguish PAQ statements from most task inventory items in addition to being worker-oriented. Each statement has just one response scale, but scales may change from one statement to the next. Scales for extent of use, importance to the job, and relative time spent (shown in boxes) are used for many statements, but by no means all. Other scales are used for several special purposes, as in statements 49 and 112 in Fig. 2.8.

Further, many statements are lengthy and somewhat detailed, with a variety of examples, and they often contain long or uncommon words.

EFFECTIVE PERFORMANCE IN THIS POSITION REQUIRES THE PERSON TO:	Not Required	Helpful	Essential
Set 1			
1. lead group activities through exercise of power or authority.	☐	☐	☐
2. take control in group situations.	☐	☐	☐
3. initiate change within the person's work group or area to enhance productivity or performance.	☐	☐	☐
4. motivate people to accept change.	☐	☐	☐
5. motivate others to perform effectively.	☐	☐	☐
6. persuade co-workers or subordinates to take actions (that at first they may not want to take) to maintain work effectiveness.	☐	☐	☐
7. take charge in unusual or emergency situations.	☐	☐	☐
8. delegate to others the authority to get something done.	☐	☐	☐
9. make decisions when needed.	☐	☐	☐
Set 2			
10. negotiate on behalf of the work unit for a fair share of organizational resources.	☐	☐	☐
11. work with dissatisfied customers or clients to achieve a mutually agreeable solution.	☐	☐	☐
12. help people in work groups settle interpersonal conflicts that interfere with group functioning.	☐	☐	☐
13. help settle work-related problems, complaints, or disputes among employees or organizational units.	☐	☐	☐
14. negotiate with people outside the organization to gain something of value to the organization.	☐	☐	☐
15. mediate and resolve disputes at individual, group, or organizational levels.	☐	☐	☐
16. negotiate with people within the organization to achieve a consensus on a proposed action.	☐	☐	☐
17. mediate conflict situations without taking sides.	☐	☐	☐

10/27/92   [Go to next page]

FIG. 2.7. A sample page from a personality-based inventory of general position requirements.

As a result, PAQ items may be less ambiguous to respondents who understand them but they can be a challenge to people who do not read well. Readability problems, coupled with what amounts to a change in instructions with each change in response scale, suggest that incumbents in jobs requiring little verbal ability may find the PAQ difficult to complete. This may be why the use of incumbents for completing the form is not strongly recommended, at least not without assistance from people trained in PAQ use (McCormick & Jeanneret, 1988). For those likely to

TABLE 2.4
An Outline of the Position Analysis Questionnaire

1. *Information input*
   1.1. Sources of job information
      1.1.1—Visual sources of job information
      1.1.2—Nonvisual sources of job information
   1.2. Sensory and perceptual processes
   1.3. Estimation activities
2. *Mental processes*
   2.1. Decisionmaking, reasoning, and planning/scheduling
   2.2. Information processing activities
   2.3. Use of learned information
3. *Work output*
   3.1. Use of devices and equipment
      3.1.1—Hand-held tools or instruments
      3.1.2—Other hand-held devices
      3.1.3—Stationary devices
      3.1.4—Control devices
      3.1.5—Transportation and mobile equipment
   3.2. Manual activities
   3.3. Activities of the entire body
   3.4. Level of physical exertion
   3.5. Body positions/postures
   3.6. Manipulation/coordination activities
4. *Relationships with other persons*
   4.1. Communications
      4.1.1—Oral (communicating by speaking)
      4.1.2—Written (communicating by written/printed material)
      4.1.3—Other communications
   4.2. Miscellaneous interpersonal relationships
   4.3. Amount of job-required personal contact
   4.4. Types of job-required personal contact
   4.5. Supervision and coordination
      4.5.1—Supervision/direction given
      4.5.2—Other organizational activities
      4.5.3—Supervision received
5. *Job context*
   5.1. Physical working conditions
      5.1.1—Outdoor environment
      5.1.2—Indoor temperatures
      5.1.3—Other physical working conditions
   5.2. Physical hazards
   5.3. Personal and social aspects
6. *Other job characteristics*
   6.1. Apparel worn
   6.2. Licensing
   6.3. Work schedule
      6.3.1—Continuity of work (as relevant to total year)
      6.3.2—Regularity of working hours
      6.3.3—Day–night schedule
   6.4. Job demands
   6.5. Responsibility
   6.6. Job structure
   6.7. Criticality of position

INFORMATION INPUT

1.1 Sources of Job Information
Rate each of the following items in terms of the
extent to which it is used by the worker as a source
of information in performing the job.

Code	Extent of Use (U)
N	Does not apply
1	Nominal/very infrequent
2	Occasional
3	Moderate
4	Considerable
5	Very substantial

1.1.1 Visual Sources of Information

1 | U | Written materials (books, reports, office notes, articles, job instructions, signs, etc.)

2 | U | Quantitative materials (materials which deal with quantities or amounts, such as graphs, accounts, specifications, tables of numbers, etc.)

3 | U | Pictorial materials (pictures or picturelike materials used as sources of information, for example, drawings, blueprints, diagrams, maps, tracings, photographic films, X-ray films, TV pictures, etc.)

MENTAL PROCESSES

2.2 Information Processing Activities
In this section are various human operations
involving the "processing" of information or data.
Rate each of the following items in terms of how
important the activity is to the completion of the job.

Code	Importance to This Job (I)
N	Does not apply
1	Very Minor
2	Low
3	Average
4	High
5	Extreme

39 | I | Combining information (combining, synthesizing, or integrating information or data from two or more sources to establish new facts, hypotheses, theories, or a more complete body of *related* information, for example, an economist using information from various sources to predict future economic conditions, a pilot flying aircraft, a judge trying a case, etc.)

40 | I | Analyzing information or data (for the purpose of identifying *underlying* principles or facts by *breaking down* information into component parts, for example, interpreting financial reports, diagnosing mechanical disorders or medical symptoms, etc.)

49 | S | Using mathematics (indicate, using the code below, the highest level of mathematics that the individual must understand as required by the job)

Code *Level of Mathematics*
N Does not apply
1 Simple basic (counting, addition and subtraction or 2-digit numbers or less)
2 Basic (addition and subtraction of numbers of 3 digits or more, multiplication, division, etc.)
3 Intermediate (calculations and concepts involving fractions, decimals, percentages, etc.)
4 Advanced (algebraic, geometric, trigonometric, and statistical concepts, techniques, and procedures usually applied in standard practical situations)
5 Very advanced (advanced mathematical and statistical theory, concepts, and techniques, for example, calculus, topography, vector analysis, factor analysis, probability theory, etc.)

FIG. 2.8. *(Continued)*

be trained as PAQ job analysts, a job analysis manual is available with detailed descriptions of each item (McPhail, Jeanneret, McCormick, & Mecham, 1991).

The recommended procedure uses job analysts as data collectors. The job analysts may be people in the organizations (or outside consultants) whose major job is analyzing the jobs of others, or they may be other employees specifically chosen for this ad hoc assignment. They interview job incumbents, their supervisors, or both; after the interviews, the analysts themselves complete the PAQ forms. Alternatively, an analyst may meet with small groups of incumbents and supervisors who fill out the form in the presence of the analyst who can answer questions about the

RELATIONSHIPS WITH OTHER PERSONS

4 Relationships with Other Persons
This section deals with different aspects of interaction between people involved in various kinds of
work.

Code	Importance to This Job (I)
N	Does not apply
1	Very minor
2	Low
3	Average
4	High
5	Extreme

4.1 Communications
Rate the following in terms of how *important* the activity is to the completion of the job. Some jobs may
involve several or all of the items in this section.

4.1.1 Oral (communicating by speaking)

99 | I Advising (dealing with individuals in order to counsel and/or guide them with regard to problems
that may be resolved by legal, financial;, scientific, technical, clinical, spiritual, and/or other
professional principles)

100 | I Negotiating (dealing with others in order to reach an agreement or solution, for example, labor
bargaining, diplomatic relations, etc.)

4.3 Amount of Job-required Personal Contact

112 | S Job-required personal contact (indicate, using the code below, the extent of job-required contact
with others, individually or in groups, for example, contact with customers, patients, students,
the public, superiors, subordinates, fellow employees. prospective employees, official visitors,
etc.; consider *only* personal contact which is definitely *part* of the job

Code | *Extent of Required Personal Contact*
1 | Very infrequent (almost no contact with others is required)
2 | Infrequent (limited contact with others is required)
3 | Occasional (moderate contact with others is required)
4 | Frequent (considerable contact with others is required)
5 | Very frequent (almost constant contact with others is required)

JOB CONTEXT

5 Physical Working Conditions
This section lists various working conditions. Rate the
average amount of time the worker is exposed to
each condition during a *typical* work period.

Code	Amount of Time (T)
N	Does not apply (or is very incidental)
1	Under 1/10 of the time
2	Between 1.10 and 1/3 of the time
3	Between 1/3 and 2/3 of the time
4	Over 2/3 of the time
5	Almost continuously

5.1.1 Outdoor environment

135 | T Out-of-door environment (subject to changing weather conditions)

FIG. 2.8. Examples of items and rating scales in the position analysis
questionnaire. From McCormick, E. J., & Jeanneret, P. R. (1988). Position
analysis questionnaire (PAQ). In S. Gael (Ed.), *The job analysis handbook for
business, industry, and government* (Vol. 1, pp. 825–842). New York: Wiley.
Reprinted by permission of John Wiley & Sons, Inc.

statements or the rating scales. McCormick and Jeanneret (1988) suggested
that the interview and subsequent completion of a PAQ for an individual
position takes about 1½ to 2 hours to complete; group meetings with job
experts were said to require about 3½ to 4 hours.

Worker Attribute Ratings. Experts in the psychological study of work
and in the study of individual differences have made judgments about
the relevance of 76 worker attributes to each of the individual PAQ items
(Marquardt & McCormick, 1972). A brief sample of the attributes is given
in Table 2.5; the sample does no more than suggest the broad scope of

TABLE 2.5
A Sample of Worker Attributes Matched to PAQ Job Elements

Aptitudes

Verbal comprehension: ability to understand the meaning of words and the ideas associated with them.

Divergent thinking: ability to generate or conceive of new or innovative ideas or solutions to problems.

Perceptual speed: ability to make rapid discriminations of visual detail.

Depth perception: ability to estimate depth or distances of objects (or to judge their physical relationships in space).

Ideational fluency: ability to produce a number of ideas concerning a given topic; emphasis is on the number, not the quality, of the ideas.

Stamina: ability to maintain physical activity over prolonged periods of time; resistance of cardiovascular system to breakdown.

Body orientation: ability to maintain body orientation with respect to balance and motion.

Continuous muscular control: ability to exert continuous control over external devices through continual use of body limbs.

Dynamic strength: ability to make repeated, rapid, flexing movements in which the rapid recovery from muscle strain is critical.

Interests or temperament traits, characterized by job situations to which people must adjust

---

Repetitive/short-cycle operations: operations carried out according to set procedures or sequences.

Influencing people: influencing opinions, attitudes, or judgments about ideas or things.

Sensory alertness: alertness over extended periods of time.

Prestige/esteem from others: working in situations resulting in high regard from others.

Dealing with concepts/information: preference for situations that involve conceptual or informative ideas and the possible communication of these ideas to others.

Note. From Mecham, R. C., & McCormick, E. J. (1969). The rated attribute requirements of job elements in the Position Analysis Questionnaire. Occupational Research Center, Purdue University, January 1969, Report No. 1 [Under Office of Naval Research Contract Nonr-1100(28)].

attributes included. The judges were instructed to rate the attributes on a 6-point scale of relevance (from none to extreme or extensive relevance) of a given attribute to the top of the response scale for a given job element. Ratings appeared to be rather reliable.

The median rating was determined for each job element, and a matrix of average attribute ratings by job elements was prepared. A very small portion of that matrix is abstracted in Table 2.6, using some job elements in Fig. 2.8 and some of the attributes listed in Table 2.5. Median ratings range from 0.0 (*no relevance*) to 5.0 (*very strong relevance*) of the attribute for the job element shown. The table is only a small sample of the larger 76 × 187 matrix, but it serves to indicate the range of importance of attributes for given dimensions.

TABLE 2.6
A Brief Abstract From the Matrix of Median
Attribute Ratings for PAQ Job Elements

Job Element	VC	PS	DP	IF	St	BO	AM	SS	RO	IP	SA	DC
Information source												
1. Written	5.0	4.0	0.5	0.0	0.0	0.5	0.0	0.0	2.5	0.0	2.5	4.5
2. Quantitative	3.0	4.0	0.5	0.0	0.0	0.5	0.0	0.0	2.0	0.0	3.0	4.0
3. Pictorial	2.0	4.5	2.5	0.0	0.0	0.5	1.0	0.0	2.0	0.0	3.0	4.0
Mental processes												
39. Combining	4.5	2.5	0.0	4.0.	0.5	0.0	0.0	0.0	0.0	0.0	3.5	5.0
40. Analyzing	5.0	2.5	0.0	3.5	0.0	0.0	0.0	0.0	0.0	0.0	3.5	5.0
49. Mathematics	3.5	2.5	0.0	2.5	0.0	0.0	0.0	0.0	1.0	0.0	0.5	4.0
Work output												
93. Finger manip.	0.0	3.0	2.5	0.0	1.5	2.0	2.0	1.0	3.0	0.0	4.5	0.0
94. Hand-arm												
manip.	0.0	3.0	2.5	0.0	3.0	3.0	4.0	2.5	3.5	0.0	4.0	0.0
Oral communication												
99. Advising	4.5	1.0	0.0	4.0	0.0	0.0	0.0	0.0	0.0	4.5	3.0	5.0
100. Negotiating	5.0	0.5	0.0	4.5	0.0	0.0	0.0	0.0	0.0	5.0	3.5	5.0
Job demands												
172. Set procedures	3.0	1.5	2.0	0.0	1.0	2.0	1.5	2.0	5.0	0.5	2.0	1.0
173. Time pressure	0.0	2.5	0.0	0.0	3.0	3.0	2.0	2.0	4.0	0.0	4.5	0.0

VC, verbal comprehsions; PS, perceptual speed; DP, depth perception; IF, ideational fluency; St, stamina; BO, bodu orientation; AM, rate of arm movement; SS, static strength; RO, repetitive operations; IP, influencing people; SA, sensory alertness; DC, dealing with concepts.

Note. From Marquardt, L. D., & McCormick, E. J. (1972). Attribute ratings and profiles of the job elements of the Position Analysis Questionnaire (PAQ). Department of Psychological Sciences, Purdue University, June, 1972, Report No. 1 (Under contract no N00014-67-A-0226-0016).

McCormick, Mecham, and Jeanneret (1989) recommended computing a composite attribute score for each attribute using the equation

$$\text{Attribute Score} = \Sigma AI / \Sigma I, \tag{1}$$

where A = the attribute relevance rating and I = PAQ job element response *for those job elements with ratings of 3 or above.* Normative data are available for converting these scores to percentile ranks, but ipsative (i.e., within job) comparisons seem more appropriate to hypothesis development than normative ones (i.e., across jobs). One need not compute attribute scores for every attribute; most will have obviously little relevance for any one job. For the several attributes rated most relevant, the computed index can be a useful decision aid.

Job Dimensions. Over the years, a series of principal components analyses has identified factors within each of the six divisions and for the PAQ as a whole.[8] Jeanneret (1990) reported the most recent analysis, based on more than 30,000 jobs. Two or more factors can be scored in each division, and only six dimensions can describe the overall dimensionality of jobs; the factor names are shown in Table 2.7.

Factor scores can be computed for each of the divisional and overall job dimensions. These scores have several purposes. One major study has shown that people tend to go into, and stay in, lines of work in which their abilities fit the demands of the work done (McCormick & Jeanneret, 1988). That is, the more that jobs can be described in terms of information input, mental processes, and other dimensions involving verbal skills, the more likely it is that people in them do in fact have higher levels of verbal aptitude. This finding has major importance for job component validity, described in chapter 8.

Another PAQ study found that the cognitive demands of the job (for information processing and decision making) moderate the validities of the cognitive tests, but that the psychomotor demands of the job have no such moderating effect (Gutenberg, Arvey, Osburn, & Jeanneret, 1983). Where cognitive demands are higher, cognitive tests are more likely to be valid predictors of performance. Stated like this, the result seems obvious. Note however, that a similar statement of the results for psychomotor demands would be false, that is, psychomotor demands did not moderate the validities of psychomotor tests. What appears to be obviously true (or obviously false) often needs empirical verification.[9]

Direct Identification of Required Attributes

In most methods of job analysis, particularly the observe-and-question methods, required worker attributes are inferred from the analysis. Some task inventories include KSA lists to be judged by job experts as job requirements, and the PAQ has its matrix like Table 2.5. A more direct method for identifying them is the *Job Requirements Inventory* (Lawshe, 1987). A quite different, but equally direct, method is the *Fleishman Job Analysis Survey* (F–JAS).

Fleishman and his associates were among the first to define and classify tasks according to their ability requirements (for summaries, see Fleishman & Mumford, 1988; Fleishman & Quaintance, 1984). The heart of the

---

[8]Note that the Cranny and Doherty (1988) objections mentioned in connection with factor analysis of importance ratings in task description inventories do not apply here. With 2,200 different jobs surveyed, much of the variance in responses must be attributed to individual differences among jobs, not simply to patterns of shared error among analysts.

[9]Note that these studies were based on *factor scores*, not on scores merely representing items defining factors. Factor scores consider responses and factor loadings on *all* items, but representational scores typically use unit weights, adding the numerical responses to only those items with high loadings on the factor.

TABLE 2.7
Job Factors From Principal Components Analyses
of PAQ Job Descriptions

Division Dimensions

Division 1—Information input
1. Perceptual interpretation, interpreting what is sensed
2. Input from representational sources, using various sources of information
3. Visual input from devices or materials, by watching
4. Evaluating or judging sensory input
5. Awareness of environmental conditions
6. Using various senses

Division 2—Mental processes
7. Decision making
8. Information processing

Division 3—Work output
9. Using machines, tools, or equipment
10. Performing activities requiring general body movement versus sedentary activity
11. Controlling machines or processes and related physical coordination
12. Skilled or technical activities
13. Controlled manual or related activities
14. Use of miscellaneous equipment or devices
15. Performing handling, manipulating, or related activities
16. General physical coordination

Division 4—Relationships with other persons
17. Communicating judgments or related information
18. General personal contacts
19. Performing supervisory, coordination, or related activities
20. Exchanging job-related information
21. Public or related personal contacts

Division 5—Job context
22. Being in a potentially stressful or unpleasant environment
23. Engaging in personally demanding situations
24. Being in potentially hazardous job situations

Division 6—Other job characteristics
25. Working a nontypical versus typical day work schedule
26. Working in business-like situations
27. Wearing optional versus wearing specified apparel
28. Being paid On a variable versus a salaried basis
29. Working on a regular versus an irregular work schedule
30. Working under job demanding circumstances or responsibilities
31. Performing structured versus unstructures work activities
32. Vigilence; being alert to changing conditions

Overall Dimensions

33. Having decision making, communicating, and general responsibility
34. Operating machines or equipment
35. Performing clerical or related activities
36. Performing service or related activities
37. Being aware of work environment; engaging in physical activities
38. Performing technical or related activities

Note. Division dimensions are from McCormick, Mecham, and Jeanneret (1989). Overall dimensions are from Jeanneret (1990).

procedure is a set of 52 abilities (Fleishman & Reilly, 1992a) for which definitions and rating scales are provided, as shown in Fig. 2.9. (Research versions of scales for 20 more potential job requirements are included.) A useful feature of the system is its distinction between the defined ability and other abilities that might be confused with it. Each ability scale is a 7-point rating scale with three tasks anchoring scale points; each one is a task that virtually everyone can understand from ordinary experiences. For each ability, one task has a high scale value, one low, one intermediate; the scale value identifies the mean ability scale value prior judges have assigned to the task. Job experts are expected to compare the tasks required by the job with the three anchor tasks and assign ability ratings; their mean ratings define the job's ability requirements. A companion volume by Fleishman and Reilly (1992b) provided information for the

1. Oral Comprehension This is the ability to listen and understand spoken words and sentences.

How Oral Comprehension Is Different From Other Abilities	
Oral Comprehension: Involves **listening** to and **understanding** words and sentences spoken by others.	*Written Comprehension:* Involves **reading and understanding** written words and sentences.
vs.	*Oral Expression* and *Written Expression:* Involve **speaking** or **writing** words and sentences so others will understand.

Requires understanding complex or detailed information that is presented orally, contains unusual words and phrases, and involves fine distinctions in meaning among words.

7

6 ← *Understand a lecture on metaphysics.*

5

4 ← *Understand instructions for a sport.*

3

Requires understanding short or simple spoken information that contains common words and phrases.

2 ← *Understand a television commercial.*

1

FIG. 2.9. Definition and rating scale for oral comprehension, one of the 52 abilities in the Fleishman job analysis survey. From Fleishman, E. A., & Reilly, M. E. (1992). *Administrator's guide: F-JAS, Fleishman Job Analysis Survey.* Bethesda, MD: Management Research Institute. Reprinted with permission.

next step, establishing operational definitions for use in decisions. For each of the 52 abilities, ability definitions are given, followed by tasks and jobs in which the ability is used and, where available, examples of tests measuring the ability.

The recommended procedure calls for job experts as raters, usually job incumbents. In most cases, a job description or task list is presented to them in preparation for rating. The job as a whole might be rated, or broad job dimensions, or selected tasks. Rating all 52 abilities is unnecessary; flow diagrams have been developed to help identify nontrivial ability requirements (Mallamad, Levine, & Fleishman, 1980).

O*NET: A Model for Occupational Analyses

A new method of large-scale occupational analysis is being developed for the United States Department of Labor for a new version of the DOT (Peterson, Mumford, Borman, Jeanneret, & Fleishman, 1995). It is a survey method; nine questionnaires measure details of several kinds of job-relevant information. In this ongoing work, the set of questionnaires constitutes a model for occupational analysis, dubbed O*NET (for Occupational Information Network). The model is intended for comparing jobs and occupations, not for providing job-specific or occupation-specific information. Nevertheless, its content includes the kinds of information useful in more narrowly focused job analysis surveys. A graphic summary of the model content is shown in Fig. 2.10.

O*NET content consists of information in six major categories; each of these is organized according to relevant taxonomies. Perhaps a brief description of two of these will whet the appetite for more detail.

Worker Requirements. Worker requirements are *developed* attributes of people. They include several kinds of skills—basic, problem-solving, social, and technical. Basic should not be confused with simple or elementary. There are ten categories of basic skills; six are in Table 2.8. Taxonomies also exist for other skills and for other worker requirements.

A taxonomy of job-related knowledge, and a system for its measurement, was developed following the precedents established by Fleishman and his colleagues (e.g., Fleishman & Reilly, 1992a). A subject area taxonomy was also developed for the educational requirements.

Worker Characteristics. The ability taxonomy also stemmed from the Fleishman work. Occupational values include interests. Work styles are work-related personality attributes; the taxonomy was informed by existing theories but, because of the work-related nature of the goals, it did not follow any existing taxonomy. It is two-tiered; seven rather

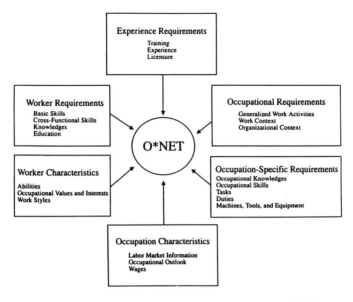

FIG. 2.10. Categories of information sought for the O*NET model. From Peterson, N. G., Mumford, M. D., Borman, W. C., Jeanneret, P. R., & Fleishman, E. A. (Eds.). (1995). *Development of prototype Occupational Informational Network (O*NET) content model* (Vols. 1–2). Salt Lake City, UT: Utah Department of Employment Security. Copyright © 1995 O*NET Content Model (Vols. 1–2). Utah Department of Employment Security. All rights reserved.

general categories have been developed, and some of these are divided into two or more subcategories for a total of 17 categories.

Other Content Categories. The remaining categories in Fig. 2.10 have similarly detailed components. I shall not describe them further, in part because some of them are described in the next chapter and in part because of the in-progress nature of the work; the taxonomies are not fixed for all time. What has been described should serve to show that this is an ambitious approach to occupational analysis, and that it can provide guidance for an extremely thorough sort of job analysis.

General Caveats and Comments on Job Analysis

Even the most careful job analysis is subjective. Job analysis is not science, even when it is used in scientific research or guided by scientific thought. It is an information-gathering tool to help managers or researchers decide what to do next. If well-developed and used systematically, it yields reliable information that leads to defensible predictive hypotheses with strong likelihood of being supported empirically. With specific reference

TABLE 2.8
Six of the Basic Skills in the O*NET Model

Construct Label	Operational Definition	High versus Low Levels[a]
Reading Comprehension	Understanding written sentences & paragraphs in work-related documents	Reading scientific journal articles vs. reading step-by-step instructions for completing a form
Writing	Communicating effectively with others in writing as indicated by needs of the audience	Writing novel for publication vs. taking a telephone message
Mathematics	Using mathematics to solve problems	Developing a mathematical model to simulate and resolve an engineering problem vs. counting the amount of change to be given a customer
Critical Thinking	Using logic & analysis to identify the strengths & weaknesses of different approaches or ideas	Writing a legal brief challenging a federal law vs. determining whether a subordinate has a good excuse for being late
Learning Strategies	Using multiple approaches when learning or teaching new things	Applying principles of educational psychology to develop new teaching methods vs. learning a new method of completing a task from a co-worker
Monitoring	Assessing how well one is doing when learning or doing something	Reviewing corporate productivity and developing a plan to increase it vs. proofreading and correcting a letter

[a]Statements anchoring high and low levels of the scale. NOTE: Four of the basic skills are omitted from this table: Active Listening, Speaking, Science, and Active Learning.

Note. From Peterson, Mumford, Borman, Jeanneret, and Fleishman (1995). Reprinted with permission. Copyright © 1995 O*NET Content Model (Vols. 1–2). Utah Department of Employment Security. All rights reserved.

to licensing examinations, Nelson (1994) placed job analysis closer to policy determination than to scientific generality. I agree; too many people expect too much from job analysis.

Insight can be legitimately expected. The insight needed to choose predictors that, when used, improve organizational functioning is more likely if one acquires correct information through well-considered job analysis. The limiting adjectives—*correct* and *well-considered*—must be satisfied to have a fully convincing hypothesis. Incorrect information is biasing. Not every job analysis must be comprehensive or even thorough, but they must be well-considered. Things can go wrong in job analysis; here are some warnings to consider in preparing to do it.

1. *Different sources of information may yield different information, at least some of it wrong.* Different sources yield different information. Observing one incumbent rather than another may get biased information. An unusually effective worker may do different things with different resources. People with strong verbal skills can describe tasks and resources more clearly than others—and, perhaps, say more to embellish their jobs.

Job analysts using panels of job experts justifiably worry about information differences among experts with different characteristics. Research on the subject is neither extensive nor well-replicated—nor wholly consistent—but some potentially influential characteristics have been studied. Examples include sex (Arvey, Passino, & Lounsbury, 1977), race (Aamodt, Kimbrough, Keller, & Crawford, 1982), performance level (Meyer, 1959; Mullins & Kimbrough, 1988), and experience (Landy & Vasey, 1991). Much more research is needed on these and other respondent characteristics before concluding that any of them matter very much.

2. *One need not use ALL of the wealth of detail a complex job analysis can provide.* Overall performance in any job, or any aspect of job behavior, can be optimally predicted by only a few predictors. After one or two variables—at most four or five—further variables rarely make more than trivial contributions to predictive accuracy. The temptation may be great to use all the predictor variables (worker attributes, abilities, or whatever) suggested by the job experts, but in the long run, judicious choice among them is likely to yield more consistently good predictions.

3. *Job analysis tends to yield static descriptions of "the way we've always done it."* Job analysis typically describes the job as it is, not how it might be, ought to be, or will be in the future. Job analyses are sometimes used, especially in human factors research, to determine needed changes in jobs and job structures, perhaps for work simplification or improved coordination across interacting jobs, but change has rarely seemed salient in job analysis for selection research. Job analyses for selection are more likely to treat jobs as static things. In fact, jobs are not static, and some changes over time can be dramatic. Less dramatic changes happen when someone on a job adapts to it by changing procedures to fit his or her own set of skills, habits, or preferences. Job analysis should, but rarely does, include planning for future contingencies and alternatives.

One approach was exemplified in a report by Arvey, Salas, and Gialluca (1992). A large inventory with both task statements and ability items was completed by more than 600 employees in diverse trades and locations; respondents rated both sets of items for importance to their jobs. Regression equations were developed to predict ability factor importance from selected task statements and for developing a decision rule for predicting whether a particular job requirement would be necessary for a future job. The study was a demonstration of an idea, not a test of a hypothesis, but the demonstration seems promising. Perhaps it will encourage others to look for ways to forecast traits required for jobs not yet in existence.

A different approach, *strategic job analysis*, was described by Schneider and Konz (1989); it builds on conventional job analysis methods. Job experts are asked to predict changes in technology, population, social values, organizational values and structure, and other elements that may affect the job. In the light of the changes they deem likely, these experts take another look at the job as it is and predict how it will change. This is surely a useful exercise, but equally surely it is best not to take it too seriously unless the basis for forecasting is better than usual. Moreover, a job redesign approach to job analysis may be much more relevant to selection problems than typically thought. With such an approach, the personnel decision maker is prepared for planned changes and need not be surprised by changes that merely happen.[10]

4. *Job analyses rarely recognize alternative ways to do the job or to qualify for it.* Most jobs can be done in more than one way. Early pioneers in work simplification sought a "one best way" to do a job, and most methods of job analysis generally describe one way, even if not necessarily the best. More attention should be given to "if–then" hypotheses: if an applicant can be expected to do the job one way, then one set of attributes will provide the best predictors, but if the applicant is likely to do it differently, then a different set of attributes may be better. "If" categories under ADA might be based on disabilities (blind people might do the job using one set of abilities, sighted people may do it with another), or on probable work styles, among others.

Dunnette (1963) noted the problem years ago: ". . . the classic prediction model is grossly oversimplified and has resulted in corresponding oversimplifications in the design of most validation studies" (p. 317). Dunnette's wisdom has too long been shelved because of the preoccupation of personnel researchers with the canonized oversimplifications enshrined in the *Uniform Guidelines*; we must look again at the Dunnette model as shown in Fig. 2.11 and Fig. 2.12. Unfortunately, job analysis methods have not emphasized options or provided the multiple hypotheses the model suggests.

---

[10]This is a suggestion from P. R. Jeanneret in personal communication dated October 26, 1995.

MODEL FOR SELECTION RESEARCH

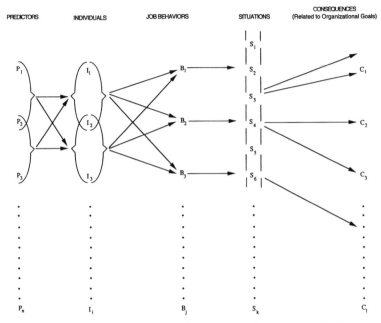

FIG. 2.11. A model for test validation and selection research. From Dunnette, M. D. (1963). A modified model for test validation and selection research. *Journal of Applied Psychology, 47,* 317–323. Copyright by the American Psychological Association. Reprinted with permission.

Figure 2.11 is not a holistic model, but it requires broader assessments of both persons and settings. A score on predictor P_1 for individual I_1 may lead to consequence C_2 if I_1 behaves in a B_2 way in setting S_4; the same score for individual I_3, who behaves in manner B_3 in setting S_6, predicts a very different outcome. Is such complexity realistic? Many think not; in fact, the trend in validity generalization research suggests not. A conclusion is premature. Little effort has yet been made to develop appropriate data for testing the idea. Job analysis methods have not explicitly looked for alternative behaviors for achieving a desired outcome, for equally desirable alternative outcomes, or for situational influences on either behavior or outcome.

5. *Job analysis is typically descriptive, not prescriptive.* It might often be useful to describe *effective* ways to do a job. Traditional job analysis methods do not distinguish between things more effective and less effective workers do on the job. They can, and they should. I have seen people using traditional methods who first divide the workers to be observed and questioned into a group of highly effective performers and another group of less effective

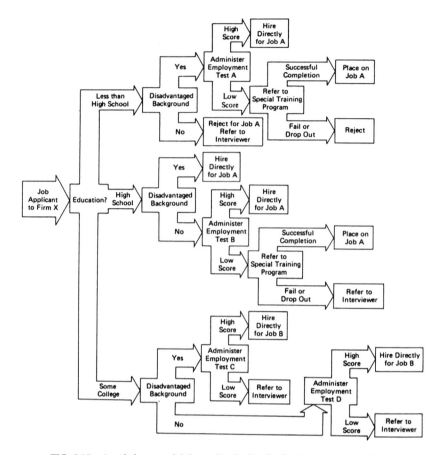

FIG. 2.12. An if–then model for individualized selection strategies. From Dunnette, M. D. (1974). Reprinted with the permission of The Free Press, a division of Simon & Schuster, from *Intergrating the organization: A social-psychological analysis*, H. L. Fromkin and J. J. Sherwood, Eds. Copyright © 1974 by The Free Press.

performers. Differences in resulting information in the two groups can highlight the actions and personal resources that lead to effectiveness. It should be done much more commonly.

6. *No one method of job analysis is clearly superior to another.* Personnel researchers should not get carried away by job analysis. Getting so involved in job analysis that one is willing to argue that one's own method of choice is better than another is to lose sight of the main purpose. There are, of course, many reasons why people analyze jobs. For personnel research, the purpose of job analysis is to understand the job well enough to form sensible, rationally defensible hypotheses about the characteristics of people that predict criterion variables of interest. That purpose is not

likely to be optimally met by any one method, nor is it likely to be met if one uses any method or set of methods uncritically.

7. *This chapter has barely scratched the surface of the topic of job analysis.* Perhaps the most important caveat of all is to point out how little information is available to the reader whose knowledge of job analysis methods is limited to this chapter. Gael's job analysis handbook (Gael, 1988b) fills two volumes and 1,384 pages of very small type; it contains methods not even mentioned here and has more information on the ones that have been described—yet the descriptions are sparse enough that a user of the handbook would need to check out specific references to get adequate information for using any of them.

REFERENCES

Aamodt, M. G., Kimbrough, W. W., Keller, R. J., & Crawford, K. J. (1982). Relationships between sex, race, and job performance level and the generation of critical incidents. *Journal of Educational and Psychological Research, 2,* 227–234.

Arvey, R. D., Passino, E. M., & Lounsbury, J. W. (1977). Job analysis results as influenced by sex of incumbents and sex of analyst. *Journal of Applied Psychology, 62,* 411–416.

Arvey, R. D., Salas, E., & Gialluca, K. A. (1992). Using task inventories to forecast skills and abilities. *Human Performance, 5,* 171–190.

Beer, M., & Spector, B. (1993). Organizational diagnosis: Its role in organizational learning. *Journal of Counseling and Development, 71,* 642–650.

Christal, R. E., & Weissmuller, J. J. (1988). Job-task inventory analysis. In S. Gael (Ed.), *The job analysis handbook for business, industry, and government* (Vol. 2, pp. 1036–1050). New York: Wiley.

Cooper, S. E., & O'Connor, R. M., Jr. (1993). Standards for organizational consultation assessment and evaluation instruments. *Journal of Counseling and Development, 71,* 651–660.

Costa, P. T., Jr., McCrae, R. R., & Kay, G. G. (1995). Persons, places, and personality: Career assessment using the revised NEO Personality Inventory. *Journal of Career Assessment, 3,* 123–139.

Cranny, C. J., & Doherty, M. E. (1988). Importance ratings in job analysis: Note on the misinterpretation of factor analyses. *Journal of Applied Psychology, 73,* 320–322.

Drauden, G. M. (1988). Task inventory analysis in industry and the public sector. In S. Gael (Ed.), *The job analysis handbook for business, industry, and government* (Vol. 2, pp. 1051–1071). New York: Wiley.

Droege, R. C. (1988). Department of Labor job analysis methodology. In S. Gael (Ed.), *The job analysis handbook for business, industry, and government* (Vol. 2, pp. 993–1018). New York: Wiley.

Dunnette, M. D. (1963). A modified model for test validation and selection research. *Journal of Applied Psychology, 47,* 317–323.

Dunnette, M. D. (1974). Personnel selection and job placement of disadvantaged and minority persons: Problems, issues, and suggestions. In H. L. Fromkin & J. J. Sherwood (Eds.), *Integrating the organization: A social psychological analysis* (pp. 55–74). New York: Free Press.

Equal Employment Opportunity Commission, Civil Service Commission, Department of Labor, & Department of Justice. (1978). Uniform guidelines on employee selection procedures. *Federal Register, 43*(166), 38290–38315.

Fine, S. A. (1955). Functional job analysis. *Journal of Personnel Administration and Industrial Relations, 2*(1), 1–16.

Fine, S. A. (1988). Functional job analysis. In S. Gael (Ed.), *The job analysis handbook for business, industry, and government* (Vol. 2, pp. 1019–1035). New York: Wiley.

Fine, S. A., & Getkate, M. (1995). *Benchmark tasks for job analysis: A guide for functional job analysis (FJA) scales*. Mahwah, NJ: Lawrence Erlbaum Associates.

Flanagan, J. C. (1954). The critical incident technique. *Psychological Bulletin, 51*, 327–358.

Fleishman, E. A., & Mumford, M. D. (1988). Ability requirement scales. In S. Gael (Ed.), *The job analysis handbook for business, industry, and government* (Vol. 2, pp. 917–935). New York: Wiley.

Fleishman, E. A., & Quaintance, M. K. (1984). *Taxonomies of human performance*. Orlando, FL: Academic Press.

Fleishman, E. A., & Reilly, M. E. (1992a). *Administrator's guide: F–JAS, Fleishman Job Analysis Survey*. Palo Alto, CA: Consulting Psychologists Press.

Fleishman, E. A., & Reilly, M. E. (1992b). *Handbook of human abilities: Definitions, measurements, and job task requirements*. Palo Alto, CA: Consulting Psychologists Press.

Freda, L. J., & Senkewicz, J. J. (1988). Work diaries. In S. Gael (Ed.), *The job analysis handbook for business, industry, and government* (Vol. 1, pp. 446–452). New York: Wiley.

Gael, S. (1983). *Job analysis: A guide to assessing work activities*. San Francisco: Jossey-Bass.

Gael, S. (1988a). Interviews, questionnaires, and checklists. In S. Gael (Ed.), *The job analysis handbook for business, industry, and government* (Vol. 1, pp. 391–414). New York: Wiley.

Gael, S. (1988b). Subject matter expert conferences. In S. Gael (Ed.), *The job analysis handbook for business, industry, and government* (Vol. 1, pp. 432–445). New York: Wiley.

Garwood, M. K., Anderson, L. E., & Greengart, B. J. (1991). Determining job groups: Application of hierarchical agglomerative cluster analysis in different job analysis situations. *Personnel Psychology, 44*, 743–762.

Gottfredson, G. D., & Holland, J. L. (1994). *Position Classification Inventory*. Odessa, FL: Psychological Assessment Resources.

Greenberg, J. (1990). Employee theft as a reaction to underpayment inequity: The hidden cost of pay cuts. *Journal of Applied Psychology, 75*, 561–568.

Gutenberg, R. L., Arvey, R. D., Osburn, H. G., & Jeanneret, P. R. (1983). Moderating effects of decision making/information-processing job dimensions on test validities. *Journal of Applied Psychology, 68*, 602–608.

Hartman, E. A., Mumford, M. D., & Mueller, S. (1992). Validity of job classifications: An examination of alternative indicators. *Human Performance, 5*, 191–211.

Harvey, R. J. (1986). Quantitative approaches to job classification: A review and critique. *Personnel Psychology, 39*, 267–289.

Howard, A. (Ed.). (1994). *Diagnosis for organizational change: Methods and models*. New York: Guilford.

Inwald, R. (1992). *Hilson Job Analysis Questionnaire*. Kew Gardens, NY: Hilson Research.

Jeanneret, P. R. (1990, August). *The Position Analysis Questionnaire: Applications based on quantitative job profiles*. In Quantitative job description and classification: Nomothetic approaches and applications. Symposium at the meeting of the American Psychological Association, Boston.

Kahn, R. L. (1977). Organizational effectiveness: An overview. In P. S. Goodman & J. M. Pennings (Eds.), *New perspectives on organizational effectiveness* (pp. 235–248). San Francisco: Jossey-Bass.

Kanter, R. M., Stein, B. A., & Jick, T. D. (1992). *The challenge of organizational change: How companies experience it and leaders guide it*. New York: Free Press.

Kleiman, L. S., & Faley, R. H. (1985). The implications of professional and legal guidelines for court decisions involving criterion-related validity: A review and analysis. *Personnel Psychology, 38*, 803–833.

Landy, F. J. (1989). *Psychology of work behavior.* Pacific Grove, CA: Brooks/Cole.

Landy, F. J., & Vasey, J. (1991). Job analysis: The composition of SME samples. *Personnel Psychology, 44,* 27–50.

Lawshe, C. H. (1987). *A practitioner's thoughts on job analysis.* Paper presented at Content Validity III, Bowling Green State University, Bowling Green, Ohio, November 15, 1984. Updated July, 1987.

Mallamad, S. M., Levine, J. M., & Fleishman, E. A. (1980). Identifying ability requirements by decision flow diagrams. *Human Factors, 22*(1), 57–68.

Marquardt, L. D., & McCormick, E. J. (1972). *Attribute ratings and profiles of the job elements of the Position Analysis Questionnaire (PAQ).* Department of Psychological Sciences, Purdue University, Report No. 1, June, 1972. (Under contract no. N00014-67-A-0226-0016)

McCormick, E. J. (1959). Application of job analysis to indirect validity. *Personnel Psychology, 12,* 402–413.

McCormick, E. J. (1979). *Job analysis.* New York: AMACOM.

McCormick, E. J., & Jeanneret, P. R. (1988). Position Analysis Questionnaire (PAQ). In S. Gael (Ed.), *The job analysis handbook for business, industry, and government* (Vol. 1, pp. 825–842). New York: Wiley.

McCormick, E. J., Mecham, R. C., & Jeanneret, P. R. (1989). *Technical manual for the Position Analysis Questionnaire (PAQ)* (2nd ed.). West Lafayette, IN: Purdue Research Foundation.

McPhail, S. M., Jeanneret, P. R., McCormick, E. J., & Mecham, R. C. (1991). *Job analysis manual for the PAQ* (rev. ed.). Palo Alto, CA: Consulting Psychologists Press.

Mecham, R. C., & McCormick, E. J. (1969). *The rated attribute requirements of job elements in the Position Analysis Questionnaire.* Occupational Research Center, Purdue University, January 1969, Report No. 1. [Under Office of Naval Research Contract Nonr-1100(28).]

Meyer, H. H. (1959). A comparison of foreman and general foreman conceptions of the foreman's job responsibilities. *Personnel Psychology, 12,* 445–452.

Moeller, A., Schneider, B., Schoorman, F. D., & Berney, E. (1988). Development of the Work-Facilitation Diagnostic. In F. D. Schoorman & B. Schneider (Eds.), *Facilitating work effectiveness* (pp. 79–103). Lexington, MA: Lexington Books.

Mullins, W. C., & Kimbrough, W. W. (1988). Group composition as a determinant of job analysis outcomes. *Journal of Applied Psychology, 73,* 657–664.

Nelson, D. S. (1994). Job analysis for licensure and certification exams: Science or politics? *Educational Measurement: Issues and Practice, 13*(3), 29–35.

Olian, J. D. (1984). Genetic screening for employment purposes. *Personnel Psychology, 37,* 423–438.

Olson, D. M., & Borman, W. C. (1989). More evidence on relationships between the work environment and job performance. *Human Performance, 2,* 113–130.

Pearlman, K. (1980). Job families: A review and discussion of their implications for personnel selection. *Psychological Bulletin, 87,* 1–28.

Peters, L. H., & O'Connor, E. J. (1988). Measuring work obstacles: Procedures, issues, and implications. In F. D. Schoorman & B. Schneider (Eds.), *Facilitating work effectiveness* (pp. 106–123). Lexington, MA: Lexington Books.

Peterson, N. G., Mumford, M. D., Borman, W. C., Jeanneret, P. R., & Fleishman, E. A. (Eds.). (1995). *Development of prototype Occupational Information Network (O*NET)* (Vols. 1–2). Salt Lake City, UT: Utah Department of Employment Security.

Rounds, J. (1995). Vocational interests: Evaluating structural hypotheses. In D. Lubinski & R. V. Dawis (Eds.), *Assessing individual differences in human behavior* (pp. 177–232). Palo Alto, CA: Davies-Black.

Sackett, P. R., Cornelius, E. T., III, & Carron, T. J. (1981). A comparison of global judgment vs. task oriented approaches to job classification. *Personnel Psychology, 34,* 791–804.

Schein, E. H. (1993). On dialogue, culture, and organizational learning. *Organizational Dynamics, 22*(2), 40–51.

Schneid, T. D. (1992). *The Americans with Disabilities Act: A practical guide for managers.* New York: Van Nostrand Reinhold.

Schneider, B. (1996). When individual differences aren't. In K. R. Murphy (Ed.), *Individual differences and behavior in organizations* (pp. 548–571). San Francisco: Jossey-Bass.

Schneider, B., & Konz, A. M. (1989). Strategic job analysis. *Human Resource Management, 28,* 51–63.

Senge, P. M. (1990). *The fifth discipline: The art and practice of the learning organization.* New York: Currency-Doubleday.

Smith, J. E., & Hakel, M. D. (1979). Convergence among data sources, response bias, and reliability and validity of a structured job analysis questionnaire. *Personnel Psychology, 32,* 677–692.

Sutermeister, R. A. (1976). *People and productivity* (3rd ed.). New York: McGraw-Hill.

United States Department of Labor. (1972). *Handbook for analyzing jobs.* Washington, DC: U.S. Government Printing Office.

United States Department of Labor. (1977). *Dictionary of occupational titles: Definitions of titles.* 4th ed. Washington, DC: U.S. Government Printing Office.

Van de Ven, A. H., & Ferry, D. L. (1980). *Measuring and assessing organizations.* New York: Wiley.

Weisbord, M. R. (1991). *Productive workplaces: Organizing and managing for dignity, meaning, and community.* San Francisco: Jossey-Bass.

3

Developing the Predictive Hypothesis

Traditional validation has always implied the hypothesis that a criterion can be predicted from one or more predictors. A practical interest in prediction requires a prior focus on criterion and predictor constructs, ideas or concepts "constructed" in an informed imagination. Scientific constructs are constructed in a scientific imagination informed by data. Constructs deserve careful definition, including relationships to or distinctions from other constructs. Definitions may include boundaries enclosing a *construct domain*.

A predictive hypothesis is a time-oriented hypothesis about the relationship of one construct, a criterion, to another, a predictor. It is more than a hunch. Binning and Barrett (1989) pointed out that developing a predictive hypothesis requires both theory building and theory testing. With some modifications in terms and numbering, I follow their presentation in Fig. 3.1.

1. A predictor construct—an idea of a way people vary—is related to a criterion construct, a form of job behavior (e.g., absence, productivity, etc.) or a result of behavior. This is the basic predictive hypothesis at a conceptual level.
2. Predictor measure X is related to criterion measure Y, a relationship expressable mathematically. This is also a predictive hypothesis, but, unlike 1, it may be empirically testable.
3. Predictor measure X is a valid measure of, reflection of, or method of inducing the predictor construct.

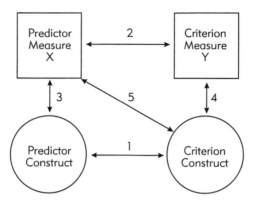

FIG. 3.1. Basic linkages in the development of a predictive hypothesis. From Binning, J. F., & Barrett, G. V. (1989). Validity of personnel decisions: A conceptual analysis of the inferential and evidential bases. *Journal of Applied Psychology, 74*, 478–494. Adapted with permission.

4. Criterion measure Y is a valid measure of, reflection of, or method of inducing the job behavior construct. Tests of Inferences 3 and 4 are used in construct validation, evaluating simultaneously the idea of the construct and a designated measure as a valid measure of it.

5. The predictor measure X is related to the criterion construct in a manner consistent with its presumed relationship to the criterion measure Y. The truth of this inference depends on the validities of Inferences 1 and 3.

Much can be added to this framework. Binning and Barrett (1989) have in fact done so, but I stop here; Inference 5 is the basic operational hypothesis.[1] It rests on the reasonableness of Inference 1, the inferred relationship between two hypothetical variables not directly measurable, and of Inference 3, the construct validity of the predictor as used.

THE BOUNDARIES OF A PREDICTIVE HYPOTHESIS

A predictive hypothesis is not a universal truth; it may be expected to hold only within some boundaries. Specifying the operational hypothesis and its boundaries requires job and organizational knowledge and, beyond that, knowledge of psychology, psychological research, and psychometric tools.

---

[1]It is Inference 9 in the full Binning and Barrett (1989) model. I have renumbered the inferences because I have limited this discussion to the five inferences of Fig. 3.1.

Specification of Operational Definitions

Predictors and criteria can be defined at two levels, conceptual and operational.[2] Hypothesis formation should ordinarily begin with constructs and conceptual definitions of them. At the level of Inference 1, for example, the hypothesis might be, "Quality of performance is a function of ability to make fine, precise manipulations of small objects." Performance quality is a criterion construct; the predictor construct is the ability to make fine, precise manipulations of small objects. The hypothesis, at this level, is not testable because no measurement operations are specified. If the predictor construct is more precisely defined as finger dexterity,[3] its operational definition may be a score on a standardized test.

Not all operational predictors stem from definitions of measurement concepts. Many inventories, tests, work samples, interviewers' judgments, and other predictors are used because they seem appropriate intuitively or because they were useful somewhere else. Even as operational definitions of unknown concepts they can be persistently effective predictors. I do not disparage predictors that work. I believe, however, that finding out what they mean can promote understanding and, eventually, better measures.

Specification of Level of Analysis

An individual level of analysis means that each variable is measured for each person; in the correlation equation, n means the number of people. At a unit level, data describe units, not individual people. By definition, turnover is a work unit variable. Conceptually, it is the rate at which employees leave and have to be replaced; operationally, it can be the proportion of new hires in a 2-year period who left the unit within 3 months after starting work. A corresponding individual level variable is the dichotomy of quitting or staying.

Specification of Population

To whom does the hypothesis apply? Anyone? Only experienced people? New entrants into the labor pool? People with required credentials (e.g., degrees or licenses)? Survivors of a hurdle, such as a basic screening test?

---

[2]Those with long memories should not assume that I refer here to the operationalism of the 1930s and 1940s. My intent is rather simplistic, merely distinguishing between having an idea about the nature of a variable (the construct) and a way to measure it (the operational definition). I *do* consider it nice if people who use measuring procedures have some idea of the nature of the variables they think they are measuring.

[3]The term, finger dexterity, is more precise than it might seem. French (1951, p. 208) defined it as "the rapid manipulation of objects with the fingers" and distinguished it from "manual dexterity" (which involves larger arm movements not part of finger dexterity), and from "aiming" (which requires accurate eye-hand positioning).

In short, who is an applicant? The question has both legal and technical implications.

Definitions of applicant populations are elusive, but the basic idea is a population to which research results should generalize. Definitions sometimes include an expected mix of demographic characteristics; population boundaries may be defined by prior conditions, such as required credentials or passing a screening test.

Specification of Time Intervals

Usually (not always), criteria collected early—after a few months or perhaps a couple of years—are more validly predicted than those collected after longer intervals. Murphy (1989) suggested that validities and most valid predictors change with changes in career stage from a *transitional* stage of new learning to a *maintenance* stage of doing more or less routinely what had been learned. Cognitive variables, for example, may be better predictors of performance in transitional stages and motivational predictors better for maintenance stages. Helmreich, Sawin, and Carsrud (1986) found that achievement motivation did not predict performance well until after a "honeymoon" period—akin to Murphy's transitional period. For some jobs, the learning period may go on and on; Ghiselli (1956) identified a job in which performance improved linearly for 6 years.

In generating hypotheses, one must decide whether they refer to predictions of performance during an early learning period, a later maintenance stage, or long term career growth and development. The time interval can be approximate, but it should make sense.

Specification of Functional Relationships

The term, *functional relationship*, implies that the level of one variable (usually Y) varies "as a function of" variation in another. The nature of the relationship (i.e., the function) may ordinarily be expressed as a mathematical equation. Functions are discussed in more detail in chapter 7, but two issues related to them should not wait to be discussed.

One is that predictive hypotheses usually assume (deliberately or by default) a linear function as the relationship between predictor and criterion. There are good reasons for the assumption, but there are also reasons for considering alternative functions. Figure 3.2 shows three examples of simple functional relationships plausible for various kinds of predictions. Panel a describes the common linear function in which any difference in X always has a corresponding difference in Y; that is, adding a point to a score implies the same added level of criterion performance whether the point is added to a low score, a moderate one, or a high one. In panel b, this is not true in the higher predictor levels;

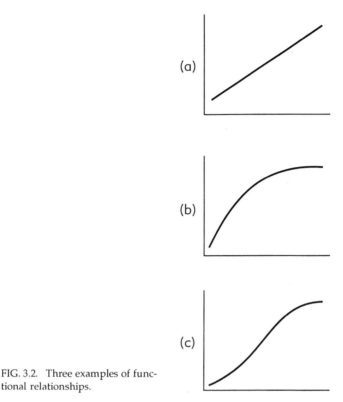

FIG. 3.2. Three examples of functional relationships.

adding a point to the lower predictor scores is associated with a bigger criterion difference than at the higher levels where the curve may be asymptotic to some criterion level. Panel c shows a similar loss of advantage at both lower and higher score levels; that is, differences in actual predictor levels in either a low-scoring or a high-scoring range have only trivial counterparts in criterion performance, whereas predictor differences in the middle range are associated with substantial criterion differences. These are by no means the only functional relationships that may be plausible; others may also deserve consideration. Failure even to think of alternatives to the linear function means failure to test them. Although linear functions will ordinarily be specified, they should be specified intentionally, not by default.

A second issue was mentioned in chapter 2, the oversimplification inherent in assuming a single best way to do a job. A combination of traits may be relevant to performance, and it may be that trade-offs exist in the kinds of traits used by different people. For example, older typists may make fewer keystrokes per minute than their younger collegues, yet they may type just as much material by absorbing more when they scan the text. This chapter is traditional in that it assumes continuous functions like those in Fig. 3.2 rather than the disjunctive and conjunctive models implied by such trade-offs (and described in chapter 7).

Symbiosis of Theory and Practice

Professional practice is the hallmark of applied psychology, but continued application without understanding never improves. Theory is understanding—or the attempt to understand. A framework like that proposed by Binning and Barrett (1989) is theoretical in calling for understanding, beginning with the constructs. When one can define the constructs with some clarity, one has an idea *why* assessment of a certain trait is likely to predict subsequent employee performance. If in fact it does *not* predict as logically expected, one must change one's understanding of the criterion, the predictor, or both; progress ensues.

Tests of Inference 2 (Fig. 3.1) are not always necessary in practice; the practical hypothesis is Inference 5. A clearly formed, theoretically sensible hypothesis (Inference 1) permits justification of a predictor for practical use if it is shown to measure validly the predictor construct (Inference 3). Moreover, some selection procedures are intended to be samples, not predictors, of actual performance content. Even defining a content domain

> is an act of theorizing. That is, the definer includes some components, and excludes others for a reason—because of an idea about the nature of the performance or the knowledge to be sampled. The resulting domain definition can be considered, in rather overly-elegant terms, a "theory of the attribute." It may not be a particularly elegant theory, it may not be based on extended prior research, but it does need some thought about the boundaries of the meaning of scores describing performance on a resulting content sample. (Guion, 1987, p. 208)

A theory of an attribute (a construct) defines (among other things) a content domain, a critically important part of criterion designation (Ilgen & Schneider, 1991).

CRITERIA

The word *criterion* is ambiguous; for a predictive hypothesis, it is simply a "dependent variable, the variable to be predicted" (English & English, 1958, p. 130). Some criteria are construct-related, others are job-related (Guion, 1987). Construct-related criteria are used in hypotheses about the meaning of scores. A job-related criterion is deemed organizationally important to predict, hypothesized to be predicted from the test scores but, as described by Austin and Villanova (1992, p. 838), not "redundant" to them. This chapter focuses on job-related criteria.

There is little virtue in trying to predict a criterion nearly everyone (or no one) does well; it is not useful, and it will not work. Prediction of individual levels of criterion performance requires individual differences—variance. If nearly everyone is at the low end of the scale, some other intervention is needed, such as better training or job redesign.

"The Criterion Problem"

"The criterion problem continues to lead all other topics in lip service and to trail most in terms of work reported." So said Wallace and Weitz (1955, p. 218); it is still true, and still commonplace to bemoan the criterion problem. What, exactly, is the problem? Austin and Villanova (1992) surveyed the criterion problem since 1917; my discussion of it draws from them and is also influenced by the writings and speeches of, and conversations with, S. Rains Wallace, who believed too much emphasis is placed on usefulness and too little on understanding (Thayer, 1992).

Criterion Dimensionality. Early studies used a variety of criteria, and the validity of a predictor depended on the criterion chosen (Severin, 1952). Should the criterion to be predicted be narrowly and homogeneously defined, should it be as inclusive and general as possible? Nagle (1953), citing Toops (1944), called single, unitary criteria "indispensable" (p. 278). However, Toops also said that criteria are *not* unidimensional, that efforts should be made to predict *profiles* of success; this widely-ignored view still seems worth developing.

Some writers have been impatient with insistence on a single, overall criterion. I urged simultaneous prediction of several criteria, arguing

> that (a) there are in many personnel situations dimensions of job performance and of performance consequences that are quite independent of each other, and that (b) the relative importance of these independent criteria ought not be judged prior to validation research—as is so commonly done in the development of "composite" criteria—but ought to instead be judged *after* the empirical data are in, at the time these data are to be used. (Guion, 1961, p. 149)

Similarly, Dunnette called on researchers to give a higher priority to understanding than to prediction:

> ... much selection and validation research has gone astray because of an overzealous worshiping of *the* criterion with an accompanying will-o-the-wisp searching for a best single measure of job success.... I say: junk *the*

criterion! Let us cease searching for single or composite measures of job success and proceed to undertake research which accepts the world of success dimensionality as it really exists. (Dunnette, 1963, p. 252)

To round out these quotations, however, one more is needed. After giving arguments for both single and multiple criteria, Schmidt and Kaplan (1971) said,

The typical practicing industrial psychologist probably seeks both economic and psychological ends in the validation process. . . . he should, ideally, weight criterion elements, regardless of their intercorrelations, into a composite representing an economic construct in order to achieve his practical goals, and, at the same time, he should analyze the relationships between predictors and separate criterion elements in order to achieve his psychological goals. (p. 432)

Practicality is in the eye of the beholder. Long-range planning committees, financial officers, design engineers, production engineers, and marketing or human resources managers may all have different views. An organization has many constituencies; differences in their practicalities may require different predictive hypotheses, each with a different criterion (Villanova, 1992). Currently, the pendulum seems again to favor a single overall criterion, but some signs suggest that it is swinging again. If so, the swing is started more by practical problems than by research or theory. The growing interest in *good citizenship* (Organ, 1988), such as willingness to help colleagues, or to put in extra time, is mainly apparent in practical selection research aimed at "bad" citizenship such as the growing interest in integrity testing (Goldberg, Grenier, Guion, Sechrest, & Wing, 1991; O'Bannon, Goldinger, & Appleby, 1989). Predictions of such criteria and predictions of job performance are independent and may not suggest the same decisions.

Measurement. P. C. Smith (1976) classed criterion measures as hard or soft. *Hard criteria* were measures based on timing, counting, or weighing something; *soft criteria* were ratings or other subjective impressions. The categories overlap; number of promotions or pay raises may seem objective but depend on subjective judgments—they are "surrogates" of ratings (Thayer, 1992, p. 101). Ratings are the most common criterion measures.

The "Problem" in Brief. Although the "criterion problem" is often thought to be simply one of finding a good, predictable criterion, it is basically a problem of definition at both the conceptual and operational levels. The measures are hard to interpret if no underlying constructs are specified. Another part of the problem is that different criterion measures may not correlate well. A composite measure may not make sense; predictions that a candidate would perform well on one criterion may be accompanied by predictions of poor performance in another, and combining the criteria dulls both predictions. At root, the criterion problem is as much a problem of meaning as of measurement. Thayer (1992) asked, "Do we understand our criteria?" We must reply, "Rarely, if at all." Improved prediction cannot be expected without firm understanding of what we want to predict.

Criterion Constructs

Criteria are measures of behavior, performance, or outcomes, or tallies or evaluations of events; they are important to the organization and to the decisions to be made. Too often, they are simply accepted as givens, without much concern for their meaning. Clarity of the constructs they represent provides clarity for the meaning of predictions.

Inferring Constructs From Measures. Events worth counting, recording, and predicting may include accidents, quitting, completion of training, or receipt of letters of commendation (e.g., letters from the public praising something done by a police officer or by a truck driver). The intended meanings of such measures are often unclear.

Absence (or absenteeism) provides a useful example of the more general problem of clarifying the meaning of criterion measures. What does it mean to count the number of days at or away from work (or the number of absences) over a given period? Psychologists once interpreted absence only as withdrawal from an aversive situation, especially if the number of days absent was greater than the number of times absent. In this view, being late is a mild form of withdrawal, being absent is a stronger form, and quitting is the ultimate withdrawal from the job or organization. Alternative interpretations can include adaptation to job demands through organizational socialization, or rational or deliberate choice between coming to work or not. In retrospective self reports of reasons for absence, nurses in two hospitals most often cited minor illness; tiredness and family demands were also named (Hackett, Bycio, & Guion, 1989).

Reasons for absence may not be readily apparent. Even classifying absences as necessary or avoidable is difficult. The day after a major blizzard in my town, a custodial employee responsible for maintaining chemical balance in the campus swimming pool managed to walk across nearly two miles of snow drifts to get to the pool. He got to work, so should the absences of others be classed as avoidable? F. J. Smith (1977) computed average scores on six attitude scales for organizational units in Chicago and in New York. Scores were correlated with percentages of people attending work on a certain day, which happened to be the day after a severe snow storm in Chicago; weather was no problem that day in New York. Mean attitude scores did not correlate well with attendance in New York, but did in Chicago. Is attendance a matter of attitude? Only, it seems, if it requires more effort than mere habit.

In both examples, and in general, the meaning of attendance or absence is unclear. Why would an organization want to predict either? One reason is economic; absence is expensive. But before the cost, absence is psychological. Withdrawal or escape from work is psychologically interesting, but is it clearly indicated by absence? Probably not; withdrawing from a situation may depend as much on the situation as on the person. A history of such withdrawal, shown both by a history of absences difficult to classify as unavoidable and other life events may suggest a generalized tendency to escape unpleasantness; perhaps a construct such as acceptance of responsibility is one reason organizations worry about absenteeism, but absenteeism may not measure it very well.

Starting with the measure (e.g., counting absences) and then trying to determine what it means is the wrong way to go. It makes more sense to decide first on the criterion *concept*; only when the concept is reasonably clear can a measure of it be tried and evaluated. With such a complex construct as responsible work behavior, a composite of several measures (maybe including attendance) may be more valid. Predicting one component, in short, may be less useful, and less well done, than predicting a *pattern* of behaviors tapping a common and clearly defined construct.[4]

A Theory of Performance. Performance is a construct, measureable in many ways. Campbell, McCloy, Oppler, and Sager (1993) defined performance as cognitive, motor, psychomotor, or interpersonal behavior controllable by the individual, relevant to organizational goals, and scalable (at least conceptually) in terms of proficiency. They explicitly excluded work outcomes, effectiveness (evaluation of outcomes), and productivity (an aggregate, not an individual, measure) from their definition. Performance is work-related activity—behavior. Their definition differs from the Society for Industrial and Organizational Psychology (SIOP) definition, "the effectiveness and value of work behavior and its outcomes" (Society for Industrial and Organizational Psychology, 1987, p. 39). Under either definition, performance is not unidimensional; it may

---

[4]Criteria may be economic; reducing costs such as absenteeism or other unwanted events can be immensely practical. However, the principle applies to economic as well to psychological constructs. There are differences in the kinds of costs to be controlled and in the mechanisms for controlling them. A clear definition of a construct, economic or psychological, permits more valid measurement of it.

have many components. Ranking employees by level of proficiency in one component may not match their rank order on another.

Performance Components and Determinants. Campbell et al. (1993) postulated three determinants to account for proficiency in any performance component: *declarative knowledge*, factual knowledge and understanding of things one must do; *procedural knowledge*, skill in knowing how to do them; and *motivation*, the direction, degree, and persistence of effort in doing them (see Kanfer & Ackerman, 1989, for background). At the workplace, both declarative and procedural knowledge may be combined as job knowledge; those with a wealth of knowledge that can be tapped by others are valued more highly than the others, but those for whom that knowledge is not accompanied by actual skill in applying it are often dismissed, somewhat contemptuously, as merely "talking a good job." A hard worker is usually valued over those who exert less effort.

The theory also suggests eight general factors of performance; with modification and abbreviation, they are shown in Table 3.1. Not all of them are relevant to every job (e.g., many jobs have no supervisory component); many may require a finer definition to be operationally useful for specific jobs (e.g., a job wherein the incumbent must communicate effectively to widely differing constituencies might require more specific communication components). They provide, however, a framework for construct definition.

Contextual Behavior. Valued behavior at work includes more than doing assigned job tasks. Regularly coming to work on time, staying with the organization rather than leaving, staying overtime on short notice when unexpected problems arise, helping others when needed, minimizing or solving conflicts within the work group, training or mentoring newcomers, justifying trust, or simply providing a good model for others—all of these form part of the context in which work is done. Borman and Motowidlo (1993), calling such things contextual activities, differentiated them from task or job performance in four ways: (a) task activities contribute directly to the technical core of an organization's production of goods and services, contextual activities contribute to the organizational or social environment in which that technical core functions; (b) task activities differ across different jobs, contextual activities are common to many if not all jobs; (c) task activities are associated with skills or abilities, contextual activities are more associated with motivational or personality variables; and (d) task activities are things people are hired to do, contextual activities are desirable but less likely to be demanded.

The latter difference poses a special problem. Clearly, selection or promotion decisions are appropriately based on predictions of required

TABLE 3.1
A Proposed Taxonomy of Higher Order Performance Components

1. *Job specific task proficiency*
   How well the person does major substantive or technical tasks central to the job, i.e., job-specific behaviors differing from one to another. Joining two pieces of half-inch wood with dovetails and glue, and joining 2 × 4 studs and sills, are different core tasks for the cabinetmaker and the carpenter.

2. *Non-job-specific task proficiency*
   Tasks performed by virtually everyone in an organization, or at least virtually everyone in a job family. In the construction example, virtually everyone at a job site—cabinetmaker, carpenter, plumbers, electricians, and various helpers—must be able to make rough cuts, drill holes, hammer nails, and clean the work area.

3. *Written and oral communication task proficiency*
   Tasks requiring formal oral or written presentations to an audience, whether of one person or many. The critical, differentiating performance component is proficiency in writing or speaking to an audience. Examples vary from formally telling the boss of the results of a planning conference to the presentation of technical data to an audience of hundreds.

4. *Demonstrating effort*
   Consistency of effort, frequency of expending extra effort when required, and the tendency to keep working even under adverse conditions.

5. *Maintaining personal discipline*
   Avoidance of negatively valued behavior: alcohol and substance abuse at work, violating laws or rules, excessive absenteeism, etc.

6. *Facilitating peer and team performance*
   Supporting peers, helping them, or acting as a de facto trainer; being a good model for facilitating group functioning by keeping the group goal directed, and reinforcing participation by other group members.

7. *Supervision/leadership*
   Influencing subordinate performance through direct interpersonal interaction: setting goals for subordinates, teaching or training, modeling appropriate behavior, and rewarding (or punishing) in appropriate ways.

8. *Management/administration*
   Management activities distinctly differing from direct supervision.

Note. From Campbell, McCloy, Oppler, and Sager (1993). Reprinted with permission.

activities. Should predictions of desirable but not required behavior influence such decisions? It is distasteful, potentially unethical, and maybe counterproductive to base personnel decisions on predictions of behavior that is nice when it happens but is not generally required.

Some contextual behaviors *are* generally required. It is, for example, required of virtually all employees in a production line to be at work on time and to stay at their work stations (or follow established procedures for getting relief) during production work; it is required of all employees that they *avoid* stealing cash or merchandise. A first question in choosing a contextual criterion, therefore, is to ask whether it represents organizationally required behavior for everyone, or at least everyone within a specified group of jobs, or whether it is merely desirable. A second question is whether the desired behaviors are more likely and more safely elicited from day-to-day managerial influence than from antecedent traits (e.g., see Organ, 1988).

Performance Outcomes. The criterion of choice is most often a result of required behavior: how much gets done, how well it is done, or perhaps how efficiently it is done. Even these outcome measures should reflect a construct of organizational interest. Suppose the construct is simple quantity of production. A simple count may suffice, but it will not mean the same thing as a composite that considers quality; the quantity of *useful* production may be the number of items produced less the number that did not pass inspection. It is not common to think of outcomes as constructs or measures of constructs. They tend to be job-specific, such as average time a troubleshooter takes to locate source of trouble, total value of insurance policies sold per year, number of new advertising accounts per month, rate of production growth based on innovative engineering, rate of scrap or breakage or use of expendable material, or number of customer complaints (or commendations) per month. Each of these is or can be made a matter of record. Each involves measurement by simply counting output or signs of output quality. Each represents a way to order employees according to their contributions to the organization that employs them. Can they, singly or in combinations, reflect a more fundamental behavioral attribute, a more important concept?

If so, many people would call that more important concept *productivity*. I would not. Productivity, especially at the level of international competition, has lately been "taking up much ink and air time" (Guzzo, 1988, p. 63). Output measures seem not to measure productivity as it is usually conceived. Moreover, productivity seems an inappropriate construct for most predictive hypotheses for two reasons. First, it refers to a ratio of output to input; from a psychological perspective, both elements of that ratio, when used to describe people (especially input), are complex and just plain mushy. Second, the concept is more applicable to higher than individual levels of analysis. That is not really a problem; more predictive hypotheses are needed for larger units of analysis, not fewer. However, for individual decisions, it seems more useful to identify aspects of individual behavior that may contribute to productivity in larger units than to bury consideration of these aspects under such a broad heading.

Some important performance constructs related causally to output may be more important to predict. Managers may prefer predictions of output, but predictions of the prerequisite behavior may do more good. The distinction was made clearly by Wallace (1965): the "results" concept of an insurance agent's sales volume differs from the behavioral concept of getting out of the office and looking for prospects. Using an earlier terminology, the performance behavior construct is a primary criterion and the outcome construct a secondary one (Guion, 1965, p. 115). The assumption, which is testable, is that a primary criterion predicts and helps explain the secondary one. Structural equation models (see chapter 8) permit evaluation of causal assumptions.

Trainability. How quickly tasks are learned may be an important construct, especially where people must frequently adapt to changing technology or assignments. Even on static jobs, the idea that anyone can become expert given enough time is a myth; those who need long learning time for complex tasks generally do not reach the level of proficiency after training reached by those who learned more quickly (Goldstein, 1986; Gordon & Cohen, 1973; Jones, 1966; Woodrow, 1938). It is organizationally useful to select or promote people who will learn their duties quickly or adapt quickly to job changes.

Status Quo, Change, and Criterion Choice

Organizations need to grow and adapt through change. Criteria should promote effective change, maintain useful stability in the face of change, and help develop an organization that continues to function effectively in a changing world (Kanter, Stein, & Jick, 1992). Simpleminded adherence to status quo, without regard for its potential dangers, does not keep organizations lively or alive.

Some years ago, William Whyte (1957) criticized American organizations who, through employment testing, choose conformers who resist change. Many of his arrows were off target but, in fact, many criteria, if predicted well, tend dangerously to maintain the status quo (B. Schneider, 1987). Avoiding criteria that merely reinforce the status quo requires intelligent recognition of the inevitability and usefulness of change. I do not refer to mindless adulation of change for its own sake or to enthusiastic pursuit of every innovation. Nevertheless, new ideas to change products, services, or ways of doing things promote growth and progress; the people who imagine and develop them are valuable to organizations and to society and should be sought at all organizational levels. Moreover, change happens in the world around the organization, even if not within it. The fact of change requires two responses in criterion development. First, change requires adaptation, and adaptability to change should be a more frequently used criterion. Second, innovation should be rewarded—and evaluated. New ideas sometimes solve problems; sometimes they create new problems. Some of them simply do not work. Measures of innovativeness should consider quality as well as quantity in evaluating ideas produced.

ISSUES IN FORMING CRITERION CONSTRUCTS

Refining a criterion construct requires some judgments and choices, some of them controversial. Despite the oversimplification, some choices are described here as dichotomies—oversimplifications to clarify them.

Typical Versus Maximum Performance

A criterion can reflect what a person *can* do under some circumstances, or what the person *will* do (is likely to do) under typical circumstances. The distinction is related to that between maximum performance and typical performance tests (Cronbach, 1970, p. 35). Can-do and will-do performance are not highly related (Sackett, Zedeck, & Fogli, 1988), and one must decide which construct is more useful in a given situation.

Complexity Versus Simplicity

Construct Complexity. Here the dichotomy is a choice between multi-dimensional and unidimensional criteria, between composites of several components and the independent components themselves. Most commonly, it is the choice between a single overall criterion and multiple, internally consistent criteria. Use of an overall, general criterion is the argument of Schmidt, Ones, and Hunter (1992), who would surely consider the criterion part of this chapter to be much ado about not much of anything. With characteristic firmness, they said,

> Criterion measures have long been considered critical because of the assumption that the nature of the criterion measure determines which predictors will be deemed valid and which invalid. It is now clear that for criteria of overall job performance . . . and tests of cognitive ability, this assumption is incorrect. . . . there are no documented cases of an aptitude or ability test being valid for one such criterion measure but not for another (i.e., zero validity). (Schmidt et al., 1992, p. 656)

This view, for which supporting evidence is considerable, clearly supports the choice of the more complex construct.

I have three quibbles, however. First, to call a predictor valid if the validity coefficient is significantly nonzero, but nonvalid otherwise, ignores differing levels of validity—that prediction can be better for one criterion component than for another, or that one predictor can be more or less valid than another. Second, this view is based on the wealth of meta-analytic research data mainly correlating cognitive test scores with overall ratings. They were, of course, explicit about this limit to their generalization, but it is reasonable to question its applicability to other kinds of criteria (e.g., contextual criteria), or to specific performance criteria studied too infrequently for meta-analysis to be feasible.

The third is more important. The quoted statement seems to treat a criterion as something used solely for validating a test. This, I contend with my own characteristic firmness, is to miss the entire point of personnel testing. The point is to effect organizational improvement through improved assessment of candidates, and the kind of change needed is reflected in the choice of the criterion. If the change needed is quite general in scope, then an overall performance criterion is best. A more specific sort of change calls for a more narrowly specified criterion. A hypothesis developer who thinks that different criterion components may require substantially different predictors has explicitly different hypotheses for the different components. If this presumption is wrong, the error will be shown because the different criteria are predicted about equally well by the same set of predictors. On the other hand, an a priori presumption of no such differences gives no opportunity to test the assumption and find it wrong.[5]

Complexity of Evaluative Evidence. When Cronbach and Meehl (1955) introduced the idea of construct validity, they referred to a *nomological network*, an integrated system of lawful generalizations within a theory. The network is never completely specified; every new piece of evidence adds information to it. Criterion evaluation does not require such a complex network. A measure of a criterion construct can be considered valid if it was carefully developed to fit a well-defined construct, and if research fails to disconfirm its validity by failing to support plausible alternative hypotheses. In short, a construct can be asserted by definition, measured in accordance with that definition, and be considered validly measured if disconfirmatory hypotheses are not supported (comments by Cronbach and Guion, United States Office of Personnel Management and Educational Testing Service, 1980, pp. 136–137). The complexity of the criterion construct determines in part the level of complexity of evidence needed to justify its measurement operations. In this sense, most practical criterion constructs are relatively simple; they are justified more by organizational relevance than by a network of scientific law, and their measures are evaluated by their construction and by demonstrations of their freedom from contaminants.

---

[5]Responding to a statement in the *Smithsonian* to the effect that no litmus test exists for distinguishing positions grounded in scholarship from those grounded in ideology, Doering (1992, p. 14), said, "there *is* a simple and reliable test. Scholarship admits the possibility of error." My view is that a hypothesis that can be shown to be wrong is preferable to one that is more likely to hide error.

Criterion Stability

Static Versus Dynamic Criteria. Ghiselli (1956) introduced the idea of dynamic criteria, in which relative rank order on any given performance dimension changes over time. It was said to occur when the rate of change in criterion performance varies for different people (i.e., when rank orders change over time) with accompanying changes in validity. Ghiselli (1956) reported that some validities were stable over time, others gradually decreased, and others changed in cycles. Subsequent reports offered further evidence of systematic validity change (e.g., Bass, 1962; Ghiselli & Haire, 1960), but some theoretical disputes have developed.

Simplex Matrices. Ghiselli (1956) noted that one form of systematic change in validity coefficients was a gradual reduction over time. In a correlation matrix showing such change, coefficients are systematically smaller as they depart from the principal diagonal. Such a matrix is termed a *simplex* (Guttman, 1955; Humphreys, 1960) or *superdiagonal matrix* (Jones, 1970). If the first variable in the matrix is an assessment of a candidate characteristic, and if the other variables are subsequent and successive measures of a criterion, the predictive validity coefficients may decline over the sequence of criterion collection times, as in Table 3.2.

Practical validation research offers few if any examples of such series of repeated criterion measures, but pairs of validity coefficients are sometimes reported, one with an early criterion and the other with a later one. Predictive validity has been lower for the later criterion in a variety of situations, for example, in education (e.g., Humphreys, 1960, 1968), in using salary to predict later salary level (Brenner & Lockwood, 1965), in pilot training (Alvares & Hulin, 1973), and in laboratory research on the learning process (e.g., Dunham, 1974; Fleishman & Hempel, 1956). Sometimes the decline does *not* occur; validities for an early criterion may even

TABLE 3.2
A Simplex Matrix of Correlation Coefficients

Variable[a]	1	2	3	4	5	6	7
1	$r_{11} >$	$r_{12} >$	$r_{13} >$	$r_{14} >$	$r_{15} >$	$r_{16} >$	r_{17}
2		$r_{22} >$	$r_{23} >$	$r_{24} >$	$r_{25} >$	$r_{26} >$	r_{27}
3			$r_{33} >$	$r_{34} >$	$r_{35} >$	$r_{36} >$	r_{37}
4				$r_{44} >$	$r_{45} >$	$r_{46} >$	r_{47}
5					$r_{55} >$	$r_{56} >$	r_{57}
6						$r_{66} >$	r_{67}
7							r_{77}

[a]Variable 1 is a predictor; variables 2–7 are the same criterion variable collected at six successive times.

be lower than those for a later one. Learning a complex job takes time; criterion data collected too early can result in lower validity than if data are collected after performance is more stabilized. With motivational predictors, validity may be trivial until the "honeymoon" period is over (Helmreich et al., 1986). Some studies of assessment center validities have shown growth, not decay, over time (Hinrichs, 1978; Mitchel, 1975). Hulin, Henry, and Noon (1990) reviewed several such studies, correlating validity coefficients with time intervals, and reported general declines in predictive validity.

What does the decline say about the criterion? Has it changed, or have the people changed differentially? Alvares and Hulin (1972) offered two alternative explanations: a *changing task* explanation, suggesting that practice changes task demands for individual workers, and a *changing subject* explanation, suggesting that patterns of abilities change with repeated exposure to a task. The changing person explanation was supported in their subsequent study of student pilots (Alvares & Hulin, 1973).

Controversy. Strong differences of opinion exist. Barrett, Caldwell, and Alexander (1985) said that evidence of dynamic dimensionality is meager and recommended instead more attention to improving criterion reliability. In effect, they argued for accepting the notion of static (unchanging) dimensionality of criteria. Austin, Humphreys, and Hulin (1989) argued that an assumption of static dimensionality is not justified and introduced examples of the simplex to support their view. Under the heading, "Does the simplex exist?" Barrett and Alexander (1989) dismissed the simplex as an example of what Barrett (e.g., 1972) liked to call a *received doctrine.*

The heading asks the wrong question. It is more important to ask whether, in given circumstances, it makes sense to hypothesize and study changes in criterion rank order and empirical validities. Relative criterion performance can be influenced over time by many variables, for example, changes in what employees are asked to do (job changes), what they have been rewarded (or punished) for doing, or in available resources (e.g., materials, tools, or technology). Optimal timing for criterion collection may depend on organizational needs. If the main consideration is success in training, then the time interval from criterion prediction to criterion assessment depends on the length of the formal training program. If the need is geared to strategic planning, then the hypothesis should apply to predictions of stable performance after learning the job, before widespread individual differences in responses to the work environment occur.

Rather than accept the alternative received doctrine assuming static dimensionality, I urge frequent, even routine, investigations of validity changes and changes in relative criterion position of employees over time.

CRITERION MEASURES

The basic predictive hypothesis is Inference 5 in Fig. 3.1, where a criterion domain is defined only conceptually. Testing the hypothesis empirically by criterion-related validation, of course, requires valid measurement of the criterion construct; moreover, considering a variety of measurement options can improve construct definition. Measurement options are discussed in later chapters, but some general criterion measurement problems should be recognized:

Unreliability may be inherent in the constructs themselves. Where behavior changes with mood swings, physical health, or fatigue, measures of proficiency will be unreliable no matter how carefully measured. Being absent, quitting, filing a grievance, or having an accident are unreliable events; Landy and Farr (1983, p. 31) listed, without being exhaustive, a dozen sources of unreliability in absence data, and similar lists could have been provided for other measures.

Judgment is always involved. Many apparently objective measures, such as counts of avoidable absences or functionally useful terminations, require judgment. It may be a rather impersonal one, but it is a judgment, nevertheless, and its reliability is not assured.

Many events have low base rates, that is, low frequency of occurrence. Even an accurate count of a low base rate phenomenon, without contaminating sources of variance, is hard if not impossible to predict.

Contextual criteria pose special measurement issues. For fuzzy constructs like honesty or organizational loyalty, construct definition may be very difficult; finding measurement operations to match the concepts as defined can be even harder. The construct validity of a measurement operation is threatened from two directions. It may be deficient, lacking variance attributable to some important aspect of the construct, or it may be contaminated by construct irrelevant variance. The best advice is to do one's best—to confer, to think critically, and then to select measures despite the lack of clarity. The worst advice is to ignore the problem, as if the problem of construct definition does not matter.

PREDICTORS AND PREDICTIVE HYPOTHESES

What variables are likely to predict the criterion? How should they be measured? Forming a predictive hypothesis is a two-part logical argument: first, that the criterion is related to certain traits and, second, that the chosen predictors are valid measures of those traits.

Constructs are inferred from knowledge of the job or organization. People with different backgrounds may infer different constructs. That is OK; no one hypothesis has a lock on good prediction. Psychologists may choose constructs from factor analysis or general theories. Managers and job incumbents may rely on their experience, using what Borman (1987) in another context called *folk theories*; if psychologists ignore ideas based on such experience, they risk ignoring some very good bets for predictors.

Folk Constructs

Job experts convened for job analysis may identify lists of variables, including personal traits, needed to carry out assigned tasks. Their lists stem from their cumulative experience, not from books or research journals; the variables can be called *folk constructs*.

A panel of higher level business executives and others met under the aegis of the United States Secretary of Labor, the Secretary's Commission on Achieving Necessary Skills (SCANS).[6] The SCANS report named five areas of competency and three foundation skills employers should expect in high school graduates (Secretary's Commission on Achieving Necessary Skills, 1991); its list can be considered, without pejoration, folk constructs. The foundation skills included (a) basic skills in reading, writing, arithmetic and mathematics, listening, and speaking; (b) thinking skills in creativity, decision making, and problem solving; and personal qualities of responsibility in exerting high levels of effort and setting high personal standards.

The five competencies—abilities to use foundation skills productively—are shown in Fig. 3.3. Headings under the five general categories of competencies add up to 20 more detailed kinds of competency.

These lists illustrate the problems and the advantages of folk constructs. The descriptions are vague and overlapping; "uses computers to process information," for example, is so inclusive as to have no meaning at all. Nevertheless, these skills and competencies offer starting points for specifying job requirements. And they show what the people interviewed and writing the report considered crucial. Reliance on folk constructs provides valuable focus, but it often needs a lot of clarification.

---

[6]The Secretary of Labor was Lynn Martin; Chair of the Commission was William E. Brock. Commission members represented business, labor, education, and governmental jurisdictions. Over a year, commission members talked to business owners, managers, union officials, and workers at different kinds of jobs and then developed a report on the kinds of skill and competency high school students need for satisfying, productive personal lives and for success in high performance, competitive industries.

FIVE COMPETENCIES

Resources: Identifies, organizes, plans, and allocates resources
    A. *Time:* Selects goal-relevant activities, ranks them, allocates them, and prepares and follows schedules
    B. *Money:* Uses or prepares budgets, makes forecasts, keeps records, and makes adjustments to meet objectives
    C. *Material and Facilities:* Acquires, stores, allocates, and uses materials or space efficiently
    D. *Human Resources:* Assesses skills and distributes work accordingly, evaluates performance and provides feedback

Interpersonal: Works with others
    A. *Participates as Member of a Team:* contributes to group effort
    B. *Teaches Others New Skills*
    C. *Serves Clients/Customers:* works to satisfy customers' expectations
    D. *Exercises Leadership:* communicates ideas to justify position, persuades and convinces others, responsibly challenges existing procedures and policies
    E. *Negotiates:* works toward agreements involving exchange of resources, resolves divergent interests
    F. *Works with Diversity:* works well with men and women from diverse backgrounds

Information: Acquires and uses information
    A. *Acquires and Evaluates Information*
    B. *Organizes and Maintains Information*
    C. *Interprets and Communicates Information*
    D. *Uses Computers to Process Information*

Systems: Understands complex inter-relationships
    A. *Understands Systems:* Knows how social, organizational, and technological systems work and operates effectively with them
    B. *Monitors and Corrects Performance:* distinguishes trends, predicts impacts on system operations, diagnosis deviations in systems' performance and corrects malfunctions
    C. *Improves or Designs Systems:* suggests modifications to existing systems and develops new or alternative systems to improve performance

Technology: Works with a variety of technologies
    A. *Selects Technology:* chooses procedures, tools or equipment including computers and related technologies
    B. *Applies Technology to Task:* Understands overall intent and proper procedures for setup and operation of equipment
    C. *Maintains and Troubleshoots Equipment:* Prevents, identifies, or solves problems with equipment, including computers and other technologies

FIG. 3.3. The five SCANS competencies.

Research and Theory

Research-oriented taxonomies provide practical starting points for hypothesis development. One example is the *Handbook of Human Abilities* (Fleishman & Reilly, 1992); it lists 52 cognitive, psychomotor, physical, and sensory/perceptual abilities. For each of them, a conceptual definition is illustrated by tasks and jobs requiring it and by some examples of measures of it. Other lists (e.g., Carroll, 1993; Ekstrom, 1973; French, 1951; Gardner, 1983; Guilford, 1959; Peterson & Bownas, 1982; Peterson, Mumford, Borman, Jeanneret, & Fleishman, 1995) differ in details, but they overlap greatly. Each list describes its authors' interpretations of available data. They all describe the major explanatory constructs, especially the cognitive constructs, common to most taxonomies.

Good hypotheses depend on prior knowledge and logic. One needs to know what has worked before, and what has failed to work, in similar situations. Some things are well-established; for example, job performance is predicted better by abilities than by other traits, and cognitive abilities predict better than noncognitive abilities, for most jobs. Not many such generalizations are so widely supported. Nevertheless, research literature (especially meta-analyses) and informal networks often describe experiences others have had predicting criteria similar to one's own.

COGNITIVE ABILITIES

Cognitive abilities are abilities to perceive, process, evaluate, compare, create, understand, manipulate, or generally think about information and ideas. Common work-relevant cognitive activities include reading verbal or graphic materials, understanding the principles that make things work, planning events or procedures, solving problems, or perceiving signs of trouble in equipment or in human interactions or in contradictions in plans. Mental abilities are diverse and somewhat overlapping. More than 50 years of factor analytic research, however, has clarified and defined many components of mental abilities.

Cognitive Factors

Factor analysis examines intercorrelations among measures to identify or infer underlying latent traits accounting for the correlations (Carroll, 1993). Several lists of mental abilities have been based on factor analyses, beginning with the Thurstone (1938) list of seven primary mental abilities: verbal comprehension, word fluency, spatial ability, perceptual speed, numerical facility, memory, and inductive reasoning.[7] Subsequent research has made finer distinctions; spatial ability, for example, divided into spatial relations, an ability to perceive spatial patterns accurately, and visualization, an ability to imagine movements of an object in space or to manipulate objects in imagination (French, 1951); both speed and accuracy components have been found for the perceptual speed factor, although they are rarely measured separately in practice. Other spatial

---

[7]Beware of names given to factors; they can be misleading because they can mean different things to different hearers. Factor analysts often avoid names, preferring to define factors more explicitly in terms of measures that have (or do not have) strong loadings on them. Here, however, the intent is to give a flavor of the varieties of factors, not to report individual researches in detail or to provide detailed definitions.

factors have been identified, as have finer distinctions of reasoning and numerical abilities. Over the years, factor analytic research has provided and replicated so many factors and operational definers of factors that some system of organizing thinking about them is necessary. One way to organize factors is hierarchical; that is, to define some factors as broader or more general than others and to identify narrower factors that fit within the broader rubric. This approach is discussed in the section on general factors.

Another organization, now generally out of style, was the *structure of intellect* model offered by Guilford (1956). Guilford classified factors in three ways: by the intellectual process or *operation* required by the tests defining a factor, by the stimulus *content* of the tests, and by the *product* or result of the process. The three-dimensional model is shown in Fig. 3.4.

The model had five operations (memory, knowing or recognizing information, evaluating information, the convergent production of ideas, and the divergent production of ideas), four content categories (figural, symbolic, semantic, and behavioral), and six products or outcomes (units, classes, relations or connections, structures or systems of ideas, transformations of information, and extrapolations or implications). In the last

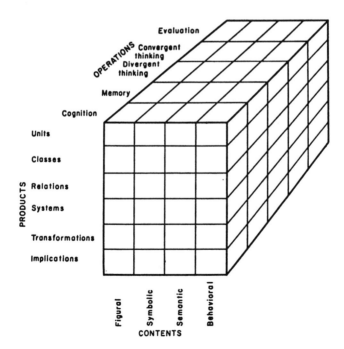

FIG. 3.4. Representation of the structure of intellect model. From Guilford, J. P. (1959). *Personality*. New York: McGraw-Hill. Reprinted with permission.

two of these, categories form a continuum of complexity. The result is a matrix of 120 cells, each representing an ability factor either found in factor analysis or hypothesized to be found. This model has been criticized, mainly for postulating too many, too narrow factors.

Ekstrom (1973) reviewed research on cognitive factors and concluded that most of it could be summarized with a dozen established factors, although Ekstrom, French, and Harmon (1975) later added three more. Her list was further abbreviated to ten by Dunnette (1976). Fleishman and Reilly (1992) listed 21 cognitive abilities. The fact that lists vary from 10 to 120 factors is no reason to reject factor analytically derived constructs. Differences in the measures analyzed, in methods of analysis, and in the focus of researchers will result in slightly different factors and differences in their specificity. The possibilities for differences make it impressive that factor analytic results have been as much alike as they are. If every nuance is treated as a difference, the lists of factors across studies can be very large. Anastasi (1988, p. 384) said that "well over 100" cognitive factors had been reported, and Carroll (1993) suggested that the number could approach infinity! I will not try to list and define them all, but I offer this illustrative (*not* definitive) short list of frequently recurring cognitive factors:

Verbal comprehension: the ability to understand words and their meanings, and to apply such understanding in verbal communications. At some level, it seems necessary in almost any job. Nearly any mental ability test yielding separate scores for distinguishable categories of ability will include a verbal comprehension score in some form. Some authors distinguish factors for understanding oral and written communication.

Fluency: the ability to produce quickly a lot of ideas or associations. Different jobs may require different kinds of fluency, such as verbal fluency, ideational fluency, or number fluency.

Perceptual speed: the ability to identify figures (such as numbers, letters, pictures, or names), make comparisons, or match visually perceived figures quickly and accurately. Perceptual speed is a generally useful predictor of clerical performance.

Flexibility and speed of closure: the ability to restructure visual perceptions and to do so quickly; for example, to remember and find a previously perceived figure embedded in distracting material, or to perceive a perceptual field as a whole, even where missing details must be supplied by the perceiver. Flexibility, a key part of Guilford's notion of divergent thinking, is related not only to sensory perceptions but to the perceptions or interpretations of ideas and events. Perceptual closure may be required for patrol officers who get only quick and incomplete glimpses of things; those with rapid speed of closure will have enough of an idea of the whole to know whether further investigation is warranted. A broader concept of flexibility and speed of closure may be relevant to an "executive decision," where a course of action must be chosen among options on the basis of limited information.

Spatial orientation and visualization: the ability to perceive spatial patterns, to orient oneself (or an object) relative to objects in space, or to manipulate or transform mentally given spatial patterns into altered patterns or arrangements. Engineers, mechanics, and others who must work from drawings need such abilities; drivers, pilots, or others who plan trips probably need it as well. Two separate factors are frequently defined in which spatial orientation involves self-reference and visualization is more object-centered.

Number facility: the ability to do elementary arithmetic operations quickly and accurately. This is an obvious requirement for jobs requiring arithmetic computation. Computers and hand-held calculators do not eliminate the need; it is easy to get vastly wrong answers with such aids, and some mental arithmetic lets one know the approximate correct answer and evaluate the answer given by the machinery.

General reasoning: the ability to understand relational principles among elements of a problem and to structure the problem in preparation for solving it; it is also the ability to work toward a conclusion or solution and to test the soundness of conclusions reached, perhaps by comparing the soundness of one conclusion with that of other possible conclusions. The very complexity of the definition attests to the complexity of the concept. Many factor analyses have identified more than one reasoning factor; distinctions, however, tend not to be very clean.

Problem recognition: the ability to tell from early and perhaps subtle warnings that something is wrong or likely to go wrong; the problems may develop in equipment, people, social systems, or data. Sensitivity to potential or existing problems seems useful in jobs such as physician, air traffic controller, or machinery operation or monitoring.

Associative memory: the ability to recall bits of information previously associated with unrelated information; for example, to remember numerical information associated with names. A typical test presents a set of pictures and names to examinees for a short time. Then, after an unrelated test or exercise is given, the pictures alone may then be shown and the examinee asked to give the names paired with them.

Span memory: the ability to recall in proper sequence a series of items (numbers, words, symbols) after a single presentation of the series, for example, looking up a telephone number and remembering it.

"Marker" tests, those consistently defining a factor in repeated analyses, are identified in the summaries by Ekstrom (1973), Fleishman and Quaintance (1984), and others. Markers help in understanding the factors, but they may not predict complex criteria as well as less "pure" measures of factor constructs. Current thinking is that broader measures of more general ability, rather than narrow tests of "pure" factors, are more likely to be useful predictors.

General Mental Abilty

Even the lowest correlations between measures of mental ability are positive, suggesting a general mental ability. Traditionally, the general trait is called *intelligence*. Sternberg and Detterman (1986) asked a couple of dozen experts to define intelligence; the disparate set of definitions, however, included core concepts such as reasoning, symbolic representation, problem solving, and decision processes. Different authors, with different perspectives, emphasize different features of behavior called intelligent. My personal favorite is this: *"Intelligence is the resultant of the processes of acquiring, storing in memory, retrieving, combining, comparing, and using in new contexts information and conceptual skills; it is an abstraction"* (Humphreys, 1979, p. 115). It is a rather unwieldy definition. So is the concept of intelligence, however defined.

Global Scores. An intelligence test may include several item types, all tapping different factors. One item might be a verbal analogies item, the next a number series, the third a mental manipulation of two-dimensional depictions of three dimensional objects, the fourth a simple arithmetic problem, the fifth an arithmetic story problem, and the next five a repetition of the same five item types at a slightly higher difficulty level, and so on through the test (the so-called "spiral omnibus test"). The only score might be the total number of items correctly answered, with no regard for the kinds of items most frequently mastered; the score is a "general mental ability" score. A different general mental ability test may have independently timed and scored homogeneous subsets of items, scores on each summed for the overall score.

Sometimes the total score is called an Intelligence Quotient, or IQ. In adult testing, an IQ score is a standard score with a mean of 100 and a standard deviation somewhere between 12 and 20, depending on the preferences of the test developer. These IQ scores depend on ability distribution in the standardizing sample and on the standard deviation chosen. The same person can have several different IQ scores if tested with several different tests. The term IQ is an old one, and it should be retired. I get upset when people—especially psychologists, who should know better—refer to IQs as traits, as in "how well he will do in life depends on his IQ." Such statements confuse the test score, IQ, with the general intelligence construct. Because an IQ score depends, among other things, on the content and structure of the particular test used, the normative sample, and the size of the standard deviation of the standard scale, IQ is clearly *not* a characteristic of the person tested. Because of the excess semantic baggage attached to it, *the term IQ simply should not be used.*

General Factors. Factor analysis can result in correlated factors; the factor correlations can be subjected to a further factor analysis to identify second-order factors, which are more general, defined by a set of the original factors. If second-order factors are correlated, a still more general third-order factor can be defined. The result is a hierarchical factor structure as diagrammed in Fig. 3.5. There are also direct methods of hierarchical factor analysis. Spearman (1927) used a method that emphasized a general intellectual ability he abbreviated *g*, a symbol once again in frequent use.

Cattell (1963) argued that the general factor had two components, *fluid intelligence* (*Gf*), involving basic reasoning, and *crystallized intelligence* (*Gc*), measured by tests such as vocabulary; eventually, he claimed five second order (general) factors, including general visualization (*Gv*), general fluency (*F*), and general speediness (*Gs*) (Horn & Cattell, 1966). Carroll (1993), in an encyclopedic re-analysis of mountains of factor analytic studies, proposed a three-stratum model. The first stratum consisted of the first

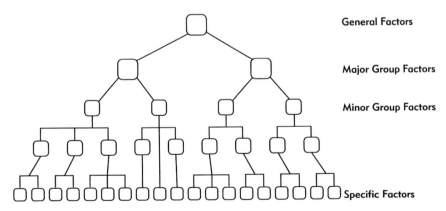

FIG. 3.5.   A hierarchical model of the factorial structure of human abilities. From Guion (1965).

order factors, somewhat like (but more narrowly and precisely defined) the list offered earlier. The second stratum included more general factors such as fluid and crystalized intelligence and others, and the third corresponded pretty well to Spearman's concept of g.

The theoretical importance of a general factor is no longer much of an issue. The major issues now are, first, whether a general factor accounts for much or little of the variance in mental ability test scores and, second, whether general factors or more specific factors are better bases for decisions. I answer neither question clearly.

Employment Tests and g. A special issue of the *Journal of Vocational Behavior* (Gottfredson, 1986) discussed the importance of g. Evidence of the predictive usefulness of g was given in several articles. Of particular interest for personnel decisions was the showing by Thorndike (1986) that, with very large samples, batteries of less general, more specific test types provided 10–15% better prediction than did general mental ability scores. In samples of moderate size, typical of employment test validation studies, the difference either disappeared or changed in favor of the more general, overall score. An exception to the latter: if a preliminary screening test was used, the relative importance of scores on specific mental abilities became greater than that of g, presumably because the preliminary screening test measured g and eliminated those with limited general ability.

Not all contributors to the issue agreed that specific cognitive abilities usually add little to the predictive power of the general factor. Linn (1986) and Tyler (1986) both sounded notes of caution, gently insisting that focus on specific abilities continue even while acknowledging the value of the more general intelligence construct.

So, should predictors be global, general constructs or more narrow, specific ones? Much heat has been wasted on this question. Different, noninterchangeable measurements can be developed for different levels of generality of the same domain, and they can be useful for different purposes (P. C. Smith, 1985). That fact is too often overlooked.

Alternative Constructs

Cognitive science may provide useful alternatives to factor analytic constructs, but it has not yet done so (Estes, 1992, p. 278). One cognitive scientist, proposing a "triarchic theory," divided intelligence, like Gaul, into three parts: (a) componential, in which cognitive tasks are analyzed into component processes, such as performance and knowledge acquisition, (b) experiential, in which dealing with novelty differs from the automatized responses likely with well-known things, and (c) contextual, in which both practical and social intelligence are invoked (Sternberg, 1977, 1985; Sternberg, Wagner, Williams, & Horvath, 1995). The two forms of contextual intelligence limit my enthusiasm; both concepts have long psychometric histories of failed attempts at measurement, and, so far, I see no historic change. The potential usefulness of the theory does not reside in currently practical assessment procedures, however, but in pushing concepts of intelligence beyond traditional psychometric constructs. Theories based on cognitive research emphasize intellectual *processes* as components; they are considered less static than traits.

The study of individual differences in cognition has not yet broadened the scope of abilities measured, a "leading priority for the intelligence tests of the future" (Sternberg, 1991, p. 265). The future is not yet here, but there is enough ferment among people interested in concepts of intelligence that the constructs they develop, insofar as they differ from traditional ones, will eventually be measurable in nonlaboratory contexts. Cognitive research on individual differences in cognition should be followed attentively, less for psychometric contributions than for new constructs.

Useful constructs can be inferred by experienced job experts, without relying on factor analysis and cognitive science. Managers, incumbents, and other job experts have their own working folk constructs. Using them, psychologists can modify well-known, well-established scientific constructs for particular responsibilities. Ad hoc constructs stemming from local wisdom, refined by an infusion of research-based knowledge, can be useful.

Creativity is an example of folk theory refined by data. Creativity is more complex than the usual first-order factors but less general than the second-order factors. It requires both fluency and flexibility in the production or invention of things, procedures, or ideas. It may also have a motivational component, a desire to do or try things that are different or unusual, the Guilford originality factor. It may also, in given situations, imply an ability to capitalize on serendipity, seeing opportunities in unplanned events or situations.

Problem-solving ability differs from creativity, a divergent thinking ability, in being a convergent thinking ability to find a right or best answer to a problem. It, too, is complex, with components like (a) problem definition, (b) systematic data gathering (identifying and going after information relevant to the problem), and (c) planning an orderly approach to analyzing the problem. Troubleshooting is an example; good troubleshooters understand the problem domain, have detailed knowledge of the systems or equipment in trouble, and follow a clear plan rather than jump willy-nilly from one approach to another. Most moderate-to-high level jobs involve at least some problem-solving activity. Raaheim (1974) suggested that solving a problem depends on prior experience with its components and with the tools available for solving it; the strong experiential component suggests that it might be related to specific job knowledge.

Planning ability seems to require elements of orderliness (i.e., the ability to arrange a set of likely events in a logical sequence) and of abilities to see implications of decisions reached, a matter of foresight.

Wisdom is a term rarely encountered in psychometric literature, but Sternberg (1990) devoted an entire book to it. Contributions of various chapter authors conceive of wisdom in terms of problem finding, of affect, of judgment, of *knowing in the face of uncertainty* (Kitchener & Brenner, 1990). The book focuses primarily on developmental issues, but it has important implications for work. Folk theory often holds that older workers compensate for loss in specific abilities by an increase in wisdom.

Ability to learn from experience seems relevant to any job with a lot of nonroutine activities. Long-term memory is probably a component, as is ability to see the implications of the knowledge it represents. It may be an ability to "restructure" knowledge (see Messick, 1984).

Verbal expression—the ability to communicate, either orally or in writing (Fleishman & Quaintance, 1984, p. 322)—may include verbal comprehension, but it is clearly more. Can one assume that a high score on a verbal comprehension test is closely associated with the ability to express oneself well? Perhaps, but the ability may require memory for what communicated well in the past, sensitivity to the targets of the communication, and much more.

Speed of information processing may be much more general than the perceptual speed factor as usually encountered. It is more familiar to refer to such an ability as *reaction time,* but I am thinking of something broader, perhaps a second-order construct like the *Broad Speediness* general factor identified by Carroll (1993). Is such an ability also related to how quickly (and perhaps how thoroughly) people can grasp complex information in such settings as briefings? If so, it would be as relevant to managerial or executive performance as simple reaction times are for cab drivers and fighter pilots. Reaction time may be influenced by the ability to focus or to divide attention. There is a strong vigilance literature (focus), but not much on speed of response where attention must be divided.

I include *common sense* in this list of commonsense constructs because the term is so common and the evidence of it so rare. Different people often mean different things by it; when job experts invoke the need for common sense, one task of the psychologist is to question them closely about what they mean. They may mean the same construct that Sternberg et al. (1995) call tacit knowledge, or experience-based knowledge.

The list could go on. All of these examples are broad, moderately general constructs. They illustrate the kinds of constructs intelligent people can infer about work requirements. They are more likely to be based on a rational understanding of the work to be done than on theory, but an understanding of relevant theory can refine their definitions.

Job Specific Knowledge and Skill

"Know-how" is a folk construct. People who have it—who know and understand thoroughly a job's requirements—are better workers than those with less of it. To be useful, the term needs cleaner definition. Job knowledge may be general or limited to specific kinds of information or skill. The O*NET system of occupational information (Peterson et al., 1995) lists skills in three categories: basic, cross-functional, and occupational specific. Some basic skills are acquired in school, but a broader view considers them capacities

> developed over a relatively long period of time that promote or provide a foundation for learning other types of material. In this sense, basic skills, although often educationally based, represent a key infrastructure needed for the ongoing development of cross-functional and occupational-specific skills as well as requisite knowledges. (Mumford & Peterson, 1995, pp. 3–8)

"Basic" does not mean elementary, as shown by those listed in Table 2.8.

Cross-functional skills are those useful in a wide range of occupations. They include a variety of problem-solving, social, technological, systems, and resource management skills. Higher order problem-solving skills include problem identification, finding information, and generating and evaluating ideas. Social skills include social perceptiveness, persuasion or negotiation, and service orientation, among others. Occupational or job specific skills, of course, focus on tasks specifically required in occupations or jobs.

The three categories are segments of a continuum from general to specific, as applicable to kinds of information as to kinds of skill. The nearer a particular skill or knowledge is to the basic or general end of the continuum, the more likely it is to be expected of all qualified candidates; the nearer to the job specific end, the more likely it is to be the content of in-house training programs. For organizational entry, hypotheses usually emphasize more general skills and knowledge; for promotions, they may emphasize skills and knowledge specific to the work to be done.

PERSONALITY CONSTRUCTS

Personality is even more amorphous than intelligence, and distinctions between specific and more general traits are harder to make. It may make more sense to refer to levels of personality description than to levels of trait generality (McAdams & Emmons, 1995). McAdams (1995) suggested three levels. Level I is descriptive, largely describing traits independently of contexts. Level II may also be descriptive, describing the kinds of actions characteristic of persons and the adaptations they typically make; at this level, descriptions "are situated in time, place, and role" (McAdams, 1995, p. 379). Level III is self-identity defined by "unity, purpose, and meaning in life" (McAdams, 1995, p. 382). Levels I and II are commonly assessed in personnel practice; Level III is considered rarely if at all. Perhaps it should be. It is the level of adult development a person has attained, and at this level it might describe, better than at the other levels, the temporal consistency and motivation of an adult job candidate.

Personality is a mixture of values, temperament, coping strategies, character, and motivation, among other things. Compared to cognitive traits, conceptual definitions of personality traits can be more easily developed for particular jobs or purposes, but finding operational definitions to fit them is more difficult.

From the 1960s to the 1980s, research on personality predictors was sparse. Some people (e.g., R. J. Schneider & L. M. Hough, 1995) attributed the demise of such research (unfairly, I think) to a review that concluded that personality test validities had not been demonstrated (Guion & Gottier, 1965). Two other influences were probably greater. First, the Civil Rights Act of 1964 explicitly permitted the use of "professionally developed ability tests," but it included no such enabling statement for personality inventories. Such inventories were targeted for severe social criticism (e.g., Gross, 1962), so many employers quietly stopped using them in fear of litigation. Second, the views of Mischel (1968), insisting that behavior is determined more by situations than by traits, were widely accepted. The idea of personality traits was widely abandoned by psychologists, but trait psychology, which never fully disappeared, reappeared in the 1980s.

Traits

A *trait* differs from a *state*, a temporary condition or mood; one may be in a good or poor mood, or anxious or not anxious, at a given time without the consistency implied by trait. A *personality trait* is a habitual way of thinking or doing in a variety of situations. It may be a general value, goal, or behavioral tendency to seek or avoid certain kinds of situations. It might be a need, even a metaphorical need, for a goal that is a state of being as well as an object or condition or experience. It may be a role that one habitually plays—the role of leader, clown, scholar, teacher, or a more nameless role having its genesis in other traits such as learned helplessness. It may be a constellation or combination of traits, a syndrome or type. The

O*NET taxonomy does not refer to personality traits but to "occupational values" and "work styles" (Peterson et al., 1995, chaps. 11, 12). These may be better descriptions of traits related to work.

Most personality inventories measure several traits; if the list of traits named in them were placed end to end, it would stretch far! Consider the variety of constructs implied in this partial list of names of scales in existing measures of personality: alienation, anxiety, coping styles, emotional empathy, hopelessness, level of aspiration, perceptions of daily hassles and uplifts, response style, rigid type, risk-taking orientation, self-confidence, self-esteem, stress tolerance, team builder, Type A, and vigor. So many possible constructs must overlap; they require some means of reduction, commonly factor analysis.

The Five-Factor Model

Languages have thousands of words describing individual personalities. Many words have overlapping meanings; for example, *timid, shy, nervous,* and *irresolute* all describe people who tend to falter in social situations. Meaningful distinctions can be made among these terms, but the more general idea of social faltering can be inferred from the similarities. The example is an "arm-chair" factor analysis. Actual factor analysis applied to such descriptive words has often resulted in five factors (e.g., Goldberg, 1981; McCrae, 1992; Tupes & Christal, 1961). The five-factor solution, sometimes called the Big 5, has been found in languages other than English (John, 1990; Paunonen, Jackson, Trebinski, & Forsterling, 1992) and in using different measurement techniques, including adjective checklists, phrases, and even a nonverbal approach (Paunonen et al., 1992). It has for some time dominated personality research; Goldberg (1993) described the domination as an "emerging consensus."

The Five Factors. Names given the factors by various researchers have differed, as listed in Table 3.3 (Digman, 1990). Some of these differences in preference can be attributed to bipolarity, with some names describing the positive and others describing the negative end of a bipolar scale. Some depend on acceptance of neologisms. Some are due to the different variables or descriptive terms used in different studies. Mainly, however, name differences seem to reflect the different nuances different researchers think most worthy of emphasis. As Goldberg (1995) said, a single descriptive term cannot capture everything in a factor defined by a whole set of descriptive words.

My preference for Factor I is *Surgency.* It suggests the interpersonal aspect associated with extraversion, the common alternative, but it also includes the dominance and visibility implied by wave-like "surging";

TABLE 3.3
Interpretative Names Given to the Five Recurring Personality Factors

---

Factor I: social adaptability, extraversion, surgency, assertiveness, exvia, social activity, sociability & ambition, power, activity, positive emotionality, interpersonal involvement.

Factor II: conformity, psychoticism, agreeableness, likeability, cortertia, paranoid disposition, friendly compliance, love, sociability, level of socialization.

Factor III: will to achieve, psychoticism, dependability, conscientiousness, task interest, superego strength, thinking introversion, prudence, work, impulsivity, constraint, self-control.

Factor IV: emotional control, neuroticism, emotionality, emotional, anxiety, emotional stability, affect, negative emotionality.

Factor V: inquiring intellect, culture, intelligence, intellect, intellectance, openness, independent.

Note. Adapted from Digman (1990, p. 423) with permission, from the Annual Review of Psychology, Volume 41, © 1990, by Annual Reviews Inc.

its positive end is partly defined by adjectives such as aggressive, assertive, unrestrained, daring, and even flamboyant (Hofstee, de Raad, & Goldberg, 1992, p. 156).

For Factor II, I prefer *Agreeableness*. It encompasses terms like likeability or friendliness without putting much emphasis on conformity or compliance or implying emotional attachment to others.

For Factor III, I prefer *Conscientiousness*; it seems the most relevant to the work context. One set of key terms identified by Hofstee et al. (1992, p. 158) includes *organized, neat, precise, exacting*; another includes terms like *conscientious, responsible*, and *dependable* clustering together, as shown in Fig. 3.6. The figure is a circumplex, a graphic depiction of the projection of pairs of factor loadings on the circumference of a circle. Words like *orderly* help define only Factor III. Words like *conscientious* help define both Factor III and, secondarily, Factor II. An emphasis on orderliness alone, implied by the first set of terms, implies obsessive attention to detail; such attention to work details has organizational value only if accompanied by conscientious regard for results, as in inspection or proof-reading. My preference here is widely shared.

For Factor IV, I prefer *Emotional Stability*. It is a familiar term, measured well by many inventories, positive rather than negative; it seems to generate no controversy, and it has frequently been a valid predictor.

Naming Factor V is not merely a matter of preference; substantive differences exist in the factors identified. "Openness to experience" is substantively different from "intellect," and neither reflects the central traits very well. In fact, Saucier (cited by Goldberg, 1995) suggested that the factor is better captured by terms like "imagination." I think the most useful term is *Intellectance*; it seems to imply, as does the collection of

Factor II and Factor III

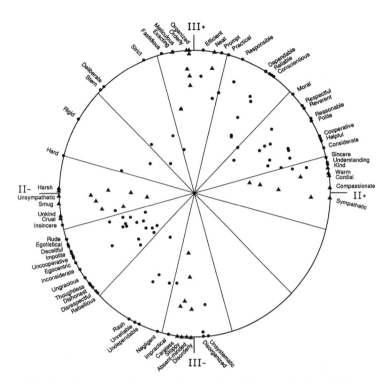

FIG. 3.6. Circumplex diagram for Factors II and III. From Hofstee, W. K. B., de Raad, B., & Goldberg, L. R. (1992). Integration of the big five and circumplex approaches to trait structure. *Journal of Personality and Social Psychology, 63*, 146–163. Reprinted with permission.

terms in Table 3.3, a liking for thinking about things, whether they be things within the culture or in personal experience, problems to be solved, or things to be created.

Conscientiousness. Factor III merits special attention. Employee theft of cash or merchandise is common enough that it has led to the use of tests to screen job applicants for honesty or integrity. These are not easy constructs to define. At first they seem to mean "theft-potential," but that is too narrow. A person of integrity is not simply a nonthief but one whose word can be trusted, whose work is reliably or dependably performed even without monitoring, who, in short, can be counted on to do the right or good thing. A closer look at honesty testing and related validation research suggests the broader construct. Some test publishers have called their instruments predictors of "counterproductive behavior," but perhaps the more common, and more positive, construct would emphasize the *dependability* or *trustworthiness* aspects of conscientiousness (Goldberg, Grenier, Guion, Sechrest, & Wing, 1991).

For a meta-analysis of personality test validities, predictors were assigned by trained judges to one of the Big 5 factors (Barrick & Mount, 1991). Predictors under *conscientiousness* had modest but useful mean correlations across criterion and occupational categories. A different meta-analysis, however, found *agreeableness* to be the most highly related and most general of the five factors (Tett, Jackson, & Rothstein, 1991).

Other Factor Taxonomies.

> An emerging consensus is not the same as universal agreement; there are those who do not accept the Big-Five factor structure. Indeed, the two most famous holdouts, Cattell and Eysenck, share little but their opposition to the five-factor model. Cattell remains convinced that there are far more factors than five, whereas Eysenck is certain that five is too many. (Goldberg, 1993, p. 31)

Eysenck (1991) described personality with just three dimensions, psychoticism, extraversion, and neuroticism. The first of these seems a blend of Factors II and III in the five-factor model, although named for the negative poles. The other "holdout," R. B. Cattell, developed *The Sixteen Personality Factor Questionnaire* (16PF). The "16" is historical. The 16PF was first published in 1949; in 1970, the 21st anniversary of the original publication of the 16PF, the opening paragraph of the 16PF Handbook (Cattell, Eber, & Tatsuoka, 1970) referred to the "thirty or so" primary personality traits. Later, 23 primary traits and 12 second-order factors were identified as comprising the structure of personality in normal behavior; more were identified for abnormal behaviors (Cattell, 1986, pp. 40–41). I will not list them; a mere list would be incomprehensible to those not already familiar with Cattell's work because it includes neologisms to avoid the excess meaning and ambiguity of common words. Those who seek alternatives to the Big Five taxonomy should study Cattell's writings seriously and in detail.

An intermediate alternative is the nine-factor taxonomy of the Personnel Decisions Research Institute (Hough, 1992, pp. 144–145), shown in Table 3.4 with abbreviated definitions.

The O*NET taxonomy of work styles (Borman, McKee, & Schneider, 1995), informed by but not directly based on factor analyses, lists seven higher order constructs, most of them divided into two or three lower order ones. In part, that taxonomy is shown in Table 3.5.

TABLE 3.4
The Nine Personality Factors in the Personnel
Decisions Research Institute Taxonomy

Dimension	Definition
Affiliation	Degree of sociability shown: liking to be with people; outgoing, participative, friendly vs. shy, reserved, and preferring to work alone
Potency	Degree of impact, influence, and energy shown: forceful, persuasive, optimistic, energetic in getting things done vs. timid about opinions or giving directions, lethargic, and pessimistic
Achievement	Tendency to strive for competence: hard worker, with high standards, concentration on and persistence in task completion, high self-confidence vs. low ego-involvement in work, self-doubting, little belief in value of hard work
Dependability	Degree of conscientiousness: disciplined, well organized, planful, respectful of rules, honest, trustworthy, orderly, thinking before acting vs. unreliable, impulsive, and rebellious
Adjustment	Emotional stability and stress tolerance: calm, even in moods; thinking clearly and rationally, with composure, in stressful situations vs. nervous, moody, irritable, worrying, functioning poorly under stress
Agreeableness	Degree of pleasantness shown in interpersonal relations: likable, tolerant, tactful, helpful, easy to get along with vs. critical, fault-finding, defensive, generally contrary
Intellectance	Degree of culture shown: open-minded, esthetically fastidious, imaginative, curious, independent in thought vs. unreflective, artistically insensitive, and narrow
Rugged individualism	Degree of fitting stereotypically masculine vs. feminine characteristics and values: decisive, action-oriented, independent, unsentimental vs. sympathetic, sensitive to criticism, subjective, feeling vulnerable
Locus of control	Perceived level of control over rewards and punishments: belief that people control what happens to them by what they do vs. belief that what happens to people is beyond their personal control

Note. From Hough (1992). Reprinted with permission.

Other alternatives mentioned by Goldberg (1993) included a two-factor model by Block, a three-factor model by Cloninger, and an alternative five-factor model by Zuckerman. Proponents of the Big 5 write convincingly of the "emerging consensus," but alternatives abound.

Commentary. The five factors may be too broad for personnel assessment. Funder (1991) asserted that global traits (like the five) are best for explanations and theory development, but that in prediction, narrower trait constructs are better. In choosing cognitive and psychomotor constructs, the trend favors more general ones, but for personality the trend seems to be toward greater specificity, favoring constructs more

TABLE 3.5
O*NET Taxonomy of Work Styles

Construct Label	Definition	High versus Low Levels[a]
I Achievement orientation	Job requires personal goal-setting and striving to succeed	Very high standards, need for success versus not very high standards or undue effort or persistence
Effort	Job requires maintaining challenging goals, exerting effort for task mastery	Continually extensive effort versus only moderate effort
Persistence	Job requires persistence in the face of obstacles	High levels when work gets hard versus few obstacles encountered
Initiative	Job requires willingness to take on job responsibilities and challenges	Volunteering to take on added challenges versus little interest in new responsibility but desire for structured, stable, responsibility
II Social influence	Job requires impact on others, displaying energy and leadership	Very energetic, preferring to lead and influence others versus rare requirements of energy or influence
Energy	Job requires energy and stamina to accomplish tasks	High levels of energy needed to get tasks done versus job not physically or mentally demanding
Leadership	Job requires willingness to take charge and offer opinions and direction	Strong preference for decision making & directing others in the organization versus little or no leader decisions
III Interpersonal orientation	Job requires pleasantness, cooperation, sensitivity, and preference for associating with other organization members	Very friendly, helpful, nonconfrontational behavior versus little requirement for such behavior
Cooperative	Job requires being pleasant and showing cooperative attitude encouraging people to work together	Smooth, cooperative work with others on the job versus little interaction with others
Caring	Job requires sensitivity to others' needs and feelings and being understanding and helpful on the job	Consistent caring and support for others on the job versus sensitivity; not highly important for this job
Social	Job requires preference for working with others (not alone), being personally connected with others	Participation and working closely with others in the organization versus usually working alone

(Continued)

140

TABLE 3.5
(Continued)

Construct Label	Definition	High versus Low Levels[a]
IV Adjustment	Job requires maturity, poise, coping with pressure, stress, and personal or work-related problems	Very calm, adaptable, avoiding overly emotional behavior versus no requirement for calmness or maintaining composure
Self-Control	Job requires keeping emotions in check even in difficult situations	High degree of self-control and nonthreatening behavior versus no challenges to self-control
Stress Tolerance	Job requires accepting criticism, dealing calmly, effectively with high stress situations	Extremely calm, tolerant of stress imposed by people or circumstances versus little stress on job
Adaptability/ Flexibility	Job requires openness to change and to considerable variety in the workplace	Being adaptible even to rapidly changing situations versus stable job and work situation needing little or no adaptation
V Conscientiousness	Job requires commitment to doing it correctly and carefully, being trustworthy, accountable, and attentive to details	Highly responsible, dependable, trustworthy on the job versus dependability not necessarily required
Dependability	Job requires reliably, responsibly fulfilling obligations	Highest levels of responsibility and dependability versus work situations permitting work that does not get done to be transferred to others
Attention to Detail	Job requires care about detail and thoroughness in completing tasks	High degree of thoroughness in handling details versus attention to detail not highly important
Integrity	Job requires being honest, avoiding unethical behavior	Highest levels of integrity and willingness to follow strict ethical code versus little involvement with ethical codes
VI Independence	Job requires autonomy, doing things in own way with little or no supervision, depending mainly on oneself to get things done	Highly autonomous with little or no dependence on others versus no requirement to work alone

(Continued)

TABLE 3.5
(Continued)

Construct Label	Definition	High versus Low Levels[a]
VII Practical Intelligence	Job requires generating useful ideas and thinking things through logically	Consistently developing useful ideas and good with job and work issues and problems versus no requirement for idea development or concern for work problems
Innovative	Job requires creativity and alternative thinking for new ideas for and answers to work related problems	A lot of creative thinking versus little or no such requirement
Analytical	Job requires analyzing information, logically addressing work or job issues and problems	Being very good at analyzing complex issues, data, or work-related problems versus no requirement for such analyses

[a]Statements anchoring high and low levels of the scales. Note that the scales describe trait requirements on a job; high and low levels refer to levels of trait requirement.

explicitly related to specific aspects of work. Examples include specific orientations such as *work orientation* (Gough, 1985) or *service orientation* (J. Hogan, R. Hogan, & C. M. Busch, 1984) or the breakdown of the Type A personality construct into two narrower constructs, achievement striving and impatience-irritability, each predicting different sorts of outcomes (Spence, Helmreich, & Pred, 1987). Even the *Hogan Personality Inventory* (R. Hogan & J. Hogan, 1992), heavily influenced by the five-factor model, includes seven scales, not five. It divides surgency into two components, ambition (the surgency emphasis) and sociability (the extraversion emphasis); intellectance is divided into one called intellectance and school success, liking academic pursuits and achievements. There is good reason to question the adequacy for applied purposes of the five broad factors. Yet two meta-analyses had positive findings on criterion-related validities for these five dimensions (Barrick & Mount, 1991; Tett et al., 1991). And Ones, Schmidt, and Viswesvaran (1994) found higher validities for broader constructs than for narrower ones (based on the curious notion that integrity tests are the broader measures of conscientiousness).

The issue is the level of abstraction at which traits are described for particular purposes. John, Hampson, and Goldberg (1991) identified three- and four-level hierarchies of terms such that each level above the lowest includes those below it. The lowest level, a subordinate level, was the narrowest (describing the most limited sort of trait) and provided the most explicit description. The middle level term included those at the subordinate one, among others. A basic level term was the broadest term that still described trait behavior. For some hierarchies, a fourth level, the superordinate level could also be identified as the most inclusive term in the hierarchy, but these terms are more evaluative than descriptive. One illustrative hierarchy, from subordinate to superordinate, consists of *tactful, polite, considerate,* and *nice.* Nice people are considerate (among other things), considerate people are polite (among other things), and polite people are tactful (among other things). Perhaps the Big 5 are basic level descriptors; for some jobs, the more restricted levels may describe traits more directly relevant. All three descriptive levels should be considered in searching job descriptions for predictor constructs.

Some critics say important personality constructs are not included in the Big 5. Apparent omissions include locus of control (Hough, 1992; Tett et al., 1991), self-esteem (Buss, 1992), activity level (Guilford, 1959), shyness (Asendorpf, 1992), "choosiness" (Riggio & Fleming, n.d.), and Type A personality (Tett et al., 1991). Some aspects of personality do not clearly fit the concept of a descriptive lexicon. Predictive hypotheses for decisions to be made among people well known in the organization may require a deeper probing of personality patterns than those where decisions are made among those new to or outside of the organization. McAdams (1992) referred to the five-factor model as a "psychology of the stranger," a psychology that does not entertain nuances among the factors or the "whole person" one comes to know when working closely together over extended time (p. 329). In short, maybe hypothesis development should consider a larger variety of constructs. In hypothesizing surgency as a predictor for potential leaders, for example, perhaps we should distinguish between the surgency in autocratic and that in transformational leadership styles.

Even the scientific merit of the five-factor model has been questioned. A special issue of the *Journal of Personality* on the five-factor model includes this comment:

> Whereas the identification of five reliable factors of trait description qualifies as a noteworthy accomplishment and one worth pursuing, ... one must not exaggerate the importance of the five factors, for an equally important task remains—*the need to understand and specify the components within (and perhaps between) the five factors.* (Briggs, 1992, p. 282, italics added)

Block (1995), among other things, criticized the model (or the approach) for excessive reliance on factor analysis without experimentation, prolonged observation, and as much concern for explanatory theory as for description. For applied use, description without theory may suffice, but McAdams (1992) and others, have argued that even an adequate description of a person's personality generally requires more information than can be found in five factor scores.

Alternative Personality Constructs

Many theoretically based constructs are available, many measured in existing personality inventories. Psychogenic needs listed long ago by Murray (1938) have inspired several inventories, such as the *Edwards Personal Preference Schedule* and Jackson's *Personality Research Form*. The *Embedded Figures Test* was based on field-dependence versus field-independence, the cognitive style or ability to disassociate perceptions or ideas from the context in which they occur. The *Myers–Briggs Type Indicator* considers the classification of people into personality types based on four dimensions: extraversion versus introversion, sensation versus intuition, thinking versus feeling, and reliance on judgment versus perception. A typology of personality types and matching types of work environments is assessed by Holland's *Vocational Preference Inventory* and its matching job analysis form, the *Position Classification Inventory*. The Millon theory, originally for abnormal behavior but now developed for normal adults, has 24 scales for 12 bipolar constructs in the *Millon Index of Personality Styles* (MIPS). These are only a few of literally hundreds of measures and constructs to be found in such periodically published directories and reviews of tests as the Buros Institute of Mental Measurements' *Tests in Print* and *Mental Measurements Yearbooks* or the Test Corporation of America's *Tests* and *Test Critiques* (e.g., Keyser & Sweetland, 1992; Kramer & Conoley, 1992; Mitchell, 1983; Sweetland & Keyser, 1991).

In General: Personality in Selection

Research Design. Too often, personality test validation for selection decisions has relied on serendipity; research has not been planned or done very well. Guion and Gottier (1965) complained that most studies reviewed used concurrent rather than predictive designs. Personality traits are enduring, but they are surely malleable by experience. Self-confidence, for example, is likely to grow for those who do well on a job and to shrink for those who have been unsuccessful; variance in self-confidence is likely to increase with experience, and so is its correlation with success. Whatever justification exists for concurrent estimates of criterion-related validity of ability measures cannot be extended to personality measures.

The review offered other criticisms and concluded that "in *some* situations, for *some* purposes, *some* personality measures can offer helpful predictions. But there is nothing in this summary to indicate in advance which measure should be used in which situation or for which purpose" (Guion & Gottier, 1965, pp. 159–160). The overall conclusion was that the research had been so poorly done that generalized confidence in personality measures was unwarranted, and without clearer evidence of their validity in the situation at hand, they should not be used to make decisions whether to hire or to reject people. The field of employment psychology is perhaps better prepared now, more than 30 years later, to study personality traits as predictors than it was at the time of that review. Meta-analyses have provided grounds for optimism.

The meta-analysis by Tett et al. (1991) classified studies as *confirmatory*, meaning a clearly stated hypothesis to be confirmed or rejected, or *exploratory*, meaning no such hypothesis. They also coded whether job analysis had been done. Generalized validity for confirmatory studies was better than for exploratory studies, and it was much better for confirmatory studies informed by job analysis. These, of course, are the studies based on a carefully developed predictive hypothesis.

Action as Content in Personality Assessment. Personality constructs tend to be unobservable descriptions of what people *are*, not what they *do*. Perhaps the emphasis needs to be reversed, and perhaps the content of personality constructs should be defined as characteristic responses to broad environmental demands, such as those of people at work or people in college. Pointing out that the psychology of college sophomores may be in part a function of the common demands they face, Dawes (1991) suggested that research questions should be rephrased to reflect those demands, asking for decription of acts rather than of traits. Botwin and Buss (1989) did so; they developed act-content inventories for 22 categories. Their research supported the five-factor model quite well, but *only* when they controlled for a general activity level. One frequently useful construct is the degree to which people are active rather than inert (Buss, 1988). When activity level was included in their analysis, the five-factor model did not fit so cleanly. General activity level is itself a construct of probable importance for many kinds of work, but not many taxonomies include it. It may be only one obvious example of work-relevant constructs not commonly assessed. Further taxonomic research is needed, and perhaps it should focus on things people persistently do in their work.

NONCOGNITIVE PREDICTORS

Distinctions between cognitive and noncognitive traits are arbitrary. Few tasks are exclusively cognitive or exclusively motor or exclusively anything else, but there are different emphases. Sometimes, the focus is on abilities and skills not ordinarily considered cognitive.

Physical and Sensory Competencies

The Americans with Disabilities Act (ADA) and the Civil Rights Act of 1964 (as amended) have dampened what little enthusiasm existed for physical and sensory competencies for personnel decisions. For many kinds of work, however, they are potential predictors of performance and may be genuine prerequisites for some jobs and therefore defensible in litigation.

Physical Characteristics. Anthropometric characteristics (mainly height and weight) may be directly useful as predictors on some jobs or as moderators. Physical traits *can* be relevant to work outcomes; accomodation for physical differences may not be as simple as it might seem. Remodeling or computerizing a work area might be prohibitively expensive; providing work aids for some people might create hazards for others. Job analysis should show just how important apparent physical requirements really are and how the job might be done differently, and it should form a foundation for imaginative thinking about potential methods of accomodation. J. Hogan and A. M. Quigley (1986) reported that height and weight requirements had been approved in litigation only where there was no adverse impact or where job-relatedness was clearly demonstrated. Common sense or the mere appearance of relevance is not and will not be enough evidence of job-relatedness. For most jobs, redesigning the work environment may be more productive than selecting people to fit the environment as it is.

Physical Abilities. Many jobs, not merely laboring jobs, require physical skills. Mail carriers, fire fighters, power line repairers, tree trimmers, construction workers, and paramedics are among those for whom strength, endurance, and balance are relevant. Nevertheless, few psychologists have studied physical abilities and their relevance in employment practices; most of what we know has come from the work of Edwin A. Fleishman and his associates, summarized in Fleishman and Reilly (1992):

Static strength: Ability to exert continuous muscular force for short periods of time. Used in pushing or lifting heavy objects.

Explosive strength: Ability to exert muscular force in short bursts. Used in running, jumping, throwing things, or striking them (as in splitting logs with an axe).

Dynamic strength: Ability to use repeated or sustained muscular force over long periods of time; muscular endurance, resistance to muscular fatigue. Used in tasks requiring climbing or digging.

Trunk strength: Ability of stomach and lower back muscles to support parts of the body in repetitive tasks or over long periods of time. Used when working with tools while partially sitting or moving heavy objects while bent over.

Extent flexibility: Ability to bend, stretch, twist or reach out; a matter of degree, not of speed. Used when working in awkward, cramped settings or extending arms to reach something.

Dynamic flexibility: Ability to bend, and so on, quickly and repeatedly. Used in tasks like shoveling substances (snow, coal, etc.) to move them.

Gross body coordination: Ability to coordinate movements of arms, legs, and torso when the whole body is in motion, as in swimming.

Gross body equilibrium: Ability to keep or recover one's balance in unstable positions or conditions. Used in construction work, or in walking on ice.

Stamina: Ability to maintain challenging physical exertion over long time periods without getting winded; an aerobic ability. Used in fighting fires or in making extensive deliveries by bicycle or on foot.

J. Hogan (1991a, 1991b) considered seven of these sufficient in personnel selection, arguing that static and dynamic distinctions rarely made sense in job descriptions. Condensing further, she identified three general fitness factors: (a) muscular strength, the ability to apply or resist force by contracting muscles; (b) cardiovascular endurance, or aerobic capacity, and (c) and coordination or quality of movement. A comparison of her taxonomy and Fleishman's is shown in Fig. 3.7. Different terms for similar abilities reflect slightly different emphases. She later combined strength and endurance factors; apparently, the physical requirements of jobs could be defined with but two factors, (a) muscular strength and endurance and (b) physical skill in movements (J. Hogan, 1991b). How general should definitions of physical abilities be? Again, it depends on the generality or narrowness of the criterion to be predicted.

Measures of physical abilities have predicted work sample criteria very well, but they can also serve as instruments of unfair discrimination (J. Hogan, 1991a). Some of the significant validities for combined groups of men and women were not significant in either group by itself. Perhaps the overall correlation is spurious, created by combining data from groups with substantially different means on both variables. If so, the apparent "validity" merely capitalizes on the mean sex differences, and sex by itself might be as good a predictor. If so, litigation seems likely.

Worry over possible sex discrimination was background for the research reported by Arnold, Rauschenberger, Soubel, and Guion (1982). All steel mill laborers used to be men; they did heavy physical work.

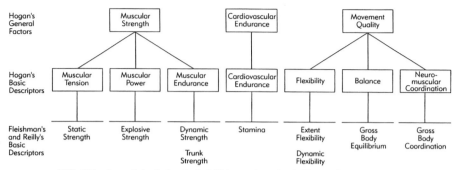

FIG. 3.7. A model of physical abilities, using the J. Hogan (1991a, 1991b) and Fleishman and Reilly (1992) descriptors.

Women applicants posed two problems. First, on average they had less physical strength, suggesting probable adverse impact and subsequent litigation. Second, abandoning physical testing to assure that those hired were strong enough risked serious on-the-job injuries. Traditional criterion-related predictive research was absurd. If avoiding personal injury is the purpose of the research, it would be worse than silly to hire lots of people and simply wait for people to hurt themselves to provide a criterion group! Arnold et al. (1982) abstracted elementary physical tasks from the various labor jobs and correlated them with performance on a general work sample. An arm dynomometer test was the best single predictor, with other tests adding very little predictive power. The muscular strength measured by the arm dynomometer test seemed the most general of the strength tests.

Physical ability, especially for strength and flexibility, can be developed by special training and exercise. Therefore, when physical abilities are predictors, opportunities for compensatory ability development and subsequent retesting should be considered. Arnold et al. (1982) were adamant that weaker applicants should be rejected, but they also insisted that those screened out be told to develop strength and improve their chances of being selected in later hiring periods.

Sensory Abilities. Vision and hearing ability are not unitary; "good vision" or "good hearing" means quite different visual or auditory skills for different jobs. Fleishman and Reilly (1992) listed 12 different visual and auditory abilities, including with near and far acuity such specialized abilities as night vision, color vision, depth perception, and a corresponding variety of sounds related to hearing. Postwar vision research at Purdue University, and others, was reviewed in Guion (1965). No such extensive research has been done on hearing. I suspect that, in both cases, strong cognitive components are involved as well as the sensory ones. A certain pitch with low volume might be emitted from a piece of machinery; two people may have the acuity to hear it, but the better worker is the one who understands its implication.

Accommodation. A candidate's abilities may have been permanently impaired by trauma, surgery, illness, or birth defects. Inspiring stories have been told of exceptional people overcoming such problems, but accommodation is typically needed for people of low physical ability. Even for less dramatic problems, such as the average lower strength levels of women, redesign of equipment to reduce strength requirements may be better than discriminatory selection practices.

Accommodation is not always initiated by the organization. The best accommodation may be done by the person. We tend to forget how very adaptable people are. Impairment of one ability is often compensated by increased skill in another. Formal hypotheses developed for most candidates may need to be replaced by job trials for a disabled candidate to see how he or she is differently abled.

We tend also to jump to conclusions. We see someone rub his or her eyes after several hours looking at a computer screen and conclude that visual skills are impaired by the work. Periodically, since computers came into wide use in offices, there have been repeated charges that they pose dangers to those who use them. The Panel on Impact of Video Viewing on Vision of Workers (1983) examined relevant research and concluded that the problems in working with video display terminals (VDTs) were more associated with stress due to job design and the work environment than with the equipment. Redesign (e.g., by using glare-reducing indirect light rather than bright banks of fluorescent tubes, or by job enrichment) can reduce the sense of stress that gives rise to most complaints. If so, it can also reduce the need to consider sensory skills in selection.

Psychomotor Abilities

The term, *psychomotor ability*, implies a combination of cognition, sensory processes, and muscular (i.e., motor) activity in task performance. Dexterity, coordination, steadiness, precision and speededness of movement, and motor response latency are categories of psychomotor ability. The general versus specific issue arises again. Fleishman and Reilly (1992), relying on Fleishman's earlier factor analytic work, distinguished hand dexterity from finger dexterity. Both require quick and accurate movements in grasping and manipulating objects, but hand dexterity requires larger arm muscle groups. Early on, Bourassa and Guion (1959) failed to find the distinction when tests were given in random rather than constant order, leading me (Guion, 1965) to question whether these are in fact independent abilities. Now I wonder if it makes much difference. I suspect that a more general dexterity factor will usually be more valid, especially if combined with sensory abilities.

Experience, Education, and Training

Some predictors are hypothesized without clearly articulated constructs; specified training or experience requirements are among them. The hypothesis justifying such requirements, if actually thought out, is that people with the desired credentials are the only ones who can do the job, or, in a less extreme view, the ones who can do it better. Credentials requirements are rarely useful; too often those with fine credentials do not have the competencies to match (Ash, Johnson, Levine, & McDaniel, 1989). They *can* be useful, if systematically evaluated and based on job analysis, (Gibson & Prien, 1977; McDaniel, Schmidt, & Hunter, 1988b). The evidence is sparse; the topic merits more research. Ash et al. (1989) suggested that education requirements, including a specific major, might be justified if (a) the job requires extended knowledge comparable to that of recognized professions, (b) the knowledge and ability requirements are hard to evaluate by other methods, (c) the consequences of *not* requiring the degree and major are likely to be severe, and (d) the degree program is the only way to acquire the knowledge demanded by the job. Even in these cases, however, it may be better to identify the competencies sought and to distinguish *preferred* from *demanded* qualifications.

Seniority is too often a basis for personnel decisions. It may be required by union contracts, although they often provide for considering qualifications as well. The justification, other than expedience, is the assumption that, as experience in the job increases over time, ability to do the job also increases. This is a linear view, or at least a monotonic view, of the relationship (see chapter 7 for these terms), a view not supported by data (Jacobs, Hoffman, & Kriska, 1990). Staying on the same job a long time may mean doing it too poorly to be promoted.

Nonlinearity may have resulted in underestimates in the relatively few empirical studies of seniority. Some research suggests that length of experience on a job, up to a few years, can be a useful consideration. Jacobs et al. (1990) suggested a limit of about 5 years, and McDaniel, Schmidt, and Hunter (1988a), in a meta-analysis, found generally low but positive validity coefficients for length of service but high ones where the mean experience in the sample was relatively brief.

ORGANIZATIONAL PREDICTORS

A useful overgeneralization: The world has become too specialized, with people in one specialty living within boundaries impervious to communication. An unfortunate example is the field of industrial *and* organizational psychology. The conjunction is often misleading; many practitioners live well within the boundaries of either side, rarely stepping across the conjunction's dividing line. Specialists on the organizational side study many influences on criteria at work, but individual differences at decision time are not often among them. Some of those called "traditional industrial psychologists" seem to specialize in selection as if it accounted for the whole of criterion variance.

A boundary-crossing article by Vicino and Bass (1978) showed that organizational variables can be predictors for promotion decisions. Using earlier research that had predicted managers' performance from a test battery, they computed the *residuals* (differences between actual and predicted criterion measures) for each manager as a new criterion. Four new predictors were then used: (a) amount of challenge on first job assignment, (b) life stability (a personal situational variable), (c) the degree to which the subject manager's and his supervisor's personalities matched, and (d) the success level of his supervisor. Three of these are organizational variables. The full set predicted the criterion residuals just as well as the original battery had predicted the original criterion data.

Vicino and Bass (1978) chided me (properly) for describing influences such as degree of urbanization, length of service, and debit size (in insurance sales) as merely criterion contaminants (Guion, 1965). Perhaps these things *do* contaminate criterion data, but treating them as predictors will permit systematic accounting for their influence on the criterion. Many other conditions of social, physical, or ideational environment may be manipulable factors that will add to predictive accuracy and therefore to improved levels of criterion performance.

> What further comes to mind is the possible usefulness at the time of hire or soon after of such measures as career certainty, career confidence, trust in the organization, significant others in one's career choices, conflict on the entry job, interdependence of supervisor–subordinate roles on the entry job, clarity of entry job objectives and commitment to them, discretionary opportunities, entry job supervisor's style of supervision, concern about community, and cosmopolitan versus local orientation. (Vicino & Bass, 1978, p. 87)

To that list may be added

> patterns of reward and reinforcement, goal-setting opportunities and goal acceptance, incentives, wage patterns, training opportunities ... disciplinary practices, opportunities for leisure or for fulfilling family responsibilities, characteristics of job design, the human-factors quality of machines and equipment, level of computerization or other technology, work schedules, level of experience or competence of co-workers, and a myriad of

other factors that, collectively, will define the situation in which a new employee will work. (Guion, 1991, p. 336)

The list of possibilities is endless; the list of demonstrated situational predictors is sparse. They should be considered systematically; people do not act independently of their environments.

Person–Situation Interaction

Most of this chapter, drawn from psychometric research, has emphasized individual differences among people as predictors. I argued further that organizational variables defining work situations may also be good predictors. An interactive perspective emphasizes the interaction of person and situation variables as part of a predictive hypothesis by Hattrup and Jackson (1996). Interactions serve a predictive purpose by moderating validities or by defining the boundaries within which generalizations hold. The validity of a measure of work orientation, for example, was moderated by perceived organizational climate (Day & Bedeian, 1991). One reason for poor predictions from personality variables, in their view, might be failure to identify organizational characteristics interacting with personality traits.

The moderating interaction was dramatic for extreme groups on climate perception—roughly the top and bottom 16% of the sample.[8] The regression of performance on work orientation was compared for these two groups. At low work orientation scores, those with negative climate perceptions performed slightly better than those perceiving a positive climate. However, at high levels of work orientation, the difference was about six times as great and *in the opposite direction*, that is, performance was substantially better for those with positive perceptions of the climate.

The slope of the regression of performance on work orientation was negative for those with a negative view of climate and positive for those with a positive view. Such a moderator variable can be used to define the limits or boundaries of a generalization. In this case, there is a discoverable point somewhere on the climate scale where the slope of the regression is neither negative nor horizontal, is positive but not usefully so; such a point could identify the lower boundary for the generalized validity of the work orientation scale.

Moderated regression, like any other, is a static prediction model; it assumes that the importance of an interaction exists today, tomorrow, and forevermore. Hattrup and Jackson (1996) want more; they proposed a dynamic interactive model with time as a factor because the effect of a

---

[8]One might suspect the climate measure and the work orientation measure to be redundant; they are not ($r = .22$).

situation is not immediate but develops over time. The model is less concerned with understanding sources of variance in a criterion than with understanding processes that influence traits, situations, and criteria.

Predictors for Team Selection

Assessment demands for teams are different for team formation than for team member replacement. Replacement seems to need traditional assessment of traits of people being considered for inclusion in an existing team, with the possible addition of interpersonal skills. Choosing people to form a neonate group, however, seems to differ from tradition in critical ways, including a group level of analysis. Assessing group attributes, especially in newly formed groups, seems a daunting task; to use once more the familiar cliché, research is needed!

Constructs Relevant to Working in Teams. In either case, individual candidates for assignment to a team must be assessed, and I stress the assessment of individual candidates for team assignments. Technical competence is surely among them, but the skills, knowledge, and motivation needed to function well in a team go beyond the core technical skills. Drawing from somewhat disparate contributions of different theorists (e.g., Cannon-Bowers, Tannenbaum, Salas, & Volpe, 1995; Guzzo & Shea, 1992; Klimoski & Jones, 1995; Landy, Shankster-Cawley, & Moran, 1995; Mohrman & Cohen, 1995; Prieto, 1993; Tziner & Eden, 1985), I suggest a set of individual traits that seem worth adding when team performance is the criterion. The list is incomplete, and not all of these are critical or even relevant in every situation, but they merit consideration.

1. *Decision-making skill.* I name this first because, of the cognitive skills that seem critical, it is the most troublesome. Without team members who can make decisions, the risk seems great that an Alphonse–Gaston routine will result in inaction.[9] On the other hand, a team member who habitually makes decisions quickly may fail to consider information from other members and in effect cut them out of the decision process. Perhaps its relation to team performance is not monotonic. In any case, it includes skill in getting information, evaluating it, knowing when there is enough of it, creating sensible or even novel options, and evaluating options.

2. *Adaptability.* The ability to adjust procedures or thoughts because of information available from others, to recognize quality in ideas or

---

[9]A half-century or so ago, in my relative youth, a widely distributed comic featured two men saying, "After you, my dear Alphonse," and "No, after you, my dear Gaston." Neither moved.

procedures different from one's own, and to accept different perspectives on a problem or issue. Perhaps the concept here is the ability to learn, to make "cognitive leaps" (Mohrman & Cohen, 1995, p. 381).

3. *Versatility*. Two concepts of versatility have already been mentioned; both are implied here: versatility in moving from one job role to another and versatility in meeting changed role demands. In the latter sense, it is the absence of resistance to change.

4. *Leadership*. An old principle of group behavior is that anyone in the group can play a leadership role, that different members serve leadership functions at different times. Such functions include deflecting a group from an unproductive path, suggesting alternative courses, raising critical questions, evaluating the group's options, planning, coordinating, monitoring progress, giving useful feedback to others—in short, influencing group activity. If a group is truly functioning as a team, each member must at times play a leadership role—and do it effectively.

5. *Situational awareness*. This label is not satisfying. I want to imply a broad ability to discern quickly and to comprehend fully changing or new circumstances in a work situation, as when one becomes aware of coming interpersonal conflict even before the potential antagonists do, or recognizes that group goals or standards have subtly changed.

6. *Interpersonal skill*. This is more familiar conceptual territory, involving skills in gaining cooperation, resolving disputes, in understanding and caring about the feelings of others. Some discussions of interpersonal skills seem to imply manipulative skills, but manipulation of others is expressly excluded here.

7. *Communication skill*. This construct also sounds familiar, but it implies in this context something quite different from elegant writing or articulate speech. It implies clarity in exchanging ideas more than clarity of one-way communication.

8. *Group orientation*. Perhaps a popular conception of extraversion might fit this construct; it implies an enjoyment of being with and collaborating with others—trusting and appreciating others—and avoiding pressure to "do it my way." It should not carry the connotation McCrae and John (1992) implied when naming the first of the Big Five factors extraversion, associating it with activity level, assertiveness, and excitement-seeking as well as gregariousness. The connotation intended includes comfort in the company of others and a willingness to be influenced by them as well as to influence them. As Mohrman and Cohen (1995) pointed out, one problem with team formation is that teamwork involves depending on others; dependency is often uncomfortable, even feared, for people who have been taught to value personal responsibility and personal achievement. The group orientation construct intended here

includes elements of emotional stability and ego-strength that make such dependency less threatening.

These constructs *seem* to be appropriate for team formation, but no one should take this seem-y side of psychology too seriously. Their appropriateness has not been demonstrated. Moreover, these constructs, as partially defined in this list, have no validated measurement operations.

DEVELOPING PREDICTIVE HYPOTHESES: A CAVEAT

I have mentioned many predictor constructs but have not suggested any "best bet" predictors for designated criteria. Linking predictors to criteria is a local hypothesis, based on local job and need analyses. Better hypotheses await massive, cross-industry, cross-occupational research and meta-analyses. The ideal of an empirically developed matrix of such linkages has not been achieved.

Without it, hypothesis development is necessarily local. Criterion constructs, other than overall performance, seem dictated by organizational needs. Choosing predictor constructs requires both local knowledge and scientific knowledge. Here is where one can get into trouble. Too much unrestrained scientific excitement leads to the use of esoteric constructs only because they are interesting—and overlooking constructs with good records. The best rule is for multivariate parsimony, the development of predictive hypotheses with relatively few predictors chosen from different categories. Cognitive constructs should always be included, but more often than is typical, the hypothesis should include personality and other noncognitive constructs. And always, the hypothesized predictors ought to make good sense to scientists and managers alike.

REFERENCES

Alvares, K. M., & Hulin, C. L. (1972). Two explanations of temporal changes in ability-skill relationships: A literature review and theoretical analysis. *Human Factors, 14,* 295–308.

Alvares, K. M., & Hulin, C. L. (1973). An experimental evaluation of a temporal decay in the prediction of performance. *Organizational Behavior and Human Performance, 9,* 169–185.

Anastasi, A. (1988). *Psychological testing* (6th ed.). New York: Macmillan.

Arnold, J. D., Rauschenberger, J. M., Soubel, W. G., & Guion, R. M. (1982). Validation and utility of a strength test for selecting steelworkers. *Journal of Applied Psychology, 67,* 588–604.

Asendorpf, J. B. (1992). A Brunswikian approach to trait continuity: Application to shyness. *Journal of Personality, 60,* 53–77.

Ash, R. A., Johnson, J. C., Levine, E. L., & McDaniel, M. A. (1989). Job applicant training and work experience evaluation in personnel selection. *Research in Personnel and Human Resource Management, 7*, 183–226.

Austin, J. T., Humphreys, L. G., & Hulin, C. L. (1989). A critical reanalysis of Barrett, Caldwell, and Alexander. *Personnel Psychology, 42*, 583–596.

Austin, J. T., & Villanova, P. (1992). The criterion problem: 1917–1992. *Journal of Applied Psychology, 77*, 836–874.

Barrett, G. V. (1972). Symposium: Research models of the future for industrial and organizational psychology. *Personnel Psychology, 25*, 1–17.

Barrett, G. V., & Alexander, R. A. (1989). Rejoinder to Austin, Humphreys, and Hulin: Critical reanalysis of Barrett, Caldwell, and Alexander. *Personnel Psychology, 42*, 597–612.

Barrett, G. V., Caldwell, M. S., & Alexander, R. A. (1985). The concept of dynamic criteria: A critical reanalysis. *Personnel Psychology, 38*, 41–56.

Barrick, M. R., & Mount, M. K. (1991). The big five personality dimensions and job performance: A meta-analysis. *Personnel Psychology, 44*, 1–26.

Bass, B. M. (1962). Further evidence on the dynamic character of criteria. *Personnel Psychology, 15*, 93–97.

Binning, J. F., & Barrett, G. V. (1989). Validity of personnel decisions: A conceptual analysis of the inferential and evidential bases. *Journal of Applied Psychology, 74*, 478–494.

Block, J. (1995). A contrarian view of the five-factor approach to personality description. *Psychological Bulletin, 117*, 187–215.

Borman, W. C. (1987). Personal constructs, performance schemata, and "folk theories" of subordinate effectiveness: Explorations in an Army officer sample. *Organizational Behavior and Human Decision Processes, 40*, 307–322.

Borman, W. C., McKee, A. S., & Schneider, R. J. (1995). Work styles. In N. G. Peterson, M. D. Mumford, W. C. Borman, P. R. Jeanneret, & E. A. Fleishman (Eds.), *Development of prototype Occupational Information Network (O*NET) content model* (Vol. 1, Chapter 12). Salt Lake City, UT: Utah Department of Employment Security.

Borman, W. C., & Motowidlo, S. J. (1993). Expanding the criterion domain to include elements of contextual performance. In N. Schmitt & W. C. Borman (Eds.), *Personnel selection* (pp. 71–98). San Francisco: Jossey-Bass.

Botwin, M. D., & Buss, D. M. (1989). Structure of act-report data: Is the five-factor model of personality recaptured? *Journal of Personality and Social Psychology, 56*, 988–1001.

Bourassa, G. L., & Guion, R. M. (1959). A factorial study of dexterity tests. *Journal of Applied Psychology, 43*, 199–204.

Brenner, M. H., & Lockwood, H. C. (1965). Salary as a predictor of salary. *Journal of Applied Psychology, 49*, 295–298.

Briggs, S. R. (1992). Assessing the five-factor model of personality description. *Journal of Personality, 60*, 253–293.

Buss, A. H. (1988). *Personality: Evolutionary heritage and human distinctiveness.* Hillsdale, NJ: Lawrence Erlbaum Associates.

Buss, A. H. (1992, August). *A personal view of personality assessment.* Invited address to the meeting of the American Psychological Association, Washington, DC.

Campbell, J. P., McCloy, R. A., Oppler, S. H., & Sager, C. E. (1993). A theory of performance. In N. Schmitt & W. C. Borman (Eds.), *Personnel selection* (pp. 35–70). San Francisco: Jossey-Bass.

Cannon-Bowers, J. A., Tannenbaum, S. I., Salas, E., & Volpe, C. E. (1995). Defining competencies and establishing team training requirements. In R. A. Guzzo & E. Salas (Eds.), *Team effectiveness and decision making in organizations* (pp. 333–380). San Francisco: Jossey-Bass.

Carroll, J. B. (1993). *Human cognitive abilities: A survey of factor-analytic studies.* Cambridge, England: Cambridge University Press.

Cattell, R. B. (1963). Theory of fluid and crystallized intelligence: A critical experiment. *Journal of Educational Psychology, 54*, 1–22.

Cattell, R. B. (1986). The actual trait, state, and situation structures important in functional testing. In R. B. Cattell & R. C. Johnson (Eds.), *Functional psychological testing: Principles and instruments* (pp. 33–53). New York: Brunner/Mazel.

Cattell, R. B., Eber, H. W., & Tatsuoka, M. M. (1970). *Handbook for The Sixteen Personality Factor Questionnaire (16PF) in clinical, educational, industrial, and research psychology.* Champaign, IL: Institute for Personality and Ability Testing.

Cronbach, L. J. (1970). *Essentials of psychological testing* (3rd ed.). New York: Harper and Row.

Cronbach, L. J., & Meehl, P. (1955). Construct validity in psychological tests. *Psychological Bulletin, 52*, 281–302.

Dawes, R. M. (1991, June). *Discovering "human nature" versus discovering how people cope with the task of getting through college: An extension of Sears's argument.* Paper presented at the meeting of the American Psychological Society, Washington, DC.

Day, D. V., & Bedeian, A. G. (1991). Predicting job performance across organizations: The interaction of work orientation and psychological climate. *Journal of Management, 17*, 589–600.

Digman, J. M. (1990). Personality structure: Emergence of the five-factor model. *Annual Review of Psychology, 41*, 417–440.

Doering, P. F. (1992). [Letter to the editor]. *Smithsonian, 23*(3), 14.

Dunham, R. B. (1974). Ability-skill relationships: An empirical explanation of change over time. *Organizational Behavior and Human Performance, 12*, 372–382.

Dunnette, M. D. (1963). A note on the criterion. *Journal of Applied Psychology, 47*, 251–254.

Dunnette, M. D. (1976). Basic attributes of individuals in relation to behavior in organizations. In M. D. Dunnette (Ed.), *Handbook of industrial and organizational psychology* (pp. 469–520). Chicago: Rand McNally.

Ekstrom, R. B. (1973). *Cognitive factors: Some recent literature* (Technical Report No. 2, ONR Contract N00014-71-C-0117, NR 150-329). Princeton, NJ: Educational Testing Service.

Ekstrom, R. B., French, J. W., & Harmon, H. H. (1975). *An attempt to confirm five recently identified cognitive factors* (Tech. Rep. No. 8, ONR Contract N00014-71-C-0117, NR 150-329). Princeton, NJ: Educational Testing Service.

English, H. B., & English, A. C. (1958). *A comprehensive dictionary of psychological and psychoanalytic terms.* New York: Longmans, Green and Co.

Estes, W. K. (1992). Ability testing: Postscript on ability tests, testing, and public policy. *Psychological Science, 3*, 278.

Eysenck, H. J. (1991). Dimensions of personality: 16, 5, or 3?—Criteria for a taxonomic paradigm. *Personality and Individual Differences, 12*, 773–790.

Fleishman, E. A., & Hempel, W. E. (1956). Factorial analysis of complex psychomotor performance and related skills. *Journal of Applied Psychology, 40*, 96–104.

Fleishman, E. A., & Quaintance, M. K. (1984). *Taxonomies of human performance: The description of human tasks.* Orlando, FL: Academic Press.

Fleishman, E. A., & Reilly, M. E. (1992). *Handbook of human abilities: Definitions, measurements, and job task requirements.* Palo Alto, CA: Consulting Psychologists Press.

French, J. W. (Ed.). (1951). The description of aptitude and achievement tests in terms of rotated factors. *Psychometric Monographs No. 5.*

Funder, D. C. (1991). Global traits: A neo-Allportian approach to personality. *Psychological Science, 2*, 31–39.

Gardner, H. (1983). *Frames of mind: The theory of multiple intelligences.* New York: Basic.

Ghiselli, E. E. (1956). Dimensional problems of criteria. *Journal of Applied Psychology, 40*, 1–4.

Ghiselli, E. E., & Haire, M. (1960). The validation of selection tests in the light of the dynamic character of criteria. *Personnel Psychology, 13*, 225–231.

Gibson, J. W., & Prien, E. P. (1977). Validation of minimum qualifications. *Public Personnel Management, 6*, 447–451, 456.

Goldberg, L. R. (1981). Language and individual differences: The search for universals in personality lexicons. In L. Wheeler (Ed.), *Review of personality and social psychology* (Vol. 2, pp. 141–165). Beverly Hills: Sage.

Goldberg, L. R. (1993). The structure of phenotypic personality traits. *American Psychologist, 48*, 26–34.

Goldberg, L. R. (1995). What the hell took so long? Donald Fiske and the big-five factor structure. In P. E. Shrout & S. T. Fiske (Eds.), *Advances in personality research, methods, and theory: A festschrift honoring Donald W. Fiske*. Hillsdale, NJ: Lawrence Erlbaum Associates.

Goldberg, L. R., Grenier, J. R., Guion, R. M., Sechrest, L. B., & Wing, H. (1991). *Questionnaires used in the prediction of trustworthiness in pre-employment selection decisions: An APA task force report*. Washington, DC: American Psychological Association.

Goldstein, I. L. (1986). *Training in organizations: Needs assessment, development, and evaluation*. Monterey, CA: Brooks/Cole.

Gordon, M. E., & Cohen, S. L. (1973). Training behavior as a predictor of trainability. *Personnel Psychology, 26*, 261–272.

Gottfredson, L. S. (Ed.). (1986). The *g* factor in employment. *Journal of Vocational Behavior, 29*(3), 293–450.

Gough, H. G. (1985). A work orientation scale for the California Psychological Inventory. *Journal of Applied Psychology, 70*, 505–513.

Gross, M. L. (1962). *The brain watchers*. New York: Random House.

Guilford, J. P. (1956). The structure of intellect. *Psychological Bulletin, 53*, 267–293.

Guilford, J. P. (1959). *Personality*. New York: McGraw-Hill.

Guion, R. M. (1961). Criterion measurement and personnel judgments. *Personnel Psychology, 14*, 141–149.

Guion, R. M. (1965). *Personnel testing*. New York: McGraw-Hill.

Guion, R. M. (1987). Changing views for personnel selection research. *Personnel Psychology, 40*, 199–213.

Guion, R. M. (1991). Personnel assessment, selection, and placement. In M. D. Dunnette & L. M. Hough (Eds.), *Handbook of industrial and organizational psychology* (2nd ed., Vol. 2, pp. 327–397). Palo Alto, CA: Consulting Psychologists Press.

Guion, R. M., & Gottier, R. F. (1965). Validity of personality measures in personnel selection. *Personnel Psychology, 18*, 135–164.

Guttman, L. (1955). A generalized simplex for factor analysis. *Psychometrika, 20*, 173–192.

Guzzo, R. A. (1988). Productivity research: Reviewing psychological and economic perspectives. In J. P. Campbell, R. J. Campbell, & Associates (Eds.), *Productivity in organizations* (pp. 63–81). San Francisco: Jossey-Bass.

Guzzo, R. A., & Shea, G. P. (1992). Group performance and intergroup relations in organizations. In M. D. Dunnette & L. M. Hough (Eds.), *Handbook of industrial and organizational psychology* (2nd ed., Vol. 3, pp. 269–313). Palo Alto, CA: Consulting Psychologists Press.

Hackett, R. D., Bycio, P., & Guion, R. M. (1989). Absenteeism among hospital nurses: An idiographic-longitudinal analysis. *Academy of Management Journal, 32*, 424–453.

Hattrup, K., & Jackson, S. E. (1996). Learning about individual differences by taking situations seriously. In K. R. Murphy (Ed.), *Individual differences and behavior in organizations* (pp. 507–547). San Francisco: Jossey-Bass.

Helmreich, R. L., Sawin, L. L., & Carsrud, A. L. (1986). The honeymoon effect in job performance: Temporal increases in the predictive power of achievement motivation. *Journal of Applied Psychology, 71*, 185–188.

Hinrichs, J. R. (1978). An eight year follow-up of a management assessment center. *Journal of Applied Psychology, 63*, 596–601.

Hofstee, W. K. B., de Raad, B., & Goldberg, L. R. (1992). Integration of the big five and circumplex approaches to trait structure. *Journal of Personality and Social Psychology, 63*, 146–163.

Hogan, J. (1991a). Physical abilities. In M. D. Dunnette & L. M. Hough (Eds.), *Handbook of industrial and organizational psychology* (2nd ed., Vol. 2, pp. 753–831). Palo Alto, CA: Consulting Psychologists Press.

Hogan, J. (1991b). Structure of physical performance in occupational tasks. *Journal of Applied Psychology, 76*, 495–507.

Hogan, J., Hogan, R., & Busch, C. M. (1984). How to measure service orientation. *Journal of Applied Psychology, 69*, 167–173.

Hogan, J., & Quigley, A. M. (1986). Physical standards for employment and the courts. *American Psychologist, 41*, 1193–1217.

Hogan, R., & Hogan, J. (1992). *Hogan Personality Inventory: Manual.* Tulsa, OK: Hogan Assessment Systems.

Horn, J. L., & Cattell, R. B. (1966). Refinement and test of the theory of fluid and crystallized intelligence. *Journal of Educational Psychology, 57*, 253–270.

Hough, L. M. (1992). The "big five" personality variables—construct confusion: Description versus prediction. *Human Performance, 5*, 139–155.

Hulin, C. L., Henry, R. A., & Noon, S. L. (1990). Adding a dimension: Time as a factor in the generalizability of predictive relationships. *Psychological Bulletin, 107*, 328–340.

Humphreys, L. G. (1960). Investigations of the simplex. *Psychometrika, 25*, 313–323.

Humphreys, L. G. (1968). The fleeting nature of the prediction of college academic success. *Journal of Educational Psychology, 59*, 375–380.

Humphreys, L. G. (1979). The construct of general intelligence. *Intelligence, 3*, 105–120.

Ilgen, D. R., & Schneider, J. (1991). Performance measurement: A multi-discipline view. In C. L. Cooper & I. T. Robertson (Eds.), *International Review of Industrial and Organizational Psychology* (Vol. 6, pp. 71–108). Chichester, England: Wiley.

Jacobs, R., Hoffman, D. A., & Kriska, S. D. (1990). Performance and seniority. *Human Performance, 3*, 107–201.

John, O. P. (1990). The "Big Five" factor taxonomy: Dimensions of personality in the natural languages and in questionnaires. In L. Pervin (Ed.), *Handbook of personality theory and research* (pp. 66–100). New York: Guilford.

John, O. P., Hampson, S. E., & Goldberg, L. R. (1991). The basic level in personality-trait hierarchies: Studies of trait use and accessibility in different contexts. *Journal of Personality and Social Psychology, 60*, 348–361.

Jones, M. B. (1966). Individual differences. In E. A. Bilodeau (Ed.), *Acquisition of skill* (pp. 109–146). New York: Academic Press.

Jones, M. B. (1970). A two-process theory of individual differences in motor learning. *Psychological Review, 77*, 353–360.

Kanfer, R., & Ackerman, P. L. (1989). Motivation and cognitive abilities: An integrative/aptitude treatment interaction approach to skill acquisition. *Journal of Applied Psychology, 74*, 657–690.

Kanter, R. M., Stein, B. A., & Jick, T. D. (1992). *The challenge of organizational change: How companies experience it and leaders guide it.* New York: Free Press.

Keyser, D. J., & Sweetland, R. C. (Eds.). (1992). *Test critiques* (Vol. IX). Austin, TX: Pro-Ed.

Kitchener, K. S., & Brenner, H. G. (1990). Wisdom and reflective judgment: Knowing in the face of uncertainty. In R. J. Sternberg (Ed.), *Wisdom: Its nature, origins, and development* (pp. 212–229). Cambridge, England: Cambridge University Press.

Klimoski, R., & Jones, R. G. (1995). Staffing for effective group decision making: Key issues in matching people and teams. In R. A. Guzzo & E. Salas (Eds.), *Team effectiveness and decision making in organizations* (pp. 291–332). San Francisco: Jossey-Bass.

Kramer, J. J., & Conoley, J. C. (Eds.). (1992). *The eleventh mental measurements yearbook.* Lincoln, NE: Buros Institute of Mental Measurements.

Landy, F. J., & Farr, J. L. (1983). *The measurement of work performance.* New York: Academic Press.

Landy, F. J., Shankster-Cawley, L., & Moran, S. K. (1995). Advancing personnel selection and placement methods. In A. Howard (Ed.), *The changing nature of work* (pp. 252–289). San Francisco: Jossey-Bass.

Linn, R. L. (1986). Comments on the g factor in employment testing. *Journal of Vocational Behavior, 29,* 438–444.

McAdams, D. P. (1992). The five factor model *in* personality: A clinical appraisal. *Journal of Personality, 60,* 329–361.

McAdams, D. P. (1995). What do we know when we know a person? *Journal of Personality, 63,* 365–396.

McAdams, D. P., & Emmons, R. A. (Eds.). (1995). Levels and domains in personality [Special issue]. *Journal of Personality, 63*(3), 341–727.

McCrae, R. R. (Ed.). (1992). The five-factor model: Issues and applications [Special issue]. *Journal of Personality, 60*(2), 175–532.

McCrae, R. R., & John, O. P. (1992). An introduction to the five-factor model and its applications. *Journal of Personality, 60,* 175–215.

McDaniel, M. A., Schmidt, F. L., & Hunter, J. E. (1988a). Job experience correlates of job performance. *Journal of Applied Psychology, 73,* 327–330.

McDaniel, M. A., Schmidt, F. L., & Hunter, J. E. (1988b). A meta-analysis of the validity of methods for rating training and experience in personnel selection. *Personnel Psychology, 41,* 283–314.

Messick, S. (1984). Abilities and knowledge in educational achievement testing: The assessment of dynamic cognitive structures. In B. S. Plake (Ed.), *Social and technical issues in testing: Implications for test construction and usage* [Buros-Nebraska Symposium on Measurement and Testing, Vol. 1, pp. 155–172]. Hillsdale, NJ: Lawrence Erlbaum Associates.

Mischel, W. (1968). *Personality and assessment.* New York: Wiley.

Mitchel, J. O. (1975). Assessment center validity: A longitudinal study. *Journal of Applied Psychology, 60,* 573–579.

Mitchell, J. V., Jr. (Ed.). (1983). *Tests in print III: An index to tests, test reviews, and the literature on specific tests.* Lincoln, NE: Buros Institute of Mental Measurements.

Mohrman, S. A., & Cohen, S. G. (1995). When people get out of the box. In A. Howard (Ed.), *The changing nature of work* (pp. 365–410). San Francisco: Jossey-Bass.

Mumford, M. D., & Peterson, N. G. (1995). Skills. In N. G. Peterson, M. D. Mumford, W. C. Borman, P. R. Jeanneret, & E. A. Fleishman (Eds.), *Development of prototype Occupational Information Network (O*NET) content model* (Vol. 1: Report, Chapter 3). Salt Lake City, UT: Utah Department of Employment Security.

Murphy, K. R. (1989). Is the relationship between cognitive ability and job performance stable over time? *Human Performance, 2,* 183–200.

Murray, H. A. (1938). *Explorations in personality.* New York: Oxford.

Nagle, B. F. (1953). Criterion development. *Personnel Psychology, 6,* 271–289.

O'Bannon, R. M., Goldinger, L. A., & Appleby, G. S. (1989). *Honesty and integrity testing: A practical guide.* Atlanta: Applied Information Resources.

Ones, D. S., Schmidt, F. L., & Viswesvaran, C. (1994, May). Do broader personality variables predict job performance with higher validity? In R. Page (Chair), *Personality and job performance*. Symposium at the Society for Industrial and Organizational Psychology, Nashville, TN.

Organ, D. W. (1988). *Organizational citizenship behavior: The good soldier syndrome*. Lexington, MA: Heath.

Panel on Impact of Video Viewing on Vision of Workers. (1983). *Video displays, work, and vision*. Washington, DC: National Academy Press.

Paunonen, S. V., Jackson, D. N., Trebinski, J., & Forsterling, F. (1992). Personality structure across cultures: A multimethod evaluation. *Journal of Personality and Social Psychology*, 62, 447–456.

Peterson, N. G., & Bownas, D. A. (1982). Skill, task structure, and performance acquisition. In M. D. Dunnette & E. A. Fleishman (Eds.), *Human performance and productivity: Human capability assessment* (Vol. 1, pp. 49–105). Hillsdale, NJ: Lawrence Erlbaum Associates.

Peterson, N. G., Mumford, M. D., Borman, W. C., Jeanneret, P. R., & Fleishman, E. A. (Eds.). (1995). *Development of prototype Occupational Information Network (O*NET) content model* (Vols. 1–2). Salt Lake City, UT: Utah Department of Employment Security.

Prieto, J. M. (1993). The team perspective in selection and assessment. In H. Schuler, J. L. Farr, & M. Smith (Eds.), *Personnel selection and assessment: Individual and organizational perspectives* (pp. 221–234). Hillsdale, NJ: Lawrence Erlbaum Associates.

Raaheim, K. (1974). *Problem solving and intelligence*. Bergen, Norway: Universitetsforlaget.

Riggio, R. E., & Fleming, T. (n.d.). *Validation of a measure of trait choosiness*. Unpublished manuscript, California State University, Fullerton, CA.

Sackett, P. R., Zedeck, S., & Fogli, L. (1988). Relations between measures of typical and maximum job performance. *Journal of Applied Psychology*, 73, 482–486.

Schmidt, F. L., & Kaplan, L. B. (1971). Composite vs. multiple criteria: A review and resolution of the controversy. *Personnel Psychology*, 24, 419–434.

Schmidt, F. L., Ones, D. S., & Hunter, J. E. (1992). Personnel selection. *Annual Review of Psychology*, 43, 627–670.

Schneider, B. (1987). The people make the place. *Personnel Psychology*, 40, 437–453.

Schneider, R. J., & Hough, L. M. (1995). Personality and industrial/organizational psychology. In C. L. Cooper & I. T. Robertson (Eds.), *International review of industrial and organizational psychology* (pp. 75–130). Chichester, England: Wiley.

Secretary's Commission on Achieving Necessary Skills. (1991). *What work requires of schools: A SCANS report for America 2000*. Washington, DC: U.S. Department of Labor.

Severin, D. (1952). The predictability of various kinds of criteria. *Personnel Psychology*, 5, 93–104.

Smith, F. J. (1977). Work attitudes as predictors of attendance on a specific day. *Journal of Applied Psychology*, 62, 16–19.

Smith, P. C. (1976). Behaviors, results, and organizational effectiveness: The problem of criteria. In M. D. Dunnette (Ed.), *Handbook of industrial and organizational psychology* (pp. 745–775). Chicago: Rand McNally.

Smith, P. C. (1985, August). *Global measures: Do we need them?* Distinguished Scientific Contribution Award (Div. 14) Address, at the meeting of the American Psychological Association, Los Angeles.

Society for Industrial and Organizational Psychology. (1987). *Principles for the validation and use of personnel selection procedures* (3rd ed.). College Park, MD: SIOP.

Spearman, C. (1927). *The abilities of man*. New York: Macmillan.

Spence, J. T., Helmreich, R. L., & Pred, R. S. (1987). Impatience versus achievement strivings in the Type A pattern: Differential effects on students' health and academic achievement. *Journal of Applied Psychology*, 72, 522–528.

Sternberg, R. J. (1977). *Intelligence, information processing, and analogical reasoning: The componential analysis of human abilities*. Hillsdale, NJ: Lawrence Erlbaum Associates.

Sternberg, R. J. (1985). *Beyond IQ: A triarchic theory of human intelligence.* Cambridge, NY: Cambridge University Press.

Sternberg, R. J. (Ed.). (1990). *Wisdom: Its nature, origins, and development.* Cambridge, NY: Cambridge University Press.

Sternberg, R. J. (1991). Death, taxes, and bad intelligence tests. *Intelligence, 15,* 257–269.

Sternberg, R. J., & Detterman, D. K. (Eds.). (1986). *What is intelligence?* Norwood, NJ: Ablex.

Sternberg, R. J., Wagner, R. K., Williams, W. M., & Horvath, J. A. (1995). Testing common sense. *American Psychologist, 50,* 912–927.

Sweetland, R. C., & Keyser, D. J. (Eds.). (1991). *Tests: A comprehensive reference for assessments in psychology, education, and business* (3rd ed.). Austin, TX: Pro-Ed.

Tett, R. P., Jackson, D. N., & Rothstein, M. (1991). Personality measures as predictors of job performance: A meta-analytic review. *Personnel Psychology, 44,* 703–742.

Thayer, P. W. (1992). Construct validation: Do we understand our criteria? *Human Performance, 5,* 97–108.

Thorndike, R. L. (1986). The role of general ability in prediction. *Journal of Vocational Behavior, 29,* 332–339.

Thurstone, L. L. (1938). Primary mental abilities. *Psychometric Monographs No. 1.*

Toops, H. A. (1944). The criterion. *Educational and Psychological Measurement, 4,* 271–299.

Tupes, E. C., & Christal, R. E. (1961/1992). *Recurrent personality factors based on trait ratings* (USAF ASD Tech. Rep. No. 61-97). Lackland Air Force Base, TX: US Air Force. (Original work published in 1961)

Tyler, L. E. (1986). Back to Spearman? *Journal of Vocational Behavior, 29,* 445–450.

Tziner, A., & Eden, D. (1985). Effects of crew composition on crew performance: Does the whole equal the sum of its parts? *Journal of Applied Psychology, 70,* 85–93.

United States Office of Personnel Management and Educational Testing Service. (1980). *Construct validity in psychological measurement.* Proceedings of a colloquium on theory and application in education and employment. Princeton, NJ: Educational Testing Service.

Vicino, F. L., & Bass, B. M. (1978). Lifespace variables and managerial success. *Journal of Applied Psychology, 63,* 81–88.

Villanova, P. (1992). A customer-based model for developing job performance criteria. *Human Resources Management Review, 2,* 103–114.

Wallace, S. R. (1965). Criteria for what? *American Psychologist, 20,* 411–417.

Wallace, S. R., & Weitz, J. (1955). Industrial psychology. *Annual Review of Psychology, 6,* 217–250.

Whyte, W. H., Jr. (1957). *The organization man.* New York: Doubleday.

Woodrow, H. (1938). The effects of practice on groups of different initial ability. *Journal of Educational Psychology, 29,* 268–278.

4

The Legal Context for Personnel Decisions

Few organizations have full discretion in making decisions. Laws often limit the personnel actions employers may take. Some occupations require licenses. Interlocking directorates are illegal in the United States under the Clayton Act. Limitations may be specified in union contracts. Legal constraints vary by country. In Sweden, selection for many occupations is limited to people who have the proper work permits issued by unions.

Some laws mandate consideration of characteristics not relevant to job performance; others require that other irrelevant characteristics *not* be considered in employment decisions. A required irrelevancy in many American civil service jurisdictions is veterans' preference. The most frequently litigated prohibited irrelevancies are based on race, sex, age, or disability. These legal requirements are based on a social policy that transcends the interests of individual employers. Most such policies are more concerned with prohibiting discrimination *against* members of designated groups than with promoting discrimination *favoring* certain groups. Laws permit going to court for a variety of reasons, and Americans seem increasingly willing to sue. In this age of litigation, personnel decisions based on whim, stereotypes, prejudices, or expediency are just plain foolish. Even apparently objective bases for decision, such as test scores or educational levels, have often been declared unacceptable if not sensibly adopted (Sandman & Urban, 1976).

This chapter emphasizes American laws promoting equal employment opportunity (EEO), particularly the Civil Rights Act of 1964, as amended. That legislation has dominated employment practices in the United States for at least three decades and is the foundation for other antidiscrimina-

163

tion laws. Its importance is widespread; it has influenced legislation in other countries, and American EEO laws apply anywhere in the world where United States citizens are employed by an American-controlled company. Businesses incorporated in other countries are subject to these laws for their operations in the United States.

A BRIEF HISTORY OF EEO REGULATION IN THE UNITED STATES

Religious discrimination is barred under the First Amendment. A person with a vested property right in employment can sue under the Fifth Amendment's protection against deprivation "of life, liberty, or property, without due process of law" if a personnel decision results in loss of employment. The Thirteenth, Fourteenth, and Fifteenth amendments, adopted during the reconstruction era and accompanied by the Civil Rights Acts of 1866, 1870, and 1871, provide collectively that all persons within the jurisdiction of the United States (citizens and noncitizens alike) shall have the same rights under the law, including property rights. Enforcement of these provisions of law was dormant during most of the 20th century. However, they were dusted off in the late 1960s to bring suits against state and local jurisdictions, exempted under the 1964 Civil Rights Act until its 1972 amendment (see, e.g., *Baker v. Columbus Municipal Separate School District*, 1971, 1972; *Washington v. Davis*, 1976).

The federal government did not lead in EEO legislation. After World War II, some states and cities enacted fair employment practices laws. Even later, employers in some states were bound by local laws more complex or stringent than the federal regulations. In the District of Columbia, for example, 13 different kinds of discrimination have been prohibited. State laws often apply to small employers. The 1964 Civil Rights Act applies only to organizations employing 15 or more for 20 or more weeks during the year, but some state laws may apply to anyone with even a single employee. State laws are not surveyed in this chapter, but they add to the complexity of the legal context within which an employer operates.

Executive Orders

Different EEO regulation came in a series of Executive Orders (EO) dating back to World War II. The first (EO 8802), issued by President Roosevelt, required federal agencies to include provisions in defense contracts obligating contractors to hire without regard to race, creed, or national origin. Similar orders were issued by Presidents Truman, Eisenhower, and Kennedy. EO 11246 was issued by President Johnson in 1965, providing that contractors (a) will not discriminate on the basis of race, color, or religion, (b) will take affirmative action to insure against such discrimination against employees or applicants, (c) will comply with the Order and with rules, regulations, and orders issued by the Secretary of Labor under its provisions, (d) will impose the same requirements on all subcontractors or vendors, and (e) will lose the contract and be declared ineligible for future government contracts in the event of noncompliance.[1]

EO 11246 had a major impact on employment procedures in the United States. The Office of Federal Contract Compliance (OFCC, now known as the Office of Federal Contract Compliance Programs, OFCCP) was established in the Department of Labor to enforce its provisions, and its provisions are applicable even to employers who do not have written contracts with the federal government (*United States v. New Orleans Public Service, Inc.*, 1974).

Affirmative action was a major feature of the Order. Enforcement regulations required contractors and subcontractors to develop affirmative action programs with detailed analyses of minority and female employment in the organization and, where such representation was weak, to establish "specific goals and timetables" for improving it—in effect, setting up targets or, arguably, quotas for specific subgroups or "affected classes." An *affected class* is a definable group of people in a "protected group" who continue to suffer discrimination or the effects of prior discrimination; contractors are not in compliance if the proportion of an affected class in the organization is less than its proportion in the available labor market.

EO 11246 was issued *after* passage of the Civil Rights Act of 1964 and the effective date of its EEO provisions in Title VII (July 2, 1965). The Executive Order may seem an odd redundancy, but its affirmative action requirement went beyond Title VII, then considered by many EEO advocates to be too weak and too slow in providing rememdies. In contrast, the Executive Order seemed like an executioner's order—swift and fatal for the employer who relied on federal contracts for business survival. In retrospect, the argument was flawed; almost no contracts were ever lifted.[2]

---

[1]Subsequent Executive Orders relevant to this discussion are not described here save to say that they have brought other groups under their protection, prohibiting, for example, discrimination based on sex, national origin, age, or conditions of handicap. Not all Executive Orders are as comprehensive as 11246; for example, reporting requirements and sanctions are not specified in EO 11141, banning age discrimination. Remedies were left to the Age Discrimination in Employment Act of 1967.

[2]The question of the social objective to be met, whether by Executive Order or legislation, has never been adequately addressed. The first OFCC Director, Edward Sylvester, asked a former colleague of mine, Dr. Richard Shore, then with the Policy and Planning Division of the Department of Labor, to draft an order concerning employment testing. It was done, and I was subsequently asked to comment on it. Among my comments, I expressed to Mr.

The Civil Rights Act of 1964

Reconstruction era attempts to provide equal rights under law had virtually disappeared by the end of the 19th century. Segregation was supported by law and the courts in much of the country—by custom in most of the rest of it. The Civil Rights Act (1964) was to social policy in the U.S. what the continental divide is to the flow of rivers. It put the full power of the federal government to work on behalf of Black citizens having equal access to schools and public accommodations as well as employment opportunities. During Congressional debate, in a misguided and unsuccessful effort to derail support for the proposed Act, a Civil Rights opponent offered an amendment to include sex as a proscribed basis for decision; another amendment added national origin. Both were accepted by the bipartisan management of the bill through Congress and became part of the Act. The Act's importance as a signal of a shifting concept of government cannot be overemphasized. Previously, the federal government had regulated things and standards (e.g., food and drugs, weights and measures). This Act regulated behavior (White, 1982, p. 108).

Unlawful Employment Practices. Title VII specifies several unlawful employment practices:

1. Employers may not fail or refuse to hire, or discharge, anyone on the basis of race, color, religion, sex, or national origin.
2. They may not segregate or classify employees or applicants so as to deprive anyone of employment opportunities on the basis of race, color, religion, sex, or national origin.
3. Employment agencies may not fail or refuse to refer candidates on the basis of any of these characteristics. This holds as well for labor unions with regard to membership or influencing employers to discriminate.

Sylvester my belief that issuance and enforcement of such an order could "eliminate unfair racial discrimination within a generation." Mr. Sylvester deemed this an appropriate objective, and work toward the issuance of the order went forward. Others, notably the staff of the EEOC, took the position that, by statute, such discrimination was to be ended immediately—specifically, by July 2, 1965. From a legal perspective, they were correct, of course. From a psychological perspective, time was needed to change attitudes, skills, levels of specific kinds of knowledge, educational foundations, and a host of other consequences of centuries of slavery and segregation. It was my belief that evidence that people were being hired on the basis of their qualifications would encourage minority youth to seek qualifications for useful and satisfying employment. The view was, without pun, a minority view that was eventually swept aside within the OFCC as well as in the EEOC in favor of goals and timetables leading to group parity as quickly as organizational growth and turnover would allow.

4. All provisions apply equally to employers, labor organizations, or joint labor–management committees controlling training programs.

5. Advertising employment or training opportunities may not indicate preferences for any group under any of these designated characteristics. Separate classified columns for "Help Wanted—Men" and "Help Wanted—Women" were stopped as were statements of preferences for characteristics that only men, or Whites, or speakers of English are likely to have.

6. It is unlawful to retaliate against people who have opposed unlawful employment practices under the Act.

Exemptions. The Act does not "apply to an employer with respect to the employment of aliens outside any State." Nor does it prevent religious organizations from hiring their own adherents to carry out religious work. Some preferential hiring is explicitly endorsed, such as preferential hiring of American Indians on or near reservations, or veterans' preference. Bona fide seniority systems were also protected. The Act does not prohibit or discourage discrimination on the basis of actual qualifications to do a job.

The Use of Employment Tests. In 1963, during Congressional debate on the Civil Rights Bill, a fair employment case in Illinois (*Myart v. Motorola*, 1964) went into the state court system, national headlines, and Congressional debate. The dispute arose when a Black applicant was allegedly refused a job, despite previous and presumably relevant experience, because of an unsatisfactory test score. He filed a complaint with the Illinois Fair Employment Practices Commission charging racial discrimination. The Commission concluded that Mr. Myart should be offered the job and that use of the test should be discontinued. It further concluded that the future use of any other test should consider the possible effects of cultural deprivation on test performance. The decision was subsequently overturned by the Illinois Supreme Court, but it engendered heated debate. Many applauded the attack on testing, but others felt that the Illinois FEPC had made an unwarranted intrusion into the business practices of a private organization. Congress feared that a federal agency, to be created under the proposed act, would also interfere with the rights of employers to establish employment standards.

In this context the Tower amendment (named after Senator John Tower who originally proposed a version of the amendment) was added to the legislation as Section 703(h). It says in part, "nor shall it be an unlawful employment practice for an employer to give and to act upon the results of any professionally developed ability test provided that such test, its administration or action upon the results is not designed, intended, or used to discriminate because of race, color, religion, sex, or national origin."

The Tower amendment was a bit ambiguous. It refered to "professionally developed *ability* tests," but not to tests of knowledge, personality, behavioral habits, or life history. It is silent on the evaluation of experience or motivation. It does not specify the requisite profession of the test developer. (May a work sample test of welding ability be developed by professional test developers or by professional welders?) In practice, courts have considered many kinds of assessments of qualifications, ranging from basic ability tests through personality inventories to assessment centers without much reference to this phrase. The emphasis is usually on determining whether the assessment procedure has had the effect of discriminating against the protected groups or has that effect without being job related enough.

Weighing Opportunity and Qualifications. What is opportunity? There is no clear definition. Enforcement has implicitly assumed that opportunity (or lack of it) is shown in outcomes. If proportions of people in protected groups who are actually hired increase, then opportunity has arguably increased. Only when various subgroups achieve parity in employment, by this view, will opportunities have been shown to be equal. A different, opposing view defines equal employment opportunity as the opportunity to develop the necessary qualifications for the kinds of work desired and, as an applicant, to be judged on those qualifications without regard for irrelevant demographic characteristics. The tension created between group-oriented and individual-oriented concepts of opportunity has bedeviled attempts to clarify public policy from the beginning; it continues to do so, especially in public controversy about affirmative action.

Many people believe that the national interest requires organizations to improve productivity to address such problems as unfavorable balance of trade, lack of market competitiveness, economic growth, and so on. Concern for national productivity has been conspicuously absent in EEO debates. The Tower amendment debates centered on the possibility of a bureaucratic intrusion into an employer's "right" to set employment policy, not on the relevance of such policy to productivity. The relative importance of equal employment opportunity and national productivity has not been debated as a matter of national policy. It should be debated and resolved if the legal context for personnel decisions is to be coherent.

The Equal Employment Opportunity Commission. The Act established the Equal Employment Opportunity Commission (EEOC), empowered to investigate charges of prohibited employment practices; to dismiss charges deemed unfounded; to use conference, conciliation, and persuasion to eliminate practices where charges were found to be true; and to work with authorities in states or other jurisdictions where the practices are prohibited by local law. Where there is a finding of "reasonable cause" to believe the charge is true, the EEOC can file suit in the federal courts. Early in EEO history, working together through "gentle persuasion" lost out procedurally to the adversarial posturing of litigants.

The Right to Sue. The Act empowers aggrieved persons to bring suit in the federal courts with or without an EEOC finding of reasonable cause. It expressly gives federal courts authority to establish appropriate remedies, including "such affirmative action as may be appropriate."[3] It gives the Attorney General the authority to bring suit, without EEOC participation, if it is believed that an employer is engaged in a "pattern or practice of resistance to the full enjoyment of any of the rights secured by this Title, and that the pattern or practice is of such a nature and is intended to deny the full exercise of the rights" provided by the Act.

Establishing Rules and Regulations. The Act created the EEOC and gave special authority to the Attorney General (i.e., the Civil Rights Division of the Department of Justice). EO 11246 created the OFCC in the Department of Labor. Other statutes placed EEO enforcement obligations in the Department of Treasury (concerning revenue-sharing funds) and in the Departments of Education and of Health and Human Services (where funds managed in these departments were involved). The nation's largest employer, the U. S. Civil Service Commission (CSC, forerunner of the Office of Personnel Management), issued its own rules for promoting equal employment opportunity within the federal government and public sector employers receiving federal grants in aid. It was a seventh agency authorized to establish rules and regulations concerning employment practices. Rules and regulations were not always consistent; employers, private or public, were sometimes subject to conflicting demands.

1972 Amendment of Title VII. The Act was amended in 1972 to bring governmental employers (federal, state, and local) under its aegis. The 1972 amendments also created the Equal Employment Opportunity Coordinating Council (EEOCC, abolished in 1978), consisting of heads (or their deputies) of the Civil Rights Commission and of the four major enforcement agencies: the EEOC, the OFCC, the CSC, and the Department of Justice. Its purposes were to promote efficiency, to eliminate contradictory requirements for employers, and to avoid duplication of effort among

---

[3]I take this to imply a broader concept of affirmative action than the "goals and timetables" (or "quotas"; the choice of term depends on one's political leanings) typically implied by the 1990s.

enforcement agencies. Its efforts culminated in the *Uniform Guidelines on Employee Selection Procedures*, identified hereafter simply as "the Guidelines" (Equal Employment Opportunity Commission, Civil Service Commission, Department of Labor, and Department of Justice, 1978).[4]

Orders and Guidelines

The Guidelines help guide employee selection aspects of the Act and Executive Orders. The course of the Guidelines development was not smooth. The history of their development may clarify them and the shortcomings they had even from the beginning.

Earlier sets of employee selection guidelines were issued from 1966 through 1974. They represented (usually imperfectly because of compromises and naiveté) the views of a variety of contributing authors.[5] Their development was characterized by controversy and acrimony among proponents and opponents of specific provisions. Moreover, each agency tended to be interested in developing regulations only when a published rule would have helped its case against a specific target industry or company. When the crisis-at-hand ended, whether by settlement or evaporation, so did progress.[6] The sequence of guidelines issuance is outlined in Fig. 4.1.

Equal Employment Opportunity Guidelines, 1966. The 1966 EEOC Guidelines (Equal Employment Opportunity Commission, 1966) were issued soon after the effective date of the 1964 Civil Rights Act and before corruption of the ordinary connotation of the word *guidelines*. It was written in narrative form, somewhat like a small textbook, providing actual guidance for employers who came under the jurisdiction of Title VII. In general, it presented orthodox requirements for the choice and evaluation of personnel selection tools, mainly tests; however, two not

---

[4]As this is written, in 1996, the Uniform Guidelines remain in force despite technical problems. I know of no plans to revise them.

[5]I am tempted, at this late date, to overlook or even deny my own involvement in this history. However, because so many people know of it, honesty seems the better policy. It requires the use of "we" where I would prefer to say "they." I refer specifically to activities associated with the development of the OFCC Testing Orders of 1968 and 1971 and the EEOC Guidelines of 1970. I was a consultant to OFCC for a few months in the beginnings of discussions about the proposed OFCC Order. After an angry hiatus, I subsequently returned as a member of an advisory committee that eventually drafted the 1968 and 1971 Orders. Despite admitted involvement, I do not accept full responsibility for the final content of these documents—and certainly not for later interpretations of them. However, that involvement did give me some insights into the processes by which they were developed. They are ideal-destroying insights I would prefer not to have had.

[6]I may be overgeneralizing here. The statement is true with regard to the development of the 1968, 1970, and 1971 documents with which I was associated. I believe it to be true more generally as well, but have no first hand knowledge to support the belief.

Evolution of Uniform Guidelines on Employee Selection
Procedures

1966	1968	
EEOC Testing Guidelines	OFCC Testing Order	
	↓ 1971	1969 CSC FPM 335.1 Supp. Evaluation of Employees for Promotion and Internal Placement
	OFCC Revised Testing Order	
1970 EEOC Guidelines on Employee Selection Procedures		↓ 1972 CSC FPM 271-1 Qualifications Standards FPM 271-2 Applicant Appraisal Procedures FPM 330-1 Examining Practices
	↓ 1974 Amended Testing Order (Documentation)	
1976 EEOC 1970 Guidelines Republished	1976 Federal Executive Agency Guidelines DOL, CSC, and Justice Department	

December 1977
Draft Uniform Guidelines on Employee Selection Procedures

↓

April 1978
Public Hearing

↓

July 1978
Proposed Uniform Guidelines

↓

August 1978	March 1979	April 1980
Published Uniform Guidelines on Employee Selection Procedures	90 Questions and Answers Issued	3 Additional Questions and Answers Issued

FIG. 4.1. Background of the Uniform Guidelines on Employee Selection Procedures. From Day, V. B., Erwin, F., & Koral, A. M. (Eds.). (1981). *A professional and legal analysis of the Uniform Guidelines on Employee Selection procedures.* Berea, OH: The American Society for Personnel Administration. Permission provided by the Society for Human Resource Management.

widely recognized departures from orthodoxy were included. One was that the concept of a test could be broader than usually recognized, including many other kinds of assessments. The other was the notion that validities might differ for different subgroups (e.g., Blacks and Whites) and that tests should be used only for subgroups for which they were valid.[7] Distribution of the 1966 document attracted little notice.

---

[7]This departure became prominent later, was studied extensively, and was later dropped as scientifically unsupportable. We consider it as differential validity, single-group validity, and differential prediction at some length in chapter 10.

Office of Federal Contract Compliance Testing Order, 1968. In 1965, the Office of Federal Contract Compliance began work culminating in the 1968 Testing Order (Office of Federal Contract Compliance, 1968). The first draft of the Order was brief, terse and, I thought, clear. Successively longer versions were distributed and discussed in ad hoc groups consisting of personnel testing experts, union officials, representatives of employers, and representatives of interested government agencies. The first distributed draft of the Order met with strenuous, seemingly defensive resistence. Later an Advisory Committee on Testing and Selection was appointed, on which I served.[8] Committee members were chosen for their expertise in employment testing and sympathy with EEO objectives. The Order is no longer in effect, but its form and some of its provisions remain in or substantially influenced the Uniform Guidelines.

The principal thrust of the Order was that contractors should validate any tests or other instruments used in selection decisions if they had an adverse impact on any group protected under EO 11246. *Adverse impact* exists if members of a protected group are proportionately less likely to be hired (i.e., have a lower selection ratio) than are members of the group proportionately most likely to be hired (i.e., whatever subgroup has the highest selection ratio).

An operational definition of adverse impact was needed. Committee deliberations initially defined it as a statistically significant difference, $p <$ .05 between the selection ratios in the two groups. (A selection ratio is the proportion of candidates actually hired in a specified time span.) Most affected employers would not know how to test for significance without expert assistance. Significance depends in part on the size of the difference in the ratios (proportions); it also depends in part on the total N, the relative ns of the groups compared, and how close the proportions are to .5. Tables were prepared showing the percentage differences needed for significance under different conditions, but they were complex. A simple rule of thumb gave a reasonable approximation: Adverse impact exists if the selection ratio in one group (presumably the minority group) is less than 80% of the selection ratio in the other.[9] Despite problems discussed in chapters 6 and 10, this remains the usual definition of adverse impact.

---

[8]The committee was jointly chaired by an academic, Raymond A. Katzell of New York University, and an industry-based psychologist, Howard C. Lockwood of Lockheed Corporation. Other members were Lewis E. Albright (Kaiser Aluminum and Chemical Corporation), Robert D. Dugan (Life Office Management Association), J. Robert Garcia (Plans for Progress, on leave from Sandia Corporation), Robert M. Guion (Bowling Green State University), C. Paul Sparks (Humble Oil and Refining Company), Mary L. Tenopyr (North American Aviation), and E. Belvin Williams (Teachers College, Columbia University).

[9]This definition appeared first in employee testing guidelines issued in the State of California, probably because Dr. Mary Tenopyr developed the tables—and served on both the OFCC and the California committees.

Adverse impact is not in itself evidence of discrimination. If actual qualifications differ in different groups, adverse impact may be inevitable in a good faith effort to hire the best qualified candidates. Moreover, affirmative action efforts, such as special recruiting, may necessarily exacerbate adverse impact. Nevertheless, where the 80% rule is not met, regardless of reason, the Order required evidence of validity for the use of the test or other procedure producing the adverse impact. Under the Order, virtually any quantitative selection procedure was subject to validation; nonquantitative selection procedures, such as interviews, could be challenged under the adverse impact concept and subsequently quantified (e.g., by ratings) and validated. If the 80% rule was satisfied, the employer had no obligation under the Order to conduct validation studies.

It was important to assure that contractors knew what was meant by *validity* and *validation*. The committee tried to outline conventional validation principles as described in existing textbooks (Albright, Glennon, & Smith, 1963; Dunnette, 1966; Guion, 1965; Lawshe, 1948; Lawshe & Balma, 1966; Thorndike, 1949). The focus in these books was on validating tests by determining correlations between test scores and job performance. We (the committee) began to fear we were writing another textbook. However, the *Standards for Educational and Psychological Tests and Manuals* (American Psychological Association, American Educational Research Association, & National Council on Measurement in Education, 1966) had appeared shortly before, describing the information needed to evaluate validity. Moreover, its conception of validity was broader. The statistical evidence familiar in conventional employment test validation was called *criterion-related validity*. The Standards added *construct validity*, applied to discussions of many kinds of clinical testing, and *content validity*, directed mainly to educational testing. These were called different *aspects*, not different kinds, of validity.

The terms had been introduced earlier, but their implications for employment testing had not been explored. The committee's principal focus remained on criterion-related validation. To simplify its work, and to avoid reinventing basic validation principles, we simply cited the APA *Standards*. We recognized, albeit hazily, their inclusion of construct and content validity and added, with virtually no serious deliberation, that "evidence of content or construct validity may also be appropriate where criterion-related validity is not feasible" (Office of Federal Contract Compliance, 1968, p. 14392). With this not-very-helpful addition, we moved on to other topics.

EEOC and OFCC Regulations in 1970 and 1971. In the 1968 Presidential campaign, Richard Nixon pledged to consolidate federal EEO enforcement. Early in the Nixon presidency, the OFCC and EEOC each named one attorney and one psychologist to a subcommittee, which met to draft a common document.[10] We took the document back to our respective agencies. It did not satisfy the OFCC committee, which sent several objections to the EEOC. Apparently, it did not satisfy the EEOC either; nothing happened for several months. Then, in 1970, the EEOC issued a new set of Guidelines (Equal Employment Opportunity Commission, 1970) following the form and outline of the OFCC Order and the subcommittee draft. It differed from the draft in major details and added provisions objectionable to the OFCC. It was consistent with the 1968 OFCC Order in defining discrimination in terms of adverse impact unless the selection procedure was properly validated. It was inconsistent in that it added an ambiguous requirement that the validation must result in a "high degree of utility" and the logically impossible requirement that the user must demonstrate that *no* "suitable" available alternative procedure exists. More problems were posed by ambiguities than by impossibilities, but reactions to the new EEOC Guidelines produced a concentrated effort in the OFCC and its advisory committee to issue a revised testing order (Office of Federal Contract Compliance, 1971). The 1971 Order contained a widely unnoticed footnote, approved by EEOC, explicitly stating that it was consistent with the 1970 EEOC Guidelines, differing only because of differing legal authority or for clarification. The footnote was an exercise of tact; many of the clarifying changes were corrections. The impossible clause (proving the absence of an alternative) was, for example, simply omitted.

These two documents gave a bit more attention to construct and content validity, but neither treated the topics very well. For many readers, they had the unfortunate effect of suggesting two unhelpful sentences, one saying that, if criterion-related validity was not feasible, evidence of content or construct validity might do, and the other that, even if criterion-related validity *were* feasible, content validity might still be appropriate. Both documents included the requirement to do and to act on differential validity studies when there were enough cases for the research.

Civil Service Commission Regulations, 1972. The federal government and local jurisdictions receiving federal funds are required by law to select employees on the basis of merit. *Merit* is usually defined by scores on competitive examinations, but "merit systems" include procedural components. To assure fair selection systems, the United States Civil Service Commission issued its own regulations in 1969 and again in 1972.

---

[10]William Enneis and Philip Sklover were EEOC psychologist and lawyer, respectively; I was the psychologist representing the OFCC advisory committee, but I no longer have records identifying OFCC's attorney.

The 1972 version (United States Civil Service Commission, 1972) seemed more a procedural manual for affected agencies at the federal, state, and local levels than an adversial list of requirements. Adverse impact was not given as a reason for requiring validation. Terms used to describe validity and the methods of validation differed from those used by the other agencies. What had been called criterion-related validation was here called "statistical validation," and content or construct validation was called "rational validation" by the CSC. Standards for both were given, consistent with existing professional standards (American Psychological Association, American Educational Research Association, & National Council on Measurements in Education, 1966). Job relatedness was said to be established by criterion-related validation *only* if the criterion had been derived from a "careful empirical analysis" of the job; otherwise, it could be "inferred but not assured" (p. 21557). Other potential limitations of statistical validation were also presented.

There were conflicts between the CSC on the one hand and the OFCC and EEOC on the other. Regulations from the latter showed a clear preference for criterion-related validation; both agencies dealt only briefly with content and construct validation. The CSC, however, was a user of tests as well as an evaluator of them. As a test developer and user, its practice was to analyze a job and then to develop a test to measure the specific KSAs inferred from job analysis as requisite for satisfactory performance. Job knowledge tests were to be evaluated in terms of content validity, and content validity arguments was thought to cover job-required skills or abilities as well. This difference, among others, set the stage for the difficulties encountered in developing a truly uniform, consensus document that could be endorsed by hiring agencies and EEO enforcement agencies.

Federal Executive Agency Guidelines, 1976. The EEOCC issued a first draft of "uniform" guidelines in 1973 for public comment. It received an "almost universally negative" reaction (Miner & Miner, 1978, p. 47), and a 1974 revision fared little better. There were strong differences of opinion among the EEOCC parties. Labor, Justice, and the Civil Service people endorsed a draft in 1975, but the EEOC would not. The major issue was that the EEOC preferred requirements for criterion-related validation that the Civil Service Commission said it (and other employers) could not afford; both the EEOC and the Civil Rights Commission felt that endorsing other validation procedures weakened existing regulations (Miner & Miner, 1978, p. 47). The impasse between executive branch agencies (the CSC and Departments of Labor and Justice) and the civil rights agencies (the EEOC and the Civil Rights Commission) persisted. In 1976, the 1975 draft was issued as the *Federal Executive Agency Guidelines* and the EEOC reissued its 1970 Guidelines, defiantly distancing itself from the other agencies.

The spectacle of the U.S. government, issuing two sets of conflicting regulations after spending so much time trying to develop a single set, seemed to stimulate further discussion; 2 years later, the *Uniform Guidelines* appeared (Equal Employment Opportunity Commission, Civil Service Commission, Department of Labor, & Department of Justice, 1978). The Uniform Guidelines and related case law now define "the legal context" for personnel decisions. Other laws proscribe other forms of discrimination, and some legal constraints are unrelated to discrimination, but the Uniform Guidelines remain the official statement of public policy on assessment in employment.

MAJOR PROVISIONS OF THE UNIFORM GUIDELINES

For a point-by-point description and discussion of the Uniform Guidelines and their implications, see Day, Erwin, and Koral (1981) and Lindemann and Grossman (1996). I offer only highlights. The document is not static. Judicial and administrative decisions have modified some interpretations. Some of them recognize developments in professional knowledge and practice, a further source of change. Some of this chapter may be out of date by the time of publication, so decision makers and their advisors must get and remain current in their knowledge of the legal context within which they work. Here, I treat the Uniform Guidelines mainly as a special case in the development of that legal context, deserving more attention than its forerunners. It is special because it is still current, has been in effect longer than any preceding document, has been a factor in developing similar documents in other countries, often guides federal actions vis-à-vis other laws, and because there seems little reason to believe it will be revised or superceded in the near future.

Adverse Impact and Disparate Treatment

Discrimination may be charged and litigated under two distinct legal theories. One is adverse impact (sometimes called disparate impact) in which discrimination is said to affect different groups differentially. Although the purpose of the law and its enforcement is to protect individual citizens from discrimination based on group identity, adverse impact refers to groups. Evidence that a group as a whole is less likely to be hired is preliminary (prima facie) evidence of discrimination against group members (but no more than that). The other theory is called *disparate treatment*, evidence that a candidate from a protected group is treated differently from other candidates in the employment process. In principle, all applicants should receive the same treatment—the same kinds of interviews, tests, application forms, and hiring standards. Singling out some people for special interviews, tests, waivers, and so forth, is different, or disparate, treatment. The provision goes further, including as disparate treatment requirements imposed "now" (at the time of negotiation or litigation) that differ from those that were imposed when alleged discrimination occurred. Even if employment standards have changed, victims of prior discrimination are not normally to be held to a higher standard than existed at the time the discrimination occurred. This would imply that a rigorous but valid employment test adopted to replace a less valid procedure determined to be discriminatory, one that made it harder to qualify for a job, could not be used to bar the victims of the prior discrimination without stringent proof of business necessity.

The Uniform Guidelines retained the principle that adverse impact requires justification in terms of business necessity. That term does not imply something necessary for the survival of the business; rather, it means that a selection procedure must be related to job behavior or performance—usually that it is a valid predictor of an important criterion—and therefore serves a useful business purpose not as well served by a known alternative with less adverse impact.

The 80% (four fifths) rule was retained. It is simply an enforcement trigger used by federal agencies. It lacks the force of law, and it must be interpreted in the light of other information. One employer might have an adverse impact ratio well under 80%, and therefore be suspected of potential discrimination, only because of vigorous affirmative action. Another employer may have an adverse impact ratio above 80% because of the chilling effect of a reputation suggesting that application to that employer would be futile for members of certain demographic groups. Although a "chilling effect" argument requires substantial proof to succeed in court (e.g., *International Brotherhood of Teamsters v. United States*, 1977), its inclusion in the Guidelines emphasizes that the four fifths rule is subject to interpretation in specific contexts.

Options Under Adverse Impact. A selection procedure having adverse impact on any protected group may be modified, eliminated, or justified by validation. These options are more easily stated than used.

Intractable technical problems may arise trying to modify tests. Changes to reduce adverse impact may also reduce validity. They could result in charges of reverse discrimination. Modification is an option to be undertaken only with carefully designed research. Elimination is not an acceptable option for procedures with useful levels of validity. To abandon the use of a valid selection procedure because of fear of litigation is to return to essentially random selection—not a wise way to run a business. Of the three, validation in support of a business necessity defense is the only organizationally sound option. The organization itself, apart from litigation, should require it. A selection procedure should be replaced if validation fails to show that it serves an important business purpose. Statistical validation is not the only way to show job-relatedness. Case law gives several examples where the business necessity defense was accepted on rational, "common sense" grounds (as cited by Day et al., 1981, p. 41).

Three options are presented in the Guidelines for using a valid selection procedure: (a) use cut scores to screen out only those deemed unqualified for the job, (b) set up bands or other methods of grouping people into categories of predicted performance levels, and (c) rank people for top-down selection. The different procedures may have differing degrees of adverse impact; the Guidelines assert that the probable level of adverse impact is least for cut scores and greatest for ranking.[11] If a cut score is used and has adverse impact, the choice of the cut score must be defended. If ranking has an adverse impact, the principle of alternatives (as presented in the Guidelines) requires the employer to consider the use of a minimum cut score as an "alternative procedure" likely to have less impact. The Guidelines are silent on the fact that it may also have substantially less validity.

Day et al. (1981, p. 41) argued that the specification of options is not simply a call for good professional practice but a requirement to search actively for alternatives—a requirement that, they said, stems from a "misreading" of case law. The misreading, if that is what it is, is widespread and raises a serious question: Does the legal context in which personnel decisions are made require the best of contemporary thought or merely minimal competence? Or, indeed, does it require *incompetent* practice? At different times, in arguments related to different cases, it has seemed to me that Guidelines interpretations favor practices of questionable competence, especially regarding cut scores and item analysis.

Alternative Selection Procedures. A further option is to substitute an alternative selection procedure with less adverse impact. Unlike the 1970 EEOC Guidelines, these Guidelines call for "consideration of alternatives"

---

[11]The list does not include or mention another option, historically used rather widely. This option, in its simplest form, involves transforming scores to percentile ranks, independently for score distributions in majority and minority groups, and then ranking applicants according to percentile scores. This would be a top-down procedure with minimal adverse impact. Separate norms, however, were prohibited by the 1991 amendment to the Civil Rights Act.

rather than a showing that no alternative exists that can do the same job. Actually, alternatives should be considered from the outset. In planning the research, a predictive hypothesis should be formed with certain applicant traits hypothesized as predictor constructs (see chapter 3). Then one must choose one or more operational definitions of the hypothesized constructs to use in the study. In making that choice, prior literature should be considered, including literature describing evidence of validity and evidence of adverse impact—and evidence of other challenges to the validity of the operations (tests, if that they be). Alternatives are considered, in good practice, independently of legal considerations.

Unfortunately, good practice is often pushed aside by the pressures of day-to-day demands on time and other resources; a legal challenge to existing selection procedures often sends employing organizations scurrying to find post hoc evidence of validity. Records rarely exist of alternatives considered when the challenged Test A was introduced and put to use, or even why it was chosen. It is simply there, like the ambient air. In this very common situation, Section V says further, "The employer cannot concentrate solely on establishing the validity of the instrument or procedure it has been using in the past" (Equal Employment Opportunity Commission, Civil Service Commission, Department of Labor, & Department of Justice, 1978, p. 38291). That is, in efforts to validate instruments in use, alternatives must also be considered. Those alternatives may include any that, at the point of threatened or actual litigation, an enforcing agency suggests: "Whenever the user *is shown* an alternative selection procedure with evidence of less adverse impact . . . the user should investigate it. . . ." (Equal Employment Opportunity Commission, Civil Service Commission, Department of Labor, & Department of Justice, 1978, p. 38297, italics added). In short, the list of alternative procedures to be considered include not only those that the employer's own judgment considers worthy but also those suggested by an adversary.

The suitable alternative requirement was surely written with criterion-related validity coefficients in mind; there is no way to say empirically whether two procedures have substantially equal content or construct validities. As a matter of fact, the Guidelines are not much help for validity coefficients, either. Are coefficients substantially equal if they do not differ significantly? If so, how much statistical power is required to test for the significance? Such questions are not answerable from the Guidelines, nor is there any recognition that even small differences in validity coefficients may indicate substantial differences in utility, the savings possible from test use.

The section on alternatives has another disquieting feature, a requirement, for a given procedure, to study "alternative methods of using the selection procedure which have as little adverse impact as possible" (Equal

Employment Opportunity Commission, Civil Service Commission, Department of Labor, & Department of Justice, 1978, p. 38297). The practical effect of this requirement for many employers has been to try to reduce adverse impact through such methods of use as differential norming, or setting up score intervals (usually called "banding"), or adding constants to scores of members of certain subgroups with little or no concern for the impact such methods have on the validity of the procedure.

If a procedure has been in use, and the user is then shown (probably in or prior to litigation) "an alternative procedure with evidence of less adverse impact and substantial evidence of validity for the same job in similar circumstances, the user should investigate it to determine the appropriateness of using or validating it in accord with these guidelines" (EEOC et al., 1978, p. 38297). On the face of it, this provision simply requires the employer to give thoughtful consideration to a suggested alternative. As a matter of experience, however, I have been involved in court cases where compliance agencies have actively (if subtly) promoted the adoption of favored tests or other alternative procedures—with greater concern for "as little adverse impact as possible" (EEOC et al., 1978, p. 38297) than for "substantially equal validity."

When the issue reaches the stage of litigation, on whom should the burden lie to consider alternatives? Day et al. (1981) believed it should lie with the plaintiff in the case:

> The agencies claim that placing the burden of seeking less adverse alternatives on the user is consistent with *Albemarle v. Moody* (1975), but *Albemarle* places the burden of demonstrating the availability of a less adverse alternative on the plaintiff in a Title VII case. It is one way in which a plaintiff can rebut the employer's showing of job-relatedness and it is no more than evidence from which triers of fact may infer that the showing of job-relatedness is pretextual. This will always be a fact question, as there are numerous factors that defy a simplistic approach. For example, the reasonableness of assuming the employer's knowledge of the less adverse alternative procedure, the degree of difference in its impact and the comparative predictiveness of the two procedures are all thorny issues going to the effectiveness of a plaintiff's effort to show that an employer's use of a validated selection procedure is, nevertheless, a pretext for discrimination. (Day et al., 1981, p. 85)

The entire issue of suitable alternatives arises because there were several court cases in the early days of litigation under Title VII in which it was quite reasonable to infer that the employer chose certain tests to be the instruments of illegal discrimination, sometimes apparently believing that the tests could be justified under the Tower amendment simply because they were professionally developed. That line of argument is no longer available, but the possibility of pretext remains real enough that plaintiffs must have the alternative procedure argument available to them. Given the ambiguities of the Guidelines provisions, however, it seems unnecessarily burdensome to require as a matter of routine that all employers liable under Title VII to consider all alternatives others may suggest.

The "Bottom Line" Argument. Sometimes, the only valid predictors may, by themselves, produce a substantial adverse impact. Efforts to reduce the adverse impact have frequently led to procedures (e.g., interviews) that would permit compensatory evaluations. At the end of the selection process, then, the "bottom line" is that the overall selection rate may be about the same for groups of applicants, reducing or eliminating adverse impact.

The Guidelines tentatively permitted bottom line arguments, identifying circumstances where such arguments were unacceptable. What these situations might be is now moot; the bottom line defense was struck down by the Supreme Court in *Connecticut v. Teal* (1982). For any assessment procedure, adverse impact analysis is required; if it exists, that procedure must be validated. If it has adverse impact, without validity evidence, it is not permitted, regardless of the bottom line.

Requirements for Validation

The Guidelines asserted that their technical requirements for validation were consistent with the existing professional standards at the time (American Psychological Association, American Educational Research Association, and National Council on Measurement in Education, 1974; American Psychological Association, Division of Industrial and Organizational Psychology, 1975). They were not entirely so; for example, the Division 14 *Principles* recognized that so-called content validity is not validity at all but an approach to test construction. Nevertheless, the requirements, especially those for criterion-related validation, were generally sensible approximations of conventional professional views. New research evidence, and the thinking stimulated largely by EEO regulations, has made some of these conventional views obsolete, and the Guidelines are inconsistent with contemporary professional views. They have treated criterion-related, content, and construct validity "as something of a holy trinity representing three different roads to psychometric salvation" (Guion, 1980, p. 386). Actually, the idea of three distinctly different *kinds* of validity has been inconsistent with professional views at least since the terms were introduced in the 1954 Technical Recommendations (APA, AERA, & NCME, 1954) and explicitly denied in the 1985 Standards (AERA, APA, & NCME, 1985). The more integrated view, that these terms refer to different aspects or varieties of evidence of validity, is discussed more thoroughly in chapter 5.

In one respect the professional community and the Guidelines authors are in full agreement; the Guidelines state, "Under no circumstances will the general reputation of a test or other selection procedures [sic], its author or its publisher, or casual reports of it's [sic] validity be accepted in lieu of evidence of its validity" (EEOC et al., 1978, p. 38299). There is no equivocation and no ambiguity; data, not reputation or hearsay, establish validity or its absence.

Criterion-Related Validation. Criterion-related validation may not be technically feasible. Three conditions are explicitly recognized in the definition of technical feasibility: (a) adequate samples (it is not clear whether this refers only to sample size or to sample representativeness), (b) adequate score ranges on both predictor and criterion (presumably enough variance that uncorrected coefficients would not be drastically different from population values; see chapter 7), and (c) an acceptable criterion (i.e., unbiased, reliable, and relevant). If it is determined that criterion-related validation is feasible, the Guidelines specify that:

1. Job information must be reviewed, or the job must be analyzed, to determine criteria; a criterion must "represent critical or important job duties, work behaviors or work outcomes. . . ." (EEOC et al., 1978, p. 38300). A full-fledged job analysis is not required if the importance of the criterion used can be shown without it; examples include production rates, errors, and absences.

2. "The possibility of bias should be considered" (EEOC et al., 1978, p. 38300) in choosing criteria. The Guidelines do not define bias, but the inference comes readily that the enforcement agencies will treat any mean difference in criterion or predictor scores of different demographic groups as bias. This is unfortunate; mean differences may reflect true population differences stemming from effects of differential experience, differential recruiting, or any of a host of other factors.

3. Samples used should be like the relevant labor market for the job in question. This seems to imply demographic similarity, but in considering concurrent studies, employers should also consider whether those in the sample have skills or knowledge acquired through experience that might influence the validities of potential predictors.

4. Relationships between predictors and criteria should be statistically expressed and should be statistically significant, typically at the 5% level of confidence. This statement is conventional.

5. Validity should not be overstated. Specifically, the provision refers to a study using several criteria, finding a significant relationship of a

predictor with only one of them, and then ignoring the possibility of a chance relationship. It also explicitly criticizes the use of multiple coefficients of correlation obtained in a sample without recognition of expected shrinkage in other samples (see chapter 8). It does *not* refer to population estimates from sample statistics.

6. If, in general, the results show that a selection procedure is a valid predictor of an important criterion, studies of fairness should be conducted (where technically feasible). This requirement marks the greatest difference between professional opinion and the Guidelines. As shown in chapter 10, the statistical models of so-called "fairness" are contradictory (if test use is "fair" by one statistical definition, it will necessarily be "unfair" by another), the Guidelines are ambiguous about the definition of fairness to be used, and the fairness models assume racial, ethnic, or sex differences in validity or prediction—differences that have rarely been reliably found.

Except for the requirements to search for bias in criteria or predictors and for evidence of unfairness—both of which are central to EEO enforcement concerns and both of which are extremely difficult to define or to demonstrate—the requirements for criterion-related validity evidence are, on their face, quite conventional.

Content Validation. The Guidelines provisions on content validity (and on construct validity) are confused and confusing. The definition of content validity in the Guidelines glossary seems to contradict the Guidelines technical standards for reporting such studies. The glossary definition seems to suggest a content domain limited to "important aspects of performance on the job" (EEOC et al., 1978, p. 38307) but not including job knowledge as job content. The Guidelines' technical standards seem to include job knowledge in the domain but require it to be more comprehensive (EEOC et al., 1978, p. 38302).[12] Further confusion comes in the statement that arguments of content validity are inappro-

---

[12]In fairness to the authors of the Guidelines, it should be pointed out that such confusion was rampant in the relevant literature of the time. It is a matter of personal embarrassment that the 1974 Standards, with which I was closely associated, had the same apparent contradiction in the two columns of a single page; the left hand column said that the content domain should be defined "in terms of the objectives of measurement, restricted perhaps only to critical, most frequent, or prerequisite work behaviors" while the right hand column said, "An employer cannot justify an employment test on grounds of content validity if he cannot demonstrate that the content universe includes all, or nearly all, important parts of the job" (American Psychological Association, American Educational Research Association, and National Council on Measurement in Education, 1974, p. 29). It is not unfair, however, to point out that the enforcement agencies have permitted this confusion to remain in the Guidelines far too long.

priate for content that may be learned on the job—a provision interpreted by Day et al. (1981, p. 159) as ruling out selection based on job experience.

Conceptual confusions aside, it is clear that the Guidelines require job analysis to identify work behaviors required for effective performance, their relative importance, and the work products expected to result. The analysis should focus on observable task behavior, although some questions about what is observable are sometimes raised (e.g., is *planning* an observable behavior?). The requirement seems to restrict options to work samples (or, perhaps, to very narrowly defined job knowledge tests). The apparent narrowness is somewhat relieved by the inclusion of tests developed previously by others, in other circumstances, if the test content matches in some convincing way the content of the job as revealed by the job analysis.

In the face of confusion, obsolescence, and naiveté, it is rather difficult to express unambiguously the Guidelines requirements for evidence of content validity. What follows must be recognized simply as one person's view of the requirements, with all the fallibility that implies:

1. A content domain must be defined on the basis of a thorough job analysis, one that not only identifies tasks and resources used in doing them but also determines their relative importance to the job overall. Implicit in this statement is the assumption that acceptable content validity arguments are job specific or at most job-family specific. That is, organization-wide content domains are unlikely to be acceptable.

2. If the defined job content is but a portion of the job, it must be prerequisite or critical to overall job performance.

3. The content of selection procedures defended on the basis of content validity must match the content defined by the job analysis.

4. Reliability estimates should be given for assessment scores (and perhaps judged according to a higher standard than required for tests developed on other grounds, particularly if adverse impact is substantial).

5. Required prior training or experience may be justified as valid content if its content closely resembles the content of the job, as identified by job analysis.[13]

---

[13]Requiring "close resemblance" may be both unlikely and unwise. I pointed out earlier (Guion, 1974) that a requirement for certain kinds of training, such as engineering training, is a requirement for knowledge that might not be applied on a given job. A mechanical engineering student, for example, takes courses in English and chemistry that may have little bearing on the design of particular pieces of heavy equipment, yet most employers hypothesize that people with engineering degrees are likely to be better at designing such equipment than people without the degrees. Although the hypothesis can be tested, it would be a silly employer—and a potentially dangerous one—who would hire a lot of non-engineers to design the equipment merely to provide data for a criterion-related validation.

6. Selection procedures defended only on the basis of content validity may be used only with a minimum cutting score; although words in the Guidelines refer to circumstances where ranking is permitted, the words necessarily imply criterion-related data. I have given the requirement as I understand it, but I must add that I consider it a silly requirement. In a typing test based on content validity, for example, it is silly to say that applicant A cannot be preferred over applicant B, who scores at the bottom edge of the acceptable range, even if applicant A completes the test without error in half the time declared acceptable. The requirement also fails to acknowledge that relationships between test scores and criteria, where they can be examined, are almost always linear or at least monotonic—a point further discussed in chapter 7. Unless there is compelling evidence to the contrary, this means that persons with higher scores can nearly always be predicted to do better on relevant criteria than those with lower scores—even if the predictor is defended by content validity alone.

Construct Validation. The Guidelines also require job analysis as the first step in a defense invoking construct validity. It should identify behavior required for effective performance and constructs believed to underlie effective behavior. Such constructs should be clearly named, defined, and distinguished from other constructs, and selection procedures chosen should be supported with empirical evidence that they are related to the intended constructs. These requirements, so far, are excellent from a professional point of view.

Unfortunately, the Guidelines go on to say, "The relationship between the construct as measured by the selection procedure and the related work behavior(s) should be supported by empirical evidence from one or more criterion-related studies involving the job or jobs in question which satisfy the provisions [for criterion-related validation]" (EEOC et al., 1978, p. 38303). In short, despite some words supporting the use of construct validity arguments, and despite the apparent understanding of them, this provision effectively rules out construct validity arguments. It is impossible to say whether this is due to the limited understanding of the topic on the part of the Guidelines authors, to some more Machiavellian manipulation, or simply to the fact that this is a committee-generated document with all the contradictions and confusions that implies; whatever the reason, the Guidelines approach to construct validity is confused and psychometrically unsound (see the discussion in Day et al., 1981, pp. 171–175). We give more serious consideration to the nature of construct validity and of its role in establishing (or failing to establish) the job relatedness of a selection procedure in chapter 5.

Use of Valid Personnel Selection Procedures

"Transportability" of Validity Information. Acceptable evidence of validity may be based on validation research done elsewhere, but only with severe restrictions. The question is whether the outside research generalizes to the user's situation; some people refer to such generalizing as "transporting" the validity evidence. This provision predates the development of validity generalization research, and discussing it now seems rather quaint. However, it is still a part of the legal context, and there are often situations where one wishes to generalize from a specific study rather than from a body of related studies.

A generalized requirement, regardless of the nature of the validity evidence, is that the documentation and reporting be available in a form "similar to" the form required by the Guidelines. (As pointed out by Day et al. [1981, p. 205], one would think the persuasiveness of the evidence would be more important than its form of presentation.) Other requirements for transporting criterion-related validity studies include:

1. There must be evidence of the similarity of the job at hand and the job in the original study, identified by the same methods of job analysis.
2. The criterion in the original study is relevant to the local job.
3. The demographic characteristics of the applicant pool or research sample in the original study must be similar to those in the new situation.

Certainly the key characteristics of the job—those for which criterion data will be sought—should match in the two situations. It is less certain that broader similarity is truly necessary, and very nearly certain (from research done in the 1970s) that demographic similarity is not necessary; nevertheless, these requirements still define part of the legal context in which personnel decisions are made.

Testing for Higher Level Jobs. Employers frequently want to hire people who will advance in the organization. The desire is defensible, but predictability of behavior tends to deteriorate over time. The Guidelines recognize this and further recognize that in many jobs advancement to higher levels is rare; in such jobs, hiring for the higher level may in effect be a pretext for discrimination. Employers are permitted to assess applicants for the higher levels only if (a) the majority of those still employed after "a reasonable period of time" (rarely more than 5 years) progress to the higher level job, (b) the higher level job will continue to require largely the same skills during that time, and (c) the original job is not likely to provide the development of the requisite knowledge or skill.

Use of Scores. Four methods of score use are recognized: ranking (both top-down selection in which the highest scoring candidates are chosen first and the less systematic procedure where of two candidates the one with the higher score is preferred over one with a lower score), banding, pass–fail with a cut score, and combination with other tests. The Guidelines imply that a method of use is chosen on the basis of the validation method and results. In good practice, however, the method of use is chosen and determines appropriate research design; the validity of a test used in combination with others, or one used with a cut score, cannot be known from a simple linear correlation coefficient. Correlations with other tests in a composite, or the placement of the cut score, affect validity.

Little is said in the Guidelines about combining predictors, but there is a clear preference for cut scores, especially low ones. Ranking requires justification by data showing that variation in scores is related to variation in performance—that is, a criterion-related validation. Although words are used to suggest acceptability of content or construct validity arguments, the justification requirement nullifies them. Not all courts have accepted the Guidelines on this point, although many do. The idea of passing a test seems so ingrained in a society using cut scores for various kinds of licenses, diplomas, grades, and certificates that reference to passing or failing tests seems natural.

Where there are differences in mean scores of demographic subgroups (and there usually are), and where variances are about the same (and they might be), there is a necessary relationship between the level of a cutting score and the degree of adverse impact. That is, a cut score can be set high enough that virtually no one in the lower scoring group can pass it. The way to reduce adverse impact, therefore, is to lower the cutting score. How low? The Guidelines themselves do not say, but some enforcement agencies in some situations have argued that the cutoff should permit hiring people at approximately the same score of the lowest-scoring employee who is retained and on that basis presumed satisfactory. This position ignores such matters as possible compensating factors, the hiring and retention of employees as part of affirmative action programs, and so on. It ignores the statistical realities of linear or other monotonic relationships between test scores and performance. It ignores Congressional intent in supporting, in Title VII, employers' rights to set qualifications. It ignores the fact that selection procedures are typically adopted for the sake of improving levels of proficiency in the workforce, not simply for maintaining what may be an unacceptable status quo.

In a different vein, it ignores the realities of selection procedures. In civil service jurisdictions, the typical pattern is to establish an eligibility list giving the names of all candidates who have exceeded a low cut score; selection is then done by ranking (top-down) those on that list until the list is "exhausted." An exhausted list typically still has names on it of people who have passed the test, but the passage of time and difficulties in finding people still interested in the job induce the authorities to initiate a new examination and start over with a new eligibility list. Even though a passing score is established, actual practice makes the de facto passing score somewhat higher.

In the private sector, the difference between a minimum cut score, if one is even considered, and the de facto score is even more pronounced. Hiring rates differ with the times. In a period of recession, for example, a company may do little hiring, and it will choose from the best of the many applicants presenting themselves for consideration; the lowest score among those hired may be quite high. When unemployment is very low, when virtually "any warm body" will do rather than leave a job totally unfilled, the de facto cutting score is reduced drastically. Such variability seems to be unacceptable to the authors of the Guidelines; they seem to assume that, unless ranking is justified, a fixed cut point will be established. Nothing is said about selection above that point. If more people score above the cut score than can be hired, how should new employees be chosen? At random? The Guidelines do not say.

Reporting and Record Keeping Requirements

The Guidelines specify stringent record keeping requirements. Although not matters of psychological or psychometric principle, these are important to management. They are so important to litigation that any employer affected by the Guidelines should study them in great detail and with informed legal counsel. Moreover, various agencies have issued (and revised) record keeping requirements independently of the Guidelines.

CASE LAW FROM MAJOR EEO COURT DECISIONS

A *statute*, such as the Civil Rights Act, is a set of words adopted after legislative debate, compromise, and amendment. Application of these words to a specific instance is not always clear. Each party in a dispute may honestly believe the words to be on its side. The courts have the responsibility of applying the words and their legislative history to the specific case. In the United States federal courts, the dispute is first heard by the judge or jury in a District Court; the judge or jury is the "trier of fact" who determines the facts of the case and interprets them in the light of the relevant statutes and prior court decisions. Attorneys' arguments, testimony from witnesses, and study of the law and interpretation developed in prior cases all contribute to the judge's decision. When a jury is involved, the judge instructs it as to the law. In the end, one party prevails; the losing party may appeal the decision to a Circuit Court of Appeals (the appellate level), which has jurisdiction over District courts in its geographical area. At the appellate level, lawyers present their cases to a panel of judges; these judges do not hear witnesses or determine facts but hear and study arguments to determine whether an error of procedure or of legal interpretation has occurred. The decision of the lower court may be confirmed, reversed, or remanded for reconsideration or retrial. Decisions at the appellate level become binding precedents for the district courts of that circuit; that is, those decisions guide district court judges in future cases involving the same or similar legal issues. A district judge does not always follow precedent, but strong and compelling reasons, based on the facts of the case and their differences from the facts in the precedent case, are needed to justify deviation. The highest level of appeal is to the United States Supreme Court. Decisions at this highest level are binding precedents for all other federal courts—with the same possibility that the triers of fact in a new case may find important differences justifying a different legal path.

At all three levels, decisions rendered become part of *case law*—the body of judicial interpretations of the statute. The relative weight of decisions in case law is greater at the higher judicial levels, so I concentrate this review mainly on a few decisions rendered by the Supreme Court. I do not give details of cases but will give implications for personnel practices. See books by Arvey (1979), Gutman (1993), Miner and Miner (1978), or Lindemann and Grossman (1996), for more on case law.

Griggs v. Duke Power Co.

When the Civil Rights Act of 1964 was enacted, the Duke Power Company had 95 employees in a North Carolina facility, of whom 14 were Black. The plant had five departments, including a labor department. The company had required a high school diploma in all departments except labor, the only department hiring Blacks. On July 2, 1965, the effective date of the Act, the company extended the high school requirement to the labor department and required acceptable scores on two aptitude tests installed at that time.

The unanimous Supreme Court decision included many far-reaching provisions (*Griggs v. Duke Power Co.*, 1971):

1. *Business necessity*: The Court said that the Act prohibits the use of practices that appear to be fair but have discriminatory effects. "The touchstone," it said, "is business necessity." Although the Court seemed to equate business necessity with job-relatedness, other cases were needed to clarify the still-controversial concept.

2. *Job-relatedness*: Whether job-relatedness is sufficient to show business necessity was not clear from this one decision; that it is a requirement

for professionally justifying use of a selection procedure was not in doubt. The Court said that the educational and test requirements were both adopted "without meaningful study" relating them to performance. When the decision was announced, many psychologists equated job-relatedness with validity, but later decisions have shown distinctions.

3. *Intent versus effect*: Unequivocally, questions of intent were said to be irrelevant under Title VII, that good intentions cannot excuse the use of procedures that establish special obstacles, unrelated to performance, for minorities. It is the consequences of a practice, not the motive behind it, that is important. Referring to tests, the decision italicized the words *or used* in quoting from the Tower amendment permitting tests that are not "designed, intended, *or used* to discriminate. . . ."

4. *Deference to Guidelines*: Only the 1966 EEOC Guidelines were available when the case was heard. The Court asserted that Guidelines issued by the EEOC were "entitled to great deference." That did not give the Guidelines the force of law, but Guidelines provisions are to be carefully considered in Title VII cases.

5. *Tests of job qualifications*: The Court found in reviewing the legislative history of the Tower amendment affirmation of employers' rights to insist that everyone, regardless of demographic identity, meet applicable job qualifications. The history declared that the specific purpose of the proposed law was to require that selection decisions be based on qualifications rather than on race or color. The Court concluded that the EEOC's requirement that employment tests be job-related was entirely consistent with Congressional intent. Its decision said that tests are obviously useful but cannot have

> controlling force unless they are demonstrably a reasonable measure of job performance. Congress has not commanded that the less qualified be preferred over the better qualified simply because of minority origins. Far from disparaging job qualifications as such, Congress has made such qualifications the controlling factor, so that race, religion, nationality, and sex become irrelevant.[14]

Albemarle Paper Co. v. Moody

The Court in *Albemarle v. Moody* (1975) supported class-action suits. It held that, as a remedy for prior discrimination, back pay could be

---

[14]One phrase that a test must be "demonstrably a reasonable measure of job performance" has always bothered me. Obviously, there can be no "measure of job performance" of an applicant who has not yet performed the job. Therefore, in the context of the rest of the decision, I've always interpreted the phrase as meaning *demonstrably and reasonably related to job performance.*

awarded to people not individually named in the suit, who did not themselves file charges, but who were members of the affected "class." The class might, for example, be all women who had unsuccessfully applied for employment for a specified job or group of jobs between specified dates. Obviously, losing a class-action suit can be a very expensive proposition for the defending organization.

The decision also strengthened the "great deference" posture vis-à-vis the EEOC Guidelines. Those Guidelines were central in the court's determination that the validation research done by the company's consultant was defective, especially regarding criterion ratings and numbers of cases for specific job titles. (Ironically, the same data today might have been analyzed by validity generalization methods; because the Guidelines predate the development of these methods, it is a matter of interesting conjecture—but only conjecture—to try to decide how the court might have reacted to this scientific advance within its great deference position.)

In a separate but concurring judgment, Justice Blackmun was concerned about "the Court's apparent view that absolute compliance with the EEOC Guidelines is a sine qua non of pre-employment test validation." He further suggested that "too-rigid application" of those Guidelines would necessarily lead to quotas—an early expression of judicial concern.

Washington v. Davis

Washington v. Davis (1976) was not a Title VII case. It began before the 1972 amendment brought governmental agencies under Title VII scrutiny, and it was therefore tried as a constitutional case. It was particularly important, however, because it showed some discontent within the Court against rigid applications of its own prior decisions. In this case, the Court emphasized validation over adverse impact. Adverse impact was clearly shown; the test (for police officer selection in the District of Columbia) was validated against scores on the final examination in a long, intensive training program. A rigid extension of prior decisions would have denied the acceptability of the validation study because the criterion was not actual job performance; because the training program had a clear relevance to job performance, the Court held that it was an acceptable criterion and declared the test to be job related.

Dothard v. Rawlinson

The Alabama legislature had established minimum weight and minimum height requirements (120 lb, 5'2") for employment as prison guards in state correctional facilities. A woman was rejected for a guard trainee position because of failure to meet these requirements; she sued. These requirements would exclude about one third of American women but only a bit over 1% of American men. Accepting these statistics as evidence of adverse impact, the Court in *Dothard v. Rawlinson* (1977) said the burden of proof then shifted to the defendent to show job-relatedness, a position consistent with the history of testing Guidelines. Virtually all federal EEO regulations had taken the position that adverse impact triggered a demand for a showing of validity; the shift in the burden of proof that was implicit in *Griggs* and *Albemarle* was made explicit in *Dothard*.

Regents, University of California v. Bakke

This case (*Regents, University of California v. Bakke, 1978*) was heard under Title VI, the educational section of the Civil Rights Act, but it had implications for debates of future amendments of Title VII. California had two independent admissions programs, a regular program for most applicants and a special one for minorities who claimed disadvantaged status. Bakke, a White applicant to the Medical College of the University of California at Davis, was rejected in each of 2 years when minorities with substantially lower scores were admitted, and he sued successfully in California courts. The United States Supreme Court affirmed that the admissions system was unacceptable and that Bakke should be admitted, but it reversed the judgment that race cannot be legally considered. Its view was that racial diversity among medical students might be a legitimate consideration among others, but that the two-track system used at Davis violated consitutional protections.

Connecticut v. Teal

The Guidelines accepted the bottom line concept for avoiding adverse impact, albeit reluctantly and only as a matter of prosecutorial discretion. *Connecticut v. Teal* (1982), however, ruled against the bottom line safe harbor in a case involving a multiple-component promotion system. First, candidates for promotion were required to pass a written test. Those who did were placed on an eligibility list from which selections were based on prior work performance, recommendations of supervisors, and (lightly) seniority. Test results had clear adverse impact under the four fifths rule, but on the bottom line more Black than White candidates were promoted. That the bottom line statistics could, at least on their face, support a charge of adverse impact against Whites entered neither the decision nor the sharply worded dissenting opinion.

The Court's view was that Title VII sought to assure every *individual* equality in employment opportunity, not to provide overall equality for racial groups. From that perspective, a Black applicant who failed the test would find little comfort in the fact that those of his brothers who passed it had equal chances for the promotion. The court ultimately held that any component of the overall process that demographically differentially precludes further consideration is subject to adverse impact analysis and the subsequent requirement for evidence of job-relatedness.

This decision was extremely important in organizations—and there are many—using a "multiple hurdles" approach to personnel decisions. In a common practice in on-campus college recruiting, for example, the first hurdle is an interview- and credential-based decision by the recruiter to send the applicant to the home or district office for further assessment. Arguably, this first hurdle might not survive a validation study.

Watson v. Fort Worth Bank & Trust

Since the 1966 EEOC Guidelines, attempts (largely unnoticed) have been made to regulate subjective assessments as well as formal tests. *Watson v. Fort Worth Bank* (1988) examined the applicability of the adverse impact trigger to a case in which promotions were based primarily on supervisors' subjective recommendations. The Court was aware of its dilemma. Requiring adverse impact analysis for every unstructured consideration could lead to the adoption of surreptitious quotas to avoid litigation. Not requiring it could mask strongly discriminatory effects of apparently benign procedures. Even objective data such as test scores or diplomas could be combined with subjective interviews, the composite therefore being subjective, and the entire thrust of *Griggs* and its adverse impact trigger could disappear as a mechanism for enforcing Title VII.

Given these poles, what should courts do about subjective practices? On this question, the Supreme Court was divided. The decision of the plurality considered the standards of proof rigorous enough to safeguard against quota-producing "chilling effects on legitimate business practices." To show discrimination prima facie, the decision said, two standards of proof are required. First, a plaintiff must identify the specific practice being challenged—not easily done when the practice is a private, subjective judgment. Second, with the practice identified, the plaintiff must also present statistical data strong enough to convince the presiding judge that the practice has the effect of *causing* loss of equality of opportunity for members of a protected group. The decision argued that a "burden of persuasion" does not transfer to a defendant; as in other matters of evidence, the defendant has the opportunity to criticize or refute either the data or the causal inference.

The Court also said that the cost of alternative procedures is a factor to be considered; cost had not heretofore seemed to be a matter of much concern to the Court and certainly not to enforcement agencies. Similarly, for the first time, the Court also said that expensive validation studies were not needed, even for tests, when common sense and good judgment affirmed the job-relatedness of the practice. Indeed, in matters of judging job relevance, lower courts were urged to defer in many matters to the greater expertise of employers in questions of business practice.

Wards Cove Packing Co. v. Atonio

In *Wards Cove Packing Co. v. Atonio* (1989), a five-justice majority affirmed most of the plurality decision in *Watson v. Fort Worth Bank* (1988). It affirmed the extension of adverse impact analysis to subjective procedures, the need to specify the practice being challenged, and maintaining the burden of persuasion on the plaintiff. It added a further requirement that evidence of adverse impact compare the demographic data *on a specific job* to the available supply of people for that job; that is, adverse impact statistics must be based on relevant labor markets. The Court also reduced the "business necessity" language to "business justification"—implicit, I think, in earlier decisions—saying that a practice need not be essential to survival of the business or in some other sense indispensable.[15]

THE 1991 AMENDMENT TO THE CIVIL RIGHTS ACT

Differences in opinions about fairness in employment were neither resolved nor clarified by 25 years of EEO enforcement and litigation. If anything, they froze as polar opposites, held not as reasoned policy but as deeply held emotional commitments. For some, Supreme Court decisions like those in *Watson* and *Wards Cove* seemed overdue statements of sanity in the EEO arena. To many others, they seemed to signal a weakening of basic EEO principles, including the Court's standards in *Griggs*. Never mind that the *Griggs* ambiguities had required nearly 20 years to

---

[15]Many observers, including those in Congress, have decried this as "reversing" *Griggs*. In my judgment, which is far from legally trained, I cannot see that it is. From *Griggs* on, business necessity has been equated with job-relatedness; the word *necessity*, insofar as it ever had anything other than rhetorical value, has always seemed to me to imply only that a procedure was deemed "necessary" (or not) for sound business practice. Reading a "plant-closing" implication has always seemed to me a fanciful, out-of-context extension of the word "necessity." Relevant labor market statistics have long been demanded in statistical evidence of adverse impact, so I am not at all sure that this represents anything drastically new, either. Detractors of the court, however, have seen the *Watson* and the *Wards Cove* decisions as severely watering down Title VII enforcement, and subsequent lower court decisions seem to suggest that the explicitness of these decisions has indeed had such an effect.

clarify. Never mind that subsequent decisions failed to clarify other fundamental issues. It is perception that determines action, and it was perceptions that led to acrimonious exchanges among columnists, political pundits, and members of Congress and, ultimately, to attempts to "rein in" the Supreme Court by amending the Civil Rights Act to reverse its more recent decisions legislatively. A first, unsuccessful attempt in 1990 was passed in both houses of Congress and vetoed by President Bush; Congress failed to override the veto. Opponents argued that the bill called for quotas; proponents said it did not. Neither view was correct, although both were loudly proclaimed. The bill did not call for quotas, but it could have led to de facto quota-resembling efforts to avoid litigation. Soon after passage of the 1964 Civil Rights Act, employers demanded—almost as a slogan—that personnel directors make sure to "get the numbers right," to hire enough minorities and women to avoid litigation. Given the ambiguities of the 1990 bill, similar efforts to get the numbers right were virtually certain, and the right numbers are most easily obtained by using a surrogate for a quota if not a quota in fact. This problem could have been avoided by careful crafting of the bill's language, but it was apparently not tried. So-called debate was hot if not well-informed or well-intended. In my cynical view, based on correspondence with Senate members, the debaters were less concerned with defining and fixing a problem than with attempts to gain partisan advantage.

A Civil Rights Act of 1991 was passed and signed into law. It amended Title VII among other things. Worries about quotas seemed to be put to rest by prohibiting "race-norming." (Race-norming is a way to get the numbers right by using percentiles or standard scores in different score distributions for different subgroups and using top-down selection based on the percentiles.) Shortly before the Congressional debates, controversy erupted over the practice in state Employment Services referrals using the United States Department of Labor's General Aptitude Test Battery (see Hartigan & Wigdor, 1989). Race norming does not seriously affect mean job performance, but making it illegal quieted the charges of a quota bill.

Of the Supreme Court decisions opposed in the 1990 bill, only the *Watson* view that defendants did not have a "burden of persuasion" was changed by the 1991 Act. Definitions of business necessity and of job relatedness were to have been codified by the 1991 Act. Nevertheless, they remain as ambiguous (some say "flexible") as before, and common sense definitions may yet prevail.

Another provision addresses intentional discrimination, providing even for jury trials and for compensatory and punitive damages. Good sense, if not morality, requires organizations to make sure that intentional discrimination on irrelevant grounds, or even the appearance of it, does not occur.

AFFIRMATIVE ACTION

Employers must not only avoid unlawful discrimination but must take affirmative action to reduce the effects of prior discrimination. Early examples of affirmative actions included recruiting efforts, special training programs, direct mentoring, or extended probationary periods. Some affirmative action programs are voluntary, but many are imposed by court orders or consent decrees. Affirmative action is not a requirement under Title VII, although it is in the Guidelines. It has been a requirement for government contractors under the various Executive Orders, including the still effective 11246, since 1961. It has been controversial since the development of the Philadelphia Plan in 1969, and the controversy is usually emotional.

The Philadelphia Plan

The affirmative action requirement in EO 11246 posed a special problem for the building trades; contractors do not generally have their own crews of skilled employees. They often hire those sent by unions. OFCC investigations found few minorities in trade unions in the five-county Philadelphia area, despite a substantial minority population. The Secretary of Labor issued an order calling for increased proportions of minorities in each of six trades in each year of a 4-year period. Any building contractor submitting a bid for a federal contract was required to submit with it an affirmative action program to show goals within these standard ranges and a plan for reaching them.

Contractors faced a dilemma when the Comptroller General of the United States issued an opinion that commitment to the plan was illegal and that disbursement of federal funds for a contract with such a program would be withheld as unlawful. An association of contractors sought help from the courts. The appellate court supported the plan; so did the Supreme Court, in effect, by declining to hear the case. Thus began the equating of affirmative action, once largely matters of recruiting and training, with numerical goals and time tables.

Reverse Discrimination

Affirmative action was initiated not to provide favoritism for groups of people, nor to reward as veterans preference rewarded prior service, but to compensate partially for the effects of past discrimination. When courts find that an employer has a history of discrimination, affirmative action programs or even outright quotas may be mandated as remedies. When an employer independently sees evidence of adverse impact on a particular job or set of jobs, that employer may voluntarily establish affirmative action plans, goals, and time tables. Doing so, however, runs the risk of a reverse discrimination charge, and the plan must explicitly correct prior discrimination (see *Weber v. Kaiser Aluminum & Chemical Corporation*, 1977).

Employers still feel that they walk a fine line in the conflict between obedience to the Executive Order and compliance with Title VII. EEOC has not seen it so and has issued affirmative action guidelines (Equal Employment Opportunity Commission, 1979). According to these guidelines, EEOC will not find an employer liable for reverse discrimination charges for voluntary affirmative action programs if (a) facts show an actual or potential adverse impact from practices in existence or planned, (b) the plan corrects for prior discrimination as shown by discrepancy between the relevant proportion of the employer's work force and the relevant labor market, and (c) the available labor pool among protected demographic groups is "artificially" limited.

Developing Affirmative Action Plans

To establish a local affirmative action program, the employer should first identify jobs with evidence of either adverse impact or disparate treatment. If there are such jobs, the responsible practices should be identified and corrective plans developed. The plans need not be (and to be effective probably should not be) restricted to hiring intentions. They may include special recruiting, educational or training programs, and plans for identifying and advancing those whose abilities are underutilized in their current positions. They must be limited, both in time and scope; they should not go beyond correction of prior adverse impact or disparate treatment either from a desire to "do good" or from fear of litigation.

Affirmative Action as Social Policy

Employment discrimination, sometimes by law and often by general practice, was rampant prior to 1964. Since then, social policy in the United States has clearly said that discriminatory practices were wrong and that employers should work "affirmatively" to right the wrong. There is now, however, some question about whether affirmative action is compensating for prior discrimination or affirming a policy of preferential hiring. The columnist William Raspberry quoted a Black lawyer as saying, "I understand my father's claim against this country, but I'm not sure I understand my son's" (Raspberry, 1991, p. 3B).[16] The effects and effectiveness of affirmative action programs deserve critical examination.

---

[16]The same lawyer also said that Black lawyers are needed. His dilemma was that stopping preferential admissions policies to law schools could result in a dearth of Black lawyers. His dilemma is society's as well, and neither he nor society has yet found a resolution.

Affirmative action remains part of the legal context for personnel decisions. It can be used to promote the employment, and therefore the economic viability, of people otherwise denied opportunity. However, 30 years after the effective date of the Civil Rights Act, the hope of Title VII for employment without regard for demographic irrelevancies is far from realized, particularly for African Americans. Their unemployment rates are much higher, and mean incomes much lower, particularly for younger people, than those in other identifiable groups; disparities seem greater now than in 1965. I conclude that affirmative action is not working as intended and that the concept needs redefinition and redirection. I am not prepared to recommend that it be abandoned. Unfortunately, the term has become the rallying point for purely partisan rhetoric and political or personal emotion. Study, debate, and possibly changes in social policy by rational and informed minds would be more fruitful.

AGE DISCRIMINATION

The Age Discrimination in Employment Act of 1967 (ADEA; Age Discrimination in Employment Act, 1967) prohibits discrimination against anyone 40 years of age or older. It encourages employment decisions about older people on the basis of ability, not age. It applies to hiring, early retirement programs and their promotion, benefits packages, and so on. It is enforced through the EEOC.

Most ADEA litigation involves terminations—firing, reductions in force, or involuntary retirement. A few companies have openly had age limits for jobs involving public safety (e.g., bus drivers), defended as bona fide occupational qualifications (BFOQs). A review by Faley, Kleiman, and Lengnick-Hall (1984) shows that courts (at least initially) were more receptive to such arguments in ADEA cases than in cases of racial or sex discrimination, apparently on the grounds that employers should not have to experiment with the safety of third persons (e.g., passengers) to develop empirical proofs. Where someone aged 40 brings suit under ADEA, a defense must show that factors other than age were determining considerations (Faley et al., 1984). For promotions, transfer, or terminations, other factors are usually rated performance. Several reviews, with inconsistent conclusions, have considered the role of performance appraisals in the outcome of such cases (e.g., Faley et al., 1984; Feild & Holley, 1982; Miller, Kaspin, & Schuster, 1990). Paradoxically, the plaintiff's age seems to be a major determinant of the outcome of litigation; plaintiffs in their 40s tended to lose (the youngest victorious plaintiff was 52), and those over 60 tended to win (Miller et al., 1990).

Systematic procedures of performance evaluation have been important. For promotion or demotion cases, employers' defenses have been strengthened where established procedures were regularly used. Where employees were victors, decisions expressed reservations about the quality of the supervisory judgments even in formal evaluation systems. In cases involving layoffs or retirement, an advantage was found in formalized systems where performance could be compared to that of others. In cases involving outright discharge, however, the question has not been one of relative performance but of whether the employee bringing suit has failed to perform adequately. This, concluded Miller et al. (1990, p. 571), "will generally be the employer's only legitimate defense. Minimal performance, rather than relative performance, is the primary issue."

This is a sobering conclusion. Performance evaluations are usually lenient, often unrealistically so. It is unpleasant to give a poor rating, especially if it is to be discussed in a face-to-face interview. It may be administratively burdensome as well, especially where special procedures are required to justify negative ratings. Requiring only a rating of "minimally acceptable" in performance ratings probably means settling for actual performance that is less than acceptable, and effectively ruling out evaluations of performance relative to performance standards.

DISCRIMINATION AGAINST DISABLED PERSONS

The Americans With Disabilities Act of 1990 (ADA; Bureau of National Affairs, 1990), prohibits discrimination against qualified people who have disabilities. A *disabled person* is defined as one with a physical or mental impairment that substantially limits one or more major life activities, or who has a record of such impairment, or who is regarded as having such an impairment. "Major life activities" include caring for oneself, walking, speaking, seeing, hearing, and working. An impairment might be a physiological or mental condition, cosmetic disfigurement, anatomical loss, mental illness, retardation, or learning disability. The ADA does not protect people whose employment on a given job would threaten the safety or property of others.

"Has a record of" is intended to protect against decisions based on unwarranted assumptions that prior disabling conditions still exist or on inaccurate records of disability. Recovering alcoholics, or people whose prior blood pressure or cardiac arrhythmia has been controlled, are still defined as disabled to prevent employers from using their history as a reason for adverse decisions. "Regarded as having" includes the protection of those at risk because of appearances or associations with others.

The law requires employers to focus on what a candidate can do, not on disabilities. For a job to be filled, the employer must be able to distinguish essential functions of the job from those that, even if important, may not have to be performed by every incumbent. A clerical job, for example, may require operation of certain machines, reaching certain file drawers or shelves, and delivering occasional materials to people in other offices. If any one of these is deemed an essential function of the job, a qualified candidate must be able to do it. The ADA prohibits only discrimination against *qualified* candidates with disabilities. It does not require preferential hiring of qualified but disabled candidates; it explicitly encourages hiring the candidates *most* qualified to perform essential functions, irrespective of disabilities.

Reasonable Accommodation

Employers must offer reasonable accommodation to overcome barriers a disability may pose for an otherwise qualified candidate. An unusually short person may be considered disabled. The disability may be a barrier to the filing function if file drawers or shelves are too high, but providing a stool may be enough accommodation to enable a short person to carry out that essential function. Thinking of accommodation as a major architectural change is often unwarranted; Jeanneret (1994) reported that about two thirds of all accommodation requests cost less than $500. Congress, EEOC, and the courts have stressed reasonableness; accommodation is not required if it would impose an undue hardship on the organization.

Job Analysis

Job analysis is not required by the ADA, but it has long included ascertaining which tasks or functions are important to effective performance and which are less so. Under ADA it is prudent to ask whether every worker must carry out all critical activities. The distinction needs to be made between important activities that are critical in the sense that they must be carried out by at least some persons on the job and those that are essential in the sense that everyone on the job must be able to do them.

General Employment Procedures

Some procedural changes are needed under the ADA. Medical examinations or background checks are frequent parts of the employment process. Under the ADA, these procedures are permitted only after making a conditional job offer (i.e., conditioned on satisfactory results of these post-offer procedures). Candidates may not be asked on application forms or in interviews about disabling conditions, although questions about their abilities to perform essential functions are permissible. Those with known disabilities may be asked to describe or demonstrate how they might (with or without accomodation) perform those functions, but they may not be questioned about the disability itself. Reasonable accommodation applies to application forms and interviews as well to the job and job environment; accommodation might include providing application forms with large type, completing them orally while someone else fills in the blanks, providing an accessible interview location for people with mobility problems, providing an interpreter to sign for deaf candidates, or readers for blind ones, and so on.

Putting off the medical examination until a tentative decision is made poses problems for some kinds of testing. Psychomotor tests might be used in medical diagnosis, and personality inventories might be used to diagnose other disabilities, but both are more often used as predictors of performance. When the evidence says that such tests have been evaluated for predicting performance on essential job functions, they need not be treated as part of the medical examination. However, a different use of personality measures seems not to have been addressed, use for organization-wide rather than job-specific criteria. Measures of conscientiousness, for example, may serve these more general purposes, but it is not clear whether the predicted criteria would be accepted as essential functions in all jobs.

Testing

A disability may interfere with test performance, and reasonable accommodation may be required. The ADA has an individual orientation; each case is a specific case to be adjudicated on its own merits. With testing, however, a potential, group-oriented adverse impact analysis should be considered if sample sizes are large enough. If so, it might lead to a general accommodation for people with disabilities like that in the analysis. Even if adverse impact can be shown, however, accommodation is not required for a selection procedure that tends to screen out candidates with the disability if that disability also interferes with carrying out essential functions of the job—even with accommodation.

Any individual may request accommodation based on a disability. Although an interviewer may not ask a candidate about visual impairment, for example, the candidate may request a test in large type, or even braille. Tests given to people with a specific impairment must not actually measure the impaired skill, rather than other KSAs, unless the job specifically requires it. A written test given to a candidate for work as a road equipment operator may be unduly difficult for a dyslexic person, but it is not intended to assess dyslexia, and the dyslexia might not interfere with performance of essential functions. Such a test would be deemed inappropriate without special accommodation, such as oral administration.

Other kinds of accommodation might include relaxed time limits, alternative modes of test presentation (oral, on computer, etc.), permitting alternative methods of responding (e.g., using a tape recorder rather than filling in circles), simplified language, more frequent rest pauses, providing isolated space (for those whose disabilities make them susceptible to distractions), using alternative methods of assessment, or simply waiving the assessment. In any case, the word "reasonable" remains operative. Philips (1993) described two court cases that suggested limits on required accommodation, holding that granting the requests would amount to preferential treatment rather than the elimination of a disadvantage.

In any case, what does accommodation do to the validity of the interpretations of the test scores? The question can rarely if ever be answered. The only safe assumption is that scores obtained under nonstandard conditions do *not* have the same meaning as scores obtained under standard conditions. Accommodation by nonstandard procedures may be about the same as accommodation by waiving the test requirements: in either case, one may have no valid assessment of an important trait.

NEGLIGENT HIRING, DEFAMATION, AND WRONGFUL DISCHARGE

EEO law has dominated the legal context for a generation or so, but other kinds of laws also need attention. Among these are laws of *torts*, that is, wrongful acts resulting in injury. If an employee does something that results in injury to a coworker, a customer, or some other third party, the employer can be sued for damages. The suit might be based on the doctrine that an employee carrying out assigned duties is an agent of the employer. More often, in states where they apply, the doctrines of negligent hiring and retention are being used. These hold that an employer can be found negligent in hiring or keeping an employee if (a) an injury was caused by an employee acting "under the auspices of employment," (b) the employee is shown to have been unfit for the job, (c) the employer knew or should have known about the unfitness, (d) the injury was a foreseeable consequence, and (e) the hiring or retention of the employee was the *proximate cause*[17] of the injury (Ryan & Lasek, 1991).

Grounds for Action Under Negligent Hiring

There must be an injury. In most litigation, the injury is physical (results of assaults or of accidents, rapes, or other physical violence). A conse-

---

[17]Proximate cause means that the injury must be a reasonably expected or probable consequence of things done or not done by the employer. If an employee with a long history of lying causes injury by threatening a potential customer, failure to learn of that history is not a proximal cause of the injury; there is no necessary or prudent connection between being a liar and threatening people (Ryan & Lasek, 1991).

quence of criminal behavior such as theft may be the injury. Emotional or psychological injuries might be litigated.

The "auspices of employment" is rarely at issue. It is not restricted to carrying out actual job duties as the employer's agent; the activities or event causing injury may include more than assigned task performance (Shattuck, 1989), although liability seems restricted to activities carried out while the employee is on the job or in some sense representing the employer (e.g., wearing the employer's uniform). An employee on his or her own time, or commuting from work to home, is not acting under the auspices of employment (Ryan & Lasek, 1991).

Showing that an employee is "unfit" is not necessarily showing incompetence on the job. Much litigation in this area involves violence, so a person with a history of violent reactions to interpersonal frustrations may be deemed "unfit" for employment in jobs where potentially frustrating contact with others is likely. Being "unfit" includes (from case law) not only mental or personality disorders but also more ordinary deficiencies. An employee's competence in driving may be considered in determining fitness in a job in which driving ability is hardly a defining characteristic (e.g., a social worker) but in which the employee must drive from one site to another. Would checking for a valid driver's license be enough to avoid liability for an employee at fault in an injury-producing accident between sites? I do not know, but a finding of unfitness seems likely if the employee had a history of multiple at-fault traffic accidents.

The most common basis for dispute in negligent hiring and retention cases is whether the employer should have foreseen the possibility of unfitness. An employer should take steps to identify potential problems. In the previous example, perhaps checking for the license would be a sufficient precaution, but greater care would be shown by checking accident or driving records or insurance papers or perhaps giving a special driving test. It is necessary to exercise prudence and identify possible consequences if a person who is unfit in any specific way is put on the job. Shattuck (1989) listed several considerations in job analysis; with some modifications that occurred to me, most of these are shown in Table 4.1.

Appropriate Methods of Assessment

Most writers on negligent hiring emphasize reference checks and background investigations—advice easier to give than to follow. Another legal doctrine, known as defamation, has made reference checks all but worthless. About the only information prudent employers give when asked about former employees is confirmation or disconfirmation of dates of employment and last job held, and some refuse even that. There is safety in the refusal. To be actionable under a charge of defamation, information

TABLE 4.1
Job Characteristics to Consider in Liability Analysis

Job Activity	Judgment Needed
Drives company vehicle	Frequency, mileage
Receives cash or checks	Frequency, amount
Receives goods from shipper, others	Frequency, cost
Responsible for property of others	Frequency, cost
Enters customers' homes, customers present	Frequency
Enters customers' homes, customers absent	Frequency
Works where children are present	Frequency, circumstances
Works with general public	Proportion of time, risk
Works alone	Proportion of time, risk
Works with hazardous materials	Risk, risk factors[a]
Works nights	Risk, risk factors
Works with machinery	Risk, risk factors
Responsible for work of others	Degree shared
Personnel Requirements	
Must hold license or other certification	Compliance
Must operate specific equipment	Nature of equipment, risk
Must have specific product knowledge	Nature of product, risk
Must have specific education or training	Nature, risk

[a]"Risk" refers to a judgment about the nature of potential risks of injury to third parties; "risk factors" refers to judgments about personal or situational characteristics that might enhance the potential of risk.

given by the previous employer must be shown to be false, but the burden of proof falls on the employer, who must show that the statement made is true. Saying that an employee was discharged because of the supervisor's *opinion* that the employee was not trustworthy can be true if the opinion is a matter of record; it is therefore not defamatory. The same information given in a context of innuendo permits the inference that the employee did in fact violate trust, without factual support, and it may be defamatory under the principle known as "slander *per quod*." Statements that do not hold up under legal scrutiny, whether false, partially true, or unsupported by evidence, also serve as the basis for suit for wrongful discharge (Ryan & Lasek, 1990). All in all, the risks are usually deemed too severe to take on behalf of inquiry from outside the organization.

Background investigations run similar risks and may also violate a candidate's rights of privacy. Many kinds of public information can be tapped, but always with some risk that the information is erroneous. Questions of validity of references and background investigations are not new (cf. Guion, 1965, p. 409). Moreover, some resulting information can not be used for employment decisions. Courts have repeatedly ruled against the use of arrest records, for example, to deny employment to those in demographic groups experiencing unusual arrest frequency—although convictions may be used. There is always a question of cost. Thorough background investigations are likely to be fruitless for young applicants and very expensive for older ones with more background to investigate.

A FINAL COMMENT

Not all aspects of the legal context for employment decisions have been described. Omissions include, for example, record-keeping requirements, rules governing immigrants, requirements for federal employment of part-time people, the polygraph protection act, state laws or laws of other countries. Moreover, what *is* described here is subject to changes in statutes, regulations, or court decisions.

What I have tried is to emphasize that personnel decisions must be made according to existing laws. The law is dynamic, ever-changing, and varies by state or local jurisdiction. Changes follow or accompany (or are accompanied by) changes in the ideas and attitudes of society in general, whether emerging spontaneously or in response to leadership. Even imperfect law is an expression of, and an instrument of, social policy. Perhaps, then, the objective of this chapter is better described as trying to emphasize that personnel decisions must be made not only according to organizational policies and interests but according to social policy and interest insofar as it can be understood.

REFERENCES

Age Discrimination in Employment Act of 1967, 29 U.S.C. Sec 621 et seq. (1967).

Albemarle Paper Company v. Moody, 422 U.S. 405 (1975).

Albright, L. E., Glennon, J. R., & Smith, W. J. (1963). *Psychological tests in industry*. Cleveland: Howard Allen.

American Educational Research Association, American Psychological Association, & National Council on Measurement in Education. (1985). *Standards for educational and psychological testing*. Washington, DC: American Psychological Association.

American Psychological Association, American Educational Research Association, & National Council on Measurement in Education. (1966). *Standards for educational and psychological tests and manuals*. Washington, DC: American Psychological Association.

American Psychological Association, American Educational Research Association, and National Council on Measurement in Education. (1974). *Standards for educational & psychological tests*. Washington, DC: American Psychological Association.

American Psychological Association, American Educational Research Association, & National Council on Measurements Used in Education. (1954). Technical recommendations for psychological tests and diagnostic techniques. *Psychological Bulletin, 51*, 201–238.

American Psychological Association, Division of Industrial and Organizational Psychology. (1975). *Principles for the validation and use of personnel selection procedures.* Dayton, OH: Hamilton Printing Company.

Arvey, R. D. (1979). *Fairness in selecting employees.* Reading, MA: Addison-Wesley.

Baker v. Columbus Municipal Separate School District, 329 F. Supp. 706 (DC Miss 1971).

Baker v. Columbus Municipal Separate School District, 462 F. 2d 1112 (CA 5 1972).

Bureau of National Affairs. (1990). ADA: Americans With Disabilities Act of 1990: Text and analysis. *Labor Relations Reporter, 134*(11), S-3–S-47. (Supplement)

Civil Rights Act of 1964, 42 U.S. Code, Stat 253 (1964).

Connecticut v. Teal, 457 U. S. 440 (1982).

Day, V. B., Erwin, F., & Koral, A. M. (Eds.). (1981). *A professional and legal analysis of the Uniform Guidelines on Employee Selection Procedures.* Berea, OH: The American Society for Personnel Administration.

Dothard v. Rawlinson, 15 FEP Cases 11 (1977).

Dunnette, M. D. (1966). *Personnel selection and placement.* Belmont, CA: Wadsworth.

Equal Employment Opportunity Commission. (1966). *Guidelines on employment testing procedures.* Washington, DC: Equal Employment Opportunity Commission.

Equal Employment Opportunity Commission. (1970). Guidelines on employee selection procedures. *Federal Register, 35*(149), 12333–12336.

Equal Employment Opportunity Commission. (1979). *Affirmative action guidelines,* 29 CFR 1608.

Equal Employment Opportunity Commission, Civil Service Commission, Department of Labor, and Department of Justice. (1978). Uniform guidelines on employee selection procedures. *Federal Register, 43*(166), 38295–38309.

Faley, R. H., Kleiman, L. S., & Lengnick-Hall, M. L. (1984). Age discrimination and personnel psychology: A review and synthesis of the legal literature with implications for future research. *Personnel Psychology, 37,* 327–350.

Feild, H. S., & Holley, W. H. (1982). The relationship of performance appraisal system characteristics to verdicts in selected employment discrimination cases. *Academy of Management Journal, 25,* 392–406.

Griggs v. Duke Power Co., 401 U.S. 424 (1971).

Guion, R. M. (1965). *Personnel testing.* New York: McGraw-Hill.

Guion, R. M. (1974). Open a new window: Validities and values in psychological measurement. *American Psychologist, 29,* 287–296.

Guion, R. M. (1980). On trinitarian doctrines of validity. *Professional Psychology, 11,* 385–398.

Gutman, A. (1993). *EEO law and personnel practices.* Newbury Park, CA: Sage.

Hartigan, J. A., & Wigdor, A. K. (Eds.). (1989). *Fairness in employment testing: Validity generalization, minority issues, and the General Aptitude Test Battery.* Washington, DC: National Academy Press.

International Brotherhood of Teamsters v. United States, 431 U. S. 324 (1977).

Jeanneret, P. R. (1994, July). *Accommodation: State of the research and practice when complying with the Americans With Disabilities Act.* Address to the American Psychological Society, Washington, DC.

Lawshe, C. H. (1948). *Principles of personnel testing.* New York: McGraw-Hill.

Lawshe, C. H., & Balma, M. J. (1966). *Principles of personnel testing* (2nd ed.). New York: McGraw-Hill.

Lindemann, B., & Grossman, P. (1996). *Employment discrimination law* (3rd ed.). Washington, DC: Bureau of National Affairs.

Miller, C. S., Kaspin, J. A., & Schuster, M. H. (1990). The impact of performance appraisal methods on Age Discrimination in Employment Act cases. *Personnel Psychology, 43,* 555–578.

Miner, M. G., & Miner, J. B. (1978). *Employee selection within the law*. Washington, DC: Bureau of National Affairs.

Myart v. Motorola (1964). 110 *Congressional Record 5662*.

Office of Federal Contract Compliance. (1968). Validation of tests by contractors and subcontractors subject to the provisions of Executive Order 11246. *Federal Register, 33*(186), 14392–14394.

Office of Federal Contract Compliance. (1971). Employee testing and other selection procedures. *Federal Register, 36*(192), 19307–19310.

Philips, S. E. (1993, June). Update on testing accommodations. *National Council of Measurement in Education Quarterly Newsletter, 2*(1), 2–3, 6.

Raspberry, W. (1991, April 28). Affirmative action needs re-evaluating. *St. Louis Post-Dispatch*, p. 3B. (Copyright, Washington Post Writers Group)

Regents, University of California v. Bakke, 438 U. S. 265 (1978).

Ryan, A. M., & Lasek, M. (1991). Negligent hiring and defamation: Areas of liability related to pre-employment inquiries. *Personnel Psychology, 44*, 293–319.

Sandman, B., & Urban, F. (1976). Employment testing and the law. *Labor Law Journal, 27*, 38–54.

Shattuck, C. A. (1989). The tort of negligent hiring and the use of selection devices: The employee's right of privacy and the employer's need to know. *Industrial Relations Law Journal, 11*, 2–17.

Thorndike, R. L. (1949). *Personnel selection: Test and measurement techniques*. New York: Wiley.

United States Civil Service Commission. (1972). Examining, testing standards, and employment practices. *Federal Register, 37*(198), 21552–21559.

United States v. New Orleans Public Service, Inc. (1974). 8 FEP Cases 1089, 1106.

Wards Cove Packing Co. v. Atonio, 109 S. Ct., 2115 (1989).

Washington v. Davis, 426 U. S. 229 (1976).

Watson v. Fort Worth Bank & Trust, 108 S. Ct. 2777 (1988).

Weber v. Kaiser Aluminum & Chemical Corporation, 563 F 2d 2126 (CA 5 1977).

White, T. H. (1982). *America in search of itself*. New York: Harper.

II

EVALUATION OF ASSESSMENT PROCEDURES

This is the most technical section of the book. The first two chapters present measurement theory, both classical and modern. The third is a fairly conventional approach to statistical prediction, but in the end it raises some questions about the conventional criterion-related approach (when is it feasible and when not; when does it fit the logic of the predictive hypothesis and when does it not; etc.). The fourth chapter recognizes that judgments often have to be used in predictions; it identifies some options for serious, empirical evaluations of the judgments reached and for improving the psychometric quality of the judgments themselves (e.g., improved reliability). The final chapter of this section deals with the twin problems of bias and fairness, in which bias is seen as a statistical problem and fairness is seen as a judgment based on values as much as on data.

5

Basic Concepts in Measurement

The word *measure* has many uses; some clarification is needed. I offer some definitions to reduce the ambiguity within this book, but other conventions are followed elsewhere.

To measure, a verb, is to use a procedure to express numerically the degree to which a specified attribute or property describes a person or object. *A measure*, a noun, is the numerical value determined by the act of measuring. *Score* and *measure*, as nouns, are synonyms even if the procedure is not a test. *Measurement* is the general process by which differing people or objects can be ordered according to scores or by which a score can be compared to a standard. *Assessment* is a broader term than measurement, when describing a process, and broader than measure when applied to a score. Assessment includes ordering, classifying, or evaluating people or objects on some basis; the basis may be only roughly defined, even undifferentiated dimensions. *Measurement* is a special case of *assessment*. It is based on a more defined scale along which scores can be ordered with relatively fine gradations. Measurement seeks precision, and improvement in precision, in measures. In contrast, many other assessment procedures are ad hoc or used for specific practical purposes where precision is not useful or perhaps not possible.

Measurement theory is the rational foundation for developing and evaluating measurement procedures. This chapter introduces classical measurement theory; the next presents more modern developments. I use *psychometric theory* as interchangeable with measurement theory, but such use is not strictly correct. Psychometric theory is explicitly concerned with developing and evaluating measurement of traits, attitudes, or specific behaviors—a narrower focus than general measurement theory. There is no corresponding theory for broader forms of assessment that do not imply measurement or scales.

BACKGROUND NOTES ON PSYCHOMETRIC THEORY

Psychophysical and Psychological Scaling

Psychophysics. Psychophysical scaling relates magnitudes of physical stimuli to scales of associated psychological experience (perception). The equal-tempered musical scale is an easy prototype. Tones on a piano are created by vibrations when the strings are hit; the faster the vibration, the higher the perceived note. Development of the scale as we know it stems from scientific experimentation in music in the late 16th and early 17th centuries (D. M. Guion, 1973). Its units (octaves, tones, or semitones) are perceived as equal intervals throughout the scale, but at the higher tones in the scale it takes a bigger difference in physical frequencies to be perceived as a unit, as shown for octaves in Fig. 5.1. Physical frequencies relate to the perception of an octave in a 2:1 ratio; the frequency of A above

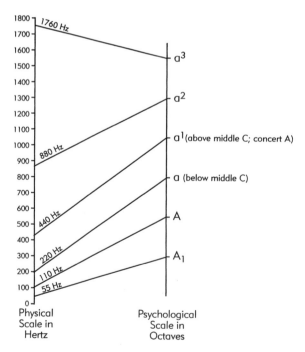

FIG. 5.1. The physical scale of frequencies and the associated musical scale of octave differences in the note A.

middle C is twice that of A one octave lower, which is twice that of A still another octave lower. The 2:1 ratio is a theory of the perception of an octave; psychophysical research attempted to develop such theories for all sensory modalities.

The general unit in psychophysical research was a just noticeable difference (*jnd*); the size of a *jnd* might vary from one observer to another. Detectable differences (*jnds*) in musical pitch are smaller for talented or well trained musicians than for those less skilled. Equations were found for individuals and averaged to develop general laws of sensory perceptions. That is, psychophysics provided formal models of the psychological processes being measured and finely graded scales with equal psychological intervals.

Attitude Scaling. Thurstone (1927) derived the law of comparative judgment from classical psychophysics; it is a mathematical statement of a theory of scale separation of stimuli in purely psychological scales, that is, scales without corresponding physical stimulus scales (e.g., attitude scales). It is a theory of judgment, not a theory of attributes measured, and it is a method of measurement based on ranking and paired comparisons.

In psychophysics, equally often noticed differences are assumed equal. A difference between stimuli 1 and 2 noticed as often as that between stimuli 2 and 3 shows the two intervals to be equal. Applying the principle to groups gave rise to the *method of equal-appearing intervals* as another procedure for developing scales to measure attitude or values (Thurstone & Chave, 1929). A different approach to attitude scaling, known as the *method of summated ratings*, was developed by Likert (1932). Both are methods of scaling requiring no theories of the attributes scaled. One must have, of course, a rudimentary theory—at least a vague notion—of the nature of the attitude one wants to measure, but a scale can be developed by following the procedural cookbook, with only the fuzziest notion of what it measures. Psychometric theory, classical or modern, still seems to emphasize method and process more than substantive content.

Reaction Times and Individual Differences

"The Personal Equation." In the 18th century, clocks at Greenwich Observatory were set on the basis of the time that stars passed a cross hair in a telescope. Near the end of the century, the Royal Astronomer fired an assistant for consistent errors, but it was subsequently learned that professional astronomers also disagreed because of individual differences in their reaction times. "Personal equations" were developed by which the observations of one astronomer could be equated with those of another with a different average reaction time. Invention of the chrono-

scope in the 19th century allowed more precise computation of individual reaction times, so more exact personal equations (or correction factors) could be used in recording observations (Boring, 1961).

Astronomy moved rapidly to measurement not dependent on personal equations, but the problem attracted the attention of Wundt, a founding father of modern experimental psychology. His "mental chronometry" measured components of mental processes in seven levels of complexity, each requiring lower levels as prior steps. The time required to carry out a given step was determined by measuring how long it took to complete the process *through* that step (level), measuring how long it took to get *to* that step, and subtracting. This line of research was abandoned, partly because of poor measures, but it has resurfaced in modern cognitive psychology with modern technology. Both the old and the new are based on measurement of reaction times as measures of the duration of psychological processes.

Psychological Testing and the Normal Distribution. Quetelet, a Belgian astronomer and mathematician, noted that, if the center of a distribution of measures were correct or represented perfection, then nature erred equally often in either direction. He later found that distributions of social and moral data also followed this "normal law of error." That law was important to Galton's studies of the inheritance of genius. Dividing the range of ability measures into 14 segments, and using Quetelet's tables to find the probability of being in each level, he concluded that one person in four might be in the lowest superior level, but only 1 in 79,000 would be in the seventh level. He believed that these levels defined equal scale intervals. He used a crude index of co-relationship to test the proposition that ability is inherited; it eventually led Pearson to develop the product–moment coefficient of correlation. It treats the standard deviation of a more or less normal distribution (the "normal law") as a useful unit of measurement (Boring, 1961). It continues to be the unit in most psychological measurement.[1]

Cattell (1890) and others of his era developed several perceptual and sensory tests and tests of memory, which Hull (1928) considered academic aptitude tests. Employment tests were developed by Munsterberg at Harvard, clinical tests by Kraepelin in Germany, and intelligence tests by

---

[1]Boring (1961) pointed out, first, that one cannot assume that a mathematical function such as the "normal law" applies to a particular variable until it has been demonstrated empirically, which Galton and most of his followers failed to do. He then went on to say, "The *a priori* assumption that the normal law applies to biological and psychological variables, and therefore provides a device for changing ordinal scales into equal intervals, has continued well into the present century. The scaling of mental tests in terms of standard deviations . . . in some ways preserves this ancient fallacy" (p. 123).

Binet, Simon, and Henri in France (Anastasi, 1982; Hull, 1928). Paper-and-pencil mental ability tests of the early 20th century used Binet's question and answer approach rather than the sensory or motor skills tested earlier; the same period saw projective personality tests and standardized school achievement testing. By mid-century, a specialized group of test experts, concerned about the proliferation of tests used with or without clear measurement properties, developed a set of "Technical Recommendations" for the development and evaluation of tests and test use (American Psychological Association, American Educational Research Association, & National Council on Measurements Used in Education, 1954).

Different kinds of psychological measurement have all emphasized individual differences in perceptions, abilities, or personalities. Some have emphasized theories of psychological processes. Few have offered theories of attributes measured. Usually the technique came first, followed later by questions of what the measures mean. Reliability was the dominant topic in measurement during much of the second quarter of the 20th century; later, validity became the dominant concern. In employment practice, validity is often equated with effectiveness of prediction, but in psychometric theory it refers to meaning (Messick, 1989, 1995b).

RELIABILITY: CONCEPTS OF MEASUREMENT ERROR

People differ. So do measures, for many reasons: flaws in measurement, the vagaries of chance, or traits measured—including traits not intended to be measured. Flaws, chance, and unintended traits are measurement errors. Concepts of reliability and validity both involve error, although in different ways.

Measurement Error and Error Variance

Errors happen in measurement. Two people using the same yardstick to measure the same table may get different results. A chemist using the most sophisticated equipment available may weigh a crucible several times, with results apparently differing only trivially, and settle for the average as the "true" weight. Mental measurements are still more subject to error. Intelligence is an abstract, complex concept, nearly defying definition, yet it is routinely measured with tests. There are always measurement errors, but despite them scores usually reflect fairly well the level of the trait being measured. It is sensible to assume, despite error, that one who scores high on an arithmetic test really is pretty good at arithmetic. The basic assumption of psychological testing is that any measure contains an element of error and an element of "truth." Classical psychometric theory begins by assuming that any measure X (obtained score) is the algebraic sum of a true measure (true score) t and a measurement error (error score) e, or

$$X = t + e \qquad (1)$$

Further assumptions are (a) that true scores and error scores are not correlated, (b) error scores in one measure are not correlated with error scores in another, and (c) error scores in one are not correlated with true scores on something else. Together, these assumptions say that error scores are truly random. In fact, however, some errors are not purely random. A true score, if really true, contains no error, but the theory defines it as the mean of an infinite number of a person's obtained scores on parallel measures of the same trait (Thurstone, 1931), that is, measures with the same means, standard deviations, and distributions of item statistics. But if every obtained score in that infinite set contains the same error, the mean is the score one would intuitively consider "true," plus or minus that repeated, constant error. The theoretical error score, in short, does not include errors the person makes constantly over repeated testing; it includes only unpredictable, random error. If errors were only random, the mean of repeated measures would approximate an intuitively "true" score. The constant error across repeated measures for each person, however, influences the mean of repeated measures precisely as it influences each individual measure.

I once had a thermometer with a glass tube attached by staples to a board showing the scale. My son (at age 4) liked to slide the tube up and down; the temperature reading depended on where he left the tube—a random error. However, if we pushed the tube down as far as it would go, we got a reading about 20 degrees too low. It was inaccurate, but it was *repeatedly, predictably* inaccurate, always with that 20-degree *constant* error.

Distinguishing systematic, repeatable errors from errors that vary randomly across repeated measures allows rephrasing the basic equation as

$$X = s + e \qquad (2)$$

Instead of t (true score), Equation 2 considers an individual's actual score X to consist of a systematic score s (a composite of an intuitive true score and any systematically repeated error), and e, the random error.

Equation 2 describes the score of just one person; the s score includes that person's own private constant error. These personal errors differ for different people, so a set of them has some variance. A different sort of error is constant for everyone in the set. It influences all measures in the set equally and therefore has no variance. Classical reliability theory is concerned with data sets and variances, so the equation is expanded to one describing variance in X:

$$\sigma_x^2 = \sigma_s^2 + \sigma_e^2 \tag{3}$$

where σ_x^2 is the total variance in a set of scores, σ_s^2 is the variance due to systematic causes, and σ_e^2 is variance due to random error.

Reliability

Reliability is often used to designate a personality trait, a pleasant characteristic of a person who can be counted on to do desirable things. The term is not commonly applied to a chronic liar, who can also be counted on—to tell lies when lies are more convenient or fun—but it could be. That thermometer can be counted on; if the tube is pushed all the way down, it will consistently be wrong by 20 degrees; it is reliably wrong.

Technically, reliability is consistency in sets of measures. Equation 3 shows where the consistency comes from: from the trait being measured and individual systematic errors, with little variance due to random errors. If the thermometer tube is wherever the child left it, the measurement errors are inconsistent, not predictable. Eliminating the random error created a large constant error, but it also created consistency. As a basic concept, then, *reliability is the extent to which a set of measurements is free from random-error variance.* In equation form,

$$r_{xx} = 1 - \frac{S_e^2}{S_x^2} \tag{4}$$

where r_{xx} is the reliability coefficient, S_e^2 is the variance of the random sources of error, and S_x^2 is the total variance. The smaller the error variance relative to total variance in obtained scores, the more reliable the measures in the distribution. In discussions of reliability, "measurement error" refers to random sources of error.

We could also define reliability as the proportion of total variance attributable to systematic sources, but it is important to recognize that it is *not* defined as the proportion of total variance due to "true" variance. Such a definition would imply a specific trait, a specification irrelevant to an understanding of consistency (cf. Tryon, 1957).

Index of Reliability. If one actually knew the systematic scores in a distribution, a correlation coefficient, r_{sx}, could be computed between systematic scores S and obtained scores X. Such a coefficient is purely hypothetical, but important to reliability theory; it is the *index of reliability*, and it helps clarify the reliability concept.

An index of reliability of 1.00 means that all of the variance in a set of measures is attributable to systematic sources (including systematic errors). One lower than 1.00 means that less than 100% of the variance is attributable to systematic sources; the proportion is the correlation squared (the coefficient of determination). If the correlation r_{sx} were .90 the coefficient of determination is .81, meaning that 81% of the total variance in X has systematic sources; the rest is random-error variance. Obviously, the index of reliability cannot be computed directly. Error scores and systematic scores are purely theoretical.

Reliability Coefficient. There are, however, methods of estimating reliability. One common method correlates two sets of measures of the same thing from the same people. The correlation coefficient approaches unity to the extent that each individual measure occupies the same relative position in each of the two sets of measures. It will be less than perfect to the extent that the two sets of data are inconsistent in ordering people.

Such a correlation coefficient is a *coefficient of reliability*, r_{xx}; it is also an estimate of the square of the index of reliability. It is therefore interpreted directly (without squaring) as the coefficient of determination of the index of reliability, estimating the proportion of the total variance accounted for by systematic sources of variance.[2] The relationship between the computed coefficient of reliability and the theoretical index of reliability can be stated as

$$r_{xx} = r_{sx}^{2} \tag{5}$$

or

$$\sqrt{r_{xx}} = r_{sx} \tag{6}$$

A reliability coefficient estimates the degree to which variance in a set of scores is systematic. The meaningfulness, and the usefulness, of a reliability coefficient for evaluating measurement depends on the sources of variance treated as systematic or random in computing it.

Validity

Reliability is often termed the sine qua non of mental measurement; if a test is not reliable, it cannot have any other merit. However, evidence of reliability is not in itself sufficient evidence that a measure is a good one. There is still the very important question of whether systematic sources of variance are relevant to the purpose of measurement. This is a matter of

---

[2]For a detailed mathematical proof of this statement, see Guilford (1954), or other statistics or test construction texts. Although derivations of formulas are important for a full understanding of them, they will not be presented in this text.

validity. Validity is the major consideration in test evaluation. Reliability is important because it imposes a ceiling for validity. The theoretical relationship of reliability to validity is shown by the formula

$$r_{x^\infty y^\infty} = \frac{r_{xy}}{\sqrt{r_{xx}r_{yy}}} \qquad (7)$$

where $r_{x^\infty y^\infty}$ is the theoretical correlation that would exist if predictor x and criterion y were perfectly reliable, r_{xy} is the validity coefficient actually obtained, and r_{xx} and r_{yy} are the respective reliability coefficients. This is known as correcting the validity coefficient for *attenuation*, that is, for unreliability.

It may be important for theoretical purposes to ask what the correlation would be if the two variables were measured with perfect reliability. That question is rarely important in personnel research. We have a test. It is imperfect. We use it anyway, use something else, or improve its reliability; in any case, we use a less than perfectly reliable test. There is little value in dreaming about the validities that might have been if only we had a perfectly reliable test.

In some situations, however, it is useful to know the level of validity with a perfectly reliable criterion, that is, to know how much of the *reliable* criterion variance is associated with predictor variance. We can find out by correcting for criterion unreliabilty only:

$$r_{xy^\infty} = \frac{r_{xy}}{\sqrt{r_{yy}}} \qquad (8)$$

where y is the criterion, y^∞ is the perfectly reliable criterion, and x is the test. This is the correction for attenuation in the criterion. Assume a validity coefficient of .40—good, better than many, but not noteworthy. Assume also a criterion reliability coefficient of .25—a terribly low reliability. Substituting in Equation 8, $r_{xy^\infty} = .40/\sqrt{.25} = .40/.5 = .80$, the estimated correlation with a perfectly reliable criterion. The coefficient of determination for this hypothetical correlation is .64; 64% of the total *explainable* variance is accounted for by the test. Clearly, this offers reasonably effective prediction, given the limits of criterion unreliability. A validity coefficient expressed as the relationship of the predictor to the explainable criterion variance is a more standardized statement than the uncorrected coefficient, is less subject to the vagaries of random criterion variance, and generally makes more sense.

Accuracy

Accuracy should not be confused with reliability. A thermometer or test may provide exceedingly inaccurate measures that are quite reliable even so. Nor should accuracy be confused with validity. Consider the thermometer example. To determine its accuracy, a set of temperature readings could be paired with criterion readings obtained for the same situations using instruments in the Bureau of Standards. If the correlation between our faulty thermometer readings and the standard readings were high, we could conclude that the thermometer gives "valid" measures of temperature—but not necessarily accurate ones. The thermometer with the 20-degree constant error could be perfectly valid, as shown in Fig. 5.2: the connected dots show perfect correlation despite the constant error. The unconnected xs show both perfect correlation and perfect accuracy. Lest this be considered a peculiar circumstance of the consistency of the error, Fig. 5.3 illustrates a possible perfect correlation where the amount of error in a test thermometer is greater at high temperatures than at low ones.

Accuracy, in relation to a standard, must be a function of both *strength* of relation (correlation) and *kind* of relation to the standard. To be accurate, a measure must be highly correlated with a standard measure of the same thing, and the relationship must be a specific form of a linear one. The general formula for a linear relationship (as in Fig. 5.2) is

$$Y = a + bX \qquad\qquad (9)$$

where a is a constant amount that must be added to (or substracted from) predictors in predicting Y, and b is a constant amount by which each value of X must be multiplied to predict Y. For perfectly accurate measurement, $a = 0$ and $b = 1$, and the regression equation is simply $Y = X$.

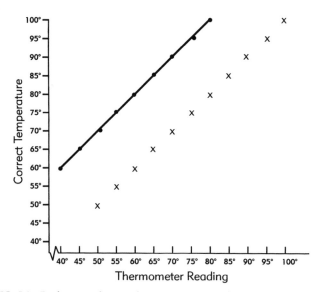

FIG. 5.2. Perfect correlation where inaccuracy is due to constant error.

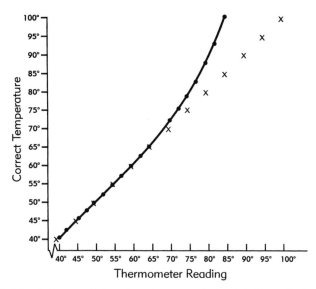

FIG. 5.3. Perfect correlation where inaccuracy is due to both constant error and scale differences.

Accuracy depends, then, on (a) the degree of correlation of a test instrument and an accepted standard, (b) the absence of the constant *a* in the regression equation, and (c) how close the constant *b* is to unity.

This is all very well for physical measures; we can refer sensibly to the accuracy of predictions or of measures defined by standards in some Bureau of Standards. There is, however, no such Bureau for cognitive or temperament traits. The concept of accuracy, therefore, is meaningless for psychological constructs.

SOURCES OF VARIANCE IN RELIABILITY ESTIMATION

Thorndike (1949) pointed out that reliability, or the lack of it, depends on the reasons for individual differences in test performance. At first glance, it would seem to be the measuring instrument (test) that has reliability. On second thought, it is clear that a test is a constant stimulus and that score variance stems from people's responses to it. Even situational considerations as heat or humidity may influence reliability if they influence the responses people make. The sources of variance in mental measurements are sources of variance in human performance.

Thorndike's categories were based on distinctions between long-lasting and temporary characteristics of people and between characteristics that

TABLE 5.1
Sources of Unreliability in Measures

I.   Lasting and general characteristics of the person
II. Lasting but specific characteristics of the person
     A. Specific to the test as a whole
     B. Specific to individual test items
III. Temporary but general characteristics of the person
IV. Temporary and specific characteristics of the person
     A. Specific to the test as a whole
     B. Specific to individual test items
V.   Factors in the administration of the test or in the evaluation or scoring of performance
     on it
VI. Chance (variance not otherwise accounted for)

---

are very general, influencing behavior in a wide variety of situations, and those that are more specific to a test or item. In a later discussion of the sources of variance, Stanley (1971) pointed out that random errors in scores can arise from aspects of test administration and scoring. He therefore added another category of variance sources, and I follow his lead. Table 5.1 shows, in reduced form, the sources of variance as identified by Thorndike (1949) and modified by Stanley (1971). The following outline expands Table 5.1 and is adapted from the Thorndike and Stanley presentations. It describes why people get different scores; with some verbal modification, it applies also to nontest assessments.

Reasons for Individual Differences in Test Performance

  I.   Reasons that are more or less permanent and that apply in a variety of testing situations.
       A. Some traits are general in that they influence performance on many different kinds of tests. Intelligence may influence performance on verbal, numerical, spatial, or job knowledge tests.
       B. Some people are more test-wise than others; that is, because of more experience or special training or insights in taking tests, they come closer to their maximum potential scores in any kind of test situation.
       C. Some people grasp the meaning of instructions more quickly and more completely than others. Some may flounder through much of a test before catching on to what is required, regardless of the nature of the task.
  II. Reasons that are more or less permanent but that apply mainly to the specific test being taken.

A. Some of these reasons apply to the whole test or to any equivalent forms of it.
   1. Some people have more of the ability or knowledge or skill or other trait being measured by the test.
   2. Some people find certain kinds of items easy while others may be more confused by them. For example, some people are good at "outguessing" true-false items.
B. Some reasons apply only to particular items on a test. Of all the items that *could* be included, only a small number actually *are* in the test. There is an element of luck here; if the test happens to contain a few of the specific items to which the person does not know the answer, that person will have a lower score than someone else who is luckier in the specific questions asked.

III. Reasons that are relatively temporary but would apply to almost any testing situation.
   A. A person's health status may influence the score.
   B. A person may not do as well when he or she is particularly tired.
   C. The testing situation is challenging to some people; they want to score high so that they can enjoy a feeling of achievement; others may feel less motivation to do well.
   D. Individuals react differently to emotional stress; the score of a person tested under stress is likely to differ from one obtained under emotionally secure conditions.
   E. There may be some relatively temporary fluctuations in test-wiseness.
   F. A person varies from time to time in readiness to be tested; such differences in set produce differences in attention to and comprehension of the test situation and, therefore, differences in scores. Readiness begets better scores.
   G. People respond differently to physical conditions (light, heat, etc.); those with the same abilities may score differently because of differences in their reactions to unusual or perhaps adverse physical conditions.

IV. Reasons that are relatively temporary and apply mainly to a specific test.
   A. Some reasons apply to the test as a whole (or to equivalent forms of it).
      1. People differ in their understanding of a specific set of instructions; understanding instructions helps maximize scores, and understanding may come more readily at one time than at another.

2. Some tests require special techniques; some people may "stumble" sooner into certain insights useful in tackling a particular test than would others.

3. Differences in the opportunities for practicing skills required in test performance produce score differences.

4. A person may be "up to" a test or "ripe" for it more at one time than at another; individual differences in readiness cause differences in scores.

B. Some reasons apply only to particular test items.

1. Momentary forgetfulness or lapses of memory while taking a test make a person miss an item that might otherwise be answered correctly.

2. The same thing can be said of momentary changes in level of attention, carefulness, or precision in detail.

V. For measures involving interactions between examiner and examinee, for measures using open-ended responses to be evaluated on a complex basis, for measures involving ratings, (e.g., performance evaluations, evaluations of work samples)—for all of these, scores may be influenced by characteristics of someone other than the examinee.

A. Conditions of testing may vary in strictness or accuracy of time limits, in lighting, in distractions, or other conditions intended to be standard or controlled.

B. Interactions between examiner and examinee characteristics (e.g., race, sex, age, or personality traits) may enhance performance for some examinees and interfere for others.

C. Bias or carelessness in rating or other evaluations of performance.

VI. Some reasons just cannot be pinned down. After everything else has been taken into account, there are still unexplained individual differences. For example, sometimes a person may simply be luckier in guessing than at other times.

Errors Reflected in Reliability Coefficients

Reliability is traditionally estimated by computing a correlation between two sets of measures presumably measuring the same thing in the same sample of people in the same way. The two sets of scores might be scores on two different but equivalent forms of the same test, scores on the same test given at different times, or scores on two halves of a test. For each person, the two systematic scores are expected to be the same; systematic variance therefore causes, improves, or at least maintains correlation. Error scores are *not* the same, being random, so error variance comes from conditions or personal characteristics that differed in the two sets of scores. Random error variance inhibits or lowers correlation coefficients. If the effect of a source of variance is consistent in the two sets of scores, it is treated as a source of systematic variance. If it differs, it is treated as a source of error variance. Different estimates of reliability differ in the sources treated as systematic (correlation-causing) or as error (correlation-reducing).

Category I variance (general and long-lasting) is certainly systematic and correlation causing. Such influences leading a person to a high or low score on the test at one time (or one form or one half) will operate in pretty much the same way and degree the second time.

Category IIA also considers long-lasting characteristics, but less general ones. They are general enough to influence responses on the whole test. They include the trait being measured, surely a source of systematic variance (intuitively "true" scores) if the trait itself is stable.

Category IIB is also concerned with long-lasting characteristics, but it is focused narrowly, even on specific items. It includes the chance element of whether a person does or does not know the proper response for a particular item. A person who happens to know the answer will score higher than one who happens not to know it. This contributes to a small but definite part of the total variance attributable to the luck of the draw in choosing items. Variance due to the particular sample of items is therefore a source of random error unless the same items are in both measures and no new learning (or forgetting) has time to occur. If reliability is computed by correlating two equivalent forms of the same test (i.e., two forms built to the same logical and statistical specifications but with different specific items), the person who knew a specific fact required for the first form will not necessarily have that advantage in the second one.

In Category III (temporary but general characteristics), some are more temporary than others. I think of these as changing slowly enough that the change will not be noticed within a testing session but rapidly enough that the change may be pronounced before a second testing session. Actually, then, the question of whether these are sources of systematic or error variance depends on the interval between testing sessions. If that time is so short that no change occurs, then these are sources of systematic variance. If the time is long enough for changes to be effective, then they are treated as error variance.

Category IVA is less general. Like Category III, it is concerned with temporary traits, so the time interval determines how it is treated. With very short intervals, it is likely to be treated as systematic.

Category IVB includes sources of variance specific to particular test items and quite temporary. These are treated as error variance in almost any method of estimating reliability. Momentary fluctuations in set, mental blocking, and other temporary characteristics have their influence on specific test items or groups of items. Such momentary characteristics are unpredictable and should be treated as error.

Category V includes some sources that may contribute to systematic variance, but most of them are more likely to be treated as sources of error. Consider test time limits. It is unlikely that the same error in timing would be made twice; timing errors should surely be treated as sources of error variance. Specific biases of an examiner, however, may be long lasting; if the same examiner tests all examinees, examiner characteristics contribute to systematic variance (i.e., they do not reduce the correlation). If different examinees are tested by different examiners, however, examiner differences can contribute to error variance. Ratings are subject to a variety of rater differences, so rater characteristics are usually sources of error. If a single rater is involved, of course, that rater's quirks are treated as systematic.

Category VI represents error variance in its purest form and is pure chance.

OPERATIONAL DEFINITIONS OF RELIABILITY

Reliability estimation methods vary in designs for data collection and in computational procedures. Each one is a specific set of procedures for defining what is meant by reliability—an operational definition of reliability. Different operational definitions emphasize different sources of error variance. Giving a test a second time in exactly the same form and manner as before, the so-called *test–retest method*, considers stability the source of consistency. This method treats Category IIB, for example, as a systematic source of variance. Another method correlates scores obtained from equivalent forms of the same measuring device. This method treats IIB as a source of error variance. Either of these methods may be varied by allowing different amounts of time to elapse between measurements. If the two measures are obtained at pretty much the same time, Category III is treated as a systematic source, but it is treated as error when the time interval between is large. Dividing a test into two equivalent halves is another method. With this technique, even very temporary characteristics, ordinarily considered sources of error in other procedures, may enhance correlation. Five kinds of operational definitions of reliability that treat variance sources differently are compared in Table 5.2.

A conservative reliability estimate (usually desirable except when used to correct for attenuation) treats many characteristics of persons and settings as sources of random error. The preferred procedure would therefore seem to be the delayed equivalent forms method, which considers Categories I and IIA as systematic and all other categories as

TABLE 5.2
Allocation of Variance in Different Estimates of Reliability

Estimate Method	Treatment of Sources of Variance[a]							
	I	IIA	IIB	III	IVA	IVB	V	VI
Immediate test–retest	S	S	S	S	S	E	E	E
Delayed test–retest	S	S	S	E	E	E	E	E
Immediate equivalent forms	S	S	E	S	S	E	E	E
Delayed equivalent forms	S	S	E	E	E	E	E	E
Split half	S	S	E	S	S	S	E	E

[a]S = systematic variance; E = error variance

sources of error. However, differences in intended uses of scores and in item domains influence judgments of appropriate treatment of variance sources. If a test is to be used to assess current readiness for training, long-term stability may not be important. If a test of job knowledge is based on a small item domain, so that all possible items appear in one form of the test, item sampling is not a source of error. Operational definitions should be sensitive to the most serious sources of error for the situation at hand.

Coefficients of Stability

Stability means scores are consistent over time. A coefficient of stability defines random error as individual differences in score change (inconsistency) over an appreciable time period. Retesting (using the same test) is useful if item sampling is not a problem. Retest correlation may be spuriously high if previous responses are remembered. (Immediate test–retest after a few minutes or hours is often encountered but rarely recommended.) Testing with an equivalent form (defined in the next section) after the time interval increases variance attributed to error, eliminating memory as an irrelevant source of systematic variance.

Coefficients of stability are useful for psychomotor or sensory tests if intervals are long enough to counteract practice or fatigue effects. Longer time intervals are needed for cognitive tests. The appropriate time interval depends on how long people remember particular content and how often the content is practiced. A lot of skill practice or information use produces overlearning; those with initial high scores would surely repeat them, but over time those with low scores would improve; differences in benefits of practice are treated as error variance.

Stability is important in performance ratings but hard to assess. Memory creates a spurious impression of stability; ratings are easy to remember, particularly when there are few ratees or when they are burned in memory in feedback sessions. Performance itself may not be stable. How much do coefficients of stability reflect stability in measurement compared to stability in the trait measured? Measures should not be considered unreliable if they detect changes in characteristics being measured. High stability may show only that the measure is not sensitive to change.

Coefficients of Equivalence

Virtually all measurement is based on data sampling. Accident frequency is sampled, for example, during a specific time period. Even a measure of one's weight is a sample of the day's varying circumstances such as heat or humidity, intake of fluids, salt, or food, or the shoes worn.

When two samples come from the same specifications and correlate well, the question of equivalence arises. Two test forms with different items are equivalent if (a) they have matching content (each has the same number of each kind of item), and (b) their means and standard deviations do not differ significantly. Equivalent forms are developed by specifying logical and statistical properties (item type and content; item difficulties, validities, or intercorrelations; or test means and standard deviations) to which each of them will conform. Such item matching should yield correlated forms with essentially the same "true score" distributions.

A coefficient of equivalence defines reliability as the extent to which a set of measures is free from errors due to sampling a test content domain (cf. Tryon, 1957). Actually, because genuine equivalence is hard to achieve, reliability coefficients computed as correlations between equivalent forms are rather conservative. The conservatism is not so great with tests of well-defined content like vocabulary or arithmetic, but it may seriously distort reliability estimates for less well-defined areas such as temperament and motivation or for measurement by ratings. Coefficients of equivalence are useful reliability estimates for test-like performance measures such as work samples or simulations or observer checklists when equivalent forms can be developed. Equivalent forms of achievement tests are likely to be needed in situations where retesting is likely.

Coefficients of Internal Consistency

Functional unity (Peak, 1953) implies homogeneity among the components of a measurement procedure so that the various parts all seem to be measuring pretty much the same thing. Related terms are *internal consistency* and *unidimensionality*. These terms are hierarchical. Of them, unidimensionality most strongly implies homogeneity. Internal consistency implies homogeneity but not necessarily unidimensionality. A test has functional unity even with clearly distinguishable components if they are positively related. For any of these, reliability estimation is called *internal consistency analysis*. Coefficients of internal consistency treat variance due to variations in item content as a major source of error variance, and they show how much the variance is systematically based on a common concept measured by the test as a whole. They are widely used because of their convenience; they need only one administration with just one test form (if there is no time limit).

Split-Half Estimation. Strictly speaking, split-half methods do not estimate internal consistency; they are more like coefficients of equivalence. They assume, not homogeneity of item content, but equivalent heterogeneity in the two halves; they do assume that the test as a whole is at least a functional unity. Splitting into halves must be carefully done. In most cognitive tests, items are arranged according to item type, content, and difficulty. A first-half versus last-half split does not give equivalent halves. A common alternative split puts odd-numbered items in one half and even-numbered items in the other. With forms so thoroughly intermixed, a temporary characteristic must be temporary indeed not to influence both scores, so Category IVB variance is treated as systematic variance, giving a spuriously high estimate of reliability. That is useful for criterion measures because it adds caution to a correction for attenuation. A period for recording performance is, in effect, a single administration, and the weeks or days of a year's production are analogous to items in a test. An odd–even split can smooth out seasonal variations with even-numbered weeks in one half and odd-numbered weeks in the other. It is preferable, however, to select items (or days or weeks) for the two halves randomly. Random selection tends to balance errors, making the halves more nearly equivalent; it also reduces somewhat the tendency to overlook heterogeneity encouraged by an odd–even split. Moreover, the number of consecutive items appearing in either half is variable, so more of the IVB variance is treated, properly, as error.

A correlation between half-scores needs correction because reliability is in part a function of number of items or observations. Correlating half-scores gives a coefficient of equivalence for half as many items as are in the full test. The relationship between reliability and test length is shown by the general Spearman–Brown prophecy formula,

$$r_{nn} = \frac{nr_{xx}}{1 + (n - 1)r_{xx}} \qquad (10)$$

where r_{nn} is the reliability expected for scores based on n times as many items or observations as those at hand, and r_{xx} is the reliability coefficient for the test as it is. If $n = 2$, as in estimating the reliability coefficient of a full test from that computed for a half-test, the formula simplifies to

$$r_{xx} = \frac{2r_{\frac{1}{2}\frac{1}{2}}}{1 + r_{\frac{1}{2}\frac{1}{2}}} \tag{11}$$

where $r_{\frac{1}{2}\frac{1}{2}}$ is the correlation computed between the two half-test measures and r_{xx} the coefficient prophesied for the full-length test. This is usually described as a Spearman-Brown "correction."

A different (I think preferable) split-half technique is the Rulon method (Rulon, 1939), stemming directly from the conceptual definition of reliability. It seeks a direct estimate of random error variance by treating score differences on the two halves as error and applying the definitional equation

$$r_{xx} = 1 - \frac{S_e^2}{S_x^2} \tag{12}$$

where $S_e^2 = \Sigma d^2 / N$ and d is the difference between the scores on the two halves. (Note that Equation 12 repeats Equation 4.) The assumption of equivalence in the two halves remains; this plan assumes that, if the two halves are truly equivalent, scores on them differ only because of variable error. Squaring these differences and dividing by N (number of cases measured) estimates the variance of assumed errors. Error variance divided by total variance is the proportional statement, returning us to the original concept of reliability as the extent to which measures are free from random error variance. No Spearman-Brown correction is needed.

Kuder–Richardson Estimates. Techniques involving analysis of item variance are more literally estimates of internal consistency. The most common of these methods were presented by Kuder and Richardson (1937) in a series of formulas; these formulas require the assumption of homogeneity (Cureton, 1958). The Kuder–Richardson formulas may be considered averages of all the split-half coefficients that would be obtained using all possible ways of dividing the test. The preferred formula (Richardson & Kuder, 1939) known as Kuder–Richardson Formula 20 (K–R 20) from the numbering of equations in the original derivation, is

$$r_{xx} = \left(\frac{n}{n-1} \right) \cdot \left(1 - \frac{\Sigma_{pq}}{S_x^2} \right) \tag{13}$$

where n is the number of items in the test, p is the proportion of correct responses to a given item, $q = (1 - p)$, and S_x^2 is the total test variance. Note that error variance is given as the sum of item variances, pq. This is a harsh assumption and may indicate why this formula gives a lower bound estimate of reliability (Guttman, 1945).

It is now more common to find references to Cronbach's coefficient alpha, a more general version of the K–R 20 equation,

$$\alpha_n = \left(\frac{n}{n-1}\right) \cdot \left(1 - \frac{\Sigma S_i^2}{S_x^2}\right) \tag{14}$$

where α_n is r_{xx}, the reliability coefficient called alpha for a test of n components (items or sets of items), S_i^2 is the variance of item responses or other component scores, and S_x^2 is the total score variance. If item responses are dichotomous, then $S_i^2 = \Sigma pq$, and the equation for alpha is the same as K–R 20. Alpha can be used for items with response scales, ratings, or scores on small sets of dependent items such as a set of items based on a single passage or illustration.

Useful as it is, the alpha coefficient should not be used merely for convenience, and it should be interpreted only as internal consistency, not confused with equivalence or stability. It is appropriate for most norm-referenced tests of abilities because these are typically constructed to provide homogeneous sets of items. It is not appropriate for domain-referenced tests constructed to represent a not-necessarily-homogeneous content domain.

Internal Consistency for Speeded Tests.   Internal consistency estimates require tests to be untimed; these methods assume opportunity to respond to every item. For speeded tests, a split-half reliability can be used only if the two halves are separately timed.

Interrater or Interscorer Agreement

Category V source includes errors attributable to raters or scorers. Two different observers seeing the same behavior or product may evaluate it differently—a source of error variance. With tests and rating scales scored by observer judgments, such a source of error can be large. The score depends not only on the behavior of the person observed or rated, but also on scorer or rater responses and characteristics.

Interrater reliability, like other operational definitions, is often expressed as correlation. If there are several raters or scorers, a correlation matrix can be computed and an average determined, or intraclass correlation can be used. With dichotomous ratings, it may be expressed as the percentage of agreement between pairs of raters.

Comparisons Among Reliability Estimates

I consider the differences among the various estimates important, but some experts think not. Estimates by various methods turn out to be similar (Cronbach & Azuma, 1962; Towner, 1956). If variance in a set of measures is generally systematic, with little of it attributable to random error, different operational definitions of reliability should agree fairly well; variance Categories I and IIA should account for the bulk of the variance in any method of estimation. However, different methods make different assumptions, procedural and mathematical, and define error differently; I believe researchers, test developers, and test users should use estimates that make sense for the circumstances they face. When a test is used to predict performance over a long period of time, stability is more important than internal consistency. If retesting is common enough to justify equivalent forms, coefficients of equivalence are needed. If production should be consistent month in and month out, an alpha coefficient over a period of several months is appropriate. The absolute values of stability, equivalence, and alpha coefficients may not differ very much, but small differences in reliability can make great differences in the appropriateness of decisions about individual people, as shown in Table 5.3 (from Wainer & Thissen, 1996). Consider very good reliability coefficients of .94 by one method and .92 by another. If the reliability is .94, retest scores differ by more than a half standard deviation for 15% of the cases; 21% of the retest scores differ that much with a coefficient of .92, an increase of 40%. If one method fits the intended use and the other does not, the difference is less trivial than a .02 difference in reliability suggests.

Standard Error of Measurement

So far, reliability has been defined and discussed in terms of distributions or sets of measurements. However, the basic datum is always a single

TABLE 5.3
Proportions of Examinees With Retest Scores Differing
by Designated Amounts for Various Levels of Reliability

Test Reliability	Percentage of cases differing by more than		
	.5 SD	1.0 SD	1.5 SD
.00	72	48	29
.60	58	26	9
.70	52	20	5
.75	48	16	3
.80	43	11	2
.85	36	7	1
.90	26	3	.1
.92	21	1	0
.94	15	.4	0
1.00	0	0	0

Note. Adapted from Warner and Thissen (1996). Copyright (1996) by the American Educational Research Association. Adapted by permission of the publisher.

measure, and the reliability of an individual score may be important—
increasingly so as ADA and selection for single positions preclude use of
large data sets. The standard error of measurement, expressed in test
score units, serves that purpose. Rearranging the definitional equation for
reliability, we get

$$S_e^2 = S_x^2(1 - r_{xx})$$ (15)

or

$$S_e = S_x\sqrt{1 - r_{xx}}$$ (16)

where S_e is the standard error of measurement.

Standard errors of measurement have three uses in personnel decisions:
(a) to determine whether scores for two people differ significantly, (b) to
determine whether a person's score differs significantly from a hypothetical true score, or (c) to determine whether scores discriminate differently
in different groups, for example, different demographic groups or groups
defined by different score ranges. The latter use should be more common
than it is. In mass employment, it is important to know whether test
scores distinguish people reliably in those regions of the distributions
where hard decisions are made. They should; one evaluation of a test can
ask whether the range with the minimal standard error of measurement
is the crucial range for decisions. Standard errors may be computed
independently for different regions, given enough cases.

INTERPRETATION OF RELIABILITY COEFFICIENTS

Some people simplify reliability interpretation by stating a minimally
satisfactory coefficient. It is not that simple. Interpretation must consider
other information, including the intended use of the measures. For basic
research, high reliability may not be critical. Decisions about individuals,
however, require highly reliable measures. A reasonably sought level of
"highly reliable" may depend on the history of a particular kind of
measurement; "high" for interviews is lower than for standardized tests.
Several other factors need to be considered in interpreting coefficients.

Homogeneity of Sample

The size of a correlation coefficient depends in part on the extent of
individual differences in the sample. In relatively homogeneous groups,
where all scores are pretty much alike, total variance is small. Because error

scores and true (systematic) scores are uncorrelated, homogeneity does not influence the size of the error variance; error variance is about the same whether the data include only average scores or a full score range. It is the ratio of error to total variance that counts (see Equation 4).

If reliability data are collected from a select group of employees, it is necessary to estimate the reliability expected in a more variable applicant group. If we can estimate total applicant variance, we can estimate reliability for applicants by the formula

$$r_{nn} = 1 - S_o^2 \frac{(1 - r_{oo})}{S_n^2} \tag{17}$$

where the subscript n refers to a new, more variable group, and the subscript o refers to the old, homogeneous group.

This equation can rarely be used in criterion measurement. Such measures are usually obtained from select groups of people who (a) are hired and (b) stay long enough to provide criterion data. There is usually no estimate of an unselected variance, hence no basis for the correction. A criterion reliability coefficient is, therefore, likely to be an underestimate—a crucial point in interpreting a validity coefficient corrected for criterion unreliability; the underestimate leads to a spuriously high correction.

Average Ability Level

The average ability level in the group studied also influences the reliability coefficient. Error variance is likely to be larger in lower-level groups where luck can influence scores. It is poor practice to use data obtained from people at one level to estimate reliability for people at a different level. A test for selecting unskilled helpers should not be evaluated by reliability data from skilled journeymen.

Sample

A reliability coefficient computed from a handful of cases is no better than any other coefficient based on inadequate data. Increasing the number of cases does not have a systematic effect on the size of the coefficient, but it does affect its dependability. Adequacy is not just a matter of numbers. The sample should represent the population for which the measure is to be used. The reliability of a temperament test planned for industrial applicants cannot be adequately determined by giving the test to mental patients or college sophomores or even employees already on the job.

Length of Test

Reliability is generally influenced by the length of a test or period of observation, as described by the Spearman-Brown formula. The generality, like others, has exceptions; added length can, in fact, decrease reliability if the added items or observers add only random variance to the pool (Li, Rosenthal, & Rubin, 1996). Reliability may also be decreased if, as in many new forms of testing, the added items have strong local dependencies, as in sets of items all referring to the same reading passage or problem situation (Wainer & Thissen, 1996). Within the generality, however, simple algebra permits transforming the Spearman-Brown formula to answer the question, "How long must the test—or criterion time period—be for adequate reliability?" The transformed equation is

$$n = \frac{r_{nn}(1 - r_{xx})}{r_{xx}(1 - r_{nn})} \tag{18}$$

where n is the number of times the existing test must be multiplied for a desired level of reliability, r_{nn} is that level, and r_{xx} is the reliability coefficient before lengthening the test. Use of the equation assumes that increments are equivalent to the existing procedure. It may be applied only to coefficients of equivalence or of internal consistency.

Reliability improvement improves validity. Properly increasing test length by a specific value of n, estimated validity will be shown by

$$r_{x_n y}{}^2 = \frac{r_{xy}}{\sqrt{\dfrac{1}{n} + \left(1 - \dfrac{1}{n}\right) r_{xx}}} \tag{19}$$

where $r_{x_n y}$ is the validity expected for the lengthened test x, and n is the factor by which the test is to be lengthened (Thorndike, 1949). Using selected values in this equation will show that, where a test is reasonably reliable to begin with, not much added validity will be gained through lengthening the test. Where, however, a low validity coefficient is due to low test reliability, lengthening the test can be useful.

Item Characteristics

Ambiguous items, or those giving extraneous hints, reduce reliability. Items with optimal difficulty levels (about .50) are more reliable than extremely easy or extremely hard items. Relatively high interitem correlations, or high correlations of item responses with total scores (discrimination indices), are needed for high internal consistency coefficients. In short, building reliability into a test (or any other measurement procedure) begins with good test development.

A Preview: Generalizability Theory

Reliability is part of classical test theory. Chapter 6 describes a more modern development, generalizability theory, which evaluates several potential sources of error simultaneously. Reliability theory is a useful aid in understanding generalizability theory. It is also useful because generalizability analysis is not always feasible.

VALIDITY: AN EVOLVING CONCEPT

Validity is another ambiguous term. Thurstone (1931), in his monograph on test theory, defined validity conceptually as the correlation of test scores with a criterion *that is a better measure of the trait* than the test. The better measure may be hard to get or otherwise costly. Hull (1928) considered the best aptitude criterion "the test of life itself" (p. 1). This classical notion of validity used criteria only to judge the excellence of tests as trait measures. A test, it was generally said, "purports" to measure something, and validity is the degree it measures "what it is intended or purports to measure" (Drever, 1952, p. 304). This view differs from a later, now common view of validity as the effectiveness of test use in predicting a criterion measuring something else and valued in its own right. The early concept of validity evaluated test scores as measures of a trait of interest; the later one evaluates test scores as predictors of something else. Investigations of both ideas have been called validation, results of either are called validity, and data collected for one of these evaluations may (but may not) be useful for the other. The distinction has not been commonly recognized.

We tend to use a verbal shorthand, referring to "test validity" as if validity were a property of the method of measurement. It is not; it is a property of the *inferences* drawn from test *scores* (Cronbach, 1971); the inferences (interpretations) may be descriptive or relational.

Three Troublesome Adjectives

Early attempts to clarify the validity concept (American Psychological Association, American Educational Research Association, & National Council on Measurement in Education, 1966; American Psychological Association, American Educational Research Association, & National Council on Measurements Used in Education, 1954) described criterion-related, content, and construct validity as aspects of validity; however, no general definition of validity was offered. Criterion-related validity was shown by the relation of test scores to an external criterion. Content validity was a matter of the fidelity of sampling a content domain in the construction of the test. Construct validity was more complex, requiring both a showing of reasons for inferring a particular construct from the test scores and for not inferring alternative constructs. The three came to be treated as if they were three different *kinds* of validity, not aspects, an error of interpretation forcefully criticized by Dunnette and Borman (1979) and by me as psychometric trinitarianism (R. M. Guion, 1980). At least since Cronbach (1971), validity concepts have emphasized the *meaning* of scores: how a score can be interpreted, or what can be inferred about a person with that score. Inferences are constructs, and the "unitarian" view that has emerged treats the notion of validity, with no modifying adjective, as an expanded view of what was called construct validity (Messick, 1989, 1995a).

Modifying adjectives have caused (or reflected) much of the mischief that has confused discussions of validity. A note in the 1974 Standards (American Psychological Association, American Educational Research Association, and National Council on Measurement in Education, 1974) identified a half-dozen other adjectives in common use; a recent unfortunate addition to the litany is *consequential validity*, a term based on a misreading of Messick (1989), who argued that consequences of test use should be considered in drawing inferences of validity. The unfortunate trouble with such adjectives is that they tend to emphasize one aspect of validity while ignoring others.

Interpretive and Relational Inferences

Interpretive inferences describe characteristics revealed by the measurement procedure itself; I call them descriptive inferences. Relational inferences interpret scores in terms of different but correlated characteristics. These are not wholly independent. The validity of descriptive inferences depends on several sources of information, relational data among them; it is closely associated with the idea of construct validity. Relational inferences are not well understood without understanding the descriptive properties of the related variables. Nevertheless, the distinction emphasizes different demands on validation: the difference between evaluating the success with which a construct is measured and evaluating its use. Both are important, but so is the distinction. For personnel decisions, the distinction is between interpreting scores as traits and interpreting them as signs of something else (Wernimont & Campbell, 1968).

A relational inference is made when one infers from a score a corresponding level of performance on a criterion; it is usually evaluated by correlations. There is almost always more than that to be inferred from a well-understood test score. Validity is more than a correlation coefficient. To be sure, a test can be designed to do no more than predict a criterion—to be an ad hoc, empirically developed measure, heterogenous in content, and wholly atheoretical, having no meaning at all if the criterion changes. A change in the job or technology or context can destroy the validity of such a limited relational inference, and no one will know why; what, if anything, has been measured is a mystery.

Usually, several constructs can be offered as plausible descriptive interpretations. One of them may be intended by the developer or user; others may be unwanted contaminants. If scores can sensibly be interpreted in terms of the intended construct or meaning, but not in terms of the intrusive others, then the intended descriptive inferences are surely valid, apart from any relational inferences that may also be valid.

Psychometric Validity

Validation for descriptive inferences seeks confirmation of the meaning of test scores intended by the test developer (or some subsequent meaning intended by a test user) and disconfirmation of plausible alternative meanings. Because such validation is procedurally different from traditional employment test validation, I distinguish evaluating (validating) descriptive inferences from validating relational ones.[3] For personnel assessment, with apology for yet another adjective, I call the result of the former *psychometric validity*. The result of the latter I call *job relatedness*, at least in personnel decision contexts—the term is admittedly parochial. Maybe it should more generally be called usefulness.

This chapter emphasizes psychometric validity. It is intended to examine classical psychometric theory and look beyond the comfortable limits that corral validity within a coefficient. Validity, whether of measurement or of use, is itself an inference—a conclusion reached from an abundance of information and data.

The simple, fundamental question of psychometric validity is, "How well has the intended characteristic been measured?" More precisely, the question asks, "With what confidence can the scores resulting from the measurement be interpreted as representing varying degrees or levels of the specified characteristic?" There is never a simple answer. Answers are judgments, not numbers, and they are to be supported by data and logical argument. They depend on the relative weight of evidence—the weight of accumulated evidence supporting an interpretation relative to the weight of accumulated evidence opposing it. One looks not at single bits of information but at the preponderance of the evidence.

---

[3]After more than a decade of making this distinction, I've discovered that it is not at all new. Cureton (1950) made even finer distinctions; he referred to the correlation between observed scores on a test and observed criterion scores as *predictive power*, reserving the word validity for the correlation between observed predictor scores and criterion true scores (i.e., correction for criterion unreliability). Correction for unreliability in both measures (i.e., correlation between predictor true scores and criterion true scores) gave what he called *relevance*. I have long admired Dr. Cureton, but not until I discovered the Angoff (1988) history did I realize that ideas I've been preaching were his, not mine.

VARIETIES OF PSYCHOMETRIC VALIDITY EVIDENCE

"The 30-year-old idea of three types of validity, separate but maybe equal, is an idea whose time has gone. . . . A favorable answer to one or two questions can fully support a test only when no one cares enough to raise further questions" (Cronbach, 1988, p. 4). In the 1985 *Standards*, it was said, "An ideal validation includes several types of evidence, which span all three of the traditional categories. . . . Professional judgment should guide the decisions regarding the forms of evidence that are most necessary and feasible in light of the intended uses of the test and any likely alternatives to testing" (American Educational Research Association, American Psychological Association, & National Council on Measurement in Education, 1985, p. 9).

Landy (1986) also questioned the usefulness of the threefold distinction. He said that some decisions in litigation under Title VII tend to be based on whether a "correct" approach to validation was used, correctness depending on which of three "kinds" of validity was being defended.

> As a result of this tendency to label validity approaches as correct or incorrect in a given situation, Title VII cases often take on the appearance of a primitive form of stamp collecting. There are only three spaces to be filled—the content space, the construct space, and the criterion-related space. The test in question is the metaphorical stamp. If it is a test of constructs, then it is pasted in the construct space, and the litigants set out to determine if all of the requirements for construct-validation efforts have been met. If it is a test of knowledges, skills, or abilities currently possessed by an applicant, then either the content or the criterion-related space is filled and the litigants consider a different checklist of requirements. These list checkers take on the appearance of the modern-day equivalent of the biblical Pharisees, checking scripture to determine if law or tradition has been violated. (Landy, 1986, p. 1184)

It is not my purpose (nor was it Landy's) to abolish these three concepts, but I do not use the traditional trinitarian terms in the discussion that follows. I suspect that the term *validity* has outlived its usefulness. I have not yet done so, but I would not mind retiring the word to the scrapheap of overused terms dying of terminal ambiguity (R. M. Guion, 1996a). Instead, we should refer to *evaluation* of tests and test uses; the very term requires us to ask questions and seek answers in making evaluative judgments. I pose, under four headings, some questions a decision maker might try to answer about an assessment procedure and its results. Answers require professional judgment; sometimes they require forming and testing hypotheses (Landy, 1986). These questions do not form a comprehensive checklist to be completed by stamp collectors or bean counters. Indeed, I have presented lists ranging from 4 to 14 questions covering pretty much the same content (e.g., R. M. Guion, 1983a, 1983b, 1987a, 1991, 1996a, 1996b). This list has nine. I hope the inconsistency in numbers confounds any simplistic, bureaucratic tendency to insist on a specific checklist.

Evidence Based on Test Development

Formal measurement consists of rules for assigning numbers to represent real relationships. For example, suppose that oranges have more of some property (e.g., acidity) than apples (they *can* be compared!) and that apples have more of it than bananas. These relationships are transitive, meaning also that oranges must have more of the property than do bananas. The rules for assigning numbers become a mathematical model of the real relationships implied. Measures are meaningful if the numbers fit the model and the model is faithful to the reality of transitive, quantitative relationships. One can never prove either, but one can show that the procedure was developed to reflect relationships consistent with the model. Validity is not usually invoked in evaluating formal measurement procedures, but evidence of it is found when intelligent efforts have failed to prove that the measures do not represent reality (Coombs, Dawes, & Tversky, 1970).

Psychological measurement is rarely based on formal models. Even so, a theory of the construct can usually be articulated, even if it is a rather vague and incomplete theory specifying only a few quantitative properties, if any. If development of the measure has been consistent with that theory, that consistency (or inconsistency if it has not) is one piece of information to consider in judging the psychometric validity of the resulting scores.

Basic Validity Questions in Test Development. Sometimes a model is so elegant and convincing (e.g., the measurement of information) or so routine and natural (e.g., measuring linear distance with a yardstick) that the measures are accepted without much question. However, most measurement in psychology lacks such models, and evaluation is needed. I suggest these questions to guide evaluation of the procedure's development:

Did the developer of the procedure have a clear idea of the attribute to be measured? This is a question of intentions; the developer of the procedure must have had something in mind to be measured. It may have been a thoroughly established construct—or little more than a vague idea of a continuum along which people or objects could be ordered. It may have been a theoretical construct such as latent anxiety, or something empirically tangible such as the smoothness of a machined surface, or something observable such as coordinated motor responses to visual stimuli. These are all abstractions, attributes of people or objects of concern. It is a small but positive sign of validity if development followed a clear conception of the attribute to be measured. It is a large, negative piece of evidence if the developer has not bothered or is unable to describe the attribute measured, how it matches or differs from other attributes under other names, or whether it is an attribute of people, of groups of people, or of objects people do something with or to. It is not enough if the developer has only provided a name for the attribute; it is still negative evidence, even damning evidence, if the developer has not gone beyond the label to a coherent rationale guiding the procedure's development. In introducing the idea of psychological constructs and construct validity, Cronbach and Meehl (1955) referred to the construct as a theory; Frederiksen (1986) referred to a theory of the criterion; I have referred to a *theory of the attribute* (R. M. Guion, 1987b). By this I mean that the developer of the measurement procedure has an idea of the boundaries of the attribute, the sorts of behaviors that exhibit the attribute and those that do not, or some variables with which the attribute may be correlated and some with which correlations would not be expected. This is less than the grand nomological network envisioned by Cronbach and Meehl (1955); it nevertheless suggests testable hypotheses about the construct (Dunnette, 1992). Not all testable hypotheses have to be tested. Test use can be justified if there is some evidence supporting the intended inference and other evidence ruling out the most plausible alternatives. Even this limited requirement is not possible if the intended inference is not identified and defined.

Are the mechanics of measurement consistent with the concept? Most psychological measurement is based on the responses people make to standard stimuli presented according to standard procedural rules. If the developer had a clear idea of what was to be measured, it should have governed a plan for procedures, and further questions like these need answers:

Is the presentation medium appropriate? Does printing a test on paper, showing it on a CRT, or recording it on a cassette fit the definition of the attribute to be measured? No one medium is inherently better than another. In evaluating a test, however, I want to know if its developer has carefully thought about the question or has simply followed habit.

Are there rules of standardization or control, such as time limits? If so, were they dictated by the nature of the trait being measured, or were they chosen for convenience (e.g., setting time limits to fit a standard class period) or out of habit?

Are response requirements appropriate? It is not appropriate to use a recognition-based multiple-choice item type for a construct defined in terms of free recall; it is not appropriate to use verbal questions and answers for constructs defined as physical skills.

Satisfactory answers to such questions provide only slight evidence of validity, but unsatisfactory answers—or no answers at all—are reasons for questioning assertions of validity.

Is the stimulus content appropriate? The content of a measurement procedure should certainly fit the nature of the attribute to be measured. This is more than so-called content validity. Of course, if the attribute to be measured implies a specific content domain, such as knowledge of the content of a training program, then content-oriented test development— with its insistence on domain definition and rules for domain sampling— constitutes useful and strong evidence of validity. But the principle applies also to more abstract constructs such as those developed by factor analyses. For tests of factorial constructs, item types defining the factor in prior research should be used, or evidence should show that the item type chosen taps the factor satisfactorily.

If the appropriateness of item content is not obvious from either the domain definition or research history, then a test user needs evidence that the developer has done some serious, creative thinking and has, moreover, some logical or empirical support for the content selected. Lack of such evidence is another big item in the list of reasons for questioning the validity of inferences that might be drawn from scores.

In some few cases, sampling a well-defined domain may be ample evidence without further study. Content sampling alone is enough to justify test use if five requirements are met (R. M. Guion, 1977):

The content must be, or be rooted in, behavior with a generally accepted meaning, such as the field test portion of a driver's license test.

The content domain must be defined unambiguously. People who understand the measurement problem should understand the domain boundaries, as defined, clearly enough to agree on whether a given topic or action falls within them, even if they do not agree on details of the definition.

The content domain must be directly relevant to the measurement purpose. It must not assume a relationship beyond that of sample to domain. It must be a sample of a much larger universe or domain, external to the test itself, that the measurement purports to represent. The distinction here is between a *sample* and a *sign* (Wernimont & Campbell, 1968).

Qualified judges must agree that the domain has been properly sampled. Two key words are *qualified* and *properly*. The major qualification of judges is a thorough knowledge of the domain to be sampled. "Properly sampled" may require proportional sampling (e.g., proportional to time spent or to importance of component parts), although differences in component difficulty, importance, or other considerations might take precedence; it avoids irrelevant content *not* in the defined domain.

The response content must be scored and evaluated reliably.

Was the test carefully and skillfully developed? After determining that the developer had a clear idea in mind at the outset, and that it stayed in mind long enough to plan the measurement operations and content, I look for evidence that the plan was carried out well. The evidence depends on the plan. If equipment is required, the evidence might include a record of the alternatives considered and the reasons for choices. More broadly, when judgments were required (and they nearly always are), they and the reasons for them should be a matter of record. Even when I do not agree with the choice, I am inclined to credit full disclosure of the reasoning as a positive sign of care, especially if judgments about test content were established by experts using a systematic plan. Useful evidence includes information about the experts chosen, their qualifications, reliabilities of their judgments, and procedures used to reconcile differences. The final set of items should fit the original plan; departures from that plan should be satisfactorily explained.

Useful evidence also comes from answers to questions like these:

Were pilot studies done to try out ideas, especially if they are unusual, about item types, instructions, time limits, ambient conditions, or other standardizing aspects of the test?

Was item selection based on item analysis? Were appropriate item statistics computed and used? Did the data come from an appropriate sample or from what I insist on calling a "scrounge sample" (to be blunter than the usual polite term, "sample of convenience")? Was the sample large enough to yield reliable statistics? Does the final mix of selected items fit the original plan, or is there some imbalance? Was the item pool big enough to permit stringent criteria for item retention?

Were methods of test construction, particularly sophisticated methods such as item response theory (see chapter 6) carried out with full awareness of the assumptions and constraints of the method?

Creating Validity. The likelihood that justifiable inferences can be drawn from scores on a test is built into the test in its planning and construction. No one has said it better than Anne Anastasi:

> Validity is thus built into the test from the outset rather than being limited to the last stages of test development.... The validation process begins with the formulation of detailed trait or construct definitions, derived from psychological theory, prior research, or systematic observation and analyses of the relevant behavior domain. Test items are then prepared to fit the

construct definitions. Empirical item analyses follow, with the selection of the most effective (i.e., valid) items from the initial item pools. Other appropriate internal analyses may then be carried out, including factor analyses of item clusters or subtests. The final stage includes validation and cross-validation of various scores and interpretive combinations of scores through statistical analyses against external, real-life criteria. (Anastasi, 1986, p. 3)

Evidence Based on Reliability

Is the internal statistical evidence satisfactory? Classical item analysis looks for two item characteristics: (a) difficulty level, usually expressed in the reverse as the percentage giving the correct item response, and (b) discrimination index, typically expressed as the correlation of item responses to total scores. Item statistics can be examined for spread and average difficulty or discrimination indices to see if they are appropriate for the anticipated measurement purposes. A test that is too easy or too hard for the people who take it will not permit valid inferences. Item statistics should be evaluated, of course, in the light of the circumstances that produced them. Their usefulness may depend on such things as sample size, appropriateness of the sample to the intended population, and probable distributions of the attribute in the sample. No universally correct statement of the most desirable item characteristics can be made. Ordinarily, one might consider a variety of item difficulties a sign of a "good" test. For some kinds of personnel decisions, however, a narrow band of difficulties might enhance discriminability in a critical region and be considered better evidence of validity than a broad band.

Responses should be somewhat related to total score on all items; otherwise, no clearly definable variable is measured. Usually, a rather high level of internal consistency is wanted. A high coefficient alpha does not provide positive evidence that the item set as a whole is measuring what it is supposed to measure, but it *does* offer assurance of systematic content. If other information (such as meritorious care in defining the construct and in developing items to match the definition) makes it reasonable to assume that most items have indeed measured the intended concept, then a satisfactory alpha is reasonable evidence that the scores reflect it without much contamination.

Constructs vary widely in specificity; some are very narrowly defined, such as any one of the 120 constructs in the Guilford structure of intellect model (Guilford, 1959), or very broadly defined, such as a construct of creativity which may include many narrower constructs. Tightly defined constructs require high internal consistency coefficients.

Internal consistency is necessary for descriptive inferences. How high should it be? Tradition looks skeptically at internal consistency coefficients lower than .70 and limits enthusiasm to those exceeding .90. The foolishness of offering specific numbers is clear when one considers internal consistency for measures justified mainly on content sampling, where internal consistency is less important. There should be some; if the internal consistency coefficient is not nonzero and positive, the overall score is uninterpretable. Nevertheless, evidence of internal *consistency* may be less relevant than evidence of internal *completeness* or *relevance* in domain sampling. A completely sampled domain may require two or more somewhat internally consistent scores for parts of it to provide meaningful assessment if the parts are not positively correlated.

Are scores stable over time and consistent with alternative measures? Stability over some not-too-brief time period seems essential, especially if internal consistency is relatively unimportant. If equivalent forms of the test have been developed, they should in fact meet at least minimal requirements of equivalence (common means and variances) as well as correlate well. If scoring is done by observers rating performance or its outcome, then certainly interrater agreement is an essential ingredient of reliability. Because reliability limits validity, evidence of high reliability suggests good descriptive validity, but consistency may be due to consistent error.

Evidence From Patterns of Correlates

Correlating scores on a measurement procedure to be evaluated with other measures may yield evidence of validity. Such research provides information of two kinds, both equally important to conclusions about validity. One is confirmatory evidence, evidence that confirms (or fails to confirm) an intended inference from test scores. It is evidence that relationships logically expected from the theory of the attribute are in fact found. The other is disconfirmatory evidence, evidence ruling out alternative inferences or interpretations of scores—evidence that relationships *not* expected by the nature of the construct are in fact *not* found. Confirmatory evidence that does in fact confirm the intended interpretation is a necessary but insufficient condition for accepting scores as valid measures of an intended trait. Evidence is also needed that plausible alternative interpretations can be rejected (i.e., disconfirmed).

Multitrait–multimethod matrices are commonly used to study correlates with other variables. Two or more traits are identified (one measured by the assessment method at hand), and they are each measured by two or more methods. Confirmatory evidence of validity exists if correlations among measures of the same trait across methods are higher than correlations among traits within common methods (Campbell & Fiske, 1959).

One form of statistical evidence that has pleased some people remarkably well is a nice *validity coefficient*; the term has been responsible for much mischief. Many people place far too much faith in a single validity coefficient. A nice validity coefficient might stem from a common contamination in both the instrument being validated and the criterion. Suppose that performance ratings of school principals are contaminated by a general stereotype that a good principal is physically tall, imposing in stature, looks like scholar, and speaks in a low, soft voice. If the measure to be validated is an assessment center rating of administrative potential, and if these ratings are influenced by that same stereotype, there will be a nice validity coefficient. It does not follow that the assessment ratings are good indicators of administrative ability.

Another problem with a single validity coefficient is that it seeks only evidence confirming (or failing to confirm) a particular inference. It says nothing to confirm or to disconfirm alternative inferences. Other problems, such as unknown third variables, are discussed in chapter 7.

Validity coefficients are, of course, valuable bits of evidence in making judgments about validity, but *one should not confuse validity coefficients with validity*, and one should not base judgments about validity on validity coefficients alone.

Does empirical evidence confirm logically expected relationships with other variables? Specifying an attribute to be measured, and maybe explicating a theory of the attribute, is the first step in planning a measurement procedure. The theory of the attribute will suggest that good measures of it will correlate with some things but not with others, and at least some of these hypotheses can be tested. Evidence supporting them also confirms the validity of the scores as measures of the intended attribute. Traditional criterion-related validation procedures follow this logic. One might hypothesize from one's theoretical view of mechanical aptitude that those with high scores on a test of it will do better in an auto mechanics school than will those with low scores. To test the hypothesis, scores are correlated with grades in the school. A significant, positive correlation is evidence of validity for both relational and descriptive inferences. Testing other hypotheses, perhaps showing correlations with the number of correct troubleshooting diagnoses in a standardized set of aberrant pieces of equipment, or the speed with which a bicycle is taken apart and reassembled, gives further evidence of psychometric validity. Every such hypothesis supported adds further confirming evidence of the validity of interpreting scores as measures of mechanical aptitude as it has been defined. Failure to support hypotheses casts doubt (a) on the validity of the inference or (b) on the match of the theory of the attribute with the operations—of the conceptual and the operational definitions of the attribute. Without such a match, either the operational definition must be modified (or replaced) or the conceptual one changed. Suppose that hypotheses about correlates of the mechanical aptitude scores were not supported (or were supported only weakly) when the external criterion involved speed. It would suggest that the ability to do mechanical things quickly cannot be inferred from scores on that particular test. Either a speed component must be added to those operations, or the theory of the attribute must explicitly exclude speed as a component. In this way, accumulated data permit the nature of potentially valid inferences to be more precisely specified.

If scores on the test at hand and measures of expected correlates and noncorrelates can be obtained in the same sample of people, a correlation matrix can be developed. It can be explored by methods described in chapter 6, but elegance of analysis is not routinely needed. What is needed is at least one well-conceived, well-conducted, and therefore convincing confirming study. Two such studies would be better, and still more would be still better. One incorporates new data when possible and examines the preponderance of the evidence in evaluations.

Does empirical evidence disconfirm alternative meanings of test scores? In practical terms, this means ruling out contaminations. Work sample scores should not be biased by the particular equipment an examinee happens to use. Performance ratings should not be biased by differential stereotypes among raters. Work attitude scores should not be biased by a social desirability response set. A test of spelling ability should not be biased by a printed format that requires excellent visual acuity. Many such problems can be guarded against during test development, but some of them need empirical study. Failure to disconfirm the more plausible contaminants may suggest validity problems.

Cronbach (1988) identified two approaches to construct validation, one a "weak program" and the other a "strong" one (although, of course, these terms represent extremes of a continuum). The weak program is exploratory, it casts about for evidence wherever it may be and, if useful, incorporates it into the judgment of the validity of score interpretations. Such a program, he said, "has some merit." If pursued doggedly, it seems bound to yield improved interpretations of scores on existing tests and improved techniques for developing further ones.

A strong program requires a more explicit theory of the attribute, one that develops deliberate challenges to the intended interpretations, suggesting confirmatory hypotheses that seriously risk not being supported and alternative interpretive hypotheses that risk confirmation rather than disconfirmation. Whether through experience, challenge from others, or one's own fertile imagination, one identifies and evaluates plausible rival inferences.

Strong programs improve the march of science; weak ones do so also, but largely by luck. Where on the continuum does the personnel decision maker want to be? In a litigious environment, trying for a strong program seems sensible. Potential plaintiffs can challenge tests by posing rival interpretations of the scores. By anticipating the more plausible rivals, and disconfirming them, one develops a defense. Anticipating them, and confirming them, is good reason to find another basis for decision before someone sues.

Evidence Based on Outcomes

Are the consequences of test use consistent with the meaning of the construct being measured? A theory of an attribute should identify outcomes or consequences of test use relevant to the construct Messick (1989, 1995a). For example, if the attribute to be measured involves flexibility in thinking about problems, the theory of the attribute may include flexibility in solving problems of malfunctioning equipment. If a test of the attribute is used to select mechanics, then one consequence of its use is that high scorers are likely to think of and try alternative explanations for mechanical problems—hence, to solve more of them. If they actually do solve more problems than do low scorers, it is evidence of valid measurement of the construct as well as evidence supporting the predictive hypothesis. Some consequences are unintended. If the test of the attribute is heavily loaded with contaminating verbal skills, the consequence may be that high scorers have to read a lot of manuals before giving up a previously inflexible approach. Such a consequence would cast serious doubt on scores as measuring a construct defined mainly by flexibility in thinking.

Unfortunately, much silliness has been written (but, in kindness, is not cited) about unintended consequences and validity. Adverse impact and ethnic differences in mean scores have been used as examples of unintended consequences and concomitant reduction of psychometric validity—without considering the possibility of actual group differences or reasons for them. What makes the example so pernicious is that it is so thoughtlessly offered when it might, if carefully considered and subjected to appropriate research, be a good example. Consider a multiple choice test of job knowledge. A test-taking strategy commonly used in one group but not in the other might account for the difference. If so, scores may not mean the same things in the two groups; the mean score difference does not truly reflect group differences in job knowledge. The validity of knowledge-level inferences from scores, both interpretative and relational, is diminished by this unintended consequence. Note that the unintended consequence in this example is not the mean difference; it is the difference in approach to the task of taking the test. The mean difference itself might be attributable to real group differences in opportunities to get the knowledge relevant to the job, a consequence that does not hurt interpretations of knowledge levels implied by the scores. One should not be too hasty in deciding that validity has been damaged because of an observed effect of test use. Neither should one be too hasty in attributing score differences to the instrument when they may more properly be attributed to differences in responding to it.

REFERENCES

American Educational Research Association, American Psychological Association, & National Council on Measurement in Education. (1985). *Standards for educational and psychological testing.* Washington, DC: American Psychological Association.

American Psychological Association, American Educational Research Association, & National Council on Measurement in Education. (1966). *Standards for educational and psychological tests and manuals.* Washington, DC: American Psychological Association.

American Psychological Association, American Educational Research Association, & National Council on Measurement in Education. (1974). *Standards for educational and psychological tests.* Washington, DC: American Psychological Association.

American Psychological Association, American Educational Research Association, & National Council on Measurements Used in Education. (1954). Technical recommendations for psychological tests and diagnostic techniques. *Psychological Bulletin, 51,* 201–238.

Anastasi, A. (1982). *Psychological testing* (5th ed.). New York: Macmillan.

Anastasi, A. (1986). Evolving concepts of test validation. *Annual Review of Psychology, 37,* 1–15.

Angoff, W. H. (1988). Validity: An evolving concept. In H. Wainer & H. I. Braun (Eds.), *Test validity* (pp. 19–32). Hillsdale, NJ: Lawrence Erlbaum Associates.

Boring, E. G. (1961). The beginning and growth of measurement in psychology. In H. Woolf (Ed.), *Quantification: A history of the meaning of measurement in the natural and social sciences* (pp. 108–127). Indianapolis: Bobbs-Merrill.

Campbell, D. T., & Fiske, D. W. (1959). Convergent and discriminant validation by the multitrait-multimethod matrix. *Psychological Bulletin, 56,* 81–105.

Cattell, J. M. (1890). Mental tests and measurements. *Mind, 15,* 373–380.

Coombs, C. H., Dawes, R. H., & Tversky, A. (1970). *Mathematical psychology: An elementary introduction.* Englewood Cliffs, NJ: Prentice-Hall.

Cronbach, L. J. (1971). Test validation. In R. L. Thorndike (Ed.), *Educational measurement* (2nd ed., pp. 443–507). Washington, DC: American Council on Education.

Cronbach, L. J. (1988). Five perspectives on validity argument. In H. Wainer & H. I. Braun (Eds.), *Test validity* (pp. 3–17). Hillsdale, NJ: Lawrence Erlbaum Associates.

Cronbach, L. J., & Azuma, H. (1962). Internal consistency reliability formulas applied to randomly sampled single-factor tests. *Educational and Psychological Measurement, 22,* 645–665.

Cronbach, L. J., & Meehl, P. E. (1955). Construct validity in psychological tests. *Psychological Bulletin, 52,* 281–302.

Cureton, E. E. (1950). Validity. In E. F. Lindquist (Ed.), *Educational measurement* (pp. 621–694). Washington, DC: American Council on Education.

Cureton, E. E. (1958). The definition and estimation of test reliability. *Educational and Psychological Measurement, 18,* 715–738.

Drever, J. (1952). *A dictionary of psychology.* Baltimore: Penguin.

Dunnette, M. D. (1992). It was nice to be there: Construct validity then and now. *Human Performance, 5,* 157–169.

Dunnette, M. D., & Borman, W. C. (1979). Personnel selection and classification. *Annual Review of Psychology, 30,* 477–525.

Frederiksen, N. (1986). Construct validity and construct similarity: Methods for use in test development and test validation. *Multivariate Behavioral Research, 21,* 3–28.

Guilford, J. P. (1954). *Psychometric methods* (2nd ed.). New York: McGraw-Hill.

Guilford, J. P. (1959). *Personality.* New York: McGraw-Hill.

Guion, D. M. (1973). *Music and experimental science in sixteenth century Italy.* Masters thesis, University of California, San Diego.

Guion, R. M. (1977). Content validity—the source of my discontent. *Applied Psychological Measurement, 1,* 1–10.

Guion, R. M. (1980). On trinitarian doctrines of validity. *Professional Psychology, 11,* 385–398.

Guion, R. M. (1983a, April). *Disunity in the trinitarian concept of validity.* In a symposium, Paul Sandifer (Chair), Clearing away the cobwebs: A closer look at content validity. At the meeting of the American Educational Research Association, Montreal.

Guion, R. M. (1983b, August). *The ambiguity of validity: The growth of my discontent.* Presidential address to the Division of Evaluation and Measurement at the meeting of the American Psychological Association, Anaheim, CA.

Guion, R. M. (1987a). Actions, beliefs, and content: Some ABCs of validity. In C. J. Cranny (Ed.), *Content validity III: Proceedings* (pp. 1–12). Bowling Green, OH: Bowling Green State University.

Guion, R. M. (1987b). Changing views for personnel selection research. *Personnel Psychology, 40,* 199–213.

Guion, R. M. (1991). Personnel assessment, selection, and placement. In M. D. Dunnette & L. M. Hough (Eds.), *The handbook of industrial and organizational psychology* (2nd ed., pp. 327–397). Palo Alto, CA: Consulting Psychologists Press.

Guion, R. M. (1996a). Evaluation of performance tests for work readiness. In L. Resnick & J. Wirt (Eds.), *Linking school and work: Roles for standards and assessment* (pp. 267–303). San Francisco: Jossey-Bass.

Guion, R. M. (1996b). The questions of validity. In J. F. Kehoe (Chair), *Whither construct validity.* A symposium conducted at the meeting of the Society for Industrial and Organizational Psychology, San Diego, April 26.

Guttman, L. (1945). A basis for analyzing test–retest reliability. *Psychometrika, 10,* 255–282.

Hull, C. L. (1928). *Aptitude testing.* Yonkers-on-Hudson: World Book.

Kuder, G. F., & Richardson, M. W. (1937). The theory of estimation of test reliability. *Psychometrika, 2,* 151–160.

Landy, F. J. (1986). Stamp collecting versus science: Validation as hypothesis testing. *American Psychologist, 41,* 1183–1192.

Li, H., Rosenthal, R., & Rubin, D. B. (1996). Reliability of measurement in psychology: From Spearman-Brown to maximal reliability. *Psychological Methods, 1,* 98–107.

Likert, R. (1932). A technique for the measurement of attitudes. *New York Archives of Psychology, 22*(140).

Messick, S. (1989). Validity. In R. L. Linn (Ed.), *Educational measurement* (3rd ed., pp. 13–103). New York: American Council on Education & Macmillan.

Messick, S. (1995a). Standards of validity and the validity of standards in performance assessment. *Educational Measurement: Issues and Practice, 14*(4), 5–8.

Messick, S. (1995b). Validity of psychological assessment: Validation of inferences from persons' responses and performance as scientific inquiry into score meaning. *American Psychologist, 50,* 741–749.

Peak, H. (1953). Problems of objective observation. In L. Festinger & D. Katz (Eds.), *Research methods in the behavioral sciences* (pp. 243–299). New York: Dryden.

Richardson, M. W., & Kuder, F. (1939). The calculation of test reliability coefficients based upon the method of rational equivalence. *Journal of Educational Psychology, 30,* 681–687.

Rulon, P. J. (1939). A simplfied procedure for determining the reliability of a test by split halves. *Harvard Educational Review, 9*, 99–103.

Stanley, J. C. (1971). Reliability. In R. L. Thorndike (Ed.), *Educational measurement* (2nd ed., pp. 356–442). Washington, DC: American Council on Education.

Thorndike, R. L. (1949). *Personnel selection: Test and measurement techniques.* New York: Wiley.

Thurstone, L. L. (1927). A law of comparative judgment. *Psychological Review, 34*, 273–286.

Thurstone, L. L. (1931). *The reliability and validity of tests.* Ann Arbor: Edwards.

Thurstone, L. L., & Chave, E. J. (1929). *The measurement of attitude: A psychophysical method and some experiments with a scale for measuring attitude toward the church.* Chicago: University of Chicago Press.

Towner, L. W. (1956). Reliability coefficients obtained under varying degrees of deviation from theoretically perfect conditions. *Educational and Psychological Measurement, 16*, 345–351.

Tryon, R. C. (1957). Reliability and behavior domain validity: Reformulation and historical critique. *Psychological Bulletin, 54*, 229–249.

Wainer, H., & Thissen, D. (1996). How is reliability related to the quality of test scores? What is the effect of local dependence on reliability? *Educational Measurement: Issues and Practice, 15*(1), 22–29.

Wernimont, P. F., & Campbell, J. P. (1968). Signs, samples, and criteria. *Journal of Applied Psychology, 52*, 372–376.

6

Further Concepts in Measurement

Classical psychometric theory has served well and is sufficient for many practical uses. Extensions of classical theory, and alternatives to it, have been developed; they are useful, but they may sometimes require more resources (e.g., subject pools, opportunities for repeated measurement, etc.) than most personnel researchers will have. Even when practical limitations make them infeasible, however, they present concepts worth incorporating even when older approaches must be used.

Chapter 5 described classical psychometrics as it has evolved, not as formulated in early writings. This chapter follows the evolution in three areas: factor analysis, generalizability theory, and item response theory. These topics deserve fuller treatment than given here, and others could have been chosen. Researchers will, of course, go beyond these introductions.

Classical theory assumed that a measure or score implied a position along a single scale measuring a single attribute, but it did not make precisely clear what a "single attribute" is. One of its most venerable procedures is split-half reliability to estimate internal consistency. A split-half procedure does not assume, and certainly does not assure, that only one attribute is reflected in the total score. A stricter notion of unidimensionality was a later goal in measurement—a necessary goal if scores are to be truly transitive. If a single trait (or construct) is to be measured, then the influence of another one introduces systematic error, preventing unidimensionality. The concept of unidimensionality stems from factor analytic methods; an early one (the method of tetrad differences, Spearman, 1927) investigated the proposition that scores on each test in a set of tests were primarily influenced by a general factor, g. Subsequent methods (e.g., Thurstone, 1947) enabled researchers to identify various sources of systematic variance ("factors") with common influences on scores of two or more tests in the set of tests studied. Factor analytic procedures have not only made it possible to study the internal structure of tests and other forms of measurement but to develop tests to maximize intended sources of variances and to minimize others. The systematic variance intended for one test may be systematic error for a different one; reading comprehension may be the intended trait in a reading test and a contaminating source of systematic error in an arithmetic test.

Systematic error may prevent literal transitivity; any given total score may be influenced by the intended trait and also by any other traits systematically influencing scores. A higher score of one person on a measure of trait A, compared to someone else, *might* mean that person does in fact have or show a higher level of trait A; but the person may be lower on trait A but get a higher score anyway because of the additive influence of one or more of the systematic sources of error. In this sense, not only random error but systematic errors reduce validity. Early concepts of reliability were deficient in assuming that only random error limited validity. Once it was recognized that both random and systematic errors influenced scores and the inferences to be drawn from them, it was only a short step to recognize further that there can be multiple sources of systematic error—and from there to generalizability theory.

All of the statistics used in classical test theory—item statistics, distribution descriptive statistics, and the various correlations of reliability and validity estimation—depend on the distribution of the measured construct in the sample providing the data. If the sample is truly representative of the population from which it is drawn, then these sample statistics can be taken as reasonable estimates of population values. However, where sample distributions of the measured traits differ markedly from population distributions, sample statistics may be poor descriptors of population values. This problem led to the development of *latent trait theory*, currently known as *item response theory*, and procedures for developing relatively sample-free estimates of population values.

FACTOR ANALYSIS

Factor analysis identifies and describes underlying dimensions or factors that produce correlations between scores. So do related procedures such as cluster analysis, linkage analysis, canonical correlation, and several methods of multidimensional scaling. All such procedures are based on the idea that variables with similar patterns of correlates are pretty much the same. They provide answers to the questions, "How many dimensions are combined or confounded in the measure at hand?" or "What dimension or dimensions account for the variance in the measure?" A *dimension* in this context is a *construct*. Dimensionality is implied because some people may "have" less or more of the construct than other people. Measurement implies unidimensionality of constructs, a somewhat elusive concept. A dimension may be broad, such as intelligence, or more restricted, such as perceptual speed, or very narrow, such as any one of the 120 factors of mental ability postulated by Guilford (1959).

Elementary Concepts

In principle, factor analysis identifies dimensions by finding clusters of highly correlated variables, which are minimally correlated with other clusters of variables. All of these methods, from the simplest to the most complex, begin with a set of variables, all measured in the same sample of people, and analyze a resulting matrix of correlations or covariances.[1]

It is useful to visualize data collection in a data matrix in which each cell contains a quantified observation. A three-dimensional data matrix is shown in Fig. 6.1. In it, variables are the columns, individual people are the rows, and occasions are the successive layers from front to back. A correlation matrix can be computed for any slice of the data matrix. We can compute correlations of test scores across persons, that is, between the columns of the face of the matrix. We could also compute correlations between persons across tests (i.e., between the rows of the face of the matrix), clustering people rather than tests. Or we could correlate scores over occasions. Any such matrix of correlation coefficients can be the basis for a factor analysis.

Some caveats apply. Observations (measures) should be reliable. There should be enough of them to permit reliable correlation coefficients. And (unless using more complex procedures than decribed here) the concept of linear correlation must make sense. To clarify the latter points: If several scores of a person are correlated across occasions, there must be enough occasions for reliable correlation and there must be some reason to think that a linear trend exists over occasions—that scores go up or down linearly, or do not change. If correlations are based on only a few observations, or if there is reason to believe that scores will change systematically over the time span involved, factor analysis is inappropriate. To be

---

[1]The sample does not have to be people; objects, animals, procedures, or other entities can be sampled. One might collect a large sample of work products, measure specified characteristics of them, and correlate the measures. The resulting matrix can be factor analyzed to identify basic dimensions of the products, perhaps for evaluating them.

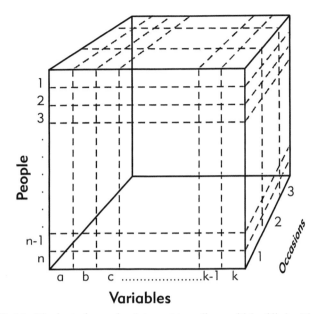

Variables

FIG. 6.1. The basic form of a data matrix; cells would be filled with the scores obtained from each of *n* people on each of four tests on four different occasions.

blunt, the data are bad data, and the result of any analysis of bad data would smell equally bad.

A typical correlation matrix is between variables. An atypically small one for illustrative purposes is shown in Table 6.1. These variables might be four different tests; each cell in the matrix shows the correlation coefficient computed for any pair of them, such as the correlation of .62 between Tests A and B.

It is easier to understand what happens in factor analysis if we work backwards from a solution, that is, from the case where underlying, latent factors have been identified and the contribution of each to scores on each test is known, as in Fig. 6.2. In this example, Test A should correlate well

TABLE 6.1
Correlation Matrix Showing Hypothetical
Relationships Among Four Tests

	A	B	C	D
A	—	.62	.63	.15
B		—	.52	.00
C			—	.17
D				—

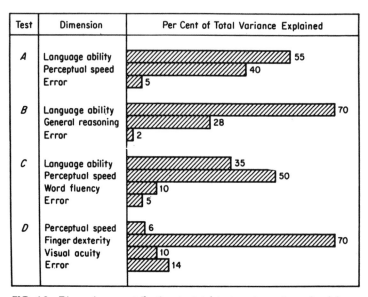

Test	Dimension	Per Cent of Total Variance Explained
A	Language ability	55
	Perceptual speed	40
	Error	5
B	Language ability	70
	General reasoning	28
	Error	2
C	Language ability	35
	Perceptual speed	50
	Word fluency	10
	Error	5
D	Perceptual speed	6
	Finger dexterity	70
	Visual acuity	10
	Error	14

FIG. 6.2. Dimensions contributing to total test variance in each of four hypothetical tests. From Guion (1965).

with Test B because a big part of the total variance in each is due to individual differences in language ability. The correlation between Tests A and C may be even higher; more of the total variances from these tests stem from common dimensions—in this case, two of them. Test D correlates only slightly with A and C (only small common sources of variance) and not at all with B (because they measure nothing in common). Error, of course, refers to the unreliable component of scores attributed to random error which, by definition, should be uncorrelated across the four tests.

This backward approach is, of course, unreal. In practice, we know only the correlations between the tests and we draw inferences about the factorial structure of the tests from those correlations. A matrix of correlations for such tests is shown in Table 6.1. Actually, the matrix in Table 6.1, although based on Fig. 6.2, would not allow us to know the full structure of these tests. In a matrix this small, one can simply look at the correlations and know that Tests A, B, and C are all measuring the same thing to some degree, and that Test D does not measure it. Knowing something about these tests, we can simply look at the matrix and draw some inference about the nature of that "same thing." If Test A is a general mental ability test, B is a vocabulary test, and C is a test of reading speed, these tests obviously have a common requirement that test takers understand verbally expressed ideas. It is therefore plausible to infer that the ability to satisfy this requirement is one underlying cause of the correlations observed; it can be tagged "language ability."

The matrix is too small, and merely looking at it is insufficient. In factor analysis, at least two variables, and preferably more, should be included in the matrix for each factor anticipated. Because three of these tests, according to Fig. 6.2, require at least some perceptual speed, an actual factor analysis would identify perceptual speed as a factor. General reasoning ability, word fluency, finger dexterity, and visual acuity are also sources of variance in the matrix, but each of these influences scores on only one test, and factor analysis of this matrix could not identify them. Although I specified them as systematic sources of variance in creating the example, factor analysis of such an inadequate matrix would treat them only as sources of error variance—as if the variance they produce were random. At a minimum, four more tests would have to be included in the set for these factors to be identified.

Cluster Analysis Methods

Elementary Linkage Analysis. The simplest of all clustering methods is elementary linkage analysis, completed in a very short time with nothing more elaborate than a correlation matrix and a pencil (McQuitty, 1957). A crude, unsophisticated procedure, it is rarely used in the age of computers. It is nevertheless a useful first approximation to a factor solution, helpful in planning a full-scale factor analysis from pilot study data.

Nonhierarchical Cluster Analysis. More formal methods of cluster analysis exist (see, e.g., Aldenderfer & Blashfield, 1984; Tryon & Bailey, 1970) and computer programs have been written for many of them. Cluster analysis was seen early by its inventor, Robert Tryon, as a "poor man's factor analysis" (Tryon & Bailey, 1970, p. vii). The basic idea is that variables measuring the same thing not only correlate well, but they tend to have the same patterns of correlations with other variables. If one draws a profile on translucent paper showing how well a given test correlates with each of the other tests in a set, and superimposes that profile on one for another test similar in internal structure, the two profiles will be quite congruent. If they are not, the two tests measure different things.

This visual look-and-see approach is easy enough with only a few variables. It is progressively more difficult for larger correlation matrices, requiring computational aids (Thomas, 1952; Tryon & Bailey, 1970). Cluster analysis, at whatever level or method, classifies cases (variables, people, or other entities, depending on the content of the basic data matrix). Every case is assigned to a class or cluster, or it is classified as a misfit, belonging with no other case. The usual methods treat the various clusters or classifications as mutually exclusive; in this sense they are all at a common level of inclusiveness, hence nonhierarchical.

Hierarchical Cluster Analysis. In hierarchical cluster analysis, a preliminary set of mutually exclusive clusters may be identified by similar profiles of correlational patterns, but they may be subsequently combined or have additional variables added to them to form larger, more inclusive clusters (Anderberg, 1973; Ward & Hook, 1963). A hierarchical analysis combines individual cases (people, objects, jobs, or whatever is being clustered) into small clusters, then combines small clusters into larger ones, and at ever higher levels keeps combining clusters until all have been subsumed under one grand heading as shown in Fig. 6.3.[2] The ordinate in such a display is some measure of cluster homogeneity. For simplicity, Fig. 6.3 shows only an undefined scale representing profile distances, but a standard index, such as a ratio of within-group variance to between-group variance, could be the ordinate in a given study.

The researcher must decide how many clusters best describe the data; it is necessarily a judgment call, albeit with help from statistical criteria set in advance. The usual rule seeks the smallest number of clusters that will assign all (or most) cases to acceptably homogeneous categories. Defining acceptable requires a trade-off of homogeneity within clusters and differentiation between clusters. Statistical decision rules can help, but researcher judgment remains the basis for the decision.

In Fig. 6.3, horizontal dotted lines are drawn at points *a*, *b*, *c*, and *d*. If the researcher thinks clusters should be tight (i.e., within-profile distances should be very small), the decision might correspond to level *a*. At this level, four clusters are identified: Cases B, C, and D; Cases E and F; Cases H, I, and J; and Cases K and L. Cases A, G, and M through R do not fit within any of the four; they are "isolated" cases, having insufficient similarity to other cases. Making Level *b* the decision point produces three less homogeneous clusters but reduces the number of isolates. Level *c* also defines three clusters, but it permits the isolates of Level *b* to enter clusters, making them more heterogeneous. Level *d* combines two of the Level *c* clusters to form one that is quite heterogeneous; it offers no advantage over Level *c*.

Cluster analysis is usually an iterative procedure. One difference between hierarchical and nonhierarchical clustering is that, in the latter, individual cases are free to move from cluster to cluster in successive iterations. In hierarachical clustering, the original clusters tend to be fixed.

---

[2]Figure 6.3 began with actual data, but they have been corrupted here for simplification and illustration.

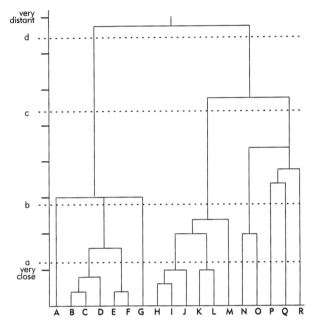

FIG. 6.3. A cluster tree for hierarchical cluster analysis. The ordinate may
be a measure of profile distances or other measure of cluster homogeneity.
Variables (or cases) are identified only by letter. Vertical lines from a letter
to the horizontal lines connecting it to another case show relative similarity
of profiles.

Multiple Factor Analysis

Few standard, universally accepted and used measurement instruments
exist in psychology. If someone develops a way to measure some new
form of reasoning, someone else will see a somewhat different and presumably better way to do it. If both get used a lot, someone else will see
a reason for still a third version. Or perhaps different investigators have
similar ideas about a construct but give it different names and develop
their own ways to measure it. Worse, different measures of a popular
construct, all under the same name, may not correlate at all well. For
whatever reasons, there is a great deal of redundancy in psychological
measurement, and it does not always occur where it might be expected.

Multiple factor analysis is a means by which redundancy in a set of
measures can be reduced to a smaller set of clearly distinguishable variables called factors (or components). As in cluster analysis, factor analysis
assumes that a high correlation between two sets of measures is caused

by some a common source of systematic variance—a latent construct called a factor. Unlike the clustering methods, factor analysis tries to isolate the factors represented in a matrix of correlations, even factors that influence measures in different clusters.

It is not my purpose to show how factor analyses are done or to discuss fully their many purposes; see Kerlinger (1979) or Bobko (1990) for introductions or Pedhazur and Schmelkin (1991) for more comprehensive and advanced treatment. It *is* my purpose to offer clues for understanding reports of factor analytic research.

Tables of Factor Loadings

Results of factor analytic research are presented in tables of factor loadings.[3] These tables show the hypothetical correlation of each measure with each of the underlying, or latent, factors identified by the analysis; such a correlation is called a *factor loading*. Table 6.2 is an example from a small study. It identifies the variables (tests), the resulting factors (by Roman numerals) accounting for parts of the total variance among the measures, the factor loadings of each variable on each factor, a value h^2 (to be discussed later) and a reliability estimate for each variable. I describe this study and its implications, partly because I know it well, and partly because it includes features I consider necessary.

The Study. The data in Table 6.2 are very old (Bourassa & Guion, 1959); they predate computerized analyses, but they illustrate some aspects of factor analytic research more simply than do larger, more modern studies. First of all, they illustrate research designed to answer specific questions, not research that is merely hunting around to see what's in a matrix. Technically, this was an exploratory study, not a confirmatory one, but it posed and tested specific hypotheses about the factors explaining variance in the set of variables.

Even more than in other kinds of research, well-designed factor analytic research has always been built on prior findings. Prior research had distinguished two dexterity factors, a hand dexterity factor involving arm and hand motions, and a finger dexterity factor involving finer movements of the fingers but not arm movement (French, 1951). Experience with transistor assemblers suggested that tweezer use might be an independent, even finer form of dexterity. Moreover, it was noted that a dexterity test requiring tweezers correlated highly with visual depth

---

[3]For most methods of factor analysis there can be two such tables. One of these is the result of the basic computations which, in many commonly used factor analytic methods, depends on an arbitrarily chosen starting point. The other consists of rotated factor loadings. Rotation, discussed in the next section, gives more interpretable information.

TABLE 6.2
Rotated Factor Loadings

Variable	I	II	III	IV	V	h^2	r_{xx}
Minnesota turning	.61	.05	−.06	.27	.14	.47	.85
Minnesota placing	.73	.12	−.06	.17	.18	.61	.88
Dowel manipulation	.60	−.04	.14	.33	.33	.60	.87
Purdue Pegboard, nonpreferred	.68	.17	.13	.03	.01	.51	.80
Purdue Pegboard, both hands	.63	.06	−.02	−.17	.17	.46	.87
O'Connor Finger Dexterity	.50	−.03	.09	.14	.43	.46	.83
Placing test, finger	.28	.08	.05	.25	.26	.22	.49
O'Connor Tweezer Dexterity	.22	.05	.34	.17	.42	.37	.85
Pin moving	.32	.10	.00	.41	.31	.38	.68
Bowling Green Tweezer	.37	.04	.20	.00	.53	.46	.71
Placing test, tweezer	.37	.03	.28	.37	.15	.38	.82
Depth Perception, Ortho-Rater	.18	.57	.12	.04	.08	.38	.88
Depth Perception II	.00	.53	−.09	.05	.34	.41	.57
Near acuity, left eye	−.19	.62	−.08	.14	.40	.61	.90
Near acuity, right eye	−.08	.65	.00	.16	.36	.58	.86

Note. From Bourassa and Guion (1959). Reprinted with permission.

perception. Although French (1951) had excluded vision from the dexterity factors, we (i.e., Bourassa & Guion, 1959) believed that vision was involved in the dexterity demands of ordinary work. The study was based on two hypotheses: (a) that a tweezer dexterity factor could be identified that differs from either hand or finger dexterity, and (b) that visual factors and psychomotor factors would be correlated. Specifically, we believed that visual factors (depth perception and near point visual acuity) would be more highly correlated with dexterity as the muscle movements became finer, that is, least with hand dexterity and most with tweezer dexterity. Although the study was driven by these hypotheses, they received no support. Expected factors did not emerge, and those that did emerge were not correlated. All in all, it was a thorough disconfirmation of our hypotheses; more sophisticated methods could not have disconfirmed them more emphatically.

The study illustrates how the variables for factor analysis can be chosen. At least two tests are required to define a factor; the tests in this study had frequently defined one of the four factors established in prior research. When a previously unknown factor is proposed, new measures must be developed and pilot tested for fit to the expected characteristics of the factor. Four tests requiring tweezer use, three of which were developed for this study, were intended to define tweezer dexterity.

Factor Rotation. The term "rotation" is somewhat archaic, based on pre-computer procedures. Thurstone (1947) developed a factor analysis method known as the centroid method; in it, the starting point was arbitrary; different people analyzing the same matrix from different starting points would have different resulting factor loadings. Rotation made the factor loadings less arbitrary, more consistent across researchers, and more interpretable.

Given a center, or origin, Cartesian coordinates show the correlation between any two variables as the cosine of an angle; like correlation, a cosine varies between ±1.0. The cosine of 90° (or 270°) is zero, so a right angle represents zero correlation; two variables or factors described with a right angle (or a zero correlation) are said to be orthogonal. The cosine of 0° is 1.0, representing perfect positive correlation; an angle of 180° represents a negative correlation of –1.0. Intermediate correlations, positive or negative, can be depicted by intermediate angles. Because the centroid method provides an origin for such graphic depiction, a table of factor loadings can be transformed to charts, two factors at a time placing each variable in its appropriate relation to each factor (the Cartesian axes) and to each of the other variables. Placing the coordinates on translucent paper gives an overlay that can be rotated to provide a less arbitrary placement of the axes. For example, one may place axes where the resulting loadings will be as close as possible to either zero or 1.0—a rule that maximizes variance of loadings on a factor, known as *varimax* rotation. Other rotational rules have been used. The advantage of rotation is to provide a more easily interpreted structure.

The angle separating two axes describes the correlation of the factors they represent. If the rotation keeps the axes at 90° angles, it depicts uncorrelated factors, and is known as *orthogonal* rotation. Graphic rotation can also move one axis at a time so that angles between axes are permitted to vary; this is known as *oblique* rotation and permits interpretation of factors as correlated. The degree of correlation may stem from characteristics of particular samples of situations, subjects, or measures chosen for research; the inferred correlations may therefore be unreliable. However, a matrix of correlations among oblique factors can be factor analyzed to look for a higher level of generality, or *second-order factors*.

The point was demonstrated in the Thurstone (1947) box study. Twenty measurements were taken from each of a sample of boxes; they included functions of the basic three dimensions, such as the square of the width, the perimeter of a side, or the diagonal across an end. Correlations were computed and the resulting matrix was analyzed. Three basic dimensions resulted—length, width, depth. Clearly, these are dimensions of physical space and may be considered independent, that is, uncorrelated (orthogonal). However, oblique rotation showed them to be *not* independent. Moreover, considering the logic of the study, we really should not expect them to be. The study was based, not on physical objects in general, but on boxes. Boxes have an expected shape. Most of them, opened from the top, have less depth than width, less width than length. Because of this common tendency, the three dimensions are correlated in a population of boxes.

Ordinarily, orthogonal rotation is preferred because it clarifies differences between factors and because it yields more reliable factor loadings than the oblique loadings influenced by sampling idiosyncracies. Often, however, oblique rotation can help avoid overinterpretation of factors and their distinctions. I often recommend oblique rotation. If the factors are truly distinct, then the estimated correlations are trivial, and orthogonality can be accepted. If only orthogonal rotation is done with data where factors are in fact correlated, the only hint of factor correlation is in high loadings on several factors for many measures. The choice may not be purely arbitrary. Although the logic of the Bourassa and Guion (1959) study demanded oblique rotation, the data did not conform; the factors turned out to be orthogonal despite the hypothesis.

Although the word "rotation" continues to be used, rotation by manipulating charts is not. Most statistical packages for computers offer several approaches for either orthogonal or oblique rotation. Programs for hierarchical factor analysis avoid some of the pitfalls of oblique rotation and subsequent analysis of factor correlations.

Factor Loadings. Factor loadings are interpreted like other correlations; squaring them gives a coefficient of determination. The loading of "Minnesota turning"[4] on Factor I in Table 6.2 is .61; the coefficient of determination is about .37. That means that about 37% of the total variance in scores on that test is due to variance in Factor I. Almost none of the variance on this test can be attributed to Factor II.

The nature of a factor is inferred from the measures with the highest loadings and is limited by (i.e., not related to) the characteristics of those with low loadings. Naming or otherwise interpreting factors is somewhat subjective. In interpreting a factor, variables may be listed in the order of their factor loadings down to some arbitrary value considered significant enough to use (usually .30), as in Table 6.3. The two factor loadings in italics mean that these are the highest loadings on any factor for these two tests. This fact, plus the further fact that these two tests are at or near the top of the list gives them special importance in interpreting the factor.

Bourassa and Guion (1959) named Factor V *Visual Feedback* and defined it as the ability to use fine visual cues in the manipulation and placement of small objects. The three tests at the top of the list all called for placing small objects into holes. Two of them, but not all three, called for the use

---

[4]The Minnesota Rate of Manipulation Test has two parts, turning and placement. In one the objects (comparable in size to checkers) are turned over; in the other, they are placed in holes in a board.

TABLE 6.3
Variables With Significant Loadings on Factor V

Test	Loading
Bowling Green Tweezer Dexterity Test	.53
O'Connor Finger Dexterity Test	.43
O'Connor Tweezer Dexterity Test	.42
Ortho-Rater, near acuity, left eye	.40
Ortho-Rater, near acuity, right eye	.36
Depth perception	.34
Dowel manipulation	.33
Pin moving	.31

Note. From Guion (1965).

of tweezers. The inclusion of a nontweezer test in this list, and the failure of a tweezer placing test to appear (a factor loading of .15 considered nonsignificant) mean that the factor is not the hypothesized tweezer dexterity factor. The inclusion of the three vision tests, and the fact that the dexterity tests with significant loadings required examinees to look closely at the objects in picking them up and placing them, made visual feedback a better interpretation of the skill represented by this factor. Note that this example shows how nonsignificant loadings can contribute to understanding constructs.

No such factor had been identified in previous factor analyses, so it was identified as "tentative," subject to verification in further research. So far as we know, no such research has been done, and, even though this is an old study, the lack of confirming or disconfirming evidence means that the factor can neither be accepted nor rejected for a taxonomy of sensorimotor skills.

Consider further the columns headed III and IV. These were considered spurious and not interpreted. Factor III has only one loading above .30; there are three for Factor IV, but they form no discernible pattern.

Communality and Uniqueness. The total variance, s^2, of any variable in a correlation matrix is a function of (a) sources of variance shared with other variables in the same set and (b) variance due to sources unique to the variable (i.e., not found in any of the others in the matrix):

$$s^2 = h^2 + u^2 \qquad (1)$$

where h^2 is the *communality* of the variable and u^2 is its *uniqueness*. Communality is the proportion of the total variance explained by correlations of a variable with other variables in the set studied, the sum of the squares of all of its factor loadings. In Table 6.2, for example, the communality of the Minnesota turning test is .47; 47% of its total variance is explained by the factors identified in the study.

The remaining 53% of its total variance is not common to other measures in the battery; it is unique. Part of its uniqueness is due simply to unreliability; random errors of measurement, according to the reliability estimate in Table 6.2, contribute about 15% of the total variance. That leaves 38% of the total variance as systematic specific factor variance, unique to this one test, in this battery.

For the Minnesota placing test, the communality is only .22; 78% of its variance is unique. Is variance in these Minnesota test scores sufficiently explained? It is in answering this question that the reliability estimate is important. For the turning and placement tests, the unique variance not explained by the factors identified in this analysis, is 53% and 78%, respectively. These seem quite different, at least until we look at the reliability estimates. 85% of the turning score variance is systematic, potentially explainable. For the placing test, only 49% is systematic. The analysis has identified factors accounting for 55% (.47/.85) of the *explainable* variance in the turning scores and for 45% (.22/.49) in the placing test scores. Clearly, these tests do not differ as much in unidentified sources of systematic variance as the communalities alone might suggest. Factor analyses rarely account for large proportions of systematic variance, especially in psychomotor tests. There are always unrecognized, untapped sources of variance in the matrix analyzed.

Some uniqueness may stem from failure to include in the study variables tapping the same sources of variance. Look again at Fig. 6.2. 70% of the variance of Test D was due to variance in finger dexterity, a source of variance not present in any of the other three tests. The only source of communality in that test—in this four-test battery—comes from the 6% of its variance attributable to perceptual speed. However, adding a fifth test, one measuring finger dexterity in a different way, would substantially increase communality. The same logic applies to the Minnesota tests.

Factor scores are based on factor loadings. A person's factor score is computed by multiplying the score obtained on every test in the study by its factor loading and summing the products. If a factor loading for a test is very small, but positive, the test score adds something to the factor score, even if not much; if the loading is negative, a nonzero score reduces the factor score. This is very different from a common procedure for developing scores to represent factors: simply adding the scores on all variables with significant factor loadings (known as *unit-weighted scores* for the factor). The difference between a factor score and the more common unit weighted score is not trivial. Factor scores maintain maximum independence between the dimensions; those based on unit weighting are usually correlated, even when rotation was orthogonal, possibly confusing interpretations.

Confirmatory Factor Analysis

In the early days (sometimes, unfortunately, even still), some people factor analyzed available data sets with no discernible ideas about the factors they might find. From the beginning, however, the best factor analytic research began with hypotheses about constructs, how they might be measured, or what other constructs ought to be different. A battery of measurement instruments would be assembled and include reference or marker variables with a history of high loadings on relevant factors. It would be administered to people in an appropriate sample, analyzed, and the results compared subjectively to prior expectations. But even a hypothesis-testing factor analysis used an exploratory method—just as if the researcher had started with nothing more than curiosity.

Confirmatory factor analysis methods are now available. The research plan specifies expected factors; it may also specify zero loadings for some test-factor combinations, nonzero loadings for others; and it may specify factor correlations. Method factors can be hypothesized (and therefore controlled for) separately from substantive factors. The fit of data to an a priori model confirms (or disconfirms) the model. This is, of course, like other statistical hypothesis testing. The model may be confirmed only in the sense that the null hypothesis is not rejected. That is, one does not really *confirm* the correctness of a model, one only fails to *disconfirm* it. Nevertheless, confirmatory factor analysis is an important research model, helping in the design and interpretation of research.

GENERALIZABILITY THEORY

Generalizability theory examines the limits or boundaries within which test score meanings generalize. Any assessment may be influenced by the particular set of circumstances and is useful only if the assessment generalizes to other circumstances (e.g., other times, other behavior samples, other test forms, other raters or interviewers). An assessment is a valuable aid to decisions only if inferences drawn from it are like those drawn under other conditions.

Many kinds of generalization are important. Cook and Campbell (1979) referred to *external validity* to mean the problem of generalizing research findings to "target" populations of people, settings, tasks, or times. Schmidt and Hunter (1977) referred to meta-analysis results as "validity generalization" when they indicated that research findings in one set of studies can be generalized to settings not included in that set. Cronbach, Gleser, Nanda, and Rajaratnam (1972) developed generalizability theory to describe principles and procedures for testing the limits of the generalizability of inferences from trait measurements.

Here I present only the basic logic and some simple designs. More detailed discussions may be found in Cronbach et al. (1972), a primer prepared by Brennan (1992), the reliability chapter by Feldt and Brennan (1989), or the general article by Shavelson, Webb, and Rowley (1989).

Elements of the Theory

Generalizability theory is a measurement theory as well as a method in that it provides both a conceptual and statistical framework for evaluating the dependability of measures. It provides evidence for evaluating how well an attribute is measured. It extends classical test theory by elaborating on potential sources of error. It also contributes to construct validation by determining the influence of unwanted sources of systematic error.

Assessments are done in given sets of circumstances—by a certain person, on a particular day or time of day, in a certain room or other location, with specific ambient temperature or noise or distractions, and so on. If score interpretations were limited to any single combination of these specific circumstances, they would have little interest to anyone; such circumstances are usually expected to be matters of indifference, variables that have at most a trivial influence on the outcome. We want to generalize the assessment inference to the one we would have made from assessment of the person on another occasion, in another setting, or with another administrator or ambience.

Classical test reliability estimation inquires into limited kinds of generalizability. Internal consistency coefficients refer to generalizing across the various items or observations. Stability coefficients tell whether inferences generalize across testing occasions. A generalizability study can answer both kinds of questions, and without the two-occasion limit, by collecting data in an experimental design for analysis of variance. It simultaneously estimates variance attributable to different sources, such as persons, items, and occasions. If all items are used for all persons on all experimental occasions, the design is "fully crossed," expressed as $p \times i \times o$, and shown by Venn diagrams as part a of Fig. 6.4. Part b depicts a design in which two (presumably equivalent) sets of items are used on two occasions, as if using equivalent forms in a test–retest reliability study. Items would be "nested within" occasions, expressed as a $p \times i{:}o$ design. These are only two of the many different designs one might choose for studies of two sources of variance other than the traits of the people assessed. Clearly, either design provides more information than does a single reliability coefficient.

Basic Concepts in a Hypothetical Application

Consider a behavioral checklist for use in interviews to assess friendliness, as required for receptionists and other positions calling for extensive public contact. As we spell out what we mean by friendliness in this

(a)

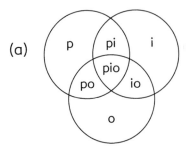

(b)

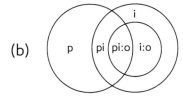

FIG. 6.4. Two designs for person, item, and occasion generalizability studies.

context, our "theory of the attribute" is that friendly people consistently smile when greeting others, give them undivided attention, and show interest in them or sympathy with their problems. It excludes emotional involvement with others, long-term relationships, or altruism. In a group meeting, job experts might add to the theory of friendliness for the job at hand, but these are enough to show how an interviewer's checklist might be structured.

Sources of Irrelevant Variance. The theory implies consistent behavior, perhaps behavior shown throughout the working day. Morning grouches may be more likely to show some of the checklist behaviors in the afternoons, and morning chirpers may tend more to show them in mornings, but the time of day of the interview should be irrelevant. Also irrelevant, if the attribute is to be measured well, is the observer or interviewer who completes the checklist. A generalizability theory analysis can be used to determine the influence of both relevant and irrelevant sources of variance. Checklist behaviors of the people observed should account for most of the variance in the assessments; time of day and the individual observer should account for none, or for very little, of it.

Variance Components. A generalizability study of checklist scores examines specified sources of variance. The example includes four obvious sources of variance: individual differences among the people observed (p), checklist items (i), time of day (t), and observer (o)

completing the checklist. A generalizability study would be designed as one would design an experiment. We might, for example, choose a fully crossed design for the study, $p \times i \times t \times o$. Perhaps 20 people might each be interviewed twice, once in the morning, once in the evening; the interviews might be taped so that maybe six observers might complete eight item checklists. Other designs might eliminate the need for taping, but this one gives us 20 people, eight items, two times of day, and six observers. The design is fully crossed in that each of the 20 people is interviewed at both times and is rated on all eight items by all six observers. The 20 people are the *objects of measurement*. People are usually the objects of psychological measurement, but other objects of measurement might be jobs or work products. The other elements of the design (items, time, and observers) would be called factors in most discussions of analysis of variance, but in generalizability theory they are known as the *facets* of the design to avoid confusion with the factors of factor analysis. Each facet in the design has two or more *conditions* or levels: eight items, two time periods, and six observers. (We do not ordinarily refer to the object of measurement as a facet in the design; if we did for this illustration, a people facet would be said to have 20 conditions.)

There are more than four sources of total variance: the four main effects, p, i, t, and o; six two-way interactions, pi, pt, po, it, io, and to; four three-way interactions, pit, pio, pto, and ito; and the residual four-way interaction confounded with random error, $pito$. The statistical significance of any single source is of no interest in generalizability analyses; the question of interest is, how much of the total variance is attributable to each source of variance?

If the attribute is well-measured, that is, if the inferences from the checklist scores generalize well across the conditions of measurement, most of the total variance will be due to individual differences among the people interviewed. A substantial variance component for time of day might mean that the attribute itself lacks desired stability. A substantial variance component for items would suggest a need for more items or, alternatively, to eliminate or revise some checklist items (although the latter poses a threat to content representativeness). A substantial variance component for observers might suggest a need for observer training or, perhaps, for averaging across a set of observers.[5] (In fact, generalizability analyses include estimates of the numbers of observations needed for acceptable generalizability, analogous to the use of the Spearman-Brown equation.)

---

[5]Averaging treats the set of observers as a fixed facet so that decision makers can generalize only for this set. That is not a disadvantage; in fact, it is wise to evaluate the observers at hand without generalizing to a universe of unknown observers.

Sampling. Generalizability theory differs from classical psychometric theory in that classical theory is based on the idea of parallel forms (i.e., with identical "true" score distributions) whereas generalizability theory requires only *randomly parallel* forms, that is, forms based on loosely random sampling from the various levels or conditions of the scorable items. I stress loosely; I am persuaded by Wood (1976, p. 249) that the term is more closely related to the Brunswikian idea of a representative sample than to the more formalized random sampling of probability theory. For the example, occasions should sample realistic interviewing times, not all possible ones.

Universes and Universe Scores. The relevant facets depend on the researcher's definition of a *universe of admissible observations*. The definition is subjective; it depends on the researcher's theory of the attribute. Two different researchers developing similar assessment procedures may have different ideas of things that belong in or lie outside that universe. Conditions of admissable observations include those that the researcher considers matters of indifference. In the example, one researcher might consider time of day irrelevant, but another's theory might treat friendliness as dependent on the time of day. For the former, an observation at any time of the work day is admissible; for the latter, only observations at specified times are admissible. Occasions of observation might be defined in several ways, such as the day of the week or now versus later. In defining a universe of admissible observations for generalizability analysis, the facet conditions to study are those that researchers think should be irrelevant but pose the greatest threats to capturing the meaning of the attribute.

In the example, checklist items define one facet of a universe of admissible observations; they constitute the observations relevant to the researcher's theory of the attribute. Admissable observations must fit the definition of the construct being assessed. Many possible kinds of behavior in an interview might reveal the level of friendliness. Any observable behavior that fits the construct definition is admissible.

Researcher preference may be especially strong in the definition or restriction of the observer facet of the universe of admissible observations. One researcher may think that any reasonably intelligent observer would do and might include volunteers from an introductory psychology class. Another researcher may assume that experience as an interviewer is essential and limit the universe to experienced interviewers, letting it be a matter of indifference which experienced interviewer makes the checklist ratings. Another may restrict the observer facet to actual interviewers, excluding those who only observe tape recordings.

The universe of admissible observations is necessarily broad, including all of the facets that the researcher (whether developer or user of the measurement procedure) wishes to consider matters of indifference. In contrast, Cronbach et al. (1972) identified a different, more restricted concept, the *universe of generalization*, the set of conditions within which a decision maker wants to make generalizations. The universe of generalization might include all of the facets and conditions defining the universe of admissible observations for the measurement process per se, but it is likely to be substantially narrower. It should not be larger. Defining a universe of generalization that goes beyond the universe of admissible observations implies either (a) the testing of a hypothesis, analogous to criterion-related validation, or (b) simply overgeneralization.

Cronbach et al. (1972) distinguished between a *G-study* and a *D-study*. A generalizability study (G-study) investigates facets and conditions of a universe of admissible observations, mainly those that have a bearing on the meaning of scores. A decision study (D-study) investigates facets and conditions involved in decision making, whether decisions about the measurement procedure or about the objects of measurement; it is based on the universe of generalization important for the intended decision making. As in other analyses of variance, a D-study is likely to identify some facets as fixed rather than random. For example, if an organization has only two interviewers for a particular purpose, those two conditions of an interviewer facet are fixed; they exhaust the possible conditions within that organization.

In a D-study, a decision maker might find it useful to obtain estimates of *universe scores* for the objects of measurement. These are somewhat analogous to true scores, without the mysticism. A person's universe score is the mathematical expected value of that person's mean performance over the facets that define the universe. As a result, the person can have as many universe scores as universes defined. A work sample test, for example, may have one universe of generalizability defined by a quality control expert and a different one defined by a production supervisor. The same product can have different universe scores for the two definitions.

Multiple Sources and Concepts of Error

Classical psychometric theory divides the total variance in a set of measures into true score variance and error variance. The idea of "true" score variance stretches the concept of true beyond reasonable limits, and the classical idea of error variance is too simplistic, allowing only for random error. These limits of classical theory have long been recognized, but its users have generally adapted to the linguistic nonsense. As Thorndike (1949) pointed out, we can mean different things by *true* or systematic and *error*, depending on which category we treat a source of variance as fitting. Gulliksen (1950) and Lord and Novick (1968) acknowledged multiple sources and concepts of error within the true score language, but they still referred to two categories. Generalizability theory extends classical theory by methodically considering multiple sources of systematic error, different kinds of error in the estimation of universe scores, and the idea that the purposes of measurement may determine what is considered an error.

Sources of Systematic Error. In the example, many different sources of systematic error can be defined in terms of the several facets of the universes defined. Random error is acknowledged, of course, but multiple sources of systematic error are identified in the universe of admissible observations. If much of the total variance is associated with facets of that universe, specific, nontrivial sources of systematic error are identified. Multiple studies may be needed to cover all facets in a universe of admissible observations, and still further studies may be suggested when ·
a developer or user of the procedure accumulates experience with it and finds previously unrecognized problems.

Errors in Estimating Universe Scores. Estimates of true scores in classical theory are based on regression equations where observed scores are adjusted for regression to the mean:

$$t = X + r_{xx}(X - M_x) \tag{2}$$

where equation components retain earlier meanings. Estimates of universe scores in generalizability theory are also based on regression equations, but necessarily more complex ones. In addition to considering the person's observed score position relative to an overall mean, it must also be considered with reference to the means for the various conditions of the various facets of the universe of generalization. Cronbach et al. (1972, p. 138) offered several alternative equations for different D-study designs. True score estimates are rarely computed when working within classical psychometrics because the observed scores and the estimated true scores are perfectly correlated. Estimates of universe scores, however, are *not* perfectly correlated with obtained scores, largely because of weaker assumptions (e.g., the assumption of randomly parallel forms instead of strictly parallel) and, for some designs, because the necessary slope parameters cannot be determined.

Estimating a specific point value by a regression equation involves some degree of error. In the statistical prediction of a criterion variable, for example, we may compute a standard error of estimate to measure the extent of prediction (estimation) errors. The generalizability theory error of estimate, denoted by ε, is analogous. A universe score is also subject to two other kinds of error, known as *absolute* error and *relative* error. The absolute error is the difference between the observed and universe score, on the original raw score scale, denoted by capital delta, Δ. It is important when decisions are made about people on the basis of domain-referenced interpretations of their own scores (see chapter 11), without reference to their relative standing in a distribution of scores. Relative error is the difference between observed and universe scores expressed in deviation score units, denoted by the lowercase delta, δ. It is important when relative standing is used as the basis for decision, as in norm-referenced measurement (see Shavelson et al., 1989).

In classical theory, errors are assumed uncorrelated. In generalizability theory, the three kinds of error are correlated, but imperfectly; knowing the magnitude of one of them does not shed much light on the others. The relative magnitudes of these errors, however, is known. Absolute error is greater than relative error, and error of estimate is less than either of the other two. The order suggests useful considerations for practice in test use. Domain-referenced interpretations are likely to be less reliable than norm-referenced interpretations; universe score estimates based on regression are likely to be more reliable than observed scores.

The latter assertion applies as well to true score estimates in classical theory. Why, then, are such estimates rarely used in personnel decisions? One reason is the belief that scores for everyone should be interpreted in the same way, with no differentiation of subgroups according to various conditions of measurement. Moreover, the overall rank order of candidates by observed scores is precisely the same as the rank order by estimated true scores. Suppose, however, that the assessment procedure is scored by observer ratings (as in interviews, individual appraisals, or assessment center exercises) and that a generalizability study found a strong variance component for an observer facet. In this case, the classical assumption that error is random does not hold, and estimating universe scores by taking observers into account would provide a different but more reliable rank ordering of people seen by different observers. If the conditions of facets resulted in socially sensitive subgrouping, with most women or minorities in a particular subgroup, the increased merit of estimated scores might not, from a practical point of view, be useful (see Cronbach et al., 1972). Nevertheless, this implication of generalizability theory should not be overlooked.

Error and the Purposes of Measurement. From classical psychometric theory, we have become used to thinking of "the" error of measurement, by which we mean only the random error component (but we frequently do not say so and almost as often do not remember). However, from Thorndike (1949), we know that estimates of a random error variance component always depend on how our research method has treated certain sources of variance. We know also that some sources of variance are not wanted, even though they are not random; these are treated by our methods of reliability estimation as systematic sources of variance, tied to the amorphous concept of "true" scores. Perhaps the greatest advantage of generalizability theory is that it forces serious thought about likely sources of variance, those that should be considered sources of error and those acceptable under the theory of the attribute.

Some Applications of Generalizability Theory

This introduction to generalizability theory has necessarily been brief and incomplete. Two examples may illustrate its usefulness and introduce features not yet mentioned.

Survey Research. An employee survey by Tombaugh (1981) was stimulated by ambiguity in the concept of job involvement; he wrote 64 new items to augment or possibly replace those in the 20-item Lodahl–Kejner Job Involvement Scale (Lodahl & Kejner, 1965). Items were one facet. The questionnaire was administered in group sessions. For some subjects, a company official led the group meetings; for others, the researcher was the group leader. Subjects were nested within administrators, a second facet. Another concern was score stability, so two administrations of the survey were scheduled (an occasions facet). As it turned out, these two occasions were dramatically different. In the interim, (a) 2 months elapsed, (b) wage and salary increases were given, (c) a plant shutdown resulted in 4 to 6 hours daily overtime during the 3 weeks preceding the second occasion, and (d) union contract negotiations had begun. Moreover, the first occasion was on a payday, and the second was midway between paydays. None of these was planned, but the cumulative effect should, it seems, have strengthened any impact of occasion on job involvement scores. Finally, differences in item content were a concern. The 84 items were factor analyzed, and three major factors were identified. These three factors were conditions of a final facet. An alternative analysis used a sample of individual items.

The only substantial variance component was for individual differences among subjects; the variance components for individual items, item factors, administrators, or occasions were zero or very nearly so. Generalizability coefficients were computed (ratio of universe-score variance to the variance of expected scores for the universe of generalization) and were uniformly high when individual items were the final facet; factor scores resulted in slightly reduced generalizability across administrators or occasions or item sets. Tombaugh (1981) concluded that the original 20-item set allowed highly generalizable, internally consistent inferences.

Estimating Required Numbers of Observations. A single observation may not be adequate, but how many observations—samples of behavior—are enough? Ratings might be obtained from a single rater, but can one have confidence in ratings by just one rater? If not, how many are needed? In evaluating the job content relevance of test items, how many job experts are required for satisfactory dependability? In classical psychometrics, these questions would be answered using the Spearman-Brown prophecy equation.

A generalizability coefficient is analogous to a reliability coefficient, although systematic variance is more precisely defined and estimated in it. Estimating generalizability coefficients for increased numbers of observations is also analogous to use of the Spearman-Brown equation. The procedure permits an estimate of the increase in systematic variance relative to error in each facet of the desired universe of generalization.

Komaki, Zlotnick, and Jensen (1986) described a behavioral observation form for supervisors. Observers were trained to a specified reliability level. They watched supervisors at work in 30-minute time periods; seven theater managers were observed 27 times, and 20 bank managers were observed 22 times each. Observations were made in a variety of circumstances and settings, and behaviors were tallied in a taxonomy of seven categories based on operant conditioning principles, shown in Fig. 6.5. Solitary activities (doing paperwork, moving to a different location, etc.) had no interactions with others. Some interactions were not work related. Work related interactions with others included discussions of the manager's own performance or those related to work other than performance (for example, telling someone "the computer is down"). Interactions concerning the performance of other people included *antecedent* behavior (e.g., giving instructions or reminders), *monitoring* (getting information about the subordinate's or other person's performance), and *consequences* (behavior evaluating the other person's performance).

Generalizability analysis gave estimates of generalizability coefficients for the various facets in the two locations. Some behavioral categories were observed more dependably than others, as shown in Table 6.4. Monitoring in the theater could be reliably assessed (i.e., with a satisfactory generalizability coefficient) with as few as five observation periods; it required 25 observations for reliable assessments of bank managers. Non-work-related behaviors could be tallied more reliably for bank managers than for those in the theater, but not very well for either.

Studies like these make useful pilot studies for determining how many observers or how many raters or how many observations will be needed

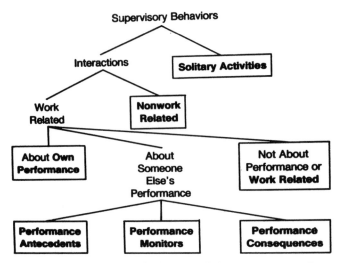

FIG. 6.5. Operant taxonomy of supervisory behavior. From Komaki, J. L., Zlotnick, S., & Jensen, M. (1986). Development of an operant-based taxonomy and observational index of supervisory behavior. *Journal of Applied Psychology, 71,* 260–269. Copyright by the American Psychological Association. Reprinted with permission.

TABLE 6.4
Generalizability Coefficients for Varying Numbers
of Observations of Supervisors in Two Occupations

	Number of Observations		
	5	15	25
Theater			
Consequences	.26	.51	.64
Monitors	.86	.95	.97
Antecedents	.62	.83	.89
Work related	.41	.68	.78
Nonwork related	.08	.20	.30
Solitary	.73	.89	.93
Bank			
Consequences	.32	.58	.70
Monitors	.34	.61	.72
Antecedents	.32	.58	.70
Work related	.49	.75	.83
Nonwork related	.30	.57	.69
Solitary	.60	.82	.88

Note. From Komaki, J. L., Zlotnick, S., & Jensen, M. (1986). Development of an operant-based taxonomy and observational index of supervisory behavior. *Journal of Applied Psychology, 71,* 260–269. Copyright by the American Psychological Association. Reprinted with permission.

in subsequent research. The Komaki et al. (1986) study illustrates the point particularly well. Note that the observations said nothing at all about *effective* supervisory behavior; that was to be the subject of subsequent research. Indeed, Komaki (1986) subsequently used the observational index to test three specific hypotheses about supervisory effectiveness, accepting 20 observation periods as acceptable for her purposes.

ITEM RESPONSE THEORY

Item response theory (IRT), earlier known as latent trait theory, is based on the commonsense idea that people with a lot of a specific ability are more likely to give the right answer to an item requiring that ability than are people with less ability. Those with the most favorable attitudes toward something are more likely to give item responses that reflect a positive attitude than are those with less favorable attitudes. Whatever the nature of the underlying, latent trait measured by an internally consistent set of items, a systematic relationship can be assumed between levels of the trait and the likelihood of a specified response. The relationship can be modeled as a mathematical function, or equation, an *item characteristic curve* (ICC). Knowledge of the equation parameters for the different items can, along with knowledge of a person's responses to the items, lead to an estimate of that person's level of the trait. This is quite different from classical measurement theory, in which an ability test score reflects only the number of items answered correctly (with or without some correction for guessing), with no regard for differing item characteristics.

There are many IRT models, multidimensional and unidimensional, linear and nonlinear, or dichotomous and polychotomous responses (e.g., points on scales or categories in a classification). The basic IRT models assume unidimensional traits, dichotomous responses, and nonlinear item characteristic curves; this introduction to IRT is limited to such models.

Local independence is generally assumed in IRT models, meaning that a person's response to one item is not affected by the response given to any other item. Local independence does not mean uncorrelated. Item responses must be correlated or there can be no internal consistency, let alone unidimensionality. At a specific level of ability, however, item responses should be uncorrelated (Hambleton, 1989, p. 151).

Problems in Classical Theory

Sample-Bound Data. Classical psychometric theory uses two item statistics, a difficulty index and a discrimination index. The difficulty index is usually the proportion of examinees who give the correct or

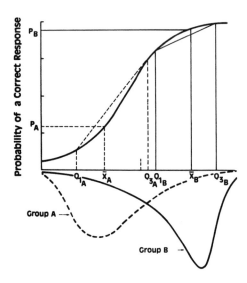

FIG. 6.6. Differences in item statistics in two groups in which the probability of a correct response is the same for given level of ability in both groups. From Guion, R. M., & Ironson, G. H. (1983). Latent trait theory for organizational research. *Organizational Behavior and Human Performance, 31,* 54–87. Reprinted with permission.

keyed response to the item. It is actually the inverse of difficulty; an item answered correctly by nearly everyone is, at least in that sample, an easy item. The discrimination index shows how well item responses are related to total scores; it might be as simple as the difference in proportions giving the correct response in high- and low-scoring halves of a distribution, or it might be a point-biserial coefficient of correlation.

These are statistics; they describe item responses in a specific sample and depend on the distribution of the trait in that sample. In a high ability sample, higher on average than the relevant population, a difficulty index erroneously suggests an easy item; the same item in a low ability sample appears hard. If sample distribution shape and level differ substantially from the population distribution, item discrimination statistics underestimate population values.[6] Samples that differ from each other in the shape and level of the underlying trait distributions yield different item statistics.

The point is illustrated in Fig. 6.6, showing an ICC. The abscissa is a theoretical scale of the latent ability, designated theta, Θ; the ordinate is the probability of a correct response. Distributions of ability in two groups are shown below the abscissa. The mean ability in Group B is much higher than the mean ability in Group A, therefore the proportion of correct responses is much greater; that is, item difficulty statistics are quite different in the two groups. The first and third quartiles (Q_1 and Q_3) in each group are also shown. The line on the curve connecting these

---

[6]In theory, but not often in practice, sample variance may be greater than the population variance, in which case the value obtained may be an overestimate. Even in such a case, a discrimination index is a correlation statistic, subject to the same vagaries of any other correlation statistic relative to the population correlation.

points for either group has a slope proportional to the point biserial correlation, or discrimination index; the slopes differ substantially, so traditional discrimination indices in the two samples also differ. The same total number of cases, divided into two samples, yields two sets of item statistics. Dividing the total into still more groups would yield still more statistics, all differing.

IRT overcomes this problem because of *parameter invariance*. A functional equation is characterized in part by its parameters, the constants of the equation (e.g., the a and b parameters of the linear equation $Y = a + bX$). In IRT computations, simultaneous estimation of item parameters and ability parameters creates ICC equations that are more stable than the characteristics of particular research samples; the item parameters are said to be invariant. In any sample, at any mean ability level, the ICC is essentially the same and specifies the probability that a person of a given trait level, Θ, will give a keyed response; that probability depends on the form and specific properties (parameters) of the curve, not on the number of people at that trait level or at any other. Parameters of the ICC are also independent of the distribution of the trait in the population of interest (Hambleton, 1989). The probability of a correct item response is therefore not a normative statement but an invariant one; groups of subjects with substantially different distributions of the trait will provide substantially the same parameters.[7] It is the invariance of item parameters that makes IRT a substantial advance in psychometric theory.

Parameter invariance permits applications not feasible under classical test theory. Large pools of items can be calibrated (i.e., have individual ICC parameters determined) by giving smaller item sets to different groups of people; it makes virtually no practical difference whether a given item was calibrated in Group A or Group Z. This fact, in turn, makes possible adaptive testing, described in chapter 11, or a more scientifically meaningful approach to adverse impact, described later in this chapter.

Further Problems. Three other classical test theory problems do not plague IRT. First, classical test theory assumed a single standard error of measurement, constant at different score levels. The assumption is generally recognized as a bit absurd; it is logical to expect a greater error of measurement at low ability levels than at high ones. In fact, methods of estimating standard errors for different score ranges have been suggested (Lord & Novick, 1968). Nevertheless, IRT eliminates the

---

[7]In practice, invariance is usually within a linear transformation. Most computer algorithms are such that the parameters calculated would in fact be different in different samples, but a linear equation could transform those in one sample to match those in the other. Correlations between difficulty indices in the two samples, for example, tend to approach unity.

apparent problem by using an information function showing the differing precision of ability estimation at different ability levels.

Second, tests developed by classical methods have no common metric. If one person is assessed with one set of items and another person with a different set, their scores cannot be compared unless the two sets of items are equivalent. In IRT, however, the theta scale provides a common metric regardless of the specific item set used.

Third, test scores in classical test theory ignore patterns of response. Two people may get the same total score (i.e., the same number of items right) and be considered alike in ability by correctly answering different specific items. In IRT, the score (the ability estimate) depends on the parameters of those items answered correctly.

Item Characteristic Curves

An item characteristic curve may have many forms; examples include linear functions, discontinuous functions such as Guttman step functions, and ascending or descending curvilinear functions, either monotonic or non-monotonic. Use of a linear function assumes that, for a given unit change on the ability scale, there is a change in the probability of a correct response—a probability change that is the same for a unit change anywhere on the ability scale. A step function assumes a discontinuity such that the probability of a correct (keyed) response is zero up to a specific trait level, at which it changes to 1.00. A monotonic curve assumes that the probability of a correct response continually increases (or continually decreases) with ability level, but not at a constant rate. People in a low ability range have little likelihood of giving a correct or keyed response, regardless of specific levels of low ability; the slope of the curve in the low range is very slight. In a middle range of ability, the change in probability increases sharply with increasing increments in ability—up to a certain point—after which there are further but progressively smaller changes; that is, the slope of the curve is increasingly steep up to the *point of inflection*, after which it begins to return to a more gradual slope until, at higher score ranges, the slope (and therefore the probability difference) is again trivial. A generally ascending nonmonotonic curve is similar except that, at very high ability levels, the probability of a correct response drops a bit.

What form is appropriate? Lord (1980) considered it an empirical matter. With enough subjects, a first approximation of an ICC can be drawn by plotting conventional item difficulty statistics against total score. In most psychological measurement, the result will look most like the positive monotonic curve. A well-established mathematical model of such a curve is given by the equation for a normal ogive,[8] and much of the early research

---

[8]Most students will have encountered ogives in association with graphs of cumulative frequency distributions.

on IRT problems used that equation. It is, however, a rather complex equation. A simpler one, the logistic function, provides a close approximation to the normal ogive and is the model most commonly used.

Three-Parameter Logistic Model. The 3-parameter logistic equation is

$$p_i(\Theta) = \frac{c_i + (1 - c_i)}{1 + e^{-Da_i(\Theta - b_i)}} \tag{3}$$

where $p_i(\Theta)$ is the probability that one with an ability level, Θ, will give a correct response to item i, where a_i, b_i, and c_i are parameters of the curve, and D is an arbitrary constant (usually set at 1.7 making the resulting curve virtually interchangeable with the normal ogive).

The three parameters in the 3-parameter model are the a, b, and c constants. Values of Θ, however, are additional, fourth parameters in the equation; if there are 500 subjects in the research sample and 20 items, then there are 560 parameters to be estimated: 500 values of theta and the 3 ICC parameters for each of the 20 items. It is easy to see why practical use of IRT had to wait for modern computers and computer programs.

The b parameter is the value of theta, Θ, at the point of inflection where the slope of the curve is at its maximum. In ability testing, it is called the difficulty parameter; the larger the value of Θ, the more difficult the item. The a parameter is a value, expressed in Θ units, proportional to the slope of the curve at the point of inflection. It is called the *discrimination parameter*, the higher values indicating greater discrimination of ability among examinees. The c parameter is the lower asymptote of the curve, the probability of a correct response from a subject of infinitely low ability. In ability testing, it is sometimes (although imprecisely) known as "the guessing parameter." In attitude measurement, it might reflect some sort of response bias (Drasgow & Hulin, 1990). If the value of c is zero, the b parameter is the value of theta corresponding to a probability of a correct answer of .5.

Figure 6.7 shows the 3-parameter ICCs for three different items. Items 1 and 3 are easy items with relatively low values of b; Item 2 is clearly more difficult, requiring a higher level of ability to have a 50–50 chance to answer the item correctly. It is also the most discriminating item, as shown by the steeper slope at its point of inflection. There is, moreover, very little likelihood of getting it right by chance, as indicated by a near-zero value of c. Items 1 and 2 have desirable ICCs in that neither item is unduly easy or unduly hard, neither is easily answered correctly by chance, and both discriminate different levels of ability well along a fairly large range of ability. Item 3 is an interesting item but not one a test developer would want to retain. The probability of a correct answer by chance is high, and the probability of a correct answer is less than

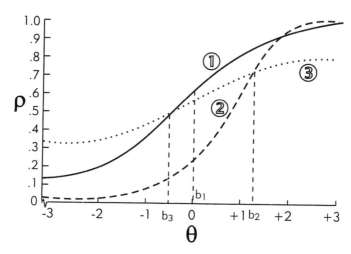

FIG. 6.7. Item characteristic curves for three items.

certain even at the highest ability level. The slope is slight, indicating that the probability of getting it right does not differ much among people of different ability levels. It is probably an ambiguous item.

Parameter invariance is not absolute. For the most commonly used computer programs, the zero point on the Θ scale is set at the sample mean, and the range from −3.0 to +3.0 depends on sample variability; the computed values of the parameters will actually be different for samples differing in mean or variance. The shapes of the ICCs will be congruent, however, and the scale used in one sample can be transformed by a simple linear regression equation to the scale used in the other; parameters set on one scale can be transformed to the other scale. An illustration is shown in Fig. 6.8. A regression equation of $B' = 1.11A + 0.6$ permits the transformation of b parameters in Group A to the scale for b parameters computed in Group B; the correlation for these data is .989—"a good, but not particularly rare, correlation" (Guion & Ironson, 1983, p. 60). In this sense, parameters are said to be invariant within a linear transformation.

The correlations between b parameters calculated in different samples can be expected routinely to exceed .95. Correlations for the other parameters are lower, dipping to .30 and below for the c parameter. The relative unreliability of c estimates is not surprising; the number of cases at the extremely low end of the ability distribution is quite small even in a large sample. For that reason, it is usually recommended that c be set at a common value or constrained not to exceed a value (such as .25 on a four-option multiple choice examination).

Figure 6.8 identifies four items that are outliers, without which the correlation would be still higher. Items circled as a and b are extremely

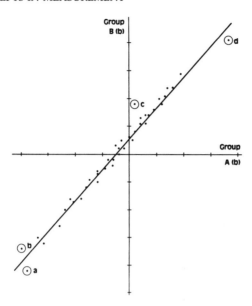

FIG. 6.8. Scatterplot of *b* values for 40 items computed independently in two samples. From Guion, R. M., & Ironson, G. H. (1983). Latent trait theory for organizational research. *Organizational Behavior and Human Performance, 31*, 54–87. Reprinted with permission.

easy, and Item d is extremely hard. Most test developers would consider deleting these items simply because they are so extreme. Item c is different. It is in a middle range of difficulty in both samples, but it is substantially more difficult in Group B than in Group A. Its *b* parameter is *not* invariant; the item functions differently in the two groups. Why? Feasible answers include the possibility that the item is biased against Group B, that it is ambiguous, that some group-related characteristic of test administration was especially important for the item—and others not yet thought of. Whatever the reason, the item does not have an invariant difficulty parameter and would probably be deleted from the test.

Alternative Models. If estimates of a *c* parameter are so unstable, why have them? If guessing or response bias is irrelevant to the trait measured, what value does a *c* parameter have? Questions like these, and the fact that for many measurement purposes the *c* parameter is not theoretically meaningful, have led many investigators to use 2-parameter models, omitting the *c* parameter from Equation 3 by setting it equal to zero. The *a* and *b* parameters are the two ICC parameters estimated.

If parameters like *c* can be ignored, why not ignore another, such as *a*? Some investigators do, and the result is a single-parameter model in which only the difficulty parameter is computed. Figure 6.9 illustrates the difference between the 2-parameter and 1-parameter models. Part a of the figure shows the 2-parameter model with two overlapping ICCs. Item 2 is considered more difficult because its point of inflection is at a higher point on the theta scale. (Note that, because $c = 0$, the value of b corresponds to $p = .5$.) It is also the more discriminating item because it has a steeper slope at that point. However, in the high ability range, the probability of a correct answer to Item 2 is greater than for Item 1, that is, Item 1 is harder for high ability people. Stated differently, Item 1 is harder for some people and Item 2 is harder for others.

In contrast, in the 1-parameter model shown in Part b, the relative difficulty of the two items remains the same; there is (and, under the assumption of equal discriminability, can be) no crossing of the curves.

The 1-parameter model is also known as the Rasch model (see Rasch, 1980) because it was developed independently by Georg Rasch, a Danish mathematician. Rasch's equation has been shown to be transformable to a logistic form in which there is no c parameter ($c = 0$) and a substitution permits the assumption of equal values of a across items (Hambleton, 1989). Despite the mathematical equivalence, proponents prefer to call it

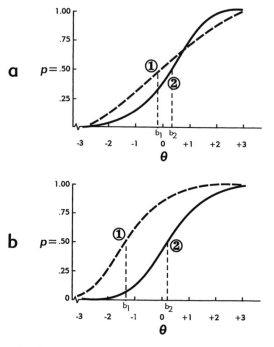

FIG. 6.9. Two-item examples of item characteristic curves under a 2-parameter model (a) and a 1-parameter model (b).

the Rasch model rather than the 1-parameter logistic. Doing so tends to separate it from the family of logistic models.

There seems ample reason to consider it independently. The logic of the Rasch model is not merely that a 3-parameter model can be simplified, but that the Rasch model, and not a 2- or 3-parameter model, truly promotes objectivity in psychological measurement. According to the Rasch model, the unweighted sum of the number of items a person answers correctly

> will contain all the information needed to measure that person and . . . the unweighted sum of right answers given to an item will contain all the information needed to calibrate that item. The Rasch model is the *only* latent trait model for a dichotomous response that is consistent with "number right" scoring. (Wright, 1977, p. 102)

Wright criticized models with a "guessing parameter" as confounding item characteristics and person characteristics. He also criticized 2-parameter models permitting ICCs to cross, contending that it is hardly objective measurement if one item is more difficult than another for some people and easier for others.

Logically, these points are well taken. Empirically, however, some items do tend to promote successful guessing, and items do in fact frequently differ in discrimination power. My view is that the question is an empirical one. Using the 3-parameter model will show whether the two less reliable parameters differ from zero or equality in any significant or important way. If generally not, the logically and mathematically simpler Rasch model may be chosen, and items not conforming to it may be deleted.

Test Characteristic Curves

A *test characteristic curve* (TCC) can be computed or drawn as an average of the ICCs of its individual items. For any given level of Θ, the mean probability of a correct response can be determined across all items; this value is an *expected true score*, defined here as the expected proportion of right answers for people at the Θ level of ability.

Relation of Theta to Expected True Scores. In IRT, the concept of a true score has no special mystery; it is simply an average of probabilities. Both expected true score and theta are theoretical expressions of the same thing, but on two different scales of measurement (Lord, 1980). The ability scale Θ is ordinarily expressed on a scale of normal deviates, not unlike other standard scores, and it is independent of the specific items in the test. The expected true score is ordinarily expressed as the proportion of the items answered correctly; it is dependent on the specific item set.

Everyone with a given level of theta, responding to the same items, has the same expected true score. The relationship between true score and theta is not linear; it follows a function similar to the ogival shape of an ICC. Theta continues to be the abscissa of the plot; the ordinate of the TCC is the expected true score.

If the TCC is steep, meaning that the test as a whole distinguishes well between people of different ability, true score variance is high. If the curve is shallow, the true score distribution will have little variance, and people with similar true scores may differ a good bit on underlying ability. If there is a specific region of ability within which test scores should distinguish ability levels as much as possible, items from a calibrated pool can be chosen for maximum discrimination at the desired levels. That brings us to the information functions.

Test and Item Information Functions. The concept of reliability is superceded in IRT by the concept of item and test information. Reliability remains a useful concept, but IRT offers a better way to think about reliability problems, especially those associated with the classical concept of the standard error of measurement.

Internal consistency is not much of a problem in tests constructed by IRT analyses. Many of the relevant computer programs use iterative models, alternately estimating person and item parameters. If items do not form an internally consistent whole, the iterative processes take a long time to converge, if in fact they ever do. I have had convergence problems in a test with a K–R 20 coefficient in the low .90s; Arnold (1980) and Koch (1983) reported serious problems of item rejection using a graded response model when internal consistencies appeared good. If the models are so sensitive to departures from the assumption of unidimensionality, internal consistency seems assured for instruments developed using them.

In classical test theory, the standard error of measurement (SEM) is a generalized index of the precision of measurement. It is score-based, therefore it depends on the set of items used, and it is a kind of average of the SEMs at all of the different scores within the distribution (or portion of it). IRT indicates the precision of measurement at different ability levels through the *information function*, a function indicating the degree of precision at any given value of Θ. Each ICC has a corresponding information curve; see Fig. 6.10. For any value of Θ, the amount of information (the value of the information function) is proportional to the square of the slope of the item's ICC.

At points on the ICC where the slope is slight, the information level is low. Where the slope is steep, the information level is high. (The actual value of the information function also depends on the conditional variance, pq, at that value of Θ.) Thus, in Fig. 6.10, the information functions

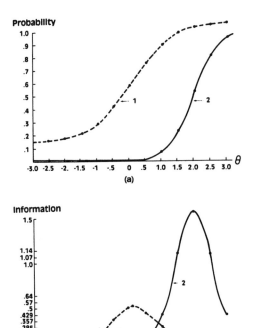

FIG. 6.10. Two item characteristic curves (a) and their corresponding item information curves. From Guion, R. M., & Ironson, G. H. (1983). Latent trait theory for organizational research. *Organizational Behavior and Human Performance, 31*, 54–87. Reprinted with permission.

of both items peak at the point of steepest slope (the point of inflection) of their ICCs, and information is particularly high for Item 2 for high ability people.

Not everyone with a specified level of theta has the same obtained score. We are dealing with probabilities. Even someone with a probability of .9 of giving a correct answer may get it wrong. Even if someone has a low probability of getting an item right, that item may call for information he or she just happens to have. Because of such happenstance, obtained scores are not mere transformations of theta; measurement is imprecise. The extent of imprecision can be estimated from the *test information function*. A test information curve is obtained by summing, not averaging, the item information functions. Test information is inversely proportional to the classical SEM and can be estimated at any given value of Θ. For a Θ associated with a high level of test information, the expected true score will be approximated closely by the obtained score; that is, the obtained score is a more precise measure of ability.

Those interested in more technical detail about IRT may find it in chapters by Allen and Yen (1979), Drasgow and Hulin (1990), or Hambleton (1989) or in books by Hambleton and Swaminathan (1985), Hulin, Drasgow, and Parsons (1983), or Lord (1980).

Applications of Item Response Theory

Validity questions are not removed by using IRT, but finding that items fit an IRT model is pretty good evidence of psychometric validity. It is rather difficult to obtain a set of items that fit the model chosen without having a fairly clear idea of the nature of the construct and without preparing items with that theory of the attribute in mind. It may be assumed, therefore, that most items in an IRT pool do in fact tap the construct to some degree. If the history of the development of the item pool makes that assumption reasonable, then the method can be trusted to weed out items that do not fit the intended construct.

Computerized Adaptive Testing. Think of an examinee on one side of a table and a test administrator, with a very large deck of cards, on the other. Each card has on it a test item and, in ink visible only to the test administrator, the item's b parameter and information level. The administrator chooses an item where $b = 0$. If the examinee answers it correctly, the administrator chooses a second, harder item with a positive b value. If the first answer is wrong, the second item chosen is easier; it has a negative b value. A few more items are similarly chosen to identify the likely region of Θ. A few more items are chosen having maximum information in that region. The result can be a very precise estimate of Θ for that person with only a few, carefully chosen items.

The scenario is unlikely. The idea of someone sitting with a large deck of cards picking out items is, frankly, boring. The scenario is not at all unlikely, however, if the examiner is a computer and the cards are entries in its data bank. A computer program can do, almost instantly, precisely what I have described. The result is called computer adaptive testing (see, e.g., Wainer et al., 1990). This is discussed further in chapter 11.

Rating Scales. The discussion so far has emphasized testing, with occasional wording to recognize that IRT is applicable to other forms of measurement, ratings among them. Models are available for graded scales such as the common 5-point response scales, for nominal response categories (e.g., county of residence), or continuous scales.

Rating scales are used for many purposes. Performance in general may be assessed by performance rating scales completed by a supervisor or peers. Performance on a simulation, work sample, or business game might be rated by observers; observers may be asked to rate products of work samples or simulations. The use of an appropriate IRT model can identify the kinds of observational items that discriminate well and have maximal information at important scale levels.

Analysis of Bias and Adverse Impact. IRT is useful for EEO concerns because item parameter estimation is independent of the ability distribution in the sample studied. If the trait measured is not itself correlated with sex, race, or idiosyncracies of a particular culture, then subgroups based on sex, race, or culture should yield the same invariant ICC parameters within linear transformations. IRT analysis is in fact sometimes used to identify items that function differently in the different subgroups. Differential item functioning is a major topic in the study of bias and is discussed in chapter 10.

Adverse impact was discussed in chapter 4, it needs to be reexamined in the light of IRT principles. The 80% rule for defining adverse impact is subject to many criticisms, among them that it fails to distinguish between adverse impact ratios due to bias and those due to genuine differences in the trait measured.

Using IRT logic, Ironson, Guion, and Ostrander (1982) argued that adverse impact should be defined in terms of the distortion—the overstatement or understatement—of actual subgroup ability differences at the ability level where decisions are made. The basis for their argument lies in the relationship of expected true scores to Θ. If the TCC has a very steep slope, the mean score difference may exaggerate a true subgroup difference in ability; if the slope is very shallow, the mean score difference may understate or hide true ability difference. Four examples of distortions of true differences are shown in Fig. 6.11. In the top half of the figure, two tests are compared; they have identical means but different slopes in the test characteristic curve. Test A, with the steeper mid-range slope, exaggerates true ability differences; Test B with a relatively slight slope, but one which is constant throughout the ability range, minimizes those differences. Both, by the Ironson et al. (1982) definition, have adverse impact. If we are more concerned about adverse impact that exaggerates rather than masks true mean differences, Test B causes little concern. (The slope should not be confused with validity.)

In the lower half of Fig. 6.11, the slopes are the same, but subgroup means differ. Test C is easier than Test D. A test that is easy masks true differences; a hard test exaggerates them.

It is important to note that discussion of subgroup mean differences is merely a convenience, unrelated to a psychometric (or other) definition of adverse impact. Adverse impact depends on the level of scores where decisions are made. If one is trying very hard to maintain or improve workforce quality, the region of decision is in the above average ability

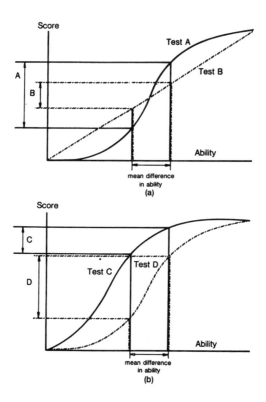

FIG. 6.11. Distorted reflections of true ability differences between groups using different tests when (a) tests are equated for ability but differ in the slopes of their test characteristic curves, and (b) when tests are of unequal difficulty but have test characteristic curves with identical slopes. From Ironson, G. H., Guion, R. M., & Ostrander, M. (1982). Adverse impact from a psychometric perspective. *Journal of Applied Psychology, 67,* 419–432. Reprinted with permission.

range. If one is trying to fill as many positions as possible while maintaining some minimal sense of standards, the region of decision is lower. In either case, it is the distortion of proportional differences at a specific ability or score level that defines adverse impact, not the distortion at the level of group means.

One final comment concerns the practice of comparing measures of quite different traits in assessing adverse impact. Some authors (Cascio & Phillips, 1979; Schmidt, Greenthal, Berner, Hunter, & Seaton, 1977) have compared paper-and-pencil tests with performance tests for adverse impact. To be sure, these researchers were investigating the feasibility of performance testing, and the comparisons were incidental. In an actual decision-making situation, however, such comparisons are not justified. To say that, under the *Uniform Guidelines,* a work sample is a preferable alternative to a test of general mental ability is meaningless because the two tests measure very different constructs. If job analysis shows that the kind of adaptability associated with general mental ability is needed in the job, such as quickness in learning new methods or tools or materials, then evidence of performance using currently known methods or tools or materials is not an appropriate alternative. Or, if experience shows that most applicants must be trained for the job, the work sample is inappropriate even with little adverse impact. The point here, however, is that even two tests of the same construct may have substantially different test characteristic curves and therefore have different kinds and levels of distortion of subgroup ability differences.

Appropriateness Measurement. Levine and Rubin (1979) introduced the term "appropriateness indices" for methods of identifying people whose scores on a test or attitude measure are likely to be invalid—even when the measurement process yields valid inferences for most, even nearly all, cases in the data set (p. 271). Several methods have been proposed for identifying such scores, one of which is based on IRT. This approach has been explored systematically by Drasgow and his associates (e.g., Drasgow, 1982; Drasgow & Guertler, 1987; Levine & Drasgow, 1982).

Various IRT methods of appropriateness measurement were described by Drasgow and Hulin (1990). All of them involve looking at patterns of responses among items in light of the individual's estimated ability level. If a person of relatively low ability gets a lot of right answers to hard items, one might suspect some form of cheating. On the other hand, if a person with a moderately high estimate of ability misses too many items with low difficulty parameter items, carelessness may be suspected.

CONCLUSION

Except for simple factor analysis, little in this chapter has been widely used in personnel selection. Nevertheless, those who willfully remain ignorant of modern psychometric theories and methods condemn themselves to the backwaters of psychological research. Without knowledge of the purposes, points of view, logic, and language of current theories and methods, they cannot keep up with the measurement literature.

Personnel decisions should be based on assessments of characteristics hypothesized to be important to job performance and other relevant behavior at work. The assessments, however made, should be evaluated critically—and often comparatively. Chapters 5 and 6 have focused on the evaluation of tests and other assessment procedures. They have both emphasized the evolving concept of measurement error. It has evolved from a concept of only random error—unreliability—to the broader concept of multiple sources of systematic error. If systematic error is to be taken seriously, traits to be measured must be clearly defined, and methods of assessment must be designed explicitly for them, applying jointly the relevant substantive theory and psychometric methods (Embretson, 1985). Without a theory to define a construct and distinguish it from others, the properties of items cannot be identified, and the descriptive value of the test cannot be evaluated.

The design and evaluation of tests is more demanding than for other methods of assessment. Nevertheless, these principles developed for testing apply equally well to other forms of assessment: constructs must be specified and assessment procedures must be relevant to those constructs. Evaluation of any assessment procedure recognizes that scores lead to descriptive inferences about the people being assessed, and that evaluation is less an evaluation of the assessment tool than of the quality of the inferences drawn from using it.

For many people, the notion of a construct is mysterious, grand to the point of grandiose, and something to be identified only after extensive research. As pointed out in chapter 5, a construct need be little more then an idea about how people differ in some important way, it should have some unity (without necessarily being unidimensional) so that transitivity is conceptually sensible, and it should be distinguishable from other ideas about how people might differ. Consider Cronbach's disavowal of the most highfalutin concepts of construct validity:

> But Lerner (1976) is right when she calls the Cronbach-Meehl (1955) formulation utopian, and says that we need to develop a line of argument reasonable to nonscientists. Construct validation is a better topic for the seminar room than for the public arena; Meehl (1971, 1977), I think, would concur. By 1969 we had realized that a test interpretation is to be validated, rather than a test, and that validating a decision rule differs from validating a descriptive interpretation. Though the developer of a test should help the user in any practical way, validation is the interpreter's responsibility. (Cronbach, 1980, pp. 99–100)

In most respects, the statement is the view presented in these chapters, but I have one difference of opinion. I argue, as shown in chapter 5, that validating the descriptive interpretation (psychometric validity) is first of all the responsibility of the developer; the organizational (interpreter's) responsibility is to validate the decision rule, which in the parochial context of personnel decisions I have called job relatedness. My position is that the predictive interpretation of a score is essentially statistical, not psychometric; a prediction of a future condition, not a description of the present condition at the time of assessment. The distinctions, in my view, are important and necessary for good decisionmaking.

Factor analysis and related approaches to identifying dimensionality in measurement are tools of description. Generalizability analysis is a tool for clarifying description by identifying potential contaminants of trait descriptions and by identifying the limits of generalizability of descriptive statements. Item response theory is a tool for examining psychometric properties of responses to items that have, in Embretson's (1985) words, "substantive properties" relevant to the descriptive construct being measured (p. 4). In short, the topics touched on in chapter 6 augment those of chapter 5 because they have introduced further, perhaps better, ways to evaluate descriptive inferences from numerical results of assessments.

REFERENCES

Aldenderfer, M. S., & Blashfield, R. K. (1984). *Cluster analysis.* Beverly Hills, CA: Sage.

Allen, M. J., & Yen, W. M. (1979). *Introduction to measurement theory.* Monterey, CA: Brooks/Cole.

Anderberg, M. R. (1973). *Cluster analysis for applications.* New York: Academic Press.

Arnold, J. D. (1980). *Measuring managers' desired roles and role demands of their positions.* Unpublished doctoral dissertation, Bowling Green State University, Bowling Green, OH.

Bobko, P. (1990). Multivariate correlational analysis. In M. D. Dunnette & L. M. Hough (Eds.), *Handbook of industrial and organizational psychology* (2nd ed.; Vol. 1, pp. 637–686). Palo Alto, CA: Consulting Psychologists Press.

Bourassa, G. L., & Guion, R. M. (1959). A factorial study of dexterity tests. *Journal of Applied Psychology, 43,* 199–204.

Brennan, R. L. (1992). *Elements of generalizability theory* (2nd ed.). Iowa City, IA: American College Testing Program.

Cascio, W. F., & Phillips, N. F. (1979). Performance testing: A rose among thorns? *Personnel Psychology, 32,* 751–766.

Cook, T. D., & Campbell, D. T. (1979). *Quasi-experimentation: Design and analysis for field settings.* Chicago: Rand-McNally.

Cronbach, L. J. (1980). Validity on parole: How can we go straight? Proceedings of the ETS Invitational Conference, *Measuring achievement: Progress Over a Decade, 5,* 99–108.

Cronbach, L. J., Gleser, G. C., Nanda, H., & Rajaratnam, N. (1972). *The dependability of behavioral measurements: Theory of generalizability for scores and profiles.* New York: Wiley.

Dragow, F. (1982). Choice of test model for appropriateness measurement. *Applied Psychological Measurement, 6,* 297–308.

Dragow, F., & Guertler, E. (1987). A decision-theoretic approach to the use of appropriateness measurement for detecting valid test and scale scores. *Journal of Applied Psychology, 72,* 10–18.

Dragow, F., & Hulin, C. L. (1990). Item response theory. In M. D. Dunnette & L. M. Hough (Eds.), *Handbook of industrial and organizational psychology* (2nd ed.; Vol. 1, pp. 577–636). Palo Alto, CA: Consulting Psychologists Press.

Embretson, S. E. (1985). *Test design: Developments in psychology and psychometrics.* Orlando, FL: Academic Press.

Feldt, L. S., & Brennan, R. L. (1989). Reliability. In R. L. Linn (Ed.), *Educational measurement* (3rd ed., pp. 105–146). New York: American Council on Education; Macmillan.

French, J. W. (Ed.). (1951). Description of aptitude and achievement tests in terms of rotated factors. *Psychometric Monographs, 5.*

Guilford, J. P. (1959). *Personality.* New York: McGraw-Hill.

Guion, R. M. (1965). *Personnel testing.* New York: McGraw-Hill.

Guion, R. M., & Ironson, G. H. (1983). Latent trait theory for organizational research. *Organizational Behavior and Human Performance, 31,* 54–87.

Gulliksen, H. (1950). *Theory of mental tests.* New York: Wiley.

Hambleton, R. K. (1989). Principles and selected applications of item response theory. In R. L. Linn (Ed.), *Educational measurement* (3rd ed., pp. 147–200). New York: American Council on Education; Macmillan.

Hambleton, R. K., & Swaminathan, H. (1985). *Item response theory: Principles and applications.* Boston: Klewer-Nijhoff.

Hulin, C. L., Drasgow, F., & Parsons, C. K. (1983). *Item response theory: Application to psychological measurement.* Homewood, IL: Dow Jones—Irwin.

Ironson, G. H., Guion, R. M., & Ostrander, M. (1982). Adverse impact from a psychometric perspective. *Journal of Applied Psychology, 67,* 419–432.

Kerlinger, F. N. (1979). *Behavioral research: A conceptual approach.* New York: Holt, Rinehart and Winston.

Koch, W. R. (1983). Likert scaling using the graded response latent trait model. *Applied Psychological Measurement, 7,* 15–32.

Komaki, J. L. (1986). Toward effective supervision: An operant analysis and comparison of managers at work. *Journal of Applied Psychology, 71,* 270–279.

Komaki, J. L., Zlotnick, S., & Jensen, M. (1986). Development of an operant-based taxonomy and observational index of supervisory behavior. *Journal of Applied Psychology, 71,* 260–269.

Levine, M. V., & Drasgow, F. (1982). Appropriateness measurement: Review, critique, and validating studies. *British Journal of Mathematical and Statistical Psychology, 35,* 42–56.

Levine, M. V., & Rubin, D. F. (1979). Measuring the appropriateness of multiple-choice test scores. *Journal of Educational Statistics, 4,* 269–290.

Lodahl, T. M., & Kejner, M. (1965). The definition and measurement of job involvement. *Journal of Applied Psychology, 49,* 24–33.

Lord, F. M. (1980). *Applications of item response theory to practical testing problems.* Hillsdale, NJ: Lawrence Erlbaum Associates.

Lord, F. M., & Novick, M. R. (1968). *Statistical theories of mental test scores.* Reading, MA: Addison-Wesley.

McQuitty, L. L. (1957). Elementary linkage analysis for isolating orthogonal and oblique types and typal relevancies. *Educational and Psychological Measurement, 17,* 207–229.

Meehl, P. E. (1971). Law and the fireside inductions: Some reflections of a clinical psychologist. *Journal of Social Issues, 27*(4), 65–100.

Meehl, P. E. (1977). Specific etiology and other forms of strong influence: Some quantitative meanings. *Journal of Medicine and Philosophy, 2,* 33–53.

Pedhazur, E. J., & Schmelkin, L. P. (1991). *Measurement, design, and analysis: An integrated approach.* Hillsdale, NJ: Lawrence Erlbaum Associates.

Rasch, G. (1980). *Probabilistic models for some intelligence and attainment tests.* Chicago: University of Chicago Press. (Originally published in 1960 by the Danish Institute for Educational Research)

Schmidt, F. L., Greenthal, A. L., Berner, J. G., Hunter, J. E., & Seaton, F. W. (1977). Job sample vs. paper-and-pencil trades and technical tests: Adverse impact and examinee attitude. *Personnel Psychology, 30,* 187–197.

Schmidt, F. L., & Hunter, J. E. (1977). Development of a general solution to the problem of validity generalization. *Journal of Applied Psychology, 62,* 529–540.

Shavelson, R. J., Webb, N. M., & Rowley, G. L. (1989). Generalizability theory. *American Psychologist, 44,* 922–932.

Spearman, C. (1927). *The abilities of man.* New York: Macmillan.

Thomas, L. L. (1952). A cluster analysis of office operations. *Journal of Applied Psychology, 36,* 238–242.

Thorndike, R. L. (1949). *Personnel selection: Test and measurement techniques.* New York: Wiley.

Thurstone, L. L. (1947). *Multiple factor analysis.* Chicago: University of Chicago Press.

Tombaugh, J. R. (1981). *The generalizability of job involvement scores.* Unpublished master's thesis, Bowling Green State University, Bowling Green, OH.

Tryon, R. C., & Bailey, D. E. (1970). *Cluster analysis.* New York: McGraw-Hill.

Wainer, H., Dorans, N. J., Flaugher, R., Green, B. F., Mislevy, R. J., Steinberg, L., & Thissen, D. (1990). *Computerized adaptive testing: A primer.* Hillsdale, NJ: Lawrence Erlbaum Associates.

Ward, J. H., Jr, & Hook, M. E. (1963). Application of an hierarchical grouping procedure to a problem of grouping profiles. *Educational and Psychological Measurement, 23,* 69–81.

Wood, R. (1976). Trait measurement and item banks. In D. N. M. De Gruijter & L. J. T. van der Kamp (Eds.), *Advances in psychological and educational measurement* (pp. 247–263). London: Wiley.

Wright, B. D. (1977). Solving measurement problems with the Rasch model. *Journal of Educational Measurement, 14,* 97–116.

7

Bivariate Prediction
of Performance

Employment testing is future-oriented, always at least implying prediction. Predictions, like measures, should be evaluated by comparing, in an accumulated record, the match of explicitly predicted and actual performance—that is, the likelihood that an assessment-based prediction is true. Traditionally, the relationship is determined and evaluated statistically through criterion-related validation.[1] The two previous chapters emphasized the validity of measurement. This one and the next emphasize the validity of prediction.

Criterion-related validation seeks answers to two basic questions. First, what *kind* of relationship exists between a predictor and the criterion predicted? This question is answered by a regression line, straight or curved, or an equation. Second, what is the *degree* of relationship? Is there any relationship at all? How strong is it? Is it significant? How accurately can predictions be made? Answers can be based on validity coefficients showing the strength of relationship specified.

The term *validity* in this sense refers to the relationship between predictor scores and the criterion used in the analysis—to the similarity of the ordering of people in the two distributions. If the criterion is job-re-

---

[1]Occasionally, someone will abbreviate the term criterion-related validity and speak or even write about "criterion validity." This vulgarization of the language causes mischief in communication and should be avoided; logically, criterion validity refers to the validity of a criterion, a psychometric evaluation of the criterion measure, *not* to the statistical concept of the degree of relationship between a criterion and another variable (or collection of variables) that predicts it.

lated rather than construct-related, this is a different concept of validity from that described in chapter 5 as psychometric validity. With a job-related criterion, it is an evaluation of the job-relatedness of the predictor, for which we can retain the term criterion-related validity. It refers to the accuracy of the statistical predictions made. Even when criterion-related validation is not feasible, the concept provides a model for other evaluations of the usefulness of predictors.

This chapter considers only *bivariate prediction*, the prediction of one variable Y from another variable X (although either may be a composite). The use of just one predictor is unlikely to be optimal, but the bivariate case illustrates most of the relevant statistical issues.

VALIDATION AS HYPOTHESIS TESTING

Criterion-related validation directly tests the hypothesis that criterion Y is a mathematical function of predictor X. It is not the only way to test a predictive hypothesis (Landy, 1986), but it offers a prototype. It specifies a criterion Y worth predicting and a way to assess a predictor trait or composite X. It points out that a time lag is inherent in prediction, at least conceptually. The information on which predictions and decisions are made is available in advance—sometimes far in advance—of the time when the criterion information becomes available. A close look at the problems and procedures of criterion-related validation can help in understanding other ways to evaluate bases for personnel decisions.

The first essential requirement for good criterion-related validation is a well-chosen, well-measured criterion. It must be important to the organization and to the decisions to be made, have substantial variance, and be measured reliably and validly. Conceptualization and measurement seem obviously important, but the habit of using whatever criterion lies at hand is so strong that these obvious requirements are often overlooked. Statistical validation should not merely assume that the criterion measure is valid. Its psychometric validity should be evaluated using the same principles (chapters 5 and 6) used to evaluate other measures.

Generalizing from a research sample to an applicant population requires caution. A research sample hardly ever is a representative sample of an applicant population, a fact often overlooked. Only those selected can provide criterion data, so a research sample is usually a biased sample of an applicant population. Researchers should try to specify and match as well as possible the population to which their results should generalize, but they must also acknowledge some imprecision in the match.

BIVARIATE REGRESSION

Regression refers to the clustering of measures around a central point. A *scatterplot*, graphically showing a point for each pair of X and Y values, will show a distribution of Y values for any given value of X. Values of Y in each X column are distributed about a central point; usually, more of them are near that central point than are far away from it. It is convenient to think of the distribution as normal, around the column mean or some other designated central point.

If the two variables are related, the central point in each column changes systematically with changes in the predictor variable. The pattern of change can be shown graphically with a smoothed regression line or curve that describes the relationship.[2] The pattern can also be described algebraically with a functional equation, $Y = f(X)$. Many functions are possible, but some may fit the data better than others. The central points are identified by whatever equation or graphic line or curve is used to describe the relationship. Explicit prediction is based on the kind of relationship, not on the degree—on the line or curve or equation describing the relationship, not by the amount or frequency of deviation from it.

Less explicitly, one can usually predict that, most of the time, performance of those who score high on the predictor will be better than that of those whose scores are low. This general statement is based on the usually reasonable assumption that the relationship is *positive* and *monotonic*. A relationship is positive if higher predictor scores are associated with higher criterion scores. It is monotonic if that statement (or the converse negative statement) is true throughout the predictor score distribution. It is both positive and monotonic if the central points in the criterion distributions are consistently higher for successively higher values of the predictor—if the smoothed curve always goes up, even if only a little bit in some places.[3] If the functional relationship is both positive and monotonic, more of X implies more of Y throughout the X range.

If actual criterion level is to be predicted (rather than relative level), the regression pattern—the kind of relationship between predictor and crite-

---

[2]It may be some kind of discontinuity, not smooth. The statistical training of psychologists is typically limited to functional equations in which the graph of the equation is smooth—a smooth straight line or (rarely) a smooth curve. As a rule, the possibility of discontinuous relationships is ignored. There may be a threshold ability level that must be reached before any functional relationship can be found, and at the threshold, perhaps, the predicted performance level might jump from nearly zero to some low but distinctly nonzero level. Such thinking is purely speculative, but not necessarily foolish speculation. Such discontinuities, if found, would provide a rational basis for minimum cutting scores.

[3]The emphasis on the smoothed curve is because random variations occur in the pattern of column means as central points; literally connecting them ordinarily yields a jagged pattern. When I refer to a consistent increase, I refer to the trend of change in central points in a functional equation or in a smoothed line or curve.

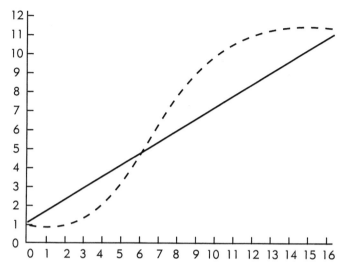

FIG. 7.1. Straight line or curve for use in predicting a criterion from assessment.

rion—must either be empirically determined or assumed. Two different kinds of positive, monotonic relationships are shown in Fig. 7.1. The equation for the linear (straight line) relationship is $Y = 0.6X + 1.0$. In a linear relationship, the incremental difference in predicted values of Y for adjacent values of X is constant throughout the range of scores in X. In the straight line in Fig. 7.1, a 1-point difference in X is always matched by a difference of .06 in the predicted value of Y.

The curve in Fig. 7.1 describes a different kind of relationship. I have not determined the equation for it, although that could be done. It is a simple freehand curve, drawn to represent a smoothed pattern approximating the mean values of Y (one definition of the central points) for narrow intervals of X. With such a curve, predicted values of Y differ very little for different scores in either the low or the high end of the X scale, but they differ a great deal in the mid-range of the X scale.

Linear Functions

The general linear regression is $Y = a + bX$. The constant b is the *slope* of the line, the incremental increase in Y with each unit increase in X, and a is the Y *intercept*, the expected value of Y when X equals zero. Values of a and b can be determined for a given data set by solving a simple pair of simultaneous equations:

$$\Sigma Y = Na + b\Sigma X$$
$$\Sigma XY = a\Sigma X + b\Sigma X^2$$

(1)

In personnel research, linear regression is typically assumed and rarely questioned, maybe because it is easily computed. Technically more important justifications for assuming linearity include:

1. In computations based on the same data set, the linear regression constants, *a* and *b*, and the associated statistics such as correlation coefficients, are more reliable than those in nonlinear equations. (A more reliable statistic is one with less variability from sample to sample.)

2. Linear regression is "robust"; its relevant statistics (*a*, *b*, *r*, etc.) do not seem to depend much on the fit of data to the basic assumptions.[4] To say a statistic is robust may suggest only that it is not particularly sensitive to violations of assumptions.

3. Evidence of nonlinear relationships is relatively rare. Hawk (1970) and Coward and Sackett (1990) found them with about chance frequency in studies using the Generalized Aptitude Test Battery (GATB); they have occurred more frequently in other data sets (e.g., Tupes, 1964).

4. Departure from linearity can be statistically significant without being important. The curve in Fig. 7.2, for example, is slightly higher than the straight line for values of *X* from 3–9; it is slightly lower at each end of the *X* distribution. The two regression patterns do not differ dramatically in mid-range values of *X*; the largest difference is about .5 on the *Y* scale. (For some criteria, this could be an important difference; for others it may not be.)

5. Some nonlinear functions can easily be transformed (e.g., with logarithmic transformations) to linear ones.

6. Correlation coefficients based on the linear assumption are required in many statistical analyses following bivariate validation. Multiple regression, factor analysis, meta-analysis, utility analysis are a few examples of procedures that usually need linear coefficients.

Nonlinear Regression

Despite the arguments favoring it, it is unwise to assume linearity automatically, without further thought. Scatterplots should be routinely examined for regression patterns. A nonlinear pattern may fit better and make more sense. Ghiselli (1964) reported a nonlinear regression that withstood several cross validations. Where a specific form of nonlinear regression is superior to linear regression in repeated replications, there

---

[4]The assumptions are, at least for linear correlation, linearity of regression and homoscedasticity, meaning equal *Y* variances in the different values of *X*. Homoscedasticity (and its opposite, heteroscedasticity) will be defined more fully later in the chapter.

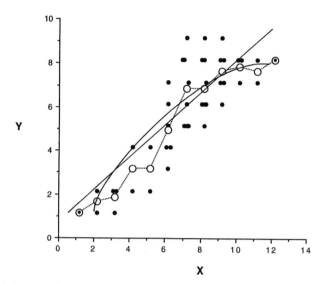

FIG. 7.2. A straight line and a freehand curve fitted to a hypothetical data set.

is little reason to use a repeatedly inferior linear regression, especially if the curve makes sense.

An Example. Consider Fig. 7.3. The criterion Y is an overall average of supervisory ratings of performance on standard scales (mean = 50); the predictor X is the score on a vocabulary test. Table 7.1 gives the data.

The best fitting linear regression is nearly horizontal. No matter what the test score, the performance predicted by the linear equation is about the same.

The same scatterplot is shown in Fig. 7.4, marked off in columns. An x in each column shows the mean rating and mean test score for the column. A freehand curve was drawn to smooth out the jagged line fitting those column means. Low scoring people tend to get low ratings—and so do high scoring people. The highest ratings go to those with moderate test scores.

Does such a relationship make sense? It can, under either of two circumstances. If authoritarian enough, supervisors may be annoyed by subordinates who are brighter than they—and give them lower ratings than they deserve. If so, the ratings are not valid; the relationship is not good evidence of predictive validity.

Alternatively, the ratings may be valid measures of performance, but the jobs may require only moderate verbal intelligence. People with low scores may not have enough verbal ability to do the job well; those with

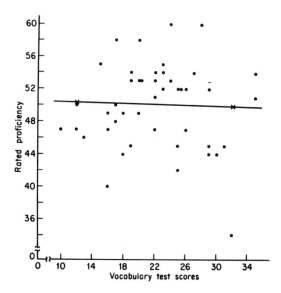

FIG. 7.3. Scattergram of vocabulary test scores and proficiency ratings in the home office of one organization. From Guion (1965).

high scores may be too bored by it to do well. This is plausible in the small community where these data were gathered; jobs that pay as well are not available. Maybe bored people keep the jobs for the sake of the money, doing them perfunctorily.

In such a situation, neither linear regression nor a curve should be accepted without replication and without determining the reasonableness

TABLE 7.1
Vocabulary and Rated Proficiency of Office Workers

X^a	Y^b	X	Y	X	Y	X	Y	X	Y
19	45	22	54	16	40	12	47	10	47
24	53	29	45	30	44	23	55	29	53
15	55	23	52	17	58	22	53	26	52
22	47	26	47	35	51	31	45	16	49
24	60	28	60	25	52	20	53	29	52
23	56	25	52	17	48	20	53	12	50
18	49	13	46	22	51	27	54	25	42
29	44	19	54	17	50	32	34	16	47
20	58	18	44	20	49	35	54	25	45
19	53								

^{a} = Scores on the word meaning section of the Purdue Clerical Adaptability Test. ^{b} = Supervisory ratings of overall proficiency on the job after 2 years.
Note. From Guion (1965).

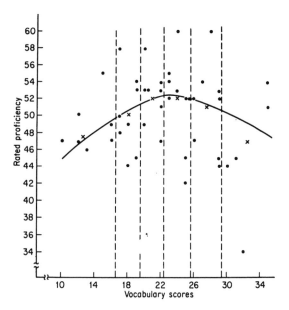

FIG. 7.4. Scattergram divided into columns showing curvilinear relation of rated proficiency to vocabulary test scores; regression curve is a freehand curve fitting the column means. From Guion (1965).

of proffered explanations. If results were replicated, and if ratings were valid, then a hiring strategy might prefer those with moderate scores, hiring only enough high scoring people to provide a pool from which promotions might later be made.

Departures From Linearity. Some curve types are shown in Fig. 7.5. If freehand curves seem somehow unscientific, one can fit exact regression equations (Ezekial, 1941; Guilford, 1954; Lewis, 1960). However, it is not necessary to compute equation parameters precisely when decision rules can be based just as well on an approximation. A freehand curve can have as much practical merit as one based on the best-fitting equation.

Polynomial trend analyses (Pedhazur & Schmelkin, 1991) are used by many researchers to consider possible departures from linearity. A first order polynomial is a simple linear equation with the term bX. A second order polynomial is the same equation plus an additional term, cX^2, a quadratic equation describing a parabolic function. A third order polynomial adds yet another term, dX^3, a cubic function. Each term raises X to a higher power and has its own constant. The more "bends" in the curve, the higher the power of the final term. Trend analysis determines the portion of total criterion variance explained at each polynomial level. If a trend (e.g., linear or quadratic) accounts for enough, the analysis

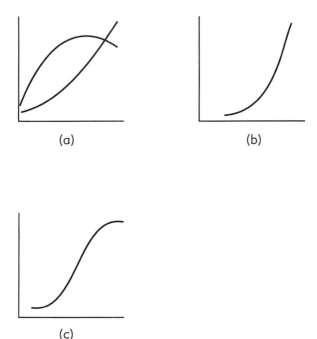

FIG. 7.5. Some examples of curve types: (a) two parabolic curves, with different signs for the parameters, (b) exponential, (c) ogival or logistic.

stops. If not, the analysis continues by determining the additional variance contributed by the next trend level.

Trend analysis is popular, but I do not use it. I am more interested in the sensibleness of a function than in the variance it may explain. In most monotonic functional relationships, a linear trend will account for most of the variance. A well-fitting curve may nevertheless be a more useful decision tool because the predictor might discriminate among individuals more effectively at some score levels than at others.

Logistic Functions. In item response theory, an item characteristic curve based on a logistic function describes the probability of a correct answer at specific ability levels. A similar equation relating ability level (as measured by score on a particular test) to the probability of achieving a specified level of job success, a *job characteristic curve*, was reported by Raju, Steinhaus, Edwards, and DeLessio (1991). Using a 2-parameter logistic regression theory of the relationship of ability to performance, they found that the proportion of people at each score level (except extremes) actually classified as successful was quite close to the predicted proportion. Of course, a single report by itself does not demonstrate generalizable value of logistic regression. I mention it because (a) the logistic model has been useful in other applications and (b) it makes sense in personnel selection situations where applicants vary widely in predictor scores. In short, it is better to consider functional relations that make good sense for defined situations than to assume linearity through force of habit.

CONTINGENCY AND EXPECTANCY TABLES

Contingency Tables

Often, there is no need for highly differentiated predictions; gross, categorical predictions can serve organizational purposes quite well. These can be developed from contingency tables, such as Table 7.2. Categories may be nominal classes or intervals of continuous data.

The example in Table 7.2 is hypothetical but merges characteristics of two actual situations. People on this job customize and install a technical product and help customers learn to use it. Training is self-paced through three levels; the criterion is the level reached within a specified period. The predictor is a four-category classification of prior work experience.

Experience in customer service work appears to be the best background for learning this job; about twice as many of those with that background, compared to candidates in other categories, completed Level 3 in the allotted time. Neither technical nor sales experience seems very helpful,

TABLE 7.2
Hypothetical Data for Prediction From Categorical Variables

| Training Level Completed | Principal Experience Category | | | | | | | | | |
| | Clerical | | Customer Service | | Technical | | Sales | | Total | |
	f^a	%	f	%	f	%	f	%	f	%
Level 3	3	12	15	56	9	25	5	20	32	28
	(7)		(8)		(10)		(7)			
Level 2	4	16	10	37	12	33	15	60	41	36
	(9)		(10)		(13)		(9)			
Level 1	18	72	2	7	15	42	5	20	40	35
	(9)		(9)		(13)		(9)			
Total	25	100	27	100	36	100	25	100	113	99

[a] Actual, observed frequencies are given on the first line for each level; below the observed frequency, in parentheses, is the chance frequency expected on the basis of marginal totals.

although people with a sales background have a good record of completing Level 2. A clerical background seems inadequate.

Contingency tables are a practical compromise between an overly simplistic pass–fail use of predictors and statistical regression; broad categories are predicted rather than predicting precise numerical values, but the categories are more informative than those in a simple dichotomy. Cell entries can be frequencies, percentages, or criterion means. The best prediction for anyone in a given predictor category is the associated criterion category with the highest value.

Empirical Expectancy Charts

Expectancy charts are typically based on contingency tables with a dichotomous criterion; they usually show the percentage of those whose scores are in a given interval who have been in some sense successful on the job. They usually have three to six predictor intervals; Lawshe and Bolda (1958) recommended five. Each interval contains about the same number of people, and the chart shows the percentages who are also in a superior or successful criterion group. An example is Fig. 7.6. The chart shows the "expectancy" of success for people in each interval.

Expectancy charts are for decision makers, not for researchers. They provide a sense of the kind and strength of relationship found but without the precision of a regression pattern or correlation coefficient. They do, however, promote understanding of the usefulness of predictors and help in making decisions about applicants. People with little statistical training can make predictions using expectancy charts.

The word expectancy is questionable in this context. It has a future connotation, but empirical expectancies are historical values from the past. If the past is a good guide to the future, these historical percentages

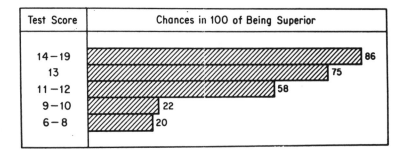

FIG. 7.6.   An expectancy chart based on empirical proportions. From Guion (1965).

are predictive, but the next set of people tested and hired are likely to have different percentages of success in the different score ranges.

Theoretical Expectancy Charts

Lawshe, Bolda, Brune, and Auclair (1958) argued that the statistical theory used by Taylor and Russell (1939) contains less error. Theoretical expectancy charts can be developed from empirical data by assuming linear regression and a normal bivariate correlation surface, the characteristic oval-shaped outline of a bivariate scatterplot when both distributions are approximately normal. If each distribution is dichotomized, as in Fig. 7.7, the proportion of superior workers above or below a specified score can be estimated. The proportion of the total area above the horizontal line (quadrants a and b) represents the proportion of employees classed as superior. The area to the right of the de facto cut score (a and d) represents the proportion of applicants who were hired: the selection ratio. The shaded quadrant a represents people who are both hired and superior. The proportion of those accepted who are also superior can be increased

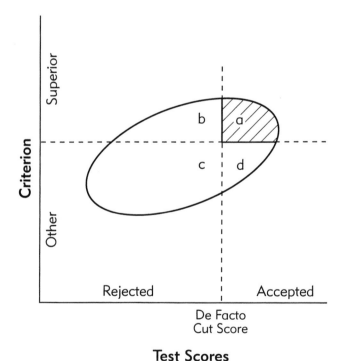

FIG. 7.7. Schematic diagram of relationship between validity, percentage superior without testing, and de facto cutting score.

by relaxing one's definition of success (i.e., by lowering the horizontal line dichotomizing the criteria), or by decreasing the selection ratio (moving the vertical line to the right) or by making the relationship stronger (i.e., increasing correlation that narrows the elliptical outline of the data). Reducing the performance level defining success does little to improve organizational functioning. Raising the de facto cut score requires more recruiting. Ideally, steps are taken to improve validity.

The Taylor-Russell tables assume the mathematical properties of the normal bivariate correlation surface. They are entered using the base rate proportion of superior employees, the expected selection ratio, and the correlation coefficient to find the theoretical proportion of those accepted who will be superior. Lawshe et al. (1958) developed tables for developing five-category expectancy charts based on that theory. Although precisely satisfying the assumptions is unlikely, the theory based on these assumptions is probably a better guide to future prospects than is the empirical past. It is, at least, likely to be less dramatic—more conservative—at the distribution extremes, as shown in Fig. 7.8. Lawshe et al. (1958) suggested use of theoretical expectancy charts if there was no evidence of a marked departure from the assumptions of the normal bivariate correlation surface; they provided a chi square test of the fit of the theoretical model to the data (but see also Guion, 1965, p. 157).

MEASURES OF CORRELATION

A coefficient of correlation describes how closely two variables are related. It is based on the tightness with which criterion values cluster around the central points that define the regression function. Various kinds of correlation coefficients describe degrees of relationship; they may differ

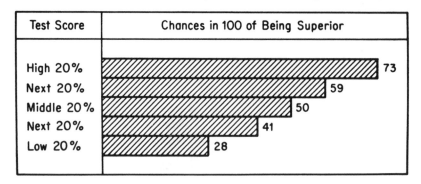

Test Score	Chances in 100 of Being Superior
High 20%	73
Next 20%	59
Middle 20%	50
Next 20%	41
Low 20%	28

FIG. 7.8. Theoretical expectancy chart showing expectancies based on a specified correlation coefficient, $r = .40$. From Guion, 1965.

on the kinds of relationship assumed, on data distributions, or on kinds of measurement scales, but they have important common characteristics.

Basic Concepts in Correlation

Any coefficient of correlation is based on a specified regression pattern. If the pattern does not fit the data very well, but is assumed in computing a coefficient, the coefficient understates the relationship. The degree of understatement can range from trivial to dramatic.

If correlation is perfect, the research subjects have identical rank orders on predicted and actual scores, and the scale distances between measures of any pair of people is the same on both scales. Perfect correlation is rare; departures from perfection are expected. The lower the correlation, the greater the prediction error. Regression functions permit prediction; correlation coefficients permit inferences about the degree of prediction error based on the specified regression function.

Residuals and Errors of Estimate. A *residual* is the difference between the observed value of Y for an individual case and Y_c, the predicted criterion level for the value of X in that case; Y_c may be found from the regression equation or from a graph of it. If a less than optimal regression pattern is used, such as the linear pattern in Fig. 7.3 and Fig. 7.4, the mean and variance of the residuals will be relatively large. When differences in Y are in fact related to those in X, the variance of the residuals is necessarily lower than the variance of Y itself. This is what is meant when it is said that X "accounts for" some of the variance in Y.

A Generalized Definition of Correlation. The basic defining equation for all correlation is

$$\text{Coeff} = \sqrt{1 - \frac{s^2_{res}}{s^2_y}} \tag{2}$$

where "Coeff" is used in place of a more specifically identified coefficient to emphasize the generality of the equation, s^2_{res} is the variance of the residuals, and s^2_y is the total variance of Y. Most coefficients of correlation can range between 0 and 1.0; for monotonic relationships, the range can be from +1.0 to −1.0, depending on whether high scores are associated with good or poor performance. (A negative slope can be changed to positive by the simple expedient of reversing the scale of one of the variables, so this discussion of basics is limited to positive values.) A coefficient of 1.0, then, indicates a perfect relationship in which every data point falls directly on the regression line or curve with no residuals at all. The ratio of residual variance to total variance indicates the degree of imperfection in the strength of relationship. If s^2_{res} equals s^2_y, that ratio is 1.0 and the coefficient is 0.0.

Coefficients of Determination. If Equation 2 is squared (i.e., the square root is not taken), the result is called the *coefficient of determination.* It estimates the proportion of shared variance in the two variables, typically expressed by saying that the proportion of variance in one of them (usually Y) is "accounted for by" the variance in the other. This means common or associated variance, but the usual parlance includes terms like "variance explained by" or "variance accounted for" despite their unwarranted causal implication. Even the term itself—determination—inappropriately implies causation.

Validity coefficients of .30 are not uncommon. The coefficient of determination is .09, or 9% common variance. Expert witnesses and attorneys in litigation are fond of intoning in such a case that "less than 10% of the criterion variance is explained by the predictor," slurring over the word variance as if it were unimportant. Many researchers, too, are obsessed with coefficients of determination, as if they were meaningful measures of effect size (they are not).

Variance is an important statistical concept. Variances can be added together; standard deviations cannot be. The standard deviation is the closer description of variability because it is a kind of average of individual differences expressed in the same units as the measurement scale. However, it has limited mathematical usefulness. You cannot add (or subtract, multiply, or divide) the standard deviation of one measure to the standard deviation of another because standard deviations are square roots of other numbers. It is obvious that $3 + 3 = 6$; it is equally obvious that $\sqrt{3} + \sqrt{3}$ is *not* equal to $\sqrt{6}$.

A common variance statement is simply not a useful description of a co-relationship; an unsquared correlation coefficient is directly useful. An even better descriptive statistic is the slope of the regression line; it is more meaningful because it gives the expected change in Y associated with a change in X (Pedhazur & Schmelkin, 1991, p. 380). This is only the first of many caveats about bivariate coefficients of correlation and their derivatives. Historically, the validity coefficient was the end product, virtually the only product, of criterion-related validation. Researchers in psychometrics and personnel decisions are increasingly skeptical of a lone correlation coefficient as an index of the value of a predictor.

Third Variables. A second caveat is familiar: correlation says nothing about causation. It is easy to presume that a variable obtained first somehow produces the second one. To do so is to forget the third variable problem. Both the X and the Y may be effects of some common third variable or collection of variables. Gulliksen (1950) gave a delightful example. He said that the number of storks' nests built each year in Stockholm correlated .90 with the annual birth rate there! Few people believe that storks bring babies, or vice versa, in Stockholm or elsewhere. If the correlation is reliable, one might speculate about third variables that may explain it, such as economic variation or perhaps the coldness of winters. Other speculation is possible, but the only sure thing is that a causal interpretation of the correlation is wrong.

The Null Hypothesis and Its Rejection. To be useful for prediction, a predictor's correlation with the chosen criterion should be greater than zero—preferably substantially greater, but at least statistically significantly greater. The significance question is discussed later.

The Product–Moment Coefficient of Correlation

Nearly all statistical computer packages include procedures for computing product–moment coefficients, also known as Pearsonian coefficients. Different programs use slightly different equations, but all are derived from the basic product–moment definition:

$$r_{yx} = \frac{\Sigma z_x z_y}{n} \tag{3}$$

This basic equation looks simple but is too complex for practical purposes. It requires transforming every value of X and Y to z-scores (once called the "moments" of a distribution), multiplying each pair of z-scores, and finding the mean of the products. A useful computational equation uses raw scores:

$$r_{yx} = \frac{n\Sigma XY - \Sigma X \Sigma Y}{\sqrt{[n\Sigma X^2 - (\Sigma X)^2][n\Sigma Y^2 - (\Sigma Y)^2]}} \tag{4}$$

where r_{yx} is the product–moment coefficient for the regression of Y on X. X and Y are the raw scores, and XY is the product of the raw scores, for each person, and n is the total number of cases. Several things influence a product–moment correlation coefficient.

Nonlinearity. A product–moment correlation coefficient assumes linear regression. To the degree the assumption is violated, the coefficient will underestimate the degree of relationship, but where evidence of nonlinearity is questionable or trivial, the linear assumption is still preferred.

Homoscedasticity and Equality of Prediction Error. It also assumes *homoscedasticity,* that is, equal residual variances in different segments of the predictor distribution. If the outline of the scatterplot is approximately an oval, the assumption may not be seriously violated. Serious violations, however, cause r_{yx} to understate the relationship seriously. Because the assumption of homoscedasticity is almost universally accepted without question, and because the product–moment coefficient seems moderately immune to violations of it (Greener & Osburn, 1980), many researchers wrongly act as if residual variance were fixed throughout a distribution. A single, overall statemant of residual variance is best considered an average of residual variances at different score intervals—and therefore the overall product–moment coefficient is best considered an average of the coefficients (corrected for range restriction, discussed later) in the different segments of the distribution.

Lord and Novick (1968) noted that violation of the assumption is likely. They thought that heteroscedasticity arose primarily because of nonlinearity; like Raju, Burke, and Normand (1990), they considered logistic functions, because of greater error in the extremes, more likely than linear ones. In personnel selection, a different and common source of nonlinearity is shown by a triangular scatterplot as in Fig. 7.9. Homoscedasticity is clearly violated; residual variance is greater at high score levels than at lower scores. This can happen if lack of a trait (e.g., an ability) prevents criterion effectiveness, but abundance of the trait makes effectiveness possible without assuring it.

Heteroscedasticity can be a more serious problem than usually recognized because it may result in correlation coefficients that markedly un-

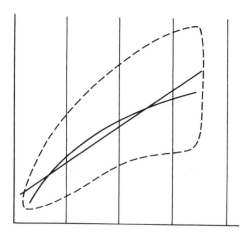

FIG. 7.9. Outline of a scattergram where the columns have distinctly unequal variances; note that the triangular scattergram tends to make the regression nonlinear. From Guion (1965).

derstate the value of a predictor. The average correlation may be poor, but if the lowest residual error is in that part of a distribution where the most critical decisions are made, the predictor may be more useful than the coefficient suggests. It may work the other way. If decisions are to be made at the extremes of the distribution (e.g., if only top candidates are to be accepted), and if residual error at the top scoring levels is great, the predictor may not be useful despite generally high correlation.

Correlated Error. Measurement errors are assumed to be uncorrelated with each other and with the two variables. If the assumption is limited to random errors, violations have little effect on the correlation of reasonably reliable measures. Safeguards against major influences of correlated random error are (a) maximizing reliabilities of both measures, and (b) replicating studies in new samples.

Systematic errors of measurement are also assumed uncorrelated, and they create more serious problems. A source of systematic contamination common to both variables may produce a spurious increase in the coefficient, as shown in Fig. 7.10. If it contributes to one variable but not both, the proportion of common variance, and therefore the correlation may be reduced.

Unreliability. As described in chapter 5, unreliability, in either variable, reduces correlation. The effect is systematic and therefore correctable. Predictor unreliability is simply a fact in the decision context as well as in research. Criterion unreliability, on the other hand, influences research findings but not individual decisions. Coefficients should therefore be corrected only for criterion unreliability. This estimates the population coefficient for the predictor as it is:

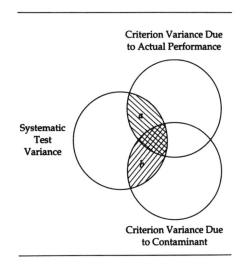

FIG. 7.10. Representation of spurious coefficient due to third variable contamination. From Guion (1991). Reproduced by special permission of the publisher, Consulting Psychologists Press, Inc., Palo Alto, CA 94303, from *Handbook of Industrial and Organizational Psychology*, Second Edition, Volume 2 by Marvin D. Dunnette and Leaetta M. Hough. Copyright 1991 by Consulting Psychologists Press, Inc. All rights reserved. Further reproduction is prohibited without the publisher's written consent.

$$r_{y\tilde{\ }x} = \frac{r_{yx}}{\sqrt{r_{yy}}} \tag{5}$$

where $r_{y\tilde{\ }x}$ is the expected correlation between a perfectly reliable Y and the fallible predictor X.[5]

Realism dictates two other actions. First, overestimate criterion reliability so that the resulting correction is an underestimate of the population value. Spuriously high corrections "may not only lead one into a fantasy world but may also deflect one's attention from the pressing need of improving the reliability of the measures used" (Pedhazur & Schmelkin, 1991, p. 114). Second, correct only coefficients that are statistically significant. Adjusting possibly zero correlations can be seriously misleading and is a bad practice. It is, fortunately, an uncommon practice, but it happens often enough to warn against it.

Reduced Variance. If variance on either variable is substantially less in the sample than in the population variance, the sample coefficient underestimates population validity. Reduced variance is commonly called *restriction of range*, associated with truncation of one or both variables.

With a high correlation, the generally elliptical scatterplot in (a) in Fig. 7.11 is narrow relative to its length; if the correlation is low, the ellipse is wide, as in (b); if the correlation is zero, the scatterplot is outlined by a circle. Removing either end of the ellipse reduces variances and makes the remaining portion wider relative to its length, that is, reduces the correlation, as in (d) in Fig. 7.11.

The problem cannot be solved by meddling with the scale, such as turning a 5-point rating scale to a 9-point scale. (I have seen it happen!) The problem is not the measurement scale but the disparity in scale variance in the sample and in the population sampled. Anything that truncates the sample distribution reduces variance and, therefore, correlation. Several things can happen to produce a research sample with lower than population variance, and corrections are available for some of them:

1. The predictor distribution can be directly truncated, for example, by accepting all those above a cut score and rejecting those below it. Variances are known both for the unrestricted group (an estimate of variance in the applicant population) and the restricted group (those hired), so the corrected correlation coefficient can be obtained by the equation

---

[5]Perhaps "correction" should be encased in quotation marks. It is the conventional word for these estimates or "adjustments," the term used in the *Standards* (AERA, APA, & NCME, 1985). One is never sure, however, that the result of applying the correction for attenuation or other similarly labeled corrections results in a correct description of the population parameter. It is, however, likely to be closer.

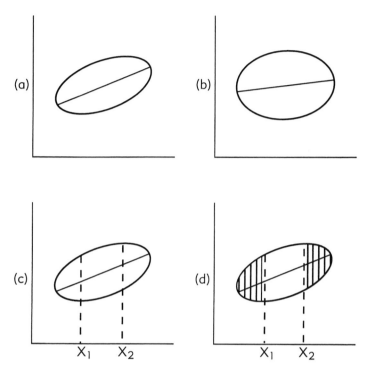

FIG. 7.11. Elliptical scattergrams showing effect of restriction of range on correlation: (a) scatterplot of high correlation, (b) scatterplot of low correlation, (c) plot of high correlation with X_1 showing where low scorers tend to be lost to the research sample and X_2 showing where high scorers are likely to be lost, and (d) the changed shape of the scattergram when the low and high scoring cases are in fact lost.

$$r_n = \frac{r_o \cdot \dfrac{S_{xn}}{S_{xo}}}{\sqrt{1 - r_o^2 + r_o^2 \cdot \dfrac{S_{xn}^2}{S_{xo}}}} \tag{6}$$

where r_n is the new estimate of the coefficient for an unrestricted sample, r_o is the old (obtained) coefficient for the available restricted sample, and S_{xn} and S_{xo} are the predictor standard deviations for the unrestricted and restricted groups, respectively (Thorndike, 1949, p. 173). Sometimes the "old" standard deviation is not known. In this equation and the two that follow, an estimate can be based on available national norms. Sackett and Ostgaard (1994) recommended an estimate 20% lower than national norms.

2. The organization may accept all applicants on probation and then terminate or transfer people below some criterion cut point. Then a test

may be given and concurrently validated. The direct restriction is on the criterion, not on the predictor, but the estimated unrestricted correlation coefficient can be found by reversing the roles of predictor and criterion in Equation 6 (Ghiselli, Campbell, & Zedeck, 1981, p. 300).

3. Indirect truncation of the predictor occurs if prior selection is based on a correlated third variable. If selection has been based on one test, and another test is being validated, variance on the new test is restricted to the extent that it is correlated with the old one. Letting X and Y be the new test and the criterion respectively, and letting Z be a third variable, the unrestricted coefficient could be estimated by

$$r_n = \frac{r_o + r_{zx}r_{zy}\left(\dfrac{S_{zn}^{\,2}}{S_{zo}^{\,2}} - 1\right)}{\sqrt{\left[1 + r_{zx}^2\left(\dfrac{S_{zn}^{\,2}}{S_{zo}^{\,2}} - 1\right)\right]\left[1 + r_{zy}^2\left(\dfrac{S_{zn}^{\,2}}{S_{zo}^{\,2}} - 1\right)\right]}} \tag{7}$$

where the notation of n, o, and S remain as in Equation 6; r_{zx} and r_{zy} are the coefficients in the selected (restricted) sample (Thorndike, 1949, p. 174).

4. Sample variance may be lower than population variance just by chance. But one would not know, and no correction is available.

5. Unknown factors may have reduced variance indirectly. Again, no correction exists.

Correction equations can be used in cases of reduced variance even with no clear point of truncation. Instead of an explicit cut score, for example, there may be a region—a score interval with fuzzy boundaries—below which no one was hired, above which most applicants were hired, and within which decisions were mixed. Several reports by Linn (e.g., Linn, 1968; Linn, Harnisch, & Dunbar, 1981) have verified that reduced variance, even without mathematically precise truncation, is associated with reduced correlation—perhaps drastically reduced in highly selective situations—reinforcing the need to correct for the effect. Equation-based corrections are conservative, giving underestimates of population values (Linn et al., 1981).[6]

---

[6]Reporting *both* the corrected and uncorrected coefficients is absolutely essential. A "primary" standard, Standard 1.17, states: "When statistical adjustments, such as those for restriction of range or attenuation, are made, both adjusted and unadjusted coefficients and all statistics used in the adjustment should be reported" (AERA, APA, & NCME, 1985, p. 17).

Corrections in Tandem. What happens when a coefficient is corrected both for unreliability in the criterion and for reduced variance? Not much. Lee, Miller, and Graham (1982) studied the effect in a large Navy sample. Corrections were made sequentially for range restriction and for criterion unreliability in each of six groups developed by assuming different selection ratios. Except at the 10% selection ratio, the estimates were somewhat higher than the population values.

Subsequently, Bobko (1983) approached the question analytically, providing an equation that makes the corrections simultaneously. Using the notation just explained,

$$r_n = \frac{\dfrac{r_o}{\sqrt{r_{yy}}} \cdot \dfrac{S_{xn}}{S_{xo}}}{\sqrt{\left(1 - \dfrac{r_o^2}{\sqrt{r_{yy}}}\right) + \left(\dfrac{r_o^2}{\sqrt{r_{yy}}} \cdot \dfrac{S_{xn}}{S_{xo}}\right)}} \tag{8}$$

With small selection ratios, small samples, and low criterion reliability, the difference between r_n and the population value can be great; however, he also showed that, on the average, this tandem correction underestimates the true underlying correlation (Bobko, 1983).

The analytic approach assumes the normal bivariate surface and samples of 100 or more. It has its own assumptions usually violated by real data. Nevertheless, tandem correction for criterion unreliability and predictor range restriction—whether sequentially using traditional equations or with Equation 8—seems a generally safe and conservative way to estimate correlation in an unrestricted sample of the population.

Distributions. Product–moment coefficients require no assumption about distributions, but some interpretations of them assume an underlying normal bivariate surface (e.g., the Taylor-Russell tables). Extreme skewness in one variable but not the other produces nonlinearity and consequent correlation reduction; in fact, any time the two distributions differ markedly in shape, correlation is markedly reduced (Edwards, 1976).

Group Heterogeneity. A large sample sometimes seems like a Holy Grail people will do anything to find, such as combining small, disparate samples. Samples may then include groups of people that differ in systematic ways. Combining them may hide important differentiating characteristics. Subgroups in the overall sample may have different means on one or both variables or different correlations. Figure 7.12 shows how combining such differing groups distorts overall correlation coefficients.

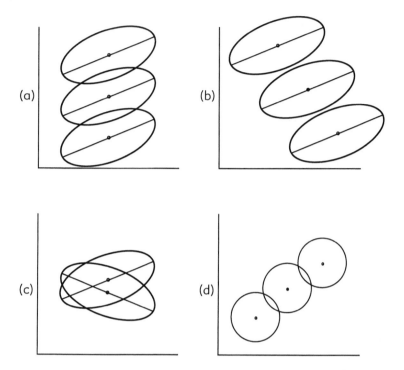

FIG. 7.12. Effects of combining groups with differing means of correlations into a single research sample: (a) combining three groups with the same correlation but with differing criterion means, (b) combining three groups with the same correlation but with differing means on both variables, (c) combining two groups with the same correlation but differing in sign, (d) combining three groups in which the correlations are all zero but the means on both variables differ systematically.

results in an approximately zero correlation. Each group in (b) also has strong positive correlation, but combining them would result in a negative coefficient. The group interaction shown in (c) would result in an overall coefficient of about zero and a triangular scatterplot. The most serious distortion is (d); here an overall correlation would be positive and probably strong despite the fact that the two variables are not related in any of the groups; the apparent correlation would be due only to the correlation of group means. Whatever might distinguish the three groups is apparently related to the criterion as well as to the predictor, but these two variables are not related at the individual level.

Questionable Data Points. Plotting data sometimes shows one or more *outliers*. An outlier is "an unusual, atypical data point—one that stands out from the rest of the data [and] may lead to serious distortion

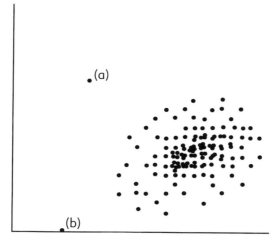

FIG. 7.13. The effect of an outlier: (a) an outlier that may reduce correlation; (b) an outlier that may increase correlation.

of results" (Pedhazur & Schmelkin, 1991, p. 398). Figure 7.13 illustrates two effects, with exaggeration for emphasis. Outlier (a) reduces correlation if it is included with the mass of data; in a small total sample, it could even turn an apparent positive relationship to a negative one. Inclusion of outlier (b) on the other hand would inflate the correlation.

Many personnel researchers believe that all data points should be retained in the analysis (Orr, Sackett, & Dubois, 1991), but I think outliers should be investigated. Point (a) might be from one who performs well on the criterion but did not line up the answer sheet properly. Point (b) might represent incomplete data. Some outliers may be due to correctable errors, such as an incorrectly scored test; the solution is obvious: correct the error and do the analysis over. Some may be due to errors that are not correctable; for example, an examiner may misread instructions and give one person nearly double the standard time. Not much can be done here beyond deleting the errant data point and do the analysis over without it. Unfortunately, deleting outliers has potentially unpleasant consequences, among them rationalizations to excuse deleting troublesome data that are not actually due to error. Any research report should identify any deletions and the reasons for them; it is the researcher's obligation to investigate outliers, to decide what to do about them, and to report fully. When in doubt, keep the outlier in the data set.

A Summary Caveat. I have identified several things that can influence or distort a product–moment correlation coefficient. Sometimes the direction of error is plain, but some influences may lead to unknown or unknowable error. Some with knowable effects can be corrected, but many of them are like incurable aches and pains: you simply have to live with them. Living with them, however, should induce caution. One should not place undue faith in a single bivariate validity coefficient. It can offer some evidence—even good evidence—of validity, but potential distortions should be considered in evaluating that evidence. One may need to gather new data, either through replications or studies of possible explanations.

Statistical Significance

Research reports typically say something like, "the correlation was not statistically significant," or "it was significant at the 5% level of confidence." These terms refer to the probability that the reported coefficient differs from zero only by chance; if it differs more than expected by chance, the "null hypothesis" of no relationship is rejected. What researchers know, and how they behave, are not always the same. Too often they act as if, having rejected the null hypothesis, they can virtually equate the sample correlation coefficient with the population value, or as if mere rejection is enough to assure that the population correlation is usefully nonzero. Neither is so. The concept of statistical significance has become so encrusted with false implications that a hard look at the subject is needed.

The Logic of Significance Testing. Statistical validation begins in a sample where both predictor and criterion data are known. Suppose $r = .20$. This is not a very strong relationship, but it can be useful. Can a similar relationship be expected in later sample where decisions have to be made without prior knowledge of criterion performance?

Part of the answer depends on the quality of the research. We cannot have confidence in the generalizability of poorly designed or conducted research where research subjects are inappropriately chosen, data collection is haphazard and inconsistent, criteria suffer contaminations, or data recording or analysis is careless. However, any sample statistic is subject to error, no matter how carefully the research was conducted. Some error may be due to idiosyncratic characteristics of people in that sample.

Part of the answer may lie in inevitable violation of statistical assumptions. Correlation analysis assumes that measurement errors are not correlated. In any given sample, however, the errors will in fact have *some* nonzero correlation, even if small.

Part of the answer may lie in sampling error. The smaller the sample size, in absolute number or relative to the population, the greater the likely error.

Clearly, the unimpressive but potentially useful coefficient of .20 is to some degree in error, even if negligibly. Different samples from a common population would provide a distribution of different coefficients; the mean of a big enough set of them would match the population correlation. Can the population, and future samples from it, be counted on to give coefficients of about the same size as the one at hand?

That is a useful question, but it is not the question answered by significance testing. Significance testing goes at it in a reverse (or perverse) process; it tests the null hypothesis that the correlation coefficient in the population is precisely zero. Now, rejection of the null hypothesis does not imply that the sample coefficient is a good estimate of the population coefficient, and failure to reject the null hypothesis does not mean that it is true. Literally, the null hypothesis "is *always* false in the real world" (Cohen, 1990, p. 1308).[7] Specifically, it estimates the probability, p, that, if indeed the population correlation is zero, a sample would capitalize enough on error to provide a correlation as large or larger than that obtained, just by chance. Part of the perversity is that significance testing asks not what that probability is, but only whether it is lower than some prestated level. It answers with a yes or no dichotomy, not with a probability level.

The purpose is laudable, but the topic is introduced with trepidation. Significance testing is fraught with mischief. Far too many researchers appear to believe that the ultimate objective of research is to reject the null hypothesis. It is not. Consider this view from a retiring editor of the *Journal of Applied Psychology*: "One of the most frustrating aspects of the journal business is the null hypothesis. It just will not go away. . . . Perhaps p values are like mosquitos. They have an evolutionary niche somewhere and no amount of scratching, swatting, or spraying will dislodge them" (Campbell, 1982, p. 698). We need a fresh, elementary (even simplistic) look at the null hypothesis.

Gremlins in Interpreting Significance Tests. Significance testing grew from controlled agricultural experiments, not from correlation analysis. If one divides a wheat field into plots, systematically using a treatment in some plots but not others, one asks if the treatment actually influences yield—a causal question. The amount of effect is of less concern than whether there is one. In designing an experiment, one specifies in advance a significance level sufficient to justify a causal inference. The results are neatly dichotomized either as reaching that preset level or not.

Significance tests do not answer causal questions in correlational work, and the yes-or-no approach is too mechanistic and rigid for my taste. I

---

[7]Chow (1991) presented a different view. Essentially, she argued that such a literal interpretation ignores the conditional nature of null hypothesis testing: that one seeks the probability of rejecting the null hypothesis contingent upon its truth; that is, *if . . . then*. For a fuller account of her views in a different context, see Chow (1988).

prefer to report estimated probability rather than to use an asterisk to indicate a significant correlation. I dislike the wrong-headed habit of many researchers to use rows of varying numbers of asterisks, shouting like latter-day Paul Reveres: one if by land (i.e., $p < .05$) and two if by sea ($p < .01$)—and perhaps three or four in a series of discrete p values. Reporting with such a galaxy of stars[8] makes it too easy to treat the number of asterisks as a measure of effect size. My preference for reporting p levels rather than significance is, of course, open to the same risk.

Experimental research also presupposes random sampling, but valida-tion samples are not often random. They are data from people assessed *and hired*. Those assessed may be a sample of people from an applicant population, but the validity coefficient is from a subsample of those assessed who were hired and therefore provided criterion data. Differ-ences between samples of the applicant population and samples of ap-plicants who get hired may be trivial or important, but one can rarely be sure which.

Many other wrong-headed interpretations are often made in signifi-cance testing. It is *not* acceptable to interpret the failure to reject the null hypothesis as evidence of no relationship. First, as shown with the data in Fig. 7.3 and Fig. 7.4, to reject or fail to reject null under one assumption about the nature of the regression pattern says nothing at all about rejecting or failing to reject null under a different one. Second, the absence of something, including the absence of a relationship, is extremely difficult to demonstrate (for a broader perspective, see Hearst, 1991). Third, failure to reject null may be due to small sample size. Fourth, rejection at one level does not imply rejection at all levels.

Levels of Confidence. Suppose the mean correlation coefficient from a lot of samples is zero. The standard deviation of the distribution is estimated by the standard error of the correlation when $r = 0$, $SE_{r=0}$. If we know, in SE units, how far a coefficient of .20 is from the mean (zero), we might use a table of normal deviates to find the areas under the curve beyond correlations of ±.20. If $SE_{r=0}$ is .12, then a coefficient of .20 is $(.20/.12)$ standard deviation units from the mean; $z = 1.67$. According to the tables, a coefficient 1.67 or more standard deviations above or below the mean has a probability of .095 of occurring by chance. That probability

---

[8] I confess that I cannot cite a source for this felicitous phrase; I no longer remember where I encountered it, but I admire the person from whom I have purloined it. I have seen large tables of correlations, based on widely different ns, where the number of asterisks (stars) went as high as 5! A large table, in which each entry is greeted with from one to five stars is indeed a galaxy! My predecessor as editor of the *Journal of Applied Psychology*, John P. Campbell, set a rule: no more than two significance levels! It was a good rule; I followed it, but the associate editors during my term did not.

is less than .10. Is $p < .10$ reason enough to reject the idea that the population value is 0.00? Maybe. If one is desperate for a predictor, or if unavoidable problems have marred the research process, or if criterion reliability is poor but unspecifiable, then one may decide that the probability less than .10 of getting a correlation as high as .20 (or whatever it might be), by chance alone, is indeed reason enough.

Different sets of circumstances may suggest that a lower probability— perhaps $p < .02$ or $p < .001$—is required to reject the null hypothesis safely. Over the years, $p < .05$ has become "sanctified (and sanctifying)" (Cohen, 1990, p. 1307) as the habitually preferred level at which one will have confidence that the null hypothesis is false and can be rejected. I accept convention and treat .05 as the confidence level of choice—unless specific circumstances suggest easing the required level or making it more stringent. The choice is arbitrary. It is sometimes rigid. Some researchers will reject the null hypothesis when $p = .049$ but will not reject it if $p = .051$.

Computing and Evaluating t. Previously, I used areas under a normal curve and values of z. In fact, significance testing uses t tests (see any elementary statistics text), where t is the ratio of a difference to the standard error of that difference and interpreted in relation to sample size. A difference between a sample's correlation coefficient and the hypothesized null value of zero is, obviously, the coefficient itself. The value of t, therefore, is the coefficient divided by the standard deviation of the distribution of t, estimated as the standard error of the statistic. For linear correlation (r), the standard error when $r = 0$, $SE_{r=0}$, is

$$SE_{r=0} = 1/\sqrt{n - 1} \qquad (9)$$

where n is the sample size. One may consult a table of t values, of which Table 7.3 is a small abstract, to determine whether the value of t is high enough for the correlation to be considered significantly different from zero at various significance levels. (Note that such a table is entered, not with n, but with df, "degrees of freedom." I do not define that term here but say only that, for correlated bivariate data, $df = n - 2$.)

Type I and Type II Errors and Statistical Power. In strict significance testing, a researcher either rejects or fails to reject the null hypothesis. If it is true and the researcher does not reject it, or if it is false and the researcher does reject it, the choice is correct. The choice is erroneous if the null hypothesis is true but is rejected, or if it is false but not rejected. These two types of errors are known as *Type I* and *Type II* errors, respectively. The chosen level of confidence is called *alpha*, α, the

TABLE 7.3
Abbreviated Table of *t*

df	Probability			
	.20	*.05*	*.02*	*.001*
5	1.476	2.571	3.365	6.869
10	1.372	2.228	2.764	4.587
15	1.341	2.131	2.602	4.073
25	1.316	2.060	2.485	3.725
40	1.303	2.021	2.423	3.551
120	1.289	1.980	2.358	3.373

Note. From Fisher, R. A., & Yates, F. (1957). *Statistical tables for biological, agricultural, and medical research* (5th ed.). Reprinted by permission of Addison Wesley Longman Ltd.

probability associated with Type I errors. The lower the α probability, the lower the probability of a Type I error.

The lower the likelihood of Type I error, the greater the likelihood of Type II error. Which is the more serious error can be determined only in the full context of a particular situation. As the probability of Type I error increases, so does the probability of hiring people on the basis of an invalid assessment. As the probability of Type II error increases, so does the probability that a valid assessment procedure will be discarded.

Statistical power "is the probability that a statistical test will lead to the rejection of the null hypothesis" (Cohen, 1977, p. 4). Power is a function of three things: (a) the size of the sample used, (b) the *effect size* (e.g., correlation) in the population, and (c) the alpha level chosen. A judgment of significance, then, is made more likely by increasing sample size, by working with intelligently developed predictive hypotheses that are very likely to result in substantial correlations, or by relaxing α. Some ambivalence is justified; we like to reduce error, but we do not ordinarily like to lose power. The complement of power (1 − power) is the *beta* probability, β, the probability of Type II error—that is, the failure to reject a false null hypothesis.

Concepts of power and Type II error received little attention in early personnel research. Usually, failure to reach traditional levels of significance (i.e., .05) was not seen as a serious problem—if the results "approached" it, the sample was small, and the correlation was fairly large. If the predictor were badly needed, an "almost significant" finding was likely to be used in decision making. It was not good science, and it was certainly not orthodox, but it might have made good business sense.

The advent of litigation under the Civil Rights Act of 1964 changed matters. Validity under the *Uniform Guidelines* became virtually synonomous with significance at the .05 level, and lack of a statistically significant validity coefficient was reason enough to abandon a predictor, regardless

TABLE 7.4
Abbreviated Power Table For Determining Sample Size,
Assuming No Restriction of Range or Criterion Unreliability

	Power When $\alpha = .01$				Power When $\alpha = .05$			
r	.50	.75	.90	.99	.50	.75	.90	.99
.10	662	1052	1480	2390	384	692	1046	1828
.20	164	259	364	587	95	171	258	449
.30	71	112	157	253	42	74	112	194
.40	39	61	85	136	24	41	61	104
.50	24	37	51	82	15	25	37	63

Note. Adapted from Cohen, J. (1977). *Statistical power analysis for the behavioral sciences* (Rev. ed.). New York: Academic Press. Reprinted with permission.

of other lines of evidence. Issues of statistical power became important; with insufficient power, one could lose the use of a good predictor; Type II error took on importance not earlier recognized.

Type II error is also important in investigating construct validity. Some studies will use construct-relevant criterion variables *not* expected by theory to be related to the measure being validated. In such cases, it would be nice to *accept* the null hypothesis, not merely fail to reject it. The logic of significance testing does not permit acceptance of null; in this case, of course, literal acceptance of null is not what the researcher seeks. To assert that a population value is zero is not as important as being able to declare it trivial. The logic of Type II error offers a probabilistic approach toward this level of acceptance. As Cohen (1977, pp. 16–17) described it, one first specifies a correlation effect considered too low to be acceptable (e.g., r = .05). Then one sets power high so the β probability is low. Finally, an α level is specified. One may then consult power tables to determine the sample size needed to detect significance when the population correlation is the level specified as trivial. Failure to reject null under these circumstances is tantamount to accepting the view that the population parameter is trivial if not literally zero.

Lawyers and managers often ask their consultants, "Well, how many cases do you need?" They seem unwilling to accept "it depends"; they want a specific number. I have developed the habit of providing an abbreviated set of power tables, like Table 7.4, and asking a set of questions of my own:

1. What do you think is a likely or useful population value for the correlation coefficient (indicated in the table simply as *r*)?
2. What level of confidence—*p* < .05 or *p* < .01—will satisfy you for this project? (Which half of the table should be used?)

3. What level of risk are you willing to accept? That is, given the correlation and confidence level you have specified, what is the minimally acceptable probability of finding significance in the sample? (Which column should be used?)

Most of the time the choices seem to be a population validity of about .30, a 5% confidence level, and at least 99 chances in 100 of finding significance—no one I have asked has ever selected a 50–50 chance. Table 7.4 tells us that, for this combination of responses, the sample size must be at least 194. However, Table 7.4 assumes perfect criterion reliability and no restriction of range—unlikely conditions. So I then abbreviate a table provided by Schmidt, Hunter, and Urry (1976). Among their tables one finds required sample sizes for population correlations of .35 or .50, power of .50 or .90, and several levels of criterion reliability and selection ratios as indications of direct restriction of range. Anticipating the choice of $\alpha = .05$, and an approximation of .35 for the population correlation, I offer a small table like Table 7.5 and ask two more questions:

4. Which level of criterion reliability is most realistic?
5. What is the probable selection ratio?

Suppose the answers are .70 for criterion reliability and a selection ratio of .20. I can then point out that a research sample as large as 518 cases will not provide quite as much power as was wanted—although .90 is fairly good power.

TABLE 7.5
Sample Sizes Required ($\alpha = .05$) for Power = .90 for Various Selection
Ratios and Criterion Reliabilities When True Validity Is .35

SR[b]	SD[c]	Criterion Reliability[a]				
		.90	.80	.70	.60	.40
.70	7.01	179	203	234	276	421
.50	6.03	240	272	314	370	567
.30	5.15	325	371	428	505	775
.20	4.68	393	448	518	611	937
.10	4.11	508	579	669	790	1213
.05	3.71	622	709	820	968	1487

[a]Reliability levels for criterion measurement in an unselected group (i.e., a group in which the selection ratio was 1.00). [b]Selection ratio: proportion of job candidates selected in strict top-down order, providing a direct restriction of range. [c]The standard deviation of scores for the selected group, smaller as the proportion selected gets smaller.

Note. Adapted from Schmidt, F. L., Hunter, J. E., & Urry, V. W. (1976). Statistical power in criterion-related validation studies. *Journal of Applied Psychology, 61*, 473–485. Copyright by the American Psychology Association. Reprinted with permission.

In short, the question, how large should a research sample be to reach significance, is by no means simple. In planning empirical validation, the researcher must estimate probable true or population validity, choose an alpha level, decide on the power level wanted (and how realistic), and estimate probable criterion reliability and restriction of range. Restriction of range may be either direct or indirect (or both), and different power tables and equations apply to the two kinds. Tables were provided by Cohen (1977) for various alpha levels, correlation levels, and power levels. Schmidt et al. (1976) provided several tables for considering alpha levels, two power levels, and two population validity levels for various combinations of criterion unreliability and direct restriction of range. Under conditions of indirect restriction of range, which may be more typical, the required sample sizes would be substantially smaller; Sackett and Wade (1983) published tables for determining these. According to Raju, Edwards, and LoVerde (1985), the tables underestimated required sample sizes under indirect restriction of range because of an error in the equations used; they provided corrected equations without rebuilding the tables. In planning research, all of these sources should be consulted to determine desired sample sizes or to evaluate the sample sizes available. After doing so, it may be decided that criterion-related validation is not feasible.

Alternative Estimates of Product–Moment Correlation

A product–moment correlation coefficient is computed with two continuous variables, linearly related, with somewhat similar distributions. Occasionally one or both variables are dichotomies, but product–moment coefficients can be estimated.

The *biserial coefficient of correlation*, r_{bis}, is used if one variable is continuous and the other a dichotomy assumed to be imposed on an underlying, normally distributed continuous variable:

$$r_{bis} = \frac{\overline{X}_p - \overline{X}_q}{S_x} \cdot \frac{pq}{y} \tag{10}$$

where $\overline{X}_p$ and $\overline{X}_q$ are the predictor mean scores for the two criterion groups, p and q are the respective proportions of the total sample, y is the ordinate of the normal curve at the point marking the separation of p and q, and S_x is the standard deviation of the full predictor distribution.

If no underlying continuum is assumed, or if it is but the assumption of normality is questionable, the *point-biserial coefficient of correlation*, r_{pbis}, offers an estimate:

$$r_{pbis} = \frac{\overline{X}_p - \overline{X}_q}{S_x} \cdot \sqrt{pq} \tag{11}$$

using the same notation. In most computer programs, r_{pbis} is simply computed as r with the dichotomized variable treated as a continuum having only the values 1 and 2.

If both variables are dichotomized and have normally distributed underlying continua, and the assumption of linear regression is appropriate, r may be estimated by the *tetrachoric coefficient of correlation*, r_{tet}. The equation is complex, with an infinite progression of successively smaller terms, and is not presented here; most statistics packages provide programs for it.

The *phi coefficient*, ϕ, may be computed for "true" dichotomies in both variables. Speaking strictly, phi is not an estimate of r, but it uses a data table like that in Fig. 7.14. It is found by the equation

$$\phi = \frac{ad - bc}{\sqrt{(a + b)(a + c)(b + d)(c + d)}} \tag{12}$$

where the letters a, b, c, and d are the frequencies in the cells as designated in Fig. 7.14.

How good are the different estimates of r? To illustrate comparisons, I have tinkered twice with a set of real data. The first time, I exaggerated criterion skewness already present. To make a second set, I reduced the skewness, providing more nearly normal distributions in both variables.

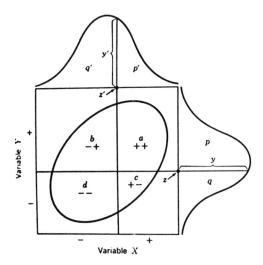

FIG. 7.14. Normal bivariate distributions divided into four categories by dichotomizing X and Y. From Guilford, J. P., & Fruchter, B. (1973). *Fundamental statistics in psychology and education.* New York: McGraw-Hill. Reprinted with permission.

I dichotomized the skewed distributions, assigning values of 2 (superior) (approximately one third of the cases) and 1 (other). Splits for the normalized data set were as near the mean as frequencies allowed without arbitrarily assigning some identical scores on both sides. Product–moment correlation coefficients provided standards for comparing the various estimates shown in Table 7.6. The product–moment correlations were, by intent, virtually the same in the two data sets (one rounded up to .41, the other rounded down to .40).

The "estimates" differ from these values, in some cases substantially. They should; dichotomizing continuous data reduces correlations (Cohen, 1983; Thorndike, 1949). Biserial correlation is much lower than r in both sets, especially the skewed data. The assumption of normality must be taken seriously; merely "normalizing"—moving toward normality—is not enough. The point biserial coefficient requires less stringent assumptions; it appropriately underestimates r for the skewed data, but it inappropriately exaggerates r for the "normalized" criterion. Note that the computer approach treating the dichotomized criterion as continuous values of 1 to 2 exactly duplicates r_{pbis} by formula. The bottom two lines of Table 7.6 use 2×2 dichotomies. Phi computed by its own equation is identical to r with two 2-point distributions and seems the most reasonable of the estimates. In general, the estimates deserve some skepticism.

Nonlinear Correlation Coefficients

Simple Computation of Curvilinear Coefficients. Curvilinear regression is rare, maybe because it is rarely looked for. When data are reliably nonlinear, the degree of relationship is underestimated by linear correlation. Statistics textbooks usually avoid discussion of nonlinear correlation, often with a footnote calling it "beyond the scope" of the book. Such frightening footnotes are not needed; nonlinear regression may be more

TABLE 7.6
Variety of Correlation Coefficients From Common Data

Method	Skewed	Normalized
Product–moment r[a]	.41	.40
Biserial r, by equation[b]	.15	.22
Point biserial r, by equation[b]	.30	.44
Product–moment r, 1 dichotomy[c]	.30	.44
Product–moment r, 2 dichotomies[c]	.32	.30
Phi coefficient, by equation[d]	.32	.30

[a]Standard computation by GB-STAT statistical package. [b]r_{bis} and r_{pbis} computed by equations 17 and 18, respectively. [c]1 dichotomy in the criterion variable or both variables dichotomized. [d]Computed by equation 20.

complex and less reliable than linear, but not so much more complex, nor so much less reliable, that it merits being ignored.

If nonlinear regression is established, the correlation coefficient can be computed by the basic definition, Equation 2. Predicted values of Y can be found by equation or graph and the residuals $Y - Y_c$ computed. The variance of the residuals is the mean of the squares of the residuals and can be substituted in Equation 2. When the appropriate form of the regression curve is unclear, such as whether a logistic function or a quadratic makes more sense, residual variances can be computed for both to give an ad hoc basis for choice.

What symbol should be used for nonlinear correlation coefficients? The Roman letter r is used for linear correlation. The Greek letter rho, ρ, is used for curvilinear correlation. It is also used for many other things. It may represent a population value estimated by a coefficient (either linear or nonlinear). It is used for rank difference correlation. In discussions to follow, I make clear with subscripts which use is intended. For curvilinear correlation coefficients as sample statistics, I use ρ_{cv}, and for curvilinear population parameters, $\hat{\rho}_{cv}$.

Significance Testing. Where ρ_{cv} is computed by dividing scatterplots into columns, the equation for computing the standard error of the curvilinear correlation coefficient is:

$$\sigma_{\rho_{cv}} = \frac{1 - \rho_{cv}^2}{\sqrt{n - k}} \qquad (13)$$

where $\sigma_{\rho_{cv}}$ is the standard error of estimate, ρ_{cv}^2 is the square of the curvilinear correlation coefficient, n is the sample size, and k is the number of columns. The standard error for the curve shown in Fig. 7.4 is .132. If $\hat{\rho}_{cv} = 0$, as assumed in significance tests, the standard error is .158. Since $\rho_{cv} = .41$, $t = .41/.158 = 2.595$. With 46 cases, there are 44 degrees of freedom, and the null hypothesis can be rejected, $p < .02$. (Note that the null hypothesis would not have been rejected had we settled for linear regression.)

Heteroscadasticity. A curvilinear coefficient of correlation, like the Pearson coefficient, assumes homoscedasticity. Violations make it overstate the relationship at some score levels and understate it at others. Kahneman and Ghiselli (1962) introduced the theta statistic, Θ, the ratio of the variance of criterion scores within an interval to overall criterion variance, to describe relationship strength within relatively narrow predictor intervals. Lower values of theta mean better prediction.

I devote unusual space to theta because, with a change in computational detail, it can have a new practical use. I focus on the study reported by Brown, Stout, Dalessio, and Crosby (1988) for the Aptitude Index Battery

(AIB). The AIB, developed for selecting life insurance agents, predicts failures quite well; it is less effective in predicting successes (Thayer, 1978), a fact Brown et al. (1988) documented with theta, as in Table 7.7.

Dividing more than 16,000 cases into 10 intervals of about equal numbers and computing theta for each interval, they found relatively low values in the lowest deciles and high ones in the highest deciles. Note the values greater than 1.0, showing that criterion variance within the interval is as great or greater than the overall criterion variance. In these intervals, the "predictor" does not predict.

Truncating the distribution to consider only cases above possible cutting scores, Brown et al. (1988) computed both theta and a corrected r in the various remaining intervals, from no restriction to only the top 10%. *Both* statistics were successively higher as the presumed cutting scores became more stringent—an apparently contradictory finding. Lower values of theta, and higher values of r, should be associated with improved prediction, so how can one study produce higher values of both?

The answer is in Fig. 7.15. The best fitting regression function is parabolic, with a sharp, positive slope in the highest intervals where the corrected correlation coefficient reflects the slope. Theta becomes progressively larger as scores increase because of the typical increase in residual variance.

TABLE 7.7
Successive Values of Theta in Using the Aptitude Index
Battery for Predicting Life Insurance Sales Success

Score Interval	Within Interval Thetas With Varying Truncation				
	0%[a]	20%	40%	60%	80%
650–793	1.43	1.35	1.28	1.21	1.07
620–649	1.23	1.16	1.10	1.04	.92
599–619	1.02	.96	.91	.86	
581–589	.98	.92	.88	.83	
564–580	.89	.83	.79		
547–563	1.03	.97	.92		
531–546	.97	.91			
512–530	.84	.79			
480–511	.70				
181–479	.75				

[a]No truncation at all, that is, 0%, provides the initial values of theta for all ten intervals. The remaining columns give theta values for the kinds of data one would have using cutting scores eliminating the bottom 20%, the bottom 40%, and so on from the data available for analysis.

Note. Adapted from Brown, S. H., Stout, J. S., Dalessio, A. T., & Crosby, M. M. (1988). Stability of validity indices through test score ranges. *Journal of Applied Psychology, 73,* 736–742. Copyright by the American Psychological Association. Reprinted with permission.

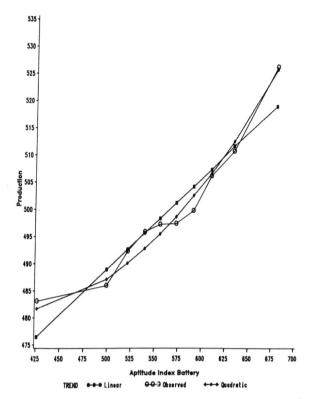

FIG. 7.15. Observed mean production and Aptitude Index Battery for ten score intervals, with linear and quadratic regression plots. From Brown, S. H., Stout, J. D., Dalessio, A. T., & Crosby, M. M. (1988). Stability of validity indices through test score ranges. *Journal of Applied Psychology, 73,* 736–742. Reprinted with permission.

Theta is not a tool for overall evaluation of relationships. It is a tool for evaluating predictor use within the score levels where the predictor is most likely to be the basis for decisions. It should be (but it is certainly not) routinely used to look for serious departures from homoscedasticity, and where they are found, to determine whether theta suggests effective prediction in those parts of the distribution where critical personnel decisions are likely to be made.

The suggestion has a glitch, also shown in Table 7.7. Values of theta do not progress in an orderly fashion from low score intervals to high. Why not? Brown et al. (1988) attributed the fluctuations to chance, a view supported by the fluctuations in observed data points in Fig. 7.15. These are column means, and even with this very large sample, they need smoothing. Ordinarily, column variance in the theta computation is based on deviation from the column mean. I suggest that it would be more useful to stay closer to the definition in Equation 2, that is, to compute residual variance from central points defined by the regression function, in this case, Y_c predicted from the quadratic equation.

UTILITY ANALYSIS

The usefulness of a predictor–criterion relationship depends on more than the size of the coefficient. Utility analysis is a formal, analytic study of usefulness or, formally, *utility*. Utility is directly related to the size of the validity coefficient. It is the slope of the linear regression equation in standard score units; the mean test score (in standard score terms) of those recommended to be selected can be multiplied by r to predict their mean criterion performance (again, in standard score terms). Without selection, of course, both mean standard scores are zero, and multiplication by any value of r yields zero. Being selective enough for the mean criterion standard score to be .1, and with a validity coefficient of .30, ‚provides a mean criterion performance in the selected group of, in standard score terms, .03, treated as a 3% gain. Utility also depends on the selection ratio. With greater selectivity allowing a standard predictor mean score of .5 for those selected, the predicted criterion performance is then .15, a 15% gain. A 15% gain is surely more useful than 3%, but the question can as surely be asked whether either gain is useful to the organization. There are other considerations. What decision rules are used—top down or something else? Does the benefit of getting the gain, whether 3% or 15%, outweigh the costs incurred?

Background Notions of Test Usefulness

Utility analysis grew from earlier work showing that usefulness (a) is directly proportional to r, (b) depends also on criterion variability, selection ratio, and criterion base rates, and (c) is an organizational, not merely psychometric, concern. The Taylor-Russell tables measured usefulness by the increase in the proportion of employees considered satisfactory (Taylor & Russell, 1939). Jarrett (1948) evaluated it as the ratio of mean output (where the criterion has a true zero) in a selected group to that in an unselected group (see also Guion, 1965).

   Utility analysis can serve many organizational purposes; I mention just three. First, it can aid decisions about using a particular procedure, comparing the benefits of its use to the costs incurred in installing and using it. Second, it offers a means for choosing between alternatives. Many assessments are based on paper-and-pencil aptitude tests. An alternative might be a hands-on assessment of existing competencies. Utility analysis might (following appropriate criterion development and assessment validation research) determine the relative utility of each form of assessment.

The number of people to be hired and existing criterion variability is the same for either program; if other considerations like costs do not differ greatly, utility analysis for comparing alternatives reduces to comparing validity coefficients (Guion & Gibson, 1988). Where considerations like costs *do* differ greatly, as they do in comparing paper-and-pencil tests with hands-on performance tests, utility analysis can be an important decision aid. Third, utility analysis is a tool for the internal marketing of a proposed program. Modern history includes many great ideas abandoned or never implemented because of a lack of compelling evidence of their worth. As a case in point, Johnson (1975), describing a book on the famous Hawthorne studies and subsequent counseling program, said that the Hawthorne plant had 5 counselors on the staff in 1936, a peak of 55 in 1948, and down to 8 in 1955; "there came a time when new management . . . began to ask questions about justifying the cost of it. Under the impact of this questioning, the program declined" (Johnson, 1975, p. 275). Perhaps, but by no means certainly, utility analysis might have saved the program.

Estimates of savings through utility equations have sometimes been staggering and even incredible. It may be that the individual level of analysis typical of most utility studies ignores the system that is the organization and therefore exaggerates expected utility (Schneider, 1996). People seeking to convince others of the value of specific programs must be as conservative as possible to make their estimates seem realistic to managers who have seen other projections of potential savings go sour.

Utility and the Consequences of Test Use

Messick (1989) included some consequences of test use as part of his view of test validity. A less limited view of consequences is surely relevant to utility. There is obvious utility in getting such intended consequences as improved production, greater safety, less time needed for training, and the like. Utility is reduced when test use has unintended consequences such as hiring people who will get bored and quit, offending candidates so that well-qualified ones do not apply, litigation, bad publicity, major capital expenditures for testing space and equipment, or high personnel costs for administering the testing program. Although the dollar benefits or costs of such consequences may be hard to estimate, they are factors in evaluation to be considered as systematically as possible. It is in directing thought to the variety of consequences of actions that utility analysis has its major benefit to an organization.

Utility analysis is most useful in considering the relative utilities of available options. When used as a relative measure, utility might be expressed in more abstract terms than dollar values, and abstract terms may prove less distracting in comparing options. One example might be to express utility as the increase in mean benefit expressed in standard score or standard deviation terms.

Estimating Utility

Modern utility analysis dates to articles by Brogden (1946; 1949) and the book by Cronbach and Gleser (1957). A basic equation known as the Brogden–Cronbach–Gleser model may be written

$$\Delta U = (N)(r_{xy})(\overline{Z}_x)(SD_y) - C \tag{14}$$

where ΔU = the increase in average dollar payoff as a result of using the selection procedure instead of random selection; N = the number of employees selected by the procedure; r_{xy} = the validity coefficient; $\overline{Z}_x$ = mean standard score of those selected; SD_y = the standard deviation of the criterion performance, in dollar units, without the x scores as selection tools; and C = the total cost of selection for all tested applicants (as presented by Boudreau, 1983).

The model shows several variables to consider in evaluating utility. Each one in the string of multiplied variables is positively, directly related to utility. N, the number of people hired, is obviously important; if hiring one person results in some savings, hiring 10 can result in more. As mentioned earlier, utility is directly proportional to r (note: not to r^2) and to the mean qualifications of those selected at a specified selection ratio. These considerations are obvious and easily computed. The joker in the equation is SD_y. Most criterion measures are not readily translated into money units, although Brogden and Taylor (1950) suggested procedures for doing so. Difficulties with SD_y account for the lack of work on utility between the introduction of the first equation (Brogden, 1949) and modern applications (Cascio & Silbey, 1979; Schmidt, Hunter, McKenzie, & Muldrow, 1979).

Roche (1965) described developing, with the help of cost accountants, a dollar criterion based on production. He concluded that it was possible, but that the resulting utility estimates may be seriously in error. Despite an apparently straightforward problem, many assumptions, estimates, and arbitrary allocations entered the system. In commenting on the study, Cronbach (1965, p. 266) said, "His reports on the employment situation in his company and on his efforts to extract the needed information from the accountants make it clear that the dollar payoff from an employee is an elusive concept, and that our theory is monstrously oversimplified." And, of course, it is—and not only because of the SD_y problem.

Schmidt et al. (1979) developed a way to estimate SD_y using the judgments of job experts. Supervisors of computer programmers in 10 federal agencies were given detailed instructions and asked to estimate the annual values of the products and services of programmers at different levels of performance: the 15th percentile (poor programmers), 50th percentile (average programmers), and the 85th percentile (superior programmers). The difference between the 50th and 85th percentiles provides one estimate of SD_y; so does the difference between the 15th and 50th. If they are about the same, an assumption of normality in the performance distribution would be justified. Because they were similar but not identical, the estimated SD_y was the average of the two.

Estimating SD_y has been the concern of much subsequent work in utility theory. The judgment method was empirically supported by Bobko, Karren, and Parkington (1983), although they proposed some procedural modifications. Later, however, in a review of relevant research, they concluded that the method was not easily applicable to many kinds of jobs and that the judgment task raised many basic research questions about the judgment processes required (Bobko, Karren, & Kerkar, 1987). Other methods of estimating SD_y in a dollar metric have been proposed (e.g., Cascio, 1982; Hunter & Schmidt, 1982), but many experts have begun to question its use relative to other metrics for expressing utility (e.g., Boudreau, 1991; Cascio, 1993; Vance & Colella, 1990). Further information on estimating SD_y appears in many articles (e.g., Judiesch, Schmidt, & Hunter, 1993; Raju et al., 1990; Raju, Burke, Normand, & Lezotte, 1993).

"THE COST OF DICHOTOMIZATION"

So Cohen (1983) titled an article showing the effect of dichotomizing a predictor X at the mean, resulting in two equal intervals. If the product–moment correlation of X with Y is r, such dichotomization necessarily results in a biserial coefficient of correlation of $.798r$, where $.798$ is the value of a multiplying constant e. With the cut score at the mean, therefore, the utility of the dichotomized X is reduced to about 80% of the utility of continuous scores (because other considerations in the utility equation stay the same). Moreover, the loss in utility is greater the further dichotomization is from the mean. If the cut score is $.5$ SD from the mean, $.5$ SD, $e = .762$. At 1 SD, $e = .662$.

The "cost" is exacerbated by the corresponding losses in values of t in testing for statistical significance and in power associated with any given sample size. In those cases where the urge for simplistic ease has also dichotomized a continuous criterion, the power loss may result in throwing out as nonsignificant a test with substantial utility if used top down. It is a practical problem in an age of litigation.

Suppose commendable validation research finds a coefficient of .30 with a very good criterion, statistically significant, $p = .045$; corrections to estimate correlation in an unselected population are therefore appropriate. The research report includes all of that information, and a regression equation and standard error of estimate that, if used by decision makers, could offer precise predictions with known margins of error. The report is filed as justification of the selection procedure.

Suppose further that, for operational use, a cut score is set at a level that will reject a bit more than 15% of the applicants, that is, about 1 *SD* below the mean. We now have a binary distribution of scores of 0 and 1 where we once had a continuous distribution of scores, and we now have a de facto validity coefficient of .662 × .30, or .1986. With the same sample size, this may no longer meet the usual 5% level of statistical significance; under a challenge to the use of the test, the nice research report fails to support that selection procedure as it is actually used. The validity of a selection procedure is its validity as it is used, not the validity of some hypothetical use that might have been.[9]

A COMMENT ON STATISTICAL PREDICTION

In regression analysis, the predicted value is a specific point on the criterion scale; a range based on the standard error of estimate can also be specified within which the criterion value for an individual may be expected at a given probability. The first specification says that, *on the average*, people with a certain score will perform at the predicted criterion level. The second specification acknowledges that most people are not going to perform at that precise average. Most researchers know both things, but in their statistical zeal, they tend to forget them. Together, these specifications are saying that the predictor variable itself leads us to expect a certain criterion performance, but that chance or other things may intervene to lead any given person to perform at a better or poorer level.

Nearly all statistical analyses are based on assumptions that (a) are rarely if ever satisfied in real data, (b) can generally (on the average) be noticeably violated without seriously affecting results, but (c) can be violated in any single situation with serious effects on results and their interpretations. One such assumption is the assumption of a normal distribution. There is no such thing in real data. Micceri (1989) examined 440 large sample distributions of test data and other distributions gleaned from published articles or reports of various kinds. *All* were in some respect nonnormal. He concluded that the normal curve, like the unicorn, is an improbable creature.

---

[9]From my distant youth, I recall these words which I cannot attribute properly: "Of all sad words of tongue or pen, the saddest are these: It might have been." Users of cut scores based only on the desire for convenience or the distrust of decision makers' abilities might frame these words and post them where they will be seen daily.

If the normal curve is improbable for one variable by itself, a normal bivariate surface is more so. To be sure, statistical analyses based on the assumption of the normal bivariate surface have, on the average, been useful in analyzing real data. That fact is not enough, however, to justify the blithe assumption that violations of assumptions never matter, that a prediction has not been affected by them, or indeed that the prediction has not been affected by other considerations not in the equation. Statistical prediction, as surely as predictions without a statistical basis, are subject to informed professional judgment.

REFERENCES

American Educational Research Association, American Psychological Association, and National Council on Measurement in Education. (1985). *Standards for educational and psychological testing.* Washington, DC: American Psychological Association.

Bobko, P. (1983). An analysis of correlations corrected for attenuation and range restriction. *Journal of Applied Psychology, 68,* 584–589.

Bobko, P., Karren, R., & Kerkar, S. P. (1987). Systematic research needs for understanding supervisory-based estimates of SD$_y$ in utility analysis. *Organizational Behavior and Human Decision Processes, 40,* 69–95.

Bobko, P., Karren, R., & Parkington, J. J. (1983). Estimation of standard deviations in utility analysis: An empirical test. *Journal of Applied Psychology, 68,* 170–176.

Boudreau, J. W. (1983). Economic considerations in estimating the utility of human resource productivity improvement programs. *Personnel Psychology, 36,* 551–576.

Boudreau, J. W. (1991). Utility analysis for decisions in human resource management. In M. D. Dunnette & L. M. Hough (Eds.), *Handbook of industrial and organizational psychology* (2nd ed., Vol. 2, pp. 621–745). Palo Alto, CA: Consulting Psychologists Press.

Brogden, H. E. (1946). On the interpretation of the correlation coefficient as a measure of predictive efficiency. *Journal of Educational Psychology, 37,* 65–76.

Brogden, H. E. (1949). When testing pays off. *Personnel Psychology, 2,* 171–183.

Brogden, H. E., & Taylor, E. K. (1950). The dollar criterion—Applying the cost accounting concept to criterion construction. *Personnel Psychology, 3,* 133–154.

Brown, S. H., Stout, J. D., Dalessio, A. T., & Crosby, M. M. (1988). Stability of validity indices through test score ranges. *Journal of Applied Psychology, 73,* 736–742.

Campbell, J. P. (1982). Editorial: Some remarks from the outgoing editor. *Journal of Applied Psychology, 67,* 691–700.

Cascio, W. F. (1982). *Costing human resources: The financial impact of behavior in organizations.* Boston: Kent.

Cascio, W. F. (1993). Assessing the utility of selection decisions: Theoretical and practical considerations. In N. Schmitt & W. C. Borman (Eds.), *Personnel selection in organizations* (pp. 310–340). San Francisco: Jossey-Bass.

Cascio, W. F., & Silbey, V. (1979). Utility of the assessment center as a selection device. *Journal of Applied Psychology, 64,* 107–118.

Chow, S. L. (1988). Significance test or effect size? *Psychological Bulletin, 103,* 105–110.

Chow, S. L. (1991). Some reservations about power analysis. *American Psychologist, 46,* 1088.

Cohen, J. (1977). *Statistical power analysis for the behavioral sciences.* New York: Academic Press.

Cohen, J. (1983). The cost of dichotomization. *Applied Psychological Measurement, 7,* 249–253.

Cohen, J. (1990). Things I have learned (so far). *American Psychologist, 45*, 1304–1312.

Coward, W. M., & Sackett, P. R. (1990). Linearity of ability-performance relationships: A reconfirmation. *Journal of Applied Psychology, 75*, 297–300.

Cronbach, L. J. (1965). Comments by Lee J. Cronbach. In L. J. Cronbach & G. C. Gleser (Eds.), *Psychological tests and personnel decisions* (2nd ed., pp. 266–267). Urbana, IL: University of Illinois Press.

Cronbach, L. J., & Gleser, G. C. (1957). *Psychological tests and personnel decisions.* Urbana, IL: University of Illinois Press.

Edwards, A. L. (1976). *An introduction to linear regression and correlation.* San Francisco: Freeman.

Ezekial, M. (1941). *Methods of correlation analysis* (2nd ed.). New York: Wiley.

Fisher, R. A., & Yates, F. (1957). *Statistical tables for biological, agricultural, and medical research.* (5th ed.). New York: Hafner Publishing Co.

Ghiselli, E. E. (1964). Dr. Ghiselli comments on Dr. Tupes' note. *Personnel Psychology, 17*, 61–63.

Ghiselli, E. E., Campbell, J. P., & Zedeck, S. (1981). *Measurement theory for the behavioral sciences.* San Francisco: Freeman.

Greener, J. M., & Osburn, H. G. (1980). Accuracy of corrections for restriction of range due to explicit selection in heteroscedastic and nonlinear distributions. *Educational and Psychological Measurement, 40*, 337–346.

Guilford, J. P. (1954). *Psychometric methods* (2nd ed.). New York: McGraw-Hill.

Guilford, J. P., & Fruchter, B. (1973). *Fundamental statistics in psychology and education.* New York: McGraw-Hill.

Guion, R. M. (1965). *Personnel testing.* New York: McGraw-Hill.

Guion, R. M. (1991). Personnel assessment, selection, and placement. In M. D. Dunnette & L. M. Hough (Eds.), *Handbook of industrial and organizational psychology* (2nd ed., Vol. 2, pp. 327–397). Palo Alto, CA: Consulting Psychologists Press.

Guion, R. M., & Gibson, W. M. (1988). Personnel selection and placement. *Annual Review of Psychology, 39*, 349–374.

Gulliksen, H. (1950). Intrinsic validity. *American Psychologist, 5*, 511–517.

Hawk, J. A. (1970). Linearity of criterion-GATB aptitude relationships. *Measurement and Evaluation in Guidance, 2*, 249–251.

Hearst, E. (1991). Psychology and nothing. *American Scientist, 79*, 432–443.

Hunter, J. E., & Schmidt, F. L. (1982). Fitting people to jobs: The impact of personnel selection on national productivity. In M. D. Dunnette & E. A. Fleishman (Eds.), *Human performance and productivity: Vol. 1 Human capability assessment* (pp. 233–284). Hillsdale, NJ: Lawrence Erlbaum Associates.

Jarrett, R. F. (1948). Per cent increase in output of selected personnel as an index of test efficiency. *Journal of Applied Psychology, 32*, 135–145.

Johnson, H. W. (1975). The Hawthorne studies: The legend and the legacy. In E. L. Cass & F. G. Zimmer (Eds.), *Man and work in society* (pp. 273–277). New York: Van Nostrand Reinhold.

Judiesch, F. L., Schmidt, F. L., & Hunter, J. E. (1993). Has the problem of judgment in utility analysis been solved? *Journal of Applied Psychology, 78*, 903–911.

Kahneman, D., & Ghiselli, E. E. (1962). Validity and nonlinear heteroscedastic models. *Personnel Psychology, 15*, 1–11.

Landy, F. J. (1986). Stamp collecting versus science: Validation as hypothesis testing. *American Psychologist, 41*, 1183–1192.

Lawshe, C. H., & Bolda, R. A. (1958). Expectancy charts: I. Their use and empirical development. *Personnel Psychology, 11*, 353–365.

Lawshe, C. H., Bolda, R. A., Brune, R. L., & Auclair, G. (1958). Expectancy charts. II. Their theoretical development. *Personnel Psychology, 11*, 545–560.

Lee, R., Miller, K. J., & Graham, W. K. (1982). Corrections for restriction of range and attenuation in criterion-related validation studies. *Journal of Applied Psychology, 67,* 637–639.

Lewis, D. (1960). *Quantitative methods in psychology.* New York: McGraw-Hill.

Linn, R. L. (1968). Range restriction problems in the use of self-selected groups for test validation. *Psychological Bulletin, 69,* 69–73.

Linn, R. L., Harnisch, D. L., & Dunbar, S. B. (1981). Corrections for range restriction: An empirical investigation of conditions resulting in conservative corrections. *Journal of Applied Psychology, 66,* 655–663.

Lord, F. M., & Novick, M. R. (1968). *Statistical theories of mental test scores.* Reading, MA: Addison-Wesley.

Messick, S. (1989). Validity. In R. L. Linn (Ed.), *Educational measurement* (3rd ed., pp. 13–103). New York: American Council on Education & Macmillan.

Micceri, T. (1989). The unicorn, the normal curve, and other improbable creatures. *Psychological Bulletin, 105,* 156–166.

Orr, J. M., Sackett, P. R., & DuBois, C. L. Z. (1991). Outlier detection and treatment in I/O psychology: A survey of researcher beliefs and an empirical illustration. *Personnel Psychology, 44,* 473–486.

Pedhazur, E. J., & Schmelkin, L. P. (1991). *Measurement, design, and analysis: An integrated approach.* Hillsdale, NJ: Lawrence Erlbaum Associates.

Raju, N. S., Burke, M. J., & Normand, J. (1990). A new approach for utility analysis. *Journal of Applied Psychology, 75,* 3–12.

Raju, N. S., Burke, M. J., Normand, J., & Lezotte, D. V. (1993). What would be if what is wasn't? Rejoinder to Judiesch, Schmidt, and Hunter (1993). *Journal of Applied Psychology, 78,* 912–916.

Raju, N. S., Edwards, J. E., & LoVerde, M. A. (1985). Corrected formulas for computing sample sizes under indirect range restriction. *Journal of Applied Psychology, 70,* 565–566.

Raju, N. S., Steinhaus, S. D., Edwards, J. E., & DeLessio, J. (1991). A logistic regression model for personnel selection. *Applied Psychological Measurement, 15,* 139–152.

Roche, W. J., Jr. (1965). A dollar criterion in fixed-treatment employee selection. In L. J. Cronbach & G. C. Gleser (Eds.), *Psychological tests and personnel decisions* (2nd ed., pp. 254–266). Urbana, IL: University of Illinois Press.

Sackett, P. R., & Ostgaard, D. J. (1994). Job-specific applicant pools and national norms for cognitive ability tests: Implications for range restriction corrections in validation research. *Journal of Applied Psychology, 79,* 680–684.

Sackett, P. R., & Wade, B. E. (1983). On the feasibility of criterion-related validity: The effects of range restriction assumptions on needed sample size. *Journal of Applied Psychology, 68,* 374–381.

Schmidt, F. L., Hunter, J. E., McKenzie, R. C., & Muldrow, T. W. (1979). Impact of valid selection procedures on work-force productivity. *Journal of Applied Psychology, 64,* 609–626.

Schmidt, F. L., Hunter, J. E., & Urry, V. W. (1976). Statistical power in criterion-related validation studies. *Journal of Applied Psychology, 61,* 473–485.

Schneider, B. (1996). When individual differences aren't. In K. R. Murphy (Ed.), *Individual differences and behavior in organizations* (pp. 548–571). San Francisco: Jossey-Bass.

Taylor, H. C., & Russell, J. T. (1939). The relationship of validity coefficients to the practical effectiveness of tests in selection: Discussion and tables. *Journal of Applied Psychology, 23,* 565–578.

Thayer, P. W. (1978). Somethings old, somethings new. *Personnel Psychology, 30,* 513–524.

Thorndike, R. L. (1949). *Personnel selection: Test and measurement technique.* New York: Wiley.

Tupes, E. C. (1964). A note on "Validity and nonlinear heteroscedastic models". *Personnel Psychology, 17,* 59–61.

Vance, R. J., & Colella, A. (1990). The utility of utility analysis. *Human Performance, 3,* 123–139.

8

The Use of Multivariate Statistics

Most jobs are complex. Effective performance requires several traits, not just one. Predictions of performance require combining or sequencing predictors in ways chosen among options. Choices are based on both statistical considerations and professional judgment.

COMPENSATORY PREDICTION MODELS

Scores on predictors can be combined in any of several models. In a linear, additive model—the most common kind of model—scores are summed to form a composite, maybe with different weights for different variables. The several predictors are assumed to be linearly related in the composite, which is linearly related to the criterion. Summing scores is *compensatory*; a person's strength in one trait may compensate for relative weakness in another. Consider Table 8.1. Candidate A has equal strength in all three traits. Candidate B is weaker than A in Trait 1 but may have enough added strength in Trait 3 to compensate. Candidate C is extremely deficient in Trait 2 but strengths in the other two may compensate. All three form the same composite score by adding the three component scores. If one trait is more important than the others, its scores get more weight (i.e., multiplied by a larger value) than the others, as in the lower half of Table 8.1. If Trait 2 is considered so important that C's deficiency in it is unacceptable despite other scores, an additive model is inappropriate.

TABLE 8.1
Composite Scores for 3 Traits for Three Hypothetical Candidates

Candidate	Trait			Sum
	1	2	3	
Without different weights				
A	10	10	10	30
B	8	10	12	30
C	15	0	15	30
With different weights				
Weights	2	3	1	
A	20	30	10	60
B	16	30	12	58
C	30	0	15	45

Regression Equations

Multiple regression analysis finds optimal weights for the several predictors, multipliers that form a composite having the best possible correlation with the criterion in the sample studied. The composite estimates with minimal error the expected criterion value for each person. Those optimal weights are optimal *only* in the research sample. In a different sample, different optimal weights would be found. The best to be expected is that the weights computed in one sample will approximate the optimal weights in most other samples.

Weights may be computed for either standardized or unstandardized scores. In conventional notation, the letter beta, β, stands for standardized weights used with standard z-scores, and the letter b refers to unstandardized weights used with raw scores or deviation scores. Both kinds of weights depend on correlations with the criterion and other predictors. Unstandardized weights also depend on relative variances.

The case of two predictors illustrates more general principles. In raw score form (with simple subscripts), the 2-variable regression equation is

$$Y = a + b_1X_1 + b_2X_2 \qquad (1)$$

where a = the Y intercept and b = regression coefficients for multiplying predictors as identified by subscripts. If the composite score C is the sum of b_1X_1 and b_2X_2, the equation can written in the familiar $Y = a + bC$ form, where a = Y intercept and b = the slope of the regression of Y on the composite score C. The regression coefficients can be computed directly from the relevant correlation coefficients and standard deviations:

$$b_1 = [(r_{yx_1} - r_{yx_2}r_{x_1x_2})/(1 - r^2_{x_1x_2})] \cdot (s_y/s_{x_1})$$

and   (2)

$$b_2 = [(r_{yx_2} - r_{yx_1} r_{x_1 x_2})/(1 - r^2_{x_1 x_2})] \cdot (s_y/s_{x_2})$$

where the values of r = a correlation coefficient, specified by subscripts, and s = a standard deviation of the criterion or of a predictor.

If $r_{x_1 x_2} = 0$, the regression weight of either predictor is its validity coefficient reduced by the ratio of the criterion standard deviation to the predictor standard deviation.[1] If raw score distributions are standardized, all standard deviations are 1.0, so standardized regression weights equal the validity coefficients. If $r_{x_1 x_2} > 0$, β weights are lower than the validity coefficients. If the two validity coefficients differ, the predictor with the higher validity has the greater weight, and the disparity increases as the intercorrelation increases. If $r_{x_1 x_2} = 1.0$, one predictor is enough; the other adds nothing.

Larger regression equations can be developed in two ways. One is simultaneous multiple regression, in which simultaneous equations are solved for the unknown regression weights. The other is a form of hierarchical analysis, identified by Pedhazur and Schmelkin (1991) as methods of variance partitioning; the most common is called step-wise regression. On the face of it, hierarchical analysis sounds great, but it is hard to interpret and has only limited usefulness.[2] Two uses relevant to personnel decisions are (a) the selection of a few predictors from many, and (b) the evaluation of moderator variables. The first of these I consider here; the second I describe later.

Hierarchical analysis sequentially enters several predictors into an equation. In one method, the first variable entered is the one with the largest validity coefficient; the next variable entered is the one that, among all others in the set, accounts for the largest share of the remaining criterion variance. Predictor standard deviations and intercorrelations influence choices of second or subsequent variables; for example, a variable highly correlated with one already chosen accounts for little incre-

---

[1]That ratio is necessarily 1.0 or less. With perfect correlation, predicted and actual criterion values will be the same and so will their standard deviations. With imperfect correlation, $r_{yx} < 1.00$, there is always some regression to the mean, meaning that predicted criterion values regress (move) toward the criterion mean, resulting in a lower variance or standard deviation. Because we virtually always have less than perfect correlation, regression weights are lower than the validity coefficients.

[2]"We would like to state at the outset that, in our opinion, the various methods . . . are of little merit. Moreover, no orientation has led to greater confusion and misinterpretation of regression results than variance partitioning. Had it not been for our wish to give you an idea of the pitfalls of this orientation, so that you may be in a better position to evaluate research in which it has been employed, we would have refrained from presenting it altogether" (Pedhazur & Schmelkin, 1991, p. 423).

mental variance, even if also highly correlated with the criterion. Some methods have stopping rules, forming a composite using only selected predictors. As the number of variables in the pool increases, the effects of error (both sampling error and chance correlations of measurement error) are magnified. If there are eight predictors and a criterion, nine variables in all, the intercorrelation matrix has $[n(n - 1)]/2 = 36$ fallible coefficients, so an unreliable sequencing of variables is likely. Informed judgment in selecting variables may be better than capitalizing blindly on chance.

Multiple Correlation

Sometimes the size of the multiple coefficient of correlation, R, is of more interest than the regression equation. It is an index of the strength of the relationship of the predictor composite and the criterion. It can be computed as a bivariate r, with the optimal composites as X, or from existing correlation coefficients. For the two-predictor case,

$$R^2_{y \cdot x_1 x_2} = \frac{r^2_{yx_1} + r^2_{yx_2} - 2r_{yx_1} r_{yx_2} r_{x_1 x_2}}{1 - r^2_{x_1 x_2}} \tag{3}$$

where $R_{y \cdot x_1 x_2}$ = the coefficient of multiple correlation for two X variables predicting Y; the various product–moment correlations are defined by the subscripts. The equation shows general principles of multiple correlation: (a) the validity of the composite is proportional to the validities of the components, and (b) the validity of the composite is inversely proportional to the intercorrelations among components.

Suppressor and Moderator Variables

Suppressors. By those principles, each test in a well-developed battery is a valid predictor of the chosen criterion and has low correlations with other variables. A valid predictor may contain an invalid, contaminating variance component. A variable that does not predict the criterion but is correlated with the contamination may improve prediction. To see how this works, look again at Equation 3. If $r_{yx_2} = 0$, but if both of the other two correlations are not zero, then the numerator of that equation becomes simply r_{yx_1} (the other two terms being zero). The denominator is less than 1.0 (because $r_{x_1 x_2}$ is *not* zero); therefore, $R_{y \cdot x_1 x_2}$ is *greater* than the validity of the one valid predictor alone. The reason is that variable X_2 removes from the composite (suppresses) the unwanted variance in X_1 not associated with the criterion. In a regression equation, it has a negative weight.

Typically, the effect is not great. If $r_{yx} = .30$ for the valid predictor, and if $r_{x_1 x_2} = .40$—these are not unrealistic numbers—the multiple correlation coefficient is raised only to .33. With a higher interecorrelation, the suppressor effect is greater; it is also clearer if all three coefficients are first corrected for range restriction and criterion unreliability. Suppressor effects are rare, but not as rare as once thought (Tzelgov & Henik, 1991).

Moderators. Moderator variables influence the relationship between other variables; they are correlated with correlation. Frederiksen and Melville (1954) found better prediction of academic performance from interests better for noncompulsive students than for those classed as compulsive. Although it is easier to think about validities in subgroups, variations in correlations associated with a continuous variable like compulsiveness "should vary continuously, . . . not jump from one value to another at some arbitrary level of compulsiveness" (Saunders, 1956, p. 209). That is, validity should change systematically and continuously as the level of the moderating variable changes. He suggested adding a term to regression equations multiplying predictor scores by moderator scores. Where there is a moderator effect to investigate, the suggested regression equation for one predictor and one moderator has the form

$$Y = a + b_1x + b_2z + b_3xz \tag{4}$$

where Y = the criterion, x = the predictor, z = the moderator variable, and xz = the product of x and z scores, the interaction or moderator term, weighted in the composite by b_3. In Equation 4, variables X and Z are expressed in deviation score units (e.g., $x = X - M_x$) with means of zero, unlike the linear Equation 1. Moderated regression is an additive (compensatory) model, but it is not linear because of the multiplicative term. A significant interaction term says that, for every value of z, there is a different slope of the regression of y on x, even though the difference may be small and gradual.

Deviation scores (or perhaps z-scores), not raw scores, should be used when variables are multiplied. The effect of raw score computation in regression analysis is to standardize all components, including the product term. Aiken and West (1991) pointed out that standardizing products of raw scores results in sometimes dramatic changes in the linear regression terms of the component variables themselves.

Like suppressor variables, examples of moderator effects for personnel decisions are rarely reported and rarely replicated. The initial surge of enthusiasm led to sweeping searches for moderators in whatever data pool was available; such reliance on exploration and serendipity was not often rewarded. Enthusiasm for demographic moderators (as solutions to fairness problems) was no more fruitful. Searches for moderators in the validity generalization paradigm have turned up only a few. As a result, many selection specialists have given up on moderators.

Such pessimism is unwarranted. Some failures to find moderators are methodological (e.g., use of raw scores). Many more are due to inadequate logic. Research agenda should abandon serendipity. Moderators seem more likely to be found after serious thinking, hypothesizing, and theory formation than after searches among variables for which there is no useful rationale. The field of industrial and organizational psychology is big. Many activities and concepts, expected to influence a variety of work outcomes, have been studied and promoted extensively. A systematic consideration of such variables surely should be a rich source of reasoned moderator hypotheses.

Other Additive Composites

Multiple regression is but one way to form a composite, and reasons for forming composites are not limited to criterion prediction.[3] Reasons might include, for example, weighting predictors to promote an organizational policy. "The general problem of the combination of measures has been obscured by the indiscriminate adoption of the multiple correlation technique as the 'best' solution, *and by the failure to investigate the properties of various weighting systems*" (Richardson, 1941, p. 379, italics added). With computers and mindless use of software, the problem is even more obscured than Richardson suspected; it easy to compute regression weights, appropriate or not.

Effective Versus Nominal Weights. In any weighting method, the weights one *thinks* one is using can differ from the actual contributions of component variables to the composite: "It does not follow that test variables with equal linear weights have actually been weighted equally. The mischievous character of arbitrarily assigned weights depends on the fact that the actual *effective* weights turn out to be quite different from the *nominal* weights originally assigned" (Richardson, 1941, p. 380). This discussion of the mischievous character, like Richardson's, is limited to linear, additive models with uncorrelated or positively correlated variables.

Suppose we have three variables to combine. The effective weight of each is its contribution to the total variance of composite scores. With the simplifying assumption of perfect reliability, the following general principles govern effective weights:

1. If component variables have equal variances (as with standard scores) and zero intercorrelations, effective weights are proportional to

---

[3]This section is taken more or less verbatim from Guion (1991). It is based largely on the unjustifiably but generally ignored work of Richardson (1941).

the *squares* of the nominal weights. If variable A is to be weighted twice as heavily as B or C, the nominal weights are 2, 1, and 1, but the effective weights of uncorrelated standard scores are 4, 1, and 1, respectively.

2. If intercorrelations are zero, but variances are not equal, the effective weight of a component is proportional to the product of the square of its nominal weight (V) and its variance s^2.

3. If nominal weights and variances are unequal, and if variables are positively correlated, the effective weight of a component is proportional to the product of its nominal weight and the weighted sum of its correlations with other variables. (Treating reliability as perfect, the self-correlation is 1.00 in these computations.) The equation for total composite variance, s_t^2, is:

$$s_t^2 = V_1 s_1 \Sigma V_i r_{1i} s_i + V_2 s_2 \Sigma V_i r_{2i} s_i + \ldots + V_n s_n \Sigma V_i r_{ni} s_i \qquad (5)$$

where V, r, and s refer to nominal weight, correlation, and standard deviation, respectively, the subscripts $1 \ldots n$ refer to the variables, and the subscript i refers to all other variables; so, r_{ni} following Σ, refers to the sum of the correlations of variable n with each of the other variables. Table 8.2 shows nominal weights, standard deviations, and intercorrelations in a three-component situation; relative nominal and effective weights are also shown. (Relative weights are computed by summing weights for all variables and dividing each weight by the sum.) Relative nominal and effective weights differ substantially.

4. To eliminate the remaining simplification, if all other considerations are equal, the effective weight of a component is directly proportional to its reliability. The common practice of weighting by the inverse of the standard deviation is justified only when differences in variances are caused by differences in construction (e.g., when one test has 10 items

TABLE 8.2
Data for a Hypothetical Three-Variable Composite

Variable	V	s	Correlations			Relative Weights	
			A	B	C	Nominal	Effective
A	1	1	1.00	.50	.80	.167	.067
B	3	2		1.00	.60	.500	.460
C	2	3			1.00	.333	.473

and another has 100). If differences in variances are associated with differences in reliabilities, weighting inversely to standard deviations (or unit weighting z-scores) may give the highest effective weight to the least reliable component—an anomoly to be avoided.

Further Purposes in Weighting. Weights can be developed for optimal prediction, or by arbitrary assignment according to judged importance. Horst (1966) identified further options for weighting schemes; weights might be assigned that maximize the reliability of the composite (but see Green, 1950), its variance, or (if intercorrelations are positive and substantial), the variance attributable to the common factor. Where only a few variables form a composite, the choice of a weighting scheme can make substantial differences in the effective weights for each variable, and the correlations of the various composites may be low enough to indicate real differences in criterion-related validity coefficients.

A weighting method should be based on rational, theoretical grounds rather than on computations alone. One important rational principle is simplicity. Studies long ago cast doubt on the value of weights determined by very sophisticated methods. Ghiselli and Brown (1949), using arbitrary weights based on results of a quite different study, reported a high validity coefficient. Lawshe and Schucker (1959) reported predictions as good for sums of raw scores as for more formal methods, including multiple regression, which are supposed to maximize predictive accuracy. Often, psychometric and statistical assumptions are not met in applied settings; it is not wise to take excessive pride in an impressive weighting system. It is wise to see if effective weights make sense.

"Unit" Weighting. "Unit" weighting means simply adding scores or standard scores, literally multiplying by 1.0, as in the top of Table 8.1. Dawes and Corrigan (1974) insisted, and demonstrated, that use of more complex models offers no more than slight improvement over simple weights, whether equal or differential, in accounting for criterion variance; their finding held even with randomly chosen weights. Others have supported the finding (Einhorn & Hogarth, 1975; Wainer, 1976). However, (Cattin, 1978) said that regression weights may predict better than unit weights if (a) patterns of intercorrelations among the predictor variables differ, (b) the regression-based multiple R is high, (c) different predictors have substantially different weights, and (d) the ratio of subjects to variables is large. He recommended an empirical comparison, computing both a cross-validated R (discussed later) and the correlation for the unit-weighted composite—and using whichever is higher. I suggest a third option to try: unequal weights that approximate or are proportional to the optimal regression weights. In general, carefully computing weights

to several decimal places may give only the appearance of precision; simpler nominal weights may do as well or better if variables are carefully selected, are positively correlated with each other and with the criterion, and do not differ greatly in validities or reliabilities.

NONCOMPENSATORY PREDICTION MODELS

A truly noncompensatory trait—one so vital to performance that no other strength can compensate—is unlikely. Psychologically, people learn to live with deficiencies and make up for them. Statistically, the idea suggests a discontinuous function with no functional relationship on either side of the point of discontinuity. I know of no such finding. Even so, some researchers have found nonadditive, noncompensatory prediction models useful (e.g., Brannick, 1986; Einhorn, 1971; Mertz & Doherty, 1974).

Multiple Cutoff Methods

A multiple cut (multiple hurdles) approach uses a cut score for each of two or more tests. An applicant scoring below the cut score on any of them is rejected; each test is a "hurdle" to clear. Two situations may justify the method: (a) if each trait is so vital to performance that other personal strengths cannot compensate for weaknesses in them, or (b) if their variance is too low to yield significant correlation.

Generally, however, objections to cut scores in bivariate prediction apply even more to multiple predictors, where even very low cut scores can result in rejecting too many candidates. A cut score about 1.5 SD below the mean of a normal distribution will reject about 7% of the candidates. If a similar cut score is set on another, uncorrelated measure, 7% will be rejected by it, also. Some people might be in the low 7% on both tests, but the percentage of the total group being rejected will approach, even if it does not reach, 14%. More hurdles mean more rejections. Many of those passing all of the hurdles will do so with scores too low to suggest any genuinely useful qualifications at all. Cut scores high enough to assure people qualified on each trait may find no one qualified on all of them.

A multiple cutoff approach is justified only when predictors are perfectly reliable (Lord, 1962, 1963). If practical considerations demand it, it can be modified by a partially compensatory model (Lord, 1963). Selection effects using compensatory, noncompensatory, and partially compensatory models are shown in Fig. 8.1; those selected score above (or to the right of) the lines applicable to both variables.

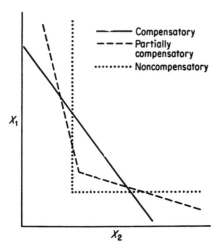

FIG. 8.1. Areas of decision within two-predictor scattergrams for compensatory, partially compensatory, and noncompensatory decision models; in each case, the area above or to the right of the line is the area within which selection is the appropriate decisions and those below and to the left of the line are rejected. From Guion (1965a).

Sequential Hurdles

In a *sequential hurdles* approach, those who "pass" one or more preliminary steps are assessed later on other characteristics. The early cut scores are often intended to reduce the size of the group to be assessed by costlier methods. There may not be a fixed cut score; a fixed number of candidates more qualified than others may move to the next stage.

Fixed cut scores transform scores to a dichotomy, 1 (*pass*) or 0 (*fail*). This is important in validating later assessments in a candidate population limited to those passing the earlier hurdles.

Conjunctive and Disjunctive Models

The equations identified jointly as Equation 6 offer one definition (there are others) of conjunctive and disjunctive decision rules:

$$\text{Conjunctive: } Y = \min(b_1X_1 + a_1, \ldots, b_kX_k + a_k)$$

$$\text{Disjunctive: } Y = \max(b_1X_1 + a_1, \ldots, b_kX_k + a_k)$$

(6)

Equation 6 supposes a battery of k predictors. As written, a linear bivariate regression equation exists for each predictor (although other functions might be justified). The conjunctive decision rule bases decisions on the predictor that minimizes the estimated criterion value; there is no cut score. No other score in the set, no matter how high, compensates for an unsatisfactory prediction based on the minimum score. A disjunctive decision rule, similarly, is based on one predictor, the one with the highest estimated value of Y. No matter how poorly one performs on some other variable, the decision is based on the candidate's strength. These models should be considered much more often than they are at present.

Identifying Situations for Noncompensatory Models

Brannick and Brannick (1989) identified six possible prediction models, two of them using equations developed earlier by Brannick (1986). He saw that conjunctive and disjunctive models dealt with profiles in which points are scattered about a central level and developed equations for detecting nonadditive (i.e., noncompensatory) components in prediction.[4] The simpler of the two Brannick equations is

$$Y = a + \Sigma b_i X_i + b_{k+1}[\Sigma(z_i - \bar{z})^2]^{1/2} \tag{7}$$

where Y = the predicted criterion value, the phrase $a + \Sigma b_i X_i$ = the conventional multiple regression term, and $\Sigma(z_i - \bar{z})^2$ is proportional to the standard deviation of the variables, expressed in z-scores, within the profile; $\bar{z}$ = the mean of the z-scores in the profile. If the scatter term adds significantly to the variance explained by the linear term, a noncompensatory model is suggested. The more powerful equation is

$$Y = a + \Sigma b_i X_i + b_{k+1}[\Sigma B_i(z_i - Y^*)^2]^{1/2} \tag{8}$$

where $a + \Sigma b_i X_i$ is the usual multiple regression equation; the full scatter term, $[\Sigma B_i(z_i - Y^*)^2]^{1/2}$, is proportional to within-profile variance, differing from the scatter term of Equation 7 in being a weighted variance. The variables within the profiles are weighted according to their contribution to the predictions. Remember that the standardized regression coefficients, in bivariate relationships, are the same as the correlation coefficients. Here they are designated B to distinguish them from the unstandardized coefficients designated b (and from the linear β weights). The central tendency in Equation 7 is the profile mean z-score, and the profile points are straightforward z-scores. In Equation 8, it is the Y score predicted for the profile values, Y^*; the differences between profile z-scores and that central tendency are weighted before summing by their standardized regression coefficients (i.e., weights). In practice, use of Equation 8 requires three computational steps:

---

[4]It should be noted that all of these are properly recognized as examples of multiple regression, even though the organization of this chapter has so far limited the term to the common linear, additive model.

1. In standard score form, estimate standardized regression coefficients and standardized criterion scores from the ordinary least squares regression equation.

2. With Y^* as a central tendency of the standardized profile of variables, z_i as the standard score of variable i, and B_i as its corresponding standardized regression coefficient, compute the scatter term, $[\Sigma B_i(z_i - Y^*)^2]^{1/2}$. (This term, despite the use of standard scores, is not itself in standard score form, so it does not have unit variance.)

3. Therefore, in simultaneous regression, apply Equation 8. A new set of linear regression coefficients, the unstandardized b_i, will be computed as will the regression coefficient for the scatter or profile term, b_{k+1}.

In both Equation 7 and Equation 8, the scatter term suggests a nonadditive model if it adds significantly to the multiple correlation. In some uses, notably in predictions of judgments, the significance test is inappropriate because of within-judge dependencies, but even in such cases, Brannick and Brannick (1989) recommended heuristic use of the significance test. Note that Equation 8 provides a basis for estimating criterion variance associated with the scatter term, and that the degree of relationship can be estimated by correlating actual and expected values of the criterion. It does *not*, however, tell the decision maker how to use the information the scatter term provides. It might be used as it is, simply as a term adding significantly to prediction. It might be used conjunctively or disjunctively, or in some other nonadditive combination. Various algorithms might be tried to see which gives the maximum R^2. One such algorithm might be, "If X_1 is below a standard level, predict from X_2."

I sympathize with frustrated readers at this point. I have said nothing about the relative benefits of these or other models that could be discussed, such as profile matching (Cattell, 1949; Guion, 1965a) or prediction from categorical variables (Guion, 1954; Wickens, 1989). The only recommendation I can offer is to continue research to develop, evaluate, and clarify uses of noncompensatory models.

REPLICATION AND CROSS VALIDATION

Error is a fact of psychometric life. Each assessment and each statistic contains some—some random, some systematic. An additive composite holds hope that random errors may cancel each other. Hope springs eternally but is not always rewarded. When scores are added, systematic errors may also be added, some random errors may be too big to be canceled by others, and some errors of either kind may by chance be correlated with error in the criterion. A simple additive combination can give a large validity coefficient in one sample that is never again repeated in another. The problem is worse with complex combinations, many variables, or peculiar nonadditive or nonlinear components. Because high validities encourage new personnel procedures promoting or requiring organizational change, it is unwise to rely on a one-shot coefficient that might have capitalized on errors. Results of validation, especially a multivariate one, need to be repeated—replicated—in a new sample when feasible.

Multiple regression requires cross validation. Loose use of language sometimes treats cross validation and replication as interchangeable, but they are different.[5] Cross validation applies multiple regression weights obtained in one sample to data obtained in a different one to see whether the multiple R found in the first sample holds up in a second or whether it was inflated by sample-specific error. Replication refers to a repetition of an original study, with or without some systematic change in measures or procedures, to see if independent results are similar.

Cross validation is required in multiple regression studies because the composite-forming regression equation developed in one sample has the highest possible correlation with the criterion in that specific research sample. In another, independent sample from the same population, using the same equation, the new correlation is almost always lower. *Shrinkage*, the reduction in the size of the multiple coefficient of correlation, is expected. If shrinkage is negligible, the weights are considered stable; if large, the weights are not reliable and the composite is not recommended.

Double cross validation combines replication with cross validation. A regression equation is developed in each of two independent samples and cross validated in the other. Predictors with strong weights in both equations have done well twice, and they can enter simultaneous regression analysis based on all cases, combining the two samples.

The logic of cross validation calls for independent samples. A common but poor practice draws a sample and divides it, either into two equal samples or into one larger sample for research and a smaller "hold-out" sample for cross validation. This practice may be better than no cross validation at all, but it lacks independence. When a sample is randomly divided into two parts, any systematic error in one part exists also in the other, making similar weights more likely. Moreover, the research sample is smaller, so weights have more sampling error than if they had been obtained with the total sample. A cross validated coefficient is sometimes higher than in the research sample—the opposite of shrinkage. Such an

---

[5]Mea culpa. In Guion and Gottier (1965), we used the term *cross validation* when we were referring to simple replication.

anomaly is more likely with interdependent samples. The practice was denounced by Murphy (1983), who titled it "Fooling Yourself With Cross Validation: Single Sample Designs."

Dividing a single sample is ill-advised, but it may not be feasible to draw two large samples. An alternative is to estimate shrinkage from a single sample by formula estimation (e.g., Cattin, 1980; Claudy, 1978; Schmitt, Coyle, & Rauschenberger, 1977). Formula estimates consider only sampling error, not measurement error, either random or systematic, but shrinkage from random error is lower in the large sample than in the smaller one resulting from dividing. However, it *is* a single sample; results should be replicated if possible.

Wherry (1931) offered the most commonly used equation for estimating the shrunken coefficient from a single sample. As presented by Claudy (1978) but with notation used earlier, and in squared form, it is

$$\overline{R}^2 = 1 - [(n - 1)/(n - k - 1)] \cdot (1 - R^2) \tag{9}$$

where $\overline{R}$ = the estimate of the shrunken coefficient, R = the computed coefficient, n = sample size, and k = the number of predictors in the equation. Other equations have been offered. Results differ little among them; simplicity is a useful basis for choosing. Conceptually, $\overline{R}$ differs somewhat from the empirically determined shrunken coefficient in two-sample cross validation. It does not estimate correlation in a second sample, it estimates the population multiple correlation. Given the option, replication is preferable.

"SYNTHETIC" VALIDITY

Lawshe (1952) introduced the term *"synthetic" validity*, distinguished from generalized or situational validity, for testing procedures in small businesses where conventional validation was not feasible. Synthetic is in quotation marks because it is a bit of a misnomer; validity can be expressed or developed or discovered, but not synthesized. What is synthesized is a valid test battery. Synthetic validity means "inferring validity [of the battery] in a specific situation from a logical analysis of jobs into their elements, a determination of test validity for these elements, and a combination of elemental validities into a whole" (Balma, 1959, p. 395). At different times, different people have viewed synthetic validity from different perspectives and with different approaches (Guion, 1965b; Lawshe & Steinberg, 1955; McCormick, Meecham, & Jeanneret, 1989; Wise, Peterson, Hoffman, Campbell, & Arabian, 1991).

In general, the results support the idea that a valid test battery can be synthesized. The U.S. Army's Synthetic Validity Project (Wise et al., 1991) was a large scale study with fairly typical findings. It compared criterion-related validity coefficients for Army occuptions to those based on synthetic validity equations; across occupations they differed hardly at all (by .01 or .02, depending on how job component importance was weighted). However, there was no discriminant validity. An equation developed for one occupation could be applied equally well to others. Validity coefficients were as high as could reasonably be expected—and discriminant validities as low as anyone could fear. Is that bad? The generalized answer, I think, depends on whether one's purpose is selection or placement. With poor discriminant validity, placement is not helped. Selection for a brand new job, or for one with infrequent hiring, may be helped by synthetic validity. If criterion components are substantially correlated, discriminant validity is not critical; an approximate equation based on synthetic validity will work. Discriminant validity may be elusive because performance on criterion components is not specific, that is, because performance is truly general. Alternatively, it may be a function of the human developmental progression from very general to more specific kinds of abilties. Perhaps greater discriminant validity exists for predictions of later criteria, such as performance on jobs to which entry-level people are promoted.

Perhaps not. Such speculation does no more than suggest that research continue. For most purposes, the lack of discriminant validity is less serious than the lack of conventional ways to evaluate selection procedures. As pointed out by Mossholder and Arvey (1984), contemporary needs are for validity evidence and documentation that can be applied to a variety of settings regardless of sample size. Moreover, the rapid evolution of jobs can make conventional validity information obsolete in short order. Rethinking the challenge of synthetic validity and the associated absence of discriminant validity may let synthetic validation address both problems.

"CAUSAL" RESEARCH

Predictive hypotheses usually imply that criterion performance is caused (in part) by the predictor trait even though the implication is untested in conventional validation. A causal chain is implied when a predictor is used to predict success in training and training success is assumed to predict later job performance. The plausibility of such causal chains (or more complex networks) can be investigated by path analysis.

Validated selection procedures are often only part, even if the core, of actual selection programs. Over time, many candidates appear; different people may make decisions about different candidates. As a matter of policy, valid prediction equations or expectancies may inform decision makers without dictating their decisions. In short, selection programs are often more complex than simply giving a test and then using an explicit, score-based decision rule. Such programs evolve or are developed in the belief that they will produce clear and measurable benefits. That is a causal statement: that the benefits are the effect of the program. Its plausibility might be investigated using quasi-experimental studies.

Path analysis and quasi-experimental field research are among so-called causal or confirmatory research methods. I use the term "causal" loosely; Pedhazur and Schmelkin (1991) reviewed the pitfalls of the term with so many contradictory quotations that I also use it fearfully. It is, however, conventional to refer to structural equation modeling as causal modeling. Let us use the term without taking it too seriously. Causal research does not confirm or prove causality; it merely tests the plausibility of a causal model. Only if plausibility is confirmed may users proceed as if the causal statement were correct.

Path Analysis

Structural equation modeling of causal assumptions is a powerful method of statistical analysis; path analysis is the popular name for one form of it. A brief glossary can help introduce the general concept.

> *Structural equations*: a set of equations specifying a theoretical model implying a set of causal relationships.
>
> *Specification error*: omission of relevant variables related to the independent variable(s). Specification is assigning variables to a place in the theory to be tested. A specification error means that the model of reality represented by a set of equations is wrong—to some degree, and in some sense. The term usually refers to omission, not to variables that do not belong in the model. A bivariate hypothesis is surely misspecified. A fully specified model is sometimes called *self-contained* (James, Mulaik, & Brett, 1982).
>
> *Identification*: information within the model necessary to represent the parameters of the equations in the model. Models are *just-identified*, *overidentified*, or *underidentified*. A just-identified (or *saturated*) model is one that provides the information needed to estimate the parameters (e.g., the right number of equations for the number of unknown parameters to be estimated). Such a model cannot be tested because it

has no degrees of freedom, no redundancy. An underidentified model is untestable because necessary information is lacking. Only an overidentified model can be tested, but knowing when a model is overidentified presents problems and controversy among experts. When results yield negative variances or correlations greater than 1.0, identification problems may be the culprit. The concept is confusing. Pedhazur and Schmelkin (1991) acknowledged that even their unusually clear exposition probably produced a "sense of frustration, if not helplessness" (p. 704).

Exogenous and *endogenous* variables: Exogenous variables are those the model accepts as given; explaining variance in these variables lies outside of the model itself. Endogenous variables are those whose variation is explained, according to the theory modeled, by other variables within the model (including exogenous variables).

Mediating variable: one occupying an intermediate position in a causal chain. James and Brett (1984) distinguished between mediators and moderators (a nonlinear interacting variable) but pointed out that a given variable *can* serve in both roles within a model.

Development of Path Models. Path analysis is theoretical; it studies a systematic theory of the events or variables that may produce one or more outcomes of interest. The theory need not be a grand, overall theory of the discipline, but it should be comprehensive enough to avoid specification errors. Any thoughtful development of a multivariate predictive hypothesis is, in a sense, theory development. Suppose one wants to predict how long it will take people to learn to repair malfunctioning electronic equipment. The traditional hypothesis is limited to personal traits such as knowledge of electronic theory, cognitive flexibility in developing and trying out possible problem solutions, or perhaps achievement motivation; it might even include the skill level of (or time with) a trainer or mentor. The usual predictive hypothesis says nothing, however, about potential causal links among these four predictors; their interrelationships are considered only in terms of intercorrelations. Figure 8.2a illustrates this traditional research model in a "single-stage model" (Pedhazur & Schmelkin, 1991, p. 311), that is, one where the dependent or criterion variable is related to each one in a set of more or less intercorrelated variables. The model implies causality in the direction of the arrow, but only because the four independent variables existed first.

Suppose, however, we propose that the motivation to achieve in this learning situation is an endogenous variable caused by both the work ethic the person brings to the job (an exogenous variable) and some

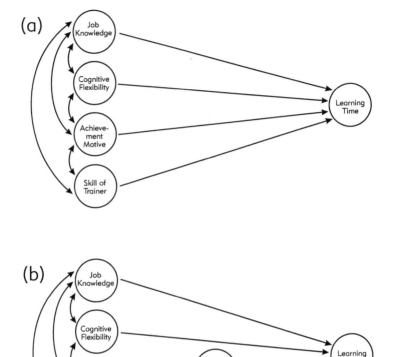

FIG. 8.2. Transformation of simple predictive hypothesis to a causal model. In (b), the causal model, some arrows between exogenous variables have been omitted to avoid making the drawing too crowded.

exogenous characteristics of the trainer, including but not limited to the trainer's skill level, or the amount of one-on-one time. The model in Fig. 8.2b hypothesizes achievement motivation as a direct influence on learning time and an effect of a general work ethic and trainer skill; it is a mediating variable. It also assumes that learning time is influenced by three learner traits but not by trainer skill. Given the content of this paragraph, the model is misspecified; the amount of one-on-one time is not included, and I offer no reason for ignoring it.

A properly specified model need not include every variable in the causal chain, nor does a model of the effect of personnel decisions require specification of every independent variable that might influence criteria.

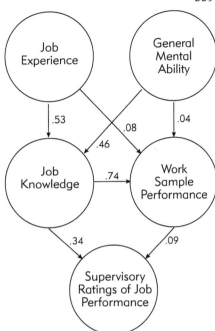

FIG. 8.3. Path coefficients for incumbents in four military specialties. Abstracted from Schmidt,
F. L., Hunter, J. E., & Outerbridge,
A. N. (1986). Impact of job experience and ability on job knowledge, work sample performance,
and supervisory ratings of job
performance. *Journal of Applied
Psychology, 71*, 432–439. Reprinted
with permission.

To model a causal understanding of a given selection program, one tries
to understand how various program elements contribute to a decision
and whether the decision has an influence on one or more criteria. The
issue is whether the program itself has been fully specified.

An Example. Schmidt, Hunter, and Outerbridge (1986) reported a path
analysis for data collected from people in four military specialties; a
synopsis of the model and their results are shown in Fig. 8.3. According
to the model, amount of job experience influences level of job knowledge
and ability to do the job, as shown on work sample tests. General mental
ability also influences knowledge and work sample performance, and
both of these influence supervisory ratings. Beside each path arrow in
Fig. 8.3 is a path coefficient, a standard partial regression weight, showing
the strength of the influence in that path.[6]

The model as a whole is confirmed, but for these incumbents, whose
job experience ranges from a few months to many years, general mental

---

[6]Partial correlation and partial regression weights have not been discussed in this book;
see Pedhazur and Schmelkin (1991). In the original report, Schmidt, Hunter, and Outerbridge
(1986) provide two sets of path coefficients, those reported here and another set for data in
which the nonlinear relation of job experience to work sample performance was transformed
to a linear coding of a grouped distribution. The purpose here is simply to illustrate path
analysis, so only one set is given.

ability has little direct impact on work sample performance. It does have an impact, however, on work sample performance via the mediating job knowledge variable. Supervisory ratings are more heavily influenced by job knowledge than by the performance typified by the work sample.

Measurement Models.   Causal models imply constructs, but the example was tested with operational measures. A measurement model specifies constructs, or latent variables, each of which is measured by several optional operations. Such a model reduces measurement error and is helpful in the search for moderator variables. The reliability of a product term is lower than the reliabilities of the constituent measures; where only one measure of each variable (construct) is used (as is typical in multiple regression), so product terms identifying moderator effects lose power. Jaccard and Wan (1995) showed that multiple indicators in a structural measurement model can help identify significant interactions.

Quasi-Experimental Designs for Program Evaluation

An assessment procedure or management program can be evaluated at an organizational level of analysis using experimental or quasi-experimental research. In a true experiment, people are assigned at random to the experimental conditions or treatments, thereby controlling for individual differences. The dependent variable in a well-controlled experiment is the hypothesized effect of the treatments. In a quasi-experiment, a causal inference is desired but not assured because, among other things, the people studied are not randomly assigned to treatments. Nevertheless, quasi-experimental research, like path analysis, can either confirm or disconfirm the plausibility of causal hypothesis. Disconfirmation is less ambiguous.

Two Quasi-Experimental Studies

Loss of inventory by theft or careless error is a serious problem in convenience stores. Terris and Jones (1982; also reported in Terris, 1985) reported a time series study of shrinkage in relation to the introduction of an integrity test. Monthly records of shrinkage, in dollars and in loss as a percentage of sales, were maintained for more than 3 years, about 2 years before and up to 19 months after introduction of the test. Results in Fig. 8.4 show improvement in two criteria. The average per store shrinkage rate was $515 before test use and $249 afterward.

Nevertheless, the results were inconclusive. One discussion of the study included this:

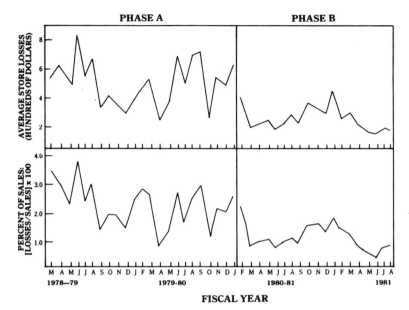

FIG. 8.4. Monthly inventory shrinkage in a convenience store chain before
and after the introduction of an integrity test for pre-employment screening.
From Terris, W. (Ed.). (1985). *Employee theft: Research, theory, and applications.*
Park Ridge, IL: London House Press. Reprinted with permission.

Perhaps the program was seen as a more general message from management that dishonesty was not to be tolerated. It is possible that employees
. . . might have assumed that additional measures were also being taken to
detect theft, and that they may have avoided stealing to ensure that they
were not caught. It is also possible that the new screening procedure sen-
sitized managers more to the issues of employee theft, resulting in higher
levels of management vigilance. The design of the study does not allow us
to identify the true nature of the effects reported. (O'Bannon, Goldinger,
& Appleby, 1989, p. 89)

The study does not clarify the true underlying reason for the desirable
results, but it is plausible to suppose that the results were attributable to
something related to the assessment procedure. The study says nothing
about the psychometric validity of the assessments; it says only that the
idea that their use leads to desired organizational results is not disconfirmed. The results justify their continued use. However, if the reason for
their usefulness is unknown, their use is continued in ignorance. In
ignorance, improvements are not likely, so the research should not stop
here. A full program might include management development meetings
with problem-solving discussions of theft and its reduction; or systematic
publicity about theft consequences; or job enrichment, particularly in pay,

responsibility, and opportunity. With such a program, path analysis could be added to the time series to identify its most effective parts and provide insight into the contribution of each.

In three groups of discount stores, records of terminations for "gross misconduct" were kept for several months (Paajanen, 1988) before and after starting a testing program to screen applicants. Group A had many such terminations before test use; Group B had relatively few; the test was not used in Group C. Results are shown in Fig. 8.5.

Group A stores had a persistent but relatively slight decrease in such terminations over the 15 months before testing. The pretesting regression line in Group B had a much more pronounced negative slope. No reason is apparent from these data, but the two groups of stores surely have different histories. After test introduction, clear discontinuity appears in both regression lines; the downward slope continues, with less random fluctuation and a slightly greater rate of change. In Group C, the rate of gross misconduct terminations was lower to begin with, and the trend is downward—a bit more marked after test use began in the other two groups of stores.

The discount store example is more informative than the convenience store example. Regression lines in Fig. 8.5 provide more perspective for the more or less random fluctuations in monthly data, and the discontinuity is more persuasive than a pattern of jagged lines. Moreover, there

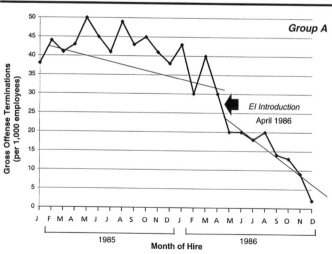

FIG. 8.5. *(Continued)*

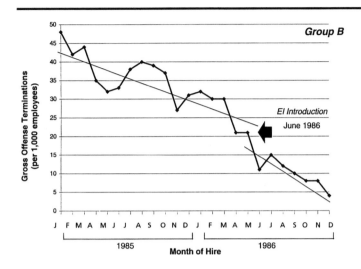

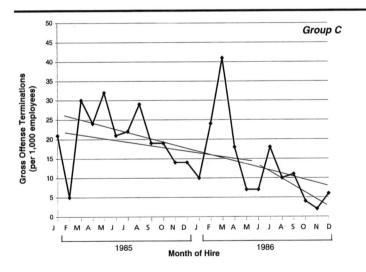

FIG. 8.5. Monthly rates and regression lines for "Gross Misconduct Terminations" in three groups of discount stores. From Paajanen, G. E. (1986). PDI Employment Inventory. Minneapolis: Personnel Decisions, International. Reprinted with permission.

were two sets of experimental stores, not just one, and the program was introduced in them at different times. The group of stores where testing was not introduced permits two comparisons of experimental and control groups.

Some questions remain unanswered. Why the downward slope in all three? Why was the downward slope so much more pronounced in one experimental group than in the other? Why were more terminations experienced in the two experimental groups than in the control? Were actions being taken, independently of the assessments being evaluated, that also were effective in reducing shrinkage?

Some Quasi-Experimental Designs

Validity and Research Design. Readers frustrated by the distinction between the validity of measurement and validity of prediction should be braced for further frustration. We now consider four aspects of the validity of causal inferences from quasi-experimental research (Campbell & Stanley, 1966; Cook & Campbell, 1979; Cook, Campbell, & Peracchio, 1990). Evaluation of designs for quasi-experimental research requires evaluations of potential threats to these aspects of validity.

Statistical conclusion validity refers to statistical significance. No one should ascribe excessive importance to statistical significance, but it is prerequisite to inferences of causality. *Internal validity* requires that the manipulated variable or "treatment" be the only plausible explanation of an outcome. Design flaws that permit other explanations of the outcomes threaten internal validity and may invalidate the research and its findings. *Construct validity* refers to interpretations of the meaning of outcome and treatment variables—largely the same meaning as before except that the constructs are not necessarily metric. *External validity* refers to the generalizability of research findings beyond the specific study itself.

Design descriptions here are illustrative but terribly brief. For better descriptions, consult Cook et al. (1990) and Cook and Campbell (1979). Using their notation, the letter X designates the treatment (or program) and the letter O designates outcome or criterion variable. Subscripts indicate the relative sequence of outcome observations.

Uninterpretable Designs. Some designs rarely if ever permit even a modest inference of causality; they have little internal validity.

Design 1: One group, posttest only

$$X \qquad O_1$$

In this design, a treatment is introduced and at a subsequent time an outcome is observed. There is no control group, there is no prior observation, there is no point in using it.

Design 2: One group, pretest and posttest

$$O_1 \quad X \quad O_2$$

In this design, one group of people is observed before the treatment and again afterward. Improvement in the measured outcome is supposed to be attributable to the treatment. But why? It could be attributed to almost any influence, recognized or not. If the design is used with an extreme group (e.g., extremely low performance), regression to the mean might account for any apparent improvement.

Design 3: Two nonequivalent groups, posttest only

$$X \quad O_1$$
$$O_1$$

This sort of thing happens when someone has implemented a program and then later asks a researcher to evaluate it. There is nothing against which to compare results in either group. Group nonequivalence pretty much precludes even a weak inference of causality.

Three Generally Interpretable Designs. These are not sure designs; each is subject to possible threats to validity. Carefully done, however, their results are likely to be interpretable, even if ambiguity remains.

Design 4: Untreated control group with pretests and posttests

$$O_1 \quad X \quad O_2$$
$$O_1 \quad \quad O_2$$

This is the most common design. Two groups are identified and initial observations, O_1, are made; only one group gets the experimental treatment. Subsequently the criterion is again measured in both groups. Four possible outcomes are shown in Fig. 8.6, the most clearly intepretable being outcome (d). In this case no outcome change occurs in the control group; initially, the treatment group is lower, catches up after treatment,

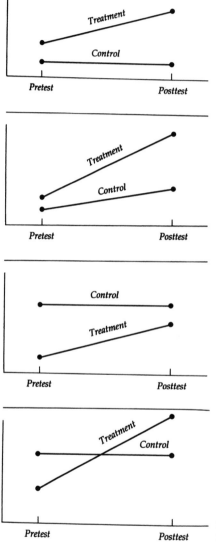

FIG. 8.6. Four possible outcomes of research with treatment and control groups and both pretest and posttest outcomes. From Cook, T. D., Campbell, D. T., & Peracchio, L. (1990). Quasi experimentation. In M. D. Dunnette & L. M. Hough (Eds.), *Handbook of industrial and organizational psychology* (2nd ed., Vol. 1, pp. 491–576). Palo Alto, CA: Consulting Psychologists Press. Reproduced with special permission of the publisher, Consulting Psychologists Press, Inc. All rights reserved.

and in time exceeds the criterion level of the controls. The figure depicts a reliable mean difference in both pretest and posttest, but the direction is switched. The pronounced interaction rules out many plausible alternative inferences. The other three patterns allow statistically significant outcomes also to be interpreted as treatment effects, even if less convincingly.

Design 5: Two groups with switching replications

O_1	X	O_2		O_3

O_1		O_2	X	O_3

This is essentially Design 4 with replication in which the roles of the groups are reversed. If the treatment works, results should be that $O_2 > O_1$ in the top group and $O_3 > O_2$ in the bottom group, with other differences trivial. This is probably stronger than an exact replication because the context for treatment is different the second time. Further improvement in design would use another group without treatment.

Design 6: One group removed-treatment design

O_1	X	O_2	X	O_3	noX	O_4

Sometimes, doing something, no matter what, brings about improvement. Suppose production was observed at O_1, after which X introduced, followed by an increase in production at O_2 and a further increase at O_3 after adding still more X. One might think that X caused the production increases unless the final step is taken: returning to the original condition. If the last observation is not about the same level as the first, results cannot be interpreted; if it is, a causal relationship is plausible.

Pragmatism and Program Evaluation

An assessment program for decision making is usually an amalgam in which the assessment procedure itself is confounded with location, unit, decision maker, and other variables. It is useful to evaluate the whole package when an assessment procedure is introduced in an organization. It may have unmeasured effects, such as changing the calibre of candidates who apply. Quasi-experiments can help managers decide whether the program as a whole produces criterion improvements.

The designs described here may not be able to answer subsequent "why?" or "why not?" questions. To get a handle on these questions, and some others, one needs a much broader program of evaluation, among other things, trying to identify unintended and perhaps undesirable consequences of program introduction (cf. Berk & Rossi, 1990). It is not easy to discover unintended consequences; one might do so through luck, prescience, formal hypotheses, social criticism, or intelligent observation.

The process is difficult; evaluating and understanding programs merits more attention in assessment than it has so far received.

META-ANALYSIS AND VALIDITY GENERALIZATION

A replicated finding is better than one from even a good single study. Science wants to know what is generally (even if not invariably) so. Scientific generalization depends more on a chain of similar findings, from different settings and methods, than on an isolated one.

Criterion-related validation tests the hypothesis that a given trait is dependably associated with a certain kind of outcome or criterion. A typical study is done in a single setting, with specific predictor and criterion measures. Supporting the hypothesis in that setting does not make it "generally so." Affirming the generality of a relationship requires a research history supporting it in different settings with different details.

Ghiselli (1966) surveyed hundreds of validity studies and found wide variation in validity coefficients for given combinations of test type, occupational group, and criterion category. That was not surprising; the variation among findings, if not the reason for it, was well known. Conventional guesses attributed it to unknown and perhaps unknowable local influences. Pleasantly surprising was that many mean validity coefficients were high, as in Fig. 8.7. If the mean uncorrected coefficient is .40 or more, the chance of finding validity in one's own situation seems good. Validities for such job-test-criterion combinations could even be considered "generalizable" (Lawshe, 1952, p. 31).

The idea of generalizable validity was dormant for years. Schmidt and Hunter (1977) revived it by showing that variability in validity coefficients in different situations could be attributed to statistical and procedural variables—they called them "artifacts"—in individual studies. They introduced *validity generalization*, a specific form of meta-analysis. *Meta-analysis* looks quantitatively for conclusions that have been generally so in independent research on the same basic hypothesis. Traditional literature surveys had the same objective but were verbal rather than quantitative, often imprecise, and subjective. Subjectivity remains in meta-analysis, primarily in coding information, but procedures are systematized and results are quantitative. Of the many approaches to meta-analysis, the one known also as validity generalization is the most directly appropriate to personnel testing.

Principles of Validity Generalization

Validity generalization (Schmidt & Hunter, 1977) assembles correlation coefficients from independent validation studies of the same hypothesis. The mean of the resulting distribution is an estimate of the mean in the

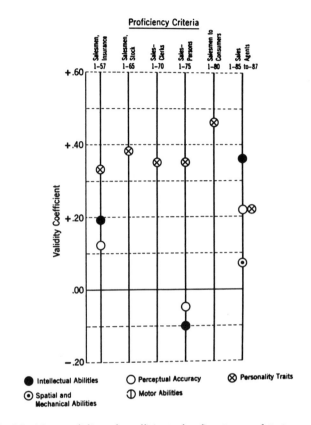

FIG. 8.7. Mean validity of coefficients for five types of tests against proficiency criteria for six sales-related occupations. From Ghiselli, E. E. (1966). *The validity of occupational aptitude tests.* New York: Wiley.

population from which the samples came. The variance of the distribution exceeds zero only to the degree to which results in the samples come from different populations, stem from different systematic influences, or are subject to different sources of error.

The validity generalization approach begins with the idea that the criterion-related validity coefficient is the same in all tests of the research hypothesis—or would be if not for artifactual influences on the results of individual studies. Coefficients can be corrected statistically for some artifacts; corrections for others are applied to the estimated variance of the distribution of corrected coefficients. If that variance can be explained largely by these artifacts, then validity is said to generalize across the diverse situations from which individual coefficients came. If not, then systematic characteristics of different studies are examined as potential moderating influences.

Validity generalization tests two hypotheses in addition to the substantive hypothesis. The *situational specificity* hypothesis is that criterion-related validity depends in part on unknown influences within research settings; it can be rejected if corrections substantially reduce the variance of the validity coefficient distribution. Corrections cannot be made for unknown or unreported artifacts, so Hunter and Schmidt (1990) advocated a rule of thumb that rejects situational specificity if 75% or more of the variance is explained by known artifacts. Unknown artifacts may account for the rest so that the corrected mean correlation may be treated as the population value across all studies.

The validity generalization hypothesis is not simply the obverse of situational specificity, although rejecting the hypothesis of situational specificity is a necessary first step. Validity generalization is supported when nearly all of the coefficients in the distribution are at or above a nontrivial level and in the same direction (all positive or all negative). Reports usually identify the point in the distribution above which 90% or more of the corrected validity coefficients lie. If validity generalizes, the mean of the distribution of coefficients (after correction for statistical artifacts) is the best single estimate of validity in the job or job family sampled in the accumulated research.

Table 8.3 presents a list of artifacts that may influence validity coefficients and their distributions. In reading the table, assume that, "in the book of the recording angel" (from a reliability discussion by Stanley, 1971, p. 361), a "true" validity coefficient exists and describes the relationship of predictor to criterion constructs. Measurement errors, of course, always exist (Artifacts 2, 3, 8, and 9). Procedural errors in the design or conduct of the study (Artifacts 4–7 and 11) are also likely. Merely taking a sample suggests a result different from the "true" result; the smaller the sample, the greater the error (Artifact 1). There is a nonzero likelihood of error in recording, analyzing, or reporting what was done and found (Artifact 10). The accumulated data may include samples from different populations with different "true" validity coefficients. All of these are sources of variance in the set of coefficients, and validity generalization research makes corrections for one or more of them.

Corrections for artifacts provide a distribution of "corrected" coefficients. Its mean is an estimate of the hypothetical "true" validity, and the variance of these estimates is less than that of the uncorrected coefficients. If the corrected variance approaches zero, the spector of unknown situational influences is exorcised. When coefficients in a corrected distribution are both positive and negative (and not close to zero), the kinds of predictors in the analysis do *not* have generalized validity; failure to reduce variance substantially by the corrections argues that something does in fact influence validities across situations. The task then changes from seeking generalizations to searching for moderators.

TABLE 8.3
Artifactual Influences on Validity Coefficients
With Examples From Personnel Research

---

1. Sampling error:
   Study validity will vary randomly from the population value because of sampling error.
2. Error of measurement in the dependent variable:
   Study validity will be systematically lower than true validity to the extent that job performance is measured with random error.
3. Error of measurement in the independent variable:
   Study validity for a test will systematically understate the validity of the ability measured since the test is not perfectly reliable.
4. Dichotomization of a continuous dependent variable:
   Turnover—the length of time that a worker stays with the organization—is often dichotomized into "more than . . ." or "less than . . ." where . . . is some arbitrarily chosen interval such as one year or six months.
5. Dichotomization of a continuous independent variable:
   Interviewers are often told to dichotomize their perceptions into "acceptable" versus "reject."
6. Range variation in the independent variable:
   Study validity will be systematically lower than true validity to the extent that hiring policy causes incumbents to have a lower variation in the predictor than is true of applicants.
7. Attrition artifacts: Range variations in the dependent variable:
   Study validity will be systematically lower than true validity to the extent that there is systematic attrition in workers on performance, as when good workers are promoted out of the population or when poor workers are fired for poor performance.
8. Deviation from perfect construct validity in the independent variable:
   Study validity will vary if the factor structure of the test differs from the usual structure of tests for the same trait.
9. Deviation from perfect construct validity in the dependent variable:
   Study validity will differ from true validity if the criterion is deficient or contaminated.
10. Reporting or transcriptional error:
    Reported study validities differ from actual study validities due to a variety of reporting problems: inaccuracy in coding data, computational errors, errors in reading computer output, typographical errors by secretaries or by printers. Note: These errors can be very large in magnitude.
11. Variance due to extraneous factors:
    Study validity will be systematically lower than true validity if incumbents differ in experience at the time they are assessed for performance.

Note. From Hunter, J. E., & Schmidt, F. L. (1990). *Methods of meta-analysis: Correcting error and bias in research findings*. Newbury Park, CA: Sage. Reprinted by permission of Sage Publications.

Three different results occur in validity generalization research. A study may (a) refute (or support) the situational specificity hypothesis by showing (or not) that the variance of the distribution of corrected coefficients approaches zero, (b) support (or refute) the validity generalization hypothesis by showing (or not) that all or nearly all validity coefficients across diverse situations are nontrivial in size and in the same direction, and (c) (if situational specificity is rejected and generalization is supported), give an estimate of population validity in the form of the mean of the corrected coefficients $(\bar{r}_c)$.[7] The quality of these findings depends on how many of the artifacts the analysis has been able to correct and on how well the corrections have been made. Research reports rarely give all the information needed for the corrections, but meta-analytic results are usually more dependable than single-study results.

Methods of Analysis

I describe here only the simplest method, omitting most of the controversy, modification, and options in a rather extensive literature. I follow, unless otherwise specified, the presentation of Hunter and Schmidt (1990), which should be consulted for details, assumptions, equations, and further procedures.

The first step is to search thoroughly for both published and unpublished research reports. Some experts recommend purging the file of bad research; others seek the most nearly complete file possible. Each report is read and coded for data points and associated information. Each validity statement is one data point. If two or more data points are reported from a sample (for the hypothesis at hand), they are not independent. A decision about handling nonindependence must be made early in the process; options include randomly choosing one data point from the lot, averaging them, or (conceivably) ignoring the problem.

Coding includes classifying and recording information about the various artifacts. Distinctive job characteristics, industry in which the study is done, sample demographics, or characteristics of work environments may also be coded. If situational specificity is rejected, much of this information will not be used, but it is practical to anticipate its use at the outset, before objectivity-destroying biases or mental sets develop. A major frustration in meta-analysis is the failure in many research reports to give even basic

---

[7]"Estimate of population validity" is a longer phrase than "true validity," but it is also more accurate. Some people have adopted the latter phrase as everyday vocabulary, but I prefer to resist it. We cannot know the mythical truth, but we can know estimates of what it might be in the population sampled. The estimate itself is subject to failures in correction and also to the fact that even with the most extensive search for studies to include in the meta-analysis, the studies included are but a sample of those that might have been done.

information. If sample size, reliability, and range restriction are given, correlation coefficients can be corrected so that the distribution of coefficients is a distribution of population estimates, not of raw coefficients. If not, judgments based on the literature can often be made about artifact distributions to get plausible values to use for corrections.

Interpretation of results is evaluative. Analyses done with only a few data points are often evaluated unfavorably. Even an excellent analysis may be rejected as irrelevant to one's own purpose if the hypothesis, jobs studied, or criteria do not fit it. Equations used in corrections may be criticized, although choices among optional equations seems a rather trivial issue relative to the advantage of the method in general (perhaps an overinterpretation of Linn & Dunbar, 1986; Raju & Burke, 1983).

"Bare Bones" Analysis: Correction for Sampling Error Only. The simplest form of meta-analysis corrects only for sampling error, the biggest artifactual source of variance in most sets of correlation coefficients. This "bare bones" analysis offers the simplest description of validity generalization. In correcting only for sampling error, other artifacts are ignored; ignoring them, of course, does not get rid of them, and the analysis should be more comprehensive if possible.

Table 8.4 presents hypothetical correlation coefficients presumably from 10 independent studies, all testing roughly the same hypothesis. The sample size is known for each study, but no information related to other artifacts is available; thus, only a bare bones analysis is possible.

Each study may be considered a replication of the others. These are not precise replications, of course, being based on different measures, or done under different conditions (e.g., predictive designs or concurrent).

TABLE 8.4
A Hypothetical Set of Correlation Coefficients From
Ten Independent Studies of the Same Hypothesis

Study No. (i)	N_i	r_i	$N_i r_i$	$N_i(r_i - \bar{r})^2$
1	23	.17	3.91	.1863
2	217	.23*	49.91	.1953
3	68	.53*	36.04	4.9572
4	141	.30*	42.30	.2256
5	92	.08	7.36	2.9808
6	30	.15	4.50	.3630
7	45	.03	1.35	2.3805
8	101	.19	19.19	.4949
9	309	.32*	98.88	1.1124
10	54	.39*	21.06	.9126
Σ	1080		284.50	13.8086

*significantly different from 0.0 at the .05 level.

They are, nevertheless, replications in the sense that each is concerned with the correlation between the same two constructs).

The best estimate of the population correlation across replications is an average. Data points based on large samples are more reliable estimates of population correlations than those from small samples, so each one is weighted by the size of the sample from which it came:

$$\bar{r} = \frac{\Sigma(N_i r_i)}{\Sigma N_i} \tag{10}$$

where $\bar{r}$ = mean correlation coefficient across studies, weighted for sample size, N_i = the size of the sample in study i, and r_i = a correlation coefficient observed in study i. Substituting the data in Table 8.4, $\bar{r}_r$ = 284.50/1080 = .26. Note that these correlation coefficients have not been transformed to Fisher's z'. An average correlation, based on the z' transformation, tends to overestimate population values, even at the modest levels of most validity coefficients.

The variance across these studies is best described in terms of the average squared deviations, weighted by the sample sizes:

$$s_r^2 = \frac{\Sigma N_i (r_i - \bar{r})^2}{\Sigma N_i} \tag{11}$$

where s_r^2 = variance of observed correlation coefficients across samples, weighted for sample size, and the other notation is as before. Substituting data in Table 8.4, s_r^2 = 13.8086/1080 = .0128. If one looks only at the range of coefficients, from .03 to .53, one might think results differed substantially. No one adequately trained in statistics would look only at those values, however, because the end points of distributions are notoriously unreliable. Further noting that half of the correlations are nonsignificant, one might have serious doubts about the generality of support for the hypothesis. However, both the extreme values of the range and the significance tests are misleading. Although small, there is some variance among these correlations. The question is whether that variance approaches zero when artifacts are considered—whether the "corrected" variance, s_{rc}^2 (variance of corrected coefficients, r_c, in the set of studies) is close enough to zero. A prior question is the variance due to sampling error, s_{ec}^2. Unless there is an anomalously large sample in the data set, Hunter and Schmidt (1990, p. 108) recommend the equation

$$s_{ec}^2 = \frac{(1 - \bar{r}^2)^2}{\bar{N}_i - 1}. \tag{12}$$

Substituting in Equation 12, $s_{ec}^2 = (1 - .0676)^2/(108 - 1) = .008$. Subtracting this from the estimated total variance from Equation 11, $s_{rc}^2 = .0128 - .008 = .0048$. In short, when sampling error is the only source of error considered, the variance of the distribution of population estimates in the 10 studies of Table 8.4 shrinks to .0048 from an initial variance of .0128—sampling error has accounted for 62.5% of the initially observed variance across studies. That does not meet the 75% rule of thumb advocated by Hunter and Schmidt (1990). This simple analysis, therefore, does not permit rejection of the situational specificity hypothesis, so the question of validity generalization does not arise.

Correcting for More Than One Artifact. There usually are other correctable artifacts; corrections for criterion unreliability and range restriction are often possible. Further corrections might lead to different results. It is not often, however, that corrections can be made for all artifacts in Table 8.3. Even individual studies that provide full statistical information rarely offer information about such matters as transcription or reporting error, so they cannot be considered in the analysis; however, we cannot rule out (or, for that matter, rule in) the possibility that these artifacts may account for a nontrivial portion of the variance.

By the rule of thumb, if more than 25% of the original variance remains after the ordinary corrections, we are justified in searching for moderators. The search is limited by the information coded from the original studies. That information may provide one or more variables, continuous or categorical, that may correlate well with the corrected coefficients. A substantial correlation identifies a moderator.

Procedures for estimating variance of corrected coefficients were given in Hunter and Schmidt (1990). These equations, however, seem to provide underestimates, so improved procedures have been proposed (Hunter & Schmidt, 1994; Law, Schmidt, & Hunter, 1994a, 1994b). These refinements are seen as more accurate and more likely to give reason to reject situational specificity; the older procedures are more conservative.

Using Artifact Distributions. Research reports in this imperfect world often provide no information about things that might have influenced the results. In any given set of studies to review, some will report certain kinds of information, but others will not. Some kinds of information (such as codable information about criterion construct validities) will rarely be mentioned. Where little or no information is available across studies, an artifact is consigned to the abyss of unknown influences—influences that may be large or small, positive or negative, common or uncommon, but contributing in unknown ways and degrees to the variance of correlation coefficients. If distributions can be developed from the studies that do report on an artifact, or perhaps from other sources, approximate correction factors can be computed from them and used in the analysis.

Representative Validity Generalization Findings

Schmidt and Hunter (1981) said, "Professionally developed cognitive ability tests are valid predictors of performance on the job and in training for all jobs" (p. 1128). This seems an overwhelming, even reckless, generalization, yet there is support for it, and it is important to note what it does *not* say. It does not suggest that all cognitive tests are *equally* valid predictors across all jobs, all criteria, or all circumstances. Estimates of population validities vary. This section describes results of several meta-analyses, with a wide range of positive, nonzero estimates of population validities. It is not intended as a critical review of individual meta-analyses; rather, it is intended only to provide the flavor of some major results.

The studies surveyed used different methods and equations. These methodological differences, however, do not make as much difference in results as do differences in criteria, job complexity, occupation, or type of predictor. Different studies report different things. Some report 90% credibility values, some 97.5% credibility values, and some give the 90% or 95% confidence intervals. Some correct only for sampling error, others correct for several artifacts. For these matters, too, this survey is silent; these details, though important, would distract from the main emphasis intended. Where data are tabled, the tables include the number of data points (K), the estimate of true validity (still denoted r_c), the percentage of original variance accounted for by sampling error and any other artifacts, and the lower bound of the confidence interval.

Clerical Occupations. Table 8.5 presents results of several meta-analyses. The different types of tests considered part of clerical aptitude validly predict clerical performance in nearly all clerical job categories. All estimates of population validities are positive, as are most 90% credibility values; in fact, only a few are less than .10. Exceptions are noncognitive tests: motor tests (for which the rationale is rather dim, anyway, for most clerical jobs) and performance tests (which are likely to be occupationally specific). Specific conclusions about generalizable validity in clerical work can be drawn from Table 8.5:

1. General mental ability tests predict proficiency in virtually all clerical work.

2. Tests of perceptual speed are valid predictors for virtually all clerical jobs; most corrected coefficients are about .40 or higher (see also Ruch, Stang, McKillip, & Dye, 1994).

TABLE 8.5
Validity Generalization Analysis of Validities in
Clerical Occupations Against Proficiency Criteria

Occupation; Test Type	K	r_c	% Variance Accounted	90% Cred. Value
General clerks[a]				
Intelligence tests	72	.67	76	.40[a]
Stenographers, typists, and related[b]				
General mental ability	76	.50	56	.19
Verbal ability	215	.39	53	.10
Quantitative ability	155	.49	80	.32
Reasoning ability	36	.38	100	.38
Perceptual speed	368	.45	53	.14
Memory	49	.38	65	.13
Spatial/mechanical ability	38	.20	74	.04
Motor ability	95	.29	50	−.02
Performance tests[c]	55	.50	25	−.05
Clerical aptitude[d]	63	.50	60	.22
Computing, account recording[b]				
General mental ability	47	.49	51	.18
Verbal ability	97	.41	54	.10
Quantitative ability	121	.52	74	.32
Reasoning ability	29	.63	87	.47
Perceptual speed	251	.50	80	.33
Memory	39	.42	100	.42
Spatial/mechanical ability	47	.42	64	.17
Motor ability	97	.30	75	.12
Clerical aptitude[d]	26	.53	53	.20
Production, stock clerks, related[b]				
Verbal ability	28	.37	100	.37
Quantitative ability	33	.60	93	.49
Reasoning ability	10	.31	66	.08
Perceptual speed	50	.45	100	.45
Memory	11	.44	79	.25
Spatial/mechanical ability	12	.48	96	.41
Motor ability	21	.27	100	.27
Information/message distribution[b]				
Perceptual speed	10	.40	57	.12
Motor ability	12	.15	56	−.14
Public contact and clerical service[b]				
General mental ability	10	.43	100	.43
Quantitative ability	17	.45	100	.45
Perceptual speed	23	.39	84	.24
Motor ability	21	.26	100	.26
All clerical job categories combined[b]				
General mental ability	194	.52	51	.21
Verbal ability	450	.39	52	.09
Quantitative ability	453	.47	77	.30
Reasoning ability	116	.39	70	.19
Perceptual speed	882	.47	77	.19

(Continued)

TABLE 8.5
(Continued)

Occupation; Test Type	K	r_c	% Variance Accounted	90% Cred. Value
Memory	117	.38	72	.17
Spatial/mechanical ability	108	.30	60	.05
Motor ability	257	.30	57	.03
Performance tests[c]	67	.44	23	−.11
Clerical aptitude[d]	142	.48	53	.18
All Clerical Job Categories[e]				
Language skills	24	.31	100	.31
Reading comprehension	24	.26	100	.26
Vocabulary	23	.27	64	.18
Computation	24	.30	94	.28
Problem solving	24	.29	100	.29
Decision making	23	.23	97	.24
Following oral directions	24	.27	100	.27
Following written directions	24	.29	100	.29
Forms checking	24	.25	97	.24
Reasoning	23	.21	90	.17
Classifying	24	.32	100	.32
Coding	24	.31	100	.31
Filing names	23	.29	68	.21
Filing numbers	23	.28	100	.28
Visual speed and accuracy	24	.23	100	.23
Memory	23	.17	82	.12
Generic Battery[f]	24	.37	94	.34

[a]From Schmidt and Hunter (1977); the 97.5% credibility value, .40, was reported. [b]From Pearlman, Schmidt, and Hunter (1980). [c]Work samples, specifically typing and dictation tests. [d]Composites of verbal, quantitative, or perceptual speed abilities. [e]From Psychological Services, Inc. [PSI] (in press). Job categories include general clerks, information clerks, administrative clerks, figure clerks, typist clerks, bookkeeping clerks, and machine operator clerks. [f]The generic battery consists of the Language Skills, Computation, Following Written Directions, and Coding Tests of Basic Skills.

3. Validity generalizes for the three major components of most clerical aptitude test batteries: verbal ability, quantitative ability, and perceptual speed.

4. Proficiency of clerks who do computational work is predicted well by tests of reasoning ability as well as tests of quantitative ability.

5. In some clerical occupations, specifically those involving information, message distribution, and public contact, memory has not been tested enough to permit meta-analysis; for others, however, the proficiency-related validity of memory tests generalizes.

Judgments about test-based predictions of proficiency may be made with greater confidence from these meta-analyses than from local validation research. There is no need to validate these kinds of tests in local clerical settings; the generalized estimates of population coefficients are based on dozens, even hundreds, of studies with the proficiencies and abilities of tens of thousands of clerical workers evaluated. One more study is unlikely to change the conclusions.

Table 8.5 also shows that validity is better in some circumstances than in others. Test and job types moderate validities; other moderators may exist but not be identified. Of the 43 comprehensive meta-analyses in Table 8.5, those reported across general test types, only 19 accounted for at least 75% of the variance. If general mental ability tests generally predict proficiency in clerical work, and if artifacts account for only 51% of the overall variance among coefficients (Pearlman, Schmidt, & Hunter, 1980), moderators may function even though the tests are job related at any moderator level.[8] Local validation is indicated only if the local situation has a remarkable characteristic distinguishing it from others and is a plausible moderator.

Professional, Managerial, and Supervisory Occupations. Ruch et al. (1994) reported rather high mean corrected coefficients for these occupations. There were few studies for these analyses, in some cases as few as six. Corrected mean correlations were over .50 for vocabulary, basic arithmetic, numerical reasoning, and verbal reasoning tests. They strongly support the importance of a set of "four r's" for high level jobs: reading, 'riting, 'rithmetic, and reasoning.

Computer Programmers. An aptitude test for selecting programmers, the three-part Programmer Aptitude Test (see McNamara & Hughes, 1961), has been used often; Schmidt, Gast-Rosenberg, and Hunter (1980) reviewed 42 studies. There are three part scores; for the total score, $r_c =$ .73 for predictions of on-the-job proficiency and .91 for predictions of success in training.

Many of the individual validations were done early in the computer era, long before computer literacy was commonplace among young adults. Has the test retained its validity in the computer era? The report does not say.

Life Insurance Salespersons. The *Aptitude Index Battery* (AIB) has long been used in the life insurance industry to select people to sell life insurance. Across 12 companies, the AIB had a corrected r_c of .26,

---

[8]Reanalysis of the Pearlman, Schmidt, and Hunter (1980) study was reported by Schmidt, Law, Hunter, Rothstein, Pearlman, and McDaniel (1993). Using methods of analysis they consider more accurate, the figure jumps from 51% to 91%, rendering this discussion off target. The earlier data gave details needed for Table 12 (not relevant to the purposes of the reanalysis) but the newer analysis gives more reason to reject situational specificity.

spuriously low considering typical nonlinearity. Corrections accounted for 62% of the original variance and suggested a moderating influence (Brown, 1981). It was found—when companies were divided into two groups differing in management of recruiting and selection. Brown (1981) concluded that the quality of management of the recruiting and selection process may either constrain or enhance test validity.

It was an interesting finding and it raised interesting questions. Would a similar moderator be found for other job-test combinations? Would more general concepts of management quality moderate validities? Such moderators are rarely investigated; the necessary data are rarely included in research reports. The life insurance industry has its own research arm and is in the rare position of having the data. Perhaps similar information could be included in consortium studies or other industry-wide efforts.

Law Enforcement Occupations. Some findings reported by Hirsh, Northrop, and Schmidt (1986) are presented in Table 8.6. They found strong validities for training criteria (not reported here), but results for proficiency criteria are quite modest despite corrections for the first five artifacts. Situational specificity is rejected under the 75% rule only for reasoning and spatial/mechanical tests. (It could be rejected also for a composite, not shown, of verbal, memory, and reasoning tests plus scores for driving skill and human relations skills.) However, generalization of these modest validity estimates cannot be recommended.

Although the authors considered their findings for training criteria consistent with those for other job-test combinations, the validities for proficiency are noticeably lower. Therefore, the meta-analysis offers little help to those in businesses and governmental jurisdictions wanting to hire the most proficient law enforcement people. There is, of course, the composite, but r_c for the 5-variable composite is only slightly better than that for quantitative abilities not included in it. The problem is not in the

TABLE 8.6
Validity Generalization Results for Predicting
Proficiency in Law Enforcement Occupations

Test Type	K	r_c	% Variance Accounted	90% Cred. Value
Memory (M)	25	.10	64	−.07
Psychomotor skill (Ps)	9	.14	66	−.01
Quantitative ability (Q)	8	.26	44	.03
Reasoning ability (R)	29	.17	90	.08
Spatial/Mechanical ability (Sp)	29	.17	100	.17
Verbal ability (V)	18	.18	63	.00
V + R + M + Sp	7	.22	34	−.07

Note. From Hirsch, Northrop, and Schmidt (1986). Reprinted with permission.

meta-analysis; validity coefficients simply seem to be low in law enforcement occupations, where the criterion problem is horrendous. Another plausible reason for low validities is that, in law enforcement, cognitive ability may play a less important role than noncognitive skills, especially interpersonal ones or personality variables. Personality tests are often used in selecting police officers, but usually as psychiatric screening devices rather than as predictors of future performance. The implied prediction is seldom validated.

Craft and Assembly Jobs. Meta-analyses reported by Levine, Spector, Menon, Narayanan, and Cannon-Bowers (1996) supported the generalization of the validity of cognitive tests for predicting performance in six craft (or craft-like) jobs in the utility industry, although support was unclear for cognitive tests of perceptual skills in one of the six categories. When composites were formed from cognitive, perceptual, and psychomotor tests, the validity for proficiency criteria generalized well.

Choosing Predictors From Meta-Analyses

Judgment is always required in choosing predictor constructs and their operational definitions; the judgment is simplified (but not eliminated) if one bases it partly on an adequate and appropriate meta-analysis. An appropriate one investigates and supports an appropriate hypothesis. Ordinarily, the constructs of the local predictive hypothesis are narrower than those of a meta-analysis, but the meta-analysis constructs, to be appropriate, must encompass if not match those of local interest. Even if meta-analysis supports one's predictive hypothesis at the construct level, it may not offer as much help in choosing a test that operationally defines the generally valid construct. For example, an appropriate meta-analysis might include both highly reliable tests and those with questionable reliability, but it is hard to identify them. It is also possible that a poor test has been used in only one of the several studies; if so, test quality does not appear as a potential moderator, identifying the good and poor bets.

To evaluate adequacy, several questions need answers:

1. Has a useful level of validity been shown to generalize across the several situations represented by the studies reviewed? That is, is the 90% credibility value positive and nontrivial?

2. Are r_c and the 90% credibility value high enough to overcome the effects of second-order sampling error? (Second order sampling error stems from having too few data points in the analysis.) Fundamentally, the question is whether the addition of another study would change r_c appreciably. Schmidt, Hunter, and Caplan (1981) suggested that adding

more data points where $K = 50$ or more would change outcomes only trivially. When K is small, however—and those reviewed here contain several analyses with fewer than 10 studies—the value of r_c may not be stable and may be a poor basis for assuming validity for the local test.

3. Are the data points themselves reasonably stable? Are the number of cases in each study large enough to assure a reasonably stable distribution of stable coefficients? I am skeptical of meta-analyses of studies with samples of only 10–20 cases, unless there are an awful lot of them. Words like reasonably and an awful lot are far too ambiguous to be helpful; what is reasonable, or enough, probably depends on how desperately one needs help in finding a predictor construct.

4. Has the analysis been carefully done? Have the researchers been systematic and objective and reliable in establishing and using categories for coding the various studies?

5. If situational specificity has not been clearly rejected, have plausible moderators been investigated? Or suggested?

Issues in Validity Generalization

Some matters still at issue, at least for me, can be reviewed quickly.

1. Does meta-analysis oversimplify the search for generalizations? Too much emphasis on the general can obscure important exceptions. A comment following a discussion generally approving validity generalization:

> The work of Schmidt and Hunter and their colleagues has broken new ground and set a new standard for integrative work in personnel psychology. Still there is a danger of overgeneralizing conclusions and carrying the implications of this work too far. Generalizations are important to any scientific area, but so too are the exceptions. . . . Our task is not only to seek generalizations, but to find and attempt to understand exceptions. (Linn & Dunbar, 1986, p. 232)

Cronbach (1982) said that

> general, lasting, definite "laws" are in principle beyond the reach of social science, that sheer empirical generalization is doomed as a research strategy. . . . In protesting against this view, some of our colleagues are beginning to sound like a kind of Flat Earth Society. They tell us that the world is essentially simple: most social phenomena are adequately described by linear equations; one-parameter scaling can discover coherent variables independent of culture and population; and inconsistencies among studies

of the same kind will vanish if we but amalgamate a sufficient number of studies. (Cronbach, 1982, p. 70)

Is meta-analysis misdirecting research? Yes, if it causes people to stop doing research on exceptions or rejects as myth or superstition the search for aptitude-situation interactions. These are not, however, necessary consequences.

2. Validity generalization is fundamentally a two-variable process; it is most often concerned with the relationship between one predictor and one criterion. It is not concerned with the "third variable" problem, the possibility that correlation may be *inflated* with contaminants common to the variables. Table 8.3 lists many artifacts that reduce correlation, but it is silent on the third-variable question, the question of pervasive contamination. In *Personnel Psychology*, Schmidt, Pearlman, Hunter, and Hirsh (1985) posed 40 questions and provided answers; Sackett, Tenopyr, Schmitt, and Kehoe (1985) inserted comments where they had reservations about the answers. One recurring theme was that of a flawed database. Sackett et al. (1985, p. 781) said, "[W]e could be in the position of 'garbage in, garbage out.' " In rebuttal, Schmidt et al. (1985, pp. 788–789) referred to outlier analysis as a basis for discarding certain kinds of flawed data, the removal of non-Pearsonian correlations from the database, and said that most flaws result in conservative rather than in inflated conclusions; they said further that common flaws would produce bizarre results far removed from those of other analyses and therefore "immediately recognized as highly suspect." I find this rebuttal unconvincing; for me, common third variables remain a haunting prospect.

3. What is learned from a meta-analysis of consistently flawed data? Hunter and Schmidt (1990) gave detailed attention to identifying and perhaps removing outliers in a distribution of coefficients, and Hedges (1990) pointed out that the seriousness of flaws may vary with the research context. These responses deal with a few individually flawed studies. The question asks about the data set as a whole. If the entire body of research is thought to be subject to one or more common flaws, the issue centers on the confidence one can have in that entire body. The allegation of universal flaws is not likely to be widely accepted, of course, but the gadfly that raises the question may be the one who points the way to better research designs and the need for a whole new data set. More probable is the allegation that everything is flawed but in such very different ways that the flaws have no chance to emerge as moderating influences.

4. I once knew a delightful lady who declared the overwhelming principle of test use to be, "Don't use rancid data." I wonder if meta-analysts should follow her dictum. Is it possible that very old studies should be excluded from the meta-analysis because their methods, data,

or subjects are so outmoded that their results have no contemporary relevance? Consider the Programmer Aptitude Test validities. Is that meta-analysis helpful to people hiring programmers today? I am not sure. Computer programming may still require the same aptitudes required in 1950, but aptitude requirements may have shifted with technological change and in the growing ubiquity of computer knowledge.

One of the 40 questions said that results based on old, outdated studies are dubious, and Schmidt et al. (1985) responded by asserting, "There is no evidence that validities of aptitude and ability tests change with time. In fact, the evidence shows remarkable stability. . . . Anyone advancing the hypothesis that validities change or have changed over time should present evidence supporting this hypothesis" (p. 722). I consider that response essentially unscientific. The only support offered is for cognitive tests in clerical selection and for unspecified military predictors (which are mainly cognitive). It fails to consider possible validity changes in other domains, it fails to show the generality of the position taken, and it fails to consider reasons one may advance for investigating a time dimension. The fact is that little research has investigated the stability of the sources of validity over time or the effect of specific environmental change (e.g., technological change) on specific test-criterion relationships. A related controversy raises the question of whether a single meta-analysis should include studies in which the time interval between predictor and criterion measurement varies from zero to a long time. This controversy was discussed in chapter 3 in the discussion of the possibility of dynamic criteria; I think the possibility should not be ignored. Perhaps validity once established is as permanent as the aquaducts of Rome, but the open-minded researcher will consider effects of circumstances that might prove an exception.

5. Meta-analysis is a procedure for analyzing sets of independent research findings for the same basic hypothesis. In practice, it is often hard to identify the variables of "the same basic hypothesis" and to know if the different studies are replications testing it. How precisely should the variables be defined? The answer depends in part on the purpose of the analysis. In the study of the predictive validity of the AIB (Brown, 1981), both the predictor and the criterion were clearly defined because the intent was to see if the validity of that particular instrument for predicting that particular criterion was constant across companies. The variables were more precisely defined than those in the clerical analysis reported by Pearlman et al. (1980), where the purpose concerned clerical work in general, jobs were defined loosely, and the predictor constructs were broad. Was "general mental ability" the same construct as "intelligence" in the earlier report (Schmidt & Hunter, 1977)? Does "spatial/mechanical ability" include a variety ranging from visualization

to knowledge of mechanical principles? The criterion construct was either proficiency or training—very broad terms. Does proficiency mean both speed and accuracy of performance? Consistency?

After a meta-analysis of unspecified constructs, the mean corrected coefficient, r_c, is the correlation between two unspecified constructs.

> In the interest of obtaining a large data set, studies of distinguishably different pairs of variables may be included: Criteria may include overall supervisory ratings, ratings on components of performance, production levels, indices of production quality, and others; predictors may include a variety of factorially different tests.... If the validity generalization hypothesis is well supported and situational specificity rejected, these differences may not be moderating obtained validities, but they obscure the meaning of the "true" validity coefficient. (Guion, 1991, p. 363)

Of course, even if the meaning is obscured or imprecisely understood, the result is nevertheless a supported generalization, and a broad one, with practical implications. But is understanding an impractical luxury?

6. When is situational specificity safely rejected? Simply by accounting for most of the variance with artifacts? The 75% rule? When the confidence interval around r_c is small? How small? When a search for moderators fails? What if no one moderator is common enough in even a large set of studies to provide much variance? The notion that unidentified variables in local situations influenced the size of validity coefficients was invoked early in history to explain the wide differences in validity coefficients found in apparently similar settings. The notion went untested for years, largely because there was no known way to test it. Meta-analysts provided and applied a method, and situational specificity has often been found wanting. Their work has shown that the variability among validity coefficients is less than previously supposed, but it has not convincingly demonstrated that validity variance necessarily reduces to zero. "Nor is this a particularly sensible proposition. The arguments advanced for situational specificity *do* have an intuitive appeal and it is hard to believe that context has no effect on test validity other than that which arises as purely technical artifacts of measurement" (Hedges, 1988, p. 200).

In spite of these issues, validity generalization must be recognized at least as one of the major methodological advances in personnel research in the final 20 years of this century. Many of the issues center on the possibility of moderators. Frank Schmidt (personal communication, November 3, 1995) has raised this practical question: Suppose we found a moderator that shows high corrected mean correlations differing by perhaps .12 or so in two kinds of organizations. That information provides better estimates of population validity coefficients, but it does not influence hiring practice. Without knowing of the moderator, users of meta-analysis would suppose, correctly, that the validity and utility of prediction is quite high in both kinds of organizations.

This leads to one final issue—or, more accurately, a final question. What sort of research program, providing the raw data for future meta-analyses, can be envisioned for, first, an improved search for moderator effects and, then, methods for determining the generalizability of the effects?

COMMENTS ON STATISTICAL ANALYSES

Chapters 7 and 8 have offered many equations relevant to the evaluation of predictors. Personnel researchers need extensive training in data analysis. A much wider variety of data analytic techniques is available to statistically well-trained people than described here, and different situations may favor different methods of analysis. The conventional statistics I have mentioned are descriptive; they permit inferences of statistical reliability, but they are not well suited to seeing how well real data fit organizational needs or theoretical models. Research related to personnel decisions, perhaps due in part to the freezing of the field in the EEO era, has given relatively little attention to newer, theory-confirming statistical methods. Those who will improve the empirical evaluation of assessment-based personnel decisions will surely develop a larger repertory of confirmatory techniques and models.

Researchers need an inclusive knowledge of statistical procedures, but there is an important caveat: *Statistics is a tool, not a religion.* Too often, researchers appear to have a blind faith in the results of statistical analysis. Statistics is a guide to judgment, not an alternative to it; results of statistical analysis merit thoughtful evaluation, not automated acceptance.

Accounting for error and exceptions deserves serious research. Ghiselli (1960a, 1960b) started to investigate systematic reasons for errors of prediction in his notion of the *prediction of predictability*, later known as the moderator concept; moderator research faltered because (a) researchers studied demographic factors extensively, concluded that they did not serve as moderators, and with magnificent illogic concluded that therefore there are no moderators, and (b) the era of pure empiricism led researchers to try any old variable that was handy as a moderator—with or without, and usually without, any systematic reasoning behind the effort. Because the moderator concept involved an accepted statistical operation (moderated regression), and because that statistical operation has not had a lot of success, the prediction of predictability became a lost idea. Neither statistical failures nor statistical successes should be accepted on faith.

REFERENCES

Aiken, L. S., & West, S. G. (1991). *Multiple regression: Testing and interpreting interactions*. Newbury Park, CA: Sage.

Balma, M. J. (1959). The development of processes for indirect or synthetic validity (A symposium): 1. The concept of synthetic validity. *Personnel Psychology, 12*, 395–396.

Berk, R. A., & Rossi, P. H. (1990). *Thinking about program evaluation*. Newbury Park, CA: Sage.

Brannick, M. T. (1986). The development and evaluation of some models for detecting the presence of noncompensatory combinations in phenomena of interest to industrial and organizational psychologists. *Dissertation Abstracts International, 47*, 3564B.

Brannick, M. T., & Brannick, J. P. (1989). Nonlinear and noncompensatory processes in performance evaluation. *Organizational Behavior and Human Decision Processes, 44*, 97–122.

Brown, S. H. (1981). Validity generalization and situational moderation in the life insurance industry. *Journal of Applied Psychology, 66*, 664–670.

Campbell, D. T., & Stanley, J. C. (1966). *Experimental and quasi-experimental design for research*. Chicago: Rand McNally.

Cattell, R. B. (1949). r_p and other coefficients of pattern similarity. *Psychometrika, 14*, 279–298.

Cattin, P. (1978). A predictive-validity-based procedure for choosing between regression and equal weights. *Organizational Behavior and Human Performance, 22*, 93–102.

Cattin, P. (1980). Note on the estimation of the squared cross-validated multiple correlation of a regression model. *Psychological Bulletin, 87*, 63–65.

Claudy, J. G. (1978). Multiple regression and validity estimation in one sample. *Applied Psychological Measurement, 2*, 595–607.

Cook, T. D., & Campbell, D. T. (1979). *Quasi-experimentation: Design and analysis issues for field settings*. Chicago: Rand McNally.

Cook, T. D., Campbell, D. T., & Peracchio, L. (1990). Quasi-experimentation. In M. D. Dunnette & L. M. Hough (Eds.), *Handbook of industrial and organizational psychology* (2nd ed., Vol. 1, pp. 491–576). Palo Alto, CA: Consulting Psychologists Press.

Cronbach, L. J. (1982). Prudent aspirations for social inquiry. In W. H. Kruskal (Ed.), *The social sciences: Their nature and uses* (pp. 61–81). Chicago: University of Chicago Press.

Dawes, R. M., & Corrigan, B. (1974). Linear models in decision making. *Psychological Bulletin, 81*, 95–106.

Einhorn, H. J. (1971). Use of nonlinear, noncompensatory models as a function of task and amount of information. *Organizational Behavior and Human Performance, 6*, 1–27.

Einhorn, H. J., & Hogarth, R. M. (1975). Unit weighting schemes for decision making. *Organizational Behavior and Human Performance, 13*, 171–192.

Frederiksen, N., & Melville, S. D. (1954). Differential predictability in the use of test scores. *Educational and Psychological Measurement, 14*, 647–656.

Ghiselli, E. E. (1960a). Differentiation of tests in terms of the accuracy with which they predict for a given individual. *Educational and Psychological Measurement, 20*, 675–684.

Ghiselli, E. E. (1960b). The prediction of predictability. *Educational and Psychological Measurement, 20*, 3–8.

Ghiselli, E. E. (1966). *The validity of occupational aptitude tests*. New York: Wiley.

Ghiselli, E. E., & Brown, C. W. (1949). The prediction of accidents of taxicab drivers. *Journal of Applied Psychology, 33*, 540–546.

Green, B. F. (1950). A note on the calculation of weights for maximum battery reliability. *Psychometrika, 15*, 57–61.

Guion, R. M. (1954). Regression analysis: Prediction from classified variables. *Psychological Bulletin, 51*, 505–510.

Guion, R. M. (1965a). *Personnel testing*. New York: McGraw-Hill.

Guion, R. M. (1965b). Synthetic validity in a small company: A demonstration. *Personnel Psychology, 18,* 49–63.

Guion, R. M. (1991). Personnel assessment, selection, and placement. In M. D. Dunnette & L. M. Hough (Eds.), *Handbook of industrial and organizational psychology* (2nd ed., Vol. 2, pp. 327–397). Palo Alto, CA: Consulting Psychologists Press.

Guion, R. M., & Gottier, R. F. (1965). Validity of personality measures in personnel selection. *Personnel Psychology, 18,* 135–164.

Hedges, L. V. (1988). The meta-analysis of test validity studies: Some new approaches. In H. Wainer & H. W. Braun (Eds.), *Test validity* (pp. 191–212). Hillsdale, NJ: Lawrence Erlbaum Associates.

Hedges, L. V. (1990). Directions for future methodology. In K. W. Wachter & M. L. Straf (Eds.), *The future of meta-analysis* (pp. 11–26). New York: Russell Sage Foundation.

Hirsh, H. R., Northrop, L. C., & Schmidt, F. L. (1986). Validity generalization results for law enforcement occupations. *Personnel Psychology, 39,* 399–420.

Horst, P. (1966). *Psychological measurement and prediction.* Belmont, CA: Wadsworth.

Hunter, J. E., & Schmidt, F. L. (1990). *Methods of meta-analysis: Correcting error and bias in research findings.* Newbury Park, CA: Sage.

Hunter, J. E., & Schmidt, F. L. (1994). Estimation of sampling error variance in the meta-analysis of correlations: Use of average correlation in the homogeneous case. *Journal of Applied Psychology,* pp. 171–177.

Jaccard, J., & Wan, C. K. (1995). Measurement error in the analysis of interaction effects between continuous predictors using multiple regression: Multiple indicator and structural equation approaches. *Psychological Bulletin, 117,* 348–357.

James, L. R., & Brett, J. M. (1984). Mediators, moderators, and tests for mediation. *Journal of Applied Psychology, 69,* 307–321.

James, L. R., Mulaik, S. A., & Brett, J. M. (1982). *Causal analysis: Assumptions, models, and data.* Beverly Hills, CA: Sage.

Law, K. S., Schmidt, F. L., & Hunter, J. E. (1994a). Nonlinearity of range corrections in meta-analysis: Test of an improved procedure. *Journal of Applied Psychology, 79,* 425–438.

Law, K. S., Schmidt, F. L., & Hunter, J. E. (1994b). A test of two refinements in procedures for meta-analysis. *Journal of Applied Psychology, 79,* 978–986.

Lawshe, C. H. (1952). What can industrial psychology do for small business? (A symposium). 2. Employee selection. *Personnel Psychology, 5,* 31–34.

Lawshe, C. H., & Schucker, R. E. (1959). The relative efficiency of four test weighting methods in multiple prediction. *Educational and Psychological Measurement, 19,* 103–114.

Lawshe, C. H., & Steinberg, M. D. (1955). Studies in synthetic validity. I. An exploratory investigation of clerical jobs. *Personnel Psychology, 8,* 291–301.

Levine, E. L., Spector, P. E., Menon, S., Narayanan, L., & Cannon-Bowers, J. (1996). Validity generalization for cognitive, psychomotor, and perceptual tests for craft jobs in the utility industry. *Human Performance, 9,* 1–22.

Linn, R. L., & Dunbar, S. B. (1986). Validity generalization & predictive bias. In R. A. Berk (Ed.), *Performance assessment: Methods & applications* (pp. 203–236). Baltimore: Johns Hopkins University Press.

Lord, F. M. (1962). Cutting scores and errors of measurement. *Psychometrika, 27,* 19–30.

Lord, F. M. (1963). Cutting scores and errors of measurement: A second case. *Educational and Psychological Measurement, 23,* 63–68.

McCormick, E. J., Meecham, R. C., & Jeanneret, P. R. (1989). *Technical manual for the Position Analysis Questionnaire* (2nd ed.). Logan, UT: PAQ Services, Inc.

McNamara, W. J., & Hughes, J. L. (1961). A review of the research on the selection of computer programmers. *Personnel Psychology, 14,* 39–51.

Mertz, W. H., & Doherty, M. E. (1974). The influence of task characteristics on strategies of cue combination. *Organizational Behavior and Human Performance, 12,* 196–216.

Mossholder, K. W., & Arvey, R. D. (1984). Synthetic validity: A conceptual and comparative review. *Journal of Applied Psychology, 69,* 322–333.

Murphy, K. R. (1983). Fooling yourself with cross validation: Single sample designs. *Personnel Psychology, 36,* 111–118.

O'Bannon, R. M., Goldinger, L. A., & Appleby, G. S. (1989). *Honesty and integrity testing: A practical guide.* Atlanta: Applied Information Resources.

Paajanen, G. E. (1988). *The prediction of counterproductive behavior by individual and organizational variables.* Unpublished doctoral dissertation, University of Minnesota, Minneapolis.

Pearlman, K., Schmidt, F. L., & Hunter, J. E. (1980). Validity generalization results for tests used to predict job proficiency and training success in clerical occupations. *Journal of Applied Psychology, 65,* 373–406.

Pedhazur, E. J., & Schmelkin, L. P. (1991). *Measurement, design, and analysis: An integrated approach.* Hillsdale, NJ: Lawrence Erlbaum Associates.

Psychological Services, Inc. (in press). *Basic Skills Tests: Technical manual* (Rev. ed.). Glendale, CA: Author.

Raju, N. S., & Burke, M. S. (1983). Two new procedures for studying validity generalization. *Journal of Applied Psychology, 68,* 382–395.

Richardson, M. W. (1941). The combination of measures. In P. Horst (Ed.), *The prediction of personal adjustment* (pp. 379–401). New York: Social Science Research Council.

Ruch, W. W., Stang, S. W., McKillip, R. H., & Dye, D. A. (1994). *Employee Aptitude Survey Technical Manual* (2nd ed.). Los Angeles: Psychological Services, Inc.

Sackett, P. R., Tenopyr, M. L., Schmitt, N., & Kehoe, J. (1985). Commentary on forty questions about validity generalization and meta-analysis. *Personnel Psychology, 38,* 697–798.

Saunders, D. R. (1956). Moderator variables in prediction. *Educational and Psychological Measurement, 16,* 209–222.

Schmidt, F. L., Gast-Rosenberg, I., & Hunter, J. E. (1980). Validity generalization results for computer programmers. *Journal of Applied Psychology, 65,* 643–661.

Schmidt, F. L., & Hunter, J. E. (1977). Development of a general solution to the problem of validity generalization. *Journal of Applied Psychology, 62,* 529–540.

Schmidt, F. L., & Hunter, J. E. (1981). Employment testing: Old theories and new research findings. *American Psychologist, 36,* 1128–1137.

Schmidt, F. L., Hunter, J. E., & Caplan, J. R. (1981). Validity generalization results for two job groups in the petroleum industry. *Journal of Applied Psychology, 66,* 261–273.

Schmidt, F. L., Hunter, J. E., & Outerbridge, A. N. (1986). Impact of job experience and ability on job knowledge, work sample performance, and supervisory ratings of job performance. *Journal of Applied Psychology, 71,* 432–439.

Schmidt, F. L., Law, K., Hunter, J. E., Rothstein, H. R., Pearlman, K., & McDaniel, M. (1993). Refinements in validity generalization methods: Implications for the situational specificity hypothesis. *Journal of Applied Psychology, 78,* 3–12.

Schmidt, F. L., Pearlman, K., Hunter, J. E., & Hirsh, H. R. (1985). Forty questions about validity generalization and meta-analysis. *Personnel Psychology, 38,* 697–798.

Schmitt, N., Coyle, B. W., & Rauschenberger, J. (1977). A monte carlo evaluation of three formula estimates of cross-validated multiple correlation. *Psychological Bulletin, 84,* 751–758.

Stanley, J. C. (1971). Reliability. In R. L. Thorndike (Ed.), *Educational measurement* (2nd ed., pp. 356–442). Washington, DC: American Council on Education.

Terris, W. (Ed.). (1985). *Employee theft: Research, theory, and applications.* Park Ridge, IL: London House Press.

Terris, W., & Jones, J. W. (1982). Psychological factors related to employees' theft in the convenience store industry. *Psychological Reports, 51,* 1219–1238.

Tzelgov, J., & Henik, A. (1991). Suppression situations in psychological research: Definitions, implications, and applications. *Psychological Bulletin, 109,* 524–536.

Wainer, H. (1976). Estimating coefficients in linear models: It don't make no nevermind. *Psychological Bulletin, 83,* 213–217.

Wherry, R. J. (1931). A new formula for predicting the shrinkage of the coefficient of multiple correlation. *Annals of Mathematical Statistics, 2,* 446–457.

Wickens, T. D. (1989). *Multiway contingency tables analysis for the social sciences.* Hillsdale, NJ: Lawrence Erlbaum Associates.

Wise, L. L., Peterson, N. G., Hoffman, R. G., Campbell, J. P., & Arabian, J. M. (Eds.). (1991, February). *Army synthetic validity project: Report of Phase III results* (2 vols. Tech. Rep. No. 922). Alexandria, VA: United States Army Research Institute for the Behavioral and Social Sciences.

9

Judgment in the Prediction of Performance

The purpose of assessment is to provide a basis for decisions. A decision is a judgment, but other judgments permeate the entire process of finding out what and how to assess, assessing, evaluating assessments, and using them. A first judgment is properly made about the assessment, not about a candidate; it is the judgment that an assessment procedures will or will not provide valid descriptions of candidates and valid predictions about their quality of functioning if chosen. Ideally, these judgments are based on research data and made by researchers.

Judgments or decisions about candidates are made by managers, not researchers. Good judgment here depends on valid assessments. Whether the assessments lead to valid decisions—whether they are even considered in making decisions—depends partly on the way assessment data are presented. Judgment aids help; managers should be trained in their use.

Judgments themselves may be the predictors, as subject to validation as other predictors. They present added problems for validation; different people making judgments can reach different, even conflicting, conclusions. Are judgments of some people more valid, as measures of traits or as predictors, than those of others? Can reasons for differences be identified? Validity and some sources of differences can be determined using judgment theory research models, especially the "lens model" (Hammond, 1966, p. 37).

Collaboration by managers and researchers can lead to better bases for judgment, better judgment processes, and more valid judgments. It also helps in other aspects of the personnel decision process. This chapter ends with a fictitious example of an integrated personnel procedure where researchers and managers work together for wise decisions.

The meaning of wise decisions can be clarified by a useful heuristic treating four words as forming a hierarchical continuum.[1] The first, at the base of the continuum, is *data*, such as scores or correlation coefficients. A step higher is *information*, an integration and interpretation of data. Still a higher step is *knowledge*, an integration of the information at hand with other information stored from prior experience. At the top is *wisdom*, where perhaps disparate sorts of knowledge must be integrated in making judgments. Wise decisions require not only data and information but the integration of them into a broader experiential framework of information and knowledge. Researchers and HR specialists should not merely pump data—assessment scores—to their managers; they should make sure that the assessments are informative and fit into a broader scheme of managerial knowledge about people, jobs, the organization, and the position at hand—a point also made by Schneider (1996).

JUDGMENTS OF VALIDITY

Validity of prediction is inferred, not merely computed. It is a judgment, inferred only if the preponderance of evidence supports the intended prediction. A validity coefficient is accepted as evidence of valid prediction only if the data and analysis are judged adequate.

Judgments of Psychometric Validity and Job Relatedness

If local validation is not feasible, and no relevant meta-analysis exists, job relatedness can be based on two sequential judgments in an option emphasizing construct or psychometric validity. First, a trait must be judged prerequisite (or at least helpful) to performance of important aspects of the job—the predictive hypothesis. Second, the test (or whatever) must be judged a valid measure of that construct (see American Educational Research Association, American Psychological Association, & National Council on Measurement in Education, 1985, Standard 10.8, p. 61). If logic and data support both judgments, the assessment is judged a valid predictor of performance of those job aspects; it is arguably a valid measure of a job-related trait. A brief reprise of the distinction between job-relatedness and psychometric validity, and slightly rephrased questions for evaluating them, may highlight the role of judgment. The first eight items are from chapter 5; the rest are from chapters 1, 3, and 7 and Guion (1991):[2]

---

[1]Thanks to Frank Landy (personal communication, February 16, 1996) for this heuristic.
[2]The list is presented as a guide to serious thought, not as a checklist for routine use. I have presented such lists in several places, with the number of listed items deliberately varied (from 4 to 18!) in an attempt to discourage the checklist mentality.

1. Did the developer of the procedure seem to have a clear idea of the attribute (construct) to be measured? Was development informed by at least a rudimentary theory of the attribute?
2. Do you consider the measurement methods—including presentation, procedures, response requirements—consistent with that idea?
3. Do you think the stimulus content is appropriate? Is the content domain unambiguous? Relevant to the measurement purpose? Was it properly sampled? Can responses be scored, observed, or evaluated reliably?
4. Can you infer care and skill in the development of the assessment instrument? Were pilot studies and item analyses done, and done well?
5. Is the score intended to reflect a single attribute or to sample a heterogeneous domain? If the former, are items internally consistent? If the latter, was the domain well defined and sampled systematically, and does it have at least a modicum of internal consistency?
6. Are scores stable over time?
7. Do the scores relate to other variables in a way consistent with the relationships expected from the theory of the attribute?
8. Do relationships disconfirm alternative hypotheses about the meaning of the scores?
9. Does the predictive hypothesis sensibly relate the attribute to job performance? Do job experts consider the attribute relevant? Is there prior research suggesting or even demonstrating its relevance?
10. Does a well-formed predictive hypothesis require other attributes of equal or nearly equal importance? If so, can the job relatedness of the attribute at hand be evaluated on its own?
11. Is there any reason to suspect that a nonmonotonic relationship exists? If so, is there any evidence suggesting the points in the assessment distribution where the relationship changes from positive to zero to negative?
12. Are criteria measured validly and predicted with reasonable accuracy? The question assumes criterion-related validation, but requires judgments about criterion validity and possible contaminants, adequacy of research design, sufficiency of sample in size and composition, and others.

Answers to the first eight questions in this list can be drawn from manuals or other documents or from local research. Favorable answers form a basis for inferring psychometric validity. Positive responses to the remaining items provide evidence of job relatedness—even where the criterion-related evidence implied by question 12 is missing. Answers to some of the questions are data-based, but they require judgment, if only to judge the adequacy of the data. If an overall judgment of job relatedness is based on good reasons for favorable responses to most of the first eleven question, it is probably better than that based on a single, local, unreplicated criterion-related validity study.

Estimates of Criterion-Related Validity Coefficients

Criterion-related validity coefficients can be estimated by informed, expert judgments. Schmidt, Hunter, Croll, and McKenzie (1983) asked eminent personnel psychologists, chosen for experience and expertise in personnel selection, to make such judgments. The pooled judgments of such experts estimated population correlations nearly as accurately as validation studies with fairly large sample sizes.

These experts were acknowledged leaders in the field of personnel selection. Not everyone with appropriate credentials has a similar level of expertise. Hirsh, Schmidt, and Hunter (1986) replicated the study using recent PhDs in industrial and organizational psychology. They substantially overestimated the coefficients, with a larger mean error, than the more established experts. Nevertheless, their pooled estimates were about as accurate as those obtained from typical small-sample empirical studies.

These are important findings. They offer an alternative way to judge job relatedness. I once used expert judgments in a slightly different way; the method has had no scientific test, but I believe it can be useful in similar situations where an estimated validity coefficient is needed and experts with the necessary qualifications are available.

A panel of 15 experts, all highly experienced in personnel selection and as carefully chosen as those in the Schmidt et al. (1983) study, was convened to evaluate a test that had been challenged in litigation.[3] Detailed job descriptions were examined; test items and item analysis results were studied. The panel members linked categories of KSAs to major job duties, linked test items both to job duties and to the KSAs, evaluated test content, scoring key, and probable psychometric properties of the items, and estimated the criterion-related validity coefficient. At each step, each panelist made and recorded his or her independent judgments; when all had done so, group discussion followed. In the final step of a detailed process, the panelists estimated the probable correlation coefficient that

---

[3]Court cases do drag on and on. So far as I know, the case for which this procedure was developed is still alive, although dormant, and will therefore not be identified.

would have been obtained in a competent validation study if it had been feasible. By this time, panelists were thoroughly familiar with the test and the job.

The first estimate of validity was direct, using a procedure like that used by Schmidt et al. (1983). Panelists were given a brief description of good but realistic research conditions: a reasonably reliable criterion, little restriction of range, and relative freedom from criterion contamination. No discussion or conversation occurred while panelists were making their estimates. The median estimate was .40.

A second estimate was based on the logic of factor analysis. A product–moment correlation coefficient is the sum of the products of the orthogonal (uncorrelated) common factor loadings in the two variables. If only one common factor contributes to variance on both variables, and it has a factor loading of .5 on one variable and .6 on the other, the product of the two loadings is .3, and so is the coefficient of correlation between them. Quantitative judgments about factors with loadings on both test and criterion can therefore give indirect estimates of validity coefficients.

Figure 9.1 shows a form for recording estimates of factor loadings and thus to obtain an indirect estimate of the validity coefficient.[4] It has been filled in as if by one of the expert judges. This hypothetical judge believed that performance on the overall job would tap all of the test factors to similar degrees and would systematically tap a set of other variance sources, none major, not included in the test (e.g., contextual criteria such as helpfulness to coworkers). The judge considered test variance to be due primarily to verbal comprehension and to judgment or general reasoning, with almost no variance due to interpersonal sensitivity. The arithmetic is shown in the margin; cross-products of factor loadings sum to .46, the judge's estimate of the criterion-related validity coefficient that might have been obtained had such a study been feasible.

Would this procedure add anything to the direct estimation procedure of Schmidt et al. (1983)? Perhaps not, when the experts are so carefully chosen. I suspect, however, that guesses about factor loadings may be more on the mark than guesses about validities when the experts know the factor analytic literature well but have less direct experience with employment test validation. If so, the pool of useful experts would be larger because more psychologists know the psychometric literature in general (including ratings and factor analytic literature) than have extensive experience with personnel tests and test validation.

---

[4]Actually, this differs from what was done; it shows what *should* have been done in the panel's meeting. The form actually used omitted the estimates of unique variance in the criterion and in the test. Because these people were indeed expert, this omission resulted in their taking unique variance into account in different ways. The form given here is more like the one recommended by the panel after discussion.

A Factorial Basis for Estimating Criterion-Related Validity

Pretend that the KSA categories previously identified were orthogonal factors resulting from a principal components analysis including both the [test name] and the overall criterion. For both test and criterion, assume a reliability of .90; no assumption need be made about communality—it may or may not approach reliability.

What would be the approximate loading of the test on each of the factors below (the KSA categories) identified by the group in earlier judgments? Likewise, what would be the approximate loading of an overall criterion on each of these same factors?

How much systematic test variance is unrelated to the criterion? (Although the above instructions do not ask for loadings to be expressed in variance terms, you may do so here; zero is entered on the corresponding line under "Overall Job Performance.") Likewise, how much systematic criterion variance is unrelated to variance in test scores? (Again, zero is entered on the corresponding line under "Total Test Score.")

Record answers in the appropriate spaces below. Remember that the sum of the squares of the factor loadings, plus the unique variance estimate, cannot exceed .90 in either column.

Overall Job Performance	KSA Factor Category	Total Test Score
.30	A. Verbal Comprehension	$.65 \times .3 = .19$
.30	B. Number Fluency	$.30 \times .3 = .09$
.35	C. Perceptual Speed and Accuracy	$.20 \times .35 = .07$
.20	D. General Reasoning, Judgment	$.45 \times .2 = .09$
.30	E. Interpersonal Sensitivity	$.05 \times .3 = .02$
		.46
0	F. Systematic Test Score Variance Unrelated to Criterion	.14
.47	G. Systematic Criterion Variance Unrelated to Test Scores	0

$r_{xy} = .46$

FIG. 9.1. A form for estimating validity coefficients by first estimating factor loadings.

MANAGERIAL USE OF ASSESSMENTS

Managers—not researchers, test developers, staff psychologists, or human resources specialists—make staffing decisions. Managers, despite wanting the best people, usually want to fill a vacancy satisfactorily as quickly as possible (Herriot, 1993); testers generally want to maximize performance and compliance with government regulation (Heneman, Huett, Lavigna, & Ogsten, 1995). Most managers have no training in psychometrics or test theory, they may not understand the constructs assessed, and they may hold unwarranted views about tests. Some managers distrust tests and place little reliance on test scores. Worse (from a tester's perspective) is a manager who believes tests are great, who defers to test scores even when evidence shows them invalid, and who simply does not hear warnings or qualifications about them. Such true believers are surprisingly common and harder to work with than the skeptics. To deal with both kinds of unwarranted views, some staff psychologists establish rules for using tests or other assessments in making personnel decisions. The rules might specify preferred score levels or patterns, circumstances to justify overlooking poor scores, or further information to consider along with test scores or other systematic assessments. Some managers may decide for themselves whether to use test information and, if so, how to use it. That seems an odd policy. Developing and validating systematic, standardized assessment programs requires an investment. It is strange to let individual whim determine how or whether the results of the investment will be used.

Strange it may be, but it is likely when managers are not satisfied with established staffing procedures (cf. Heneman et al., 1995). Those responsible for the assessment programs should take active steps to gain program acceptance and to assure proper use of scores.

Use of Critical Scores or Cut Scores

Many managers think of test scores as passing or failing. That habit, coupled with a staff psychologist's view that managers cannot be trusted with test scores, often leads to cut scores. The manager is free to choose among passing candidates at random, by whim, or on the basis of information available by chance. This may help gain acceptance (although I do not know that it does), but it means that decisions are based less on valid assessments than on information that may be interpreted and valued differently by different managers.

Use of Expectancy Charts

An alternative is to develop expectancy charts and train managers in their use. These aids to judgment will be considered later. I emphasize here that they may also be training aids. I think a staff psychologist's or researcher's responsibility includes assuring that decision makers are trained in (a) the nature of the constructs being assessed, (b) why they are important, (c) the fundamental principles by which the assessment of them was evaluated, (d) the nature of defensible and indefensible inferences from scores, and (e) acceptable limits of individual judgments to override ordinarily defensible inferences. Expectancy charts can help. They help teach that prediction of either success or failure is rarely certain but is instead probabilistic. They usually show that the probability of success is greater at higher score levels. Good training would also teach the limits of predictions such as those imposed by the criterion chosen; an expectancy of a superior level of production gives no clue about probable performance on a criterion the decision maker might have preferred, such as a dependability or ingenuity.

Incompatible Expectancies. Probabilities annoy managers who want definite answers, and annoyance is enhanced when two or more probabilistic statements are not compatible—when the probabilty of being satisfactory on one criterion is high but is accompanied by a low probability of being satisfactory on another. Training in the use of assessments should stress that people do not necessarily function at the same level in all aspects of work-related performance. People who work carefully and make no errors may not get much done. Incompatible predictions require reconciling judgments, not denunciation of the assessments. Where research permits predictions of independent criteria, managers should be trained to expect incompatibility and given guidance for dealing with it in decision making.

Monitoring Assessment Use. Training wears off. Personnel decisions like selection, promotion, or transfer are not everyday events for individual managers, and the training may be old when test scores are reported to them for a pending decision. Human resources (HR) specialists, if themselves competently trained, can work with the manager, refreshing the principles of expectancy chart use, when decisions are to be made.

Use of Score Bands

Banding (discussed in chapter 10) establishes a score interval of indifference, a band of scores in which some score differences are considered too trivial to use for decisions. Decisions within the band are therefore based on information other than the test score.

Acceptance of banding by decision-making managers seems not to have been addressed in the banding literature. Resistance might be expected if managers dislike the bases for choice within bands, such as random choice or choice based on demographic variables. To gain acceptance, managers should get training in the meaning of bands and in the variety of work-relevant considerations that might drive their decisions. Making decisions collaboratively with (or monitored by) HR specialists seems useful and probably necessary. Managers, trainers, and testers should recognize that letting work-relevant factors influence choices among people whose test scores differ only trivially might enhance, not reduce, the usefulness of assessment. As Kriska (1995) put it, "Banding does not guarantee that better decisions will be made, but it does provide a rational, cost effective way of considering additional information. Better personnel decisions obviously will result in an increase in utility" (p. 94). But better decisions require help in making judgments within bands.

Use of Narrative Interpretations

For higher level or nonroutine jobs, expectancy charts and score bands may not be sensible; individual assessments of multiple characteristics are more likely than individual tests or composite scores. The results of comprehensive assessment are more likely to be reported in narrative, descriptive interpretations. The report can be both instructional and a judgment aid; it can define the constructs assessed, distinguish them from other constructs with which they might be confused, and provide detailed descriptions of the inferences that can (and cannot) be drawn from the assessments of them. When possible, I prefer that the report writer and recipients meet together to go through the report point by point to assure that those who use it as a basis for decision understand it well.

JUDGMENTS AS PREDICTIONS AND DECISIONS

Personnel decisions are judgments that imply prediction. Most often they have no research foundation and may follow no known plan. Typically, they are not seriously evaluated beyond vague statements like, "Joe really knows how to size people up." We can do better.

Statistical Versus Judgmental Prediction

Many judgmental predictions are not even recognized as such; that is, no clear statement identifies the basis for judgment or hypothesizes that it is somehow related to a predictable outcome. One might, of course, formally frame and test a hypothesis that a firm handshake, looking one squarely in the eye, or some other form of body language indicates that the candidate will work hard or be conscientious. More often, I think, such cues are not even recognized as the basis for judging that "this person is a good bet."

Clinical and counseling psychologists make "clinical predictions"—judgments—of likely future behavior. In evaluating a convict being considered for parole, a psychologist's duty may be to predict whether the person, if paroled, will be a repeat offender. Such predictions are not made lightly; the psychologist responsible for them gathers much data about the person, considers much data about recidivism in general, and gives these data much thought before making the prediction.

So also the personnel decision maker may make informed judgments about candidates and the performance expected of them if hired. Candidates might be tested, interviewed, and evaluated in assessment centers; their backgrounds might be checked and people who have known them in various contexts might be interviewed for still more data. Much of the data about a candidate might be useless, and the decision maker may not know the value of specific pieces of information. Yet a decision must be made, it can be made on the basis of informed and explicit judgments, and those judgments are more or less well-informed predictions.

Statistical analysis can be misleading, too, particularly when data are poor or greatly violate statistical assumptions. Nevertheless, Meehl (1954) demonstrated long ago that statistical prediction is consistently superior to clinical (judgmental) prediction. Later, he suggested six circumstances that might, perhaps, favor clinical prediction. Among them was the idea that optimal prediction might be based more on patterns of relationships among predictors than on the linear, additive relationships assumed in the multiple regression equations (the most common statistical prediction); perhaps well-informed clinicians (judges) could identify salient patterns better than arithmetic processes could (Meehl, 1967). People making judgments might be using information in a "configural" way (i.e., using algorithms that may be nonlinear, nonadditive, or even noncontinuous). It was an interesting idea, but in subsequent research, it did not pan out. It has been a well-accepted view that statistical prediction is almost always, some even say necessarily, better than prediction by human judgment (see, e.g., Goldberg, 1991).

That view needs to be qualified a bit. In general, research does show that statistical prediction works better than judgments, but I think this is not necessarily so. The persistent finding may be explained by conventions in the design of judgment research that favor linear, additive models for predicting judgments. I go into more detail on the design problem in a later section on judges' insight into their judgment policies. For now, considering the relative merit of statistical and judgmental prediction, I consider Meehl's original position to be plausible still: where there is substantial configurality—a condition not addressed in most of the research on the relative validities of statistical and judgmental prediction—statistical prediction is not necessarily better. The condition, however, may be exceptional; where there is not substantial configurality, statistical prediction probably is superior.

Prediction and Decision Without Statistics

Statistical prediction is feasible when common criterion and predictor data can be collected for a lot of people. In these cases, employment decisions can be evaluated in terms of mean performance of those selected. However, many decisions must be made without the luxury of research data. For unusual jobs, many high level jobs, or lower level jobs in small organizations, many candidates may be assessed but only one (or a few) may be chosen. The cost of error in these cases, and the reward for being right, may be greater than in those where statistical predictions are feasible. If only one person is chosen, that person's performance is the crucial evaluation of the decision. In small organizations or large, the higher the organizational level, the fewer the incumbents. Even with dozens of keepers of accounts, there is but one comptroller. When that comptroller retires, moves to a different organization, gets fired, or dies, another one person must be chosen to fill the position; perhaps a dozen people or more may be considered. There is no choice between judgmental and statistical prediction; judgment is the only option.

That judgment may be made by one person, or it may be collaboratively made in a selection or screening committee. Despite the old saw about a camel being a horse assembled by committee, group judgments tend to be more reliable than individual judgments, and it usually seems appropriate to use committees comprised of members of various constituencies. Each member should make an independent judgment, as if he or she were the only person making it; the group, meeting as a whole, can then reconcile differences.

Some circumstances permit candidate comparisons; others do not. Perhaps a candidate must be assessed and either accepted or rejected without further ado. Examples may occur under the Americans with Disabilities Act (ADA). Suppose a candidate protected under ADA applies for a job for which a test and an expectancy table are ordinarily used; suppose further that the candidate has a history of epilepsy (or cardiac arrhythmia or whatever) and that the condition has for some time been controlled by appropriate medication. The disability is not likely to interfere with either job performance or assessment. The expectancy chart can be used (even if with slight misgivings); accommodation is not needed.

Suppose instead that the candidate's condition is a form of learning disability, and that accommodation in assessment requires someone to write down the candidate's answers to orally administered test questions. Or perhaps the candidate requires a test form in large print. In either case, validities may differ in unknown ways from those based on standard conditions. One can only hope that judgments about scores, other information, and associated probabilities may provide rational grounds for adjusting expectancy chart probabilities subjectively. A rating or a subjectively adjusted probability is surely less valid than an appropriate score on a valid, standardized test, but we cannot be so sure that it is any less valid than an inappropriate test score. When standard testing procedures are changed, scores are likely to be inappropriate; validity information is no longer applicable; and some degree of error, direction and extent unknown and unknowable, has contaminated the resulting scores. A disabled candidate's score might be nudged up or down a bit, depending on a psychometric judgment of the validity retained in the accommodation, but so far, no clear principles for making such adjustments are available.

Judgment Aids

Clarifying Judgments To Be Made. Those who are to make the judgments need a clear idea of the major responsibilities of the position to be filled and the qualifications required for it. The clarification serves to define and document the judgments required and the expected sequence in making them. Clarification is the first and perhaps most essential aid to reliable judgments, but it is not easily achieved.

Procedural Planning. Detailed plans for information and procedures can make the judgment process more systematic and therefore more reliable. The larger the pool of potential candidates, the greater the need for logistical planning. For wide-ranging search committees, I recommend planning both a sequence of judgments and the steps to follow in making them. For each candidate, at each step, the decision may be to move the candidate to the next step—which may mean getting new information or new assessments—or to drop the candidate from further consideration. The plan should clearly state the qualifications to be assessed at each step and the procedures to be used in assessing them. Procedural justice argues for a plan used as consistently as possible across candidates.

Developing Assessment Scales. Test scores are assessments; so are ratings in assessment centers or interviews, or from files. Some file information may be quantitative, some narrative, and both kinds can be useful. Information can be assessed on more than one dimension. Prior responsibilities, for example, might be assessed in terms of the cost of error, the scope of the responsibility accepted, or the quality of the achievement in fulfilling it—or something else. If the dimension is not specified, different people may evaluate the same information on different dimensions, giving an unwarranted appearance of disagreement.

To assure procedural justice and reliability, the information to be used should be specified as unambiguously as possible and measurement scales developed. Some people want to have all assessments made on the same scale, whether based on test scores, interviews, or information in files or credentials. I tend to use 9-point scales, such as shown in Fig. 9.2, for no better reason than the unsupported idea that it encourages raters to make two sequential ratings on easy 3-point scales: first, choosing the high,

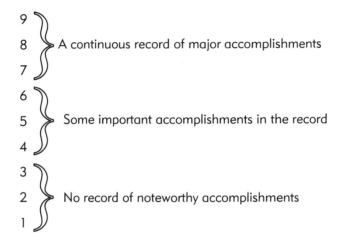

9
8   } A continuous record of major accomplishments
7

6
5   } Some important accomplishments in the record
4

3
2   } No record of noteworthy accomplishments
1

FIG. 9.2. A 9-point scale for rating a history of achievements using data from interviews, references, and application materials.

middle, or low third of the scale and, second, choosing the specific high, middle, or low point within that range as a rating. In Fig. 9.2, the rater may have found no record of accomplishment deemed worthy of being designated "major" or "important" and so rated the record in the bottom third of the scale; however, the rater may have noted a fairly persistent record of getting things done, even if not noteworthy things, and therefore used the highest value within that lower third as the assessment of accomplishment.

At some point, at least some candidates are likely to be interviewed. A structured interview plan can standardize the interview and the related assessment scales. Interviews are notoriously lacking in evidence of validity—unless they are well structured (Arvey & Campion, 1982). Predeveloped assessment scales help specify and standardize the nature of the judgments to be made. What kinds of information are wanted? Why is such information appropriate or relevant to the position to be filled? What is the nature of the dimension reflected by the information? How should it be evaluated? What relative weight should it have? Preparing the rating forms can provide answers to such questions ahead of time and assure a degree of procedural justice in turning from one file to another, from one interview to another, or from one evaluator to another. Procedural justice is important to candidates; its corollary, reliable judgment, is essential to the validity of the final decision.

Using Expectancy Charts. When tests are used but not empirically or locally validated, theoretical expectancy charts (described in chapter 7) can be useful aids if an acceptable validity coefficient is available or can be estimated. They can be developed using a validity coefficient (a) reported in a manual or other research report based on a comparable situation, (b) estimated from an appropriate meta-analysis, (c) estimated less formally from a body of prior research where each study fits only part of the situation at hand but the accumulated data fill it reasonably well, or (d) estimated by panels of experts.

Consider a situation where the assessment plan for a specialized sales position includes assessment by tests of two traits, general intelligence and surgency. Suppose that, for both psychometric and theoretical reasons, the Watson-Glaser *Critical Thinking Appraisal* (*CTA*; Total Score) and the *Hogan Personality Inventory* (*HPI*; Sociability Score) are used (among other things). Assume that no relevant validity coefficient was found for the *CTA*, but that an expert panel linked component scores to job duties and concluded that a total score validity coefficient, appropriately corrected, would not be less than .35. A validity coefficient .51 reported in the Hogan Manual (Hogan & Hogan, 1992) for advertising sales, a position making interpersonal demands similar to those in the position at hand, was rounded down to .50. These estimates permit theoretical expectancy charts for these two tests, shown in Fig. 9.3. Score intervals on the *CTA* were derived from the full norms for upper division college students (Watson & Glaser, 1980); those for the HPI are based on total sample norms (Hogan & Hogan, 1992), although a truncated distribution might have been better (cf. Sackett & Ostgaard, 1994).

One might assume, reasonably in this case, that the two tests are uncorrelated. One might also assume, although less reasonably, that neither is correlated with ratings of information obtained from interviews, letters of endorsement, work histories, and accomplishments. Assuming orthogonal information may simplify judgments, but if the assumption is unwarranted, it is likely to reduce the validity of judgments.

Assessments can be compared more easily on a common scale. Expectancies on a 5-bar expectancy chart can be translated to the 9-point scale by assigning a rating of 1 to all scores in the bottom interval and dividing each higher interval at roughly the median to provide the other eight categories.

Combining Information for Overall Assessment

Systematic procedures, with the aids described, seem idealistic, but they can save a great deal of grief. I think ad hoc judgments and decisions in these low-frequency selection decisions are usually inconsistent in procedure, unreliable in result, and difficult to explain by the people who make them. The predictions have unknown validity; they may not even be recognized as predictions. Matters can be helped by careful planning, and methods of consolidating information can be part of the planning.

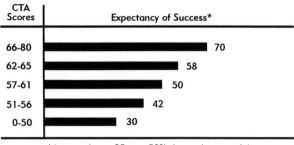

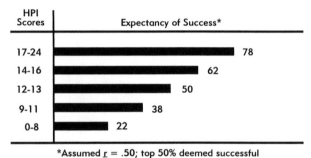

FIG. 9.3. Theoretical expectancy charts for two tests for a hypothetical specialized sales position.

Conventional Models. With common scales, the several assessments of a candidate can simply be averaged, with or without differential weights (see chapter 8). I recommend the mean assessment, rather than the sum, to ease the problem of missing data—often severe with interviews or credential files. Disjunctive, conjunctive, and other noncompensatory combinations described in chapter 8 may also make sense.

Use of Empirical and Subjective Probabilities. An expectancy chart (as in Fig. 9.3) gives empirically based, theoretical probabilities of meeting a performance standard associated with different categories of information. The probability is the proportion of people meeting a specified standard, Y, (or possibly an event) given prior predictor information such as the score interval, X; it is written formally as $P(Y \mid X)$, the probability of Y given X. Probability statements can help make judges more careful.

At the opposite extreme is the joker who thinks he knows it all and who makes statements like "Nine times out of ten a man who can't look you in the eye spells trouble." Forget the silliness of the statement;

examine it for what it illustrates. Two features merit attention. First, it is imprecise. "Spells trouble" has no clear meaning; neither the nature nor level of trouble is specific. Equally imprecise is the complaint: "can't look you in the eye." Eye contact can vary between none at all to unwavering; either extreme can be disconcerting. Second, it is a statement that $P(Y \mid X)$ = .9, a probability pulled from thin air. It is merely a verbal habit, uttered with neither data nor logic, based on simple prejudice or stereotype. It may sound like a probability statement, and it may influence decisions, but it is not the mark of a careful judge.

In Fig. 9.3 the top score interval on the CTA is between 65.5 and 80.5. Would anyone seriously believe that the success expectancy is precisely .70 for those with scores of 68 and of 78? A thinking person, even with no training in statistics, might expect a higher probability of success for the higher score. Such a person might assign a probability of .64 or .65 to the lower score and .77 to the higher one. These guesses do not rely on a table of areas under the normal curve; they simply illustrate that subjective probabilities can be based on general information and empirical data.

Consider an applicant whose CTA score is 63 and whose HPI score is 15. Assume also that this applicant is a paroled felon and that company policy is to give employment to deserving ex-convicts. From test scores alone, remembering that these are probably uncorrelated, the success probability must be greater than .62; my guess is about .68. A different probability to consider is the likelihood of the candidate committing another crime. To estimate that probability one might consult empirical literature on recidivism, particularly where prior research considers the type of crime, socioeconomic variables, and other relevant data. If that probability is estimated to be nonzero to an important degree, the subjectively estimated probability of success on *both* criteria may be lower than that based on test scores alone. If the selection ratio is about .50, and the resulting sucess probability estimate remains better than .5, the decision maker may decide to hire the candidate, despite the prison record.[5]

------

[5]Technically, there are two different questions. First, what is the probability of success, defined as being in the top half, given the scores on the CTA and the HPI? Let $P(Y)$ be the probability of being in the top 50%; with no prior information, $P(Y) = .5$. If the score on the CTA is 63, $P(Y \mid CTA) = .58$ from Figure 3. With an HPI score of 15, $P(Y \mid HPI) = .62$. Both of these values exceed $P(Y)$, so $P(Y)$ must be greater than .62—but I have not made up enough information to say how much greater. To assert subjectively that $P(Y \mid CTA, HPI) \approx$ .68 is a pure guess. The second question is easier: Given $P(Y \mid CTA, HPI) \approx .68$, and given $P(S \mid D)$ (where S is being satisfactorily free of further crime and D is the accumulated basis for a subjective probability) of .85, the probability of being both in the top half of the performance distribution and free of further criminality is a multiplicative function, about equal to .68, .85, or about .58. It is not necessary, however, to be so precise; it *is* necessary to provide heuristics that can keep decision makers thinking in probabilistic terms without requiring training in probability theory.

In short, it is possible to combine empirical probabilities and informed guesses in making probabilistic predictions about the outcomes of personnel decisions. That is, the cardinal rule of psychometrics—standardization—may be set aside; different information for different candidates can be combined when it can be expressed probabilistically.

This sort of intuitive speculation has been systematized in Bayesian statistics, a branch of statistical thought based on conditional and joint probabilities. Discussions of Bayes's theorem and of the statistical procedures it has spawned may be found in references such as Lee (1989) and Smith (1988), both of whom have brief and relatively easy coverage, and Novick and Jackson (1974), a more extensive book on general statistics from a Bayesian perspective.[6] One value of a Bayesian approach is that it can provide important guidance for making subjective probability statements systematically (see especially Smith, 1988) and for incorporating empirical probabilities from small samples.

Reliance on subjective probabilities can pose some dangers. Dawes, Mirels, Gold, and Donahue (1993) showed experimentally that people who know better (that is, people who know the base rates for the occurrence of certain events) ignore their knowledge and act as if $P(Y \mid X) = P(X \mid Y)$. An EEO example using data from *Connecticut v. Teal*, provided by DeGroot, Fienberg, and Kadane (1986), was cited in Lee (1989). Of 48 Blacks taking a promotion test, 26 were selected; the others failed. Of the 259 Whites tested, 206 passed; the others failed. The question of adverse impact asks whether the selection ratios for the two groups differ. In probability terms, is the probability of being selected different for Blacks and Whites? Let S = number selected within a group, B = number of Blacks, and W = number of Whites; the adverse impact question is whether $P(S \mid B) < P(S \mid W)$. Substituting numbers, $P(S \mid B) = 26/48 = .54$, and $P(S \mid W) = 206/259 = .80$. Under the 80% rule, the answer is yes, but the answer is quite different from that one gets by asking whether those selected are more likely to be Black or White: $P(B \mid S) = 26/232 = .11$, and $P(W \mid S) = 206/232 = .89$. The adverse impact ratio is .68 using the correct question and .098 using the irrelevant inverse. The error is not trivial and has appeared in several EEO discussions. A further example in clinical medicine shows the same error, and unfortunately it is common (Eddy, 1982); physicians reported assuming that the probability of cancer, given a

---

[6]Bayesian statistics have been used very little in personnel research. Early approaches to validity generalization were Bayesian, and much of the early decision theory under the lens model, discussed in the next section of this chapter, were Bayesian; in both instances, more traditional and conventional statistics have replaced the earlier models. For this reason, and because my understanding of the complexities of Bayesian analysis is so limited that my subjective probability of a gross error is about .99, I've elected to say virtually nothing about Bayes's theorem and the statistical enterprise it permits.

positive X-ray, is about equal to the probability of a positive X-ray in a patient already known to have cancer! Data show that the likelihood of cancer given an X-ray showing a mass was about 8%; the erroneous probabilistic reasoning led to an estimate of about 75%. Again, that is not a trivial error. The inverse in each example answers a question of no real interest. That is precisely the importance of the work by Dawes et al. (1993); in their experiment, intelligent judges did indeed equate the relevant probability statement with its inverse even though knowing that it answered an inappropriate, irrelevant question.

This is but one example of the dangers inherent in the use of personal or subjective probabilities: in general, they are subject to many sources of bias. Little is known about procedures that can be fairly sure of reducing bias and enhancing the accuracy of such probability statements. Therefore, I can advocate subjective "nudging" of empirical probabilities or expectancies, but I cannot advocate any greater reliance on subjective probabilities.

JUDGMENT THEORY AND LENS MODEL RESEARCH

Candidate qualifications or broader fitness for employment, promotion, or special training may be assessed by judgments. Judgments may be made about products, work sample quality, markets, the safety of work environments, performance, or work procedures. Are judgments any good? Are they useful for personnel decisions? If only some of them are, how do you know which ones? How do people who make certain kinds of judgments arrive at them? That is, how do they use information in making the judgment? How valid are their judgments as predictors of important criteria?

The Lens Model

Many research paradigms are used to study judgment and decision making; one, particularly well suited to personnel assessments, is called the *lens model* (Brunswik, 1956; Hammond, 1966, 1993).[7] The metaphor is that a designated set of variables, or cues, serves somewhat like a lens through which an object (or person) in the environment may be perceived and judgments made about it. A basic principle of lens model research is the Brunswikian principle of representative design, especially important in applied settings. That principle differs from the experimental research ideal of manipulating one variable, observing another, and allowing noth-

---

[7]I do not discuss the lens model in the detail it deserves, and I do not mention other approaches at all. I recommend reading the presentation by Stevenson, Busemeyer, and Naylor (1990).

ing else to vary. Representative design recognizes both the multivariate nature and the uncertainty of the perceived environment and of the judgments people make about things in it. Failure to present cues reasonably realistically poses threats to the external validity of the research.

A diagrammatic description of the lens model, stripped to essentials, is shown in in Fig. 9.4a. On the left is a criterion, the dependent variable of interest, something to be evaluated or predicted. On the right is a judgment about the criterion. In the center is a set of k variables thought to be related either to the criterion or to judgments about it—"cues" that make up the metaphorical "lens" through which events or conditions are perceived. They may be predictors of the criterion, and they may influence or predict people's judgments about it.

The criterion may be job performance; the corresponding judgments may be predictions of performance or assessments of job candidates intended to predict performance. Profiles of the lens variables are accumulated for many candidates, actual or hypothetical; the "judge" makes predictions or assessments of each candidate based on the cues in the lens.

The lens model is usually used to study the judgments of individuals. Each judge, even where there are several, is studied individually. For each one, each cue variable is correlated with judgments across profiles, yielding $r_{j1}, r_{j2}, r_{j3}, \ldots r_{jk}$, or with the criterion itself, yielding $r_{c1}, r_{c2}, r_{c3}, \ldots r_{ck}$. Cues can be combined in any of the ways described in chapter 8; multiple regression is typical (but not necessarily the best or most descriptive model). The judgment side represents the judge's judgment policy, and the environmental side is, in effect, the policy of the real world. A judge's policy can be evaluated by comparing it to the real-world policy.[8]

Policy Capturing

Different people with the same information make judgments differently. One may consider some information and ignore other, giving implicit weights to some pieces of information but no weight to others. Another may use all information but consider some of it more important than other, implicitly using differential weighting. Another might treat it all as equally important. Still another may consider one piece of information so crucial that, if it is missing or inadequate, no other information will compensate for the deficiency. Or there may be an "if–then" judgment in which different categories of one sort of information call for consideration of different secondary information. These various patterns of

---

[8]Calling this a real-world policy may stretch credulity; for example, the criterion might be simply another judgment, perhaps pooled, or a very imperfect approximation of some sort of empirical reality. But this language provides a quick taste of an environmental policy, to use an alternative expression.

(a) The lens model:

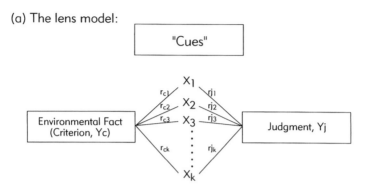

(b) The policy-capturing model:

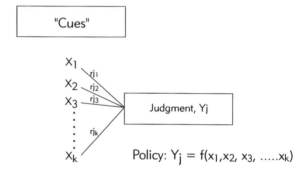

FIG. 9.4. A simplified description of the lens model and of policy capturing.

judgment are individual policies. They are not necessarily conscious or deliberate, but they can be captured by a mathematical model. Most often, a multiple regression equation is used as the model. Policy capturing is depicted in Fig. 9.4b, the right-hand side of the full lens model.

Policy-capturing research can be used to identify differences among decision makers, such as interviewers. If two or more distinctly different policies are found, it may be possible in conference to consolidate them into a single organizational policy that the judges can learn to use. It is, however, useful to think of it as part of the lens model in which the policies themselves can be evaluated.

The Lens Model Equation

A more complete depiction of the lens model is shown in Fig. 9.5. Actual judgments, Y_j, can be correlated with those predicted from the policy, Y'_j. In effect, this is done in computing the multiple coefficient of correlation

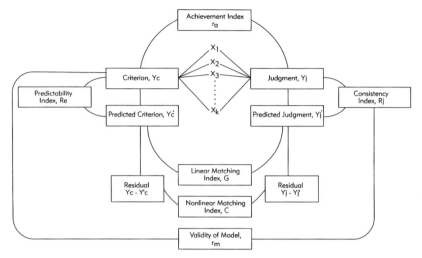

FIG. 9.5. A more detailed description of the lens model and of the indices that may be computed.

between cues and judgments, so we denote it simply as R_j, identified in Fig. 9.5 as the consistency index, sometimes considered an index of cognitive control (Hammond & Summers, 1972). On the environmental side, the corresponding index is the criterion predictability index, R_c.

The correlation of judgments across profiles, Y_j, with the criterion, Y_c, is called the *achievement index*, r_a; it is a criterion-related validity coefficient for the judgments. Judgments made by different people may differ in validity. Judgments predicted by the policy equation can also be correlated with the criterion; this correlation, which I designate r_m, is the validity of the judgment model or policy equation. It is typically larger than r_a.

A general equation integrates the lens model (Tucker, 1964):

$$r_a = GR_cR_j + C\sqrt{1 - R_c^2}\sqrt{1 - R_j^2} \tag{1}$$

where G is the correlation between predicted criterion values and judgments predicted from the policy, a linear matching index. C is the correlation between residuals; if it is substantial relative to G, the linear additive model is unlikely to be optimal. The Brannick (1986) equation (in chapter 8) may also be used to check appropriateness of an additive model.

Lens Model Research Design

Cue Profiles. A common approach to lens model research gives the judge a booklet containing the set of profiles of variables (cues). Many profiles are needed; many researchers want at least a 10:1 ratio of profiles to cues. Profiles may describe real or hypothetical people, perhaps combining situational and personal characteristics. Tasks vary. For each profile, the judge may predict the criterion level expected for people with such a profile (e.g., whether such a person will or will not quit within 6 months, or an expected level of performance), indicate an appropriate decision (e.g., to hire or not), or provide a more global evaluation (e.g., skill level, readiness for promotion). Profiles in booklets are "paper people" and may not be representative (Gorman, Clover, & Doherty, 1978)—unless profiles come from actual files and operational decisions are also based on file data.

Cue Weights in a Policy Equation. The achievement index, r_a, offers one evaluation of the judgments. Another is the correlation between the criterion and the judgments predicted by the captured policy, r_m, in which validity depends on the judgment model assumed. In the linear, additive model most often assumed, validity depends on the weights for the various cues.

Subjective weights might be used; that is, judges may be asked to estimate subjectively the weights they have used (or intend to use) in making their judgments. Empirical weights are more often developed, usually by multiple regression to optimize the correlation between cues and judgments or criteria. These weights are optimal only in that they maximize (within the profiles sampled) the correlation between the composite and the criterion. Or one might pursue simplicity and simply add cue values together; if so, all cues should be oriented to have a positive correlation with the criterion and be expressed in a common metric.

Policies captured by multiple regression are generally more valid than the judgments they predict (Dawes, 1979; Dawes & Corrigan, 1974; Dudycha & Naylor, 1966; Goldberg, 1970). When the most valid policy of a group of decision makers is found, the implication is that the equation of that policy should be used instead of the actual, unreliable judgments of the decision makers. It is an easy implication, supported by tremendous amounts of evidence, but it is hard to put into practice in an organization. False pride in our abilities to size up people makes most of us unwilling to be replaced by an equation.

A Lens Model Application

Roose and Doherty (1976) developed profiles of 360 life insurance agents from company personnel records. Of these, 160 were held back for cross validation; the remaining 200 were presented to 16 agency managers who predicted whether the person described would survive the first year. The profiles included 64 variables, combining listed variables and narrative statements as shown in Fig. 9.6. A confidence scale incorporated with the predictions generated a 10-point scale to represent the judgment. Multiple regression was used throughout. Results included these:

1. The survival criterion was clearly predictable from cues in the profiles. Estimating R_c by two methods gave values of .32 and .43, validity coefficients typical of more standardized predictors.

2. Judges' policies consistently overused the Aptitude Index Battery (AIB). Its regression weights were consistently greater than merited by the test's validity coefficient in this sample—for an interesting reason. Some judges treated it as a nonlinear relationship. Given that managerial training emphasizes the historic nonlinearity of AIB validity, the finding that at least some of them remember it is hardly surprising. The more sobering finding is that most judges treat it as linearly related to survival, and therefore inflate the importance of the AIB.

3. The judges did not agree much. Differences in judgments (on the 10-point scale) may have been partly due to differences in base rates of hiring decisions; they ranged from 12% to 71%.

4. Unit weights provided more valid predictions of the criterion than did the judgments themselves or the models of the managers' policies. As the researchers pointed out, however, the variables that were chosen for unit weighting were chosen through the use of traditional multiple regression procedures.

The wide variability in decisions led the researchers to look at those profiles on which there *was* agreement to hire or reject among 13 of the 16 managers. Treating these managers as a single group making dichotomized judgments about this limited set of profiles, a consensus policy equation was derived. The consensus policy is not necessarily an organizational policy, but it provides useful information for a policy development conference. For example, the consensus equation, like most individual ones, overemphasized the AIB relative to its empirical validity for these profiles (Roose & Doherty, 1976). The managers were clearly influenced by the amount of deviation of an individual score from an established cut score, and this influence is grist for the group discussion mill. The group may decide to give less attention to large deviations—or it may recommend, as Roose and Doherty did, that decision makers be given only dichotomous pass–fail test results. Or it may recommend that expectancies associated with the scores be given. Whatever the final recommendation, a consensus policy equation can provide a basis for the explicit development of a corporate policy.

Age	*26*
Source	*Employment Agency*
Marital Status	*Married*
Wife's Activities	*Working at a permanent job*
Number of Children and Ages	*None*
Housing	*Rents a house*
Face Amount of Life Insurance on Self (Not Including Group)	*$45,000*
Annual Premium Paid for Above	*$444*
Present Monthly Needs	*$798*
Savings	*$4800*
Equity in Home if Owned	*N/A*
Net Worth	*$9300*
Occupational Classification	*Proprietor, executive, or official*
Number of Full Time Jobs Held	*2*
Number of Years Had Full Time Job	*3*
Presently Employed - Full Time	*No*
Aptitude Index Battery Score	*16*
Recommended Starting Salary	*$800*

The applicant has been married for 1 year and has lived in the local area for 1 ½ years. He and his wife are in good health. He is serving in the Marine Reserves and will be discharged in 1973. He enjoys lake activities and spectator sports and belongs to the Elks. He and his wife entertain in their home about 2 times per month and are entertained by others approximately 2 times a month.

The applicant maintained a B average in high school and served as Class Vice-President. He attended college and received his B. A. degree in 1970. He paid all his college expenses by working. He majored in Finance in which his grade point average was 2.0-3.0; his overall average was 1.6. He received his worst grades in English. While in college he pledged a social fraternity but eventually dropped out because of his heavy work load.

The applicant worked for the State Highway Department 2 years before beginning college. While in school he held several part-time jobs—a boat rigger, oil field roustabout, and ambulance driver. After graduating from college he became a partner in a landscape company and earned $10,000. He recently sold out to his partner because he wanted a career more in line with his college training. It is thought he has an upper-middle class market.

☐ Yes, I think this applicant will still be employed as an SRT at the end of his first year in business.

☐ No, I don't think this applicant will still be working as an SRT at the end of his first year.

How confident are you of this decision?

I could be easily swayed by other field supervisors	1	2	3	4	5	If my manager disgreed, I would argue my position strenuously

FIG. 9.6. Sample profile for judgmental predictions of success in life insurance sales work. From Roose, J. E., & Doherty, M. E. (1976). Judgment theory applied to the selection of life insurance salesmen. *Organizational Behavior and Human Performance, 16,* 231–249. Reprinted with permission.

Some Key Concepts in Judgment Theory

Cognitive Control. In introducing their concept of cognitive control, Hammond and Summers (1972) distinguished knowledge from the ability to use the knowledge. Within the lens model equation, G was taken to represent the judge's knowledge of the relationships of cues to the criterion. If a least squares prediction of the criterion from the cues matched closely, and the match might approach unity, the subject has substantial knowledge or understanding of the environment about which judgments are to be made. It does not necessarily follow that the judgments will be very consistent, as measured by R_j, because that consistency is a function of criterion predictability (Brehmer, 1976). The consistency index is a measure of the cognitive skill, or cognitive control, one has in using the knowledge.

The superiority of predicted over actual judgments may be reduced by increases in cognitive control. Task characteristics can influence a judge's level of cognitive control, and attempts to clarify the nature of the judgment task—to improve understanding of it—may improve control. For example, judges show more control in judgment tasks where the relationships between cue and criteria are simple rather than requiring complex inferences (Hammond & Summers, 1972). More generally, however, cognitive control is a learned cognitive skill.

Cognitive Feedback. Learning a cognitive skill requires knowledge of results, or feedback, but effectiveness depends on the kinds of results or feedback received. *Outcome feedback* tells how well a judgment matched the criterion value. *Cognitive feedback* gives information about the judgment process being used and the relationships among the components of the process, such as the environmental validities and intercorrelations of cues, differential cue weights, functional relationships of cues to criteria, and so on. There is consistent evidence that outcome feedback offers little if any improvement in either judgment or policy validity—that it may even hinder skill development in making judgments (Balzer, Doherty, & O'Connor, 1989); Hammond (1993) characterized the result of outcome feedback as "slow, 'stupid' learning" (p. 213). Cognitive feedback has seemed more useful.

Cognitive Conflict. Different people in an organization may have access to precisely the same information, be asked to make a recommendation based on it, and come to wholly different conclusions. Differences may be due to differences in organizational perspectives or responsibilities, personality differences, different interpretations of information, or something else. For whatever reason, differences in judgment all involve conflict in cognition. Conflict is not necessarily dramatic or emotional; different observers may make conflicting judgments quite cheerfully.

Conflict can be useful, but unresolved conflict can be damaging. Carl Rogers said there would less conflict between people if each person would express, in his own words, the other person's point of view, to the other person's satisfaction, before offering an evaluation or an opposing view (Rogers & Roethlisberger, 1952). When potential antagonists come to that level of understanding, differences may disappear, become less important, or stand out clearly enough to be amenable to resolution. Disagreements sometimes stem from positions so firmly held that resolution is impossible; even then, however, clearly understanding an opponent's point of view clarifies the differences and seems to make them less threatening. Judgment theory offers a parallel view. Using the lens model, with one judge on each side (instead of the environment on one side), the lens model statistics can be computed and offer some insight into the nature of the differences. If those with different judgments understand each other's judgment policies, sources of real difference can be extracted from the mass of cues considered. Maybe the differences cannot be wholly resolved, but they can be clearly isolated from perceptions and policy components that do not differ. A focus on similarities of policy may not eliminate conflict, but it might substantially reduce the emotional content of the conflict.

There is another, positive way to think about cognitive conflict. Two different judgments can simply be different—different readings of the information available (e.g., wholly different weights for the cues)—and both can be valid predictors. This is analogous to different constructs, and we know from multiple regression principles that two valid but poorly correlated predictors will do a better job than either one alone.

A Cognitive Continuum. Experts asked to explain their judgments sometimes have difficulty in doing so and instead call them intuitive. Judgments are sometimes rational or analytic, breaking a problem down into its components and then following some rule or algorithm to a logical conclusion. Sometimes people think of these as independent but opposing processes; Hammond and Brehmer (1973), however, saw them as two ends of a cognitive continuum. At the analytic end, thinking was said to be "explicit, sequential, and recoverable"; at the intuitive end, it was said to be "implicit, nonsequential, and nonrecoverable." Most thinking, it was said,

> is neither purely analytical, nor purely intuitive; rather it combines analytical and intuitive components. Information is transformed according to explicit rules, but the conclusions reached through these transformations are

checked, revised, and even distorted by past experience; indeed, past experience may even substitute for some of the steps in the thinking process. It is this process we refer to as *quasi-rational*. (Hammond & Brehmer, 1973, p. 340)

Characteristics of the judgment task tend to move the processing of information toward one end of the continuum or the other. If one wants judgments to be more analytical, the judgment task, among other things, should have (a) relatively few cues, that is, the amount of information to be processed should be limited, (b) measurements as objective and reliable as possible, (c) little redundancy in information presented, (d) environmental relationships beteen cues and the criterion different from a simple linear one, (e) an environmental policy with unequal weights among the cues, (f) plenty of time to arrive at the judgments (Hammond, Hamm, Grassia, & Pearson, 1987).

Resist the temptation to assume that analytic processes are necessarily superior to intuitive ones. In their study of judgments of highway engineers, conducted to test the implications of the cognitive continuum theory, Hammond et al. (1987) found that analytical cognition did not form a ceiling which achievement based on intuitive or quasi-rational processes could not exceed. Moreover, errors in judgment, as assessed by r_a, were far more variable in analytical cognition; that is, both the highest and lowest values of the achievement index occurred under analytical processing. In fact, the biggest errors are likely to appear under the use of analytic processes. To me, the most important finding is that when task characteristics and cognitive characteristics are congruent (i.e., both the nature of the task and the person's approach favor either analytic or intuitive processes), achievement is maximized. Adaptation to task demands seems to promote the best judgment.

Some Questions to Consider. The following questions seem important:

1. What form should a policy model take? The most common is multiple regression. Nonlinear or nonadditive models are sometimes proposed, but Dawes and Corrigan (1974) argued that complex models account for little or no more variance than simpler ones. Practical researchers, however, may be less interested in variance than in recognizable judgment policies. Some attention has been given to this question already; more is given later.

2. Do judges understand their own policies? The level of insight people have about their judgments is questionable. Interviewers, for example, tend to make up their minds about interviewees within the first few

minutes of the interview (Webster, 1964), but they continue on for extended periods gathering new information, apparently unaware that they have already made up their minds. Moreover, the subjective weights that judges assign to the variables bear little resemblance to the beta weights of a multiple regression equation. Efforts to get people to talk through their reasons for a judgment or decision often provide only unreliable data.

3. Are judgment policies so idiosyncratic that people will continue to use a policy even under contrary instructions; can people learn to use an alternative policy? From an organizational point of view, the question is extremely important. If procedural justice is to be perceived in selection, for example, judgments made by interviewers after the collection of several kinds of data (e.g., test scores, biodata forms, background checks, references, and information gathered in the interview itself) should be consistent; the decision about a candidate should not depend on which interviewer was seen. A uniform organizational policy should be reflected in the judgments of the several interviewers.

These questions are important for a coherent organizational policy. They deserve closer scrutiny.

The Policy Model

Suppose one must hire a company physician. The judgment in a typical design might be an HR specialist's rating of a candidate's acceptability by the current dispensary staff. Cues might include age, years of experience, perhaps an index of medical school quality, classification of internship or practice experience, and maybe a couple more. A lot of profiles would be developed. Judgment policies would be modeled by multiple regression to use the profile cues to predict the ratings. Note that all profiles make the ordinarily valid assumption that each candidate has a legal license to practice medicine, so possession of a license would not be included; it would have little or no variance and therefore could not account for variance in ratings. But suppose that one or more of the actual candidates did not have, for whatever reason, a valid license. None of the other variables would matter, the unlicensed candidates would be rejected, and a compensatory model of judgment policy would not fit that judgment. A less fanciful alternative example substitutes the practice category. The company physician is necessarily a generalist; one who has specialized in one area, especially an esoteric one, might be passed over regardless of other virtues. Both examples are configural judgments, one based on a variable not included in the research because it seems unlikely, the other included but inappropriately modeled.

Insight into Policies

The absence of self-insight is often inferred from the discrepancies between modeled and subjectively stated weights. Reilly and Doherty (1989, 1992) found, however, that many students judging the desirability of potential job offers or of potential roommates could indeed recognize their own policies. Why did these results differ from the common view that insight is rare? One reason might be that the judgment tasks were genuinely relevant to the ordinary concerns of student subjects.

One plausible reason for apparent lack of insight is that an additive policy model does not recognizably represent the way a person thinks in reaching judgments. That possibility was illustrated by Ikomi (1987, 1989), a commercial pilot and flight instructor as well as a psychologist, who wondered whether instructors in a flight school had similar policies for sending student pilots for their first solo flights. Before solo flight, student pilots must do preflight checks of the airplane, use the rudder in taxiing, take off properly, stall and recover, turn or climb or descend smoothly, handle radio communications, and above all land the airplane safely without stressing it with bounces, excessive speed and braking, or going off the runway. A compensatory decision model seems inappropriate. A flight instructor would not say, "this student can't be counted on to land the plane safely but traces beautiful figure eights over a road intersection, so I might as well send him or her on a solo flight."

Traditional linear modeling was used. Both the C index of nonlinear matching and Brannick's equation (Equation 8 in chapter 8) were used in a pilot study to test for nonadditive judgment policies, and both suggested substantial nonlinear, nonadditive components. In a further study, flight instructors declared their policies, essentially various noncompensatory algorithms; in general, declared policies predicted judgments as well or better than regression policies. It seems safe to say that judges can have some degree of insight into their judgment policies, particularly where making such judgments is a realistic, important, and essentially daily task.

To suggest that people making judgments understand how they arrive at their judgments flies in the face of a lot of contrary evidence. However, methodological problems may account for much of that evidence. People may weight different cues inconsistently. Weighting variables in multiple regression equations is tantamount to saying, "In general, these variables are weighted in this way." Inconsistency in individual judgments may be deliberate. In a specific case, a particular fact may stand out as more important than usual, and get more weight in reaching the judgment than it would in other cases. This is inconsistency, but it is not necessarily error, although the inconsistency reduces the correlation based on more reliable averages. That does not mean that the judge does not understand how he or she considers data in arriving at a judgment—only that the judge is not as rigidly consistent as the equation.

Moreover, there is no good psychological reason (as opposed to a statistical one) for judgment research to assume automatically that a regression model is a good model of the judgment process. If a person has a judgment policy, can express it in words, equations, or algorithms, then that policy can be modeled, the model can be validated, and the stated model may have greater reliability and validity than the individual's raw judgments. This approach assumes that the person does have some insight into important judgment policies, and it models the research accordingly.

Judgment situations and judgment policies, unlike validated tests, are not standardized; they may vary more than the research model assumes. Most policy capturing research presupposes a constant set of variables with the same information available for all candidates. In judgment situations, however, the missing data problem is often greater in information files or interviews than in profile booklets, the data available for a given candidate can be relatively good or poor, and additional data may be available for some candidates. Where there is a judgment model, whether captured or created, it can be used—and then the judgment it dictates can be modified in the light of evaluations of additional information (as in the example of the unlicensed physician). Standard research models, of course, do not anticipate such nonstandard judgment conditions, so we do not know how this approach would work. Logically, however, it has to be better than the unexamined, unmodeled judgments ordinarily made.

Training in Policy Use

Balzer et al. (1989) asked why judges are needed once the model is developed if the judgment model is truly superior to actual judgments in consistency and achievement. They pointed out that such an Orwellian act as letting a computer make judgments is unlikely in most social organizations; it follows that, rather than waste time on the question, efforts should be directed toward finding better ways to train judges to make consistent, valid judgments. Cognitive feedback seems to be a useful approach.

In an assessment center, assessees complete tasks while being observed by assessors. The assessors usually rate aspects of exercise performance and, when all exercises have been completed, provide overall ratings. A set of completed assessments is likely to be more reliable if assessors all look for the same behavioral cues and weight them in pretty much the same way. Can judges be trained to follow consistently the same judgment policies?

The question has not been addressed directly, but Galbraith (1985) presented the desired judgment policy to each of his subjects (all experienced assessors) giving them the rank orders of the importance of the cues (task information). Half of the subjects received the same information at a session the next day; the other half received cognitive feedback. People in *both* groups learned to use the policy. Why did cognitive feedback not show the expected superiority? He suggested the plausible explanation that the judges were experienced enough that a ceiling effect existed in the very first set of judgments. Perhaps task information is enough for experienced judges who understand the nature of the judgments required.

In a related study for judgments in job evaluation, Stang (1985) developed an interactive computer program to provide cognitive feedback. She found that (a) judges developed and learned to use a consistent policy, (b) they learned to use consistently a policy other than their own, and (c) they remembered either policy well enough to use it consistently without further feedback. In this case, cognitive feedback helped. Some of these judges were highly consistent from the outset, but most of them began with ample room for improvement.

Training interviewers can change interviewing policies. Dougherty, Ebert, and Callender (1986), in a policy-capturing field study tapping the judgments of three full-time interviewers, successfully provided such training. The three taped their interviews over a period of several months, and these tapes provided the profiles. Midway through the study, they were given special training. This was not training in the use of a weighted policy. Rather it was training in how to interview to assess three different applicant characteristics: compatibility, attitude toward the job, and responsibility. These were three of eight dimensions on which each judge rated each applicant based on the taped interview. Using only these three dimensions, policy equations (with differential weights) were computed for the period before training and for the period after training. All three interviewers benefited from training; in policy equations predicting 10 criteria, post-training equations generally did better than pre-training equations, and judgments were more consistent.

In short, through lens model research, managers' judgment policies can be identified (captured); the policies can be evaluated, discussed, and even argued over; and one of them, or a modification based on several of them, can be agreed on as desired organizational policy. If the full lens model were used, choosing an appropriate policy could consider cue validities; broader organizational concerns may also influence the policy, for example, workforce homogeneity or diversity, or responsibilities of the organization within the larger community in which it operates. When a policy is agreed on, all decision makers can be trained in its use, more consistently making similar basic judgments. Perhaps more important, the policy can be used to say what the judgment should be in *most* cases like one at hand; users who understand the reasoning and algorithm of a policy-demanded judgment may more effectively consider additional information in modifying that judgment.

A HYPOTHETICAL INTEGRATED PROGRAM
FOR PERSONNEL DECISIONS

What follows is imaginary, not a report of an actual program; it pretends, however, to be literal reporting of a personnel decision system. To develop a system like this requires much conferring, writing, and revision to make it operational, even on a pilot basis. Obviously, such a complex system cannot be fully described in a few pages. I intend only to illustrate what an integrated system might be like, the many judgments it would require, the kinds of research needed to systematize those judgments, the place of assessment in it, and procedures for evaluating it. Because the system is a product of my imagination (prodded by actual experiences with organizations that do some of the things my imagination suggests), I invite readers to add to it from their own imaginations. Someone, some-day, will develop a well-integrated system analogous to this one. In the meantime, here is a description of what one might be like.

An Overview

The program is for salaried personnel in a corporate setting. The corpo-ration has several thousand employees in multiple locations. It is decen-tralized in many respects, but the ever-present possibilities of litigation have resulted in strong central office influence (but not control) on HR policies and practices. Many people participated in developing the basic program, but procedural details were worked out at the central office level. The program calls for decisions to be made locally, not centrally. A first line supervisor is responsible for initiating the procedure and for decisions within his realm. The program can be activated by individual employees, whether salaried or hourly, permanent or temporary, when they apply for positions, training opportunities, or career planning.

Program Objectives

The over-arching objective is to improve unit performance throughout the corporation through a systematic and persistent improvement in workforce and individual qualifications; this more detailed statement of objectives is a collection of ways to reach that goal:

1. To stabilize the workforce by maximizing both work force stability and job security. This objective is met, in part, by personnel transfer and personnel development. Temporary employees are occasionally used (and included in a personnel inventory), but a lengthy study has found more lasting advantages in a long-term permanent workforce.
2. To base decisions on the best possible predictions of outcomes, whether empirical or implied. This objective is met, and meeting it is documented, by an initial and continuing program of research.
3. To minimize the time required to fill vacancies. This objective is met by a computerized, corporation-wide human resources inventory system that can identify people, both within the organization and outside of it, who meet the qualifications for a specific opportunity.
4. To help employees increase the scope of opportunities for which they are qualified and to strengthen their existing qualifications. This objective is met through diagnostic performance evaluation, opportunities for specialized training or more general personal development and career planning, and information systems publicizing them.
5. To assure procedural justice—that all candidates for opportunities have equal treatment and equal opportunity. This objective is met by unambiguously spelling out procedures, including procedures for making judgments, and monitoring to assure compliance.

System Requirements

In a work unit headed by a supervisor (first line or higher), a vacancy occurs or is anticipated. It can be filled by a lateral transfer of someone currently working at about the same level somewhere (anywhere) else in the corporation, by promotion, or from outside the organization. The supervisor and a local HR representative work together to find suitable candidates, but the final decision is the supervisor's responsibility.

A *personnel requisition* form is completed on the basis of a job analysis or detailed job plan; it describes critical components, or key elements, of the position to be filled using a common vocabulary developed as part of the system. Research has established the qualifications required for standard key elements and methods for assessing them. Qualifications are entered on the requisition form. Some supervisors, unchecked, would build empires. Some, excessively cost-conscious, would add mercilessly to the workloads of others rather than bring in someone new. Some would probably not fully understand, even after extensive training and work with a personnel specialist, the materials, terms, and procedures of the system. Therefore, a personnel requisition is completed with the advice, assistance, and consent of the supervisor's own supervisor, and it is approved or rejected by still higher authority in both the line management where the supervisor may work and the HR function.

A *personnel inventory* system within the corporation provides data on the qualifications of each employee at, or aspiring to be at, the salaried level. Searching it is the first step in filling the vacancy. As many vacancies as possible are to be filled from within the organization, but the inventory also includes people who have applied for work in the corporation.

Some qualifications are matters of record; others require formal assessment. Assessment is the mutual responsibility of the supervisor and the HR representative; formal testing or assessment center activity are undertaken by HR staff in face-to-face meetings with supervisors to discuss and evaluate the results. Some qualifications are assessed by jointly developed simulations or work samples. Some are assessed by ratings. Recent performance ratings are included in the inventory record. Some are assessed by interviewing; the supervisor conducts the interview using a structured interview plan approved by HR staff.

A system like this can be detailed on paper, bound in a handsome notebook (loose-leaf, of course), given a prominent place on the supervisor's desk and in general be very impressive—and utterly useless. It is useless if critical components of positions are defined idiosyncratically by each individual supervisor, each time a vacancy occurs. It is useless if qualifications are specified by hunch or unverified common sense. It is useless if qualifications are assessed by ad hoc methods treating principles of validity and validation as completely foreign. But a system such as this can be very useful indeed if vacancies can be described in well-understood, standard terms also used by other supervisors who contribute to the personnel inventory records; if qualifications are linked to position requirements systematically, reliably, and validly; and if the assessment of those qualifications is demonstrably job relevant and psychometrically valid. These are tall orders, and often they are only partially met. Explicitly stating and operationally encouraging the ideal, however, is a start toward meeting them more fully.

Position Analysis. In the personnel requisition, the supervisor describes the position to be filled and the qualifications it requires. A task-oriented checklist was developed for corporation-wide use. Based on research, it lists critical components found in salaried positions, yet it is short enough for general use. It identifies standardized entries in the list of critical components, but it has space to enter critical components in unique positions as well.

Using the checklist, the supervisor identifies the critical components and records them on the personnel requisition form, such as in Fig. 9.7. Prior research also standardized a thesaurus of job components, identifying,

Personnel Requisition

Plant:	Dept:	Date Issued:	Date Needed:	Req. No.:
7	15	10/1/95	1/2/96 or before	

Issued By: ___B. V. Helmquist___

Reason for Need: ___Planned retirement of present incumbent___

Position Title and Description: ___Technical Report Production Editor.___
___Enters draft reports in personal computer from hard copy or disk; edits___
___reports for format, grammar, spelling, style, and content consistency.___
___Creates graphics as needed. Prepares final file for production.___

Critical Job Components	Code	Qualifications	Code
Uses personal computer to edit documents.	8D143	Level 3 knowledge of major programs for:	
		word processing	AC614
		spreadsheets	AC615
		graphics	AC617
		desktop publishing	AC619
Edits executive level documents	8F519	Memory for verbal content	MC127
		Memory for numerical content	MC128
		Level 5 knowledge of English usage	VE210
Maintains confidences	2A116	General trustworthiness	PC001

FIG. 9.7. Part of a sample personnel requisition form for use in the hypothetical integrated program for personnel decisions; only the most critical components and qualifications are listed. Code numbers refer to entries in the system thesaurus giving full definitions of job components and preferred methods of assessment. Requisitions include other information such as salary levels, EEO constraints, and so forth.

defining, and classifying them in language generally familiar among supervisors. If a vacant position is truly unique, its most critical component may not appear in any other job in the corporation, but its absence from the thesaurus is no reason to ignore it. Nevertheless, departures from the standard list are inevitable topics of conversation between the supervisor and the HR specialist.

Standardized definitions of job components in the thesaurus contain statements of required or desired qualifications: the kinds of abilities, skills, training, experience, or other qualifications required (or helpful) for excellence in performance. Panels of experts (industrial psychologists specializing in the study of individual differences) developed these statements. For components where prior research was unavailable or inadequate, panels of psychologists and panels of job experts worked together with an HR specialist to develop predictive hypotheses.

The psychologist panels also specified ways to assess qualifications in the standard list. Methods were diverse, specifying various kinds of tests, personality inventories, specially developed biodata forms, elements of qualifying training or experience, performance appraisals, performance or other behavioral exercises, and structured interviews with candidates, references, prior supervisors, and others.

The Personnel Inventory. Information is not included in the inventory merely because it is available or because someone thinks it might be nice to have. It must include:

1. Identification data: name, identification code numbers, current employment status (company location and operating unit; whether employed full-time, part-time, share-time, etc.), birthdates, date of initial employment, and various EEO codes.

2. Prehire employment history: job and occupation codes, type of industry, tenure on previous jobs, and employment status (e.g., was a prior job held full-time or as part-time student employment?).

3. Company employment history: dates of hire and employment status or job changes; job and location codes, salaries and salary changes (with reasons), and summary evaluation of performance status at the time of each job change; recent performance evaluations. The emphasis is on recent.

4. General qualifications: scores on tests, assessment center results, and other centralized, standardized assessment procedures administered or administratively controlled by the corporate HR function; educational background, including specific kinds of courses taken and grades received; and special abilities, such as abilities in different languages, or those associated with active hobbies or other avocational activity.

5. Job-related qualifications associated with the critical components of jobs held and satisfactorily performed: knowledge or skills acquired through specialized training and development programs; results of job-specific testing or other assessment programs; any known qualifications in the standardized list but not required in the employment history; and rated characteristics, where outstanding, of contextual work behavior.

6. Disabilities: ADA accommodations requested.

7. Preferences: the person's preferences for fields of work, locations preferred in the event of transfer, special family-related accommodations.

8. Career path data: Career suggestions may have been designated by management (e.g., potential sequence of and rated readiness to begin career-path promotions) or by the individual (transfer or promotion preferences, training and development opportunities wanted, etc.).

Recruiting. The principal recruiting source is the personnel inventory, but only in the sense of providing a list of potential candidates. Turning a potential candidate into an actual candidate who wants serious consideration for the position may require more. The personnel requisition should provide basic information for a realistic job preview (Rynes, 1991; Wanous, 1980). Recruiters in the corporation's ongoing program of college recruiting have current vacancy lists, but they know that many vacancies are filled from within. Therefore, they seek candidates willing to be placed on a list if not on a job.

Assessment Procedures. Assessment of some qualifications may be inferred and accepted from the data in the inventory report. Generally, however, the inventory identifies people who might be, rather than who clearly are, qualified to fill the vacancy; further candidate assessment is usually needed. All assessment procedures, including the supervisor's interview prior to decision or assessments for qualifications for nonstandard critical components, are the responsibility of HR specialists. They administer, score, and interpret most standardized tests. They share responsibility with the work unit for performance tests such as work samples. Interviews are ordinarily conducted by unit personnel, but planning for them (structuring, setting up rating scales, etc.) is assisted by someone from the HR staff.

Each selection decision is certified by a responsible HR specialist to be in compliance with legal requirements (especially EEO and ADA requirements) and with the corporate policy of procedural justice.

Employee-Initiated Procedures. An employee—even a well-satisfied and productive one—may seek a transfer for the sake of more money, more responsibility, more interesting work, less commuting time, or something else. For whatever reason, employees are encouraged to request a local or corporate-wide search of the inventory for vacancies, either current or anticipated, for which that employee is or can become qualified. This includes vacancies in in-house training programs or training or educational opportunities through a related company-sponsored tuition refund program.

Decisions. Decisions are made jointly by several people. For the organization, the ultimate decision responsibility lies in the hands of a hiring supervisor or the head of a training program; if the opportunity is offered, however, the employee or trainee decides to accept or to reject it. These are the central decision roles, but others are usually involved. The supervisor's own supervisor and other officials in the operating unit play advisory roles, as do HR specialists. They do not have veto power; the supervisor may hire someone others think less than the best. Supervisors who consistently ignore the judgments of others, however, are not wise. To minimize controversial conflicting judgments, the program offers guidance in the form of a policy model emphasizing categories of variables to be considered and appropriate sequences or weights to use in considering them. These models have been developed through prior policy-capturing research and subsequent policy conferences.

Evaluating the System

Major details of the program are summarized in Fig. 9.8. This program is fiction but not implausible. It incorporates most of the procedures so far described in this book, and it does so as a system rather than as a set of isolated functions. It incorporates a solid empirical foundation and many kinds of judgments. If it were an actual program, how well would it work? And how would one find out?

Overall Evaluation. Quasi-experimental research seems appropriate. Because the system was envisioned for a corporation with units in many geographical areas, and because it takes time in even one location to get

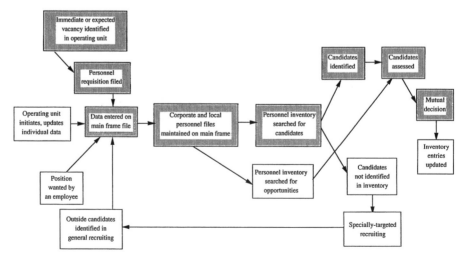

FIG. 9.8. Flowchart for the integrated personnel system.

it operational, the research design might be similar to that designated as Design 4 in chapter 8. It would need at least two periods of observation, rather than one, before putting the system to work, and the design might consider three groups of locations rather than two. Certain of the various corporate locations could be considered more or less matched, providing two corporate groups somewhat similar in function, size, work force stability, or some other information. Unmatched locations would form a third group.

Observations at location level would be dictated by the program objectives. They call for a unit level of analysis and might include:

1. *Mean unit productivity*: Different things are produced at different locations or in different operating units, so a common measure of unit productivity may be hard to develop. Some cost/benefit ratio might be feasible. Maybe an engineering or financial standard could be computed and the productivity assessed as a percentage of that standard. Whatever it is, a productivity construct must be defined and operationalized to take differences into account and provide valid assessment across locations.

2. *Work force characteristics*: These might include several things: work force stability (turnover), mean level of job satisfaction or other employee attitude (company identification, intention to stay or quit, etc.), diversity, or a measure of work force quality.

3. *Mean time of unfilled vacancies*: This is a straightforward, direct measure of the achievement of one of the program objectives.

4. *Growth in employee initiatives*: Perhaps a measure such as the number of requests for transfer, training, or personal development opportunities per hundred employees would serve. The construct here is the degree to which employees seize the opportunities the system can provide.

Some people would urge the development of a composite measure of all these outcomes—the development of which would be an exercise in group judgment. One necessary judgment is whether a particular outcome is sufficiently under company control; that is, can any company-initiated program influence it directly? The answer would differ for different outcomes. My own judgment, however, is that each measure should be treated individually as an observation and the design used to test, diagnostically, any pattern of strengths or weaknesses in program outcomes (similar to the logic in Guion, 1961).

For each outcome measure, then, the modified design would have four periods of observation—the length of the observation period depends on several things such as criterion stability, seasonal variations, or the patience of management. The first one would be before work began on program development, providing a baseline set of observations. The second would be a period of program development in the first set of locations. The third would be the time of program introduction, a period of debugging. Fourth would be a period after the program is declared fully operational. In each period, observations might be recorded monthly for the group of locations with the system, the matched group without it, and the third group which did not match the others. Each period of observation in each group of locations could be treated as a time series for analysis and comparison:

O_1	O_2	X,O_3	O_4
O_1	O_2	O_3	X,O_4
O_1	O_2	O_3	O_4

Process Evaluation. Developing such a program would use principles outlined in earlier chapters for developing position descriptions, linkages of qualifications to critical position components, evaluations of assessment procedures, and so forth. Much of it is amenable to evaluation by expert judgment or lens model research. The integrated personnel system is basically judgmental, and evaluation asks whether judgments are or are not generally good. Does wisdom reign, or is the system only superficially integrated and thoughtful? Many smaller diagnostic studies are possible and needed, but an overall evaluation seems indispensible for practical purposes. Make no mistake: In most organizations, even where validation studies are routinely done, actual personnel decisions are reached in a model somewhat like this imaginary one—at least as judgmental in character but less systematic, less well-informed by research, and not evaluated as total programs.

REFERENCES

American Educational Research Association, American Psychological Association, & National Council on Measurement in Education. (1985). *Standards for educational and psychological testing*. Washington, DC: American Psychological Association.

Arvey, R. D., & Campion, J. E. (1982). The employment interview: A summary and review of recent research. *Personnel Psychology, 35*, 281–322.

Balzer, W. K., Doherty, M. E., & O'Connor, R., Jr. (1989). Effects of cognitive feedback on performance. *Psychological Bulletin, 106*, 410–433.

Brannick, M. T. (1986). *The development and evaluation of some models for detecting the presence of noncompensatory combinations in phenomena of interest to industrial and organizational psychologists*. Doctoral dissertation, Bowling Green State University, Bowling Green, OH.

Brehmer, B. (1976). Note on clinical judgment and the formal characteristics of clinical tasks. *Psychological Bulletin, 83*, 778–782.

Brunswik, E. (1956). *Perception and the representative design of psychological experiments* (2nd ed.). Berkeley: University of California Press.

Dawes, R. M. (1979). The robust beauty of improper linear models in decision making. *American Psychologist, 34*, 571–582.

Dawes, R. M., & Corrigan, B. (1974). Linear models in decision making. *Psychological Bulletin, 81*, 95–106.

Dawes, R. M., Mirels, H. L., Gold, E., & Donahue, E. (1993). Equating inverse probabilities in implicit personality judgments. *Psychological Science, 4*, 396–400.

DeGroot, M. H., Fienberg, S. E., & Kadane, J. B. (Eds.). (1986). *Statistics and the law.* New York: Wiley.

Dougherty, T. W., Ebert, R. J., & Callender, J. C. (1986). Policy capturing in the employment interview. *Journal of Applied Psychology, 71*, 9–15.

Dudycha, L. W., & Naylor, J. C. (1966). Characteristics of human inference process in complex choice behavior situations. *Organizational Behavior and Human Performance, 1*, 110–128.

Eddy, D. M. (1982). Probabilistic reasoning in clinical medicine: Problems and opportunities. In D. Kahneman, P. Slovic, & A. Tversky (Eds.), *Judgment under uncertainty: Heuristics and biases* (pp. 249–267). Cambridge, England: Cambridge University Press.

Galbraith, J. T. (1985). Training assessment center assessors: Applying principles of human judgment. *Dissertation Abstracts, 45*, 3104-B.

Goldberg, L. R. (1970). Man versus model of man: A rationale, plus some evidence, for a method of improving on clinical inferences. *Psychological Bulletin, 73*, 422–432.

Goldberg, L. R. (1991). Human mind versus regression equation: Five contrasts. In D. Cicchetti & W. M. Grove (Eds.), *Thinking clearly about psychology. Volume 1: Matters of public interest (Essays in honor of Paul E. Meehl)* (pp. 173–184). Minneapolis: University of Minneapolis Press.

Gorman, C. D., Clover, W. H., & Doherty, M. E. (1978). Can we learn anything about interviewing real people from "interviews" of paper people? Two studies of the external validity of a paradigm. *Organizational Behavior and Human Performance, 22*, 165–192.

Guion, R. M. (1961). Criterion measurement and personnel judgments. *Personnel Psychology, 14*, 141–149.

Guion, R. M. (1991). Personnel assessment, selection, and placement. In M. D. Dunnette & L. M. Hough (Eds.), *Handbook of industrial and organizational psychology* (2nd ed., Vol. 2, pp. 327–397). Palo Alto, CA: Consulting Psychologists Press.

Hammond, K. R. (1966). Probabilistic functionalism: Egon Brunswik's integration of the history, theory, and method of psychology. In K. R. Hammond (Ed.), *The psychology of Egon Brunswik* (pp. 15–80). New York: Holt, Rinehart, & Winston.

Hammond, K. R. (1993). Naturalistic decision making from a Brunswikian viewpoint: Its past, present, and future. In G. A. Klein, J. Orasanu, R. Calderwood, & C. E. Zsambok (Eds.), *Decision making in action: models and methods* (pp. 205–227). Norwood, NJ: Ablex.

Hammond, K. R., & Brehmer, B. (1973). Quasi-rationality and distrust: Implications for international conflict. In L. Rapoport & D. A. Summers (Eds.), *Human judgment and social interaction* (pp. 338–391). New York: Holt, Rinehart, & Winston.

Hammond, K. R., Hamm, R. M., Grassia, J., & Pearson, T. (1987). Direct comparison of the efficacy of intuitive and analytical cognition in expert judgment. *IEEE Transactions on Systems, Man, and Cybernetics, 17*, 753–770.

Hammond, K. R., & Summers, D. A. (1972). Cognitive control. *Psychological Review, 79*, 58–67.

Heneman, H. G., III, Huett, D. L., Lavigna, R. J., & Ogsten, D. (1995). Assessing managers' satisfaction with staffing services. *Personnel Psychology, 48*, 163–172.

Herriot, P. (1993). Commentary: A paradigm bursting at the seams. *Journal of Organizational Behavior, 14*, 371–375.

Hirsh, H. R., Schmidt, F. L., & Hunter, J. E. (1986). Estimation of employment validities by less experienced judges. *Personnel Psychology, 39*, 337–344.

Hogan, R., & Hogan, J. (1992). *Hogan Personality Inventory: Manual.* Tulsa, OK: Hogan Assessment Systems.

Ikomi, P. A. (1987). *Models of flight instructor decisions.* Unpublished manuscript, Bowling Green State University, Department of Psychology, Bowling Green, OH.

Ikomi, P. A. (1989). *The prediction of judgment in realistic tasks: Do judges have self-insight?* Unpublished doctoral dissertation, Bowling Green State University, Bowling Green, OH.

Kriska, S. D. (1995). Comments on banding. *The Industrial-Organizational Psychologist, 32*(3), 93–94.

Lee, P. M. (1989). *Bayesian statistics: An introduction.* New York: Oxford University Press.

Meehl, P. E. (1954). *Clinical versus statistical prediction.* Minneapolis: University of Minnesota Press.

Meehl, P. E. (1967). What can the clinician do well? In D. N. Jackson & S. Messick (Eds.), *Problems in human assessment* (pp. 594–599). New York: McGraw-Hill.

Novick, M. R., & Jackson, P. H. (1974). *Statistical methods for educational and psychological research.* New York: McGraw-Hill.

Reilly, B. A., & Doherty, M. E. (1989). A note on the assessment of self-insight in judgment research. *Organizational Behavior and Human Decision Processes, 44,* 123–131.

Reilly, B. A., & Doherty, M. E. (1992). The assessment of self-insight in judgment policies. *Organizational Behavior and Human Decision Processes, 53,* 285–309.

Rogers, C. R., & Roethlisberger, F. J. (1952). Barriers and gateways to communication. *Harvard Business Review, 30,* 46–52.

Roose, J. E., & Doherty, M. E. (1976). Judgment theory applied to the selection of life insurance salesmen. *Organizational Behavioral and Human Performance, 16,* 231–249.

Rynes, S. L. (1991). Recruitment, job choice, and post-hire consequences: A call for new research directions. In M. D. Dunnette & L. M. Hough (Eds.), *Handbook of industrial and organizational psychology* (2nd ed., Vol. 2, pp. 399–444). Palo Alto, CA: Consulting Psychologists Press.

Sackett, P. R., & Ostgaard, D. J. (1994). Job-specific applicant pools and national norms for cognitive ability tests: Implications for range restriction correlations in validation research. *Journal of Applied Psychology, 79,* 680–684.

Schmidt, F. L., Hunter, J. E., Croll, P. R., & McKenzie, R. C. (1983). Estimation of employment test validities by expert judgment. *Journal of Applied Psychology, 68,* 590–601.

Schneider, B. (1996). When individual differences aren't. In K. R. Murphy (Ed.), *Individual differences and behavior in organizations* (pp. 548–571). San Francisco: Jossey-Bass.

Smith, J. Q. (1988). *Decision analysis: A Bayesian approach.* London: Chapman and Hall.

Stang, S. W. (1985). *An interactive judgment analysis of job worth.* Doctoral dissertation, Bowling Green State University, Bowling Green, OH.

Stevenson, M. K., Busemeyer, J. R., & Naylor, J. C. (1990). Judgment and decision-making theory. In M. D. Dunnette & L. M. Hough (Eds.), *Handbook of industrial and organizational psychology* (2nd ed., Vol. 1, pp. 283–374). Palo Alto, CA: Consulting Psychologists Press.

Tucker, L. R. (1964). A suggested alternative formulation in the development by Hursch, Hammond, and Hursch and Hammond, Hursch, and Todd. *Psychological Review, 71,* 528–530.

Wanous, J. P. (1980). *Organizational entry: Recruitment, selection, and socialization of newcomers.* Reading, MA: Addison-Wesley.

Watson, G., & Glaser, E. M. (1980). *Watson-Glaser Critical Thinking Appraisal.* San Antonio, TX: The Psychological Corporation.

Webster, E. C. (1964). *Decision making in the employment interview.* Montreal: Industrial Relations Centre, McGill University.

10

Analysis of Bias

Bias was not a big concern in the early days of employment testing. After the Civil Rights Act of 1964, a set of so-called fair employment models dominated attention for a while. Many issues in these models now seem dormant, but they keep popping up in pronouncements of politicians, pundits, and reporters, and sometimes, almost surreptitiously, in the technical literature. Fairness and freedom from bias are not the same thing, but there is some overlap. Bias is technical; fairness is more a matter of opinion, policy, and power. During the civil rights debates of the late 1950s and early 1960s in the United States, words like bias, fairness, discrimination, and prejudice seemed to be used almost interchangeably; definitions and distinctions are still not universal.

Popular use treats bias and prejudice as synonyms, but they have different dictionary definitions (e.g., Flexner, 1987). Bias may be either positive or negative; prejudice is stronger and usually negative. Psychologically, prejudice is an attitude, but bias is a distortion in statistics or measurement. *Bias* refers to systematic group differences in item responses, test scores, or other assessments for reasons unrelated to the trait being assessed—a form of the more general third variable problem in which one or more sources of unwanted systematic variance function differently in the groups compared. Bias is more easily alleged than demonstrated; it is easier to imagine the various kinds of third variables that may bias scores than to show their influence.

If a test item requires knowledge common in one group but not in another, and if that knowledge is irrelevant to the trait, then the item is biased. It is culturally biased if an acceptable response depends on skills

433

or information common in one culture but not in another. Cultural bias can be expected across countries in multinational organizations, but it is less certain for subcultures (e.g., Black and White) within a single national experience where the same media of mass communication (movies, television, print media, school curricula, etc.) give subcultures much in common despite some profound differences. Subcultural differences may be differences in habits, especially habits of thought. If most members of one subculture are very conscious of time and time constraints, and most of those in a different subculture are less concerned about the passage of time, then tightly timed tests may be approached differently by most members of each subculture. Time awareness might be a biasing third variable, but it might also be related to the purpose of measurement. If the trait to be measured includes a speed component, then time awareness is a relevant component of the construct. If the construct definition stresses capacity or power, such as a kind of reasoning ability, then a speed component indicates bias.

Discrimination means making distinctions. It is not always pejorative; to call someone a "discriminating person" has a favorable connotation. Assessment procedures are supposed to help their users make distinctions—to discriminate between those with much of a trait and those with less (or those with even more), or to discriminate between those who can do the job acceptably and those who cannot (or who can do it better). The word has an unfavorable connotation when distinctions are based on prejudice, stereotypes, procedures, or policies unrelated to the trait or to the performance it predicts. Such discriminatory (not discriminating) practices are poor organizational policies, and many are illegal.

In employment, fairness refers to the job relevance of a potentially biasing or discriminatory practice. An item in a job knowledge test for decorators or furniture finishers may ask about japanning; answers may distinguish those with prior understanding of the activity from those without it, fairly and without bias: It discriminates precisely on the basis of knowledge relevant to the job, and that is the intent of the test. The item is not relevant to a house painter's job; if answers are related to socioeconomic status, the item is biased, unfair, and discriminatory.[1]

In short, fair discrimination distinguishes those highly likely from those less likely to achieve a performance standard. Unfair discrimination exists "when persons with equal probabilities of success on the job have unequal probabilities of being hired for the job" (Guion, 1966, p. 26).[2] The distinction will not be labored. In this chapter, the word "unfair" will usually

---

[1] "Japanning" refers to coating an object with a hard, black, glossy varnish or lacquer of a sort originally associated with Japan.

[2] The definition is somewhat ambiguous and was later cleaned up by Einhorn and Bass (1971).

be implied; frequent repetition is unnecessary. Analysis of bias tries to ferret out instances of unfair discrimination.

DISCRIMINATION

Discrimination Based on Group Membership

It is illegal in the United States to discriminate against any person on the basis of race, color, religion, sex, or national origin.[3] Groups of people identified on such bases (and in some other laws) are called *protected groups*. Discrimination need not be intentional to be illegal. A procedure (e.g., tests or interviews) with the effect of unfairly discriminating against people in a protected group is discrimination under the law, even if inadvertent. Procedures with only a "chilling effect," discouraging applications, may also constitute illegal discrimination. Organizational decision makers must be alert to inadvertent or chilling discriminatory practices—even if only to avoid litigation—and be aware that unfair discrimination that is not illegal is nevertheless unwise.

In the United States, group-based discrimination is so entangled with legal issues that groups defined in other ways are often overlooked. Socioeconomic groups, groups defined by cultural or intellectual habits, and other kinds of groups without legal or political protection may be discriminated against with no threat of litigation. Such discrimination is nevertheless poor management; it can rob the organization of people with excellent qualifications. Many kinds of people are, perhaps routinely, discriminated against on grounds not protected by law: people with unusually long or short hair, people who are unusually tall or short, people who are not well-dressed or are too well-dressed—in short, people

---

[3]The law prohibits discrimination based on sex, but many people prefer to say "gender"—thereby engendering (pun intended) spirited debate. In dictionaries (e.g., except for archaic or etymological entries that relate *gender* to *genre*), gender is equated with sex, although entries for sex do not identify gender. If they are synonyms, insistence on *gender* instead of *sex* is a neo-Victorian waste of a syllable. Distinctions are made in psychology, however. I follow Deaux (1993, p. 125): "use sex [when comparing people] on the basis of the demographic categories of male and female. . . . Use gender when one is making judgments or inferences about the nature of femaleness and maleness, of masculinity and femininity." The law does not prohibit discrimination against feminine people, it prohibits discrimination against women or men, that is, on the basis of sex. I shall stay with the word sex. However, I am inconsistent. A similar distinction between biological and social implications can be made between race and ethnicity. Nevertheless, about the only time I use these terms differently is when I speak of ethnicity as broader than race, including both the racial and national origins proscriptions. I regret any displeasure my choices, or failures to make choices, may cause.

with characteristics that displease the decision makers. Focusing on valid, job-related assessment can reduce such instances of bias in decisions.

Distributional Differences

Statistical analysis of bias and discrimination is necessarily group oriented. Analyses can examine group differences in score distributions, in validity, or in predictions. Unfortunately, the only commonly considered distributional difference is the difference in mean scores. This is not enough; differences in variance, skewness, other distributional characteristics, and psychometric differences that influence the distributions should also be considered in analyses of bias.

Group Mean Differences. A lower mean test score in one group compared to another is not by itself evidence of bias, nor is use of test scores with group mean differences evidence by itself of discrimination. Nevertheless, too often a mean difference is the only basis for allegations of discrimination. Markedly different mean scores can occur for many possible reasons other than bias. Consider just four of them:

1. The two groups are biased samples of their respective populations. One group is among the best in its population, the other from those in the lower tail of its population distribution.
2. The two groups are representative samples of populations that actually differ on the trait being measured.
3. Many of the test items require background experiences not common in the lower scoring group.
4. Conditions of test administration differed in the two groups.

The first of these is plausible if the higher scoring group was subjected to stringent screening and the lower scoring group came from extensive, uncritical recruiting. If the second is plausible, different means may not indicate bias at all. The experiences in the third may be job related. The fourth may describe an error in administering a test in one of the groups. The many reasons for mean differences are extremely difficult to evaluate. A conference on civil rights reached agreement on this if on little else: "Average group differences in test scores do not necessarily reflect bias arising from test construction or use. . . . Average group differences in test scores may remain in tests even if all bias is removed" (United States Commission on Civil Rights, 1993, p. 7). Referring to mean differences as bias, without even thinking about nondiscriminatory potential causes, is simplistic and misleading; citing mean differences as bias and denying a genuine possibility of true differences is dishonest.

Differences in Other Distributional Characteristics. Distributions may differ in variance. Protected groups may include people from disadvantaged, even dysfunctional, backgrounds—and people with more education and higher socioeconomic heritage. A plausible hypothesis is that minority groups have higher variance on tests of occupational skills and information influenced by personal background experiences, as illustrated in Table 10.1. The group means are different, but the difference in variability is greater. If it were possible to hire all people with scores of 16 or more, with top-down selection, 50% of Group A would be hired but only 22.5% of Group B. However, at a smaller selection ratio, the effect may disappear or even reverse because of the differences in variance; if only the top-scoring 10 of the 120 candidates are hired (those with scores of 18 or more), then the proportions hired are 7.5% in Group A and 10% in Group B.

If Group A has a higher mean, less variance, and less skewness than Group B, is the test biased against either group? Only if these differences stem from causes unrelated to the trait being measured. Nothing in the distributional statistics, however, speaks clearly to that point; the only clarity is that the relative proportions receiving favorable decisions is affected by a combination of these statistics and the selection ratio.

TABLE 10.1
Hypothetical Distributions for Two Groups Differing
in Test Score Means and Standard Deviations

Raw Score	Group A		Group B	
	f	cum f	f	cum f
20	1	80	1	40
19	2	79	2	39
18	3	77	1	37
17	9	74	1	36
16	21	65	2	35
15	23	44	2	33
14	10	21	5	31
13	6	11	6	26
12	3	5	7	20
11	1	2	6	13
10	1	1	4	7
9			1	3
8			1	2
7			0	2
6			0	2
5			1	1
M	15.3		12.6	
SD	1.7		3.6	

Discrimination as Systematic Measurement Error. Distributional differences may stem from true differences or from systematic sources of measurement error related to group membership. The latter can happen when groups are defined or influenced by unmeasured third variables such as test-taking habits. If the influence of a third variable is greater in one group than in others, it can be a source of unintentional, unknown, and unfair discrimination—even if not illegal.

A test user who was too cheap and unethical to buy her tests used poor quality photocopies instead. It was easy to show that this user not only violated copyright laws but also reduced the validity of her intended inferences; visual acuity was a strong influence on the scores. Scores were biased against people with even mild visual disability; that constituted unfair discrimination. The incident occurred long before ADA, so using the scores for decisions was unfair and unwise, but not yet illegal.

Unfair discrimination denies jobs to qualified people and denies the services of qualified people to organizations. Unfair discrimination due to unknown and unmeasured third variables, may reduce both psychometric validity and job relatedness.

Differential Validity and Prediction

The same terms often refer to different concepts. To military researchers during and after World War II, *differential validity* meant that the validity coefficients for predicting performance differed for various jobs. Early in the EEO era, differential validity meant different validity coefficients for a given job in different groups. The earlier concept was associated with different criteria, not different groups of people; the more recent usage referred to different constructs measured in different groups and is therefore related to unmeasured third variables (Cole & Moss, 1989).

"FAIRNESS" MODELS

A large test fairness literature developed in the 1970s proposing "fairness models" of prediction. The models were group-oriented, focusing on protected classes. Unfairness, sometimes considered a property of the test, was usually a matter of the way a test was used. The 1985 *Standards* supplanted the term *fairness* by the term *selection bias* (American Educational Research Association, American Psychological Association, & National Council on Measurement in Education, 1985).

The Regression Model

In linear regression, the sum of the residuals is zero. If the sample with which the regression equation is computed is divided into two groups, using a common regression line, the sum of the residuals in the subgroups is not necessarily zero; indeed, these sums may be substantially nonzero. Cleary (1968) defined a test as biased if prediction of an appropriate criterion results in nonzero errors of prediction in the subgroups. That is, she considered a test biased if the criterion score predicted from the common regression line is consistently too high or too low within subgroups. Her concept has become known as the *regression model*, or the *Cleary model* of fairness. Fairness by this definition is illustrated in Fig. 10.1a[4] where a common regression line fits both groups (i.e., zero sum of residuals) despite mean score differences. All other conditions in this figure, b, c, d, and e, are cases where mean subgroup residuals are not zero when the common regression line is used. The subgroups have different regression lines, and therefore the residuals from a common regression line cannot cancel out to an average of zero (as they would for the combined groups). In Fig. 10.1, because scores are given in z-scores, the slopes of the lines are the correlation coefficients, so subgroup validity coefficients are the same in cases a, b, c, and d. In e, where regression lines cross, use of the common regression line instead of the crossed regression lines also shows nonzero sums of errors in the subgroups as well as differences in validity. In short, in all cases except a, test use was unfair under the regression model if the common regression line were used as a basis for decisions for both groups. The remedy might use each group's regression line and base selection decisions on predicted criterion performance.

Such a remedy, however, is unlikely to result in more employment opportunities for people in lower scoring groups. When the model was proposed, experience with differential prediction was limited. Minority groups were expected to have the higher regression line, as in b, so that their performance would be underpredicted by test scores. To the contrary, in accumulated evidence, minorities (almost always Blacks in the early studies) had the lower regression lines, as in c and d; their performance was overpredicted by a common regression equation. In retrospect, it is hard to know why it was ever thought otherwise; it would be strange indeed if a 400-year history of slavery and enforced economic deprivation were to depress test scores but no other area of performance. Examples of differential validity, as in e, are rare; parallel regression lines, when found, seem often to be attributable to factors other than bias, such as unreliability or unmeasured third variables (Linn & Werts, 1971). Never-

---

[4]It should perhaps be known as the Humphreys model because it was given in essentially the same form by Lloyd Humphreys: "In these validation studies, it is important not only to determine whether standard errors of measurement are equal, but also whether the same score has the same meaning in the groups being compared, i.e., *whether the regression lines are identical or merely parallel*" (Humphreys, 1952, p. 134, italics added). During the era of controversy about models of fairness, that almost casual contribution was overlooked.

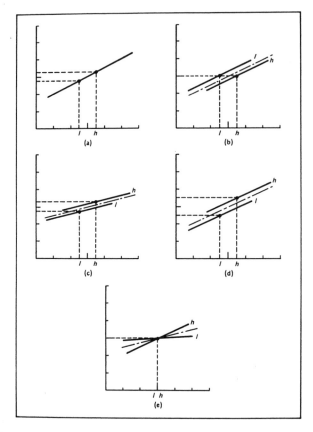

FIG. 10.1. Five examples of possible validity of regression differences for two subgroups; axes in standard score scales. From Guion, R. M. (1976). Personnel selection and placement. In M. D. Dunnette (Ed.), *Handbook of industrial and organizational psychology* (pp. 777–828). Chicago: Rand-McNally. Reprinted with permission.

theless, differential validity and differential prediction were virtually canonized in federal regulations and case law.

Professional canon, in the testing *Standards*, also supports the idea of investigating differential prediction, both in the sense of differentially predicting different outcomes and differentially predicting a given outcome for different groups (American Educational Research Association, American Psychological Association, & National Council on Measurement in Education, 1985). The bias–fairness distinction is made in the introduction to the standards on validity:

Several proposed ways of evaluating selection bias rest on different definitions of the fairness of a selection procedure. Unlike selection bias, however, fairness is not a technical psychometric term; it is subject to different definitions in different social and political circumstances. At present a consensus of technical experts supports only one approach to selection bias as technically appropriate. This approach is adopted in the *Standards* with the understanding that it does not resolve the larger issue of fairness. (American Educational Research Association, American Psychological Association, & National Council on Measurement in Education, 1985, p. 13)

The one approach, defined under the heading *predictive bias*, is consistent with the Cleary definition of fairness: "The systematic under- or over-prediction of criterion performance for people belonging to groups differentiated by characteristics not relevant to criterion performance" (AERA, APA, & NCME, 1985, p. 93).

Group Parity Models

Thorndike (1971) said that a fair test requires that the proportion in each subgroup that would have been hired on the basis of the criterion be matched by the proportion of those actually hired on the basis of test performance. Figure 10.2 is the familiar bivariate scattergram outline for one group. If one knew criterion levels in advance, and selected only those who were superior on the criterion, the proportion selected would be the areas $(a + b)/(a + b + c + d)$. Call that ratio p_c. Knowing only the test score, only those above some de facto cut score would be selected. So, the proportion actually hired, p_t, is $(a + d)/(a + b + c + d)$. Only if the ratio $p_c:p_t$ is the same in both (or all) subgroups is test use fair, a state that can often be achieved or approximated by manipulation of cut scores in the different groups.[5]

Cole (1973) carried the argument further. Her model, with notation in Fig. 10.2, required the ratios $(a + d)/(a + b)$ to be the same in the different groups, or in her terms, the same conditional probability of selection given success. To achieve fairness, as with the Thorndike model, the effective cut scores in the groups need to be adjusted. Both models are included in the term *group parity*.

Group parity and regression models are incompatible. Except under the unlikely condition of perfect correlation, fairness under one model is unfair under another. For example, in Fig. 10.1, assuming normal distributions for both groups, d and e are fair under the Thorndike model, but they are unfair under the Cleary model; only a is fair under the Cleary model, but it is unfair under group parity models. Other models were proposed (for a summary, see Petersen & Novick, 1976), any one being inconsistent in some respects with the others.

---

[5]Worth noting is that Thorndike (1971) pointed out that, in standard score terms, test score mean differences are often about twice the criterion mean differences, as in Fig. 10.1c.

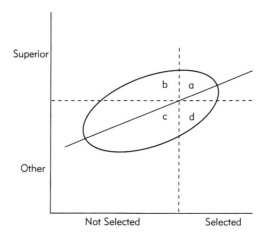

FIG. 10.2. Quadrants of the normal bivariate scattergram for identifying components of the group parity models.

The Fates of the Models

A special issue of the *Journal of Educational Measurement* (Jaeger, 1976) may have stilled debate over the models; it demonstrated the futility of looking to statistical models to answer political or social questions. Most participating authors looked to more rational, explicit values and the development of decision algorithms to maximize both organizational and social utilities. Except for a few attempts in the regulatory agencies to match Guidelines requirements to group parity definitions, the Cleary model has generally been accepted as perhaps the best of a poor set of choices.[6]

Note that the fairness models are models of test use, not models of bias inherent in test scores or assessment instruments. They are more likely to raise questions of cutting scores, whether actual or de facto, than of bias due to systematic error variance from third variables. Indeed, little effort has yet been directed toward the identification of third variables, beyond obvious demographic categories, that might contribute differentially to test score variance in different demographic groups.

ANALYSIS OF BIAS AND ADVERSE IMPACT IN TEST USE

Test bias is a psychometric term referring to distortion from different unwanted sources of variance in scores from different groups. *Adverse impact* is a social, political, or legal term referring to an effect of test use.

---

[6]"Generally" is the correct qualifier; not universally. Wigdor and Sackett (1993) rejected the Cleary model and supported the Cole model (without mentioning either by name or reference).

Table 10.1 illustrates adverse impact if the test is used to select a lot of people, but none for filling only a few positions.

Test Bias as Differential Psychometric Validity

Test bias produces scores with different meanings for people who are alike on the characteristic being measured. To define bias more precisely, the interpretation of test scores is biased against members of a group if groups of people matched on the trait measured have different scores because of one or more sources of variance related to group membership. Several features of this definition merit attention. First, it is the meaning inferred from scores that may or may not be biased, not the test per se, although intrinsic test characteristics may contribute to biased inferences. Second, it is group-related. The score of an individual test-taker may be invalid, but bias is only one possible source of invalidity. A score can lead to a wrong inference if the person misunderstands the instructions; bias exists only if the instructions are presented so that many people in the group have a common misunderstanding. Third, the definition requires reason to believe that the groups of people being compared are equal with respect to the trait being measured. A measure of bias that does not disentangle itself from genuine group differences is not interpretable. Finally, the definition places the emphasis on sources of group variances, not on group means. Sources of variance are potentially identifiable. Variance is supposed to be due to the same source—the characteristic being measured—in all groups. Bias exists when other sources of variance influence scores in one group but not in another. An example offered by Steele and Aronson (1995) is *stereotype threat*—for example, the degree to which Blacks or females are vulnerable to general stereotypes about their abilities and to which that vulnerability affects scores in testing where consequences are important (see also Spencer & Steele, 1994; Steele, 1992).

A definition of bias offered by Cole and Moss (1989) treats it as *"differential validity of a given interpretation of a test score for any definable, relevant subgroup of test takers"* (p. 205). This definition of bias, and its accompanying call for discriminant and convergent validity evidence "within a hypothesis-generating orientation that requires the examination of plausible rival hypotheses" (Cole & Moss, 1989, p. 205), might be called *differential construct validity*. Investigation of bias from this perspective includes much more than merely comparing correlation coefficients. Test developers and users must think carefully through the maze of complexities, contradictions, and ambiguities possible in any evaluation of psychometric validity. These requirements are exacerbated when one subgroup is to be compared with all others to decide whether the construct inferences from scores in that group differ from the inferences from scores in the others.

A given research setting may involve several groups, but it is easier to think of bias analysis as comparing them two at a time. The convention in bias analyses refers to a *focal group*, potentially a victim of bias, and a *reference group* (often all others) used for comparisons by any of a variety of statistical tools. Simple factor analysis can be used, but simultaneous factor analysis comparing factor structures in different groups simultaneously is more directly relevant (Drasgow & Kanfer, 1985). Analysis of variance methods have been in use for many years. And, of course, the item response theory (IRT) models, particularly at the item level, are widely recommended and appropriate for the differential validity context.

Factor Analysis. An example of exploratory factor analysis is shown in Table 10.2. It shows, in three groups of Israeli students, factors accounting for variances in each of the subtests of a Hebrew version of the SAT (Zeidner, 1987). Means were substantially lower for the Oriental students. Should the difference be attributed to bias?

It is clear by inspection that the three groups have essentially the same factor structures; moreover, nothing in the analyses suggests an additional factor in any group. Without a differing systematic source of variance, the suggestion that the Hebrew SAT is biased against Oriental Jewish students is not supported.

Item Response Theory (IRT). Overall test bias can be studied by IRT, although it is more often used at the individual item level. Groups with different ability distributions should provide (within a linear transforma-

TABLE 10.2
Factor Loadings on a Hebrew SAT for
Three Groups of College Applicants

Subtest	Israeli			Oriental			European		
	$F1^a$	$F2$	h^2	$F1$	$F2$	h^2	$F1$	$F2$	h^2
Information	.83	.16	.70	.81	.20	.70	.79	.14	.70
Figures	.08	.79	.63	.16	.78	.64	.08	.77	.59
Mathematics	.23	.63	.44	.26	.60	.43	.20	.59	.40
Vocabulary	.70	.18	.52	.67	.17	.48	.76	.15	.52
Analytic	.27	.66	.50	.19	.64	.44	.23	.59	.41
English	.51	.39	.41	.51	.43	.44	.51	.35	.42
% total variance	26	28		25	27		24	27	

[a]F1 and F2 are Factors 1 and 2, designated Verbal Ability and General Reasoning, derived from principal factor analyses with varimax rotations.

Note. From Zeidner, M. (1987). Test of the cultural bias hypothesis: Some Israeli findings. *Journal of Applied Psychology, 72,* 38–48. Copyright by the American Psychological Association. Reprinted with permission.

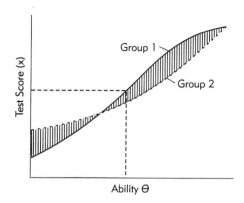

FIG. 10.3. Test characteristic curves with parameters estimated for two groups; the shaded area is the area between the curves.

tion) the same item parameters in test of that ability and the same test characteristic curves. Figure 10.3 depicts test characteristic curves for two subgroups. The two curves are not the same; test performance interacts with group membership; the degree of bias is considered proportional to the area between the curves. The total area is infinite if the lower asymptotes differ—as they typically do—so the area measured has a restricted definition, for example, between Θ values of -3 to $+3$.

Adverse Impact Under the 80% Rule

Under some circumstances, test scores have adverse impact—a legal term, not a statistical or psychometric one. Although adverse impact ratios are often cited, along with mean differences, as if they provided evidence of bias, they do not. They may be confused because adverse impact is a term with an attitude problem—a negative attitude forcing adversarial roles. It is "fraught with inferences and implications that there is some kind of inherent biasing characteristic of tests that accounts for different selection ratios among candidate subgroups" and "Instead of selecting a neutral term (e.g., 'pass–fail' ratio), the agencies chose 'impact,' which carries the clear connotation that tests intrinsically have an impelling or compelling effect on candidates from one subgroup" (Lawshe, 1987, p. 493).

Adverse impact can occur for several reasons, of which bias is but one. Other reasons include (a) chance, (b) measurement problems inherent in the test, (c) the nature of test use, (d) differences in distribution sizes, (e) reliable subgroup differences in general approaches to test taking, or (f) true population differences in distributions of the trait being measured. Adverse impact may be said to be due to bias *only* if one or more of the first five of these is shown and if the sixth one can be rejected.

The use of an adverse impact ratio depends on changing candidate sample characteristics and is therefore unstable (Lawshe, 1979, 1987). And again, adverse impact ratios do not consider true population differences.

TABLE 10.3
Selection Ratios and Adverse Impact Ratios for a Hypothetical Case

Basis for Decision	Proportion Selected[a]		Adverse impact Ratio
	Group 1	Group 2	
True ability	.72	.62	.86
Method A	.76	.58	.76[b]
Method B	.67	.67	1.00

[a]Assume all "qualified" candidates are selected. [b]Adverse impact under the 80% rule.

Note. From Ironson, G. H., Guion, R. M., & Ostrander, M. (1982). Adverse impact from a psychometric perspective. *Journal of Applied Psychology, 67*, 419–432. Copyright by the American Psychological Association.

Table 10.3 illustrates the problem. If we knew true ability levels, we would know that Group 1 has a higher proportion of qualified candidates than does Group 2, that is, that selection ratios based on true abilities are truly different, although the impact ratio would be greater than 80%. What we have, however, is two different methods of measuring the ability that give fallible results. Use of Method A results in adverse impact under the 80% rule; use of Method B does not (Ironson, Guion, & Ostrander, 1982). But is Method B truly superior? Observed selection ratios under either method differ only trivially, yet only Method A implies adverse impact. In fact, it can be argued that Method B adversely affects employment opportunities in Group 1 because it fails to recognize Group 1's greater likelihood of having truly qualified members.

The need for a mechanism for triggering enforcement machinery is clear, but it is not clear that the Guidelines definitions offer the right kind of mechanism. There must be a better way. Ironson et al. (1982) proposed "that the concept of adverse impact be redefined in terms of the degree of distortion of underlying differences in ability at the ability level where decisions are made" (p. 430). The basis for their argument, described in chapter 6, lies in the nature of the relationship of expected scores to theta, Θ, the underlying latent trait. If the test characteristic curve has a very steep slope, any true subgroup difference in ability may be exaggerated. If the slope is very shallow, the difference may be minimized.

Criterion Bias

In criterion-related validation, the criterion should be reliable, valid, and free from third-variable biases. It is amazing how easy that sentence is to write and how difficult it is to accomplish. Reliability is often exceedingly difficult to ascertain for criterion measures; sometimes nothing short of a generalizability analysis will do it, and often such analyses are not feasible in working organizations. A serious attempt to assess criterion validity may in itself be a way of assessing criterion bias. Evidence of valid measurement of the intended criterion construct is the sort of evidence most appropriate; a major question in construct validation is whether extraneous sources of variance influence the measures. If so, and if the numbers of cases allow, it should be possible to determine if the extraneous sources are related to subgroup composition.

DIFFERENTIAL ITEM FUNCTIONING (DIF)

Some litigation has centered on a concept of bias in individual items. Psychometricians prefer the term *differential item functioning (DIF)* to *item bias* (Holland & Wainer, 1993). Traditional item statistics, such as the proportion of the sample giving a correct answer, are inappropriate for studies of DIF because of their dependence on the trait distribution in the sample studied. Because they reflect group differences in that trait, they cannot disentangle genuine differences from bias. Some litigants, however, have called tests biased merely because of group differences in item pass rates. Drasgow (1987) described out-of-court settlements of two court cases on the basis of this simple-minded item difficulty statistic. In one case, *Golden Rule Insurance Company v. Washburn* (1984), the settlement stipulated that, on future tests, group item difficulties should differ by no more than .15. The second, *Allen v. Alabama State Board of Education* (1985) was more restrictive, specifying a maximum difference of .05.

Item difficulty differences on a widely used test exceeded the .15 maximum of the Golden Rule agreement on 90% of the items when responses of Black males and Black females were compared to those of White males (Drasgow, 1987)—one of those apparently interesting facts that is uninterpretable, without meaning, because genuine group differences in these statistics are confounded with bias. An IRT-based method (described by Lord, 1980), however, identified fewer than half of the items as biased—and inconsistent in direction of effect; the numbers of items harder for minorities nearly equal the numbers of items easier for them. In short, the cancelling effect of these differing directions made the cumulative effect on total test scores very low. With similar findings for other subgroups, Drasgow concluded that no measurement bias existed in total test scores in the six groups studied. This is not an unusual finding.

Expert Judgment and Sensitivity Review

In early research on subgroup differences in item responses, focal group representatives were asked to read items and identify those biased against their group. Obvious problems arose: judgments were often unreliable, very large numbers of items were called biased, and reasons for judging them to be biased were often labored or not given. Such judgments may be more important, however, than these problems might suggest. A test, like Caesar's wife, must not only be above reproach but must appear to be above approach—must not only be unbiased but must be perceived as unbiased. A person who considers an item biased or offensive may respond to it differently from other test takers; if enough people in a group see it similarly, the effect can be group related. If members of a focal group think an item perpetuates negative stereotypes about their group, they may respond quite differently from people in other groups. We do not know that this will happen; research on the reasons for DIF is sparse. But the possibility is strong enough that most test developers will not take the risk. Many commercial test developers have therefore established sensitivity review guidelines and systematized procedures for making judgments about proposed items.

Members of item or sensitivity review panels should be demographically heterogeneous, but that does not mean that each member "represents" a demographic group. Suppose a panel is to have male and female Whites, Blacks, Hispanics, and "others"—eight categories in all. Suppose further that the panel will have one member for each category. It is terribly hard to believe in one "representative" White female, Spanish-speaking male, or either kind of "other." It is easier to believe that panel members should be intelligent and well-trained in procedures and the kinds of cues to consider in making their judgments.

Training is based on the task set for the panel. Each panel member may be required in advance to answer yes or no to several questions, write a reason for the answer, and be prepared to discuss the reason with other panel members to try to achieve consensus. The following list of questions is illustrative, but only the first two are commonly used:

1. Does the item include content that may be deemed offensive to most members of identifiable sexual, racial, cultural, ethnic, disability, religious, or age groups?
2. Does the item perpetuate sexual, racial, cultural, ethnic, disability, religious, or age stereotypes?
3. Does the item contain language that might be offensive to potential examinees, irrespective of subgroup membership?
4. If the item requires knowledge or skill not essential to the purpose of measurement, are members of different groups equally likely to have had opportunities to learn it?
5. Will words or phrases used in the item have different meanings for members of different sexual, racial, ethnic, disability, religious, or age groups?

6. Will vocabulary level or complex sentence structure pose problems for some groups, problems not related to the purpose of the test?

7. If the item alludes to experiences members of some subgroups are more likely than others to have had, would the experience or lack of it contribute to different probabilities in responding correctly?

8. Does the item describe activities or situations, unrelated to the trait measured, likely to be unfamiliar to some groups of examinees?

9. Is the item format unusual and likely to be unfamilar to some groups of examinees?

Answers to questions like these require research not yet done. How does one know, for example, the words likely to mean different things in different groups? Panel members are expected to make judgments without factual information. However, they can come together for preliminary training. Collectively, they can develop rules and examples to justify yes or no answers, to distinguish important from trivial item characteristics. Unfortunately, such panel-developed protocols result from shared ignorance; we lack firm knowledge of item characteristics that matter. The following referred explicitly to references to minorities or women in an item set, but it could apply to answers to any of these illustrative questions:

> Does it make a DIF difference? If it does, to whom? And how much difference does it make? Do we find, as I suspect, that if we build the optimal test for one group as defined by the relevance of its content or the DIF statistics of its items, we build a less optimal test for another group? How "biased" is such a test against that other group? If there is no optimal test for all groups, how do we balance a test so that it is as fair as possible to all test takers? Although the sensitivity review process would not permit such items in a test, it would be useful to know whether and, if so, how negative or offensive items affect a test taker's performance. (Ramsey, 1993, p. 385)

Lacking answers to questions like these, I suspect that the principal virtue of review panels lies in public relations or political correctness, not in psychometrics—in problem prevention, not problem solving.

Statistical Methods for Detecting DIF

Transformed Difficulty Statistics. Angoff (1972, 1982) presented a rather simple procedure for identifying potentially biased items when responses are scored dichotomously:

1. Within each subgroup, compute item difficulty levels for all items on a test and express them as probabilities of a correct answer, p.

2. Using tables of areas under the normal curve, transform all values of p to z-scores.
3. Transform z-scores to Deltas using the equation $\Delta = 4z + 13$; thereby eliminating negative values. With two subgroups, there is a pair of delta values for each item.
4. Plot the pairs of delta values, as in Fig. 10.4, and compute the correlation.
5. Identify items where Deltas are out of line, measuring location vertically from the regression line.

Figure 10.4 is hypothetical to show the effect in an easily visible exaggeration. The correlation of Delta values in the two groups is .90, somewhat lower than usual; correlations of .98 or even .99 are not unusual. Three correlation-reducing outliers are identified: items 13, 21, and 28. The method offers no clue why these items do not fit the pattern, but items tagged as biased might be removed from the scoring key if not from the test itself.

The method is easy to use, has freqently been useful, and has therefore been popular. However, it has some problems. Results can be misleading if the discrimination indices are not fairly uniform across the plotted items. High discrimination items might be identified as biased only be-

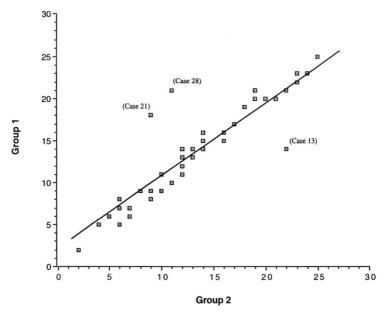

FIG. 10.4. A plot of transformed item difficulty statistics for the detection of biased items.

cause they discriminate better, and those with relatively low discrimination indices may mask bias (Holland & Wainer, 1993). Another problem is that delta values are not uniformly reliable.

Contingency Methods. Methods based on contingency tables require matching groups on ability; the matching may help distinguish DIF from group trait differences. Different methods of matching may be used. Angoff (1982) suggested matching on an external variable. IRT methods may match on the basis of estimated latent traits. Some methods match on total test scores. The latter may seem risky; paradoxically, however, total test scores seem relatively free from bias even when many items appear to be biased in one direction or the other (recall Drasgow, 1987).

Contingency methods compares item functioning in groups of people with comparable scores. The basic data matrix for investigating DIF is shown in Fig. 10.5. With two groups to compare, a reference group (i) and a focal group (j), and responses that may be keyed either correct (c) or not (w), the basic contingency table is the familiar 2×2 matrix. Comparisons may be made in each of several (k) trait levels within which the focal and reference groups are more or less matched. As further shown in Fig. 10.5, the cell entries may be either frequencies or proportions.

Early contingency models used ordinary chi square analysis. It now seems less favored, but it has the twin virtues of being both easy to use and easy to understand.

Conventional chi square (χ^2) compares frequencies actually observed to those expected by chance in a contingency table in which each variable is usually expressed in two or more categories. For example, variable A may have a categories and variable B may have b categories; a may or may not equal b. The table has $a \times b$ cells; each cell contains the observed frequency of occurrence (f_o) for the designated pair of categories and the frequency expected (f_e) on the basis of the marginal totals. In Fig. 10.5b, the expected frequency for the upper right cell would be $(n_c \times n_i)/N$. The statistic χ^2 is generally computed by the equation

$$\chi^2 = \Sigma \frac{(f_o - f_e)^2}{f_e} \tag{1}$$

where f_o and f_e are the observed and expected frequencies, respectively. Chi square is interpreted for statistical significance (from tables) for specified degrees of freedom (df); ordinarily, $df = (a - 1)(b - 1)$.

For item analysis, consider an $a \times b \times k$ contingency table for each item, a in Fig. 10.5, where variable A has two categories (the reference group i and the focal group j), variable B has two categories (correct responses to the item, c, and incorrect responses, w) and where there are $k = 5$ matched levels of the trait being measured—a $2 \times 2 \times 5$ contingency table.

(a) Full contingency table for DIF analysis:

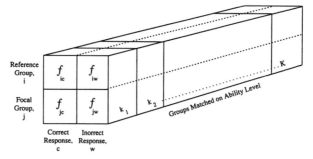

(b) Slice of contingency table for each ability group, with marginal totals:

	Correct Response, c	Inorrect Response, w	Totals
Reference Group, i	f_{ic}	f_{iw}	n_i
Focal Group, j	f_{jc}	f_{jw}	n_j
Totals	n_c	n_w	N

(c) Similar slice of table, expressed in proportions:

	Correct, c	Inorrect, w	Totals
Reference Group, i	p_{ic}	p_{iw}	1.00
Focal Group, j	p_{jc}	p_{jw}	1.00

FIG. 10.5. Contingency tables for investigating differential item functioning; (a) diagram of basic data matrix, (b) 2 × 2 frequency matrix for each of k matched groups, or (c) 2 × 2 proportions matrix for each of k matched groups.

For an unbiased item, the proportion of people answering it correctly is the same for each subgroup when all people in both groups have the same general trait level (e.g., approximately matched on total score). In proportional (rather than frequency) form, the equation for χ^2 is

$$\chi^2 = \Sigma n_i \frac{(p_{ck} - p_{ci})^2}{p_{ck}} + \Sigma n_j \frac{(p_{ck} - p_{cj})^2}{p_{ck}} + \Sigma n_i \frac{(p_{wk} - p_{wi})^2}{p_{wk}} + \Sigma n_j \frac{(p_{wk} - p_{wj})^2}{p_{wk}} \quad (2)$$

where n_i and n_j are the total sizes of the reference and focal groups, p_{ck} and p_{wk} are the expected proportions of correct and incorrect responses in each k interval, and subscripts c, w, i, and j refer to correct responses, incorrect responses, reference group, and focal group, respectively.

The equation provides a *full* chi square which can be tested for statistical significance. Scheuneman (1979) proposed a *modified chi square* approach. Her modification is intended to be analogous to an item characteristic curve, so it includes only the terms for correct responses. Many researchers, however, prefer the full chi square because the distribution of the modified chi square is unknown, interfering with the determination of significance. A biased item is one yielding a statistically significant full chi square.

The *Mantel-Haenszel* method, a chi square procedure for studying differences in matched groups (Mantel & Haenszel, 1959), is a widely used method of studying DIF. Holland and Thayer (1988) recommended it as a natural extension of chi square procedures that provides a powerful test of significance and a measure of the degree of differential item functioning. The extension, or modification, is somewhat different from the ordinary chi square, partly because it provides a "continuity correction"; as reported by Holland and Thayer (1988, p. 134), it takes the form, across the k slices of the $2 \times 2 \times k$ contingency table, of

$$\chi^2_{MH} = \frac{(|\Sigma f_o - \Sigma f_e| - \frac{1}{2})^2}{\dfrac{\Sigma n_i n_j n_c n_w}{N^2(N-1)}} \tag{3}$$

where the subscripts o and e refer to observed and expected frequencies, respectively, n and N are cell frequencies and total number of cases in the interval, and other notation is consistent with Fig. 10.5. The Mantel-Haenszel chi square is interpreted from the usual tables of chi square with one degree of freedom within each of the k slices; across all of the k matched groups, $df = k$.

The statement of the null hypothesis is somewhat different from the usual expression. Instead of stating it as the hypothesis of no difference between obtained frequencies and those expected from marginal totals, the Mantel-Haenszel null hypothesis (in DIF) is expressed as an equal ratio in each of the matched groups of the proportion of correct answers to the proportion of incorrect responses. In Fig. 10.5 notation, $p_c + p_w = 1$, and the basic null hypothesis is that $p_{ic}/p_{iw} = p_{jc}/p_{jw}$ in each of k matching categories. The test of the null hypothesis is

$$p_{ic}/p_{iw} = \alpha(p_{jc}/p_{jw}) \tag{4}$$

where α is identified as a common odds ratio across all of the k matching categories; the null hypothesis is that $\alpha = 1$. Alpha in this equation is the odds ratio $p_{ic}p_{jw}/p_{jc}p_{iw}$ for each of the k categories, and it provides a measure of the degree of differential item functioning. Holland and Thayer (1988) proposed a logarithmic scale, comparable to Angoff's delta scale, which will be symmetrical around an estimated alpha of zero:

$$\Delta_{MH} = - (2.35)\ln(\alpha_{MH}) \tag{5}$$

The interpretation of these values is not difficult. α_{MH} is the average factor by which the odds that a reference group member will get the item correct exceeds the odds for a member of the focal group. If the value is greater than 1.0, the reference group generally did better on the item; if it is less than 1.0, the focal group was correct more frequently. Likewise, positive values of delta indicate how much more difficult the item was for the reference group, and negative values indicate how much more difficult it was for the focal group. At the Educational Testing Service, MH DIF levels have three categories (Dorans & Holland, 1993). An item is assigned to Category A (negligible DIF) if Δ_{MH} from Equation 5 is not significantly different from zero, $p < .05$, or in absolute terms is less than one delta unit. It is assigned to Category C if $\Delta_{MH} > 1.5$ *and* is significantly, $p < .05$, greater than 1.0 in absolute value. All others are in the intermediate category B.

In his brief survey of item bias methods, Hills (1989) cited among its advantages that the Mantel-Haenszel method is a particularly useful procedure with small groups (defined as 100–300 cases), that it is one of the few methods offering a significance test and the only one offering both a significance test and a measure of effect, and that its results are relatively stable. Among the disadvantages: it might not do well with small groups having large mean score differences, and it is influenced by the manner of grouping score categories.

Significance is not a problem with the *standardization method*. Because it requires an enormous number of cases, thousands or tens of thousands of cases in each group, significance tests are irrelevant. Because it requires more cases than any but the largest research organizations can muster, I do not describe it in any detail. A desirable feature of the method, however, deserves mention: It permits identifying the ability levels where bias exists.

Dorans and Kulick (1986; reported also by Dorans & Holland, 1993) illustrated it with total scores on the SAT-Verbal standard scale, ranging from 200 to 800. Figure 10.6 shows a plot of the percentage of women and the percentage of men, in each of 61 intervals, responding correctly to an item. The item clearly is functioning differently, especially in a score range from about 320 to 450. The percent responding correctly increases as scores increase; in both groups, the relationship is nonlinear, markedly so for men. In both groups, at the very low or the very high scores, the differences in the percentages of correct responses are small, if any at all. But in the large range between the extremes, between 250 and slightly more than 600, the proportion of men giving the correct answer is noticeably higher than the corresponding proportion for women.

The differences in percentages giving the correct answers at each score level are shown in Fig. 10.7, part (a). Differences are the percent correct among women minus the percent correct among men; therefore, a negative difference means that a greater proportion of men were responding correctly. A zero difference in percents would represent the null hypothesis in more conventional methods, so a straight vertical line of data points at the zero level would indicate an absence of differential item functioning. For the data in Fig. 10.6, graphed in Fig. 10.7(a), the data points do not at all form a straight line at zero; most

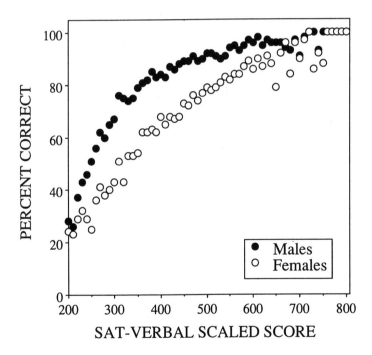

FIG. 10.6. Proportion of correct responses given by men and women at the same score levels on an item on the Scholastic Aptitude Test. From Dorans, N. J., & Holland, P. W. (1993). DIF detection and description: Mantel–Haenszel and standardization. In P. W. Holland & H. Wainer (Eds.), *Differential item functioning* (pp. 35–66). Hillsdale, NJ: Lawrence Erlbaum Associates. Reprinted with permission.

(a)

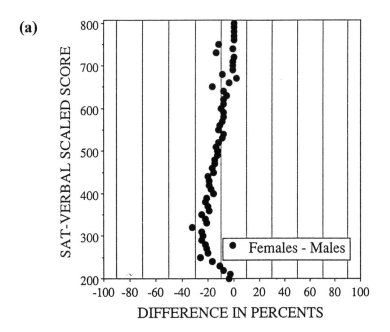

(b)

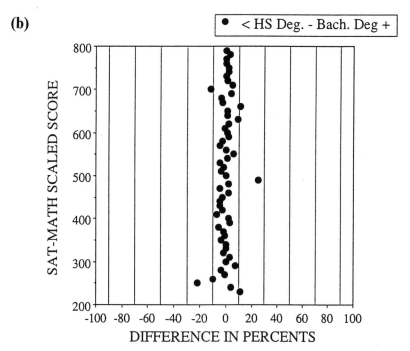

FIG. 10.7. (a) Plot of standardized differences scores ($X_{women} - X_{men}$), corresponding to data shown in Fig. 10.6, and (b) plot of standardized differences for a different item (comparing responses of people whose fathers differed in educational level). From Dorans, N. J., & Holland, P. W. (1993). DIF detection and description: Mantel–Haenszel and standardization. In P. W. Holland & H. Wainer (Eds.), *Differential item functioning* (pp. 35–66). Hillsdale, NJ: Lawrence Erlbaum Associates. Reprinted with permission.

of them are substantially to the left in negative differences, one of them exceeding −.30.

Figure 10.7, part (b), describes differences in a different item, for a different comparison, one based on socioeconomic status as measured by father's educational level. It shows a plot with a quite different appearance. Except for scores at about 250, deviations from the zero line tend to be very small, and they fall on either side of zero. It is easy to see, simply from the visual plots, that the item in part (a) is functioning in a way unlike that of the item in part (b). Part (a) shows an item functioning differently for men and women, but part (b) shows no differential item functioning for groups with high and low socioeconomic status as indicated by father's educational level. One might infer that the item in part (a) is biased against women, but one would infer that the item in part (b) is not biased against either high or low socioeconomic groups. Certainly the number of cases effectively rules out the possibility that these conclusions, or that the differences in inferences about them, are due to chance.

The advantage of the standardization method lies in the large number of ability intervals that can be examined. For most practitioners, however, the number of cases needed to get reliable data points for all of those intervals, especially at the extremes of a distribution, makes the method wholly infeasible.

IRT Methods. Just as potential bias in total test scores can be evaluated using IRT, so also can DIF be examined by measuring the area between item characteristic curves when item parameters are estimated independently in focal and referent groups. As with total scores, some limits must be set (e.g., ±3.0 on the Θ scale). For discussion of related computational procedures, see Hambleton and Swaminathan (1985) or Linn, Levine, Hastings, and Wardrop (1981).

If the area between the curves is zero, then the probabilities of correct reponses are the same at all levels of Θ, and all ICC parameters are equal, regardless of subgroup membership; the item does not function differently in the compared groups. An alternative procedure, then, is to test for the significance of the difference between item parameter estimates in the focal and reference groups. For these, and for other procedures for assessing the fit of the model in each group, see Hambleton and Swaminathan (1985) and Thissen, Steinberg, and Wainer (1993). The advantages and disadvantages listed in the Hills (1989) review depend on the specific IRT model used.

An Evaluation of DIF Research for Personnel Decisions

An early comparison of four methods of DIF detection (Ironson, 1977; Ironson & Subkoviak, 1979) found significant but low correlations between results of three of the methods described here (the transformed difficulty, chi square, and IRT methods).[7] Subsequent comparisons have sometimes shown higher correlations between DIF indices, high enough to lead Burrill (1982) in her review of comparative studies to call them "moderately highly correlated" (p. 174). It is nevertheless discouraging that items differentially functioning by one method may not be so identified by another one. Such findings raise the as-yet-unanswered question, which method is best?

It seems that most researchers would answer that, in theory, a method based on IRT is most logically associated with the problem of item bias; by definition, IRT methods most clearly control for the attribute being measured. But is it the Rasch model or a 3-parameter model—or one of the multidimensional models not described in this book? The answer may depend on strongly held preferences for one model over another. Is the issue to be resolved on the basis of statistical or psychometric theory or on the basis of cost effectiveness? If the latter, IRT methods or the related empirical method called the standardization procedure are pretty well out of the running with their demands for more cases than most researchers can muster.

Burrill (1982) reviewed several studies comparing methods. I offer some tentative generalizations, informed by hers but not identical to them:

1. All of the methods give relative statements of DIF. Even where there are measures of the degree of DIF, the measures cannot be safely interpreted in absolute terms. One implication is that DIF may depend quite a bit on the item pool in which it is studied; an item looking good in one context may be a candidate for the biased label in another.

2. It is almost impossible to control for confounding trait differences when assessing DIF. IRT models, of course, do better at this than do other methods, but not universally successfully.

3. Correlated results of the several procedures suggest only moderate convergence. Burrill (1982) called for more research on this issue, and I concur. If two methods are compared for a 50-item test, the correlation is based on 50 pairs of item difference statistics, and at least some of them will probably suggest little or no DIF. Such coefficients verge on being uninterpretable; they are based on severely skewed distributions with low variance, so the correlations are low. If a correlation is moderately high, is it because the two methods really do converge or because a couple of common outliers produce the correlation? The evidence of convergent validity I would find satisfying is a simple tally of the number of items suspected of bias by both methods compared to the number identified by one method alone—and that over a wide variety of tests compared.

---

[7]A fourth method, based on item discrimination values, did not correlate significantly with any of the other three.

In short, I have yet to be convinced by a rapidly growing literature that these diverse methods do in fact tap characteristics of items and item responses that are both uniform and important with respect to an underlying construct.

4. Methods of DIF identification give no useful conclusions about the reasons for the different functioning of the items so identified. This is a still-echoed theme in many of the chapters in Holland and Wainer (1993).

Identifying Versus Explaining DIF.

Sigmund Freud was notorious for his peculiar approach to science: He could explain everything, but he could predict nothing. I think just such an approach characterized *item bias* research 15 to 20 years ago, in its infancy. We could invent elaborate and persuasive reasons for why a particular item was biased, but could not apply this reasoning to new items and predict whether or not they would be biased. . . . We could define precisely (that is, mathematically) an item that was performing differentially for two specified groups of examinees, but we could not recognize it when we saw it.

[This] was brought home painfully to me some years ago while working with a graduate student. She and I spent the better part of an afternoon devising elaborate and ostensibly convincing theories about why six particular items were behaving differently for Black examinees, only to discover that, because of a programming error, we had been examining the wrong items. (Bond, 1993, p. 277)

This passage is dear to me because I have had a similar experience, but I appreciate it mainly because of its generality. Too often in the interface of practice and science we successfully explain an observation because we profit from doing so in a mutation of the old aphorism to believing is seeing.

Some explanations invoke supposed characteristics of groups of examinees. In a verbal analogies item cited by O'Neill and McPeek (1993), the examinee needed to know that hockey:ice::soccer:grass, and that four other athletic pairs of words were not related in the same way. Because these words all pertain to stereotypically male pursuits, it is thought, they are more difficult for women and are to be avoided. In another item where the topic concerned stereotypically female pursuits, giving a correct response requires knowing that tile:mosaic::stitch:sampler. Both items are shown in Fig. 10.8.

The correct response was clear to me in both of these items. For the first of them, which by stereotype is expected to be easier for me, a male, I knew the correct response—but not from athletic pursuits. I am not, and have never been, athletically inclined; I do not participate in, go to, read about, or watch sporting events. Nevertheless, I have somehow learned

HOCKEY : ICE ::

*(A)   soccer : grass

(B)   diving : board

(C)   skiing : lodge

Item that contains   (D)   baseball : bat
content that stereotypically in-
terests men.   (E)   archery : target

TILE : MOSAIC ::

(A)   wood : totem

*(B)   stitch : sampler

(C)   ink : scroll

Item that contains   (D)   pedestal : column
content that stereotypically interests women.   (E)   tapestry : rug

FIG. 10.8. Two items involving opposing sex stereotypes. From O'Neill &
McPeek (1993). Reprinted with permission.

that hockey is played on ice, that soccer is played on grass, and that
baseball is a game *not* played on a bat. Likewise, although I've never
made a mosaic or a sampler or an architectural column, I picked up the
ideas somewhere that a mosaic has a lot of tiles, and that a sampler has
a lot of stitches, but that a column does not have a lot of pedestals. A
verbal analogies item is, at its heart, dependent on a vocabulary acquired
through the general experience of living and on the ability to ascertain
the relationships between pairs of words. Whether the stereotypes are
relevant depends, I suppose, on the definition of the construct measured
by verbal analogies. If it is defined as a consequence of direct personal
experience, it might be reasonable to think of such items as biased (but
I doubt it). If, however, it is defined in terms of knowledge gleaned
through very general experience, or even experience-seeking (e.g., visiting
an art gallery where mosaics and samplers are exhibited), DIF seems less
expected; in fact, it seems likely only when most people in one group
engage in experience-seeking, knowledge-expanding behavior and most
people in the other do not.

Perhaps eliminating or avoiding writing items for which a stereotype
can be identified results in a biased stereotyping of items. If these items
are either very difficult or very easy (DIF is often correlated with difficulty), then only the bland inner range of items will survive the judgmental and mathematical reviews. The result, I fear, would be severe

restriction in the abilty of testers to make distinctions among people who are very able or very poor with respect to a measured ability.

Returning to Bond:

> In general, however, theories about why items behave differentially across groups can be described only as primitive. Part of the problem, as I see it, is that *the very notion of differential item functioning by groups implies a homogeneous set of life experiences on the part of the focal group* that are qualitatively different from the reference group and that affect verbal and mathematical reasoning. (Bond, 1993, p. 278; italics added)

The implication is silly.

Reasons offered for DIF are not limited to the life experiences of the people tested; structural characteristics of the tests and items themselves have been studied. Scheuneman (1982, 1987) long involved in such research, found support for a series of hypotheses about item format, wording of item stem, required inferences, placement of distractors, and others, but went on to say, "Although the complexity of the results of this study clouds their interpretations, a few possible guidelines are implied that may be useful"—a less than enthusiastic conclusion.

> What emerges most clearly from this study is how little we know about the mechanisms that produce differential performance between black and white examinees. Still, the study has demonstrated that item elements exist that are common to some number of items measuring different content that do affect differently the performance of blacks and whites. Further investigation of these elements should be fruitful in increasing our knowledge concerning the causes of bias and their eventual remedy. (Scheuneman, 1987, p. 117)

It is hard to be critical of such a statement; Scheuneman is one of very few people trying to harvest this fruit; so far, the fruit seems small and not very tasty. Those few possible guidelines consisted of three: (a) unless the options in a multiple choice item include more than one correct answer, avoid superlatives like "most" or "best" in the stems, (b) use as few words as possible in quantitative items to explain the task, substituting figures for words where possible, and (c) do not ask for the one false option. These are good rules, but they are general, not specific to bias reduction. They are familiar, long-standing rules for writing multiple-choice items (e.g., see Ebel, 1972). They offer little of value to the question of bias in test construction.

Some Unresolved DIF Issues. There are many issues, but these seem critical to me:

1. *Do internal matching procedures compromise the credibility of DIF analysis results?* Most widely used DIF methods match criterion groups on total test score. Is this a problem? Most experts think not. Most DIF studies use large enough samples to have reliable statistics, and there is little evidence that total scores suffer much bias if any. Most tests have enough items that the apparent circularity is not really a problem (Zieky, 1993). But there is that old problem with Caesar's wife. . . .

2. *On what basis should the compared groups be defined?* Probably not demographic. Demographic moderators have rarely been found, the fairness debates based on demographic comparisons led only to utility discussions, and item differences seem to go about equally often in either direction. Yet, we still have the problem Thorndike (1971) identified: for many demographic variables, group differences in test performance are greater than differences in criterion performance. In Black–White group comparisons, for example, the predictor differences are often about double (in standard deviation units) the criterion differences. Part of the discrepancy can be explained as statistical and psychometric artifacts (e.g., regression effects alone will account for part of it). Nevertheless, I suspect that much of it is due to group-related characteristics not yet identified, such as differences in test-taking strategies or response styles more likely to be found in some demographic groups, and some kinds of items, than in others. Searches for these characteristics should depend, not on serendipity, but on development and investigation of relevant theories. Ben-Shakhar and Sinai (1991) focused on tendencies to guess in multiple-choice tests; from theory on risk-taking behavior, they hypothesized that boys are more prone to take risks than girls, that guessing is a form of risk taking, and that therefore boys would get higher scores because of their greater willingness to make guesses on items where they do not know the answers. If so, their advantage from this source could be wiped out by using a formula to take guessing into account rather than a straight number-right score. They found that girls omitted more items than did the boys. Formula scoring reversed the pattern of differences in favor of girls, although the effects were generally small, from .01 to .15 *SD*. A theory-driven basis for grouping respondents should be more common.

3. *Do DIF analyses succeed in "unconfounding" trait differences from other sources and kinds of response differences?* Not really. Using data provided by Burton and Burton (1993), Linn (1993) charted the percentage of items that favored majority subjects (against protected demographic groups) at the B or C DIF levels against item difficulty and item discrimination values. Figures 10.9 and 10.10 show clearly that DIF values are associated with basic item statistics; they do not succeed in controlling for differences in the trait the items measure.

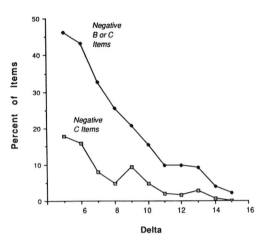

FIG. 10.9. Percentage of items with negative DIF decreasing as item difficulty increases. From Linn, R. L. (1993). The use of differential item functioning statistics: A discussion of current practice and future implications. In P. W. Holland & H. Wainer (Eds.), *Differential item functioning* (pp. 349–364). Hillsdale, NJ: Lawrence Erlbaum Associates. Reprinted with permission.

4. *What does differential item functioning say about bias?* We simply do not know. The number of possible reasons for DIF is great, and they probably include bias with its original social connotation of prejudice. But we simply do not know.

5. *Is detection of differential item functioning reliable?* No, not very. Several different methods comparing boys' and girls' responses to mathematics items were correlated with themselves. The best correlation between administrations, for any method, was .69 for the Mantel-Haenszel delta; the correlations were as low as .18 for a nondirectional chi square based on a 3-parameter IRT model. The correlations "are by any standards quite low and raise serious doubts about the ability of the indexes to identify biased items with any degree of consistency" (Skaggs & Lissitz, 1992, p. 233).

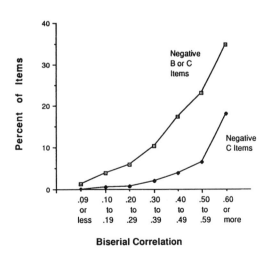

FIG. 10.10. Percentage of items with negative DIF increasing with item–test correlation. From Linn, R. L. (1993). The use of differential item functioning statistics: A discussion of current practice and future implications. In P. W. Holland & H. Wainer (Eds.), *Differential item functioning* (pp. 349–364). Hillsdale, NJ: Lawrence Erlbaum Associates. Reprinted with permission.

6. *Should items functioning differently in different groups be automatically eliminated from tests or scoring keys?* Of course not. When a differently functioning item is found, explanations are usually sought. When an explanation is developed, it should be applied to other items to see if they are also DIF items; I have not exhaustively searched the literature, but I do not recall mention of such comparisons in the DIF reports I have read. Besides, differences in item functioning are relative. If most of a test is in fact biased against members of a group, then DIF items may be the only ones that are not. Even if most items are unbiased, evidence of DIF for some of them is not necesarily evidence of bias. If the interest is in detecting and minimizing sources of bias in a test—and it generally is—then studies of DIF offer no more than a tentative first assault on the problem. For this reason alone, action should not be automatic if a DIF statistic reaches a pre-ordained level. A further reason is that items that function differentially may be important contributors as well as important threats to test validity (Linn, 1993). Statistical data should be used in decisions, but not dictate them; judgment is needed, and it should be a technical judgment focused on validity—not the sort of judgments made by sensitivity panels. Sensitivity issues and content importance issues are different and should be handled differently.

7. *So what use should be made of DIF results?* In my view, DIF analysis is important mainly if it raises answerable questions. Attempts to explain a differentially functioning item seem less important to test users than attempts to determine the implications of retaining or eliminating the item. These include implications for psychometric validity, for job relatedness, or for attitudes of test takers.

A "Discouraging Word." A man with the same last name as mine wrote about a place "where seldom is heard a discouraging word." This is not that place. So far in this chapter on bias, I have reviewed the literature on fairness; it has pretty much disappeared with no recorded resulting improvement in assessment. I have reviewed questions of test bias and have found little credible evidence either way. I have reviewed notions of adverse impact and have found the 80% rule essentially silly, ambiguous, and unreliable—even though it is taken with deadly seriousness. I have reviewed a technical set of developments on differential item functioning and found that we do not know precisely how to account for it or how it relates, if at all, to bias. Once again, I am reminded of those words of Wherry's in another context and another era: "We don't know what we're doing, but we are doing it very carefully, and hope you are pleased with our unintelligent diligence" (Wherry, 1957, p. 1). Much very careful, diligent, sophisticated work has been done, and it can hardly be called unintelligent. Yet after reviewing reams of material on the subject of bias in assessment, I find the concept ever more ethereal.

So why have I given so much attention to these attempts to identify bias? One reason is that the concept of bias is ubiquitous and cannot be ignored; it is central to much litigation, social critics focus on it, minority communities are greatly concerned about it, and the literature about it in psychological and educational measurement and research is extensive. Another reason is that various methods have articulate, insistent advocates. Another is that only those who are aware of the pitfalls of these methods can dispassionately make judgments about their usefulness in specific situations. However, the major reason is that bias, in its technical sense, is a real problem, socially and psychometrically. Our existing methods may not let us detect bias without ambiguity, but they do not let us say that bias is never a problem.

The concept of bias and the approaches proposed for identifing it need to be examined carefully and critically. Without such examination, rampant and enthusiastic acceptance of assertions of bias can cause much mischief, of which the Golden Rule decision is only one example. If the methods used for identifying bias are unsatisfactory, we should acknowledge the fact and start over with fresh thinking.

ACTING ON THE FINDINGS

Despite the problems, researchers attempt to analyze for bias or fairness, especially if there is adverse impact. The Guidelines continue to call for evidence of differential validity, and professional judgments have to be made, even with flawed data. What should be done when it is reasonable to suppose that test scores are biased against a group?

Before anything else, clarify needs. Is the top priority to maximize criterion performance or to avoid even the appearance of discriminatory practice? Is either of these the only priority, or is a balancing trade-off needed? The answer is neither universal nor self-evident; it depends on many things, including the costs of error in the situation at hand.

Corrective Action Under the Uniform Guidelines

Guidelines Provisions. The Guidelines recognize adverse impact as prima facie evidence of discrimination, and a discriminatory procedure is treated as biased. Four options are available under the guidelines.

1. *See if the procedure can be justified by law, such as the business necessity argument.* A large body of case law has developed over the years, modifying some aspects of the Guidelines and supporting others. After much confusion, which resulted in the 1991 Amendment, reasons justifying procedures gradually became clearer.

2. *Abandon the procedure.* This eliminates one possible source of discrimination (or of litigation) but it begs the question of how to choose among candidates. Ideally, choices are based on valid assessment with no adverse impact. The ideal is hard to find. Too many employers have abandoned reasonably good approximations of it in favor of selection procedures that are invalid or have no known validity but are not targeted in litigation. Critics of testing argue against test use but are strangely quiet about alternatives and their evaluation by similar rules.

3. *Modify the procedure to reduce adverse impact.* One modification uses compensating procedures so that the bottom line is absence of adverse impact. Another adjusts scores to eliminate adverse impact. These options are no longer available; see discussions in chapter 4 of *Connecticut v. Teal* and the 1991 Civil Rights Act amendment.

4. *Offer convincing evidence of job relatedness.* Valid testing is not discriminatory under the Guidelines, although different levels of validity are balanced against different levels of adverse impact. Validity requirements are based on the ambiguous, archaic idea of criterion-related, content, and construct validities as different kinds of validity. Some of the ambiguities are due to evolving professional conceptions of validity, but others were questionable from the beginning. Testers and lawyers must work together to figure out how to use this option; it seems to be the best one.

Conflicting Social Policy Objectives. Personnel decisions often require resolving conflicting values and predictions. Employers and the larger society may have competing objectives. Employing organizations want their personnel decisions to improve, or even maximize, performance and productivity. The larger society wants personnel decisions to increase employment of people who, historically, were excluded systematically from consideration. Emotion, cant, inflated rhetoric, or hypocrisy do not help. Inconsistent objectives should be faced frankly and the competing values balanced openly, according to policies and procedures clearly acknowledging required trade-offs. Wigdor and Sackett (1993) urged the federal government to use the conflicting opinions in the Departments of Labor and of Justice as a basis for a potentially more effective public policy on employment testing, advancing both the goals of employers and the goals of bringing minorities into the mainstream workforce.

It is, in fact, silly to consider these objectives as competing. Dropping old policies of exclusion and competently assessing the qualifications of all candidates, including those formerly excluded, can yield genuine benefit, both in jobs for those otherwise not considered and in enlarged pools of well-qualified job candidates. Moreover, hiring people formerly excluded can contribute to overall utility in ways not usually included in the criteria for test validation. Consider, for example, a metropolitan police force in which community political leaders have decreed that police will spend much of their time walking a beat. The objective is to reduce crime and improve the quality of life in the neighborhoods—in part by catching and arresting criminals, in part by a watchful presence, and in part by knowing the people on the beat. Knowing the people implies more than knowing their faces or even their names. It implies knowing the common values and experiences of people in the neighborhood, and beyond that, knowing those of neighborhood leaders. Neighborhoods in a city are diverse, creating a real, not just ideological, requirement for police force diversity. Hiring policies might require hiring to fill gaps in the kinds of community insights currently available. One police class might need over-representation of low-income ethnic neighborhoods; another might need recruits who know and understand those with affluence. Hiring should not follow rigidly the traditional top-down policy required in most civil service jurisdictions, even though it would maximize criterion utility.[8]

In short, three concepts are too often confused in arguments related to EEO and personnel decisions: (a) psychometric concepts, which include the reliability and validity of scores; (b) statistical concepts, which include the predictive utility of scores as well as the predictions themselves, and (c) social policy concepts, such as affirmative action. If organizational and social goals are to be met, these concepts must be kept as distinct, well-defined, unconfused, and balanced as possible.

Substantially different score distributions for different groups of candidates, a low selection ratio, and a psychometrically sound predictor with good criterion-related validity, can combine in effect to shut out members of a smaller group with a lower distribution. To whatever extent policy rejects shutting out groups of people, alternative or adjunct procedures may be necessary. Policies should be explicit so they can be debated and their implications thoroughly understood. The alternative or adjunct procedures

---

[8]Utility, it should be remembered, is usually estimated in terms of the criterion used in validating the test that predicts it. A predictive hypothesis (chapter 3) incorporates a criterion that applies to *all* officers (e.g., a composite of promptness in answering calls, skill in settling disputes or "apprehending perpetrators," general perceptiveness in noticing small differences in the way things are now compared to the way they were yesterday, etc.). It also implies that the assessment procedures used to predict the general criterion be logically related to it but not necessarily to other performance or proficiency considerations not included in the composite. There may well be other utilities beyond that based on the general criterion. Perhaps we should distinguish validation criteria from decision criteria. Decision criteria might include unique utility to be realized from a given candidate, such as might stem from a personal knowledge of a community and the people in it. These considerations provide no numbers as convenient for utility equations as validity coefficients, but estimates *can* be incorporated.

should be evaluated in terms of their effectiveness in balancing differing policy values. Frankly, I grow weary of people using statistical or psychometric arguments for certain social policies—or against those they dislike—without designing directly relevant research. I distrust ideological declarations that a favored procedure will virtually assure high validity and very nearly get rid of adverse impact, bias, or general unfairness—in short, declarations without data that a procedure being advocated for universal use will simultaneously maximize performance and minimize impact in any situation. *Understanding the effect of a procedure on each objective should precede advocacy.*

Score Adjustments

Adjusting scores to give preference to a group of candidates is not a new idea. Civil service laws have long provided for adding points to the test scores of veterans. Adding points to the scores of those in an adversely affected group is one way to reduce adverse impact—but doing so might be illegal in the United States. Sec. 106 (1) of the 1991 Civil Rights Act provides: "It shall be an unlawful employment practice for a respondent, in connection with the selection or referral of applicants for employment or promotion, to adjust the scores of, use different cutoff scores for, *or otherwise alter the results of,* employment related tests on the basis of race, color, religion, sex, or national origin" (italics added).

Race-Norming in the United States Employment Service. The prohibition is the direct result of controversy over "race-norming" in the use of the General Aptitude Test Battery (GATB) in the United States Employment Service (USES). The GATB was developed as a job counseling and job referral tool. The controversial procedure (as described by Hartigan & Wigdor, 1989) was based on factor analysis and validity generalization (Hunter, 1983). It reduced scores on 10 individual subtests to 3 aptitude scores: cognitive, perceptual, and psychomotor composites. These scores were added with weights derived independently (based on regression analysis) for each of five job families. The composite scores were expressed as percentile ranks in the applicant's population group: Black, Hispanic, or other. A given score in a group with a lower distribution of scores would have a higher percentile rank than it would if based on all three groups combined. In effect, the separate norms added points to scores of minorities.

Employment Quotas. The USES procedure was denounced in many quarters, including Congress and the executive branch, as a quota system. It reduced adverse impact, and its effect was that of a quota. In an area where the labor market is 20% Black and 10% Hispanic, and nearly all the rest White, a true proportional quota would call for hiring two Black and one Hispanic applicant for each seven White applicants hired. Such a quota need not be filled at random. Many employers have used within-group, top-down selection to avoid adverse impact; applicants are listed in rank order within groups according to their scores, and those hired are the most qualified in their respective groups.

Quotas have long been anathema in American society, where the prevailing view has been that each individual should be considered for opportunities on the basis of his or her own merit.[9] Those who used group norms to fill quotas did so less for ideological reasons than to avoid litigation. It was considered the surest way to reduce adverse impact; moreover, it is the ultimate group parity fairness method. Is its effect on mean performance level detrimental to the hiring organization? There is no strong evidence that it is, although finding people who would admit to having the requisite data may not be easy.

A Monte Carlo study, however, suggested that the effect on the mean performance of those hired is not great (Jones, 1974). Two kinds of quotas were used, one with random choice and the other top down within groups; four fairness models were simulated. Selection ratios, mean predictor and criterion differences, minority group validities, and levels of predictor or criterion skewness were varied. In various comparisons, the mean criterion performance of those selected by the test-based quota system was less than .2 SD below nonquota models and consistently less than .1 SD for the Cole group parity model. Thus a literal quota system, if based on valid assessments, can provide a balance between the frequently opposing values of increasing minority representation and of improving criterion performance. In some jobs, of course, the utility differences associated with these standard score criterion differences are important, but that is no reason to indict all score adjustment techniques. Moreover, utility computation should take into account impact on society and the community as well as corporate effectiveness.

Ambiguities in the 1991 Amendment. The amendment remains ambiguous (Kehoe & Tenopyr, 1994). Do its prohibitions, for example, apply to diagnostic testing (likely to increase under ADA) or only to predictive uses? Do they include practices that do not add points but have the effect of increasing scores in protected groups, such as manipulating content before there is anything to score (e.g., eliminating items functioning differently in one direction only)? Is that prohibited? I hope not; the practice can sometimes improve validity, especially in interest, personality, or computerized adaptive testing. Suppose, for the latter example, that an IRT DIF study showed several items functioning differently at

---

[9]An embarrassing chapter in American history is the now nearly forgotten period when colleges and universities used quotas to restrict admissions of Jews.

certain theta levels for men and women. In a computerized adaptive testing program using these data, would a program choosing items on the basis of subgroup ICC parameters be illegal?

Who knows? Provisions of the 1991 Civil Rights Act were adopted after spirited but psychometrically uninformed political debates. Answers to questions like these will probably emerge from new case law; we can only hope that developing case law is better informed than the Congressional debates. Score adjustments are thought by some people to have genuine advantages, technically and socially; others disagree sharply. The issues are too important to ignore or to bury under irrelevant rhetoric.

"Ranges of Indifference" in Test Score Bands

One procedure uses score bands, intervals within which score differences are in some sense trivial, or *ranges of indifference*. Within a band, selection decisions may consider diversity. The procedure is often considered a means of compensating for adverse impact. I have introduced it in that context, but it can serve much broader purposes.

The practice of banding has been needlessly controversial. Arguments favoring or opposing banding are based partly on psychometric grounds (e.g., assessment reliability) and partly on statistical grounds (e.g., statistical significance levels). Framing arguments in these terms is a distraction. The purpose is to transform a raw measurement scale into one that groups unit raw score intervals into larger ones where raw score differences do not matter; within such an interval choices can be based on other, perhaps competing, considerations.

In a sense, all score use involves banding. The raw measurement scale has bands, albeit of unit width; for example, statistical analyses consider a raw score of 10 to be the midpoint of the 9.50–10.49 score interval, or band. Use of a cut score creates two bands, one passing, the other not. Most banding is between these extremes. Generally, banding sets score intervals greater than raw scores but smaller than the entire region above or below a cut score. Whatever the size of the interval, the same two problems must be faced: how to define band width, and how to choose within a band where candidates outnumber openings.

Band Width. Scores contain error. Two people with the same raw scores may differ in ability, and two people of the same ability may have different scores. When faced with two candidates of somewhat (but not dramatically) different scores, it is reasonable to ask whether the scores differ significantly, statistically. The standard error of the difference, s_d, between two scores may be defined as $s_d = s_m \sqrt{2}$, where s_m is the standard error of measurement. A band interval might be defined as $1.96s_d$, within which a score difference is not (at the 5% level) significantly different from

0. A broader interval might be defined as $2 \cdot s_m$. Or one could use the standard error of estimate, s_e, to define an interval of scores within which differences in predicted criterion values might be considered trivial.

The basis does not have to be statistical; a score distribution might be divided arbitrarily into four or five or a dozen intervals with nearly equal frequencies and these might be treated as bands. Statistical definitions of band limits provide an appearance of scientific objectivity, but appearance masks the arbitrariness involved. Even with statistical definitions, arbitrary choices determine whether band width is based on predictor unreliability or on unreliability of predicted criterion performance and the level of confidence used.

The definition might be based on managerial judgments of how much loss in utility (a band width greater than 1.0 *does* involve some loss) can be sacrificed to other considerations. Managers might agree in conference on a band width they consider about right. They may decide that band width is not constant, making bands narrower (or broader) in the middle of the distribution than at the extremes. All of these are arbitrary, but no more arbitrary than the choice of statistical definitions.

Decisions Within Bands. Within a band, decisions can be based on other information. They might be based on information not routinely available, on assessments of traits not part of a general or common predictive hypothesis, or on affirmative action or diversity goals. Contextual criteria, not used in test validation or implicit in the predictive hypothesis, could be considered within bands. Choices could be based on additional assessment; one may have a very desirable selection procedure that is not cost effective if used for all applicants, but is if used only with those applicants within a band. Choice could, of course, be random, but I do not recommend it.

Fixed Bands. Table 10.4 shows a plausible distribution of scores. It has a plausible mean and standard deviation (79.7 and 5.14, respectively), it has some gaps (but not many), and it comes fairly close to a normal curve—a little flatter, not quite smooth, not quite symmetrical, but fairly close. Arbitrarily, without recourse to any statistic, it has been marked off in intervals of 4 points on the score scale.[10] The top band has a top score of 98. There is only one such score, and no one scored 97, 96, or 95—the remaining three values in the arbitrary interval. The next interval would include values of 91–94, also with only one case, so I have started over (again, quite arbitrarily) with 91 as the top of the second band. That

---

[10]Okay, technically, the interval is five points, from 98.5–94.5. This is not a case, however, where the distinction between continuous and discrete score variables is very important.

TABLE 10.4
A Hypothetical Frequency Distribution Marked Off in Bands

Score	f
98	1
91	1
90	1
89	2
87	3
86	2
84	3
83	4
82	6
81	10
80	12
79	7
78	8
77	9
76	5
75	2
74	3
72	2
70	2
67	1
60	1

band has four cases; the third band has eight cases, and so it goes. How should selection from bands differ from selection according to raw scores?

Let us accept as given that the top scoring person gets hired. That score is substantially higher (better) than any other, so barring some disqualifying fact, the predicted performance of the person with that score is surely good enough to get the job. What about the four people in the next band? Suppose there are only two openings. Which two get hired? The decision might be based on a random draw; it might be based on information not included in validation because it is not routinely available. Perhaps the candidate scoring 91 has a history of repeated felony convictions. That person might be rejected despite the high score if repeated convictions are considered a disqualifying characteristic. (Disqualifying characteristics, of course, can also operate in top-down decisions.) If one of those people scoring 89 is a minority person, and if the organization has not hired very many minorities, it may give the offer to that person. If that person accepts, which of the two remaining people in the band will fill the one remaining vacancy? Without a strong reason to prefer one over the other, the decision may be made with a coin toss. One person remains in the band. If the next opening does not occur for several weeks, that person may no longer be available, and the next opening may be filled from the third band. Otherwise, that person must be considered before others; hiring options stay limited to the band until everyone in it has been hired, disqualified, or otherwise withdrawn from consideration—that is, until the band has been "exhausted" (Cascio, Outtz, Zedeck, & Goldstein, 1991, p. 243).

By this practice, it is hard to see that banding differs in any practical way from top-down selection. It is also hard to see, if each band must be exhausted before going to the next lower one, that banding leads to quotas or does much to reduce adverse impact unless (a) band intervals are very wide and (b) bands near the top of the total distribution have many more people in them than there are openings. With reasonably narrow bands, most decisions are based on scores on the presumably valid, demonstrably job related assessment predicting a valued criterion; a smaller number of decisions are based on other considerations.

The discussion so far may seem to imply that everyone is assessed at the same time, but that is not necessarily the case. As new candidates are assessed, they can be placed in the band in which they score. In Table 10.4, for example, after the first two bands have been used up, a new examinee might get a score of 90 and enter the second band. Unless there is a disqualifying characteristic, that candidate would be virtually assured of the job regardless of subgroup identification.

Neither of these patterns of use fits the way I have seen banding work in organizations I have known. In them, banding has been chosen to increase minority hiring; within a band, minorities get preference, either totally or by quota. Nevertheless, the band must be used up; nonminorities in the band eventually are selected.

The pace of minority selection depends on the overall selection ratio, mean differences, and the relative variance in minority and nonminority distributions. Most Monte Carlo studies have assumed equal variances, but minority variance may be greater than that for nonminorities when the numbers of cases are fairly large. James Outtz (personal communication, December 13, 1993) reported that he had examined test score distributions for Black and White applicants in the federal government, in New York City, and in some other large samples—and found standard deviations of the Black distributions larger than those of White distributions—as much as 1.5 times the White standard deviation. If the selection ratio is small, and the minority group mean is lower, its members may not be chosen unless its variance is larger. If the minority mean score is a full standard deviation below that of the larger group, if the variances are equal and the distributions alike in shape, and if selection is top-down, then about 16% of all candidates would be chosen from the nonminority group before reaching the highest scoring minority. Several bands, depending on their widths, would be exhausted before coming to one with a minority representative. Under these conditions, if the selection ratio is less than 16%, no minority person would be chosen without some system of score adjustments. If Outtz's findings generalize, the problem is somewhat eased by the larger variances in the minority groups. In any case, fixed bands do not lead to quotas or reductions in criterion performance unless they are very large.

Sliding Bands. Sliding bands differ from fixed bands in that they more or less slither down the distribution rather than going down in jumps. As with fixed bands, the highest scoring person is deemed the candidate most likely to perform well on the criterion; an interval can be defined, with that score at the top, in which score differences are trivial. When the highest scoring person is out (selected, disqualified, or refused offer), the sliding band concept notes that there is now someone else at the top of the distribution, and the next step is to identify the people whose scores differ only trivially from the one now on top.

The distribution in Table 10.4 can also illustrate sliding bands. Instead of the 4-point band width, however, I pretend to be less arbitrary and use the s_m as the basis for definition. Assuming a reliability coefficient of .85 (neither very good nor very bad) and a 5% alpha level, the band width can now be rounded conveniently to 5.5. (See Cascio et al., 1991, for computational detail.) Assume that predictive validity is high and that the job is technical and requires supervision of less well-trained technicians.

Table 10.5 provides some information about the 17 people at the top of the score distribution. The top band, with a 5.5 band width, would extend down from 98–92.5; it is still home to just one person who surely seems likely to be hired. Then the band slides down to the second person; he scored 91. This is now the highest score, so the band extends down to 85.5 and includes nine people whose scores on a highly valid test differ only trivially. There is one opening; one of these nine people must be selected. It will not be the one who scores 91 as long as the policy frowns on repeat felons. Not many women study in this technical area, and there are few minorities in this company and in this job. The White male scoring 89 may be passed over on that basis alone, but his apparent brashness and relative inexperience may also argue against choosing him. Another White male and a Hispanic male, both scoring 87, have relevant technical training and experience but lack supervisory experience. Without behavioral evidence, pro or con, about the effect of the White male's family status on his work, it is not a relevant consideration—and maybe not in any case. The two White females may have more relevant work experience; one has some supervisory experience. The Black male with a score of 86, while taking a relevant course of study and getting further study after graduation, was not a very good student. It does not say why not—and finding out why not would surely be useful.

TABLE 10.5
Characteristics of Top Scoring Candidates in Distribution in Table 10.4

Score	Ethnic Group	Sex	Further Information
98	White	M	BS + special seminars in the field; handled self well in interview, good impression; known to company official as expert in the field.
91	White	M	BS + special study in the field; seemed very sure of self in interview, too cocky; has repeated felony convictions; has relevant experience in the field.
90	White	F	BS, good GPA; no problems in the interview; has some limited but appropriate experience; school and experience came after children (2) were in college.
89	White	M	currently in last year of 3-year technical school program; seemed brash to interviewer; getting some part-time experience on current day job.
89	Black	F	Some college, relevant, and fairly good GPA; seemed nervous in interview, not self-confident; useful but limited experience; has grown in job responsibilities.
87	Asian	M	Graduate degree in history; diffident during interview; no relevant job experience; active volunteer in community organizations.
87	White	M	Technical school diploma and 12 years technical experience in reputable company; expressed clear goals in interview; divorced, single father.
87	Hispanic	M	Technical school diploma and 11 years technical experience in reputable company; expressed clear goals in interview.
86	White	F	Graduate degree in art; no interview problems; has had some technical and supervisory experience in commercial computer art and sculpture.
86	Black	M	BS + special seminars; marginal GPA; clear goals in interview; extended experience but in company not known for quality.
84	Black	M	in 2nd year of 3-year tech college program; apparently doing well according to faculty reference letters; did not communicate well during interview; no relevant experience.
84	Black	F	BS, good GPA, went to school 6 years while working full time; lacked social skills in interview; has 7 years relevant experience, moving up from labor pool to supervision.
84	White	F	BS, good GPA; understood importance of technical questions in interview; 3 years experience; excellent performance ratings.
83	White	M	BS + special seminars; was an undergrad lab assistant; no problems in interview; reputation as technical expert known to company officials; 12 years experience in different companies.
83	Hispanic	M	BS + graduate courses in South America; interview went poorly because his English is inadequate; some relevant experience but unevaluated.

(Continued)

TABLE 10.5
(Continued)

Score	Ethnic Group	Sex	Further Information
83	Asian	F	BS + graduate courses; interview rating of "promising"; 2 years experience under technically excellent supervisor.
83	Black	M	High school drop-out, GED diploma; interview failed to learn much about early work experience, but uncovered major work achievements during last decade, including the last 3 years with good experience in this field.

The best that can be said at this point is that the choice will be from one of these five, but that more information is needed before a nonrandom choice is made. Calls to listed references with explicit questions, perhaps a better, more structured interview with each candidate, and possibly additional testing of constructs deemed important to the work might provide important information required for a satisfying decision.

Note the many red herrings in the further information column. Some of the information seems as if it might be helpful, but serious thought would show much of it to be the unvalidated folklore it is.

When the choice is made, it will not be the top scoring person; he was considered disqualified. Therefore, the band slides again, just as if the top scoring person had been hired. Disqualified is a key term. Procedural justice demands that reasons for disqualification be clear and consistently applied. Some decisions can be based solely on predicted job performance; some can be based on policies that reasonable people would be likely to accept (e.g., unwillingness to hire people repeatedly convicted of felonies). There is danger, however, of disqualifying for reasons that are ad hoc, prejudicial (not necessarily a proscribed prejudice), and invalid.

In most practical situations, sliding bands seem no more likely than fixed bands to promote increased minority hiring. The only real difference is in defining a "used up" band; the sliding band shifts when the top score is taken out, and all scores must be removed before shifting a fixed band. Either procedure can allow consideration of other information; the decision process calls for judgment. The role of judgment in decision making has already been emphasized, and the quality of judgment is not a unique consideration. Use, or possible abuse, of the judgment opportunity is to be evaluated where it exists. The question of banding, sliding or otherwise, is whether the exercise of managerial judgment is a good idea. I happen to think it is necessary.

Banding in General. In the special issue of *Human Performance* on banding, Schmidt (1991) called these procedures "fatally flawed," leading "to the absurd conclusion that the only justifiable form of selection is random selection" (Schmidt, 1991, p. 265). Perhaps I have not read his article carefully enough, but somehow his reasoning takes him in a direction the polar opposite of mine (that banding merely detours top-down selection). In the same issue, Sackett and Roth (1991) reported a Monte Carlo comparison of various methods of test use. Except for the now illegal use of separate top-down lists for different groups, the methods they used differ from those I have seen used in practice. Random selection, in particular, is unacceptable in most organizations I know although most will use surrogates for random selection like first come-first served.

In short, I think proponents of banding (e.g., Cascio et al., 1991) are overly enthusiastic about the technical and social policy merits of banding, opponents (e.g., Schmidt, 1991) are overly negative, and Monte Carlo researchers (e.g., Sackett & Roth, 1991) study computer models instead of real decision makers. Arguments about banding bring to mind the famous last words of *Gone With the Wind*: "Frankly, my dear, I don't give a damn."

Changing the Research Agenda

The research agenda for the past 25 years has focused largely on statistical fairness models and demographic moderators; it has been driven more by social problems than by basic measurement issues related to them. I suggest that it now focus on relevant problems of validity. Specifically:

1. *Seriously study error.* Even presumably internally consistent measures are often multidimensional with several systematic, contaminating influences. A new research agenda, therefore, should abandon the idea that all variance not accounted for by a major factor is due to random error; it should call for programmatic studies of the sources of error.

2. *Investigate Person Characteristic Curves.* Carroll (1983) showed that multifactorial findings can be artifactual. He proposed the latent trait idea of a "person characteristic function" that "focuses on the responses of single individuals to items of different difficulties rather than responses of individuals of different ability levels to single items" (Carroll, 1983, p. 259). The person characteristic function can be influenced by two sorts of error; *topastic* variance stems from chance success through guessing, and *scedastic* variance stems from the random variation of scores from one administration to another exclusive of the guessing component. Could different combinations of such errors, with systematic differences in person characteristic curves, be typical of different demographic or socioeconomic groups? If so, could such differences provide cues to the difficulty levels most likely to produce DIF? I have no idea, but I find the idea intriguing enough for a place on the psychometric research agenda.

3. *Identify test-taking strategies as possible third variables.* Much of what passes for bias, adverse impact, and the like is really the third variable problem. That is, it is due to unknown and unmeasured variables that directly influence criterion measures, predictors, or both, or that moderate the predictor–criterion relationship. Two common findings are that criterion mean differences are about half those on cognitive predictors, and that fairness studies show parallel subgroup regression lines. I suspect the third variable problem in both examples, and I further suspect that the third variables will be defined largely in terms of test-taking behaviors. I strongly urge that test-taking strategies have a prominent place on the research agenda. The notion of individual differences in test-taking strategies is not new, but research on them has not been well publicized if it has occurred. Over a period of 6 years or so I have searched old literature and watched new—and have done better in finding suggestions of what such strategies might be than clear discoveries of them. Examples might include group differences in willingness to guess, to skip items and return to them if time permits, or to consider all multiple choice options before responding rather than to respond with the first option that seems OK. Identifying strategies persistently used by individual examinees could then lead to a further agenda item: Are such differences in strategy associated with membership in various protected groups?

4. *Continue research on the new and different.* The research agenda should include psychometric and statistical investigations of new approaches to assessment, of new models of intelligence and personality, and of new approaches to old technology. Opportunities for exciting new research initiatives moving toward the unbiased prediction of behavior at work are neither disappearing nor routine. They do, however, require more focused energy among psychologists, more courage and far-sightedness among managers, and less adversarial punitiveness among lawyers and EEO regulators.

REFERENCES

Allen v. Alabama State Board of Education, No. 81-697-N (consent decree filed with United States District Court for the Middle District of Alabama Northern Division, 1985).

American Educational Research Association, American Psychological Association, & National Council on Measurement in Education. (1985). *Standards for educational and psychological testing.* Washington, DC: American Psychological Association.

Angoff, W. H. (1972). *A technique for the investigation of cultural differences.* Presented at the annual meeting of the American Psychological Association, Honolulu, September, 1972. (ERIC Document Reproduction Service No. ED 069686).

Angoff, W. H. (1982). Use of difficulty and discrimination indices for detecting item bias. In R. A. Berk (Ed.), *Handbook of methods for detecting test bias* (pp. 96–116). Baltimore: Johns Hopkins University Press.

Ben-Shakhar, G., & Sinai, Y. (1991). Gender differences in multiple-choice tests: The role of differential guessing tendencies. *Journal of Educational Measurement, 28,* 23–35.

Bond, L. (1993). Comments on the O'Neill & McPeek paper. In P. W. Holland & H. Wainer (Eds.), *Differential item functioning* (pp. 277–279). Hillsdale, NJ: Lawrence Erlbaum Associates.

Burrill, L. E. (1982). Comparative studies of item bias methods. In R. A. Berk (Ed.), *Handbook of methods for detecting test bias* (pp. 161–179). Baltimore: Johns Hopkins University Press.

Burton, E., & Burton, N. W. (1993). The effect of item screening on test scores and test characteristics. In P. W. Holland & H. Wainer (Eds.), *Differential item functioning* (pp. 321–335). Hillsdale, NJ: Lawrence Erlbaum Associates.

Carroll, J. B. (1983). The difficulty of a test and its factor composition revisited. In H. Wainer & S. Messick (Eds.), *Principles of modern psychological measurement: A festschrift for Frederic M. Lord* (pp. 257–282). Hillsdale, NJ: Lawrence Erlbaum Associates.

Cascio, W. F., Outtz, J., Zedeck, S., & Goldstein, I. L. (1991). Statistical implications of six methods of test score use in personnel selection. *Human Performance, 4,* 233–264.

Cleary, T. A. (1968). Test bias: Prediction of grades of Negro and white students in integrated colleges. *Journal of Educational Measurement, 5,* 115–124.

Cole, N. S. (1973). Bias in selection. *Journal of Educational Measurement, 10,* 237–255.

Cole, N. S., & Moss, P. A. (1989). Bias in test use. In R. L. Linn (Ed.), *Educational measurement* (pp. 201–219). New York: American Council on Education/Macmillan.

Deaux, K. (1993). Commentary: Sorry, wrong number—A reply to Gentile's call. *Psychological Science, 4,* 125–126.

Dorans, N. J., & Holland, P. W. (1993). DIF detection and description: Mantel-Haenszel and standardization. In P. W. Holland & H. Wainer (Eds.), *Differential item functioning* (pp. 35–66). Hillsdale, NJ: Lawrence Erlbaum Associates.

Dorans, N. J., & Kulick, E. (1986). Demonstrating the utility of the standardization approach to assessing unexpected differential item performance on the Scholastic Aptitude Test. *Journal of Educational Measurement, 23,* 355–368.

Drasgow, F. (1987). Study of the measurement bias of two standardized psychological tests. *Journal of Applied Psychology, 72,* 19–29.

Drasgow, F., & Kanfer, R. (1985). Equivalence in psychological measurement in heterogeneous populations. *Journal of Applied Psychology, 70,* 662–680.

Ebel, R. L. (1972). *Essentials of educational measurement.* Englewood Cliffs, NJ: Prentice-Hall.

Einhorn, H. J., & Bass, A. R. (1971). Methodological considerations relevant to discrimination in employment testing. *Psychological Bulletin, 75,* 261–269.

Flexner, S. B. (Ed.). (1987). *Random House dictionary of the English language* (2nd ed., unabridged). New York: Random House.

Golden Rule Insurance Company et al. v. Washburn et al., No. 419-76 (stipulation for dismissal and order dismissing cause, Circuit Court of Seventh Judicial Circuit, Sangamon County, IL, 1984).

Guion, R. M. (1966). Employment tests and discriminatory hiring. *Industrial Relations, 5,* 20–37.

Guion, R. M. (1976). Recruiting, selection, and job placement. In M. D. Dunnette (Ed.), *Handbook of industrial and organizational psychology* (pp. 777–828). Chicago: Rand-McNally.

Hambleton, R. K., & Swaminathan, H. (1985). *Item response theory: Principles and applications.* Boston: Kluwer-Nijhoff.

Hartigan, J. A., & Wigdor, A. K. (Eds.). (1989). *Fairness in employment testing: Validity generalization, minority issues, and the General Aptitude Test Battery.* Washington, DC: National Academy Press.

Hills, J. R. (1989). Screening for potentially biased items in testing programs. *Educational Measurement: Issues and Practice, 8*(4), 5–11.

Holland, P. W., & Thayer, D. T. (1988). Differential item performance and the Mantel-Haenszel procedure. In H. Wainer & H. I. Braun (Eds.), *Test validity* (pp. 129–145). Hillsdale, NJ: Lawrence Erlbaum Associates.

Holland, P. W., & Wainer, H. (Eds.). (1993). *Differential item functioning*. Hillsdale, NJ: Lawrence Erlbaum Associates.

Humphreys, L. G. (1952). Individual differences. *Annual Review of Psychology, 3*, 131–150.

Hunter, J. E. (1983). *Test validation for 12,000 jobs: An application of job classification and validity generalization analysis to the General Aptitude Test Battery (GATB)* (Test Research Report No. 45). Washington, DC: United States Employment Service, United States Department of Labor.

Ironson, G. H. (1977). *A comparative study of several methods of assessing item bias* (Doctoral dissertation, University of Wisconsin–Madison). *Dissertation Abstracts International, 1978, 38*, 7285A.

Ironson, G. H., Guion, R. M., & Ostrander, M. (1982). Adverse impact from a psychometric perspective. *Journal of Applied Psychology, 67*, 419–432.

Ironson, G. H., & Subkoviak, M. J. (1979). A comparison of several methods of assessing item bias. *Journal of Educational Measurement, 16*, 209–225.

Jaeger, R. M. (Ed.). (1976). On bias in selection [Special issue]. *Journal of Educational Measurement, 13*, 3–99.

Jones, D. P. (1974). *An examination of six fair selection models.* Unpublished master's thesis, Bowling Green State University, Bowling Green, OH.

Kehoe, J. F., & Tenopyr, M. L. (1994). Adjustment in assessment scores and their usage: A taxonomy and evaluation of methods. *Psychological Assessment, 6*, 291–303.

Lawshe, C. H. (1979). Shrinking the cosmos: A practitioner's thoughts on alternative selection procedures. In P. Griffin (Ed.), *The search for alternative selection procedures: Developing a professional stand* (pp. 1–26). Los Angeles: Personnel Testing Council of Southern California.

Lawshe, C. H. (1987). Adverse impact: Is it a viable concept? *Professional Psychology: Research and Practice, 18*, 492–497.

Linn, R. L. (1993). The use of differential item functioning statistics: A discussion of current practice and future implications. In P. W. Holland & H. Wainer (Eds.), *Differential item functioning* (pp. 349–364). Hillsdale, NJ: Lawrence Erlbaum Associates.

Linn, R. L., Levine, M. V., Hastings, C. N., & Wardrop, J. L. (1981). Item bias in a test of reading comprehension. *Applied Psychological Measurement, 5*, 159–173.

Linn, R. L., & Werts, C. E. (1971). Considerations for studies of test bias. *Journal of Educational Measurement, 8*, 1–4.

Lord, F. M. (1980). *Applications of item response theory to practical testing problems.* Hillsdale, NJ: Lawrence Erlbaum Associates.

Mantel, N., & Haenszel, W. (1959). Statistical aspects of the analysis of data from retrospective studies of disease. *Journal of the National Cancer Institute, 22*, 719–748.

O'Neill, K. A., & McPeek, W. M. (1993). Item and test characteristics that are associated with differential item functioning. In P. W. Holland & H. Wainer (Eds.), *Differential item functioning* (pp. 255–276). Hillsdale, NJ: Lawrence Erlbaum Associates.

Petersen, N. S., & Novick, M. R. (1976). An evaluation of some models for culture-fair selection. *Journal of Educational Measurement, 13*, 3–29.

Ramsey, P. A. (1993). Sensitivity review: The ETS experience as a case study. In P. W. Holland & H. Wainer (Eds.), *Differential item functioning* (pp. 367–388). Hillsdale, NJ: Lawrence Erlbaum Associates.

Sackett, P. R., & Roth, L. (1991). A Monte Carlo examination of banding and rank order methods of test score use in personnel selection. *Human Performance, 4*, 279–295.

Scheuneman, J. D. (1979). A method of assessing bias in test items. *Journal of Educational Measurement, 16*, 143–152.

Scheuneman, J. D. (1982). A posteriori analysis of biased items. In R. A. Berk (Ed.), *Handbook of methods for detecting test bias* (pp. 180–198). Baltimore: Johns Hopkins University Press.

Scheuneman, J. D. (1987). An experimental, exploratory study of causes of bias in test items. *Journal of Educational Measurement, 24,* 97–118.

Schmidt, F. L. (1991). Why all banding procedures in personnel selection are logically flawed. *Human Performance, 4,* 265–277.

Skaggs, G., & Lissitz, R. W. (1992). The consistency of detecting item bias across different test administrations: Implications of another failure. *Journal of Educational Measurement, 29,* 227–242.

Spencer, S. J., & Steele, C. M. (1994). *Under suspicion of inability: stereotype vulnerability and women's math performance.* Unpublished manuscript. Palo Alto, CA: Stanford University.

Steele, C. M. (1992). Race and the schooling of black Americans. *Atlantic Monthly, 269*(4), 68–78.

Steele, C. M., & Aronson, J. (1995). Stereotype threat and the intellectual performance of African Americans. *Journal of Personality and Social Psychology, 69,* 797–811.

Thissen, D., Steinberg, L., & Wainer, H. (1993). Detection of differential item functioning using the parameters of item response models. In P. W. Holland & H. Wainer (Eds.), *Differential item functioning* (pp. 67–113). Hillsdale, NJ: Lawrence Erlbaum Associates.

Thorndike, R. L. (1971). Concepts of culture-fairness. *Journal of Educational Measurement, 8,* 63–70.

United States Commission on Civil Rights. (1993). *The validity of testing in education and employment.* Washington, DC: U.S. Commission on Civil Rights.

Wherry, R. J. (1957). The past and future of criterion evaluation. *Personnel Psychology, 10,* 1–5.

Wigdor, A. K., & Sackett, P. R. (1993). Employment testing and public policy: The case of the General Aptitude Test Battery. In H. Schuler, J. L. Farr, & M. Smith (Eds.), *Personnel selection and assessment* (pp. 183–204). Hillsdale, NJ: Lawrence Erlbaum Associates.

Zeidner, M. (1987). Test of the cultural bias hypothesis: Some Israeli findings. *Journal of Applied Psychology, 72,* 38–48.

Zieky, M. (1993). Practical questions in the use of DIF statistics in test development. In P. W. Holland & H. Wainer (Eds.), *Differential item functioning* (pp. 337–347). Hillsdale, NJ: Lawrence Erlbaum Associates.

III

METHODS OF ASSESSMENT

This part of the book describes the major methods of trait assessment through tests, inventories, ratings, and various forms of individual and group assessment programs. It may seem strange that "Evaluation of Assessment Procedures" comes before "Methods of Assessment." However, the technical material of Part II provides the basis for comparing different methods of assessment in terms of such things as propensity to error, backgrounds of validity, and the theoretical bases for development of the assessment instruments.

11

Assessment by Testing

Of all assessment methods, testing has the best foundation in research, measurement theory, and the development of standards of evaluation. Other methods of assessment may be preferred for some purposes, but the development and use of tests provides a prototype for the development, use, and evaluation of assessment in other forms.

A *test* is an objective and standardized procedure for measuring a psychological construct using a sample of behavior. A test is objective in that responses can be evaluated against external standards of truth or of quality—correct or incorrect, or better or poorer than a standard. Measuring implies quantification. Tests are scored quantitatively, with measurable precision, on numerical scales representing levels of a construct to be inferred from the scores. A *construct*, as I use the term, is a fairly well-developed idea of a trait; most constructs in testing are abilities, skills, or areas of knowledge. Tests use a standardized procedure with the same stimulus component for all test takers. *Standardization* refers primarily to controlling the conditions and procedures of test administration, that is, keeping them constant—unvarying. If scores from different people are to be comparable, they must be obtained under comparable circumstances. If people tested in one room have 30 minutes in which to complete a test, and those in another have only 20 minutes, neither the circumstances nor the scores are comparable. Any circumstances of test administration potentially influencing scores should be standardized. More than anything else, it is attention to standard procedure that distinguishes testing from other forms of assessment. The distinction is fuzzy. In this chapter, I describe a variety of procedures for assessing KSAs, ranging from highly standardized tests to assessments with little or no standardization, with no clear line distinguishing tests from other assessments procedures.

Defining a test as a sample of behavior means that the examinee is not passive but does something. In other kinds of testing (e.g., blood tests) the object of measurement sits passively while something is done to it. In psychological tests, the examinee responds to test stimuli by writing answers to questions, choosing among options, recognizing or matching stimuli, performing tasks, ordering objects or ideas, or producing ideas to fit requirements—and this is not an exhaustive list.

TRADITIONAL COGNITIVE TESTS

Cognitive tests allow a person to show what he or she knows, perceives, remembers, understands, or can work with mentally. They include problem identification, problem-solving tasks, perceptual (not sensory) skills, the development or evaluation of ideas, and remembering what one has learned through general experience or specific training. They include intelligence tests, achievement tests, and job knowledge tests, among others.

Some History: Oral Trade Tests

Oral trade tests were among the earliest of employment tests. Many were developed in the Army during World War I and in industrial locations in the years immediately after (Chapman, 1921; Link, 1919; Poffenberger, 1927). Trade tests were needed, in part because many applicants genuinely thought they had expertise in a trade when, in fact, they knew only a limited aspect of it; oral tests were needed because many applicants could not read. The problems increased in the depression years and were addressed with excellent test development work in the United States Employment Service (USES). The work, described by Osborne (1940), is unfortunately no longer well-known.

USES job analysts in different regions made detailed observations and developed questions about a wide range of topics fundamental to the trade. Questions and the correct answers were reviewed regionally and nationally for adherence to specified principles, such as brevity. Research compared scores in three groups of subjects. People in the A group were highly skilled in the trade with at least four years of post-training experience. The B group included apprentices, helpers, or beginners. The C group consisted of people in other occupations whose work gave them contact with workers in the targeted trade. The proportion of correct

FORM I

Score	Expert Bricklayers (n = 65)	Apprentices and Helpers (n = 25)	Related Workers (n = 35)
15	xx		
14	xxxxxxx		
13	xxxxxxxxxxxxxxxx		
12	xxxxxxxxxxxxxxxxxxxxx *		
11	xxxxxxxx	x	
10	xxxxx	xx	
9	xx		x
8	xx	x	
7		xx	
6		x	x
5		xxxxxx *	
4		xxxxx	x
3		xx	xxx
2		xx	xx
1		xxx	xxxxxxxxxxxx *
0			xxxxxxxxxxxxxxx

FORM II

Score	Expert Bricklayers (n = 65)	Apprentices and Helpers (n = 25)	Related Workers (n = 35)
15	x		
14	xxx		
13	xxxxxxx		
12	xxxxxxx		
11	xxxxxxxxx		
10	xxxxxxxxxxxx *		
9	xxxxxxxxxxx		
8	xxxxx	x	x
7	xxxx		x
6	x	x	x
5		xx	
4	x	xxx	x
3		xxxxx	xxx
2	x	xxxxx *	xxxxx
1		xxxx	xxxxxxxxxxx *
0		xxxx	xxxxxxxxxxxx

* median score

FIG. 11.1. Distribution of scores on two forms of the oral trade test for bricklayers. From Osborne (1940).

answers should be significantly higher in group *A* than in groups B or C.[1] An example of the results for bricklayers is shown in Fig. 11.1.

Traditional Tests

Most tests now used are called paper-and-pencil tests, but materials do not define traditional tests. The defining features of traditional tests are that they are well-standardized, that their items can be reliably scored, and that they can be administered to groups of people.

---

[1]Later, as experience demonstrated that response patterns varied little between groups B and C, only one "control group" was used. It was designated group C, mainly apprentices, helpers, or beginners but augmented as needed by workers in related occupations.

Commercially Available Versus Homemade Tests. It is almost always cheaper to buy a test than to develop one; moreover, commercial publishers are likely to do a better job of writing, calibrating, and evaluating items and empirically evaluating the resulting test. When there is a choice, commercially available tests have clear advantages.

A commercial test may have less face validity, and therefore less acceptance by the people tested, than a locally developed test that refers explicitly to specific jobs or sets of jobs within the organization. Job-specific local tests developed by people well-trained in psychometrics can be as reliable and valid as commercially available ones. One study paired three subtests of the *Differential Aptitude Test Battery* (DAT) with related job specific tests (Hattrup, Schmitt, & Landis, 1992). For example, the DAT Verbal Reasoning test, a measure of the verbal comprehension factor, was paired with a technical reading test based on manuals used on the job. Confirmatory factor analysis showed that the same constructs were measured in each of the three pairs of tests. Hattrup et al. (1992) concluded that test users do not gain much, psychometrically, by building homemade, job-specific tests, even good ones, but that they do not lose anything, either, and may gain considerably in testing program acceptance. I see a third implication. No matter how much a test developer tries to make particular tests highly specific to particular uses, general cognitive constructs still account for most of the variance. Those who think they are doing things that are new or highly specific may only be fooling themselves.

Tests may have to be developed by local people to serve local purposes. I am not as skeptical of homemade tests as I was before studying a test of electronics knowledge developed by an inspection supervisor. The company, fearful of litigation but unwilling to challenge the supervisor, called for an outside evaluation of the test. It met every reasonable expectation. I have seen other examples of psychometrically good homemade tests (and some that were not). Well-informed job experts can make good tests, especially if helped by someone trained in test development principles.

Traditional Item Types. Responses to questions on the earliest tests, such as oral trade tests, were the examinee's own, not chosen from a limited set. These free responses are not usually called traditional; in general, *traditional* items permit reliable scoring. It is reliable scoring that typifies tests called traditional, not the response format. Figure 11.2 gives examples of reliably scored item types.

Multiple-choice items are prototypical traditional items; they provide reliable, valid tests. They allow an examinee to choose one correct (or best) response from perhaps three to six options. They are versatile; they can test

Sentence Completion

General assumptions about the sources of random error variance in a set of test scores are involved in the estimation of _____.

Short Answer

Estimates of reliability are intended to partition total test score variance into two components, What are they?

True-False

T   F   Reliability refers to a contaminating source of variance in a set of test scores.

Multiple Choice

An estimate of reliability that treats the choice of items presented as a source of error variance is known as
   A.   a coefficient of stability
   B.   a coefficient of equivalence
   C.   an internal consistency coefficient
   D.   a conspect reliability coefficient

Multiple Choice

Several assessment methods are used in a day-long assessment process: a 50-item multiple-choice test of job knowledge, a performance exercise rated by observers, a brief essay test with 5 items, and one large essay. Standard scores on the parts are added to provide a composite overall assessment. Considering both reliability theory and experience with estimation methods, which of the following estimates of reliability do you consider most appropriate for the overall score?

   A.   Internal consistency within the total assessment procedure
   B.   Stability of performance from time to time during the day
   C.   Equivalence of the components used in developing the overall score
   D.   Level of agreement of observers and scorers

FIG. 11.2. Examples of objective item types (i.e., types of items that incur little or no random error in scoring) for an examination on measurement theory.

for grasp of factual information (at abstract or at simple levels) or for abilities to reason from given premises, calculate, evaluate optional courses of action, identify causes or effects or associations, detect errors, infer operating principles, or comprehend principles, sequences, or arguments.

The multiple-choice format has many advantages. It permits testing at a variety of levels of cognitive functioning, from simple recognition to the analysis of problems and evaluations of solutions. It permits wider sampling of relevant content than possible with free responses, thereby providing better coverage of content domains. It may encourage guessing, but it reduces the bluffing encouraged with some constructed response forms. It reduces subjectivity in scoring and generally has higher reliability.

Multiple-choice testing is often criticized, usually as superficial. Superficiality is the item writer's fault; it is not inherent in the format. Figure 11.2 shows two multiple-choice items. One demands only recall; the other demands understanding of theory and accumulated results of applying the theory. Many criticisms, such as that multiple-choice formats inhibit the expression of creativity, can be valid—if the purpose of testing is to assess creativity. It may be. It is unwise in selecting managers, for example, to select those unlikely to show any originality (although it happens); the assessment of potential managers should include assessments of abilities to think unconventionally, to produce ideas readily and in volume, and to change ways of looking at problems—all part of creativity. However, managers should also be able to do arithmetic in their heads (to spot substantially wrong computations), choose words to convey special meanings, or perceive details quickly and accurately—all of which may be assessed best with traditional multiple choice tests. Choosing a method of assessment should be based on its purpose, not on some overgeneralized preference for one sort of test over another. Other item types in Fig. 11.2 have less to recommend them and are subject to similar criticisms. Perhaps that is one reason why the multiple-choice items are more widely used.

PRINCIPLES OF TEST DEVELOPMENT

People responsible for assessments in organizations need to understand how tests are developed. This includes people who must pass judgment on a proposed testing program, administer such programs, take administrative actions relative to or based on such programs, and develop ways to assess aptitude, performance, knowledge, or ability of others. Many assessment procedures are developed locally, even if not tests, and they will be better assessments if developed with awareness of test development principles.

Testing implies assessment with reliably fine gradations along a scale. Not all assessment programs seek that level of measurement precision, but at any level, an assessment procedure important to the organization deserves to be developed with care and understanding—even if it seeks no more than assignment of assessees to a few ordinal categories. The process of developing traditional tests illustrates basic principles applicable as well to other assessment methods.

The Basic Construct and Content Domain

Conceptual Definition of Purpose of Measurement. Test development starts by clearly saying what is to be measured, the construct that gives intended meaning to the scores. When the intended construct is vague, when one has no clear idea of what is to be measured, one cannot know whether it has been measured well. The idea of a construct need not be daunting. For practical purposes, a construct is any idea or concept of an attribute of people, jobs, behavior, environments, or other entities. Clarification of the idea may distinguish it from some other ideas and relate it to still others. A clear idea is more than a name for the construct; it is an idea defined in detail. Its definition should clearly identify its boundaries, that is, what the construct is and what it is not, and there should be some unity of concept within those boundaries. When fully defined, with boundaries and distinctions, it becomes a theory of the attribute to be measured—essential for understanding the basis for practical decisions. It should be potentially useful, from either an organizational or a scientific perspective—preferably both. To be useful, it must imply important individual differences, be subject to empirical quantification, and remain reasonably stable over a substantial time period.

Test Specifications. Construct boundaries enclose a *universe of admissible observations* (Cronbach, Gleser, Nanda, & Rajaratnam, 1972, p. 20). Boiled down, that phrase means that a test developer specifies some observations that fit the construct and some conditions or circumstances appropriate for making them. As the aphorism about skinning cats has it, a construct can be measured by more than one kind of observation or circumstance. The words *universe* and *domain* are often used interchangeably, but I find it useful to distinguish between them, considering a domain a nonrandom sample of a defined universe (Guion, 1979; Lawshe, 1975). Knowing construct boundaries and test purposes can aid in defining a universe of all acceptable kinds and conditions of measurement that may satisfy those purposes; specifying a test content domain narrows the universe and provides a test plan or set of specifications. The following should be part of test planning that continues to clarify the construct:

1. *Specify the kinds of behavior to be observed and the kinds of stimulus materials that will elicit that behavior*—in short, specify test content. Test content is not simply information or tasks; it includes all stimulus characteristics (form, time limits, and other aspects of standardization). Some tasks or behavior fit the construct better than others, but good choices usually require long thought. Choices might be based on psychometric experience (knowing tasks that have a good track record for the construct), practical considerations (e.g., cost, time requirements, or likely attitudes of the examinees), or expected social or legal consequences.

2. *Specify intended inferences as norm- or domain-referenced.* Most test scores are interpreted normatively—in standard deviations above or below the mean, or in centile units—in the distribution of scores from a specific group. Such interpretations answer the question, "How well did I do relative to other people?" An alternative question, "How well did I

do relative to some standard of excellence?" is answered in domain-referenced interpretations. Domain-referenced inferences should be used for personnel decisions more often than they are. For norm-referenced testing, item statistics are particularly important. If domain-referenced interpretations are intended, domain sampling rules are more important.

3. *Specify test components and their intended psychometric characteristics.* Test components are usually items or sets of items (testlets).[2] Characteristics such as difficulty or discriminability can be targeted in advance. For normative interpretations, psychometric theory suggests an average difficulty of .5, but that is not necessarily the best level for every application. If constructed responses are used, or if the test is to differentiate only among the highest scoring candidates, perhaps the average difficulty level should be .3 with a range from .1–.5.

4. *Specify the medium of presentation.* Options include presenting stimulus components orally, on paper, on audio- or videotape, or via a computer. The choice should be made after carefully considering alternatives, and it should make sense in the light of the construct measured.

5. *Specify the medium of response.* There is no compelling reason for the medium of presentation to be the medium of response, although (for the convenience of almost everyone, including examinees) that is typical. Written questions can be answered orally; responses to videotaped situations can be entered on machine-scored answer sheets. Whatever, the response should not violate the nature of the construct.

6. *Specify constraints on responses.* Should responses be constrained or relatively free? The answer should depend on the theory of the attribute, not on the convenience of testers or managers.

7. *Specify appropriate population characteristics.* Some reasons are obvious. Verbal items should be written to be understood by people in the intended population. A test item for tool and die makers may ask about the properties of metals—but not phrased in the jargon of metallurgical engineers. A less obvious but more important reason is that pilot studies should use relevant samples.

8. *Specify content allocations.* Domain boundaries may include several components, some more important, complex, or informative than others. Boundary judgments imply a desired distribution in the final test and the proportion of items, testing time, or points given to each. The intended allocation may be hard to keep during development; items for some topics may not have the desired difficulty statistics, or judgments of the content

---

[2]Testlets were introduced as homogenous item sets used in computerized adaptive testing (Wainer & Kiely, 1987); I use the term more broadly, meaning any internally consistent subset of items within the larger set that is the test.

relevance for some topics may be less consistent than planned; whole component topics can be lost if this specification is not met.

9. *Specify time limits, if any.* Practicalities may impose some time limits; a test given during a training class, for example, may have to be completed, with instructions and collection of papers, within a 50-minute period. Time limits may be set because speed is part of the construct. *Speeded* tests differ from *power* tests, the latter show what examinees can do without the constraints of imposed time limits. If the intended construct is defined by power, but administrative considerations impose a time limit, the specified time should allow nearly all examinees to complete the test; this effectively limits test length.

10. *Specify other standard circumstances of testing.* Establishing time limits, specifying instructions, offering sample items, limiting explanation, arranging the items in sequence, sizing the type, adjusting the video display resolution or color-coding materials for assembly, establishing scoring procedures, and the required qualifications for test administrators, among others, may need standardization. Where specifications require pilot studies, the test development plan should include plans for them.

These 10 points are not exhaustive, but they offer a flavor of things to consider in test development—the statements, decisions, and clarifications needed for a workable plan. A test plan, like a house plan, can be changed as the work moves along; a particular part of the plan might prove ambiguous, esthetically unpleasing, too time consuming, or have some other unanticipated flaw. For the most part, however, both houses and tests are constructed according to the basic plan, even though deviations in details can be anticipated. However, the plan should include procedures for recording deviations and the reasoning behind them. Such records are useful in evaluating psychometric validity.

Developing Items or Other Components

Good professional judgment is required for developing any kind of item, and good judgment requires experience. Because test development experience is greatest for multiple-choice items, I concentrate on them.

A multiple choice item has three parts: stem, a correct response, and a set of distractors. One way to write a multiple choice item is to (a) write a true statement, (b) delete a word or phrase as one would in writing a completion item, (c) write some words or phrases that would be unacceptable but plausible answers in a completion item, and (d) list them, with the correct one, as a set of options. These items assume that people who know the correct answer will choose it and that there is no widespread *mis*information on the item's topic (Horst, 1966). The first assumption is fairly safe in most employment settings. The second assumption is less safe, especially with some job knowledge items; not often, but often enough to merit concern, people will talk about experiences, build on them, and build on the comments of others so much that they know things that simply are not true. Items influenced by widespread misinformation can generally be identified in item analysis.

Several authors have offered useful rules for writing multiple-choice items; they should be studied carefully before trying to build a multiple-choice test (Ebel, 1972; Hopkins & Stanley, 1981; Millman & Greene, 1989; Osterlind, 1989; Thorndike & Hagen, 1955). Examples include:

1. Give each item some "face validity." Make items obviously relevant to the announced purpose of the test; use language that is appropriate in word choices and reading levels.

2. Be sure the item content is suitable for the purpose of the test and for the examinee population intended.

3. Write in clear and simple language and style; keep vocabulary level as simple as the problem allows.

4. Avoid negative words or words that exclude something (e.g., not, except); if they cannot be avoided, emphasize them with capital letters *and* italics or boldface type.

5. Be sure that there is just one correct (or best) answer; be sure that options are false (or, if all are partly true, that there is a clear principle for declaring one better than the others). If the item involves controversial matters, ask for the position held by a specified authority (or, better, ask about the nature of the controversy).

6. Be sure the problem for the examinee is clear in the stem. Phrasing the stem first as a question may help the test developer clarify the examinee's task, and that clarity may spill over to an item edited to another form such as an incomplete sentence.

7. Put as much of the item as possible in the stem, avoiding repeated use of a phrase in each response option (unless repetition provides more clarity); options should be as brief as possible. The stem should be as brief as consistent with clarity; excess verbiage creates ambiguity.

8. Avoid *specific determiners*—cues within items giving away the correct answer, that help an examinee who lacks the desired knowledge identify the preferred option anyway. An example is a stem ending with the article "an." If only one option begins with a vowel, that option is most likely to be chosen. Other specific determiners include variations in length or grammatical structure of the options, use of the same word in the stem and an option, implausible conditions such as never or always, or consistent placement of correct options within the sets.

9. Keep the number of options constant. If this cannot be done, vary the number of options early in the test to avoid establishing spatial sets.

10. Be sure distractors are plausible. In a good item, incorrect responses are distributed rather evenly. Good distractors can come from a pilot study giving stems as questions and calling for written responses.

11. Keep distractors similar in content. If all options refer to different aspects of the problem, each one is a true–false item; answers depend more on cleverness in eliminating options than on knowledge or understanding of the test material.

12. Keep options independent of each other; if two options are merely different ways to say the same thing, they can both be discarded quickly by an alert examinee.

13. Avoid "none of the above" or "all of the above" as options when examinees are to choose the best rather than the correct answer.

14. Keep items independent; do not let information in one item provide a cue to the answer to another one.

Some psychometrics text books give similar rules for other item types. For some, however, there has been too little experience to form generally acknowledged rules. When a relatively rare item form is needed, guidelines or rules developed in advance can make item development more systematic, even if the wisdom of individual rules is uncertain.

Pilot Studies

Choices are made at nearly every step in test development. Some can be made rationally, considering one's options and the relevant arguments for or against them. Other choices need data, and sometimes data must be developed locally. Choices need to be informed by answers to one or both of two kinds of questions: Is this working? What if?

Preliminary Studies. Pilot studies need not be elaborate or sophisticated; they may be simple trials of procedural ideas or choices. Simple studies can usually show whether enough time is being allowed to complete a power test, or whether instructions are clear enough. Structural glitches may be suspected and lead to "is it working" questions. The more novel the test, the more important such questions are. Some of them may require full-scale experiments, but many of them can be answered by trying out the instructions, or the time limits, or purely physical aspects of the test to see if they work. A useful study can be done asking a few people to think out loud as they take the test, and the listening test developer can learn where instructions go awry, or how distractors do not distract. The trials should, of course, use appropriate samples, but the samples need not be large. Such trials are easy, but should not be dismissed as trivial luxuries. It is terribly arrogant and even self-defeating, to assume that one's expertise assures a good, workable plan.

Conventional Item Analyses. Likewise, it is terribly arrogant and surely self-defeating to assume that items developed or chosen work as intended; item analysis is neccessary. Where possible, samples should be large enough to provide reliable item statistics, they should be similar to the population for whom the test is intended, and the trait measured should be distributed somewhat as it is in that population. These are tall orders, unlikely to be fully satisfied in most do-it-yourself test development, but they provide goals to be approximated as well as reality permits. Doing the best one can, even if imperfectly, is preferable to doing nothing.

Two kinds of item statistics are traditionally computed. The easier of these is item difficulty, computed (in reverse) as the proportion of those tested who give the keyed response. Conventionally, .50 is considered an optimal proportion, but other target levels can sometimes be better. Conventional wisdom also suggests that item difficulties should be essentially equal and that item responses should be highly correlated (to produce an internally consistent test).

Such "wisdom" needs to be tempered with good judgment. If all items are perfectly correlated, and if all items have difficulty indices of .50, then this test yields a 2-point distribution where half of the scores are zero and the other half are perfect. The result is classification, not measurement. To develop a fairly internally consistent, homogeneous test with scores distributed along a scale, item difficulties must vary. If the intended examinees define a general population, perhaps the average around which that variation occurs should be .50. For homemade tests, however, the intended use may require that distinctions be most reliable at higher or lower levels of the trait, and the average item difficulty around which specific item difficulties are distributed may therefore be higher or lower.

The other traditional item statistic is a discrimination index. For dichotomously scored items, a preferred index is a point biserial correlation coefficient. The criterion in computing this coefficient is usually the total test score (minus the item being analyzed); sometimes an external criterion is used. Both were used in developing the *Purdue Mechanical Adaptability Test*. Internal consistency was one goal, so one item analysis pitted item responses against total scores. Another goal was to have a test that measured mechanical knowledge, not general intelligence; therefore, a second item analysis pitted item responses against scores on a test of general mental ability. To be retained, an item had to correlate well with total score but not at all well with general mental ability. I do not know why this excellent example is so rarely followed.

Ideally, item statistics are computed in two or more independent samples; only those items in the final test that meet the specifications in double cross validation are retained. However, one sample large enough for reliable statistics is hard to get, let alone two. A less sophisticated approach divides one sample into both a high criterion group and a low criterion group. Differences in proportions giving the keyed answers in these groups is a simple item discrimination index.

Item Analysis by Item Response Theory. An IRT model with two or more parameters for the item characteristic curve provides corresponding item statistics. The slope of the curve at the point of inflection provides the item discrimination index (a) and the location of that point along the Θ scale is the item difficulty index (b).

Reliability and Validity Analyses. Further pilot studies provide data for the preliminary evaluation of tests. Some of these might be major undertakings; for example, a full scale generalizability analysis encompassing the traditional aspects of reliability (stability, equivalence, internal consistency, and interscorer reliability) requires large samples and careful planning. Full scale construct validation requires reliable testing of several confirmatory, disconfirmatory, and competing hypotheses. Even where large scale studies are not feasible, however, they can be outlined conceptually and doing so can suggest plausible sources of random or contaminating error. Even modest research can permit opportunity to address serious problems while there is opportunity to change the test before making it operational.

APPROACHES TO TAKING TESTS

Individual differences in ways people take tests may be a source of irrelevant variance. Differences in test-taking strategies have long been recognized, at least anecdotally, but data are sparse. The relevant literature seems limited to attitudes toward testing, the influence of cognitive styles, and the concept of test-wiseness.

Attitudes

A 9-scale *Test Attitude Scale* (TAS), developed and used by Arvey, Strickland, Drauden, and Martin (1990), accounted significantly for variance on other tests; mean attitudes differed significantly for job applicants (as in predictive or follow-up validation designs) and incumbents (as in concurrent designs) on seven of the scales. Scores on some scales correlated significantly (but not highly) with race, sex, or age.

Schmit and Ryan (1992) used a TAS composite score (reflecting positive test-taking dispositions) in a study using ability and personality tests to predict GPAs of college students. TAS scores moderated predictions—but in different directions. A positive motivation composite score was associated with higher validity for the ability test; a negative motivation composite was associated with higher personality test validity.

Test-Taking Styles and Strategies

Other research has studied individual differences in test-taking strategies such as changing answers. Contrary to popular thinking, people who change answers usually improve their scores, especially if they had initially high scores (Pike, 1978, p. 31). Some people answer all multiple choice items in sequence, but most skip some items and return to them later. In one study, more than 70% of the students omitted items for later consideration (Schwarz, McMorris, & DeMers, 1991).

Willingness to guess may account for some variance in scores, perhaps associated generally with individual differences in risk-taking propensities (Ben-Shakhar & Sinai, 1991; Pike, 1978). Individual differences in cognitive style also contribute some systematic error variance. Acquiescent response styles (tendency to say "yes" or "true" regardless of wording) pose a problem for true–false items. Positional response styles pose a similar problem in multiple-choice items. These are tendencies to choose either extreme or nonextreme responses: in a four-option item, some people choose extreme A or D positions when guessing; others choose the central B–C positions. Other cognitive styles also influence scores. Long ago, French (1965) identified several problem-solving styles that could be subsumed under the contrasting poles of analyzing versus a more global way of perceiving. More recently, Armstrong (1993) found field dependence versus field independence related to performance on poorly constructed test items, especially those with specific determiners. Field dependent people must be taught to look for cues in items, and to know that they are not part of the "total field" of the item that field independent people see spontaneously.

People may also differ in their sensitivity to language and language patterns. Items containing specific determiners are indeed poorly written—but not equally so. The most blatant of them seem likely to point to the correct answer for everyone. More subtle ones, however, may be helpful mainly to those more sensitive to the nuances of the language.

Test-Wiseness

All of this comes under the general heading of test-wiseness, a topic that has been talked about a lot but rarely studied systematically. *Test-wiseness* is the ability to use test and situational characteristics to improve test scores (Millman, Bishop, & Ebel, 1965). This does not imply trickery; the psychometric problem is mainly that errors are made when people lack test-wiseness and have substantially reduced scores because they missed cues others might perceive. Despite the lack of research, I think a test-wise person will, among other things:

1. Pay careful attention to instructions, oral and written, and be sure of understanding the task posed by the test and the basis for responses. A test-wise person will *not* expect simply to pick up insights into the nature of the test while taking it.
2. Ask for clarification of instructions if needed.
3. Begin working without delay and work steadily and as rapidly as possible without risk of misreading or clerical error in responding.
4. Read items carefully enough to be sure what is required.
5. Work rapidly enough to have time to check answers for errors in reading items or recording responses—and do so.

The list could be very long, but it would include little that has been empirically studied. I repeat the earlier call for more research on individual differences in test taking methods and their relative frequencies in different demographic categories.

NORM-REFERENCED AND DOMAIN-REFERENCED TESTING

Test scores are often *norm-referenced*, that is, interpreted relative to the scores of people in a comparison (norm) group. Whether a score is considered good or poor depends on the distribution of scores in the norm group. Figure 11.3 shows percentile ranks associated with raw scores in three hypothetical distributions. An examinee with a score of 12 has answered half of the items correctly. It is a magnificent score compared to those in Group C, better than more than 99% of the scores in that group. Compared to those in Group B, it is about average, neither very good nor very bad. It is not good at all—in the bottom quarter—in Group A, the group with the best set of scores.

Norm tables are rarely consulted in employment testing. Expectancy tables are more useful, but they too are norm-referenced, comparing

	Percentile Rank in		
Raw Score	Group A	Group B	Group C
24			
23	99.9		
22	99.4	99.9	
21	97.7	99.6	
20	94.3	98.5	
19	88.4	96.4	
18	79.9	93.0	
17	70.2	88.6	
16	60.0	83.1	
15	50.0	76.9	
14	40.8	69.9	
13	32.3	62.1	99.9
----	----	----	----
12	24.6	54.0	99.2
----	----	----	----
11	18.1	45.5	97.2
10	12.7	36.7	94.1
9	8.5	28.2	89.3
8	5.4	23.9	82.6
7	3.1	16.7	73.9
6	1.7	10.6	63.2
5	.8	5.7	51.0
4	.3	2.5	37.5
3		.7	23.7
2		.2	11.9
1			4.0
0			.4

FIG. 11.3. Differences in interpretations of a given test score with different norm groups; a raw score of 12 is in the bottom quarter of the distribution in Group A, slightly above average in Group B, and outstanding in Group C.

candidates with each other. In a set of candidates, those with higher scores at any level are preferred over those with lower scores. Hiring the best of a poorly qualified lot, however, is poor management. In a test of prerequisite job knowledge, if every examinee should have a very high score, it is not helpful to say that someone with a very low score is less ignorant than a lot of other people and should therefore be chosen.

An alternative to normative interpretations was originally called criterion-referenced interpretation. In it, scores are interpreted relative to the content domain being tested; like Green and Wigdor (1991), I think it is more appropriately known as *domain-referenced interpretation*.[3] Under

---

[3]Not everyone shares this preference. Linn (1994) considered "domain-referenced" to require domain specifications too rigid to be feasible for any but extremely narrow, finite domains; he said that "criterion-referenced" refers to "broader, fuzzier, but more interesting achievements" (p. 13). Glaser (1994), who introduced criterion-referenced testing (Glaser, 1963; Glaser & Klaus, 1962), prefers the original term, pushing aside the barnacles of misinterpretations of his idea that occurred over the years.

either term, the basic idea is that a domain of accomplishments is identified and defined. It should be defined clearly enough that people, even those who disagree about the domain, can generally agree on whether a specified fact or achievement is in or outside of it. Measures of the domain should fit the definition, and scores should be explicitly interpretable in terms of it (cf. Hambleton, 1994).

In domain-referenced testing, the domain, not a point in a score distribution, is the criterion for referencing or interpreting an obtained score. A score of 12 on a 24-item test may mean knowledge of half of the content, but a better, fuller interpretation can identify the half not known. Content domains are rarely homogeneous, a fact permitting diagnostic uses of domain referencing.

Developing Domain-Referenced Tests

In theory, any test can be used for either norm- or domain-referenced interpretation. In practice, tests may be developed differently for these differing purposes.

Clarity of test purpose, always important, is especially so in domain-referenced testing (Popham, 1974, 1978, 1994). It is not enough to say that a test's purpose is to measure knowledge of repair procedures for electronic typewriters. Defining "knowledge of repair procedures" requires clarity about component content areas; components should be assigned relative weights, and the kinds of items to be used for each component should be specified (Popham, 1994).

Internal consistency, and the reasonable assumption of transitivity it permits, is a basic requirement in norm-referenced testing; people being compared should be compared on a common basis. It is less important in domain-referenced testing; in fact, if it is very high, the content domain may be too restricted. Of course, without some minimal internal consistency, scores have no meaning. Components of a content domain that are uncorrelated, or negatively correlated, should be separately scored.

Evaluating the validity of a norm-referenced test is primarily correlational, either in the sense of criterion-related validation or of confirming and disconfirming construct interpretations. Evaluating the validity of a domain-referenced test calls for expert judgment of the match of items to the specified content domain.

Mastery or Nonmastery

I began the discussion of tests with a domain-referenced example, the old oral trade tests. Cut scores distinguishing journeymen from apprentices or people in related occupations were interpreted as minimal levels

of content mastery. Setting a standard for designating mastery is judgmental, even when aided by empirical data. My general aversion to
unnecessary cut scores applies here as well. Degrees or areas of mastery
may be important for many personnel purposes. If so, such global des-
ignations as master or nonmaster may preclude useful flexibility and the
diagnostic potential of a valid sample of a well-defined domain.

TESTS REQUIRING CONSTRUCTED RESPONSES

Some Criticisms of Traditional Testing

Critics of traditional testing find much to dislike. Some cognitive theorists
complain that multiple-choice tests ignore thought processes. Some social
critics consider them biased. Some educators agree with both and, further,
blame testing for many educational problems. A general theme is that
traditional tests, especially in multiple-choice form, are superficial measures of the wrong things. For some critics, the cure requires tests using
free or constructed responses.

Contemporary educational thought seeks improved education for work
readiness—education that teaches students to think clearly and creatively,
produce ideas, evaluate information, and be cognitively effective—and it
considers constructed-response testing to be the best way to assess success.
American government initiatives (like Goals 2000, 1994) follow the crusade.
The agenda is laudable, its perspective myopic.

An older tradition in employment psychology fits this new movement
in salient respects. In it, standardized, objective, multiple-choice tests have
coexisted with short answer tests, work samples, written statements of
career objectives, problem-solving exercises, and other kinds of constructed responses. Three points should be clear before going on. First,
"construction versus choice"[4] is not a distinction between new and old
ideas. Second, freely constructed response and multiple choice are methods
in a continuum from tests greatly constricting responses an examinee can
make to those posing hardly any constraint at all. Third, the choice of a
method should be based on the purpose, not on some all-encompassing
merit supposed for one option over all others.

Levels of Constraint in Item Response

Bennett, Ward, Rock, and LaHart (1990) developed a taxonomy of item
types (also presented in Bennett, 1993a). I follow it somewhat, but the
presentation here is also influenced by other sources (mainly Snow, 1993).

---

[4]"Construction Versus Choice in Cognitive Measurement" is the title of the edited volume
from which much of this section is taken (Bennett & Ward, 1993).

Multiple-Choice Items. Multiple choice and related item types anchor the maximum constraint end of the scale. Multiple-choice items differ. Some require only easy recognition; some require intervening construction in that the examinee must construct at least an approximate response before being able to make an informed choice among the options (Snow, 1993).

Selection or Identification Problems. These are also multiple-choice items, but quite different from the customary sort. An example (Bennett et al., 1990) is a passage of about 100 words, with several words underlined. Below the passage is an alphabetized list of more than 50 words, plus the phrases "no change needed" and "no appropriate replacement listed." Each underlined word is a "possibly inappropriate word choice"; the examinee is to decide if it really is inappropriate in its context and, if so, to pick a word from the list that would be more appropriate. There are far more options than a traditional multiple-choice item, so guessing is unlikely to help much. Moreover, it seems to call for mental reconstruction before searching for a replacement word.

Reordering or Rearrangement. The task here is to arrange items in a correct sequence; examples include solving anagrams, ordering sentences to make a logical paragraph, or ordering pictures to make a story, among others. Components can be arranged according to size, merit, complexity, chronology, or other principles.

Substitution or Correction. These items require the examinee to identify and correct a problem in material presented. In verbal materials, the problem may be a word that does not fit. The substitution comes not from a prepared list but from the examinee's own knowledge. Similar items could be nonverbal (e.g., wiring diagrams or abstract mechanical gadgets).

Short Answer Items. These typically require writing a word or phrase. It might be a word or phrase omitted from a written passage, a definition, a solution to a problem, or an answer to a question.

Construction or Production. These items require the examinee to produce something: a paragraph, a list, a graph, an architectural drawing, a gadget, an essay, and so forth. Work sample tests are common examples.

Oral Descriptions of Production Processes. These might include a teach-back procedure in which the examinee explains concepts, procedures, structures, or systems—usually but not necessarily orally.

Demonstration, Presentation, or Performance. These assessments require observing actual (or recorded) task performance. Auditions are obvious examples; others might be repairing a malfunctioning engine, diagnosing an illness, or giving a lecture. The assessee usually knows the nature of the required performance ahead of time and has time to practice it. Procedures might be standardized (e.g., all musicians playing the same composition), or the required performances may differ for different assessees.

Achievement Samples Collected Over Time. A person may be asked merely to develop and bring in samples of his or her best work. Standardization is truly minimal, "best work" being the assessee's own judgment. These usually are products of creative thought or skill, such as paintings, essays, short stories, recordings of performances, ad layouts—whatever is to be assessed. They ordinarily do not include intangible products like negotiated settlements between conflicting parties or reorganized production systems, but they might include written descriptions of the history of such problems, procedures used in working toward the outcome, and a reasonably objective evaluative summary of it. Note that this and the two or three methods just mentioned do not fit the definition of *test* given at the chapter beginning; they are neither standardized nor objective enough to score very reliably; they do not measure specific constructs, and the assessments may not even be ordinal in nature.

Scoring Constructed Responses

Only rarely can constructed responses at the extreme of the continuum be dichotomously scored as right or wrong, acceptable or unacceptable, safe or dangerous, workable or unworkable. The responses range widely from very poor through ordinary to excellent, even elegant; the place of a response in that continuum is a matter of judgment, often expressed as a rating.

Interrater or inter-scorer reliability is a problem. It should not matter which rater scores a response. For example, it should not matter whether it is scored early or late in a scoring session, or whether the test was taken on one date or a later one. Such unwanted sources of variance might be studied by generalizability analysis.

Some free responses can be scored reliably against a key or standard identifying acceptable and unacceptable responses. Partial credit might be given. A good (correct or acceptable) response might be given a score of 2, a poor one scored 0, and one in between scored 1. Items to be scored might be task components, whether an essay, work sample, or portfolio.

Performance on a driver's license examination may be a sum of scores on parallel parking, changing lanes, stopping, turning, and other parts.

The choice of an overall score versus component scores depends on the purpose. An overall score is useful if an either–or decision is to be made (as in selection or licensing decisions), but analytic scores are more useful for training. I think the analytic process can improve final score reliability in any case.

Scoring Keys for Essays. Keys can be prepared for essays. Those developing the scoring key may have in mind a list of content topics that should (or could) be included in a response to the stimulus question. A short rating scale (perhaps three levels) might be used in evaluating the quality of the coverage of each topic; the score may be the sum of the quality points awarded to the listed topics discussed in the written essay, perhaps giving more weight to some topics than to others. Such a key enhances scorer reliability. If the key includes all appropriate content, no one will come close to a maximum score; with even liberal time for completion, examinees are not likely to think of everything the content experts developing the key could include. A domain-referenced score of only half the possible score might be considered excellent performance.

Where possible, essays should be scored by two or more different people, each with the same understanding of the key and its use. If only one scorer is available, responses should be rescored at a later time, in a different order, without knowing the examinee's identity or earlier score. The process may improve reliability, but it does not show how to use the double scores. They might be summed or averaged; where discrepancies exceed an accepted level, some procedures require scorers to meet and reconcile differences, or a third scorer might contribute to the average.

Computer Scoring. New developments permit less freely constructed responses, scored dichotomously, or even completion items, to be scored using a computer or a scannable answer sheet. A word or number can be encoded on an answer sheet in a grid like those used for recording the examinee's name or identification number (Braswell & Kupin, 1993; Bridgeman, 1992). Computers may be feasible for even less constrained responses. A system developed by Bejar (1991) showed promise for scoring constructed solutions to architectural design problems, Braun, Bennett, Frye, and Soloway (1989) developed an expert system approach for problems on computer programming, and Bennett (1993b) incorporated artificial intelligence and expert systems in yet another proposal. Such scoring systems, of course, are not yet operational for most users.

Scoring Models. Whether items call for short answers or essays, or are scored dichotomously or with partial credit, scores on each item may be added to form a total score. Such scoring is a compensatory model, probably useful for scoring end products like essays, typewritten letters, or welded assemblies. However, where testing objectives focus on process, conjunctive or disjunctive models may be more appropriate. A compensatory model may not even be feasible if process components are sequential.

An appropriate score on a set of work sample tasks may be the poorest score for any component. In another setting, for another job, the important consideration may be doing something well, so the score may be the best of all component scores. Or the scoring model may involve some combination of models. Conceivably, a work sample could include a variety of tasks, some of which are enough alike to combine. Within groups of tasks, compensatory scoring might be used, but the total score across those groups might be based on a much different algorithm.

Comparisons of Constructed and Multiple-Choice Items

Several studies have compared relatively constrained free response and more traditional multiple-choice testing. A common assertion is that multiple-choice items measure superficial constructs and that constructed-response items measure deeper constructs. That is, the two formats are said to measure different things. Is this a tenable hypothesis? Much evidence rejects it. Bridgeman (1992) reported little difference in the abilities measured when free responses are numbers or just a few words. Ward (1982) showed that open-ended forms of some verbal aptitude item types can be as reliable as multiple-choice items and that they require only slightly greater time limits. Testing the hypothesis that multiple choice and free response define different verbal aptitude factors, he found only a single factor—no evidence of different constructs. After comparing a 50-item multiple-choice test in computer science with five essay components in the same test, Bennett, Rock, and Wang (1991) also reported a single factor, concluding that the evidence did not support the stereotype of multiple-choice and free-response formats as measuring different levels of ability. In general, the rhetoric of the constructed response movement is not empirically supported.[5] Even the least constrained response formats seem unlikely to measure constructs differing greatly from those measured by the most constrained response formats. It seems more likely that they have more contaminating sources of variance, diluting validity (Snow, 1993).

For any measurement method, it is important to formulate carefully, and investigate systematically, rival hypotheses about constructs measured. One contaminant commonly invoked is test anxiety; its effect is

---

[5]Bennett (1993a, p. 2) attributed to C. R. Reynolds the motto, "In God We Trust; All Others Must Have Data." It seems fitting here.

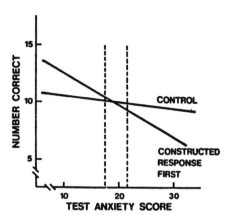

FIG. 11.4. Regression slopes of achievement test score on test anxiety score where (a) conventional multiple-choice format is used and where (b) responses were first constructed and then recorded as multiple-choice responses; differences between the dotted lines are nonsignificant. From Snow (1993).

shown in Fig. 11.4, adapted by Snow (1993) using data from Schmitt and Crocker (1981). For the typical multiple-choice format, test scores were slightly negatively related to test anxiety. Different instructions, telling the examinee to construct a response before choosing one of the options, produced the more severely negative slope. The constructed response form includes more unwanted variance due to anxiety.

Multiple-choice items typically yield more reliable scores than do even similarly constrained free-response items; Wainer and Thissen (1992) estimated that it cost $30.00 to get enough testing time and items in the free-response format to equal the reliability per penny for multiple-choice items. Martinez (1991) found multiple-choice items easier but somewhat less discriminating (i.e., lower biserial rs), but constructed-reponse items were more likely to be omitted. Student examinees (and, maybe, candidates for employment opportunities) prefer multiple-choice items but think open-ended questions measure abilities better (Braswell & Kupin, 1993; Shepard, 1991).

A Tentative Conclusion

There is much hope but little evidence that constructed-response testing is superior to more constrained responses. The rhetorical excesses may have inhibited research. Some rhetorical arguments may be worth pursuing—for example, a distinction between the traditional concern with the examinee's level of proficiency and what Mislevy (1993) called the *architecture of proficiency*:

> The ascendent view [i.e., the constructed response view] originates *from a perspective more attuned to instruction than to selection or prediction.* Learners increase their competence not simply by accumulating new facts and skills ... but by reconfiguring knowledge structures, by automating procedures

and chunking information to reduce memory loads, and by developing strategies and models that tell them *when and how* facts and skills are relevant. (Mislevy, 1993, p. 75, italics added)

And,

Rather than seeking long-term, stable characteristics that are immune to change, a test in this context is meant to provide information about characteristics of an examinee that are *ripe for change. The problem of interest is one of diagnosis* or optimal assignment to instruction; the decision is viewed as shorter term; the options are cast not in terms of level of persistent proficiency but of *architecture of current proficiency.* (Mislevy, 1993, p. 79, italics added)

Forget the straw-person reference to characteristics immune to change. Ignore also the education-specific reference of the quotations. What is left is a potentially important distinction between level and structure of performance achievement. One hypothesis might suggest that a person who has moderate if not particularly high levels in several components of proficiency, and can be readily trained in others, may be a better bet for growing requirements for flexible personnel than one who has demonstrated a high level of proficiency within a much more limited set of procedures. I do not know of any test of the hypothesis, but it is testable. If it is supported, the diagnostic value of contructed response testing may have much practical value for personnel decisions.

Some constructed response testing may have further advantages. Consider again the model of personnel decisions suggested by Dunnette (1963). If two candidates present themselves for consideration for the same job, and if one of them claims several years experience on similar jobs and the other claims no more than ability and willingness to learn, the Dunnette model suggests that these candidates be assessed in different ways for different characteristics. The latter should be assessed on relevant stable, long-term aptitudes; a work sample or job knowledge test can assess the proficiency claimed by the former.[6] If concern for the architecture of proficiency does no more than encourage a reappraisal of the Dunnette model, it will have proven worthwhile for HR assessment needs.

There is surely something valuable for employment testing in the resurgence of interest in constructed responses. However, people doing measurement and assessment for personnel decisions must not be stampeded into their premature adoption, either by academic rhetoric or by

---

[6]The legality of this sort of differential testing has yet to be determined, but in principle it seems consistent with the ADA concept of accommodating those who are differently abled.

government activities that urge uncritical transfer of educational assessment ideas to employee or job candidate assessment.

PERFORMANCE TESTS

Performance testing in the workplace means assessing proficiency in some aspect of job performance. Performance tests may be cognitive or noncognitive, paper-and-pencil or "hands-on," and anywhere from the most to the least constrained kinds of responses. They may be criteria or predictors intended to predict no further than the immediate future. An applicant who does well on a welding test may be expected do good welding the first day at work; situational variables like equipment, materials, supervision, coworkers, or personal traits like motivational level, may determine whether a good beginning is continued. Although prediction is always implied, performance tests are used mainly to assess proficiency, skill, or knowledge at the time of testing—here and now, not at some future time. Unlike low aptitude candidates, those lacking knowledge or skill may acquire it through special training and reapply when ready.

Performance tests can be used (a) to predict performance on a higher level job requiring similar kinds of proficiency, (b) to identify outside candidates who need no training beyond a general orientation, (c) to identify training needs, (d) as a criterion in validation, (e) to provide proficiency-related interpretations of predictors, and (f) in performance evaluation. Only the first of these has a strong future orientation; the principal orientation of all the other purposes is here and now. Use as a criterion should be more common than it is, but its value as a criterion can be overstated. Performance testing usually describes how well tasks can be performed when the person is doing his or her best. Where testing is intended to predict actual performance, not a hypothetical maximum level, performance test scores may be inappropriate criteria. Again, the method of assessment should fit its purpose.

Work Samples and Simulations

The most common "hands-on" performance tests may be work samples. They are well-established as predictors. Their criterion-related validity is consistently shown in reviews (e.g., Asher & Sciarrino, 1974; Cascio & Phillips, 1979; Robertson & Kandola, 1982; Schmidt, Greenthal, Hunter, Berner, & Seaton, 1977).

A work sample test is a standard sample of a job content domain taken under standard conditions. Aspects of the work process, the outcome, or both may be observed and scored. In a flight test for a pilot's license, the focus is on process; a check pilot has a checklist of required maneuvers and evaluates how well each is performed. A candidate for an office job may be given a typed manuscript with many scribbled changes on it, be seated at a word processor, and told to prepare final hard copy; perhaps only the result is observed and scored. In either case, the work sample is a *standardized abstraction* of work actually done on a job. There are degrees of abstraction. A work sample might be faithful reproductions of actual assignments, sanitized simulations of critical components, or the extreme abstraction, here and now measures of isolated skills used on the job.

Simulations imitate actual work but omit its trivial, time consuming, dangerous, or expensive aspects. They may imitate a task almost exactly, as in some simulations of aircraft cockpits. They may imitate only the general flavor of reality, as in assessment center management exercises.

Other possibilities carry abstraction still further. Performance tests might use *talk-through* interviews (Hedge, Teachout, & Laue, 1990) to describe the steps, tools used, and decisions made in doing the job. A work diary might be used. A collection of product examples (a "portfolio") may be evaluated. Even a multiple-choice test may abstract from overall performance the knowledge and understanding of processes, tools, and choices that make up performance on the job. Simulations that are not highly abstracted are known as *high fidelity* simulations; the greater abstractions may be *low fidelity* simulations (Motowidlo, Dunnette, & Carter, 1990).

All of these are performance tests. In all of them, components, tasks, or required behaviors are drawn (i.e., abstracted) from overall job demands. They may be manipulative, sensory, or cognitive; they may be faithful, obvious samples of work done or abstractions recognizable as samples only by knowing the logic leading to their use. They may test knowledge, understanding, or skill. In short, they vary widely in nature, in content, and in fidelity of imitating real job performance.

Most people seem to assume that the more faithful the simulation, the better it will predict future performance. As Sportin' Life in Porgy and Bess said, "it ain't necessarily so." Prediction may be better when faithfulness of simulation is set aside to focus on the more enduring essence of a job. Low fidelity simulations have been good predictors when they represent the essence of both the job and the simulation (Motowidlo et al., 1990; Motowidlo & Tippins, 1993). Perhaps the ultimate abstraction was reported by Arnold, Rauschenberger, Soubel, and Guion (1982) who abstracted simple arm strength from steel mill labor jobs. The arm dynamometer test was not a faithful imitation of any real task, but most of them demanded arm strength, so it measured a critical aspect of job performance.

Developing Work Samples. Work sample development begins with job analysis, although not everything the analysis identifies is included. Distinguishing a "universe" from a "domain" (Lawshe, 1975), I described choices in developing tests of content samples in four stages (Guion,

1979). A complete job analysis identifies a job content universe. The part of the universe to be assessed is a job content domain. Related assessment possibilities (including scoring methods) make up a test content universe, and the choices among them define the intended test content domain.

Proficiency is the construct measured by a work sample, but it takes many forms. For a criterion, it should identify all tasks critical for overall performance. For selection, it omits critical tasks learned on the job. Ordinarily, tasks defining proficiency should be those that many, but not all, examinees are likely to perform well. Most work samples use only frequent tasks; rarely performed tasks might be in the domain to identify those who can handle unusual job situations.

Equipment or material used should match that actually used on the job (instead, as so often happens, of stuff not yet thrown away). Tolerances and procedures for monitoring equipment should be established; if holes into which things are inserted get larger over repeated testing, monitoring hole size may be an important aspect of standardization. As always, pilot studies should evaluate the clarity of instructions, scoring procedures, and characteristics of test components (e.g., items) as well as overall reliability and validity of scores.

Work Sample Scoring. Scores are usually ratings. An overall rating of process, product, or component part can be dichotomous (e.g., satisfactory or unsatisfactory) or a scale point. A work sample product might be matched to one of a set of samples previously scaled from very poor to excellent (Millman & Greene, 1989); the score being the scale value of the sample it most closely matches. More objective measures can be used. A score on machine set-up might be the time required to do it. The score can be the pounds of pressure required to break a weld. A computer might count the number of corrections made in a sample word processing task. Ratings predominate, however, and their associated problems (see chapter 12) can be helped with procedures like these:

1. Job experts should choose work sample content, specify desired performance, and provide at least a preliminary scoring key or protocol.
2. Scorers should be trained to use the protocol: what to look for and how to evaluate specific events or product components.
3. The same performance or product should (if possible) be evaluated by two or more independent observers; impermissible differences in ratings should be defined and the procedures for reconciling differences prescribed.
4. All possible procedural safeguards of reliability should be built into the scoring system.

Evaluation. Evaluation of a completed work sample test follows the set of questions given in chapter 5. Guion (1996) restated these questions explicitly for performance tests; three further questions, drawn from Mehrens (1992), should be added for performance assessment:

1. Are the content domains sufficient for the purposes declared? "In general, performance assessment measures a narrower domain than multiple-choice testing but assesses it in more depth. Is this good?" (Mehrens, 1992, p. 7).
2. Are domains defined tightly enough? Do experts agree on whether a given test component belongs in the domain, as defined?
3. Is there evidence that performance on the work sample generalizes to the larger content domain?

Noncognitive Performance

Physical Abilities. Measuring strength, muscular flexibility, stamina, and related abilities usually requires equipment and individual testing. Equipment needs described by Fleishman and Reilly (1992) are often simple. Assessing stamina may require an electronically monitored treadmill with an accompanying electrocardiograph, but a simple step test can also assess stamina, although with less precision.

Fitness Testing. Task performance, physical fitness, and health may be related. Task performance, as measured by a work sample, may be supported by physical abilities (e.g., stamina). Abilities are supported by biological systems (e.g., cardiorespiratory systems), which may be impaired by health problems. A person with emphysema suffers cardiorespiratory impairment, resulting loss of stamina, and difficulty in tasks like climbing stairs. Poor fitness is a problem for both the person and the employer.

Medical and physical testing should have higher than typical priority, if for no other reason than protection from litigation. Litigation can spring from many directions (including getting hurt in fitness testing). An organization may be legally liable for hiring unhealthy or physically inept employees (under the concept of negligent hiring); there is an opposing liability for discrimination against the disabled. Employees who hurt themselves or develop health problems because of physically demanding jobs add to worker's compensation costs. Performance errors or accidents stemming from fatigue or clumsiness may bring suit from fellow employees, customers, or the general public. Rejected or underplaced applicants may sue under civil rights laws.

The potential cost is too great, both in the risk of litigation and the risk of physical pain, to continue using arbitary, poorly assessed standards of fitness or physical skills. Some perennial questions must be faced. For example, a physically demanding task may not be performed often but, when it is, injury might result. Should employment decisions be based on the ability to perform that task? Because of its infrequency, a worker may have little opportunity on the job to develop or maintain the necessary physical skill. On the other hand, infrequency may give time for rest and recovery between occasions. Should the job be redesigned, with the rare but risky task assigned to another job with similarly demanding tasks regularly done? Or should such tasks be spread around? Sometimes there is no option. In police work, sometimes defined as boredom occasionally interrupted by panic, the need to meet unusual physical demands is always present. Should physical fitness testing look at the job as a whole or at its maximum requirements? Should it be assessed periodically?

How much loss of musculoskeletal flexibility, cardiovascular impairment, or hearing loss must be experienced before job performance deteriorates? In medical examinations, answers to such questions are usually left to the judgment of the individual physician—but they are rarely validated. Fleishman (1988) offered a promising approach to systematizing such judgments. A guide to impairment evaluation published by the American Medical Association (1977) was tied to his scales for analyzing physical job demands; guides were developed for physicians to use in determining whether a given level of impairment would prevent effective performance of specific job tasks.

In many jobs, recurring personnel decisions may be made almost daily on employees' here-and-now readiness to work; for example, is this pilot fit to fly today? Is there an impairment that would make this construction worker's job especially dangerous today? Temporary proficiency impairments may be due to medication or drugs (including alcohol), fatigue, illness, or preoccupation with nonwork stresses. Drug testing is increasingly widely used, but drug tests or tests for blood alcohol level or body temperature do not assess impairment. It may be more useful to use performance tests of the specific proficiencies required, or perhaps physiological measures of performance impairment. Rizzuto (1985) found that even a mild dose of Valium resulted in slower neurological transmission and deficits in visual acuity, attention, and intensity perception; he found performance deficits in a visual tracking task using neurological measures of evoked responses that also identified the processing areas affected.

Olian (1984) offered a unique suggestion to reduce health hazards: genetic testing for people expected to work in environments where they risk disorders stemming from specific hazards (e.g., hazardous chemicals); some people, genetically, may be at higher risk than others. Her suggestion deserves consideration; as Murphy's Law says, where something can go wrong, some day it will, and the possibility of harm to people especially sensitive to a given hazard is real. Maybe one reason why the suggestion has not been considered further is the justifiable paranoia employing organizations experience when trying something that has not yet been tested in court.

Sensory and Psychomotor Proficiencies. Work combines cognitive, muscular, sensory, and attitudinal components; a useful work sample might focus on the sensory component. Requisite here-and-now job performance may include sensory proficiency such as correct identification or distinctions of distant shapes, colors, musical pitch, or unseen but touched objects. Except for some classic studies (e.g., occupational vision; see Guion, 1965; McCormick & Ilgen, 1980), little research has addressed the assessment of sensory skill for personnel decisions. Fleishman and Reilly (1992) identified assessment methods for a few sensory abilities; more importantly, perhaps, they identified some important skills (e.g., night vision) for which no existing measures were identified; these, too, are ripe areas for research.

Psychomotor skills, especially dexterity and coordination, are more widely tested. Especially common is the use of dexterity tests, usually requiring examinees to insert pegs or pins in holes, as in Fig. 11.5. Scores can be the number of pins (or assemblies) inserted within a time period or the amount of time required to fill the board.

Examples of tests for other psychomotor skills are provided by Fleishman and Reilly (1992). Commercial psychomotor tests are available, but sometimes manipulations imitating those required on a job should form

FIG. 11.5. Testing dexterity with the Crawford Small Parts Dexterity Test. From Guion (1965).

the test. Job analysis can identify the recurring stimulus patterns and the kinds of coordinated responses required.

High skill levels in some sensory or psychomotor areas may compensate for deficiencies in others, in work as in more general life skills. The compensatory development of unusual auditory skills among the legally blind is one example; the extraordinary skin and muscle sensitivity of the deaf and blind Helen Keller is legendary. Examples need not be so dramatic to have implications for personnel management. Rehabilitation counselors tell about people lacking certain sensory (or motor) skills performing well on jobs many employers would have denied them. Hope for finding compensatory skills is based more on anecdotes than on research. Evidence does not yet lead to general propositions about genuinely compensatory patterns.

Assessment of Basic Competencies

It is hard, and maybe not useful, to distinguish between ability and competency, but more and more frequently, calls are made for testing competencies rather than general abilities (but see Barrett & Depinet, 1991). Some distinctions may be sensible. *Competency* may refer to here-and-now performance, *ability* to aptitude for future performance. Competency scores are likely to be domain-referenced, ability scores to be norm-referenced.

There is much contemporary talk about basic competencies, especially those required in "workplace readiness" (cf. Resnick & Wirt, 1996, p. 21). I propose defining *basic competencies* in employment as the acceptable performance of simple things a person must do on a job, things like adding whole numbers, reading simple instructions, writing notes on problems or activities, or reading blueprints, among other examples— things an employee on a particular job may be expected to do without help, instruction, or accumulated job experience. The nature and complexity of a basic competency, so defined, differs for different jobs. A cashier must count money accurately. So must a pizza deliverer, who must also drive a car. An electrician must read wiring diagrams. An office clerk must read, alphabetize, and maybe type. These are basic competencies, defined by these jobs, not for work in general.

"Authentic" Performance Assessments

The phrase, "authentic performance assessment," currently popular in education, known also as *performance-based assessment*, has spilled over into legislation and regulation. According to some (e.g., Barton, 1996), its use was mandated in Goals 2000: Educate America Act (Goals 2000, 1994).

Saying it is a mandate is debatable, but Section 207(a) of the Act calls for "alternatives to currently used early childhood assessments"—a phrase reflected in other parts of the Act as well—if they are "valid, reliable, and consistent with relevant, nationally recognized, professional and technical standards" (Goals 2000, 1994, Sec. 211[5][B]). The concept of authenticity has been defined in many ways, not always consistently. The common thread may refer to assessment based on physical and cognitive challenges actually faced in the school (and, by extension, the job; cf. Linn, 1994). Performance assessment always implies that someone has done something evaluated by someone else; in that sense it is hard to imagine an inauthentic assessment, even if an invalid one is quite easily imagined. Authenticity seems to refer mainly to the match between the stimulus content of the assessment material and the stimulus content of performance in the classroom or job site. If this is correct, authenticity in performance assessment is little more than a buzzword for fidelity of simulation. In that sense, the degree of authenticity may be inversely proportional to the degree of abstraction. As in other testing, authentic performance assessment should not be used when the assessment procedure can result in harm to the assessee, others, equipment, or the services the assessing organization provides. Lower fidelity assessment may be more valid and less dangerous. Work sample, simulation, and special skill testing are all performance measures, successsively more abstract; perhaps, but not certainly, the less abstract ones may more authentically match critical job stimulus content.

Probationary Assessment. Authentic assessment of job performance should assess day in–day out performance; maybe the test is performance in probation. It may be authentic, but it has pitfalls. Probationary tasks that faithfully sample later assignments surely provide a representative, job-related, authentic job sample. However, in assessment, inferences are drawn from evaluative scores (usually ratings), not assignments, and validity depends on those inferences. Valid inferences about performance can be based on less than fully representative probationary work; a highly representative set of assignments can be spoiled by invalid evaluations.

Records and Portfolios. A current icon of authenticity is portfolio assessment. A *portfolio* is a performance record consisting of documents attesting to performance, descriptions of performance, or products of performance. It can include indirect reflections of real-world performance such as awards, production records, or commendations or disciplinary actions. A letter to an interstate trucking firm commending a driver for an exemplary action is an observation and evaluation of the driver's work; a record with several such letters may be evaluated more highly than a file with several letters of complaint. In a quite different sense, job-related biographical data such as achievement records may find a place within a portfolio. A supervisor's diary of observations of employee performance—an *incident file*—can be in the record (Guion, 1965). All of these have been used in performance evaluation, but they are more likely to be called an employee's personnel file than a portfolio.

The portfolio concept seems different. A portfolio may be assembled by the person whose performance is being evaluated. It is likely to consist of content that is best rather than representative, so it assesses maximum, not typical, performance. An assessee may choose examples of his or her best work and submit them for critique and evaluation. Note the sequence of evaluations. The first is the assessee's, who uses a personal conception of excellence in assembling the portfolio. Later a teacher or HR specialist evaluates the quality of the items collected. The disparity in concepts of excellence introduces an uncontrolled source of variance.

Portfolio assessment may help in some employment decisions. If several managers are being considered for a promotion to the executive level, each of them may be asked to submit reports on two or three programs he or she has initiated and considers noteworthy managerial achievements. In choosing people for so-called "talent" jobs, (e.g., writing advertising copy, designing consumer products, etc.) portfolios representing relevant prior work might be required. The manager of a dinner theatre might ask for a portfolio of prior stage experience before deciding which applicants for a new play will be auditioned. An investment counselor might be asked for a portfolio of portfolios. These are not commonplace jobs, but principles of assessment for personnel decisions ought not be limited to the ordinary. It may be instructive in such jobs to evaluate assessees' ideas of the best.

Enthusiasm for portfolio assessment is largely due to dissatisfaction with traditional tests. It is inappropriate, however, to criticize traditional testing by one set of rules while justifying a preferred approach by different rules. Authentic performance assessment needs to satisfy, minimally, some common evaluative requirements. Foremost among them is that the assessment should accomplish its objectives. An assessment program may be intended to shed light on how well the person assessed can do what is expected in a curriculum or a job. It may be deficient if too much of the total domain goes unassessed (Mehrens, 1992).

Second, there must be *some* standardization. When people are compared, the comparisons should be (in the overworked cliché) on a "level playing field." When assessment of different people is based on different kinds or levels of performance demands, the assessments may not be comparable at all. Standardization sometimes seems to be a dirty word to some people, but it is essential for fair personnel decisions in which some candidates come out ahead of others. Standardization may be a dirty word, but procedural justice is not. In the litigious climate in which employment decisions are made, the playing field of unstandardized assessments seems legally dangerous, quite apart from its contribution to unreliability.

Reliable assessment is the third requirement. Koretz (1993) reported low interrater reliability coefficients for the Vermont portfolio project, ranging from .33 to .43, although later estimates were somewhat improved (Koretz, Stecher, Klein, & McCaffrey, 1994). With experience, of course, scoring procedures will be improved and so will reliabilities. Reckase (1995) has shown analytically that acceptable reliability is possible. But it will require a great deal of work.

Finally, cost should be considered. "Authentic" assessment is extremely expensive. Providing equipment for simulation, for example, can cost more than the working equipment it simulates. The costs of finding, training, housing, and paying essay or portfolio readers are far greater than the costs of more traditional programs. The evaluative question is both psychometric and economic: Is the assessment benefit worth the cost? There is no general answer for all occasions; benefits and costs must be estimated in the light of specified purposes, conditions, and alternatives.

ELECTRONIC TESTING

Technological change can make tests obsolete (e.g., stenographic tests used circa 1940) or create opportunities. Electronic technologies offer new ways to do conventional testing and new ways to do unconventional testing.

Motion Picture and Videotape Tests

In large public jurisdictions, several thousand candidates might be tested simultaneously in different locations with different test administrators. Beyond logistics challenges, mass testing may pose psychometric problems only for tests requiring rigid time limits; differences among examiners in timing accuracy is a source of error. Even appropriate speeded tests are avoided because a timing error may unfairly disqualify or give unfair advantage to examinees in at least one location.

Putting a test on film, videotape, or slides, projecting items under controlled conditions, can solve the practical problem of controlling instructions and time limits. There are other psychometric advantages as well. By controlling the time for individual items, rather than an overall time limit, all subjects can attempt all items, and internal consistency analysis is feasible. Individual item characteristics can be changed, such as changing item difficulty by changing the item's exposure time.

A movie was the medium for a test of perceptual skill for the selection of police officers in a large midwestern city.[7] Perceptual accuracy is important in police work, but the police skill differs from that usually tested. An officer may look for something specific, such as a license number; more often, the officer must simply be alert to things that merit curiosity. A police officer on patrol or doing investigative work must attend to detail without knowing which details might be important. Perception must be accurate, and it must be quick.

The first section of the film gave instructions and some illustrative but very brief scenes narrated by an off-screen voice; these scenes were the basis for a subsequent memory test. The rest of the film showed several brief episodes, each followed by a set of multiple-choice questions about it. Some scenes had a story line; some were simply camera shots, for example, of people enjoying themselves on a summer day at the park. The format permitted use of behavioral stimuli (Guilford, 1959) that could not have been included in traditional tests, but it was otherwise fairly traditional. As in any other test development, we should have built the test in stages, basing each stage on pilot study data from the one before. For each scene we should have had pilot studies for item analysis and have chosen the best items; we did, perfunctorily, but we did not do an analogous pilot to choose scenes. The script was written, and the film was shot, edited, assembled, and declared a take-it-or-leave-it test. Time pressure and economic constraints forced a development process that was less than optimal. Nevertheless, construct-oriented studies led us to conclude that the scores measured a "perception-on-the-run" construct; they disconfirmed both plausible contaminants and the expected independence of three component constructs. Several criteria were predicted as well from the movie scores as from tests with more nearly complete research backgrounds.

Some Video Tests. I described the movie test because of firsthand knowledge of its construction and evaluation and because its research flaws could be described without embarrassing others. Videotaping is more up to date and has the further advantage of permitting more experimentation with alternative scenes and scripts.

Video tests have been reported for assessing situational judgment in customer service jobs, among others, with gratifying validity coefficients (Curtis, Gracin, & Scott, 1994; Dalessio, 1994). These tests generally use the vignette and question approach; sometimes the effectiveness of depicted behavior is rated. A video test to measure work habits and team

---

[7]Kenneth M. Alvares and I did the research reported here; it has not been previously published. The work was quite extensive, but it was done under court jurisdiction and could not be published until the case was settled. I believe the case, like an old soldier, just faded away.

skills showed interpersonal problem situations typical of those that can arise in a factory setting—differences in adherence to work standards, responsibility, and interpersonal conflict. In pilot studies, correlations with traditional ability tests were nearly zero, but correlations with a combined productivity–quality scale and with contextual criteria (ratings of communicating and solving problems and work habits) were significant. Corrected for criterion unreliability, the validity coefficient of the video test was virtually identical to that of a composite of five predictors (the video test and four standard ability tests), optimally weighted![8] Except for significantly higher mean scores for Asians, no statistically significant mean differences were found among ethnic groups or between two age groups; women did somewhat better on the average than men.

Computerized Testing

Medium Effects. Early computerized testing (computer-based testing, or CBT) did little more than put the items of a traditional test in a computer, presenting the items one at a time, getting a response (perhaps with a built-in time limit), and moving on to the next item. CBT tests usually differed from paper versions in that (a) items could not be skipped and tried again later, (b) time limits were set for items rather than for the tests as a whole, and (c) scores could be reported immediately. Another difference was physical; printing methods gave the paper versions a readability advantage over early, relatively low-resolution monitors. It is worth asking whether such differences matter in test characteristics such as mean scores or variances or the constructs measured.

Because computer use was especially important in clerical work, Silver and Bennett (1987) thought the pre-eminent Minnesota Clerical Test should itself be computerized. Two versions using computers were developed. One was a simple shift from paper to computer; the other, used as a criterion, put the original left-hand column on paper and the right-hand column on the computer—requiring the back and forth focus between hard copy and screen that characterizes many data entry and data checking jobs. The hypothesis that CBT tests were necessary for computerized jobs was not supported; validity coefficients were not significantly different for the paper test and the computer translation of it. Significant mean score differences, however, suggested that the computerized version was more difficult. Moreover, correlations were not high enough to suggest identical constructs. Other studies have reported similar findings (e.g., Green, 1988; Mazzeo, Druesne, Raffeld, Checketts, & Muhlstein, 1991).

---

[8]Further information may be obtained from Dr. David P. Jones, President, HRStrategies, Inc.

A meta-analysis reported by Mead and Drasgow (1993) found the computer versus paper effect moderated by test speededness. Where a test is essentially a power test (i.e., time limits are generous enough that nearly all examinees can finish), the mean correlation (corrected for attenuation) between scores obtained with the two media was .97. However, highly speeded tests did not correlate as well across media; the mean correlation for speeded tests was .72.

Bell Atlantic's Universal Test Battery. If a paper-and-pencil test is working well, there is little point in fixing it with a computer. If the special advantages of computerized testing make it the medium of choice, one may as well develop a new test, and evaluate it, using the computer format from the start. A wide range computerized test battery developed for Bell Atlantic has been used for more than 100 nonmanagement jobs (Hough & Tippins, 1994). Traditional test batteries, well-validated, were available for many of these jobs, but the program was administratively burdensome.

A single test battery was developed for administration on laptop computers. It consisted of nine timed cognitive ability tests and a six-scale, virtually untimed, noncognitive inventory (with an added response validity scale). It required about 2 hours to complete. All candidates for hire or transfer were to complete the entire battery although only parts of it were expected (and found) to be valid for any one job. This feature permitted placement and job counseling as well as selection and transfer decisions. The tests were essentially conventional except that they were developed, analyzed, and validated in computer form. The system used modem connections with the central office mainframe, permitting scoring to be centrally controlled regardless of the remoteness of the testing location. Computerization also permitted computer-generated reports for examinees.

Advantages of Computer-Based Testing. CBT is not necessarily superior to traditional testing; the Silver and Bennett (1987) experience shows that translating a perfectly good paper test into a computerized one may be a waste of resources. A beginning testing program, however, might well be governed by the advantages of computer forms. Among them:

1. Testing conditions are more completely standardized. Variations in clarity and manner of speaking are not controlled when different examiners present instructions or test items. Most of all, readiness of examinees to begin is not controlled by the usual "Are there any questions?" routine. CBT instructions can, as on paper tests, provide samples of what is to come; on the computer, however, incorrect responses to sample items can delay the start of the test until a sequence

of sample items, developed to address differing problems in under-standing, is handled satisfactorily. That such care in developing instruc-tions is rarely used does not remove the possibility from the list of potential advantages.

2. Examinees usually enjoy CBT more than more traditional forms. One was quoted after taking a computer adaptive test as saying, "It's faster, it's funner, and it's more easier" (quoted by Green, 1991, p. 246).

3. Johnson and Mihal (1973) found lower CBT mean differences in scores of Black and White examinees. They suggested that novelty and the reduction of negative expectations might account for the finding; I hypothesize that computer presentation reduces variance due to test-tak-ing strategies.

4. Different kinds of items can be used. Computers can present changing visual and auditory stimuli. As just one example, a mechanical knowledge test could be devised with items showing equipment in motion with questions about forces, problems, or errors in the graphic display.

5. Different, but potentially important, constructs can be measured. For example, response latency can be recorded, either to measure something akin to reaction time or as an item characteristic to be considered in scoring. Where special skills are used, mean response latency toward the end of the test can be compared to mean latency at the beginning to measure learning during the test.

6. Programs can be developed that permit consultation of reference materials (e.g., dictionaries, procedures manuals), in turn permitting items posing more complex problems. A computer-based simulation of archi-tectural practice used two monitors (Braun, 1994). One provided access to resources: excerpts from standard reference materials, prints and drawings relevant to the test projects, and a "file cabinet" with project-rele-vant written material one might find in an office filing cabinet. The other monitor represented the architect's work place where the examinee does design work according to the task posed in a project vignette. The examinee can access either monitor at any time with simple mouse use.

7. Test taking strategies can be studied on computerized tests, and perhaps scored and considered in interpreting the trait scores.

8. Test security is easier to maintain. A few computer disks can be held secure more easily than can a few hundred printed tests. Moreover, the order of items in the sequence can be scrambled.

9. Item banks can be created, calibrated according to stable item characteristics (either those of classical test theory or IRT), from which computers can draw items according to specifications to make up unique test forms for each examinee, permitting a large number of psychomet-rically equivalent forms to be generated from the bank. Item banking

therefore offers a potential advantage for both test security and the common problem of retesting. Two different candidates may see *some* common items, but item differences would be substantial enough to reduce the test security problems associated, for example, with item memorization (Bergstrom & Gershon, 1995; Gibson & Weiner, 1996; Vale, 1996).

There are, of course, disadvantages as well. One is cost—more in programming than in hardware. Another is examinee computer anxiety, either because of unfamiliarity with computers or with the type of software used. However, these disadvantages seem to be decreasing over time.

There are special problems of standardization. A full keyboard can be daunting to people unaccustomed to computer use; special keyboards are often provided to match response needs. All examinees should be provided the same basic keyboard configuration—movable to make it maximally convenient for both left- and right-handed users—or alternative response methods (e.g., touch-sensitive screens, mouse pointers, etc.). Programs should be the same, with the same hardware demands, for all candidates. Displays should have the same resolution, color, and other features. All testing stations should use the same make and model of microcomputer. These and other considerations are described in detail by Green (1990). The speed of computer obsolescence exacerbates ordinary standardization problems.

Computerized Adaptive Tests (CAT)

Conventional testing is also known as *linear testing*; all items are presented one after another to all examinees. A high ability person flies through the easy items; only hard items show just how able that person is. Linear testing is therefore an inefficient use of testing time.

Adaptive testing, on the other hand, uses a branching algorithm and, therefore, fewer items. It begins with one item of moderate difficulty; the next one chosen depends on the response given to the first one—and so on until a predetermined criterion for stopping the test has been reached. If the first item is answered correctly, the next one may be more difficult. If the next one is answered incorrectly, the third item may be between the first two in difficulty. Adaptive testing has long been used in individually administered ability tests, but it required the combination of modern computers and the development of item response theory to bring it to its current level of sophistication.

Use of IRT in CAT. When a large set of items is stored in the computer, each with the parameters of its item characteristic curve and information function, a first item can be one of several with a moderate, mid-range difficulty level. If it is answered correctly, the next item is harder. When it is answered, correctly or not, the information function of the two-item set and the person's ability level can be estimated. A third item can be chosen, based on its information function, that measures ability at that level with the greatest precision. The combined information from the three items provides a new, more precise estimate of ability and the basis for choosing the next item. This continues until the person's ability estimate does not change, or changes only within a narrow range according to a prescribed stopping rule, as shown in Fig. 11.6. The score is not the number of questions answered correctly; it is the estimated ability level. CAT abandons the idea of a standard set of items but not the idea of standardization. Item selection and scoring algorithms are standardized, as are testing conditions, instructions, and hardware specifications—so different examinees are treated by the same rules.

This oversimplified capsule of program design in CAT software has made it appear (for the sake of focus) that only item statistics are considered in item choice. Content may be considered, too. If the first few items in a test of elementary arithmetic skill have all been addition items, the program may specify that the next item is chosen not only for an appropriate difficulty parameter or information peak but also for content—it must not

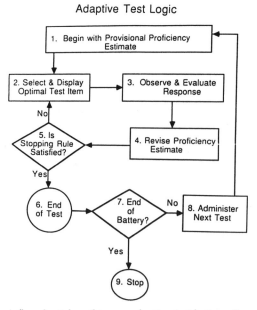

FIG. 11.6. A flowchart describing an adaptive test battery. From Thissen, D., & Mislevy, R. J. (1990). Testing algorithms. In H. Wainer et al. (Eds.), *Computerized adaptive testing: A primer* (pp. 103–135). Hillsdale, NJ: Lawrence Erlbaum Associates. Reprinted with permission.

be another addition item. Moreover, item choices should not result in overuse of some items; some algorithms have allowed some items to be ignored and others to be chosen too often.

Testlets as Items.   CAT is long past its infancy, but problems remain. A potentially serious one is the assumption that it does not matter how an item relates to other items. Despite the local independence assumption of IRT, context does matter. Location within a fixed-order test has been shown related to estimated difficulty parameters; so also may information gleaned or highlighted by a different item appearing earlier in the sequence. Despite the important concept of parameter invariance (across samples with differing ability distributions), parameter estimates are unstable enough to be influenced by such context effects (Wainer & Mislevy, 1990).

Wainer and Kiely (1987) suggested the concept of testlets as a test component with more stable characteristics. A *testlet* may consist of perhaps a half-dozen items with homogeneous content. It can be scored; the score is not the simple dichotomy of correct or incorrect responses, but graded response IRT models exist for determining the relevant parameters. The test can be initiated with a testlet of mid-level difficulty, followed by testlets chosen on the basis of score on the first one, and continuing until a stopping rule is satisfied. Testlets can be linear (items arranged in order of increasing difficulty) or hierarchical (branched as in a CAT based on individual items).

An example of a six-item testlet hierarchy is shown in Fig. 11.7. Item numbers reflect the order of difficulty, Item 7 being the hardest. The testlet is hierarchical in that, after the first level, items actually administered are chosen just as they would be in an ordinary CAT. That is, although seven items are in the testlet, the examinee responds to only three of them. Individual item responses are either correct or incorrect; the upper path results from a correct response, the lower one from an incorrect response. The eight different outcomes represent the eight possible patterns of responses to three items actually seen. Each pattern sets an ability estimate for the testlet as a whole.

The first testlet establishes an initial estimate of ability level from which the adaptive program continues from one testlet to another. Because the ability estimates from a testlet are more reliable than those from a single item, the number of testlets required to meet a reasonable stopping target is likely to be fairly small—but the total number of items used will be somewhat larger than in an item-based CAT.

CAT for Personnel Decisions.   The discussion of CAT procedures has been brief, partly because of uncertainty about its relevance to personnel assessment and decisions. Adaptive testing can maximize the precision of ability estimation at any point on the ability scale. In personnel

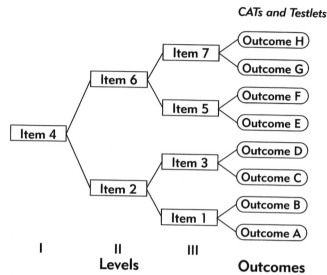

FIG. 11.7. A 3-level, 7-item, hierarchical testlet with eight possible outcomes. From Wainer, H., & Kiely, G. L. (1987). Item clusters and computerized adaptive testing: A case for testlets. *Journal of Educational Measurement, 24,* 185–201. Reprinted with permission.

decisions, however, precision is important mainly at that part of the scale where most decisions are made. If about 20% of those who apply for a job will actually be hired, and most of those offered a job will accept, precise measurement would not be very important below the 75th or above the 90th percentile. With good item parameter estimates, a brief conventional test can be developed that distinguishes well within that narrow region, but not in the low or very high scores where such differentiation amounts to little more than a nice psychometric exercise. One implication of all this is that CAT is probably not useful where cut-score use is likely, as in domain-referenced testing for mastery.

SOME SPECIAL ISSUES

Setting Cut Scores

A cut score effectively dichotomizes a score distribution, loses information, and, if not near the mean, substantially reduces validity. Dichotomization is costly and rarely recommended. Some situations, however, justify and even require a cut score:

1. Civil service jurisdictions commonly give a test to masses of candidates at one time and do not test again for a year or more. Candidates

are listed in an "eligibility list" ordered from those with the highest score to a minimum score. The minimum is a cut score below which examinees may not be listed and no one will be hired. Without a cut score, anyone who sat for the test might eventually be offered a job even if seriously unqualified; the cut score provides one basis (there are others) for deciding when to develop a new exam.

2. Licenses or certification are intended to certify a useful level of knowledge or skill, a degree of competence presumed to protect the public against incompetence. Certification is not limited to governments. Private organizations, including trade associations, may elect to certify the competence or knowledge of sales people, technical advisors, repairers, or others whose work affects customers or the public. A candidate for a job claiming certain expertise may be given performance tests or job knowledge tests to certify that expertise. Licenses and certificates are not awarded on the basis of relative standing in a distribution; in theory, at least, scores are evaluated relative to a prior standard.

3. Hiring may be cyclical. For example, if there is a policy of hiring new graduates from high schools or colleges to work as trainees, most hiring will be done at about graduation time in the spring. Openings may arise at any time through the year. By forecasting the number of openings likely to be needed before the next hiring phase, and with a fairly accurate notion of the score distribution, one can establish a cut score that will provide the necessary number of trainees who can then be assigned to more permanent positions that become available.

4. Assessment may be sequential; an assessment may be scored on a pass–fail dichotomy to decide who gets to the next step. Where many candidates compete for one or a few positions, preliminary screening may be used for all candidates, saving complete assessments (e.g., assessment centers or complex simulations) for the most promising ones. For some jobs, the preliminary assessment may look for intrinsically disqualifying considerations (e.g., poor spelling among proofreader candidates).

Cut scores are too often established merely for convenience. With them, managers getting a candidate's test score need make no judgment more taxing than whether it exceeds the cut point or not—and no HR person need try to explain more valid decision processes to the managers. This bad habit would not be worth mentioning were it not so common, so unnecessary, and so costly in terms of assessment usefulness. I say again,

> A major frustration for me these days is the almost universal and axiomatic use of cutting scores. . . . I'm referring to the kind of cut score above which anyone who comes can be hired and below which no one will be—the kind that changes a continuous score distribution to a dichotomy. A major part

of my frustration is with the reason most often given for setting cut scores: "My managers just can't handle anything more complicated than a pass-or-fail score." *I wish I knew why and when we stopped assuming that decision makers had any brains.* (Guion, 1991a, pp. 14–15)

The *Principles* (Society for Industrial and Organizational Psychology, 1987) distinguished between critical score and cutoff score. A *critical score* optimally distinguishes satisfactory (or acceptable, or successful) employees from those who are not. A *cut score* is a decision point, perhaps fluctuating as circumstances change. If applicants abound, it may be higher than a critical score; if they are scarce, it may be lower. A critical score can be used as a cut score, but they are not the same. A related term is *standard*; in educational testing, determining critical or cut scores is called "setting standards."

The Predicted Yield Method. Distributions of candidate qualifications fluctuate from week to week. Availability of openings also vary. The two may not coincide; the best applicants may present themselves when there are no immediate openings. One large company in a small town had such a problem in hiring skilled clerical workers. The best applicants graduated from high school and community colleges in the spring and usually moved away. The solution was to hire good applicants when available, place them in clerical pools, and promote or transfer employees as positions opened up. (That the pool became an excellent training program was an added bonus.)

The plan required fairly accurate prediction of the number of openings likely over the coming year and knowledge of the probable distributions of qualifications. A cut score could then be found to permit hiring enough people at graduation to meet the organization's needs for that year. This kind of cut score is not a costly dichotomization; it is based on a top-down policy. In effect, it is an answer to, "If all these people were available when we wanted them, and if we hired from the top-down as positions opened up, how far down the distribution would we go?"

Thorndike (1949) termed this the *predicted yield policy*. One need not have the limitation of hiring only in the spring to use the predicted yield method, and the time span need not be so long. The need is for reasonably accurate forecasting of positions to be filled and of score distributions. These require good record keeping and research. Number of openings is estimated by knowing of planned retirements and transfers or promotions. Records of past experience with turnover due to sickness, death, or family-related resignations can help. Reasonably accurate forecasts are more likely if informed by research on subsamples; reasons for turnover, for example, may be related to age or sex. Expected organizational changes must also be considered.

Estimating the number of available applicants requires knowledge of economic and employment trends. Local influences should be considered, such as the possible closing of a major business or arrival of a new one. Such factors influence not only an overall number of applicants but the pattern of applicant flow. Test score distributions may be different for different groups of people; they may differ substantially in different local communities. Setting useful cut scores requires realistic knowledge of local distributions, requiring reliable local norms. As time goes by, the original cut score may prove too high or too low to provide the predicted yield—or the predicted number of openings is too high or low—and adjustments may be appropriate.

Regression-Based Methods. Figure 11.8 shows four kinds of relationships. Panel *a* shows a positive, linear regression. Panel *b* shows a positive but nonlinear monotonic regression. In either case, top-down selection is appropriate; a critical score can be based on predicted criterion level.

Panel *c* is a positive monotone up to a point, after which the curve levels off and differences in X have no associated differences in Y. Above that point, people with different scores should all be considered the same.

Panel *d* (relatively rare) is nonmonotonic. The curve is positive up to a point, after which increases in X are associated with criterion *decreases*.

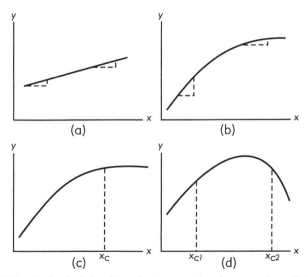

FIG. 11.8. Kinds of relationships of test scores to performance. From Guion, R. M. (1991). Personnel assessment, selection, and placement. In M. D. Dunnette & L. M. Hough (Eds.), *Handbook of industrial and organizational psychology* (2nd ed., Vol. 2, pp. 327–397). Palo Alto, CA: Consulting Psychologists Press.

In such a case, both low and high critical scores might be set to screen out extreme scorers likely to be unsatisfactory. Such patterns seem more likely with personality than with cognitive tests.

In any of these cases, it is possible to base a cut score or two on predicted levels of performance. If a criterion level can be identified that is too low, such as not being able to keep up with a work flow and resulting in lost time for others, the regression equation can be used to identify an associated critical test score or minimum qualification.

Standard Setting by Expert Judgments About Test Items. Very often standards (cut scores) must be set where no regression patterns are known. Methods for setting standards have been developed in educational testing so that performance can be measured against a performance standard rather than normatively (i.e., domain-referenced testing), and more recently, to satisfy state-mandated certification of educational attainment. More information than given here can be found in two major sources: a special issue of the *Journal of Educational Measurement* (Shepard, 1978), and a comprehensive chapter by Jaeger (1989).

Two procedures most often mentioned for setting standards are the Nedelsky and the Angoff procedures. The older Nedelsky procedure applies only to multiple-choice tests. As described by Jaeger (1989), it requires defining, identifying, and sampling a population of judges who are clearly expert in the test subject matter and also understand the kinds of applicants who would be minimally competent in their grasp of the content. *Minimally competent* may be defined in terms of local needs, and may mean minimally acceptable. Each judge must decide which response options a minimally competent person could eliminate as clearly wrong, and then, on the basis of that judgment, compute a minimum pass level for the item—the probability of a correct answer by a minimally competent person. Summing minimum pass levels across items gives the test score the expert expects from a minimally competent person. The mean of these scores across judges is a preliminary cut score.

The Angoff method has the same concerns for defining and drawing from an appropriate population of judges and for conceptualizations of minimally competent persons. It also requires for each item a direct judgment of the probability that the minimally competent person will answer the item correctly. The method is used with multiple-choice, true–false, or short-answer tests, or even work samples scored from checklist items. For each judge, summing these probabilities across all items gives that judge's estimate of the appropriate cut score; an operational cut score could be the mean of the estimates of the several judges.

A modification of the Angoff procedure adjusted judgments by including items previously used (Management Scientists, Inc., 1982). After comprehensive training, job experts made judgments about sets of items, mostly new, but including some from previous exams. For each item, they judged the percentages responding correctly among three groups: those whose performance would be unacceptable, acceptable, or better than acceptable. The average of the three judgments was compared to actual difficulty indices of the previously used items, and judgments were adjusted accordingly. Adjusted judgments defined the cut score that would best differentiate the acceptable from the unacceptable. Projected mean and variance were also computed for the new test; projections were so close to actual data that the procedure was accepted as a realistic estimate of an appropriate cut score (*Cuesta v. NY Office of Court Administration, 1987*).

Tests and Controversy

Testing, and personnel assessment generally, is and has been controversial. There are controversies among psychometrically trained experts, among people trained in different test-using disciplines, between psychometric professionals and people outside of these professions, and in society generally. In the face of all the fuss, it is strange that testing remains an important basis for so many kinds of decisions. Few people would want to get rid of various kinds of licensing exams, despite their sometimes serious deficiencies. The cry for educational proficiency exams has been translated into law in many states. Government civil service procedures using merit examination concepts grew out of disenchantment with less objective bases for selection.

In the face of controversy, it is well to remember that tests have compiled a good track record. They have successfully predicted performance on jobs and other kinds of criteria as well. Put together in a battery of tests measuring different things, groups of tests have even better records.

They are good, they are useful, but they are imperfect. Perfection cannot reasonably be expected; too many other things influence criteria for test scores to predict them perfectly. Even so, there is room for improvement. Many things we do well with tests can be done better and with greater understanding. Things we do not do so well with tests provide still greater challenges. The search for new and better ways to measure candidate qualifications, and for new and better definitions of the nature of the qualifying traits, should go forward. However, a lot of bright new ideas, once thought promising, have been tried and have withered. Psychometric history is strewn with the remnants of once grand new ideas. Many tests that were supposed to measure more important constructs than those traditionally measured have gone out of print with only negative findings resulting from their use. Item types once hailed as panaceas have left the scene in ignominious defeat. Enthusiasm for new ways, commendable as it is, is no substitute for data.

New ideas usually build on old ones. As we approach a new century, there is strong urging for new approaches to measurement and assessment, approaches that do not build on old principles but seek to replace traditional testing with new constructs and methods. Many new ideas are not as different as their enthusiastic proponents assume. Proponents should amass data to show that the expected merits of the new ideas do in fact obtain, that they match or exceed those of the old ones, and that the substitution of the new for the old does not result in losing valued merits of the old without compensating new merits. In short, new ideas in measurement should be sought, articulated, and tried. But we should not allow them to be embraced, adopted, and swallowed whole without competent trial and empirical comparison with the old.

Benefits of Coaching

In most major cities in the United States, organizations exist that purport to teach people how to take tests, especially public sector tests, and get better scores. Such training is called coaching. Does it help?

Professors persist in telling students that they should get ready for the final exam from the very first assignment on, that it represents material learned over a period of time, and that a short session of cramming (make that coaching) cannot compensate for a failure to have had the continuous learning experience. Does this apply to employment tests?

Actually, the question is simplistic, in part because such different things are called coaching. Some coaching teaches people the answers to actual items and perhaps some techniques for answering others like them. Other coaching uses long-term preparatory courses with extended instruction to enhance the abilities or knowledge being measured. Messick (1982) identified three potential aims of coaching: (a) score gain because of test familiarity and subsequent anxiety reduction, (b) gain because of improvement in the skills measured, and (c) gain because of learning test-specific strategies. The latter is probably harmful. The other two may be useful. In reviewing the research, Messick and Jungeblut (1981) found that the amount of coaching time was related to the amount of score improvement. The relationship was not linear; geometric increases in coaching time were accompanied by only equal unit increases in score gain.

To coach or not to coach is an issue not soon to be settled. Many civil service administrators and other employers oppose coaching for their tests, but many entrepreneurs produce new programs. Each new idea for coaching deserves a trial. Nevertheless, my current thinking is that job candidates are not often well-served by coaching programs. I think, admittedly without adequate evidence, that test familiarization procedures, comparable in logic to realistic job previews, should be provided to try to reduce test anxiety. For the same purpose, I recommend take-home study materials, if test content can be studied. However, such study (cramming) for a few days is not likely to increase actual abilities, or even scores on any but simple tests, and it might increase rather than reduce anxiety. Perhaps the best skill improvement will occur with physical or psychomotor abilities, but the needed training is not a simple matter of a few days with a coach and a set of weights.

Test User Qualifications

Who should buy, handle, and use tests? Are the same qualifications needed for all kinds of tests and inventories? Eyde et al. (1993) developed a book of case studies indexing cases by 86 "elements" of user responsibility and seven factors summarizing those elements (examples are in Fig. 11.9). The booklet includes not only case studies and the full list of 86 elements, but it has much more. Test users should read and follow it.

Translations of Psychometric Instruments

Multinational organizations, and some within a single country, face a special problem in testing people who speak different languages. Mere translation is not the simple matter it would appear. I was once given the example of translating a verbal test item in English into an equivalent French item. The English item depended on the ambiguity of the word *trunk*, meaning either a piece of luggage or the front end of an elephant. No corresponding French word has both meanings. Literal translations, even if possible, may not have the same psychological meaning in two languages; score equivalence is unattainable with literal translation. Translation by "centering" (getting the gist of the meaning) and acceptable back-translation into the original language seems to give equivalent meaning, but that does not assure equivalence in inferences from scores; centering may change psychometric properties dramatically, including constructs measured. Cultural differences can influence scores and their interpretation at least as much as language differences. Cross-cultural testing faces at least three kinds of problems: differences in approaches to tests, problems of test administration, and score equivalence (van de Vijer & Poortinga, 1991).

Two psychometric considerations should govern test translations. First, test item parameters must match in the original and translated versions. Item matching is best done by IRT (Hulin, Drasgow, & Parsons, 1983). Perhaps not every item would be translated to achieve precisely the same

Factor	Elements
1. Comprehensive Assessment Following up testing to get pertinent personal history data to integrate with test scores to enhance accuracy of interpretation.	23. Psychosocial history. 35. Considering patient's state. 37. Teaching research evidence and test limitations. 45. Choice of test to sample relevant behaviors. 77. Follow-up with psychosocial history. 79. Use of tests to generate hypotheses. 82. Proper reporting of clinical observations during testing.
2. Proper Test Use Accepting the responsibility for competent use of the test; exercising appropriate quality control procedures over all aspects of test use.	1. Acceptance of responsibility for competent use of the test. 7. Refraining from helping a favored person earn a good score. 8. Appropriate training and quality control over operations for all users of tests and test results.
3. Psychometric Knowledge Knowing and using correctly basic statistical principles of measurement (e.g., standard error of measurement, reliability, validity).	20. Considering errors of measurement of a test score. 32. Considering the standard error of measurement. 44. Understanding the standard error of measurement.
4. Maintaining Integrity of Test Results Correctly applying psychometric principles to the actual interpretation of test results; understanding the limitations of test scores.	39. Advising administrators about limitations of grade equivalent scores and percentile ranks for specific situations. 49. Making clear that absolute cut-off scores are questionable because they ignore measurement error.
5. Accuracy of Scoring Ensuring that all aspects of test scoring (e.g., recording, checking, correct reading of tables) are performed correctly.	55. Avoiding errors in scoring and recording. 56. Using checks on scoring accuracy. 57. Checking frequently during scoring to catch lapses. 58. Following scoring directions.
6. Appropriate Use of Norms Understanding and using different types of norms correctly, particularly in employment settings.	31. Matching person to job on aptitude validities. 59. Not assuming that a norm for one job applies to a different job.
7. Interpretive Feedback to Clients Providing correct interpretations of test scores to test takers.	71. Willingness to give interpretation and guidance to test takers in counseling situations. 72. Ability to give interpretation and guidance to test takers in counseling situations. 73. Having enough staff to provide counseling.

FIG. 11.9. Seven factors of proper test use with illustrative elements of competent test use. From Eyde, L. D. et al. (1993). *Responsible test use: Case studies for assessing human behavior.* As originally appeared in Eyde, Moreland, Robertson, Primoff, & Most (1988). Washington, DC: American Psychological Association. Copyright by the American Psychological Association. Reprinted with permission.

parameters in a 3-parameter model, but the distributions of item parameters could be kept comparable (Hambleton & Bollwark, 1991). Second, the two versions should be pretty much equally valid measures of the same constructs. Do various antecedent and subsequent correlates behave similarly? Do both versions escape the same contaminating sources of variance? Positive answers say that the tests are measuring the same constructs.

Alternatively, multinational companies can treat operations in each country as independent and develop locally valid assessment procedures. With this option, the entire test development process can take place within the culture, cultural factors influence construct definition, item writing, instruction development, and all of the developmental research. This option makes sense only if "home country" and local personnel are not competing for the same opportunities, such as promotion to a specified position. Where cross-cultural comparisons are to be made, care must be taken to make the assessments as culturally and psychometrically equivalent as possible.

REFERENCES

American Medical Association. (1977). *Guide to the evaluation of permanent impairment.* Monroe, WI: Author.

Armstrong, A. M. (1993). Cognitive-style differences in testing situations. *Educational Measurement: Issues and Practice, 12*(3), 17–22.

Arnold, J. D., Rauschenberger, J. M., Soubel, W. G., & Guion, R. M. (1982). Validation and utility of a strength test for selecting steelworkers. *Journal of Applied Psychology, 67,* 588–604.

Arvey, R. D., Strickland, W., Drauden, G., & Martin, C. (1990). Motivational components of test taking. *Personnel Psychology, 43,* 695–716.

Asher, J. J., & Sciarrino, J. A. (1974). Realistic work sample tests: A review. *Personnel Psychology, 27,* 519–533.

Barrett, G. V., & Depinet, R. L. (1991). A reconsideration of testing for competence rather than for intelligence. *American Psychologist, 46,* 1012–1024.

Barton, P. E. (1996). A school-to-work transition system: The role of standards and assessments. In L. B. Resnick & J. G. Wirt (Eds.), *Linking school and work: Roles for standards and assessments* (pp. 125–143). San Francisco: Jossey-Bass.

Bejar, I. I. (1991). A methodology for scoring open-ended architectural design problems. *Journal of Applied Psychology, 76,* 522–532.

Ben-Shakhar, G., & Sinai, Y. (1991). Gender differences in multiple-choice tests: The role of differential guessing tendencies. *Journal of Educational Measurement, 28,* 23–35.

Bennett, R. E. (1993a). On the meanings of constructed response. In R. E. Bennett & W. C. Ward (Eds.), *Construction versus choice in cognitive measurement: Issues in constructed response, performance testing, and portfolio assessment* (pp. 1–27). Hillsdale, NJ: Lawrence Erlbaum Associates.

Bennett, R. E. (1993b). Toward intelligent assessment: An integration of constructed-response testing, artificial intelligence, and model-based measurement. In N. Frederiksen, R. J. Mislevy, & I. I. Bejar (Eds.), *Test theory for a new generation of tests* (pp. 99–123). Hillsdale, NJ: Lawrence Erlbaum Associates.

Bennett, R. E., Rock, D. A., & Wang, M. (1991). Equivalence of free-response and multiple-choice items. *Journal of Educational Measurement, 28,* 77–92.

Bennett, R. E., & Ward, W. C. (Eds.). (1993). *Construction versus choice in cognitive measurement: Issues in constructed response, performance testing, and portfolio assessment.* Hillsdale, NJ: Lawrence Erlbaum Associates.

Bennett, R. E., Ward, W. C., Rock, D. A., & LaHart, C. (1990). *Toward a framework for constructed-response items* (Resch. Rep. RR-90-7). Princeton, NJ: Educational Testing Service.

Bergstrom, B. A., & Gershon, R. C. (1995). Item banking. In J. C. Impara (Ed.), *Licensure testing: Purposes, procedures, and practices* (pp. 187–204). Lincoln, NE: Buros Institute of Mental Measurement.

Braswell, J., & Kupin, J. (1993). Item formats for assessment in mathematics. In R. E. Bennett & W. C. Ward (Eds.), *Construction versus choice in cognitive measurement: Issues in constructed response, performance testing, and portfolio assessment* (pp. 167–182). Hillsdale, NJ: Lawrence Erlbaum Associates.

Braun, H. I. (1994). Assessing technology in assessment. In E. L. Baker & S. H. O'Neil, Jr. (Eds.), *Technology assessment: Vol. 1, Education and training* (pp. 231–246). Mahwah, NJ: Lawrence Erlbaum Associates.

Braun, H. I., Bennett, R. E., Frye, D., & Soloway, E. (1989). *Developing and evaluating a machine-scorable constrained constructed-response item* (Resch. Rep. 89-30. Princeton, NJ: Educational Testing Service.

Bridgeman, B. (1992). A comparison of quantitative questions in open-ended and multiple-choice formats. *Journal of Educational Measurement, 29,* 253–271.

Cascio, W. F., & Phillips, N. F. (1979). Performance testing: A rose among thorns. *Personnel Psychology, 32,* 751–766.

Chapman, J. C. (1921). *Trade tests.* New York: Holt.

Cronbach, L. J., Gleser, G. C., Nanda, H., & Rajaratnam, N. (1972). *The dependability of behavioral measurements: Theory of generalizability of scores and profiles.* New York: Wiley.

Cuesta v. State of New York Office of Court Administration, 42 EPD Section 36,949 (SD, NY, 1987).

Curtis, J. R., Gracin, L., & Scott, J. C. (1994, April). *Non-traditional measures for selecting a diverse workforce: A review of four validation studies.* Presented at the meeting of the Society for Industrial and Organizational Psychology, Nashville, TN.

Dalessio, A. T. (1994). Predicting insurance agent turnover using a video-based situational judgment test. *Journal of Business and Psychology, 9,* 23–32.

Dunnette, M. D. (1963). A modified model for test validation and selection research. *Journal of Applied Psychology, 47,* 317–323.

Ebel, R. L. (1972). *Essentials of educational measurement.* Englewood Cliffs, NJ: Prentice-Hall.

Eyde, L. D., Moreland, K. L., Robertson, G. J., Primoff, E. S., & Most, R. B. (1988). *Test user qualifications: A data-based approach to promoting good test use.* Washington, DC: American Psychological Association.

Eyde, L. D., Robertson, G. J., Krug, S. E., Moreland, K. L., Robertson, A. G., Shewan, C. M., Harrison, P. L., Porch, B. E., Hammer, A. L., & Primoff, E. S. (1993). *Responsible test use: Case studies for assessing human behavior.* Washington, DC: American Psychological Association.

Fleishman, E. A. (1988). Some new frontiers in personnel selection research. *Personnel Psychology, 41,* 679–701.

Fleishman, E. A., & Reilly, M. E. (1992). *Handbook of human abilities: Definitions, measurements, and job task requirements.* Palo Alto, CA: Consulting Psychologists Press.

French, J. W. (1965). The relationship of problem-solving styles to the factor composition of tests. *Educational and Psychological Measurement, 25,* 9–28.

Gibson, W, M., & Weiner, J.A. (1996, April). Automated test construction: A novel application of classical test theory. In W. M. Gibson (Chair), *Classical versus IRT methods: Applications in automated test construction.* Symposium at meeting of the Society for Industrial and Organizational Psychology, San Diego, CA.

Glaser, R. (1963). Instructional technology and the measurement of learning outcomes. *American Psychologist, 18,* 519–521.

Glaser, R. (1994). Criterion-referenced tests: Part I. Origins. *Educational Measurement: Issues and Practice, 13*(4), 9–11.

Glaser, R., & Klaus, D. J. (1962). Proficiency measurement: Assessing human performance. In R. Gagné (Ed.), *Psychological principles in system development* (pp. 421–427). New York: Holt, Rinehart, & Winston.

Goals 2000: Educate America Act (1994, March 31), Public Law 103-227, 108 STAT. 125.

Green, B. F. (1988). Construct validity of computer-based tests. In H. Wainer & H. I. Braun (Eds.), *Test validity* (pp. 77–86). Hillsdale, NJ: Lawrence Erlbaum Associates.

Green, B. F. (1990). System design and operations. In H. Wainer (Ed.), *Computerized adaptive testing: A primer* (pp. 23–39). Hillsdale, NJ: Lawrence Erlbaum Associates.

Green, B. F. (1991). Guidelines for computer testing. In T. B. Gutkin & S. L. Wise (Eds.), *The computer and the decision-making process* (pp. 245–273). Hillsdale, NJ: Lawrence Erlbaum Associates.

Green, B. F., & Wigdor, A. K. (1991). Measuring job competency. In A. K. Wigdor & B. F. Green, Jr. (Eds.), *Performance assessment for the workplace* (Volume II: Technical issues, pp. 53–74). Washington, DC: National Academy Press.

Guilford, J. P. (1959). *Personality*. New York: McGraw-Hill.

Guion, R. M. (1965). *Personnel testing*. New York: McGraw-Hill.

Guion, R. M. (1979). *Principles of work sample testing: III. Construction and evaluation of work sample tests*. TR-79-A10. Alexandria, VA: United States Army Research Institute for the Behavioral and Social Sciences.

Guion, R. M. (1991a, June). *What I wish I knew about assessment*. Paper presented to the International Personnel Management Association Assessment Council, Chicago, IL.

Guion, R. M. (1991b). Personnel assessment, selection, and placement. In M. D. Dunnette & L. M. Hough (Eds.), *Handbook of industrial and organizational psychology* (2nd ed., Vol. 2, pp. 327–397). Palo Alto, CA: Consulting Psychologists Press.

Guion, R. M. (1996). Evaluation of performance tests for work readiness. In L. R. Resnick & J. G. Wirt (Eds.), *Linking school and work: Roles for standards and assessment* (pp. 267–303). San Francisco: Jossey-Bass.

Hambleton, R. K. (1994). The rise and fall of criterion-referenced measurement? *Educational Measurement: Issues and Practice, 13*(4), 21–26.

Hambleton, R. K., & Bollwark, J. (1991). Adapting tests for use in different cultures: Technical issues and methods. *Bulletin of the International Test Commission, 18*(1,2), 3–32.

Hattrup, K., Schmitt, N., & Landis, R. S. (1992). Equivalence of constructs measured by job-specific and commercially available aptitude tests. *Journal of Applied Psychology, 77*, 298–308.

Hedge, J. W., Teachout, M. S., & Laue, F. J. (1990). *Interview testing as a work sample measure of job proficiency*. AFHRL-TP-89-60. Brooks Air Force Base, TX: Air Force Systems Command.

Hopkins, K. D., & Stanley, J. C. (1981). *Educational and psychological measurement and evaluation* (6th ed.). Englewood Cliffs, NJ: Prentice-Hall.

Horst, P. (1966). *Psychological measurement and prediction*. Belmont, CA: Wadsworth.

Hough, L., & Tippins, N. (1994, April). New designs for selection and placement systems: The *Universal Test Battery*. In N. Schmitt (Chair), *Cutting edge developments in selection*. Symposium at meeting of the Society for Industrial and Organizational Psychology, Nashville, TN.

Hulin, C. L., Drasgow, F., & Parsons, C. K. (1983). *Item response theory: Application to psychological measurement*. Homewood, IL: Dow-Jones-Irwin.

Jaeger, R. M. (1989). Certification of student competence. In R. L. Linn (Ed.), *Educational measurement* (3rd ed., pp. 485–514). New York: American Council on Education/Macmillan.

Johnson, D. F., & Mihal, W. L. (1973). Performance of blacks and whites in computerized versus manual testing environments. *American Psychologist, 28*, 694–699.

Koretz, D. (1993). New report on Vermont portfolio project documents challenges. *National Council on Measurement in Education Quarterly Newsletter, 1*(4), 1–2.

Koretz, D., Stecher, B., Klein, S., & McCaffrey, D. (1994). The Vermont portfolio assessment program: Findings and implications. *Educational Measurement: Issues and Practice, 13*(3), 5–16.

Lawshe, C. H. (1975). A quantitative approach to content validity. *Personnel Psychology, 28,* 563–575.

Link, H. C. (1919). *Employment psychology.* New York: Macmillan.

Linn, R. L. (1994). Criterion-referenced measurement: A valuable perspective clouded by surplus meaning. *Educational Measurement: Issues and Practice, 13*(4), 12–14.

Management Scientists, Inc. (1982). *Development/validation of written examination for uniformed court officer/senior court officer, Office of Court Administration, State of New York* (Vol. III). Philadelphia: MSI.

Martinez, M. E. (1991). A comparison of multiple-choice and constructed figural response items. *Journal of Educational Measurement, 28,* 131–145.

Mazzeo, J., Druesne, B., Raffeld, P. C., Checketts, K. T., & Muhlstein, A. (1991). *Comparability of computer and paper-and-pencil scores for two CLEP general examinations* (College Board Report No. 91-5). New York: College Entrance Examination Board.

McCormick, E. J., & Ilgen, D. R. (1980). *Industrial psychology* (7th ed.). Englewood Cliffs, NJ: Prentice-Hall.

Mead, A. D., & Drasgow, F. (1993). Equivalence of computerized and paper-and-pencil cognitive ability tests: A meta-analysis. *Psychological Bulletin, 114,* 449–458.

Mehrens, W. A. (1992). Using performance assessment for accountability purposes. *Educational Measurement: Issues and Practice, 11*(1), 3–9, 20.

Messick, S. (1982). Issues of effectiveness and equity in the coaching controversy: Implications for educational and testing practice. *Educational Psychologist, 17,* 67–91.

Messick, S., & Jungeblut, A. (1981). Time and method in coaching for the SAT. *Psychological Bulletin, 89,* 191–216.

Millman, J., Bishop, C. H., & Ebel, R. (1965). An analysis of test-wiseness. *Educational and Psychological Measurement, 25,* 707–726.

Millman, J., & Greene, J. (1989). The specification and development of tests of achievement and ability. In R. L. Linn (Ed.), *Educational measurement* (3rd ed., pp. 335–366). New York: American Council on Education/Macmillan.

Mislevy, R. J. (1993). A framework for studying differences between multiple-choice and free-response test items. In R. E. Bennett & W. C. Ward (Eds.), *Construction versus choice in cognitive testing: Issues in constructed response, performance testing, and portfolio assessment* (pp. 75–106). Hillsdale, NJ: Lawrence Erlbaum Associates.

Motowidlo, S. J., Dunnette, M. D., & Carter, G. W. (1990). An alternative selection procedure: The low-fidelity simulation. *Journal of Applied Psychology, 75,* 640–647.

Motowidlo, S. J., & Tippins, N. (1993). Further studies of the low-fidelity simulation in the form of a situational inventory. *Journal of Occupational and Organizational Psychology, 66,* 337–344.

Olian, J. D. (1984). Genetic screening for employment purposes. *Personnel Psychology, 37,* 423–438.

Osborne, H. F. (1940). Oral trade questions. In W. H. Stead & C. L. Shartle (Eds.), *Occupational counseling techniques: Their development and application* (pp. 30–48). New York: American Book.

Osterlind, S. J. (1989). *Constructing test items.* Boston: Kluwer.

Pike, L. W. (1978, January). *Short-term instruction, testwiseness, and the Scholastic Aptitude Test: A literature review with research recommendations.* Research Bulletin RB 78-2. Princeton, NJ: Educational Testing Service.

Poffenberger, A. T. (1927). *Applied psychology: Its principles and methods.* New York: Appleton.

Popham, W. J. (1974). An approaching peril: Cloud-referenced tests. *Phi Delta Kappan, 56,* 614–615.

Popham, W. J. (1978). *Criterion-referenced measurement.* Englewood Cliffs, NJ: Prentice-Hall.

Popham, W. J. (1994). The instructional consequences of criterion-referenced clarity. *Educational Measurement: Issues and Practice, 13*(4), 15–18, 30.

Reckase, M. D. (1995). Portfolio assessment: A theoretical estimate of score reliability. *Educational Measurement: Issues and Practice, 14*(1), 12–14, 31.

Resnick, L. B., & Wirt, J. G. (Eds.). (1996). *Linking school and work: Roles for standards and assessment.* San Francisco: Jossey-Bass.

Rizzuto, A. P. (1985). *Diazepam and its effects on psychophysiological and behavioral measures of performance.* Doctoral dissertation, Bowling Green State University, Bowling Green, OH.

Robertson, I. T., & Kandola, R. S. (1982). Work sample tests: Validity, adverse impact, and applicant reaction. *Journal of Occupational Psychology, 55,* 171–183.

Schmidt, F. L., Greenthal, A. C., Hunter, J. E., Berner, J. G., & Seaton, F. W. (1977). Job samples vs. paper and pencil trades and technical tests: Adverse impact and examinee attitudes. *Personnel Psychology, 30,* 187–197.

Schmit, M. J., & Ryan, A. M. (1992). Test-taking dispositions: A missing link? *Journal of Applied Psychology, 77,* 629–637.

Schmitt, A. P., & Crocker, L. (1981, April). *Improving examinee performance on multiple-choice tests.* Paper presented at the convention of the American Educational Research Association, Los Angeles.

Schwarz, S. P., McMorris, R. F., & DeMers, L. P. (1991). Reasons for changing answers: An evaluation using personal interviews. *Journal of Educational Measurement, 28,* 163–171.

Shepard, L. (Ed.). (1978). Setting standards [Special issue]. *Journal of Educational Measurement, 15*(4), 237–327.

Shepard, L. (1991). Interview on assessment issues with Lorrie Shepard. *Educational Researcher, 20*(2), 21–23, 27.

Silver, E. M., & Bennett, C. (1987). Modification of the Minnesota Clerical Test to predict performance on video display terminals. *Journal of Applied Psychology, 72,* 153–155.

Snow, R. E. (1993). Construct validity and constructed-response tests. In R. E. Bennett & W. C. Ward (Eds.), *Construction versus choice in cognitive testing: Issues in constructed response, performance testing, and portfolio assessment* (pp. 45–60). Hillsdale, NJ: Lawrence Erlbaum Associates.

Society for Industrial and Organizational Psychology. (1987). *Principles for the validation and use of personnel selection techniques* (3rd ed.). College Park, MD: Author.

Thissen, D., & Mislevy, R. J. (1990). Testing algorithms. In H. Wainer (Ed.), *Computerized adaptive testing: A primer* (pp. 103–135). Hillsdale, NJ: Lawrence Erlbaum Associates.

Thorndike, R. L. (1949). *Personnel selection: Test and measurement technique.* New York: Wiley.

Thorndike, R. L., & Hagen, E. (1955). *Measurement and evaluation in psychology and education.* New York: Wiley.

Vale, C. D. (1996, April) Generation of equivalent unique conventional test forms. In W. M. Gibson (Chair), *Classical versus IRT methods: Applications in automated test construction.* Symposium at meeting of Society of Industrial and Organizational Psychology, San Diego, CA.

van de Vijer, F. J. R., & Poortinga, Y. H. (1991). Testing across cultures. In R. K. Hambleton & J. N. Zaal (Eds.), *Advances in educational and psychological testing* (pp. 277–308). Boston: Kluwer.

Wainer, H., & Kiely, G. L. (1987). Item clusters and computerized adaptive testing: A case for testlets. *Journal of Educational Measurement, 24,* 185–201.

Wainer, H., & Mislevy, R. J. (1990). Item response theory, item calibration and proficiency estimation. In H. Wainer (Ed.), *Computerized adaptive testing: A primer* (pp. 65–102). Hillsdale, NJ: Lawrence Erlbaum Associates.

Wainer, H., & Thissen, D. (1992). *Combining multiple-choice and constructed response test scores: Toward a Marxist theory of test construction* (Program Statistics Research, Tech. Rep. 92-23). Princeton, NJ: Educational Testing Service.

Ward, W. C. (1982). A comparison of free-response and multiple-choice forms of verbal aptitude tests. *Applied Psychological Measurement, 6,* 1–11.

12

Assessment by Ratings

Ratings are ubiquitous. Ratings of job performance are common; they are also used in many other assessment methods. Raters may be peers, superiors, or subordinates; they may be outsiders used for special purposes or used because of their special expertise. One person or several, working independently or as a panel, may do the rating.

Performance ratings may be criteria or predictors. More research has been done on ratings of job performance than on ratings for other purposes, but it is relevant to other purposes and settings. This chapter emphasizes performance ratings. The focus is on ratings as assessment methods, not on their use in performance management.

Performance rating predates scientific psychology. Robert Owen, an early 19th century English industrialist and Utopian, developed a "silent monitor," a tapered wooden object about 4 inches long painted and numbered on the four sides. Each day, the supervisor would turn one side forward for each employee to indicate conduct the day before. Conduct consisted of hard work, being on time, producing well, and so forth. The black side, numbered 4, was shown for "bad" conduct; "indifferent" was blue, numbered 3; "good" was yellow and 2, and "excellent" was white with a 1. A rating could be appealed to Mr. Owen; after time for appeal elapsed, the rating was recorded in a "book of character" (Cole, 1953, p. 56).

Rating requires at least three things: (a) a source of information, preferably observation or records, (b) organizing and remembering that information in preparation for rating, and (c) quantitatively evaluating what was remembered according to some rule. Remembering observations is central. In rating a product, the time from observation to evaluation is a few minutes; for annual job performance ratings, it might be a full year.

Whatever the use, ratings are psychometric measurements, even if not very precise. Ratings are often held in low esteem as measurements. They are victim to countless forms of error, both random and systematic. Kane (1987) claimed the field of personnel psychology was stagnant because it cannot adequately measure its major dependent variable, work performance. Concerned about the many validity coefficients based on ratings as criteria, Wallace (1974) said,

> Ratings are not independent events. Each rater knows what others have said, either directly or from records, or indirectly from reputation and advancement history. Nothing succeeds like success in a business organization. ... Reliability stems not from consistency in performance but from criterion contamination.... We can do a better job of predicting what people will say about an individual's performance than the performance itself. (p. 403)

However, Campbell, McCloy, Oppler, and Sager (1992, p. 55) said, "Although ratings generally have bad press, the overall picture is not as bleak as might be expected," and claimed that ratings are more likely to be explained by ratee performance than by contaminants. Yet they agree that there are problems. Ratings need all the help they can get, and most of the attempts to help has come mainly in three forms: (a) to improve rating formats, (b) to train raters, and (c) to influence the rating process.

RATING METHODS

Ratings can be based on scales, comparisons, or checklists. They can be used for overall assessment or for assessment of more specific dimensions. Sometimes diagnostic ratings of relative strengths and weaknesses are made. Some hypotheses specify that a predictor should be related more to some aspects of work rather than others. Some call for a global, overall rating. Methods and formats should fit needs.

Graphic Rating Scales

Graphic rating scales are the most common of all rating methods. They can be used for overall ratings, but they are used more often to rate different aspects or dimensions of overall performance. Variants of graphic rating scales are shown in Fig. 12.1. The basic form is *a*, with *b* showing how ratings become numbers. Some users prefer to give more

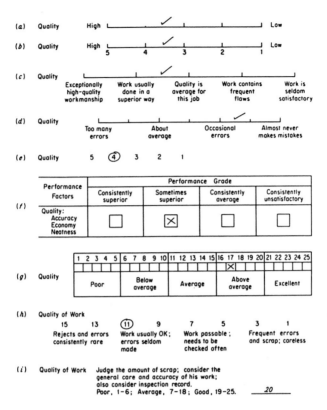

FIG. 12.1. Some variations of a graphic rating scale; each line represents one way in which a judgment of the quality of a person's work may be recorded. From Guion (1965).

structure to the scale by using verbal phrases instead of numbers, as in c. Numbers or words anchor the scale points.

The number of scale divisions varies widely; it is usually an odd number with "average" occupying a central position in the scale. More discrimination may be needed at the "above average" levels, so scales like d can put average somewhat off center. Eliminating the basic line, as in e, eliminates problems in knowing where a rater means to put a sometimes hasty check mark, as does scale f, which includes verbal anchors and more definition of the performance trait being rated. The numerical and verbal anchors are combined in g, which also uses more and finer gradations from the low to the high end of the scale. How many response categories is an optimal number? Little discrimination is possible with only two or three (although this may be enough when several ratings are added for an overall rating). It is probably absurd to ask raters to make distinctions along a 25-point range (although scale g simplifies the task by asking, in effect, for sequential judgments identifying first a group of five units). The 5-point scale is so widely used that it seems as if it had been ordained on tablets of stone. Some writers put the limit at nine scale points (Jacobs, 1986; Landy & Farr, 1980), but it is an arbitrary decision; there is little evidence that the number of scale units matters much, and the choice comes down to the researchers' preferences.

Scale *h* also combines verbal and numerical anchoring for eight possible responses. Numerical values of the responses can be changed according to the relative importance of the dimension being rated. In the example, "quality" has been prejudged to be worth a maximum of 15 points; other dimensions might have a maximum value of 8 or 10 or 30 or more points in a differential weighting scheme. If, for example, "cooperation" is deemed worth 25 points, the scale would have different numerical values, but still placed in eight response positions. Scale *i* entirely abandons the visual scale; it does not aid the rater by dividing the scale visually into five broader categories. It does, however, further structure the rating task by defining more clearly what is to be rated.

These variations show that the rater's task can be changed by changing (a) the nature and clarity of the anchors that define the values at points along the scale, (b) the nature of the required response, and (c) the clarity of the definition of the dimension to be rated. The developer of a graphic rating scale should try to avoid ambiguity; beyond that, the research literature gives little help in choosing one format over another.

But format can influence ratings. Using a 9-point scale, Madden and Bourdon (1964) asked groups of raters to rate 15 different occupations on seven dimensions. Each group was given a different scale format, but the differences were not dramatic. Some lines were horizontal, some vertical; some had clearly marked scale points, others did not. Some vertical scales used values from +4 through 0 to –4; others used 1–9; one of the latter put 1 (*very much less than average*) at the top, and another at the bottom. Main effects were found for occupations and dimensions, but the biggest main effect was for scale format despite the relatively trivial differences!

Employee Comparisons

Another well-established practice compares the ratee to others, either on global, overall performance or on multiple dimensions. The usual result is a ranking of ratees, achieved in different ways by different methods.

Method of Rank Order. Ratees might be listed on a sheet of paper, and raters may be asked to put the number 1 by the name of the best of the lot, a 2 by the next best, and so on through the list. Names might be placed on cards to be arranged. One recommended procedure is alternation ranking.

(I have used it with good interrater reliability with more than 40 people to be ranked.) Names of ratees are placed on cards and arranged in random order. When the dimension to be rated (e.g., conscientiousness, or overall job performance) is understood, the rater first identifies the best of the lot on that dimension and then the poorest. Cards with these names are pulled and the sorting has begun. Of the remaining names, the rater again selects the best and the poorest and places those cards accordingly. The process of alternating from best to worst continues until all have been ranked. The task gets progressively harder; extreme judgments are easy, but differences near the center of the distribution are harder to identify.

Ranking provides only an *ordinal* scale; one that ranks people (or objects) but gives no information about the extent of differences between them. The difference between the person ranked 1 and the one ranked 2 may be enormous or trivial; there is no way to know. *Interval* scales have units of measurement and show the degree of separation between cases. If one may assume a normal distribution of the dimension in the group, ranks can be converted to an interval scale with the standard deviation (in z scores) as the assumed unit of measurement. For example, Fig. 12.2 shows what happens in normalizing the ranks of 10 actors. A "correct" rank order (based on rank ordering by 100 judges) is shown in *a*. Ranks assigned by a rater whose rankings were correct are shown in *b* as equal steps to suggest the ordinal nature of the rankings.

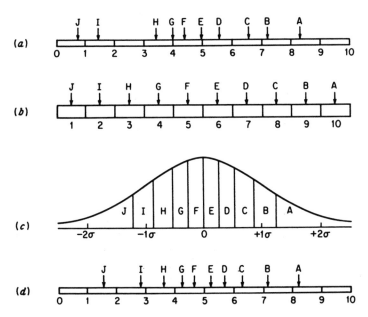

FIG. 12.2. Normalized-rank scaling. From Guilford, J. P. (1954). *Psychometric methods* (2nd ed.). New York: McGraw-Hill. Reprinted with permission.

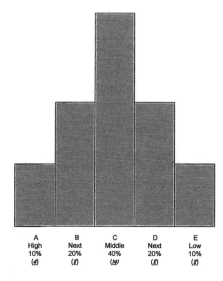

A	B	C	D	E
High	Next	Middle	Next	Low
10%	20%	40%	20%	10%
(4)	(8)	(14)	(8)	(4)

FIG. 12.3. A sample form for forced distribution ratings; numbers in parentheses show how a rater with 38 people to rate should distribute them. From Guion (1965).

Assuming normality, the 10 positions can also be shown, as in c, by dividing the area under the curve into 10 equal areas. The center of each area, projected to the base line, gives an actor a z score; convertible to any preferred standard scale, in this case, a C scale with a mean of 5 and a standard deviation of 2, shown in d (Guilford, 1954).

Method of Forced Distribution. When many people are to be rated and fine distinctions are not needed, gross ranking can be done with a forced distribution. This is a variant of graphic rating scales in that each person is assigned to a category in frequencies that mimic the assumption of a normal distribution. A number of categories is chosen (typically five, rarely more than nine), and proportions of distributions (translated into frequencies) to be placed in each category are specified. A 5-category example is shown in Fig. 12.3. A rater with 38 names to rank writes the names of the four top people in column A, the names of the next best eight people in column B, and so on.

Method of Paired Comparisons. Each ratee can be compared to each of the others in a set. For each pair of names, the rater indicates the better one on some specified dimension; the top of the rank order is the one chosen most frequently. The same name should not appear in two consecutive pairs; each person should be listed first and second equally often. There might be a lot of pairs; if five people are to be compared, there are 20 pairs of names. Ten people require 45 pairs, 190 pairs for 20 people.[1] Lawshe and Balma (1966)

---

[1]These numbers assume that each pair is compared only once; the number of pairs is $n(n - 1)/2$, where n is the number of people to be ranked. Every pair can be listed twice using both orders of presentation, but this requires twice as many pairs.

provided tables for setting up such pairs. The number of times a given name is preferred can be transformed into a standard score scale, often with a mean of 50 and standard deviation of 10.

With a long list of people to be compared, the amount of time required can get out of hand. Reasonable people disagree about how long is too long. Guilford (1954) put the limit at about 15, but Lawshe, Kephart, and McCormick (1949) reported that a list of 24 names (276 pairs) was rated reliably in 30 minutes—not an excessively wearying task. However, the required number of pairs can be reduced (see, e.g., McCormick & Bachus, 1952; McCormick & Roberts, 1952).

Prescaled Checklists

Ratings can be based on attitude scaling methods; the two most widely used are the method of equal-appearing intervals (Thurstone, 1928) and the method of summated ratings (Likert, 1932). They both apply psychometric methods to ratings, although differing in sophistication, and both may serve as foundations for other rating procedures.

Method of Equal-Appearing Intervals. A checklist can be given to a rater who simply checks the items that describe the person being rated. The items are previously scaled on the idea that equally often noticed differences are equal (Thurstone, 1928). In this procedure, a judge sorts statements into piles representing steps judged to be equal on, say, an 11-point scale.[2] A very favorable statement may be placed in pile 10 or 11; a very unfavorable one belongs in pile 1. When all judges in a group have recorded their judgments, the mean and standard deviation of judged scale values (or median and semi-interquartile range) are computed for each statement. The item's scale value is the mean (or median); the standard deviation (or semi-interquartile range) indicates the item's ambiguity. The least ambiguous statements throughout the scale are assembled into a checklist. An example is shown in Fig. 12.4. The rater would see the statements within the frame of Fig. 12.4, not the scale values or variances; an operational checklist would not include the high variance item, "conduct borders on insubordination."

After descriptions have been checked, a final score (rating) is computed. The recommended scoring procedure requires the neutral value (6 in the 11-point case) to be subtracted from the scale value of each item checked; the score is the algebraic sum of these positive and negative

---

[2]The sorting procedure described here is traditional but not really necessary. Scales are often smaller, and judgments can be obtained equally well by listing the statements, following each with the number series from 1 to 7 (or whatever range of values is being used); the judge simply circles the desired number (Prien & Campbell, 1957; Seigel & Seigel, 1962). Many other variations have been used.

Item	Scale value		Variance
___ Makes costly errors of judgment in the work	1.4		.33
✓ Does as little as possible	1.9	−4.1	1.39
✓ Plays favorites...	2.6	−3.4	1.45
___ Makes unreasonable requests....................................	3.0		1.60
✓ Sizes up people poorly..	3.4	−2.6	.93
___ Conduct borders on insubordination	3.6		5.35
✓ Is inclined to be impatient with others	4.2	−1.8	.66
___ Is self-conscious in the presence of superiors...............	5.0		2.15
___ Is very outspoken..	5.7		3.01
___ Conceals own weaknesses very effectively......................	6.4		3.14
✓ Is almost never late for work..................................	6.8	+.1	2.16
___ Can stand criticism without feeling hurt.....................	7.4		1.94
___ Keeps a firm hold without becoming unreasonable	7.8		2.19
___ Praises good work without becoming flattering	8.4		2.04
✓ Understands the problems of other departments well.......	9.0	+3.0	2.10
___ Shows remarkable clarity in thinking a problem through...	9.4		1.64
___ Is a "born leader"..	10.0		1.65
___ Is destined for a brilliant future	10.6		.94

Total score ___−8.1___

FIG. 12.4. Checklist statements scaled by the method of equal-appearing intervals. Adapted from Uhrbrock, R. S. (1950). Standardization of 724 rating scale statements. *Personnel Psychology, 3*, 285–316. Reprinted with permission.

values (Jurgensen, 1949). The numerical rating is determined by someone with a scoring key, someone other than the rater.

Measuring item ambiguity is a key feature of the method. If a word means different things to different people, it is a source of unreliability. For example, the statement, "conduct borders on insubordination," may mean troublemaker behavior to one rater and to another a commendable independence that does not cross the border. In contrast, the statement, "does as little as possible," means about the same to everyone.

Preliminary scaling may be unnecessary; Uhrbrock (1950, 1961) published, first, 724 statements and, later, 2,000 more, each with mean and variance of judgments. The statements are a mixed set of descriptions of behavior, personality, and general impressions.[3] Prien and Campbell (1957) checked the stability of the scale values of a sample from the first set of items, using a different method and judges from a different population; their scale values correlated .97 with those reported by Uhrbrock (1950). Social changes in the intervening years may have changed scale values of some items appreciably; new research may be needed to identify stable

---

[3]Earlier (Guion, 1965), I recommended using only the descriptions of behavior. Subsequent cognitive research, described in a later section of this chapter, suggests that ratings apparently based on behavioral statements may actually be based mainly on general impressions, so perhaps these statements would be just as useful.

Performance Rating Form
for
Patrol Officers

Officer's Name_____Badge No._____

Rater's Name_____District _____

(Job Competence Scale)

1. This officer's reports are clear and to the point.

   Strongly Agree   Agree   Unsure   Disagree   Strongly Disagree

2. This officer gives court testimony completely and precisely, with good recall.

   Strongly Agree   Agree   Unsure   Disagree   Strongly Disagree

3. When confronted with a set of completely new circumstances, this officer grasps the situation very quickly.

   Strongly Agree   Agree   Unsure   Disagree   Strongly Disagree

4. This officer knows how and when to search a suspect in making an arrest.

   Strongly Agree   Agree   Unsure   Disagree   Strongly Disagree

5. This officer has a firm working knowledge of police procedures as outlined in general orders, special orders, etc.

   Strongly Agree   Agree   Unsure   Disagree   Strongly Disagree

FIG. 12.5. Sample items for a rating procedure based on the method of summated ratings.

items. Drastic changes may be few; scale values tend to be independent of the attitudes and biases of the judges (cf. Prothro, 1955).

Method of Summated Ratings. Item responses may use a graphic rating scale, as in Fig. 12.5. The rater indicates (a) a level of agreement with the statement as a description or perhaps (b) frequency of behavior described with categories. Each response has a numerical value; those for desirable behavior may range from 5 (*always*) to 1 (*never*). Values are reversed for undesirable items. Neutral items give no hint of the appropriate direction for scoring, so items must clearly be either favorable or unfavorable; Pedhazur and Schmelkin (1991) recommended equal numbers of favorable and unfavorable items. The final numerical rating is the sum of the values of the response categories chosen by the rater—hence, summated ratings.[4]

---

[4]In measuring attitudes, the item response scale is often given as ranging from "Strongly Agree" through "Undecided" to "Strongly Disagree"; the abbreviations for a five-response scale are typically SA, A, U, D, SD. Many people refer to a single item using the SA to SD response scale as a "Likert-type scale." This is a betrayal of ignorance. A Likert-type scale is a multiple-item, summated-response scale. It is better simply to call it a summated response scale.

Item analysis is required, usually item-total correlations, with poor items deleted. A dubious advantage of the method is that it can be used without prior pilot studies; the item analysis can use the same data used in hypothesis testing.

Items for performance ratings should be based on job analysis defining a content domain to be assessed. Items written to fit aspects of a job content domain can be interpreted with reference to the defined domain, that is, domain-referenced interpretations are feasible. Ranking or scaling by equal-appearing intervals lead generally to norm-referenced inferences.

Behavioral Descriptions

It seems reasonable to assume that raters can offer better assessments if they avoid glittering generalities or ambiguities and describe specific on-the-job behavior or outcomes. In their landmark article, Smith and Kendall (1963) described the use of relatively unambiguous behavioral anchors for graphic rating scales. Their method is more than just another format; it is a system of domain sampling, of engaging raters in the rating process, and of developing anchors for rating scales that are likely to be meaningful and clear to the raters who use them. A trend toward a behavioral focus was already apparent (e.g., Kirchner & Dunnette, 1957; Sisson, 1948). The Smith–Kendall approach was unique and uniquely influential, not because the behavioral emphasis was new, but because it was thoroughly embedded in a systematic process.

Behaviorally Anchored Rating Scales (BARS). Smith and Kendall (1963) described a logic of rating and a procedure for developing a rating system. Many rating scales have been said to follow the Smith and Kendall approach, but they do only if using a full system of supervisory observation, recording, and rating of behavior. It was the form, and its use of scaled behavioral anchors, that attracted attention and resulted in the generic term *behaviorally anchored rating scales* or BARS. The many rating methods called BARS, and some criticisms of BARS not relevant to the procedures recommended by Smith and Kendall, called forth a clarification by Bernardin and Smith (1981). They pointed out that the Smith–Kendall approach was a sequence beginning with observation followed in order by inference, scaling, recording, and summary rating.[5]

Supervisors do not rate performance in a vacuum; the evaluation process is not confined to the time spent completing a rating form. The Smith–Kendall procedure assumes that supervisors are fairly bright peo-

---

[5]Some say that the method has evolved, and that evolution accounts for the variety. It can be said more accurately that it has been distorted by treating it merely as another rating format, without treating the form as part of a system.

ple, who know the demands of the jobs involved, who can articulate those demands in terms of performance characteristics or dimensions, who have watched people meet or fail to meet the performance demands, and who can draw reasonable inferences about the kinds of job behavior various workers might exhibit. Moreover, the procedure assumes that these bright people can approach consensus on interpretations of performance behaviors without having them imposed by an outside researcher. This implies not only the assumption but acceptance of the idea that potential raters may have valid implicit theories of performance. The procedure therefore calls for potential raters to make implicit theories explicit by expressing, in their own terms, the kinds of behavior that represent different levels or kinds of performance.

Several approaches to rating were rejected. Ordinary graphic scales, with ratings limited to specific points on the 5- or 7- or 9-point scale were rejected as too confining; a continuous scale, where raters could assign values other than the anchored scale points, was preferred. Scaling of critical incidents was rejected because a specific incident might not occur in a specific situation, and critical incidents tend toward extremes rather than in the ordinary range where most people do their work. Forced choice, a procedure popular among researchers at the time, was rejected largely because of user resistance to it.

For supervisory ratings of nurses, they chose a vertical graphic rating scale with behavioral descriptions appearing as anchors at different heights to indicate differing levels of the performance characteristic being rated. Performance characteristics (the dimensions to be rated) and the behavioral descriptions related to them were to be developed, not by the researchers, but by supervisors. Smith and Kendall (1963) did not use the term, "behaviorally anchored rating scales"; their title referred to reducing anchor ambiguity and to "retranslation of expectations," identifying key provisions of their method. First, the behavioral anchors were not intended to describe behavior a rater had actually observed; they were descriptions of behavioral "expectations" at different levels of performance on specified dimensions—examples that might be anticipated or "expected" of a ratee at any of these levels, even if they did not actually occur. They were "expectations" in the sense of "That's just the sort of thing you come to expect from Joe."[6] These examples

represent not actual observed behaviors but inferences from observations. Raters are asked to decide whether a given behavior they have observed

---

[6]I've experienced some difficulty with an ambiguity in the term "expect." Raters have told me that they *expect* every ratee to perform at the top of every scale; the implication is that they expect this even from ratees who are unlikely to perform that well. Expectations, in the Smith–Kendall sense, are anticipations of reality more than idealistic dreams of job demands or obligations.

would lead them to expect behavior like that in the description. Instead of statements such as "shows interest in patients' description of symptoms," the anchors consist of expectations such as "If this nurse were admitting a patient who talks rapidly and continuously of her symptoms and past medical history, could be expected to look interested and listen." Calling for the rater to make such predictions implies that he is willing to infer from observations of behavior, that he has his own—at least implicit—belief about the intercorrelation of behaviors. The present procedure gambles that among a relatively homogeneous group of judges such as head nurses, these beliefs will be reasonably well standardized. (Smith & Kendall, 1963, pp. 150–151)

The second key provision is *retranslation*—a procedure to assure that behavioral statements originally written for a certain dimension are seen by others as illustrations of that dimension. The procedure is analogous to that in translating a passage from one language into another. A first group of judges writes behavioral expectations to fit each dimension. A second, independent, group of judges (a) reads statements for all dimensions, mixed together in random order, (b) discusses definitions of the dimensions for a common understanding, and then (c) independently allocates each statement to a dimension. A "good" item is allocated by most judges to the dimension for which it was developed. If there is no modal agreement about where it belongs, the statement is dropped. An entire dimension may be dropped if items written for it are not generally assigned to it.

The third key provision minimizes ambiguity of scale value using the method of equal-appearing intervals. The variance of judgments is a measure of the ambiguity of the statement; high variance statements are eliminated.

A fourth feature of the Smith–Kendall procedure is usually ignored. It permits, and I think should require, raters to give at least one example of ratee behavior actually observed for each dimension rated. It could be inserted at that place on the scale that appropriately identifies its position relative to the defining anchors. With this feature, it is clear that the Smith–Kendall procedure is more than just another rating format; it is a system of stimulus material (the form) being developed from the informed observations and inferences of potential raters and used with records of continued observations by actual raters.

The procedure, in general terms, can be outlined as follows:

1. *Convene one or more groups of potential raters.* These may be some of the first line supervisors who will ultimately use the rating system and who represent various organizational locations or entities.

2. Using conference procedures, *develop a list of the performance characteristics (dimensions or constructs) that should be evaluated.* Reduce the

list to the most common or most important ones, but retain terminology used and agreed on by the potential raters.

3. In each group, *develop definitions of high, low, and acceptable performance for each dimension.*

4. In each group, for each dimension, *develop lists of behavioral examples of high, low, and acceptable performance.* For many examples, a brief account of the situation in which the behavior occurred may be necessary for clarity. Edit the behavioral examples into the form of behavioral expectations. Some such editing might be done within groups, but much of it is likely to be done later by the researchers. In any case, the key words of potential raters should be retained.

5. *Give the lists of behavioral expectations and the dimension definitions to one or more new groups of potential raters not included in the first groups.* These groups may meet physically to discuss definitions, or the lists may be mailed to them; each person in the group should work independently. The lists should be in more or less random order. A prior criterion of agreement might be a set percentage (e.g., 80%) of the judges allocating the item to its original dimension; items not meeting the criterion are eliminated. Likewise, a prior criterion can be set to identify the proportion of behavioral examples written for a dimension that must be allocated to that dimension; dimensions that fail to meet the criterion may be eliminated. This process should not be excessively mechanical; judgment is useful. Dimensions may be combined, definitions may be edited, and some intermediate data collection may be needed.

6. *Designate judges among potential raters to identify the behavioral examples, within each dimension, that describe a worker whose performance is outstanding and another whose performance is unsatisfactory.* The difference in the frequency of mention is an index of item discrimination power.

7. *Give statements that survived the preceding steps to judges from another group of potential raters for scaling by the method of equal appearing intervals.* Provide the scale definition and definitions of high, low, and acceptable levels of performance; a 9-point scale is convenient. It is useful to offer distinctions between the dimension at hand and other dimensions with which it might be confused. Items with relatively large variances are eliminated. Items retained should have minimal overlap in the dispersions of scale value judgments.

8. *Develop and distribute a final rating form to raters before ratings are due.* This provides time for familiarization with the dimensions, for observing behavior among the workers to be rated, and for recording observations. The form typically uses a vertical scale with limiting values (in the Smith–Kendall report) of 0 and 2.0, marked off in increments of .25. This is a 9-point scale, but the decimal notation seems to encourage the use

of intermediate values not explicitly identified or anchored by scaled expectations on the printed form. The form should give definitions (definition of the dimension generally and of high, low, and acceptable performance), the array of scaled expectations, space to write in some actual observations, and space to record the rating.

The procedure is clearly time consuming. When an ordinary graphic rating scale can be developed by one person in a matter of minutes, the convening of groups of experts, often from distant locations, the mailing of materials and the follow-ups required to get them back, and the time spent in data analysis may seem excessive. Perhaps it is. But if the result is a set of performance assessments that are more reliable, more valid, and more easily interpreted, it may well be worth the extra effort. Many people have used shortcuts in developing BARS. I admit (with embarrassment) to having had the item allocation and scaling done simultaneously by the same judges. The effects of such shortcuts are unknown.

Figure 12.6 is an example of a rating form developed by using in part the methods proposed by Smith and Kendall (1963). It is a bad example because it is based on some procedural shortcuts and because it used only those parts of the system that lead to a form, not the system as a whole. It has no provision for recording actual observations, for example. The research leading to it was described by Landy and Guion (1970); it was designed for peer ratings of work motivation among engineers. In calling it a bad example, I am not disclaiming the research; indeed, it is a good example of a behaviorally anchored rating scale. It is a bad example only because of the overall Smith–Kendall approach.

This is not contradictory. The term BARS has come to mean a kind of rating scale format that uses only some of the Smith–Kendall procedures. Figure 12.6 illustrates a BARS format; it used the Smith–Kendall procedures for scale definitions and for generating, retranslating, and scaling behavioral expectations. It does not illustrate a procedure for getting continuous observations and recording them as part of the rating process (Bernardin & Smith, 1981). Note, however, a difference in the form from traditional graphic scales: the scale separation marks are not the scale points that are anchored. True, there are very general descriptions apparently anchoring the top, bottom, and midpoint of the scale (shown on the left).[7] Instead, the scale values anchored are those of the behavioral examples, shown by the arrow pointing from the statement to the scale. A rater can decide which statements exemplify the kinds of behavior one

---

[7]For no good reason, I now wish that we had laid this out so that the three general descriptors were identified with top, mid, and bottom thirds of the scale instead of using these more precise-appearing arrows. I am not at all sure that it matters, however.

Persistence

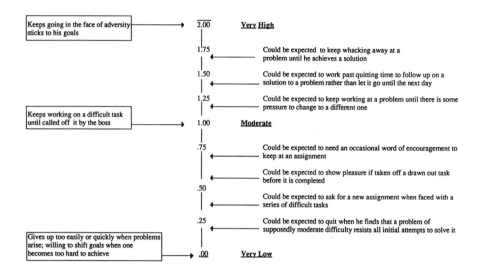

Rating:_____

FIG. 12.6. One example of a behaviorally anchored rating form devised using some key features of the retranslation of expectations; it is a form for measuring an aspect of motivation, work persistence, in a group of engineers.

might expect from the ratee. There may be one such statement, or there may be several. If several, the rater might do some sort of rough mental averaging, with some sort of rough mental weighting. (Phrases such as "some sort of" or "rough" are intended to convey the subjectivity and judgment required in the use of this form.)

A different format, still based in part on the Smith and Kendall (1963) method, is shown in Fig. 12.7. Like the other example, the rating scale is vertical, and it has nine points, ranging in this case from 1 to 9. There are eight behavioral statements, but these differ in that (a) they are explicit rather than "expected" behaviors (implying that the rater should have observed them if the ratee behaved in that way), and (b) there are no arrows—the behavior statements do not anchor precise points on the scale. Many other examples, all different, could be offered.

We must not overemphasize the form over the system. Patricia Smith and I have developed a performance evaluation system for a local police department. Ratings are made after each 28-day duty cycle. In addition to the rating forms, the system requires supervising sergeants to keep

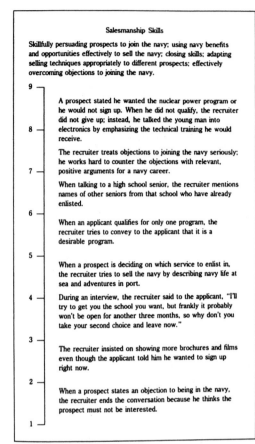

FIG. 12.7. A behaviorally anchored rating scale for assessing "salesmanship skills" of Navy recruiters. From Borman, W. C. (1986). Behavior-based rating scales. In R. A. Berk (Ed.), *Performance assessment: Methods and applications* (pp. 100–120). Baltimore: Johns Hopkins University Press. Reprinted with permission.

records of observations of good and poor behavior on the job; sergeants are evaluated by their own supervisor on how well they have made those observations. Sergeants are expected to discuss the observations with the officers involved, as soon as feasible, to encourage continued development of police skills. At rating time, they record on the rating form at least some of these observations of the ratee (and perhaps observations from other sergeants), and assign scale values to them before making summary ratings.

Behavioral Observation Scales (BOS). Instead of largely unobserved behavioral expectations, Latham and Wexley (1981) rated actually required job behaviors, grouping them for specific job dimensions. Their scales are called *Behavioral Observation Scales* (BOS). Where Smith and Kendall (1963) used Thurstone's method of equal-appearing intervals for scaling behavior expectations, the BOS approach used Likert's method of summated ratings to rate aspects of job performance. The response scale is frequency of observation, a 5-point scale ranging from 1 (*almost never*) to 5 (*almost always*) as shown in Fig. 12.8. The five points are defined in terms of the percent of the time the behavior is observed. Latham and Wexley (1981) suggested percentages of 0–64% for (*almost never*) through 65–74%, 75–84%, 85–94%, and 95–100% (*almost always*); they have also reported using a straightforward 20% increment for each scale point.

The response scale does not have to be a frequency scale. In skilled trades, for example, it might refer to the cost of errors attributed to not carrying out the behavior or carrying it out poorly. For customer service personnel, it might call for a judgment of impact on customer relations.

BOS can be developed in less time than BARS because prior item scaling is not needed. If job analysis is well-done and well-organized, behavioral statements should be prepared with minimal effort and time. Job analysis surveys may be too elemental; if so, job experts may consolidate elementary items into broader, more comprehensive statements. Items are usually considered equally weighted, but differential weights could be assigned by expert judgment. The job relevance of the ratings is obvious.

---

1. Overcoming resistance to Change*

  (1) Describes the details of the change to subordinates.

       Almost Never   1   2   3   4   5   Almost Always

  (2) Explains why the change is necessary.

       Almost Never   1   2   3   4   5   Almost Always

  (3) Discusses how the change will affect the employee.

       Almost Never   1   2   3   4   5   Almost Always

  (4) Listens to the employee's concerns.

       Almost Never   1   2   3   4   5   Almost Always

  (5) Asks the employee for help in making the change work.

       Almost Never   1   2   3   4   5   Almost Always

  (6) If necessary, specifies the date for a follow-up meeting to respond the employee's concerns.

       Almost Never   1   2   3   4   5   Almost Always

                            Total=_____

Below Adequate	Adequate	Full	Excellent	Superior*
6-10	11-15	16-20	21-25	26-30

*Scores are set by management.

FIG. 12.8. A behavioral observation scale for assessing a manager's skill in overcoming resistance to change. From Latham, G. P., & Wexley, K. N. (1981). *Increasing productivity through performance appraisal.* Reading, MA: Addison-Wesley. Reprinted with permission.

When ratings have been collected, item analysis (variability and item-total correlations) can identify nondifferentiating items. Removal of these can result in spreading out the range of actual ratings (Latham & Wexley, 1981). The method is generally norm-referenced; its purpose is to differentiate between people who perform at different levels. If the ratings form a criterion measure for validation, norm-referencing is fully appropriate. If, however, the purpose is to determine adequacy of individual performance or to serve as a reference in developing standards (for hiring, for promotion, for tenure, etc.), then a domain-referenced interpretation seems better; in such cases, item analysis may be unwise if it eliminates important items which nearly everyone does frequently or well.

Behavior Summary Scales (BSS). Assume a rating scale like row *h* in Fig. 12.1, where each of a few descriptors covers a range of scale values. Now replace those relatively vague descriptors with a set of behavioral statements, each of which consolidates or summarizes a larger number of highly specific behavioral examples. The result could be a *Behavior Summary Scale* (BSS) like that shown for Navy recruiters in Fig. 12.9 (Borman, 1986).

To develop these scales, expert recruiters generated hundreds of examples of specific behavior in a 2-day workshop; others were derived from stories told by recruits about experiences with recruiters. Content analysis resulted in nine performance categories. Eliminating redundancies and retranslating the remainder resulted in a pool of 352 examples. In BARS development, a few of these with the least variance in scale values, with scale values scattered nicely throughout the range, would be used. Instead, the group described by Borman tried to write more general summaries so that the summaries would represent, as much as possible, the content of all 352 examples. It took two steps. First, all examples were grouped into four levels as shown in Fig. 12.9; then, three statements were written describing the content of examples at each level.

Other Proposed Rating Methods

Several other approaches to rating, especially to rating performance, are briefly mentioned; these approaches appear in the literature but may need some description. They are not widely used, in some cases because early enthusiasm for them has not endured.

Forced Choice Scales. Finding at the outbreak of World War II that performance ratings used by the United States Army did not help distinguish officers ready for promotion from others, Sisson (1948) developed a new, more differentiating system known as *forced choice*

Establishing and Maintaining Good Relationships in the Community

Contacting and working effectively with high school counselors, newspaper editors, radio and TV personnel, and others capable of helping recruiters to enlist prospects; building a good reputation for the navy by developing positive relationships with persons in the community; establishing and maintaining good relationships with parents and family of prospects; presenting a good navy image in the community.

9 or 10
Extremely Effective Performance

Is exceptionally adept at cultivating and maintaining excellent relation-ships with school counselors, teachers, principals, police, news media persons, local business persons, and other persons who are important for getting referrals and free advertising	Is innovative in informing the public about the navy; actively promotes the navy and makes friends for the navy while doing it; always distributes the most current navy information	Volunteers off-duty time to work on community projects, celebrations, parades, etc.

6, 7, or 8
Effective Performance

Spends productive time with individuals such as police, city government, or school officials; may lunch with them, distribute calendars, appointment books, buttons, etc., to them, and/or invite them for cocktails	Arranges for interested persons such navy activities as trips to the Naval Academy; keeps relevant persons informed of navy activities	Encourages principals, counselors, and other persons important to a prospect to call if they have any questions about the navy

3, 4, or 5
Marginal Performance

Contacts school officials only sporadically; keeps them waiting for information they want; relationships with counselors, teachers, etc., and persons important to an applicant or recruit are distant and under developed	Is not alert to opportunities to promote the navy; rarely volunteers off-duty time to promote the navy and is unenthusiastic when approached to do something for the community; rarely accepts speaking invitations	Is, at times, discourteous to persons in the community; for example, sends form letters to persons who assisted him or other navy recruiters; is not always alert to the family's desire for more information about the navy and the program in which their son or daughter enlisted

1 or 2
Ineffective Performance

Does not contact high school counselors; does not accept speaking engagements; drives around in car instead of getting out and meeting people	Alienates persons in community or persons important to an applicant by ignoring them, not answering their questions, responding rudely, demanding information, encouraging high school students to drop out of school; sometimes does not appear at recruiting presentations for which he or she is scheduled	Presents negative image of the navy by doing things like driving while intoxicated or speeding and honking impatiently at other drivers; may express dislike for the navy or recruiting

FIG. 12.9. A behavior summary scale to rate Navy recruiter performance. From Borman, W. C. (1986). Behavior-based rating scales. In R. A. Berk (Ed.), *Performance assessment: Methods and applications* (pp. 100–120). Baltimore: Johns Hopkins University Press. Reprinted with permission.

ratings. The method used tetrads of four descriptive statements, each with two statements about equally favorable and two equally unfavorable. Prior research determined, for every statement, a preference index (P) for favorability and a discrimination index (D) of how well the statement distinguished between those independently identified as superior and others. Let + indicate high preference or discrimination and − indicate low; every tetrad had statements described as P+D+, P+D–, P–D+, and P–D–. The rater chose one statement as most descriptive and another as least descriptive, without knowing the scoring key (which was limited to discriminating items). The method gave valid ratings, but raters resisted use of a system they could not control.

Distributional Rating Method. Performance is not uniform in any respect from week to week, or day to day, or even hour to hour. It varies over time on all performance dimensions, yet virtually all of the rating methods that have been described give a most typical sort of rating. It is like giving exclusive attention to the mean of a distribution with no attention at all to its variance.

Kane (1986) developed performance distribution assessment based on the obvious notion of variability in job performance over time. It is quite complex and not widely used; I do not describe the method. Its logic stems from a presumed distribution of outcome efficacy levels, implying a scale from least to most effective outcomes of performance. A record of outcomes (in memory, diary, or whatever) provides an outcome distribution and the foundation for this model of the nature of performance.

Comment: Methods and Moratoria

At this point, a proper textbook author would offer lists of relative advantages and disadvantages of the several methods and, perhaps, recommend some of them over others, at least for some purposes. I cannot do so. Few comparative studies have been done, and those few have not consistently shown certain methods superior to others. Conventional wisdom is that the choice of method does not matter, that format makes no difference in ratings. Conventional wisdom treats differences between a 5-point graphic scale, a Thurstone scale, and the Smith–Kendall approach as mere differences in format. It is true that "in spite of the fact that people may have preferences for physical arrangements, . . . these preferences seem to have little effect on actual rating behavior" (Landy & Farr, 1980, p. 89), but it may be less true that differences in rating systems have little effect. Conventional wisdom endorsed a Landy and Farr proposal for a moratorium on rating format research. More than 10 years later, I resist conventional wisdom and have acquired two objections to the moratorium idea. First, although Landy and Farr referred literally to format, the moratorium that happened has stopped research on systematic procedures for obtaining a set of ratings as well as preferences for physical arrangements on a page. Impatience with the proliferation of rating forms is understandable, but so also is the concern within working organizations for some way to get on with the business of rating performance. I suspect that ratings developed from an ongoing system are better than ratings acquired without such a system, but this is not the topic that has been studied. Research on systems of evaluation, in realistic settings, has not genuinely been done, so a moratorium on such research is premature.

Second, comprehensive research, even on a single approach to developing a rating form, has rarely been reported. In the decade or so following the Landy–Farr contribution, researchers assumed that understanding the rating process requires only cognitive research. There are other facets of the performance rating process; for example, little attention has been given to the moderating influences of traits, although Härtel (1993) found field independence a moderator of rating accuracy. Even less has been given to backgrounds, settings, or continued experience over long periods of time.

A series of studies directed by E. K. Taylor began with one by Taylor and Manson (1951). They built graphic scales using every available suggestion for improvements, supervised the ratings, and insisted on following prescribed procedures. Results were pleasing; classical rating errors were not found. Further research refined the structure of the format, and then, in a grand final study, all of the good results of that structure faded; the research team expressed disenchantment with graphic rating scales (Taylor, Parker, & Ford, 1959). In commenting on the series (Guion, 1965), I rejected their pessimism, pointing out that most of the successes in the series—the studies where format mattered—were done with relatively inexperienced and unmotivated raters. The final set of raters were highly experienced raters and had long considered performance rating an important component of their jobs. For them, and for similarly experienced raters in an earlier study (Taylor & Hastman, 1956), format choice was trivial; in less experienced samples, structure mattered.

The best procedures for one rating purpose may not fit a different one. Rating people on behavior shown only during the course of an audition or interview is different from rating performance over the span of a year; rating aspects of objects, such as work samples or portfolios, is different from rating people or aspects of their behavior. They may differ in time span of observations or of memory, in complexity of dimensions rated, in organization of data, in opportunity to reconsider, and in many other details. Effects of such differences have not been studied.

For performance rating, research needs to consider differences in treating ratings as "relative" or as "absolute."[8] Despite a few related comments in my descriptions of rating methods, the literature on rating, unlike the

---

[8] I use these two words here only to point up a distinction. Although some authors use the two words without self-consciousness, there really is no such thing as an "absolute" rating.

testing literature, does not distinguish domain-referenced from norm-referenced assessment. Prescaled checklists and graphic rating scales, especially those with behavioral anchors, tend to be domain-referenced in construction and can be in interpretation; employee comparison, on the other hand, is strictly norm-referenced. The distinction is not trivial, and greater attention should be given to the possibilities and demands for domain-referencing in rating scales—especially those used as criteria.

If validation is to do no more than determine the variance in a predictor associated with variance in the criterion, a common aim, norm-referenced rating is fine. For demanding jobs, however, an average candidate may not be adequately qualified. Knowing that someone is above the average of a generally unqualified group is not helpful; the decision maker needs to know if the person is qualified to do the job at a designated performance level. Predictor scores validated against a criterion can be interpreted in terms of that criterion. If the criterion can be interpreted only normatively, the predictor scores can not be associated with specific performance levels. Clear definitions of the performance domains rated, clear statements of proficiency levels within the domains (expressed either behaviorally or in terms of outcomes, depending on domain definitions), and procedures that match ratings to proficiency levels—in short, domain-referenced rating— permit interpreting predictor scores in performance level terms. Research on psychometric properties of rating methods should not be abandoned; it should move toward procedures that can more clearly establish meaningful domain-referenced assessments of performance.

PSYCHOMETRIC RESEARCH ON RATINGS

Regardless of purpose or quality, ratings are measures. Questions and issues in the psychometric evaluation of tests and other assessments apply also to ratings, with added ones as well.

Measurement implies individual differences in the trait measured, and they imply variance and the evaluation of possible sources of variance in the resulting measures. Variance in ratings (or "scores") should, of course, be mainly associated with variance in the actual performance of ratees. Variance in the ratings also stems from influences of the measurement procedure, irrelevant worker characteristics, characteristics of the situation in which performance is measured, and characteristics of the raters. In short, common psychometric problems are exacerbated in ratings.

Constructs Assessed

Constructs rated are rarely well-defined. Without defining them, investigation of validity is difficult. Ratings are often evaluated by multitrait– multimethod matrices. The traits are the dimensions rated (the poorly defined, perhaps inconsistent constructs); the methods might be different rating formats, for example, or perhaps different people. They may be different organizational levels: supervisors, peers, or subordinates all rating the same people on the same scales. The implication, unstated and unrecognized, is that a performance dimension is the same construct at all three levels of relationships. However, raters at different levels are not just different sources or methods of ratings; they may be rating different things. They may have different ideas about what is important in performance or have different definitions or different weights for the various rating dimensions; they may work from different samples of ratee behavior.[9] The potential differences in construct can be illustrated by questions raters at the three levels might ask about a ratee. The supervisor might ask, "How much of my time must be spent with this ratee giving instructions or correcting errors?" A peer might ask, "Does this ratee carry his share of the workload?" A subordinate might ask, "Does this ratee treat me fairly?" The supervisor's construct involves declarative and procedural knowledge, the peer's construct may be work motivation or job competence, and the subordinate's construct is related to concepts of justice. A general caveat is that evidence of convergent validity, or of interrater reliability for that matter, may be little more than evidence of converging biases.

Agreement, Reliability, and Generalizability

Interrater Reliability and Interrater Agreement. Interrater agreement is often treated as a form of reliability, but agreement and reliability are different (e.g., Lawlis & Lu, 1972; Tinsley & Weiss, 1975). Judges agree if they make the same ratings; they are reliable if they put ratees in roughly the same relative order. The distinction is clear in Table 12.1. Reliability can be high without agreement about the degree to which the characteristic being judged describes the ratees (Case 2). It can be low without necessarily meaning much disagreement among raters (Case 3). Both agreement and reliability are useful information about a set of subjective ratings (Tinsley & Weiss, 1975).

Which statistic do you want? The answer depends on the intended use. If the ratings are used as validation criteria, interrater reliability (or "rate–rerate" reliability of a single rater) is more important because reliability limits validity. If the ratings are to be used for decisions based on level of proficiency, or if they are to aid interpretations of correlated test score levels, agreement is more important.

---

[9]Thanks to Walter Borman for these observations.

TABLE 12.1
Hypothetical Ratings Illustrating Different Levels of Interrater
Agreement and Interrater Reliability for Interval-Scaled Data

| | Case 1: High interrater agreement and high interrater reliability | | | Case 2: Low interrater agreement and high interrater reliability | | | Case 3: High interrater agreement and low interrater reliability | | |
| | Rater | | | Rater | | | Rater | | |
Ratee	1	2	3	1	2	3	1	2	3
A	1	1	1	1	3	5	5	4	4
B	2	2	2	1	3	5	5	4	3
C	3	3	3	2	4	6	5	4	5
D	3	3	3	2	4	6	4	4	5
E	4	4	4	3	5	7	5	4	3
F	5	5	5	3	5	7	5	5	4
G	6	6	6	4	6	8	4	4	5
H	7	7	7	4	6	8	5	5	4
I	8	8	8	5	7	9	4	5	3
J	9	9	9	5	7	9	5	5	5
M	4.8	4.8	4.8	3.0	5.0	7.0	4.7	4.4	4.1
SD	2.7	2.7	2.7	1.5	1.5	1.5	.5	.5	.9

Note. From Tinsley, H. E. A., & Weiss, D. J. (1975). Interrater reliability and agreement of subjunctive judgments. *Journal of Counseling Psychology, 22,* 358–376. Copyright by the American Psychological Association. Reprinted with permission.

Estimates of Interrater Agreement. With two raters, each rating all ratees, and only a few rating categories, an easy index of agreement is the percentage of ratees assigned to the same categories by both raters. Suppose, for example, that the manager and assistant manager of a restaurant independently classify every candidate for entry level work; a candidate might be considered further for kitchen work, dining area work, or neither; assume the pattern of agreements and disagreements in Table 12.2.

Summing actual proportions in the diagonal cells shows 46% agreement. Is 46% substantial, reasonable, or poor agreement? To answer, consider the expected (chance) proportion of agreement. The corresponding sum based on marginal proportions is 38%. Is 46% agreement enough greater than chance (38%) to justify further this way to assess candidates? The answer to this, too, is a judgment call, but several indices of rater agreement have built in consideration of chance agreement. An early index was *kappa* (Cohen, 1960), appropriate for the case with two raters and nominal ratings:

$$kappa = (p_a - p_c)/(1 - p_c) \tag{1}$$

TABLE 12.2
A Matrix of Agreements, Expressed as Proportions

		Manager					Marginal Total
		K^a		D		N	
	K	.06	$(.02)^b$	.10	(.08)	.04	(.10)	.20
Assistant	D	.04	(.04)	.15	(.16)	.21	(.20)	.40
Manager	N	.00	(.04)	.15	(.16)	.25	(.20)	.40
Σ Margin			.10		.40		.50	1.00

[a]Raters indicated (a) that the candidate should be considered further for kitchen work (K), (b) that the candidate should be considered further for dining area work (D), or (c) that the candidate need not be considered further for either area. [b]Actual proportions of assignments to a cell are given first; proportions in parentheses are expected proportions based on the marginal totals.

where p_a = actual proportion of agreements, and p_c = expected or chance proportion of agreements. (*Kappa* can also be computed directly from frequencies, substituting the corresponding frequencies for proportions, and using the number of ratees, *N*, instead of 1.) For Table 12.2, *kappa* = .13. For perfect agreement, *kappa* = 1.00, so this is not at all a pleasing level of agreement, quite apart from questions of statistical significance.

These indices of agreement work well for a few nominal categories but are less satisfactory for an array of scaled categories (as in a rating scale). On a 9-point scale, such as in Table 12.1, a constant difference between two raters (e.g., all ratees are in the same rank order, but one rater uses scale values of 1–8 and the other uses 2–9), prevents any literal agreements at all. No ratee is rated at the same scale point by both raters, yet it makes no sense to say the raters are not agreeing at all.

A more realistic statement could come from dividing the 9-point scale into three categories, each a third of the original scale; the statement could say how many ratees (or what proportion of them) were rated in the same third by both raters. Another option asserts that some discrepancies are trivial and can be ignored. If two or more raters use adjacent scale values for the same ratee, for example, they might be considered in essential agreement; agreement might be accepted if the same ratee is rated within a single scale point by both raters. If three raters all give the same ratee a rating of 4 on a 7-point scale, they have obviously agreed. If agreement is defined as any pair of ratings that differ by no more than one scale point, then two raters giving a rating of 4 and the third giving a rating of 5 or 3 would also be counted as an agreement (but three ratings of 4, 3, or 2 would not because one pair of ratings differs by more than one scale point). A still more relaxed range of indifference could be set. Such definitions of agreement are, of course, wholly arbitrary; they should be defensible by arguments based on scale length, on the portion actually used by raters, and on clear reasons why small discrepancies can be considered unimportant.

The question of statistical significance of such agreement statistics has been addressed (e.g., by Lawlis & Lu, 1972; Tinsley & Weiss, 1975). I do not address it here; it seems to me that a level of agreement that must be checked for significance is too low for practical use.

A General Model of Agreement. Kenny (1991) offered a general mathematical model of agreement, or consensus, among raters. Six parameters of the model are postulated as determining the level of agreement: (a) the amount of information available to the judges, (b) the extent to which the two judges have seen the same behaviors, (c) the degree to which the various judges view an observation as meaning the same thing, (d) consistency of the ratee's behavior, (e) the degree to which one person's ratings are based on irrelevant information, and (f) communication of the impressions each rater has gathered. Most agreement research focuses on the number of available observations and on ratee consistency. Kenny sees two others as at least equally important: overlap and similarity of meaning of observations.

Estimates of Interrater Reliability. If the ratings can be considered to fit an interval scale reasonably well, reliability can be estimated by ordinary methods (i.e., correlation, analysis of variance). For multiple raters, most experts agree that interrater reliability can best be estimated by intraclass correlation (see chapter 5). Some warnings of potential misuse of the statistic have been issued. For example, "There are numerous versions of the intraclass correlation coeffficient (ICC) that can give quite different results when applied to the same data. Unfortunately, many researchers are not aware of the differences between the forms. . . ." (Shrout & Fleiss, 1979, p. 420). Similar warnings were issued by Fagot (1991). It is very popular, but I recommend that intraclass correlation be used only by those who are thoroughly familar with the variety of intraclass coefficients and the considerations required for their appropriate use.

Reliability can be increased by pooling raters. Using the Spearman–Brown equation, "If the reliability of a single rating is .50, then the reliability of two, four, or six parallel ratings will be approximately .67, .80, and .86, respectively" (Houston, Raymond, & Svec, 1991, p. 409). I like this quotation because the word *approximately* recognizes that statistical estimates are "on the average" statements of what might be expected if all goes as assumed. Beyond that, however, the operative word is *parallel.* Averaging ratings (or using Spearman–Brown) if one rater is, for example, systematically lenient, simply does not fit the assumption. If essays are each rated by two raters, one more lenient than the other, the problem is like that of using two multiple choice tests of unequal difficulty (nonparallel forms). Scores based on different (unequated) test forms are not comparable. So it is with mixing lenient and difficult raters; the reliability of the pooled ratings is incorrectly estimated by the Spearman–Brown equation of classical psychometric theory. Matters are worse if each judge rates a slightly different construct.

Generalizability Studies. The path model shown in Fig. 12.10 suggests classes of variables that might affect ratings, whatever their nature. The ratee trait or performance is the construct that provides the meaning of the ratings. Settings include those in which ratings are made or ratees are observed, circumstances in which rating is done, or the purposes of rating. Some of these variables may have an influence on the trait being rated. Others may have an influence but should not; they are systematic errors that Wherry (readily accessible in Wherry & Bartlett, 1982) called *bias*. They might include some but not all characteristics of the setting that may influence some but not all aspects of the rating procedure, including whether explicit procedures are followed or not, opportunities to observe, the specific situations in which ratee behavior was observed, time span to be covered, instructions given to raters and when given, whether ratings are to be overall or diagnostic, and how and in what form the ratings are recorded. The examples are not exhaustive. Some procedural variables may interact with the ratee trait to influence the ratings; some procedures may be more appropriate for rating some things, and others may be better for other rating purposes.

Ratings may be, even if they should not be, influenced by ratee characteristics other than those to be rated: demographic characteristics, physical characteristics, general mental ability, street smarts, or personality.

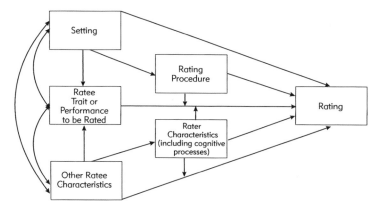

FIG. 12.10.   Path model of classes of variables affecting ratings.

Rater characteristics may include all of these and also a rater's under-standing of the characteristic rated, knowledge of the rating procedures, prior impressions of ratee characteristics, prejudices or response biases, general intelligence, or ability to do whatever behavior is rated or pro-duces the product rated. Interaction of rater and ratee characteristics may provide its own source of variance.

With so many potential sources of variance added to the usual sources of random error variance, the logic of generalizability analysis seems essential in the psychometric evaluation of ratings. Where more than one rater is required, raters are a facet in such an analysis. Frequently, raters are not independent (Wallace, 1974), so good generalizability across raters can be an artifact of common information about ratees, whether relevant to the ratings or not. In diagnostic ratings, much of the overall variance should be associated with variance across dimensions. If this expectation is confirmed, further generalizability analyses should be done within dimensions or groups of correlated dimensions.

In short, Fig. 12.10, despite depiction as a path model, may be at least as useful as a guide to choosing facets one might put into generalizability studies. The facets chosen depend primarily on the purposes of rating and the most serious threats as unwanted sources of variance.

As part of the Job Performance Measurement Project in the military services of the United States, Kraiger (1990) studied experimental per-formance ratings in each of four Air Force specialties. Generalizability analyses were basically three-facet designs: rating forms (with individual items nested within forms), rating sources (self, peer, or supervisor), and ratees. The major source of variance in all four specialties was not ratees but the interaction of ratees with rating sources. Increasing the number of raters, if they are reasonably independent and parallel, will increase reliability; Kraiger (1990) concluded, on the basis of his full data, that the generalizability of these ratings (unlike their classical reliability estimates) can best be improved by averaging ratings from more sources. Raters with different perspectives will see different pieces of information about any given ratee; averaging across these perspectives can give opportunity for more relevant information to influence composite ratings.

Validity of Ratings as Predictors

Performance ratings are often criteria but can be predictors. Ratings are incorporated in interviews, assessment centers, work samples, portfolios of past achievements, auditions, or free-response tests; note that the predictor in these assessment methods is not the interview, assessment center, or whatever; it is the rating summarizing someone's judgment

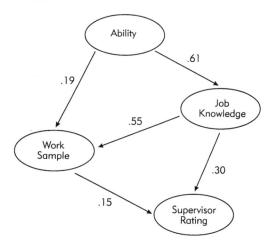

FIG. 12.11. A path model fitting average correlations across 14 studies, $N = 3264$. From Hunter (1983).

based on observations. Evaluation of job relatedness of ratings is done just as it is for other predictors.

Psychometrically, validity describes inferred meaning. Ratings are too often accepted uncritically as meaning whatever the rating scale label says, even when raters, if challenged to define the label, would not agree. Competent evidence of psychometric validity is rarely sought; in fact, most often, no psychometric evaluation occurs at all beyond possible checks on interrater agreement or reliability. Three approaches have been used, however, to study ratings as psychometric instruments. One of these, the study of convergence over organizational levels of the raters, is postponed for consideration with other rater characteristics influencing ratings. Another is the study of bias as a source of invalidity. The third is use of multivariate path models. I begin with the latter.

Path Models of Performance Ratings

Hunter (1983) presented a meta-analysis of 14 studies and placed the results in a path model, Fig. 12.11.[10] Clearly, supervisory ratings were influenced by job knowledge (as demonstrated in tests) and proficiency (as demonstrated in work samples). The corrected coefficients were not great (.40 and .35 respectively), showing "that factors other than job performance and job knowledge account for a very large part of the variation in ratings" (Hunter, 1983, p. 265). But these two variables did account for a nontrivial part of it.

---

[10]Later, Schmidt, Hunter, and Outerbridge (1986) added job experience to the model. It contributed by influencing work sample performance and, more heavily, job knowledge.

I was assigned to discuss that paper and had to confess that "one important implication, at least for me personally, is that performance ratings are not as invalid as they have seemed" (Guion, 1983, p. 267). Because the effect was modest, I suggested expanding the model to include some added variables; Borman (Borman, 1991, p. 298; Borman, White, Pulakos, & Oppler, 1991, p. 869) called it "the Guion challenge." Specifically, I suggested including at least some of the following (Guion, 1983, pp. 269–274):

1. Ratee appearance, meaning more than facial attractiveness. Tall people, not fat, not skinny, who are clean and well-groomed, with voices in a low register, seem to make better impressions and may get higher ratings than short, fat (skinny), messy people with squeaky voices.

2. "Annoyance syndrome," suggesting that supervisors may tend to give poorer ratings to people who bother them.

3. Frequency of employee communication to the supervisor; excessive frequency might belong in the annoyance package, but perhaps frequently communicating employees get better known and, if reasonably competent, may receive better ratings.

4. Ratee's interpersonal skill, or whatever sort of charm that amorphous term implies.

5. Rater bigotry, including but going beyond unreasonable racial or sex prejudice; for example, a rater might give a low rating to a ratee who actually produces quite well but does it "wrong"—meaning in a manner other than that the rater would use.

6. Cognitive complexity—an idea which subsequent research has made less attractive (to be discussed later with other rater characteristics).

7. Leadership roles, including the degree to which the rater sees rating as part of the supervisory job.

8. Levels of peer performance—a context effect for ratings. A reasonably competent person will look very good when other ratees are incompetent—or poor if compared to some truly outstanding workers.

9. Quality of equipment and material.

10. Incentives.

Each of these is a plausible source of variance in ratings and, therefore, merits a place in multivariate research. The list is brief, illustrative only. The real challenge is the challenge of multivariate, gestalt-oriented research: to identify the immense variety of variables, each of which may have only a weak effect by itself but may contribute to a strong cumulative effect, that may influence ratings.

FIG. 12.12. A revised version of the Hunter path model, based on Project A data. From Borman, W. C., White, L. A., Pulakos, E. D., & Oppler, S. H. (1991). Models of supervisory job performance ratings. *Journal of Applied Psychology*, 76, 863–872. Reprinted with permission.

Borman's Models. Borman et al. (1991), using Project A data, replicated Hunter's original path analysis with four components, but some differences in results led them to pose a linear model of the 4 components, as in Fig. 12.12.

That linear model provided the centerpiece of a model expanded by including achievement motivation and dependability as ratee characteristics, along with awards and disciplinary actions (see Fig. 12.13). The expanded model accounted for more than twice the variance accounted for by Hunter's original model (for these data, $R^2 = .31$ versus Hunter's .14) and reinforced the view that ratings are indeed more valid than I had once supposed. Their model for supervisory ratings continued to fit ratings in

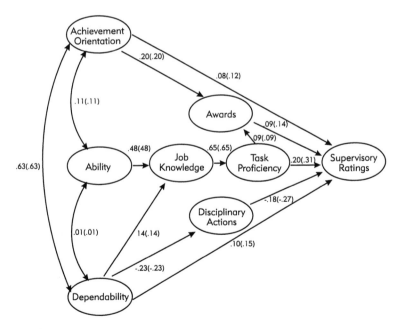

FIG. 12.13. An expanded path model based on Project A data. From Borman, W. C., White, L. A., Pulakos, E. D., & Oppler, S. H. (1991). Models of supervisory job performance ratings. *Journal of Applied Psychology*, 76, 863–872. Reprinted with permission.

differing sex and racial groups without significant differences, but fit was less good and more varied for peer ratings (Pulakos, Schmitt, & Chan, 1996).

Borman, White, and Dorsey (1995) continued. They omitted achievement motivation, awards, and disciplinary actions but included dependability and some interpersonal variables, shown in Fig. 12.14.

The 4-component linear model fit well, as before. Dependability had a direct influence plus an indirect influence through job knowledge; because dependability is important to organizations, the results again add credence to the validity of overall performance ratings. In my suggested list of potential influences, friendliness and obnoxiousness should not influence performance ratings; they did not, adding still further credence.

Comment. These studies do not suggest that performance ratings have high and generalized validity; they do increase confidence that performance appraisal systems, designed and conducted well, can be valid. I hope researchers will provide further data for meta-analyses and that the line of research begun by Hunter (1983) will continue to be expanded.

Bias as Invalidity

Ratee characteristics not being rated are sources of bias if they influence ratings; they reduce validity. One possible source of bias in performance rating is the simple matter of how well rater and ratee (e.g., supervisor

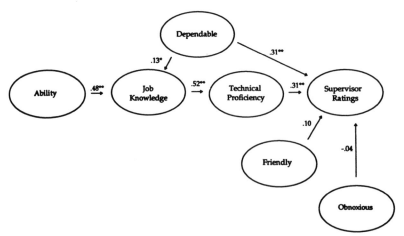

FIG. 12.14. An expanded path model of supervisory ratings including interpersonal factors. From Borman, W. C., White, L. A., & Dorsey, D. W. (1995). Effects of ratee task performance and interpersonal factors on supervisory and peer performance ratings. *Journal of Applied Psychology, 80,* 168–177. Copyright by the American Psychological Association. Reprinted with permission.

and subordinate) get along and work with each other (Duarte, Goodson, & Klich, 1993). Somewhat different is the "same as me" effect. Although similarity of ratee to rater may be a source of bias, it should not be automatically assumed without considering alternatives. In one study, ratings of interviewees apparently had a small but significant "same-as-me" effect for race (Lin, Dobbins, & Farh, 1992). The researchers' alternative interpretation was that minority candidates may have been more comfortable in a same race setting and therefore gave more information to the interviewer. If so, the resulting ratings are not necessarily biased, at least not by the raters.

Sackett, DuBois, and Noe (1991) noted attention to sex stereotyping as a bias in performance evaluation, especially where few women are in the group rated. They examined the relationship of differences in mean ratings and the proportion of women in the group and found that, where the proportion of women was high, their mean rating was higher than that of men. Their mean ratings were a good bit lower if fewer than 20% of the ratees were women.

In a widely cited meta-analysis, Kraiger and Ford (1985) found that raters gave higher ratings to ratees of their own race. A possible moderator was the "salience" of race; as the percentage of Blacks among ratees increased, the race effect was less pronounced, just as in Sackett et al. (1991). Later, however, Sackett and DuBois (1991) compared the Kraiger and Ford (1985) findings with those in gigantic USES and Project A data sets (the Project A data from Pulakos, White, Oppler, & Borman, 1989). In the USES data, and in the Army technical proficiency and personal discipline ratings, both White and Black raters gave higher mean ratings to Whites. For military bearing, Blacks received higher ratings from both Black and White raters. Why did these big studies differ from that by Kraiger and Ford? Sackett and DuBois (1991) wondered and looked at the studies by Black raters in the Kraiger-Ford meta-analysis. Two were lab studies, four used peer ratings; of the eight supervisory ratings studies, four were done before 1970. The four post-1970 entries had a +.03 effect size (corrected) compared to −.23 in the pre-1970 items. The largest effect differences were in the peer rating studies (−.80) and the lab studies (−.60). The conclusion:

> White and Black raters differed very little in their ratings of White ratees but differed much more in their ratings of Black ratees.... We conclude by noting that the patterns of findings from Kraiger and Ford's (1985) meta-analysis is often presented in textbooks.... "Blacks rate Blacks higher; Whites rate Whites higher" has become an accepted finding. This study suggests that such conclusions are premature. (Sackett & DuBois, 1991, p. 876)

A similar suggestion followed the research reported by Pulakos et al. (1989), in which the same ratees were rated by both Black and White raters, thereby controlling for true performance differences; they found the same effect for White raters, but to a much lower—indeed, trivial—degree, but not for Black raters. In still another big study, Waldman and Avolio (1991) did a hierarchical regression analysis with more than 21,000 employees in 10 occupational categories to see if race effects moderated validities of GATB scores against supervisory ratings. There was no significant race-of-rater-by-race-of-ratee interaction.

However, the question of the interaction was extended to ratings in interview panels for police promotions by Prewett-Livingston, Feild, Veres, and Lewis (1996). They found the same-race effect as reported in the original Kraiger and Ford (1985) study in the interviews; moreover, they found that the majority race on the panel had a similar effect, that is, candidates of the same race as the majority of those on the interview panel had higher ratings. Will some future meta-analysis, either of police interviews or of panels generally, support the finding? I do not know, but I am sure the interaction question will not go away any time soon.

The Sackett and DuBois (1991) comparison of pre- and post-1970 studies suggests that research findings, particularly when major social issues are involved, are specific to the times, to the zeitgeist, in which they are obtained—as Cronbach (1975) warned. Perhaps this presumed interaction is another example where social change—greater acceptance of diversity—has resulted in a change of what is scientifically demonstrable.

Does variance in a set of job performance ratings validly reflect variance in actual job performance, however that might have been defined? From the research reported, some of which is based on remarkably reliable data sets, the answer seems to be, "it depends." It depends on a variety of moderators. The concept of a moderator, however, is quite different from that of contaminating bias; it refers to factors influencing relationships, not to factors influencing or interfering with the interpretation of ratings. Unfortunately, the concepts are more easily distinguished than the effects; we cannot tell whether a demographic moderator is or is not due to a demographic bias.

Accuracy

Accuracy was defined in chapter 5 as the degree to which the identity, $Y = X$, describes the relationship between a measure X and a given standard, Y. Research on rating accuracy is restricted to experimental situations where a target rating can be developed and used as the standard, Y. Targets are usually set by panels of experts who have virtually unlimited opportunity to study the materials to be rated—typically videotapes of someone doing something or "paper people" vignettes. Simpler ways to get target ratings include (a) averaging all ratings in a set, (b) averaging ratings on pre-scaled items, or (c) the ratings of a specially identified group of expert raters (Sulsky & Balzer, 1988).

Cronbach (1955) identified four aspects of accuracy in subjective judgments; Borman (1991) suggested examples of practical uses of them. Other conceptions of accuracy have appeared in rating research (Sulsky & Balzer, 1988). During most of the period from 1980–1992, much of the research on ratings used some concept of accuracy as a dependent variable, usually focusing on the effect of cognitive processes. Most experiments have used short-term periods of observation and evaluation, such as in rating work products, interview behavior, or performance in assessment center exercises. I have serious reservations about their generalizability to long-term performance rating.

CONTEXTS FOR RATING

Actual Versus Simulated Settings

My reservations were expressed well by Landy and Farr (1983): "Rather than throwing the baby out with the bath water, they [paper-people experiments] ultimately drown the baby with experimental control" (p. 95). They also said,

> Typically, a supervisor is asked to consider the past performance of one or more subordinates. The period of past performance is typically one year. During that period of time, the supervisor and the subordinate have interacted frequently and probably know each other reasonably well.... We conceive of the prototypic performance rating as a retrospective synthesis by one individual of the efforts or performance of another. Thus we are dealing with the appraisal of a long string of actions rather than a single one; in addition, we are dealing with a constellation of activities rather than with single physical or mental operations in isolation. (Landy & Farr, 1980, p. 74)

The comment identifies several context variables that may influence ratings. Foremost among them is the time span covered. Rating performance over a year's time is a different task from rating performance in a 10-minute assessment center exercise. Frequency of interaction is another. In a factory or office setting, interactions of supervisors and subordinates may occur many times every day, but some people in sales or skilled trades may work anywhere over a large area and see the boss only occasionally; their ratings may be based on very small samples of worker behavior.

Fromkin and Streufert (1976) called such things *boundary variables*— variables that define the conditions to which research must generalize.

Experimental research is usually done at some remove from the conditions it simulates; some boundary variables can be represented among the controlled conditions, but rarely can experiments include the long time span and the possibly critical consequences of an annual performance appraisal. They can help one understand what can happen in the rating process (Mook, 1983), but they lead to better performance ratings only through presenting further questions to answer under more realistic conditions.

Problems addressed by researchers differ from those that raters or those rated think important. Researchers train raters on rating errors, or on frame of reference; ratees think raters should be trained to understand the nature of the performance they are rating and to recognize work factors beyond the individual worker's control. (In research settings, performance is so simplified that raters understand it easily.) Researchers study rater motivation in terms of the purpose of rating; raters point to deliberate distortion of ratings as a greater problem in rater motivation (Bernardin & Villanova, 1986). I recall, many years ago, a personnel manager who told me that his selection and placement decisions were 96% accurate. His evidence was that 96% of the employees hired were rated 3 on a 5-point scale, meaning satisfactory. Talking to supervisors, I learned that 3 was the only safe rating: employees with ratings of 4 or 5 were likely to be promoted out from under them, and they would not be able to get rid of anyone rated 1 or 2.

The criticism must not be carried too far. Most of the experiments are done within boundary conditions that match reasonably well the conditions of short-term rating procedures, those for assessment centers, work samples, or interviews (Bernardin & Villanova, 1986). Even for these, however, the problem of external validity remains. The lack of real consequences in a research setting can make the applicability of the findings doubtful.

Administrative Versus Research Purposes

Ratings have administrative consequences. The consequences can be severe; raters seem to be more lenient in "for real" ratings than in making ratings for research use only (Landy & Farr, 1980). In research, a constant leniency effect matters only if it results in substantially decreased variance. The problem is differential leniency in administrative ratings. Although lacking convincing evidence, I think that administrative ratings may often be lenient for those who have been loyal employees for a long time, or maybe for employees with special family or health problems—and severe for those who annoy the rater. Such factors seem less likely to influence ratings to be used for research only. They lead one to expect a relatively low correlation between ratings where administrative consequences are expected and the research ratings where honesty hurts no one.[11]

Other Contextual Variables

Other aspects of the rating context can cause trouble (Landy & Farr, 1980). Different ratees can suffer or profit from special backgrounds or credentials. A supervisor without exposure to higher education may have an unwarranted but favorable impression about college graduates even when the college work has no relevance to performance. This can work both ways; another supervisor may be biased against what he calls "college kids."

We know from studies on the salience of demographic variables that the proportions of women or men or specific ethnic groups among ratees influence their ratings. Men or women who do not fit traditional gender roles may not be rated as highly as those who do. An incentive system may be an influence; if pay is based on ratings, with a ceiling for a given time in rank, the raters may be more lenient in rating subordinates who have not yet reached the ceiling (Rothe, 1949). Organizational characteristics are influences. Zammuto, London, and Rowland (1982) reported significant organization effects across hospitals in one case, across residence centers in another. Organizational climate or culture can influence the behavior rated or the ratings themselves. "Setting" occupies an attention-getting position in Fig. 12.10, but it has not attracted much attention among rating researchers.

Rating research needs a change in direction. Research should study the influence of the physical, social, policy, and ideational environment on (a) the trait or performance to be rated, (b) procedures followed in making ratings, (c) rater characteristics, and (d) the resulting ratings. Distinguishing among these effects is not easy, but until we learn how to distinguish effects on traits from effects on ratings, we will deal effectively with questions of bias in ratings.

THE RATER IN THE RATING PROCESS

The Classical Psychometric Errors

Central Tendency. Some raters cluster all ratings around a central point on the scale, a midpoint or a subjective average, resulting in low variance.

---

[11]I was once retained to do research under court supervision. The client informed me, with reasonably compelling arguments, that the judge was biased against testing. In testimony about what we might do, I received support from that judge simply by declaring that we would not consider administrative ratings as criteria but would, thank you, develop our own! He had never clearly articulated his objection to validation research with administrative ratings as criteria, but it turned out to be the source of his anti-testing bias.

Central tendency seems to indicate raters who avoid unpleasant consequences by avoiding extreme ratings.

Leniency or Severity. Some raters are easy, some hard; some lenient, others severe. Early discussions of the leniency error (e.g., Guilford, 1936) described it as giving higher ratings to people the rater knows; the more general idea of habitual leniency or severity in rating has long been included in the definition (e.g., Guilford, 1954) and is now dominant. Raters with very high mean ratings are considered systematically lenient; those with low means, systematically severe.

Halo. E. L. Thorndike defined *halo error* as a "marked tendency to think of the person in general as rather good or rather inferior and to color the judgments of the [specific performance dimensions] by this general feeling" (Thorndike, 1920, p. 25, as quoted by Balzer & Sulsky, 1992, p. 975). According to Balzer and Sulsky (1992), his work used contradictory definitions of halo: (a) correlations of ratings on specific scales with overall ratings, and (b) intercorrelations among dimension scales. The one operational definition assumes that a general impression influences ratings on dimensions; the other assumes that raters simply fail to distinguish dimensions. Both assumptions of halo lead to spurious intercorrelations.

Dimensions to be rated are ordinarily not orthogonal, so some observed correlations are not errors. The decades of research have "provided documentation that the phenomenon is ubiquitous. More recently, a great deal of effort has been expended on reducing halo, a modest amount on articulating the sources of halo, and surprisingly little on whether haloed ratings are inaccurate" (Cooper, 1981, p. 219). Intercorrelations may be influenced by reality or by the rater's implicit theory of personality or performance; they may also be due to error.

The Balzer and Sulsky (1992) review found a variety of operational definitions of halo. None of them (they concluded) were consistent with either of the Thorndike concepts; moreover, they questioned the utility of halo in evaluating rating quality.

Their conclusion must be tempered by the results of a series of studies by Lance, Fisicaro, and others. They identified three possible causal models for halo error (Fisicaro & Lance, 1990): a general impression model, a salient dimension model, and an inadequate discrimination model (see Fig. 12.15). Lance, LaPointe, and Fisicaro (1994) compared the three models and found that the general impression model fits observed halo error better than do the other two. They found good fit for it even in contexts specifically designed to induce different concepts of halo and recommended the general impression concept in future research.

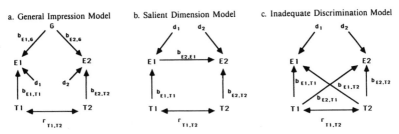

FIG. 12.15. Three causal models of halo error. From Fisicaro, S. A., & Lance, C. E. (1990). Implications of three causal models for the measurement of halo error. *Applied Psychological Measurement, 14,* 419–429. Copyright 1990, Applied Psychological Measurement, Inc. Reproduced by permission.

Halo has been considered important enough to merit many hours of research. What should be done about it? Most answers fall under headings of training raters and increasing their experience and motivation. Effective training is expected to assure that ratings of the dimensions are meaningfully distinguished, at least as well as the raters think they need to be. Experience can augment training. Most of all, I think, raters must be convinced that the differences between dimensions are important enough to maintain and use. This may be one excellent reason for asking potential raters to define the dimensions they think are important rather than imposing the dimensions from psychological or organizational theory.

Other Psychometric Errors

Prior information about a ratee may have a biasing effect, although the effect seems to diminish over time (Hanges, Braverman, & Rentsch, 1991). Prior impressions may be based on knowledge of prior ratings. An experiment by Murphy, Balzer, Lockhart, and Eisenman (1985) found that knowledge of a ratee's previous performance rating influenced ratings of subsequent performance. This well-replicated finding has important implications in assessment centers where ratings are made on several dimensions, then discussed in sequence by the panel of raters. A similar concept (called *escalation bias*) was studied by Schoorman (1988). Raters had prior information about ratees; some of them had participated in decisions to hire them, and some of these had agreed with the decision or not. The bias effect of participation and agreement with the hiring decision accounted for fully 6% of the rating variance.

Individual Differences in Ability to Rate

Rater Qualifications. Some raters are more qualified to rate than others. The main qualification is relevant knowledge, including knowledge of demands on the ratee as well as understanding ratee behavior. It may include knowledge of the work process and of both desirable and flawed product characteristics. Qualifying knowledge comes from observation or experience, not from hearsay, prejudice, or stereotypes. Typically, although not always, immediate supervisors are more qualified to rate job performance than second level supervisors who are more removed from the person and the work being rated (Landy & Farr, 1980); the relevance of the contact, not merely its frequency, seems to be the key qualification (Landy & Guion, 1970). For some work samples, the most qualified raters may be people who have demonstrated a high level of skill at the work, although highly skilled people may have automatized their skills too thoroughly to observe clearly.

Training. Minimal rater training should include instruction in the meaning of words used on the rating form, the procedure to be followed in making the ratings, and aspects of the judgment process such as avoidance of rating errors. Much can be added.

Borman (1979a, p. 418) suggested that rater training might produce, and be evaluated by, three kinds of outcomes: (a) reduction in classical rating errors, (b) improved validity and interrater agreement, and (c) improved accuracy. Of these, I think the most practical efforts are those to increase psychometric validity, but most research emphasis has been placed on the other two. According to Bernardin and Buckley (1981), efforts to replace classical errors have amounted to little more than trading in one kind of response set for another. They advocated training that emphasizes observation of behavior, such as:

1. Diary keeping, in a formal system, with top support assuring that supervisors are themselves evaluated on how well they keep diaries.
2. Frame of reference (FOR) training. FOR training involves identifying raters whose ratings are peculiar and helping them develop a common understanding of the dimensions to be rated and of the observations that support different levels of ratings.
3. Training raters how to be critical. Many raters hate to give negative ratings. Training might increase ability to handle encounters resulting from negative appraisals. Its value could be tested in both field and laboratory research, but it has not been tried much in either.

Classical errors can be reduced by rater training, but the effect is neither long lasting (Bernardin, 1978) nor simple (Borman, 1979a; Pulakos, 1984). The effect seems stronger for some dimensions and some types of scales than for others.

Different people may observe a worker's performance from different perspectives, or frames of reference (Bernardin & Beatty, 1984). Usually there is a dominant, modal frame of reference in an organization, maybe not deliberately. With a common frame of reference, raters can define levels of performance effectiveness for different performance dimensions with a common language. To see if there is one, raters can be asked to rate the relative effectiveness of each item in a list of critical behaviors and the importance of job dimensions. Raters who do not agree with most other raters are considered idiosyncratic and targeted for FOR training. They are brought together to consider the job description, to discuss the important performance dimensions, and to understand the differences between "correct" (modal) evaluations and various idiosyncratic ones. Such training uses a conference method of group problem-solving techniques to arrive at a consensus about how rating should be done. Two studies using FOR training cited by Bernardin and Beatty (1984) found increased interrater agreement and accuracy, both with paper-people vignettes and live ratings of actual job performance. Day and Sulsky (1995) considered FOR training the most promising of all rater training methods.

I question training only the idiosyncratic raters. I would have those with a common view and those with uncommon views included in training together. Both groups can contribute to the discussions, and the common or modal view can be questioned and defended or modified.

Organizational Level. Self, supervisory, and peer performance ratings typically do not correlate well. People at different organizational levels may have different qualifications to rate. Oppler, Peterson, and McCloy (1994) found that peer and supervisory ratings were predicted by different things and were not interchangeable. They attributed the differences to the greater exposure of peers to fellow trainees, especially in Army settings. Differences in the constructs measured might also explain their results.

Research on performance ratings may not apply to other rating problems; self or peer ratings may work better (i.e., be more valid) for some purposes. In assessment centers, assessors are not necessarily supervisors, but they do occupy a hierarchical position of authority; peers may be in a better position to rate some kinds of assessment center performance. Peers may be better judges of certain traits (e.g., work motivation). For some purposes, self ratings may be more valuable, such as self ratings of confidence. For other purposes, other raters may be better: customers can rate service; experts can rate work sample results; or professional people can rate readiness for something (such as readiness to return to work after trauma or to profit from specific training).

Rater Traits. We have already noted such things as individual differences in field independence. Closely related are differences in selective attention (Cardy & Kehoe, 1984). Intelligence is a factor in ratings

(Borman, 1979b; Hauenstein & Alexander, 1991), but the relationship to rating accuracy may be nonmonotonic (Smither & Reilly, 1987). Implicit theories about an occupation may interact with intelligence; Hauenstein and Alexander (1991) found a nonlinear relationship of intelligence to accuracy, moderated by raters' implicit theories.

Cognitive complexity and its opposite, cognitive simplicity, are terms suggesting individual differences in the tendency to construe things, persons, and ideas multidimensionally; more simply put, it is the ability to recognize (perhaps to fabricate) complexity. Several people have suggested cognitive complexity as an important characteristic in rating, especially where multiple dimensions are rated (e.g., Dunnette & Borman, 1979; Feldman, 1981; Guion, 1983; Jacobs, Kafry, & Zedeck, 1980; Landy & Farr, 1980). One researcher, Schneier (1977), found that raters whose cognitive complexity levels were "compatible" with the cognitive demands of the rating scale gave psychometrically superior ratings. Perhaps because the idea is intuitively appealing, several attempts to replicate these findings have been reported—and have failed. Why? Reasons might lie in the difficulty of measuring the construct; the problem might be a lack of clarity in the construct itself. Whatever the reason, I would not join those who would simply drop the idea; its logical sense makes it worth pursuing—by anyone who has a better idea of how to define it or measure it.

Rater Motivation. Poor, invalid ratings may be expected from a rater who lacks confidence in the purpose of the ratings, distrusts the researcher, or simply "has other fish to fry." Understanding and acceptance of purpose is crucial; a supervisor who sees the request for ratings as "still more paperwork" is likely to look on the request more as an infringement on his or her time than as a positive means of achieving personal or organizational goals.

Rater motivation might differ for different rating purposes. A rater might be more highly motivated to rate people where a "deservedness" decision is to be made, where the ratings may determine who gets merit pay or special recognition, or where "designation" decisions are the outcome, such as picking out one ratee among others for promotion or a special training opportunity (Williams, DeNisi, Blencoe, & Cafferty, 1985).

Aids to Observation and Memory

Records. In many settings, daily production records are kept. Review of such records can jar the rater's memory and point out aspects of performance such as level and consistency of production, recorded errors, and related facts. If the problem is to assess performance quality, and if such factual information is available, why rate? A part of the answer is that information in the files may be uneven in quality and relevance. A simple thing like the number of widgets produced each day may be tempered by a rater's knowledge of the specific equipment a ratee uses; some pieces of equipment are more prone to breakdown, slower in function, and so on. The best assessment may still be a subjective judgment—but it must be an informed judgment reached by getting and considering an array of factual information.

Incident Files or Diaries. Some appraisal forms list job duties on one side of the page and require the rater to write an anecdote or critical incident illustrating a ratee's performance of each of them. The principle is similar to that in the Smith–Kendall BARS approach of assigning ratee behavior examples to appropriate points in the scale: the rating given is supported with specific behavioral evidence. A problem with this is that the evidence recalled at the time of rating may not be a good summary description of the ratee or ratee behavior. The rater is more likely to remember the dramatic, salient example of a single brilliant achievement or major blunder than more typical incidents (of these the blunder is more likely to be remembered). Recent events are more likely to be recalled than those that happened earlier.

I once suggested that supervisors keep an incident file—records of observations of effective and less effective behavior. Remembering is easier if the rater has regularly kept an incident file. I suggested that supervisors schedule time to record, each week at least, one or two of the best things each subordinate has done that week and one or two of the worst. The best may not necessarily be very good, the worst may be satisfactory; with 52 weeks of such incidents, the range of subordinate behavior will be documented and potentially helpful in rating. If trained to strive for descriptive objectivity, supervisors can learn to replace glittering generalities such as "is a good leader" with behavioral evidence of leadership such as "delegated authority to subordinate" (Guion, 1965, p. 110, p. 468). I admit that I did not think supervisors would ever keep such records, but the idea actually has been used. Most users of it refer to the file as a "diary."

Bernardin and Buckley (1981) recommended diary keeping as a training method, but only if it is systematic and has support from the top of the organization. Top support for diaries implies that supervisors themselves are evaluated on how well they keep diaries; I think it would also imply that their bosses keep records of *supervisors'* behavior—including diary keeping. Raters, they said, will find better things to do if diary keeping is not viewed as important.

Diaries offer no panacea. In an experiment, Balzer (1986) found that a diary system can slip badly for those who have good impressions of the ratee but do not see the rating task as very important; it will work best for those who have good impressions *and* see the task as central to their jobs. This field testable hypothesis deserves testing.

Bernardin and Beatty (1984) offered recommendations for training people to maintain such records. Among them: (a) Tie training in recording observations to scale familiarization training so that observations are recorded relative to the behavioral dimensions to be rated. (b) Record objectively, not evaluatively. (c) Record a predesignated minimum number of observations per scale. (d) Make the diary-keeping system a formal part of organizational policy and practice. (e) Require the rater's supervisor to monitor the diary keeping.

COGNITIVE PROCESSES IN PERFORMANCE RATINGS

The Promise of Cognitive Research

In an influential article, Feldman (1981) proposed a cognitive model of the performance appraisal process. That process, he said, requires attention to and categorization of information, recalling it, and integrating it, either through automatic or controlled cognitive processing. He described research in cognitive psychology and its potential importance for understanding what happens when one person rates the performance of another. The article made sense.

A cognitive process is unobservable; to understand it, one must hypothesize something about that process that can be explained in terms of observable antecedents and consequents and tested under controlled conditions. The response to Feldman's article begat a large body of experimental research, the purposes of which were more to promote understanding of a process than to generalize to workplaces.

Several studies done during the decade or so following Feldman have already been cited and described. The purpose here is not to reprise them, or to debate lab versus field research, but to describe some principles and findings that have emerged from this body of research and to consider where it has brought us in a search for understanding what happens when one person rates another and for performance appraisal procedures useful in organizations (Ilgen, Barnes-Farrell, & McKellin, 1993).

Major Findings from Cognitive Research

1. The quality of ratings depends at least in part on the quality of observations. Observations tend to be selective; raters attend to some behavior but not all (Ilgen et al., 1993). It is not clear whether the observational set can be influenced by training.

2. Impressions formed, especially early ones, have strong effects on ratings, possibly through influencing what the observer believes has been observed (Ilgen et al., 1993). Impressions may have more influence than actual observations (Nathan & Alexander, 1985; Nathan & Lord, 1983).

3. Impressions are as likely to be formed from stereotypes or prototypes as from direct observations; direct observations may be distorted because of stereotypes or prototypes (Borman, 1991). Prototypical or stereotypical implicit theories of performance may explain some apparent demographic biases, but the directions of effects (for sex, at least) are unclear (Cochran & Olsen, 1994).

4. Implicit personality or implicit performance theories have strong effects on the rater's observations and on the factor structure of the resultant ratings (Johnson, 1994; Nathan & Alexander, 1985).

5. Differing implicit theories can result in different patterns of the validities of predictors when the ratings are the criteria (Sager, 1994).

6. Raters are extremely limited in their abilities to provide accurate ratings—a finding more important than it may seem, because most people seem to expect too much from a rating system (Ilgen, Barnes-Farrell, & McKellin, 1987). A case in point may be my recommendation that incident files be kept; cognitive research has shown that storing events puts observations into categories, often distorting them.

7. The purpose of the rating influences the observational set and the development of rater defenses and, in turn, rating errors (Bernardin & Villanova, 1986; Ilgen et al., 1993).

8. Diaries, or incident files, increase contrast effects in ratings; so also do behavioral checklists (Maurer, Palmer, & Ashe, 1993).

Major Issues in Cognitive Research on Ratings

There is growing skepticism about the value of much of the cognitive research. Effect sizes are usually small, but this is not surprising. Figure 12.10 showed that ratings are influenced from many sources; controlling nearly all of them leaves little room for strong effects of the variables studied; in field studies, with lots of environmental factors as well as rater characteristics uncontrolled, weak effects are further diluted.

However, the research has led to remarkably little advice on improving ratings. Recommendations based on the research differ little from the advice that would have been given prior to 1980: know the job, the standards of performance, and the reason for rating; observe often; and focus on the purpose so that extraneous considerations have minimal effect on ratings. The generalization problem is broad; Ilgen and Favero (1985) surveyed three basic kinds of theory: attribution, implicit personality theory, and social cognition, and found that none of them, as studied in a relatively common paradigm, generalizes well. The article by Ilgen et al. (1993), which may well be the new watershed influencing rating research into the next century, said that the cognitive process research has "reached a point of diminishing returns" (p. 362); it recommended more attention to the content of cognitive variables. Emphasis on content suggests a more integrated, multivariate approach to research on ratings, such as path models. Cognitive processes must be included, but so must rater characteristics, ratee characteristics (including that to be rated and likely contaminants), situational variables, and the content of formal and informal procedures followed in providing the ratings.

REFERENCES

Balzer, W. K. (1986). Biases in the recording of performance-related information: The effects of initial impression and centrality of the appraisal task. *Organizational Behavior and Human Decision Processes, 37*, 329–347.

Balzer, W. K., & Sulsky, L. M. (1992). Halo and performance appraisal research: A critical examination. *Journal of Applied Psychology, 77*, 975–985.

Bernardin, H. J. (1978). Effects of rater training on leniency and halo errors in student ratings of instructors. *Journal of Applied Psychology, 63*, 301–308.

Bernardin, H. J., & Beatty, R. W. (1984). *Performance appraisals: Assessing human behavior at work*. Boston: Kent Publishing.

Bernardin, H. J., & Buckley, M. R. (1981). Strategies in rater training. *Academy of Management Review, 6*, 205–212.

Bernardin, H. J., & Smith, P. C. (1981). A clarification of some issues regarding the development and use of behaviorally anchored rating scales (BARS). *Journal of Applied Psychology, 66*, 458–463.

Bernardin, H. J., & Villanova, P. (1986). Performance appraisal. In E. A. Locke (Ed.), *Generalizing from laboratory to field settings* (pp. 43–62). Lexington, MA: Lexington Books.

Borman, W. C. (1979a). Format and training effects on rating accuracy and rater errors. *Journal of Applied Psychology, 64*, 410–421.

Borman, W. C. (1979b). Individual differences correlates of accuracy in evaluating others' performance effectiveness. *Applied Psychological Measurement, 3*, 103–115.

Borman, W. C. (1986). Behavior-based rating scales. In R. A. Berk (Ed.), *Performance assessment: Methods and applications* (pp. 100–120). Baltimore: Johns Hopkins University Press.

Borman, W. C. (1991). Job behavior, performance, and effectiveness. In M. D. Dunnette & L. M. Hough (Eds.), *Handbook of industrial and organizational psychology* (2nd ed., Vol. 2, pp. 271–326). Palo Alto, CA: Consulting Psychologists Press.

Borman, W. C., White, L. A., & Dorsey, D. W. (1995). Effects of ratee task performance and interpersonal factors on supervisory and peer performance ratings. *Journal of Applied Psychology, 80*, 168–177.

Borman, W. C., White, L. A., Pulakos, E. D., & Oppler, S. H. (1991). Models of supervisory job performance ratings. *Journal of Applied Psychology, 76*, 863–872.

Campbell, J. P., McCloy, R. A., Oppler, S. H., & Sager, C. E. (1992). A theory of performance. In N. Schmitt & W. C. Borman (Eds.), *Personnel selection in organizations* (pp. 35–70). San Francisco: Jossey-Bass.

Cardy, R. L., & Kehoe, J. F. (1984). Rater selective attention ability and appraisal effectiveness: The effect of a cognitive style on the accuracy of differentiation among ratees. *Journal of Applied Psychology, 69*, 589–594.

Cochran, C. C., & Olsen, H. E. (1994, April). *Gender interaction effects on the level and structure of performance ratings.* Presented to Society for Industrial and Organizational Psychology, Nashville, TN.

Cohen, J. (1960). A coefficient of agreement for nominal scales. *Educational and Psychological Measurement, 20*, 37–46.

Cole, M. (1953). *Robert Owen of New Lanark.* New York: Oxford.

Cooper, W. H. (1981). Ubiquitous halo. *Psychological Bulletin, 90*, 218–244.

Cronbach, L. J. (1955). Processes affecting scores on "understanding of others" and "assumed similarity". *Psychological Bulletin, 52*, 177–193.

Cronbach, L. J. (1975). Beyond the two disciplines of scientific psychology. *American Psychologist, 30*, 116–127.

Day, D. V., & Sulsky, L. M. (1995). Effects of frame-of-reference training and information configuration on memory organization and rating accuracy. *Journal of Applied Psychology, 80*, 158–167.

Duarte, N. T., Goodson, J. R., & Klich, N. R. (1993). How do I like thee? Let me appraise the ways. *Journal of Organizational Behavior, 14*, 239–249.

Dunnette, M. D., & Borman, W. C. (1979). Personnel selection and classification systems. *Annual Review of Psychology, 30*, 477–525.

Fagot, R. F. (1991). Reliability of ratings for multiple judges: Intraclass correlation and metric scales. *Applied Psychological Measurement, 15*, 1–11.

Feldman, J. M. (1981). Beyond attribution theory: Cognitive processes in performance appraisal. *Journal of Applied Psychology, 66*, 127–148.

Fisicaro, S. A., & Lance, C. E. (1990). Implications of three causal models for the measurement of halo error. *Applied Psychological Measurement, 14*, 419–429.

Fromkin, H. L., & Streufert, S. (1976). Laboratory experimentation. In M. D. Dunnette (Ed.), *Handbook of industrial and organizational psychology* (pp. 415–466). Chicago: Rand McNally.

Guilford, J. P. (1936). *Psychometric methods.* New York: McGraw-Hill.

Guilford, J. P. (1954). *Psychometric methods* (2nd ed.). New York: McGraw-Hill.

Guion, R. M. (1965). *Personnel testing.* New York: McGraw-Hill.

Guion, R. M. (1983). Comments on Hunter. In F. Landy, S. Zedeck, & J. Cleveland (Eds.), *Performance measurement and theory* (pp. 267–275). Hillsdale, NJ: Lawrence Erlbaum Associates.

Hanges, P. J., Braverman, E. P., & Rentsch, J. R. (1991). Changes in raters' perceptions of subordinates. *Journal of Applied Psychology, 76*, 878–888.

Härtel, C. E. J. (1993). Rating format research revisited: Format effectiveness and acceptability depend on rater characteristics. *Journal of Applied Psychology, 78*, 212–217.

Hauenstein, N. M. A., & Alexander, R. A. (1991). Rating ability in performance judgments: The joint influence of implicit theories and intelligence. *Organizational Behavior and Human Decision Processes, 50*, 300–323.

Houston, W. M., Raymond, M. R., & Svec, J. C. (1991). Adjustments for rater effects in performance assessment. *Applied Psychological Measurement, 15*, 409–421.

Hunter, J. E. (1983). A causal analysis of cognitive ability, job knowledge, job performance, and supervisor ratings. In F. Landy, S. Zedeck, & J. Cleveland (Eds.), *Performance measurement and theory* (pp. 257–266). Hillsdale, NJ: Lawrence Erlbaum Associates.

Ilgen, D. R., Barnes-Farrell, J. L., & McKellin, D. B. (1987, July). *Performance rating accuracy.* Presented at the 21st International Congress of Applied Psychology, Jerusalem, Israel.

Ilgen, D. R., Barnes-Farrell, J. L., & McKellin, D. B. (1993). Performance appraisal process research in the 1980s: What has it contributed to appraisal in use? *Organizational Behavior and Human Decision Processes, 54*, 321–368.

Ilgen, D. R., & Favero, J. L. (1985). Limits in generalization from psychological research to performance appraisal processes. *Academy of Management Review, 10,* 311–321.

Jacobs, R. (1986). Numerical rating scales. In R. A. Berk (Ed.), *Performance assessment: Methods and applications* (pp. 82–99). Baltimore: Johns Hopkins University Press.

Jacobs, R., Kafry, D., & Zedeck, S. (1980). Expectations of behaviorally anchored rating scales. *Personnel Psychology, 33,* 595–640.

Johnson, J. W. (1994, April). *The invariance of the structure of performance due to rater implicity theories.* In M. D. Dunnette (Chair), Rater and ratee influences on the structure of performance ratings, symposium at Society for Industrial and Organizational Psychology, Nashville, TN.

Jurgensen, C. E. (1949). A fallacy in the use of median scale values in employee checklists. *Journal of Applied Psychology, 33,* 56–58.

Kane, J. S. (1986). Performance distribution assessment. In R. A. Berk (Ed.), *Performance assessment: Methods and applications* (pp. 237–273). Baltimore: Johns Hopkins University Press.

Kane, J. S. (1987, April 22). *Wish I may, wish I might, wish I could do performance appraisal right.* Unpublished manuscript, School of Management, University of Massachusetts, Amherst, MA.

Kenny, D. A. (1991). A general model of consensus and accuracy in interpersonal perception. *Psychological Review, 98,* 155–163.

Kirchner, W. K., & Dunnette, M. D. (1957). Identifying the critical factors in successful salesmanship. *Personnel, 34*(2), 54–59.

Kraiger, K. (1990, April). *Generalizability of performance measures across four Air Force specialties* (Technical Paper AFHRL-TP-89-60). Brooks AFB, TX: Air Force Systems Command.

Kraiger, K., & Ford, J. K. (1985). A meta-analysis of ratee race effects in performance ratings. *Journal of Applied Psychology, 70,* 56–65.

Lance, C. E., LaPointe, J. A., & Fisicaro, S. A. (1994). Tests of three causal models of halo rater error. *Organizational Behavior and Human Decision Processes, 57,* 83–96.

Landy, F. J., & Farr, J. L. (1980). Performance rating. *Psychological Bulletin, 87,* 72–107.

Landy, F. J., & Farr, J. L. (1983). *The measurement of work performance: Methods, theory, and applications.* New York: Academic Press.

Landy, F. J., & Guion, R. M. (1970). Development of scales for the measurement of work motivation. *Organizational Behavior and Human Performance, 5,* 93–103.

Latham, G. P., & Wexley, K. N. (1981). *Increasing productivity through performance appraisal.* Reading, MA: Addison-Wesley.

Lawlis, G. F., & Lu, E. (1972). Judgment of counseling process: Reliability, agreement, and error. *Psychological Bulletin, 78,* 17–20.

Lawshe, C. H., & Balma, M. J. (1966). *Principles of personnel testing* (2nd ed.). New York: McGraw-Hill.

Lawshe, C. H., Kephart, N. C., & McCormick, E. J. (1949). The paired comparison technique for rating performance of industrial employees. *Journal of Applied Psychology, 33,* 69–77.

Likert, R. (1932). A technique for the measurement of attitudes. *Archives of Psychology, 140,* 44–53.

Lin, T. R., Dobbins, G. H., & Farh, J. (1992). A field study of race and age similarity effects on interview ratings in conventional and situational interviews. *Journal of Applied Psychology, 77,* 367–371.

Madden, J. M., & Bourdon, R. D. (1964). Effects of variations in rating scale format on judgment. *Journal of Applied Psychology, 48,* 147–151.

Maurer, T. J., Palmer, J. K., & Ashe, D. K. (1993). Diaries, checklists, and contrast effects in measurement of behavior. *Journal of Applied Psychology, 78,* 226–231.

McCormick, E. J., & Bachus, J. A. (1952). Paired comparisons ratings: 1. The effect on ratings of reductions in the number of pairs. *Journal of Applied Psychology, 36,* 123–127.

McCormick, E. J., & Roberts, W. K. (1952). Paired comparison ratings. 2. The reliability of ratings based on partial pairings. *Journal of Applied Psychology, 36,* 188–192.

Mook, D. G. (1983). In defense of external invalidity. *American Psychologist, 65,* 379–387.

Murphy, K. R., Balzer, W. K., Lockhart, M. C., & Eisenman, E. J. (1985). Effects of previous performance on evaluations of present performance. *Journal of Applied Psychology, 70,* 72–84.

Nathan, B. R., & Alexander, R. A. (1985). The role of inferential accuracy in performance rating. *Academy of Management Review, 10,* 109–115.

Nathan, B. R., & Lord, R. G. (1983). Cognitive categorization and dimensional schemata: A process approach to the study of halo in performance ratings. *Journal of Applied Psychology, 68,* 102–114.

Oppler, S. H., Peterson, N. G., & McCloy, R. A. (1994, April). *A comparison of peer and supervisory ratings as criteria for the validation of predictors.* Paper presented to the Society for Industrial and Organizational Psychology, Nashville, TN.

Pedhazur, E. J., & Schmelkin, L. P. (1991). *Measurement, design, and analysis: An integrated approach.* Hillsdale, NJ: Lawrence Erlbaum Associates.

Prewett-Livingston, A. J., Feild, H. S., Veres, J. G., III, & Lewis, P. M. (1996). Effects of race on interview ratings in a situational panel interview. *Journal of Applied Psychology, 81,* 178–186.

Prien, E. P., & Campbell, J. T. (1957). Stability of rating scale statements. *Personnel Psychology, 10,* 305–309.

Prothro, E. T. (1955). The effect of strong negative attitudes on the placement of items in a Thurstone scale. *Journal of Social Psychology, 41,* 11–17.

Pulakos, E. D. (1984). A comparison of rater training programs: Error training and accuracy training. *Journal of Applied Psychology, 69,* 581–588.

Pulakos, E. D., Schmitt, N., & Chan, D. (1996). Models of job performance ratings: An examination of ratee race, ratee gender, and rater level effects. *Human Performance, 9,* 103–119.

Pulakos, E. D., White, L. A., Oppler, S. H., & Borman, W. C. (1989). Examination of race and sex effects on performance ratings. *Journal of Applied Psychology, 74,* 770–780.

Rothe, H. F. (1949). The relation of merit ratings to length of service. *Personnel Psychology, 2,* 237–242.

Sackett, P. R., & DuBois, C. L. Z. (1991). Rater-ratee race effects on performance evaluation: Challenging meta-analytic conclusions. *Journal of Applied Psychology, 76,* 873–877.

Sackett, P. R., DuBois, C. L. Z., & Noe, A. W. (1991). Tokenism in performance evaluation: The effects of work group representation on male-female and white-black differences in performance ratings. *Journal of Applied Psychology, 76,* 263–267.

Sager, S. E. (1994, April) *Individual implicit performance theories.* Presented at Society for Industrial and Organizational Psychology, Nashville, TN.

Schmidt, F. L., Hunter, J. E., & Outerbridge, A. N. (1986). Impact of job experience and ability on job knowledge, work sample performance, and supervisory ratings of job performance. *Journal of Applied Psychology, 71,* 432–439.

Schneier, C. E. (1977). Operational utility and psychometric characteristics of behavioral expectation scales: A cognitive reinterpretation. *Journal of Applied Psychology, 62,* 541–548.

Schoorman, F. D. (1988). Escalation bias in performance evaluations: An unintended consequence of supervisor participation in hiring decisions. *Journal of Applied Psychology, 73,* 58–62.

Seigel, L. C., & Seigel, L. (1962). Item sorts versus graphic procedure for obtaining Thurstone scale judgments. *Journal of Applied Psychology, 46,* 57–61.

Shrout, P. E., & Fleiss, J. L. (1979). Intraclass correlations: Uses in assessing reliability. *Psychological Bulletin, 86,* 420–428.

Sisson, E. D. (1948). Forced choice: The new Army rating. *Personnel Psychology, 1,* 365–381.

Smith, P. C., & Kendall, L. M. (1963). Retranslation of expectations: An approach to the construction of unambiguous anchors for rating scales. *Journal of Applied Psychology, 47,* 149–155.

Smither, J. W., & Reilly, R. R. (1987). True intercorrelation among job components, time delay in rating, and rater intelligence as determinants of accuracy in performance ratings. *Organizational Behavior and Human Decision Processes, 40,* 369–391.

Sulsky, L. M., & Balzer, W. K. (1988). Meaning and measurement of performance rating accuracy: Some methodological and theoretical concerns. *Journal of Applied Psychology, 73,* 497–506.

Taylor, E. K., & Hastman, R. (1956). Relation of format and administration to the characteristics of graphic rating scales. *Personnel Psychology, 9,* 181–206.

Taylor, E. K., & Manson, G. E. (1951). Supervised ratings: Making graphic rating scales work. *Personnel, 27,* 504–514.

Taylor, E. K., Parker, J. W., & Ford, G. L. (1959). Rating scale content: IV. Predictability of structured and unstructured scales. *Personnel Psychology, 12,* 247–266.

Thorndike, E. L. (1920). A constant error in psychological ratings. *Journal of Applied Psychology, 4,* 25–29.

Thurstone, L. L. (1928). Attitudes can be measured. *American Journal of Sociology, 33,* 529–554.

Tinsley, H. E. A., & Weiss, D. J. (1975). Interrater reliability and agreement of subjective judgments. *Journal of Counseling Psychology, 22,* 358–376.

Uhrbrock, R. S. (1950). Standardization of 724 rating scale statements. *Personnel Psychology, 3,* 285–316.

Uhrbrock, R. S. (1961). 2000 scaled items. *Personnel Psychology, 14,* 375–420.

Waldman, D. A., & Avolio, B. J. (1991). Race effects in performance evaluations: Controlling for ability, education, and experience. *Journal of Applied Psychology, 76,* 897–901.

Wallace, S. R. (1974). How high the validity? *Personnel Psychology, 27,* 397–407.

Wherry, R. J., Sr., & Bartlett, C. J. (1982). The control of bias in ratings: A theory of rating. *Personnel Psychology, 35,* 521–551.

Williams, K. J., DeNisi, A. S., Blencoe, A. G., & Cafferty, T. P. (1985). The role of appraisal purpose: Effects of purpose on information acquisition and utilization. *Organizational Behavior and Human Decision Processes, 35,* 314–339.

Zammuto, R. F., London, M., & Rowland, K. M. (1982). Organization and rater differences in performance appraisals. *Personnel Psychology, 35,* 643–658.

13

Assessment by Inventories and Interviews

Testing and scaling (including rating) are two basic psychometric procedures; other kinds of assessment procedures are derived from one or both of these approaches. Some of the less constrained constructed response tests are derivatives of both, developed like tests and using rating scales in scoring. Others evolved from the two psychometric foundations and also from forms of assessment that developed outside of the psychometric tradition. Commonly used derivative approaches to assessment, derived both from testing and rating traditions, include inventories and interviews.

INVENTORIES

Inventories are usually self-report measures of interests, motivation, personality, and values. Most of them are developed using test construction principles and, like tests, are scored by summing scores for item responses. Unlike tests, responses are based on opinions, judgments, or attitudes, not on externally verifiable information. Responses may be dichotomous, multiple choice, forced choice, constructed response (as in sentence completion tests), or on rating scales with three or more levels (e.g., agree, uncertain, disagree).

Inventories often have scores for more than one construct; sometimes items for different constructs are mixed throughout a total set. Scoring interpretations may be ipsative rather than normative. The latter is the familiar norm-referenced interpretation expressed as a standard score or percentile rank. An *ipsative interpretation* compares a person's score on a dimension or construct to that person's scores on the other dimensions (Cattell, 1944). In ability testing, ipsative inference scores would be interpretations of relative strengths and weaknesses; the interpretation in inventories is analogous. It may not be enough in trying to predict turnover, for example, to know that an applicant has a strong need for security; it may be important to know the strength of that need relative to the applicant's other needs such as needs for prestige or self-actualization.

Hughes and Dodd (1961) reported a case where ipsative scoring was valid and normative scoring was not. A stereotyped view of salesmen is that they are highly sociable; normative scoring reflected the stereotype. In their case, however, the salesmen were computer sales people who had to learn a customer's problem and devise a computer system to fit it. Ipsative scoring showed the sociability scale on the Gordon Personal Profile to be negatively related to performance criteria.

Ipsative scoring is relatively rare, partly because of technical problems in using it. Most statistical analyses require operational independence of variables; ipsative scales are not independent. Ipsative and normative scales should not be mixed in regression analysis: in fact, using a set of two or more ipsative variables in a multiple regression analysis is generally unacceptable practice. Moreover, scores to be compared must be on a common scale. If all subscores in an inventory are based on scales developed with the same specifications to produce a common metric, ipsative scoring will work. Scales from different instruments, developed at different times with different people and different specifications, have a common metric only with a common standard score scale, which confounds normative and ipsative measurement. Of course, if this gives valid prediction, practical people will not be upset about it.

Varieties of Inventories

Checklists. Lists of words or phrases can be assembled, and people can be asked to check those that describe them and leave blank those that do not. Items (the words or phrases) usually represent several traits, interspersed to avoid cues to the traits of interest; words can be listed alphabetically, for example; longer phrases can appear in random sequence.

Items might be chosen to fit a theory. Panels of experts may judge whether an item fits a designated trait or not, and a decision rule (e.g., 80% agreement or more) may be set for retaining items. Theory-based checklists are unusual; most are purely empirical. That is, people are classified on an external criterion (e.g., psychiatric judgment, performance level, or staying on the job or not for 2 years), a pool of items is prepared (using ideas formed in the item writers' imaginations or by raiding ideas in other inventories), and item responses are empirically compared across criterion groups. If response differences reach a specified level, the item is retained. Item choice might also be based on less arbitrary statistical procedures like factor analysis.

Scaled Response Inventories. Choosing a response from three or more categories in an ordinal sequence is a scaled response. The Minnesota Multiphasic Personality Inventory (MMPI) may be the oldest of these still in use; its response options are "true," "false," and "cannot say." Such a scale amounts to little more than a dichotomy with an escape clause. Many commonly used scales have more categories, such as a 5-point scale ranging from low to high in appropriateness as a self description of the respondent.

Multiple-Choice or Forced-Choice Instruments. Many inventories are multidimensional; items may have multiple response options, each reflecting a different construct (e.g., the Edwards Personal Preference Schedule, the Kuder Preference Record, or the Sixteen Personality Factor Questionnaire). Options may be responses to a question or simply sets of words or phrases arranged in sets of three or four from which respondents choose one that is the most (or least) descriptive. Items like these are ipsative in that they force the respondent to compare traits for self description.

Alternatives to Inventories. Interest inventories have received relatively little criticism, except criticisms based on distinctions between interests of men and those of women. Personality inventories, on the other hand, have been criticized for many reasons. For employment use, criticisms include invasion of privacy (when items ask questions about religion, sexual attitudes, or transgressions like theft), the encouragement of conformity, prevention of progress by encouraging banality, producing a race of liars,[1] and invalidity. Such criticisms, like the tide, ebb and flow over time, but they do not go away. They call for considering possible alternatives.

Some alternatives can look like tests. One of these was the Michigan Vocabulary Profile, a measure of vocabulary in several areas of activity: human relations, commerce, government, physical sciences, biological

---

[1]The criticism, technically, is of faking in inventory responses. There are other versions of why faking occurs, but the strongest rhetoric equates it with lying: "In the world of smooth conformists there is no room, it would seem, for genius. But there *is* room ... for the man of unusual ability in one direction. Among the elect of the modern age, the chosen of the professional choosers, the man most highly regarded will be, beyond question, the Liar" (Parkinson, 1962, p. 33).

sciences, mathematics, fine arts, and sports. It is now out of print and probably archaic in its definitions, but I describe it as a useful approach, worth bringing up to date. It was not intended to measure verbal comprehension; it was intended to measure interests. The rationale was that people tend to learn about things that interest them. Scores were normative for each scale, but a profile could show the areas of the examinee's best vocabularies, hence strongest interests.

More common alternatives for personality assessment were (and are) projective techniques. These consist of ambiguous stimuli ranging from ink blots and vague pictures to cartoons and picture arrangement tests to sentence completion forms. They are based on the idea that a person will "project" his or her own personality characteristics on an ambiguous stimulus. Many of them do not measure specific traits; that and other problems make psychometric validation difficult. Personality assessment has generally declined in employment practice, and projective testing has virtually disappeared. Interest in personality assessment seems to be returning, but I doubt that projectives will be part of the resurgence.

Another alternative derives measures from other measures. An example is the achievement motivation measure reported by Albright, Glennon, and Siegert (1963). In their setting, a short mental ability test was routinely administered, and it was possible to obtain rank in high school graduating class from local high schools for nearly all applicants. Both test scores and high school rank were converted to percentiles. Candidates were identified as "overachievers" if the high school rank was one or more deciles higher than the test scores. The classification validly distinguished those who stayed with the organization for at least 2 years from those who terminated within that time.

That study, of course, was done in an era when a telephone call to a school or previous employer would get actual information about a person; perhaps such a measure could not be obtained now. However, the same principle was also applied comparing scores on two tests. The first example used a speeded reading test and an unspeeded vocabulary test to classify people as compulsive or noncompulsive (Frederiksen & Melville, 1954). Scores on the two tests were correlated and a regression line was plotted in a scattergram as in Fig. 13.1. Those whose rate of reading was slower than predicted from their vocabulary scores were thought to read slowly to avoid errors and were dubbed the compulsive group; those whose reading speed was faster than predicted from vocabulary were considered noncompulsive.

These examples resulted in dichotomous classification, but there is no reason why such procedures could not provide continuous scores: the ratio of percentiles for the achievement motivation measure, or the size and direction of the prediction residual for the compulsiveness measure.

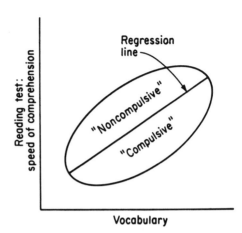

FIG. 13.1. Schematic diagram of a scattergram showing a basis for classifying people according to compulsiveness using two tests. From Guion (1965).

Problems in Inventory Measurement or Assessment

The accuracy of self descriptions can be questioned. When applying for a job, people like to make a good impression. Sometimes they are not very truthful in describing themselves, deliberately faking to make a favorable impression. Sometimes more general habits cause unintended distortions in the self-pictures they describe. Sometimes people lack real insight into their own behavior.

Faking. A *response set* (also called *response style* or *response bias*) is a tendency to follow a particular habit in responding to such stimuli as inventory items. A very common example is a *social desirability response set*, the tendency to say things one thinks others want to hear, the tendency to try to look good to other people. Candidates for a job usually want the job; they are motivated to present themselves favorably during interviews, when taking tests, or when completing inventories. A social desirability set can slip into a deliberate attempt to look good known as *faking*. Faking has been a particular concern in employment offices. It would not be remarkable if an applicant for a position requiring much alertness, even one with distinct Walter Mitty tendencies, were to respond "no" to the question, "Do you daydream frequently?" An applicant for a sales position is unlikely to say "yes" to the question "Do you dislike talking to other people?"

Some inventories have special scales to try to detect faking. The MMPI has a "Lie Scale." Hough and Tippins (1994) had a similar scale they called "Unlikely Virtues." With high faking scores, and maybe very low ones as well, one loses confidence in inferences drawn from personality scores. Sometimes scores on faking are used for score adjustments on the trait scales, but the adjustments rarely enhance prediction of job performance. If a candidate understands the demands of a job well enough to fake appropriately, it is quite possible that on-the-job behavior will be appropriate, regardless of the person's behavior away from work. I am more concerned about the people who conscientiously avoid faking their responses and can be penalized for honesty (see, e.g., Rothe, 1950). Faking is, incidentally, only one of several kinds of social desirability response set. Nine social desirability factors were identified among the 42 Edwards Personal Preference Schedule items (Messick, 1960). Probably at least some of these, unlike deliberate faking, are inadvertent.

A response set contributing variance to scores intended for inferences about something else is a validity-reducing contaminant. Several attempts have been made to reduce the influence of the social desirability set in inventory construction; I mention just two. One is to write items that are subtle or neutral with regard to social desirability. This places a restriction on item writing or selection that produces validity problems; the content domain of a trait (e.g., friendliness) is broad and includes many behaviors that nearly everyone, or hardly anyone, would consider desirable. Thus a concentration of purely neutral items discards a large portion of the content domain.

Another attempt uses forced-choice items, those in which choices must be made between equally desirable or favorable options. Several personality inventories have used forced-choice principles. Some offer a choice between equally attractive alternatives, each measuring a different trait. Some offer a choice between equally attractive alternatives for the same trait but differing in item discrimination indices, somewhat like forced-choice performance ratings (Sisson, 1948). The logic is that social desirability contributes no variance to the trait scores. The logic has not worked as well as anticipated in practice (Anastasi, 1988).

Alliger, Lilienfeld, and Mitchell (1996) did an experimental study of both faking and coaching on integrity test performance. Coaching, in this instance, can be seen as teaching faking. Faking under instructions to do so did not seem successful, perhaps because of poorly chosen strategies; coaching did improve scores on an overt test of integrity but was not successful for a covert method.

Acquiescence. The tendency to accept or agree with an item regardless of what it says, the *acquiescent response set*, has been well-documented (e.g., Jackson & Messick, 1958). Suppose a set of positively stated inventory items were rewritten in a second form as negatively worded statements. Responses to the positive and negative forms should logically be negatively correlated. Agreement with any positively worded item should ordinarily predict disagreement when the item is reversed and worded negatively, for example, when the positively worded item is "I like my job" and its negatively worded counterpart is "I do not like my job." A person who says yes to the first statement is generally expected to say no to the second. However, for many inventories, such reversals of item content often result in the same responses for both and, over several items and several people, the correlation of scores is positive, not negative. That is, no matter whether the item is worded in one direction or its opposite, people tend to respond in the same way—to acquiesce, however it is worded.

Response Set and Predictive Validity

When response sets distort the interpretations of scores for enough people, and with enough variability among people, they produce an unwanted, contaminating source of variance and lower the psychometric validity of score interpretations. It does not necessarily follow that they have similarly dysfunctional effects on statistical prediction. Ruch and Ruch (1967) once offered two explanations for the moderate predictive validities of self inventories: either they work *despite* their fakability or *because* of it. Their research supported the latter; uncorrected MMPI scores that were valid for predicting sales success lost much of that validity when the K scale for detecting faking was applied. Another example used the Gordon Personal Inventory (GPI), ordinarily used to measure four personality traits in a forced-choice format. Kriedt and Dawson (1961), however, used a simple overall score, the number of favorable self descriptions regardless of the trait scale they fit. It correlated .47 with performance ratings; trait scales did not predict ratings, even when the total score (taken as a measure of the social desirability response set) was partialed out. These findings do not say that the GPI is not a useful predictor; maybe it is—precisely because it measures recognition of the most desirable choices. Of course, the criterion ratings can be questioned. Maybe they, too, reflect the employees' abilities to look good—to make favorable impressions.

We tend to think of response sets as psychometric nuisances. A more appropriate view may consider them characteristic "styles" or modes of behavior influencing many substantive areas (Messick, 1993). They may be consistencies that integrate and control other behavior. Understanding such stylistic tendencies, in work as well as in tests and inventories, should be a high research priority.

Examinee Reactions

An applicant for a position as cashier is unlikely to object to an employment process using an arithmetic test including items on addition and subtraction. The same applicant may be bitterly offended, however, if the process includes an inventory intended to measure trustworthiness or asks questions about one's religious background. The example shows one of the kinds of reactions that concern people using inventories for employee selection; it is the "What business is this of yours?" reaction. Civil liberties and civil rights groups are wont to support offended applicants, contending that many interest and personality inventories contain material that is prurient, illegal, and an invasion of privacy.

People may feel offended by personality inventories for other reasons. Certain words—some more than others—may be offensive to some people and especially to some groups of people. Insistence on "politically correct" phrases may have been (or being) laughed into obscurity—at least, the number of examples being reported seems to have diminished—but some inventories are apparently being edited anyway to eliminate potentially offensive terms. Such editing is discussed in places like convention corridors, but it is not published—partly because, I am sure, it is done without benefit of research on its effect on validities.

Some research suggests that the problem may not be large. There was much concern in the 1980s about integrity tests (which are better described as inventories) and the reactions of those who take them. However, Ryan and Sackett (1987) found that subjects in an experimental trial generally (with a few exceptions) considered integrity testing an appropriate management tool. In general, the problem seems to be exacerbated when candidates see no relevance of the inventory items to the job sought. Some very personal questions may be relevant to some jobs, and the relevance may have been verified by competent research. Perhaps candidates should be told in advance that some questions may seem irrelevant to the job but have been shown to differentiate between those who succeed and those who fail (Schneider & Schmitt, 1986). It seems likely that a candidate who wants a job, and is given the courtesy of an explanation of an inventory's relevance to that job, will be less likely to take offense at individual items. If so, such courtesies may further safeguard validity.

PERSONAL HISTORY ASSESSMENT

The best predictor of future behavior is past behavior—a cliché, to be sure, but true. A candidate who performed well on a job in the past is likely to perform well on a similar job in the future; one who has behaved responsibly in the past is likely to be responsible in the future. The assessment problem is to learn about and evaluate past behavior of candidates. An internal candidate might be known by others in the organization. In an earlier, less litigious era, one could learn about an outsider's past behavior from reference checks; such queries now produce little more than verification of dates of enrollment or employment—if that. Candidates can be asked about their own past behavior, performance, or experience. Whatever the source, the first problem is to get information that is neither distorted nor unreliable. The second problem is to turn the information into a useful assessment. Information can come from answers to questions of limited scope, whether asked of candidates (the usual way) or others who have known them. It can become an assessment method by treating answers like inventory responses.

Neither the principle nor the method is new; similar methods were used in 1894 (Stokes, 1994). They were prominent in the 1920s, used again in the military during World War II, and then regained and retained prominence—largely (I think) because of the persistent research efforts of William Owens and his students and colleagues at the University of Georgia. Application blanks traditionally included background questions, at least about educational background and prior work experience. Some of them (before it became so easy to get sued) went much further, asking about hobbies, aspirations, family matters, financial status, or organizational memberships; sometimes the developers of these forms would have a hard time explaining why some questions were asked but, in time, many of them became items scored to assess such traits as energy level, persistence, specific job skills, or relevance of prior experience.

In many organizations scoring keys were developed for what became known as "weighted" application blanks. Several of these were developed and described in publications in the 1950s and 1960s; a variety of methods for assigning weights to responses was described in Guion (1965). Since then, the use of weighted application blanks has waned. More and more of their questions now resemble personality inventory items more than application blank items, asking about early home life, entertainment habits, educational goals for children, or nontangible rewards sought in employment. Super (1960) used that kind of information to develop what he called a *biographical inventory*. To assess independence as a trait, for example, he asked respondents to indicate the age when they first drove an automobile.[2] Such inventories, called Biographical Information Blanks (BIBs), are now more common than scored application blanks and are scored more like tests or other inventories. *Biodata* has replaced BIB as the more conventional term.

EEO regulations now prohibit or discourage some traditional application blank questions, but information about past behavior and achievement remains a useful approach to prediction.

---

[2]This may seem obscure to today's readers, familiar as they are with the rite of passage marked by getting a drivers' license at age 16. Age requirements for licenses in an earlier time varied more widely from state to state and, particularly in rural areas, some youngsters drove within a restricted area (such as a family farm) standing up so they could see out!

The Boundaries of Biodata

Biodata includes items about prior events or behaviors, but is it a biodata item or a personality inventory item if it asks about prior feelings or attitudes? An item such as "How did you feel when . . . ?" may be found in either. Is there a genuine difference between items that tap the personality domain and those of biodata? Does it matter?

There is a substantial overlap in the kinds of constructs measured with biodata and those measured by personality inventories, but there are differences, too. Both reflect personality attributes, but biodata is the larger domain, reflecting interests, attitudes, skills, and abilities in a single set of questions. Even where they overlap, the difference in approach probably matters little when validity coefficients are compared; the one that gives the better prediction is the one used. It matters much more when trying to explain or to understand the validity coefficients. What makes biodata predictive? What constructs does it measure? Answers to such questions are more elusive for biodata, so defining the boundaries of biodata content may be useful.

A guide to those boundaries provided by Mael (1991) is shown in Table 13.1. It is more than a guide to what may be considered biographical in nature; it is also a guide to kinds of items that can be used sensibly in biodata questionnaires. Briefly, these are the meanings of the headings:

1. Biodata must be *historical*, the items referring to events or experiences that have taken place in the past (in some cases, continuing to occur). Intentions, or presumed behavior given hypothetical circumstances, are not biographical and therefore are outside the boundary.

2. Biodata items are *external* actions. They may involve others. They may be observable by others. They do not involve events solely within one's own head. This restriction seems not to be widely followed; many forms identified as biodata forms ask questions of the "how did you feel?" variety. In my judgment (and, I think, in Mael's) such questions lie outside the biodata domain.

3. The biodata domain is *objective* in the sense that there is a factual, not interpretative, response. It follows that it should be first-hand information, not attributions to others. An item like "I think my parents were disappointed in me" lies outside the domain on both counts. It attributes to others (the parents) attitudes they may or may not have held, and it probably does so because of subjective interpretations of words, facial expressions, or actions—or of false memories.

4. *Discrete* actions or events have beginnings and endings; a driver's license was in fact obtained (or not) within a time period. This differs

TABLE 13.1
A Taxonomy of Biodata Items

Historical	*Future or hypothetical*
How old were you when you got your first paying job?	What position do you think you will be holding in 10 years?
	What would you do if another person screamed at you in public?
External	*Internal*
Did you ever get fired from a job?	What is your attitude toward friends who smoke marijuana?
Objective	*Subjective*
How many hours did you study for your real-estate license test?	Would you describe yourself as shy?
	How adventurous are you compared to your coworkers?
First-hand	*Second-hand*
How punctual are you about coming to work?	How would your teachers describe your punctuality?
Discrete	*Summative*
At what age did you get you driver's license?	How many hours do you study during an average week?
Verifiable	*Nonverifiable*
What was your grade point average in college?	How many servings of fresh vegetables do you eat every day?
Were you ever suspended from your Little League team?	
Controllable	*Noncontrollable*
How many tries did it take you to pass the CPA exam?	How many brothers and sisters do you have?
Equal access	*Nonequal access*
Were you ever class president?	Were you captain of the football team?
Job relevant	*Not job relevant*
How many units of cereal did you sell during the last calendar year?	Are you proficient at crossword puzzles?
Noninvasive	*Invasive*
Were you on the tennis team in college?	How many young children do you have at home?

Note. From Mael (1991). Reprinted with permission.

from an item calling for a summary of an entire flock of such events. Market researchers have long noted that questions answerable without implicit manipulation of information are better than those that ask the respondent to compute something; "how many bags of potato chips did you buy last month?" is a better question than, "On the average, how many bags of potato chips do you buy each month?" By asking for discrete information, the recollection task of the respondent is simplified and, besides, there is always the possibility, even if remote, that someone might know or can find out whether the answer given is correct. *Verifiable* answers, even if no one is likely to take the trouble to verify them, seem less likely to be faked.

5. There is no point in asking people about things over which they had no *control*. Past experiences that have shaped and influenced present or future behavior are within the boundaries; even if the experiences themselves are beyond the person's control, reactions to them are controllable. If *access* to means of control is unlikely, the experience is outside the appropriate boundaries for biodata. Concepts of what is fair, ethical, or effective must be considered as well as the personal history concept. Fairness excludes, in this sense, items where different people have had differences in access to the kind of event or experience described. Items with specific historical inequalities in accessibility seem inherently discriminatory, such as experience opportunities that have traditionally been closed to girls and women or to certain ethnic minorities.

6. Employment assessment procedures should be seen as *relevant to the job* sought, or the nature of their relevance should be clearly explained; they should have face validity. Items appearing irrelevant to the job are not likely to be very effective even if within biodata boundaries.

7. Items should be *noninvasive*. As a matter of ethics, empathy, or good sense, the boundaries should draw the line excluding background actions or events people are likely to consider none of an employer's business. Invasion of privacy is a topic more frequently encountered in social criticism than in research, but research exists (e.g., see E. F. Stone & D. L. Stone, 1990). Some topics are more acceptable than others in a biodata questionnaire, and some topics are more acceptable for some purposes than for others. In an experiment reported by D. L. Stone and G. E. Jones (1994), items in job applications about scholastic standing or job preferences seemed acceptable, but questions on family backgrounds were not. Interestingly, the family background items were considered more acceptable if asked for research purposes in a career tracking study. Maybe the perception of fairness depends not only on their relevance to the purpose but on possible consequences. Family income is nobody's business and is an "unfair" question when there is a risk of being rejected for a job; however, it was not criticized as "unfair" for career tracking where nothing bad happens as a result of giving the information.

Developing Biodata Forms

Biodata items, like others, can be found by plundering forms used by others. Imagination will add a few more, the whole set can be given an empirical trial, and those with "good" item statistics can form the "new" questionnaire. This unpleasant procedure is fairly typical, but the result can be pleasant; Reilly and Chao (1982) found biodata validity coefficients on par with those of standardized tests. Nevertheless, such biodata forms are criticized as excessively empirical, with no clear understanding of what is measured or why it might be working. The alternative is to specify a construct (or several) to be assessed, to develop its theory or rationale, and to generate systematically the kinds of items believed to tap it.

Efforts to enhance both prediction and understanding begin by clarifying the measurement purpose. For selection, transfer, or promotion, this begins with job analysis. For training and development purposes, it may begin with a diagnostic analysis of problems. Russell (1994) offered further points of departure based on personality and vocational choice theories and suggested procedures for generating items for the constructs identified as likely to be predictive. For example, Big Five personality theory can guide construct definition; at least one biodata form has explicitly developed scales for each of the Big Five factors (Curtis, Gracin, & Scott, 1994).

How should the items be generated? Russell (1994) pointed out that researchers themselves may be poor sources; he said he was in the "thirty-something generation," and he had trouble generating life history events as item content for those who were recently teen-agers. He suggested life history interviews with job incumbents, who have the twin advantages of knowing the job and of being closer in relevant background experiences. Incumbents, of course, can be anywhere between new entries and those close to retirement; those interviewed should probably be recently hired.

With content in mind, item type is the next decision. Owens (1976) listed seven kinds of items ranging from those with a simple yes–no response to a complex of several items using a common stem.

Scale Construction. Early approaches to biodata forms, like those for weighted application blanks, were purely empirical. Items were chosen from a pool by comparing responses to an external criterion, such as attendance or ratings of performance. Items that correlated well with the criterion, or more typically, items with significantly different response frequencies in high and low criterion groups, were chosen for the scoring key. This procedure (and others like it) became known pejoratively as *dustbowl empiricism*, lacking any theoretical or logical basis for choice. Many sources have provided procedures for such analyses (e.g., Devlin, Abrahams, & Edwards, 1992; Guion, 1965). It should be obvious that the validities of the resulting scales must be established by cross validation.[3]

---

[3]At least it should be obvious since the publication of the wryly funny, memorable address by Ted Cureton, "Validity, Reliability, and Baloney" (Cureton, 1950). It was precisely this procedure that led him to insist that only cross-validation evidence is sufficient.

More theoretically based alternatives exist. Relevant theory might be derived from factor analysis. Biographical scales can be developed to represent certain factors (Russell, 1994), and they will surely be internally consistent. Hough and Paullin (1994) argued, however, that factor scales lose important information and that factor analytic taxonomies are inadequate. They preferred construct-oriented scale construction, beginning with construct definition in the context of a job performance domain and continuing by identifying and defining the trait constructs hypothesized as related to certain aspects of performance. Items should be logically and empirically relevant to the construct as defined and, moreover, should have a kind of face validity, in the sense of obvious relevance to the trait construct; items with keying that go against one's expectations given the trait definition are especially undesirable. Differential item weighting, in their well-supported judgment, is rarely worth the trouble and may cause trouble if the weights are unstable.

Schoenfeldt and Mendoza (1994), however, preferred factor analytic approaches. Factor analysis, especially exploratory analysis, is an empirical approach, but the factors provide rational meaning to their scores. Obviously, factor analytic results depend on the content of the item pool, but factor structures are not purely ad hoc. For example, Table 13.2 lists factors found for customer service occupations; some of these may be job-specific examples of broader constructs, such as the Big Five personality constructs.

The construct-oriented approach advocated by Hough and Paullin (1994) was reflected in the *rainforest empiricism* used by Mael and Hirsch (1993) for one of two biodata forms developed for military academy leadership research. The "rainforest" approach (so-called to isolate it from the pejoratively termed "dustbowl" empiricism) required items with clear relevance to an intended construct, with cumulative empirical data across studies, consistent patterns of item relationships, and multifaceted profiles of criterion performance. The other form, they said, was developed by a quasirational approach. It specified a personality construct, the development of objective personal history items believed relevant to that construct, and items keyed directly to an external personality inventory validly measuring the construct. In short, the quasirational method did not lack empirical data, nor did the empirical method lack rationality. Both forms added incremental predictive validity to existing assessments, although the rainforest approach added more validity with less social desirability effect. Whether called construct-oriented or rainforest empiricism, a combination of data and thought is surely superior to either thoughtless empiricism or naive theorizing.

The "Individual Achievement Record." The development of a biodata form for use in selection for the United States federal government, as described by Gandy, Dye, and MacLane (1994), offers a prototype for an

TABLE 13.2
Factor Scales Derived From a Biodata Form for
Occupations With Customer Service Orientation

Dimension	Number of Items	Alpha Reliability	Example Item
1. Sociability	10	0.77	Introduce oneself to strangers
2. Group Membership Participation	10	0.79	Volunteer with service groups
3. Impatience	10	0.76	Upset while waiting
4. Parental Interest	10	0.66	Parents taught hobby
5. Previous Employment	10	0.78	Number of sales jobs
6. Work Ethic	10	0.63	Distracted by family problems at work
7. Male Orientation	11	0.68	Response to competition
8. Work Responsibility	10	0.64	How often late for class in high school
9. Hurry/Accomplishments	11	0.45	Earned major purchase in high school
10. Family Orientation	8	0.36	Assisted with care of family

Note. From Schoenfeldt, L. F., & Mendoza, J. L. (1994). Developing and using factorially derived biographical scales. In G. S. Stokes, M. D. Mumford, & W. A. Owens (Eds.), *Biodata handbook: Theory, research, and use of biographical information in selection and performance prediction* (pp. 147–169). Palo Alto, CA: CPP Books. Reprinted with permission.

empirical method that is not atheoretical. Development and validation of the form followed these steps:

1. Reviewed information from job analysis of federal nonsupervisory professional and administrative positions and available biodata taxonomies.

2. Established criteria for acceptable biodata items, essentially consistent with Table 13.1 with added concern for use in the public sector.

3. Wrote multiple-choice items with five response options; in most cases, the options represented a quantitative continuum. No preliminary list of constructs guided item development; rather, items reflected "loosely formed hypotheses" that the experiences were related to job performance. Experiences in school, work, and interpersonal areas were included in the pool and believed to tap a variety of constructs. Some items reported factual information; some reported perceptions of the respondent from the perspectives of others.

4. Designated a criterion (supervisory performance ratings) and subjects (entry level professional and administrative people hired over a 4-year period) and collected data.

5. Selected items and developed a scoring key based on double cross validation.

6. Validated scores empirically and analyzed for fairness (using the Cleary method) with data from more than 6,000 employees.

7. Did exploratory and confirmatory factor analyses, identifying four factors among the scored items (also evaluated construct validity by analyzing relationships to reference tests).

Other evaluative studies were done with the completed form, including some designed to promote greater understanding of the factor scores. The project shows the sort of work that can be done with a large sample.

The "Accomplishment Record." Professional people dislike being tested, believing that personnel decisions about them should be based on their records. Lawyers in a federal regulatory agency might also have objected to a test look-alike, for example, a biodata inventory. For them, Hough (1984) developed what she called an *accomplishment record* form and scales.

The critical incident approach to job analysis was used to generate examples of effective and ineffective job behavior; these were sorted by psychologists into dimensions of job performance. An open-ended form was developed for attorneys to use in describing their major accomplishments in each dimension. An example of part of the form is shown in Fig. 13.2.

Responses were scored using BARS. The retranslation procedure was used to assign accomplishment descriptions to the eight dimensions. (Two dimensions seemed confused in the retranslation and were consolidated.) Sixty accomplishments were scaled for each of the resulting seven dimensions by expert judges; descriptions were chosen from those scaled to anchor points on a rating scale, as shown in Fig. 13.3.

The method is time-consuming for researchers, administrators, and examinees, but it is unarguably job related, it does not rely on statistical subtleties, it is a reasonably valid promotion tool, and it seems not to have different effects for men and women or for people of different ethnic groups. In short, it is well worth the time it takes.

INTERVIEWS

Judgments are made during interviews, whether formally recorded as ratings or not, and judgments include assessments, predictions, and decisions. These judgments are often intuitive and haphazard. Assessment may be no more than "sizing up" an interviewee, and prediction may be no more than a vague hunch that the person, as sized up and if hired (retained, promoted, or whatever), will be great, will not be bad, or just would not

---

USING KNOWLEDGE

Interpreting and synthesizing information to form legal strategies, approaches, lines of argument, etc.; developing new configurations of knowledge, innovative approaches, solutions, strategies, etc., selecting the proper legal theory; using appropriate lines of argument, weighing alternatives and drawing sound conclusions.

Time Period: *1974-75*

General statement of what you accomplished:

I was given the task of transferring our anti-trust investigation of ___ into a coherent set of pleadings presentable to ___ and the Commission for review and approval within the context of the Commission's involvement in shopping centers nationwide.

Description of exactly what you did:

I drafted the complaint and proposed order and wrote the underlying legal memo justifying all charges and proposed remedies. I wrote the memo to the Commission recommending approval of the consent agreement. For the first time, we applied anti-trust principles to this novel factual situation.

Awards or formal recognition:

none

The information verified by: *John*   *Compliance*

FIG. 13.2. One dimension of the "Accomplishment Record" inventory and an example of a response. From Hough, L. M. (1984). Development and evaluation of the "accomplishment record" method of selecting and promoting professionals. *Journal of Applied Psychology, 69,* 135–146. Copyright by the American Psychological Association. Reprinted with permission.

work out. Assessments are often secondary to decision; some interviewers want only to reach a decision and then get on with other matters. Herriot (1993) criticized psychometric orientations in interview research; he said that the purpose is to make a decision and that evaluating decisions through statistical prediction is of more interest to academics than to managers. I suppose, with regret, that is true, but good decisions require both competent assessment and explicit (but not necessarily statistical) prediction. Predictions merely implied are rarely articulated or evaluated. My view is that interviews intended for personnel decisions *are* psychometric devices, are based on assessments, and should be evaluated by rules applied to other psychometric devices. Decision making with no concern for quality of assessment and prediction is irresponsible.

Researchers often refer to "the" interview as if all interviews were alike. Just as there are many different tests, there are many different

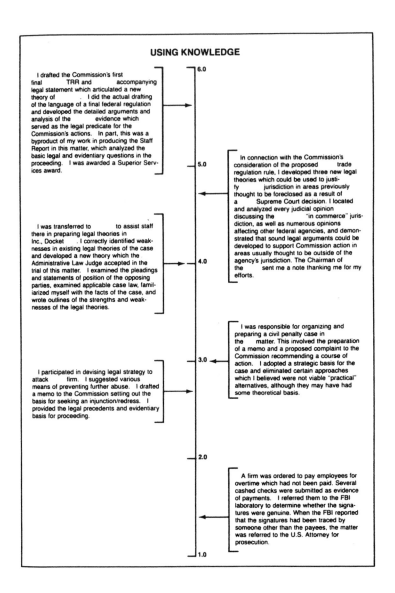

USING KNOWLEDGE

6.0

I drafted the Commission's first final TRR and accompanying legal statement which articulated a new theory of . I did the actual drafting of the language of a final federal regulation and developed the detailed arguments and analysis of the evidence which served as the legal predicate for the Commission's actions. In part, this was a byproduct of my work in producing the Staff Report in this matter, which analyzed the basic legal and evidentiary questions in the proceeding. I was awarded a Superior Services award.

5.0

In connection with the Commission's consideration of the proposed trade regulation rule, I developed three new legal theories which could be used to justify jurisdiction in areas previously thought to be foreclosed as a result of a Supreme Court decision. I located and analyzed every judicial opinion discussing the "in commerce" jurisdiction, as well as numerous opinions affecting other federal agencies, and demonstrated that sound legal arguments could be developed to support Commission action in areas usually thought to be outside of the agency's jurisdiction. The Chairman of the sent me a note thanking me for my efforts.

I was transferred to to assist staff there in preparing legal theories in Inc., Docket . I correctly identified weaknesses in existing legal theories of the case and developed a new theory which the Administrative Law Judge accepted in the trial of this matter. I examined the pleadings and statements of position of the opposing parties, examined applicable case law, familiarized myself with the facts of the case, and wrote outlines of the strengths and weaknesses of the legal theories.

4.0

I was responsible for organizing and preparing a civil penalty case in the matter. This involved the preparation of a memo and a proposed complaint to the Commission recommending a course of action. I adopted a strategic basis for the case and eliminated certain approaches which I believed were not viable "practical" alternatives, although they may have had some theoretical basis.

3.0

I participated in devising legal strategy to attack firm. I suggested various means of preventing further abuse. I drafted a memo to the Commission setting out the basis for seeking an injunction/redress. I provided the legal precedents and evidentiary basis for proceeding.

2.0

A firm was ordered to pay employees for overtime which had not been paid. Several cashed checks were submitted as evidence of payments. I referred them to the FBI laboratory to determine whether the signatures were genuine. When the FBI reported that the signatures had been traced by someone other than the payees, the matter was referred to the U.S. Attorney for prosecution.

1.0

FIG. 13.3. The rating scale for the "Using Knowledge" dimension of the Accomplishment Record Inventory for attorneys. From Hough, L. M. (1984). Development and evaluation of the "accomplishment record" method of selecting and promoting professionals. *Journal of Applied Psychology, 69,* 135–146. Copyright by the American Psychological Association. Reprinted with permission.

608

interviewers, looking for many different things, and using many different methods. Some are entirely unplanned; others are as tightly structured as any test. Assessment is the avowed purpose of some; it is a hidden purpose in others. Some are short; some are long. Some use one interviewer; others use panels. Some are done by highly skilled interviewers; others are done by people who do not have a clue to useful procedures. Interview content consists partly of the questions or tasks posed and partly of the medium, the individual interviewer. Interviewers are not as standardized as questions; the same questions can be asked in different ways by different interviewers. Stimulus content consists partly of the attitudes interviewers present or the interviewee perceives.

PSYCHOMETRIC EVALUATIONS OF INTERVIEWS

Research Reviews

Interviews have been considered too unreliable to be valid since Hollingworth (1923) reported rank orders assigned to 57 candidates by each of 12 sales managers—with virtually no agreement. A 20-year series of narrative reviews (Mayfield, 1964; Ulrich & Trumbo, 1965; Wagner, 1949; Wright, 1969) consistently identified unreliability as a major problem. Not until Schmitt (1976) was much said about lumping together data from interviewers varying in skill. Early reviewers also tentatively proposed that *structured interviews*, those with pre-planned procedures and sets of questions to be asked, would be better. The idea was later supported in reviews by Arvey and Campion (1982) and Harris (1989).

It would be nice to conclude from the chronology that interviews have improved. I think not. Early research pretty much accepted interviews as they were—haphazard, idiosyncratic, spur-of-the-moment events. The literature was sparse, and reports of even the most ordinary interviewing found their way into it. But so also did the development of interview guides. Hovland and Wonderlic (1939) reported a four-page, 34-question interviewers' guide covering work history, family history, social history, and personal history; McMurry (1947) developed a simpler patterned interview. Others were also developed, and these developments probably influenced researchers without having much influence on the way most interviews were—or still are—conducted: haphazard, idiosyncratic, and spur of the moment. My hunch is that interviews in general are no better but that the literature available for reviewers to survey has improved. If so, we probably know a lot more about assessment by interviewing, and how to make valid, interview-based decisions, than we have communicated to the world at large—where (I suspect) poor interviews remain the rule.

Experimental Studies. Webster (1964) reported a series of experiments at McGill University on variables influencing interviewers' decisions. He and his associates reached several conclusions, among them:

1. Interviewers sharing similar backgrounds develop a stereotype of a good candidate and try to match interviewees and stereotypes.
2. A favorable or unfavorable bias appears early in the interview, and decisions are generally consistent with it. (One finding was that most decisions are actually made within the first 4 minutes of the interview, even if the interview continues well beyond that time.)
3. Interviewers are more impressed by unfavorable information than by favorable information. It is more likely that an early favorable impression will turn into an unfavorable decision than the reverse. Interviewers are "not prepared to take a chance" (Webster, 1964, p. 87).
4. Interviewers seek information to support or refute hypotheses about candidates. When satisfied, they attend to something else.

The McGill studies, well-replicated, were experiments intended to describe the process of reaching a decision, not to evaluate the decision or the reasons for it. It is worth remembering, however, that a decision is itself an assessment; a candidate who gets a favorable decision is deemed ordinally better in some sense than one with an unfavorable decision.

Meta-Analyses. Beginning with Hunter and Hunter (1984), a series of meta-analyses have augmented the narrative reviews and provided explicit generalizations about the validity of (generally) aggregated interviews as predictors of job performance and other criteria. Mean validity coefficients reported in early studies were low but positive; in later analyses, mean coefficients were substantially higher as the literature grew and, perhaps, reported research with better interviews. A reasonable figure is a corrected coefficient (for criterion unreliability and range restriction) of about .36 or .37 (Huffcutt & Arthur, 1994; McDaniel, Whetzel, Schmidt, & Maurer, 1994); Conway, Jako, and Goodman (1996) used upper limits of about .56 for moderately structured interviews and as high as .67 for those that are highly structured—and .34 for poorly structured ones. Interview validity may not be as bad as once believed.

Six possible moderators were studied by Marchese and Muchinsky (1993); the most significant was structure, structured interviews being more valid. Others were length of interview (longer interviews were less valid) and sex (better validities in pools with mostly female applicants). The authors also correlated moderators with year of publication. More recent articles were more likely to report relatively good validity coefficients, to be based on structured interviews, to be primarily female samples, to be blue collar samples, and to use just one interviewer. The latter may be a function of structure; perhaps the older consensus favoring multiple interviewers was formed when interviews were more likely to be unstructured.

A dramatic difference in mean coefficients (corrected for criterion unreliability and restriction of range) was reported by Wiesner and Cronshaw (1988): .20 for unstructured and .63 for structured interviews. Huffcutt and Arthur (1994) considered structure a probable moderator, dividing it into four levels: (Level 1) wholly unstructured, (Level 2) constraints limited (typically) to topic standardization, (Level 3) prespecifiction of questions (with varying probes allowed), and (Level 4) all applicants asked precisely the same questions without deviations or follow-up questions—essentially an oral test. The four levels of structure, respectively, had mean validities of .20, .35, .56, and .57, all corrected for criterion unreliability and range restriction. The close coefficients at Levels 3 and 4 suggest a point of diminishing returns from structure. McDaniel et al. (1994) reported a mean corrected validity coefficient of .51 for job-related, structured interviews for research (versus administrative) criteria, but removing structure reduced the mean coefficient in that category to .00.

Meta-analytic conclusions evaluate interview validity more favorably than did the narrative reviews. That may be an artifact of the demands of meta-analytic research; a correlation coefficient serving as a data point implies some degree of structure. If validity coefficients for the casual conversations called interviews could be computed, they would probably be lower on average than those with correlation coefficients computed but still called unstructured (McDaniel et al., 1994). My admittedly cynical conclusion: Interviews, if well structured, can be quite valid predictors, but too often are neither structured nor valid.

Varieties of Structured Interviews

It is not easy to define what is meant by structured. Structured versus unstructured is a rhetorical, not a realistic, dichotomy; there are big differences in the degree and the rigidity of structure. In fact, the descriptive term of choice has changed over the years. Wagner (1949) did not call for *structured* interviews; he called for *standardized* interviews. By the time meta-analyses were examining moderators of interview validity, Wagner's term had almost disappeared, although some authors used both terms interchangeably. They are not synonyms; structure does not necessarily mean standardization. Every time an interviewer decides before an interview what questions will be asked, what judgments will be made, and how they will be recorded, some degree of structure exists; if such structure is developed uniquely for every interview, it is certainly not standardized. It is structured only to fit an individual candidate. It is preparation for the interview, usually done after examining a candidate's credentials—application form, résumé, any letters of recommendation that might be available, and so forth—and noting some concerns worth exploring.

However, the term *structured* more typically refers to interviews tailored to fit a job, not an individual candidate. Structuring in this sense begins with the job description, pay classification, promotion patterns, and related data. From such information, traits relevant to performance may be inferred and appropriate questions identified, to be asked of all candidates. This form of structuring implies at least some standardization.

Different people have different ideas of how interviews should be structured. Four general procedures are described here. The first uses minimal structure, guiding rather than dictating an interviewer's progress through an interview. The second is more tightly structured yet relatively flexible, permitting different candidates to be asked different questions. The other two are more firmly structured, allowing little deviation.

Patterned Interviews. McMurry (1947) developed patterned interviews, a precursor to many lightly structured procedures. It required stating clear, acceptable bases for selection—such as desired traits, background experiences, or training. An interviewer's guide provided kinds of questions that might be asked for each of these, and training was supposed to assure understanding of its questions and the selection standards. Appropriate rating scales were provided for recording summary evaluations. McMurry's rating scales were simple; in a later modification, Maas (1965) used Smith–Kendall scaled expectation ratings for each critical trait.

Behavior Description Interviewing. A more complex modification was called the *Patterned Behavior Description Interview* (Janz, 1989; Janz, Hellervik, & Gilmore, 1986). Janz et al. (1986) gave examples of the interview patterns of questions for 16 jobs. The method is based on the aphorism that the best predictor of future behavior is past behavior; all questions in a pattern ask about past behavior, making it an oral personal history inventory. Question development begins from critical incidents classified into dimensions of behavior. Questions (initial and follow-up questions) are written for each dimension unless that dimension can be assessed better by an alternative to an interview (e.g., tests, biodata, credentials). The correspondence of question to dimension need not be one-to-one; the same initial question can, with appropriate follow-up probes, provide information for more than one job dimension. For example, a critical incident for an employment test specialist might have been "Developed a valid hands-on performance test to measure problem-solving skills when informed under court order that written tests would not be permitted." The initial question might be, "Tell me about a time when you solved a measurement problem that precluded conventional testing procedures." Follow-up questions might include, "What was unusual about your solution?" and "How did you get your solution accepted by others?" If the job dimensions included creative problem solving and persuasiveness, this question and its probes can tap both. After the interview, the candidate is rated on each job dimension on a simple 5-point graphic rating scale. The sum of the dimension ratings provides a total score.

Situational Interviews. Situational interviews are based on goal-setting theory that states that behavior depends in large part on goals or intentions. Theoretically, if people are asked to say how they would respond to critical situations others have faced on a job, their answers reveal their behavioral intentions. Responses can be systematically scored using a scale anchored by behavioral responses.

Latham (1989) outlined the steps in developing a situational interview:

1. Conduct a job analysis using the critical incident technique. . . .
2. Develop an appraisal instrument such as behavioral observation scales (Latham & Wexley, 1977, 1981) based on the job analysis.
3. Select one or more incidents that formed the basis for the development of performance criteria (e.g., cost consciousness) which constitutes the appraisal instrument.
4. Turn each critical incident into a "what would you do if . . ." question.
5. Develop a scoring guide to facilitate agreement among interviewers on what constitutes a good (5), acceptable (3), or an unacceptable (1) response to each question. If a 2 and 4 anchor can also be developed, do so.
6. Review the questions for comprehensiveness in terms of covering the material identified in the job analysis and summarized on the appraisal instrument.
7. Conduct a pilot study to eliminate questions where applicant/interviewees give the same answers, or where interviewers cannot agree on the scoring.
8. Conduct a criterion-related validity study when feasible to do so. (Latham, 1989, p. 171)

An example of a question and scoring guide is shown in Figure 13.4.

You are in charge of truck drivers in Philadelphia. Your colleague is in charge of truck drivers 800 miles away in Atlanta. Both of you report to the same person. Your salary and bonus are affected 100% by your costs. Your buddy is in desperate need of one of your trucks. If you say no, your costs will remain low and your group will probably win the Golden Flyer award the the quarter. If you say yes, the Atlanta group will probably win this prestigious award because they will make a significant profit for the company. Your boss is preaching costs, costs, costs as well as cooperation with one's peers. Your boss has no control over accounting who are the score keepers. Your boss is highly competitive, he or she rewards winners. You are just as competitive, you are a real winner!

Explain what you would do?

Record answer:

_____

_____

_____

_____

Scoring Guide
(1) I would go for the award. I would explain the circumstances to my buddy and get his or her understanding.
(3) I would get my boss' advice.
(5) I would loan the truck to my buddy. I'd get recognition from my boss and my buddy that I had sacrificed my rear-end for theirs. Then I'd explain the logic to my people.

FIG. 13.4. An example of a question and scoring guide for a situational interview. From Latham, G. P. (1989). The reliability, validity, and practicality of the situational interview. In R. W. Eder & G. R. Ferris (Eds.), *The employment interview: Theory, research, and practice* (pp. 169–182). Newbury Park, CA: Sage Publications. Reprinted with permission.

Noteworthy in this sequence is an early focus on performance appraisal, calling for developing criteria first—good advice for any approach. Equally noteworthy is the explicit provision for pilot research. It is noteworthy because people who would never dream of developing written tests without pilot studies often do not hesitate to develop interview guides without them. Building a psychometric device without pilot studies displays unwarranted arrogance—or ignorance of the many things that can go wrong. Among things that can go wrong with this method is anchoring the ends of the 5-point rating scales with examples that do not get used because they are too ridiculous or idealistic. Pilot studies can identify such items.

Like behavior description patterns, situational interviews begin with critical incidents but use them differently. Situational interviews emphasize the future, not the past: "what would you do if . . . ?" rather than "what did you do when . . . ?" Situational interviews usually use panels of two or more interviewers. According to Latham, the typical panel has two managers from the job area and one human resources staff member.

One person reads the questions, but all of them record and evaluate the answers.

Comprehensive Structured Interviews. I have borrowed the term comprehensive structured interview from Harris (1989) to distinguish the specific procedures desribed by Campion, Pursell, and Brown (1988) from the generic term, *structured interview.* Campion et al. (1988) described their procedure as "more highly structured" than most other approaches.

The procedure begins with job analysis to identify KSAs from which interview questions can be developed. Acceptable questions might include those used in behavior description or situational interviews, job knowledge questions, simulations or walk-throughs, and "willingness" questions presenting aspects of realistic job previews. If job requirements differ in importance, the difference is supposed to be reflected by the relative number of questions related to the different ones. Responses are to be rated on 5-point scales, anchored at extremes and the midpoint.

The development of the interview guide does not, at this point, indicate much structure; it offers more freedom than the two preceding methods in studying the job and in the content of the questions. However, the form of the questions is simpler, more like those in a printed test; all candidates are asked precisely the same questions, and no prompting or follow-up questions are permitted (although a question may be repeated if necessary). Moreover, scores of all candidates should be available before the decision is made; this is an explicitly norm-referenced procedure. If feasible, 3-member panels are used; the same panel and the same process is to be used for every candidate. The same panel member is to conduct all interviews and ask all questions; all panel members are to take extensive notes. Questions, answers, and candidates are not to be discussed between interviews, but, after all candidates have been interviewed, large discrepancies in ratings may be discussed and changes made if appropriate. Candidates may not ask questions during the interview, although the procedure calls for a later nonevaluative interview with a personnel representative in which questions are permitted.

Comparison of the Examples. These examples have been presented to show variety, not as prototypes to be matched. All of them have shown reasonable reliabilities and validity coefficients, statistically significant and competitive with other predictors. All have been defended as practical.

There are, of course, unanswered questions. How much structure is necessary? In comparing the four examples, one should keep in mind the diminishing returns of structure as identified by Huffcutt and Arthur (1994). In doing so, however, other questions surface. The most highly structured interview guides are essentially oral tests with constructed responses. Is test-like standardization an essential feature of interview structure? The same questions could be asked and answered in written form, the responses scored by readers. Would oral and written versions be alike in reliability and validity? Would one form or the other be more susceptible to contaminating sources of variance? Would examinee reaction be the same? We do not know; it is worth investigation. As Hakel (1989) pointed out, we do not know why structured interviews are superior to unstructured interviews, or why they may be about as good as other structured forms of assessment. Again: more research is needed.

Validity

Criterion-Related Validity Coefficients. Interview validity is usually described only with criterion-related validity coefficients; they are apparently higher than formerly supposed. Pooling data across interviewers who differ in individual validity, who make different systematic errors, and whose judgments are not independent, may have seriously underestimated validity coefficients; methods have been offered for unconfounding such data (Dreher, Ash, & Hancock, 1988; Kenny & La Voie, 1985).

Incremental Validity in Prediction. Incremental validity, the increase in variance accounted for when a new predictor is added to those already accounting for some of it, is ordinarily determined by stepwise multiple regression analysis. Tests (and related assessments) are entered first to determine their validity; interview data are entered in the next step to see how much the interview adds. This order of entry arose because tests were more likely to be valid than interviews. As time went by, and structured interviews gave evidence of predictive validity, questions of their incremental validity became important.

Interviews *will* be used, in most organizations, for most jobs. Unless the word gets out about the values of structured interview procedures (Hakel, 1989), many of them will be psychometrically poor. When properly pretested, well-structured interviews are used, however, they usually predict job performance. Are they good enough predictors to add validity?

Maybe not. Walters, Miller, and Ree (1993) developed a structured interview for pilot trainees. It led to seven ratings with, individually, validity coefficients that were modest but comparable to validities for scores on written tests. Equations for written tests with or without the interview ratings did not give significantly different coefficients, perhaps because traits rated by interviewers were also measured by the written tests. Shahani, Dipboye, and Gehrlein (1991) also found no incremental validity for interview assessments. On the other hand, criteria such as client relations and cooperation were predicted better when interviews were added to the equation reported by Day and Silverman (1989), and interviews provided incremental validity in predicting criteria of leadership, military bearing, and personal discipline (McHenry, Lough, Toquam, Hanson, & Ashworth, 1990).

Sometimes, in my dreams, I reverse the order, asking what incremental validity tests add to interviews. So did Campion, Campion, and Hudson (1994). With a 30-item structured interview and a nine-test battery, they found that interviewer scores added 8% to the criterion variance accounted for by tests; reversing the order in which variables entered the regression equation, tests accounted for only 4% more than interviews alone! Remember, however, that this sort of structured interview is more like an oral test than a conventional interview; maybe it was simply a better test.

Where does such disparate information take us? To the conclusion we already knew: We do not know enough about the incremental validities even of well-structured interviews. Until better accounts of the incremental validities of interviews are available, well-informed decision makers will rely more on tests than on even their own interviewing skills.

Psychometric Validity. Very little attention has been given to the psychometric validities of interviewers' ratings. What inferences, if any, can be validly drawn about interviewees from interviewers' judgments? General answers are unavailable, so no general principles can be offered for improving the meaningfulness of interviews as assessments.

Questions of meaning are questions of constructs and return us to the problem of identifying appropriate constructs for interview assessment. Schmitt (1976) called for research to identify variables best assessed by interviews, but it has not yet happened on any useful scale. Many interviews call for ratings on several dimensions. Sometimes factor analysis of them results in only one factor (e.g., Roth & Campion, 1992). Shahani et al. (1991) reported a factor analysis of interviewer ratings on seven motivation items and five oral communication skill items (the items were developed by committee, apparently without pretesting, which might be the problem). Only one factor accounted for variance among the 12 items. The interviewers could not or perhaps did not distinguish these clearly distinguishable constructs. So what can be said to have been assessed by them?

There are exceptions. Landy (1976) found three factors among nine dimensions (manifest motivation, communication, and personal stability). Rynes and Gerhart (1990) found four factors among 10 dimensions rated.

Nevertheless, they suggested that interviewers were assessing person–job "fit," which, in an understatement, they said is an "elusive construct" (p. 14).

Although interviewer ratings are made in a context different from many other ratings, they are, after all, subject to the problems of other ratings. We will not clearly understand what interviewers can assess until the research enterprise starts to develop theoretical statements of constructs appropriate for interview assessment, train interviewers in their meanings and manifestations, appropriately structure interviews, collect data, and conduct the confirmatory and disconfirmatory research needed to determine whether interviewers' ratings on these constructs lead to valid inferences about them.

Does it matter? Can the decisions be valid even in ignorance of the constructs used in reaching them? Of course. But at this point in the history of employment psychology we should be getting tired of not knowing what we are doing, no matter how carefully we do it.

Content-Oriented Considerations. Interview guides, rating scales, and general structure of interviews are often content-related, relying on job analysis in their development. Lawshe's content validity ratio (CVR; Lawshe, 1975) was computed for items in each of three structured interview guides developed by Carrier, Dalessio, and Brown (1990). One of the guides was for use with experienced applicants, the other two for inexperienced ones. For experienced candidates, the approach worked quite well; the highest CVR items combined to form the best criterion-related validity. Not so for the inexperienced ones. Is content sampling, then, a useful approach to structuring interviews only for experienced people?

I think so. Interview questions and ratings can be informed by the job analysis or derived from it as content samples. The former is like the choice of predictors in a predictive hypothesis and may lead to more appropriate questions for inexperienced applicants. The latter, like work samples and the old oral trade tests, may distinguish truly experienced candidates from those who merely claim the experience. Inexperienced applicants need to be assessed for aptitudes for the work they have yet to learn; aptitude is surely assessed better by tests than by interviewers' ratings.

The Lens Model in Interview Research

Policy capturing and the lens model have shown individual differences in the way interviewers use information to reach overall judgments and in the criterion-related validity of those judgments, and the studies have shown that treating different interviewers as mere replications of each other (i.e., pooling data across interviewers) is unwise. Some examples:

1. Zedeck, Tziner, and Middlestadt (1983) reported overall validity coefficients of "the" interview (aggregated over 10 interviewers) at barely greater than zero. There were too few cases for individual interviewers to compute corresponding coefficients, but Zedeck et al. showed that individual interviewers had distinctly different decision policies; they wisely concluded that aggregating data (lumping different interviewers together) is inadvisable.

2. In a unique study by Dougherty, Ebert, and Callender (1986), three interviewers audiotaped interviews used in initial screening for entry clerical and technical jobs. Each interviewer saw some applicants and rated them on eight job-related dimensions and on an overall rating scale. All three interviewers rated all applicants from the tapes. Those hired were subsequently rated by their supervisors on ten dimensions, including overall performance. Validity coefficients are shown in Table 13.3. ("Live" judgments are those of the actual interviewer at the time of the interview; all other columns refer to judgments based on the tapes.) Again, aggregated interviewer overall judgments were not significantly correlated with supervisory ratings of overall job performance; neither were ratings from two of the interviewers. The third, however, significantly and substantially predicted all supervisory ratings but one. The study went beyond demonstrating individual differences in interviewer validity; it also showed that interviewers can be trained to use more effective policies.

3. The situation seemed reversed in a study by Kinicki, Lockwood, Hom, and Griffeth (1990). They found significant validity for aggregated data but not for individuals. Again, only a couple of their interviewers had enough cases for appreciable statistical power, and correlations for these disappeared under cross validation.

What conclusion can be drawn? With my predilection for seeing the world as a complex and individualistic environment, I think that policy-capturing research has demonstrated important individual differences in interviewing skill and in the validities of assessments made by individual interviewers; evaluating interviewing by lumping together interviewers who differ in policies and in effectiveness is not useful. Against that predilection, however, must be placed three cautions.

First, the best of these studies used only three interviewers, and very little data from individual interviewers were presented in the others.

Second, where there are several interviewers, clustering techniques show that some interviewers are quite similar in the information they

TABLE 13.3
Validity Coefficients for "Live" Overall Judgments, Mean of Overall
Judgments, and Individual Interviewer Judgments

			Interviewer		
Criterion Dimension	Live[a] judgments (n = 57)	Mean of[b] judgments (n = 57)	1 judgment (n = 56)	2 judgments (n = 54)	3 judgments (n = 56)
Learning tasks	.10	.17	.09	.07	.24*
Minimal supervision	.05	.32**	.19	.09	.41**
Organizing	.09	.18	.13	−.05	.26*
Judgment	−.05	.24*	.23*	.07	.26*
Job knowledge	−.09	.12	.07	−.11	.23*
Cooperation	−.04	.09	.13	−.01	.08
Productivity	.03	.19	.12	−.05	.32**
Accuracy	.18	.28*	.25*	.19	.27*
Involvement	.06	.28*	.27*	.04	.34**
Overall performance					
Actual	.06	.21	.15	.02	.26*
Predicted[c]			.23*	.19	.26*

[a]Overall judgments made by interviewers in the actual, live interviews; all other columns are correlations based on judgments from the tape recordings. [b]Mean of the judgments based on tapes by the three interviewers. [c]Using judgments predicted from the interviewer's own policy equation.
$*p < .05; **p < .01$
Note. Adapted from Dougherty, T. W., Ebert, R. J., & Callender, J. C. (1986). Policy capturing in the employment interview. *Journal of Applied Psychology, 71,* 9–15. Copyright by the American Psychological Association. Reprinted with permission.

consider in making their judgments. Moreover, the similarities can be enhanced by training interviewers to use designated policies.

Finally, meta-analyses have provided no reason to assume serious individual differences, even while making it clear that structure is extremely important. Maybe the importance of individual differences among interviewers is greatly reduced with well-structured interviews.

FACTORS INFLUENCING INTERVIEWER DECISIONS

Interviewer Experience and Habit

Most managers like people with lots of experience, but sometimes we learn things from experience that are not so, including bad habits. Gehrlein, Dipboye, and Shahani (1993) demonstrated that experience is not necessarily helpful to interviewers. Admissions officers (experienced interviewers) interviewed college applicants; other applicants were interviewed by alumni, faculty, and others termed inexperienced. Validity coefficients of interviewer ratings against GPA were nonsignificant for all of the individual experienced interviewers; surprisingly, inexperienced interviewers did much better. The authors suggested that experience tends to breed confidence even if it is unwarranted. Perhaps the less experienced people compensated for less confidence by planning their interview strategies—in effect, by developing a personal structure for their interviews.

Some interviewers habitually talk too much. Daniels and Otis (1950) found that interviewers generally do most of the talking, sometimes two or three times as much as the interviewees. Moreover, it has been shown that interviewers talk more with applicants they accept (C. W. Anderson, 1960). That finding is hard to interpret. Do interviewers talk more to applicants who show signs of success early in the conversation? Or do they simply feel good about themselves when they talk more, thereby feeling kindly toward the listening applicant?

If the interviewer is seen as an instrument for assessing candidate characteristics through conversation, it seems logical that the interviewer's contributions to the conversation would be relatively brief, encouraging the candidate to speak freely. When the purpose of the interview is to persuade the candidate to accept an offer, perhaps the interviewer should in fact talk more. But in nearly all other purposes, for example, where public relations is to be enhanced, the interviewer is likely to make a better impression on the interviewee by listening than by talking.

Apparently, the amount and kind of talking done by interviewers depends in large part on prior impressions of the candidates. In a decision-making interview, an interviewer often gets prepared by checking out application materials. If this preparation produces a favorable impression, the interviewer is likely to talk more and listen less; there are other first impression effects that bring the validity of interviews into question (Dougherty, Turban, & Callender, 1994).

Experience should lead to skill, not to bad habits. Examining a variety of reviews, Graves (1993) concluded that individual differences in interviewers' skills were likely; she recommended that researchers study individual interviewers to determine what accounts for differences between the effective and less effective ones. She proposed a model of interviewer effectiveness that covers most of the categories of variables described earlier as influencing ratings. She also gave 19 propositions for a research agenda. From some of these, I offer four principles that, admitting the need for research, seem supportable enough to be followed (the language is mine, and she might not approve):

1. Interviewer effectiveness depends on the richness of the interviewer's job-related cognitive structure, and this richness depends

on the experience of the interviewer. In addition to thorough training and supervised experience, interviewers should accumulate a wealth of other experiences to enrich their understanding of the jobs to be filled.

2. Interviewers should be bright, intelligent, analytical people.

3. Interviewers should have a clear, job relevant prototype of an ideal applicant for a job to be filled (more on this later). Interviewers might be encouraged to deviate modestly from the prototype, but not to make extreme deviations. That is, they should not be too rigid about it, but should look for people who fit the prototype reasonably well.

4. The interview should be structured and include only topics of clear job relevance.

Nonverbal Cues

Much has been written about nonverbal communication, especially as used by interviewees to make a good impression on interviewers (N. R. Anderson, 1991). Interviewers should know that they can be unduly influenced by such behavior, but many of them base judgments on it, anyway. Experienced (not necessarily good) interviewers have told me that they rely on a variety of nonverbal candidate behaviors: leaning back after making a statement (reason for distrust), firm handshake (strong character), catching one's breath (sign of lying), clean clothes (sign of neat work habits). They have not, however, given me validity evidence. Neither has research. At present, at least, interviewer reliance on interviewee nonverbal behavior must be treated as a potential source of error.

Stereotypes, Prototypes, and Biases

In the Netherlands, Van Vianen and Willemsen (1992) asked 307 employees in university scientific and technical jobs to check adjectives describing attributes identified in job advertisements. One group of subjects filled out the checklist from the point of view of evaluating a future colleague. The other half responded to the items as generally associated with men, with women, or with both genders. An item was classed as "masculine" or "feminine" or "sex neutral" by rather stringent criteria. The final, abbreviated list was dubbed the "Sex Stereotype Attribute List." Its scoring key, applied to future colleague evaluations, showed gender stereotypes for ideal applicants for various jobs, and interviewer judgments were consistent with them.

The notion of an ideal applicant need not be stereotypic. Prototypes of ideal candidates can be developed by deliberation, perhaps from job descriptions or with the help of supervisors and senior employees.

> How do different interviewers develop and use prototypes of desired candidates? ... I distinguish between a stereotype (which develops willy-nilly, is widely accepted, and seems implicitly to apply to all members of a group) and a prototype, by which I mean something like a car designer's prototype, a carefully and systematically developed ideal to be achieved; for selection, the prototype should be defined by a set of attributes that not only describe the desired candidates but distinguish them from those less desired.... I suspect that work on the idea of a prototype as a planned ideal will be more fruitful than work on more or less generally accepted stereotypes of what is." (Guion, 1987, p. 202)

"Similar-to-me" is a bias. "Similar-to-ideal candidate" seems a useful match to an ideal prototype; if the prototype is valid, matching it should imply valid assessment as well. After interviews, Dalessio and Imada (1984) asked each interviewer in a five-member panel to complete a descriptive rating form including seven college majors, 10 personality traits, 11 interests, and six preferences. Three weeks after all interviews were completed, the interviewers filled out the same form describing (a) an ideal applicant and (b) themselves. Actual interview decisions were more closely related to the ideal applicant match than to the self-applicant match.

Interviewers' biases potentially include demographic variables like sex, race, ethnicity, or age, although research generally reports little or nonsignificant differences in interviewers' ratings of men and women, or of different ethnic groups. However, a more general "similar-to-me" bias could inflate tendencies toward bias. In one study, racial similarity effects were stronger in conventional than in structured interviews, although mixed-race panels of interviewers avoided the effect (Lin, Dobbins, & Farh, 1992); similarity effects were not found for age. Another study of panels of interviewers showed a similar racial effect, giving higher ratings to candidates of the same racial identity as the majority of the panel (Prewett-Livingston, Feild, Veres, & Lewis, 1996).

Interviewee Characteristics

Obviously, characteristics of the person interviewed should influence decisions; they include the characteristics sought. Two special cases, however, merit concern as potential sources of error.

Memory. Interviews generally consist of questions requiring the interviewee to respond with a remembered event, state, or behavior. Personal recall may not be accurate (Pearson, Ross, & Dawes, 1992). People may have

have implicit theories of their own personalities that emphasize stability (e.g., This is how I think now, so I must have thought similarly then). Other people, or the same people for other questions, have implicit theories that lead them to exaggerate changes that have occurred. That is, people make the implicit assumption that behaviors match attitudes. If a person recalls behavior (e.g., leaving a job) associated with an attitude, and if the attitude has changed, the response may describe behavior more in line with the present attitude than with the earlier reality.

Impression Management. Candidates try to make good impressions, and some are better at it than others. *Impression management* is the attempt to influence the impression made on others. There are surely individual differences in self-presentation skills, but there is little information about kinds of job performance these skills may predict or the kinds of assessments they may contaminate (Fletcher, 1990). Interview research needs to study the effect of impression management. Does behavior successfully creating the desired impressions with one interviewer work equally well with another? Can interviewers learn to detect the deceptions the term "impression management" implies? If so, can they successfully ignore it in making job-relevant assessments or decisions. In a widely cited article, Kinicki et al. (1990) found that two factors described interviewer ratings on six dimensions. One they labeled "interview impression," the other was called "relevant qualifications." The terms are adequately descriptive; only the relevant qualifications factor validly predicted independent job performance ratings.

In General

A large body of research on interviewing has, in my opinion, given too little practical information about how to structure an interview, how to conduct it, and how to use it as an assessment device. I think I know from the research that (a) interviews can be valid, (b) for validity they require structuring and standardization, (c) that structure, like many other things, can be carried too far, (d) that without carefully planned structure (and maybe even with it) interviewers talk too much, and (e) that the interviews made routinely in nearly every organization could be vastly improved if interviewers were aware of and used these conclusions. There is more to be learned and applied.

REFERENCES

Albright, L. E., Glennon, J. R., & Siegert, P. A. (1963). Measuring achievement motivation at the time of employment. *Journal of Industrial Psychology, 1,* 59–65.

Alliger, G. M., Lilienfeld, S. O., & Mitchell, K. E. (1996). The susceptibility of overt and covert integrity tests to coaching and faking. *Psychological Science, 7,* 32–39.

Anastasi, A. (1988). *Psychological testing* (6th ed.). New York: Macmillan.

Anderson, C. W. (1960). The relation between speaking times and decision in the employment interview. *Journal of Applied Psychology, 44,* 267–268.

Anderson, N. R. (1991). Decision making in the graduate selection interview: An experimental investigation. *Human Relations, 44,* 403–417.

Arvey, R. D., & Campion, J. E. (1982). The employment interview: A summary and review of recent research. *Personnel Psychology, 35,* 281–322.

Campion, M. A., Campion, J. E., & Hudson, J. P., Jr. (1994). *Structured interviewing: A note on incremental validity and alternative question types.* Presented by M. A. Campion at the meetings of the American Psychological Association, August, 1994, under the title *Cutting the Edge in Personnel Selection with Structured Interviews.*

Campion, M. A., Pursell, E. D., & Brown, B. K. (1988). Structured interviewing: Raising the psychometric properties of the employment interview. *Personnel Psychology, 41,* 25–42.

Carrier, M. R., Dalessio, A. T., & Brown, S. H. (1990). Correspondence between estimates of content and criterion-related validity values. *Personnel Psychology, 43,* 85–100.

Cattell, R. B. (1944). Psychological measurement: normative, ipsative, interactive. *Psychological Review, 51,* 292–303.

Conway, J. M., Jako, R. A., & Goodman, D. F. (1996). A meta-analysis of interrater and internal consistency reliability of selection interviews. *Journal of Applied Psychology, 80,* 565–579.

Cureton, E. E. (1950). Validity, reliability, and baloney. *Educational and Psychological Measurement, 10,* 94–96.

Curtis, J. R., Gracin, L., & Scott, J. C. (1994, April). *Non-traditional measures for selecting a diverse workforce: A review of four validation studies.* Presented at the meeting of the Society for Industrial and Organizational Psychology, Nashville, TN.

Dalessio, A., & Imada, A. S. (1984). Relationships between interview selection decisions and perceptions of applicant similarity to an ideal employee and self: A field study. *Human Relations, 37,* 67–80.

Daniels, H. W., & Otis, J. L. (1950). A method for analyzing employment interviews. *Personnel Psychology, 3,* 425–444.

Day, D. V., & Silverman, S. B. (1989). Personality and job performance: Evidence of incremental validity. *Personnel Psychology, 42,* 25–36.

Devlin, S. E., Abrahams, N. M., & Edwards, J. E. (1992). Empirical keying of biographical data: Cross validity as a function of scaling procedure and sample size. *Military Psychology, 4,* 119–136.

Dougherty, T. W., Ebert, R. J., & Callender, J. C. (1986). Policy capturing in the employment interview. *Journal of Applied Psychology, 71,* 9–15.

Dougherty, T. W., Turban, D. B., & Callender, J. C. (1994). Confirming first impressions in the employment interview: A field study of interviewer behavior. *Journal of Applied Psychology, 79,* 659–665.

Dreher, G. F., Ash, R. A., & Hancock, P. (1988). The role of the traditional research design in underestimating the validity of the employment interview. *Personnel Psychology, 41,* 315–327.

Fletcher, C. (1990). The relationships between candidate personality, self-presentation strategies, and interviewer assessments in selection interviews: An empirical study. *Human Relations, 43,* 739–749.

Frederiksen, N., & Melville, S. D. (1954). Differential predictability in the use of test scores. *Educational and Psychological Measurement, 14,* 647–656.

Gandy, J. A., Dye, D. A., & MacLane, C. N. (1994). Federal government selection: The individual achievement record. In G. S. Stokes, M. D. Mumford, & W. A. Owens (Eds.), *Biodata handbook: Theory research and use of biographical information in selection and performance prediction* (pp. 275–309). Palo Alto, CA: CPP Books.

Gehrlein, T. M., Dipboye, R. L., & Shahani, C. (1993). Nontraditional validity calculations and differential interviewer experience: Implications for selection interviewers. *Educational and Psychological Measurement, 52*, 457–469.

Graves, L. M. (1993). Sources of individual differences in interviewer effectiveness: A model and implications for future research. *Journal or Organizational Behavior, 14*, 349–370.

Guion, R. M. (1965). *Personnel testing*. New York: McGraw-Hill.

Guion, R. M. (1987). Changing views for personnel selection. *Personnel Psychology, 40*, 199–213.

Hakel, M. D. (1989). The state of employment interview theory and research. In R. W. Eder & G. R. Ferris (Eds.), *The employment interview: Theory, research, and practice* (pp. 285–293). Newbury Park, CA: Sage.

Harris, M. M. (1989). Reconsidering the employment interview: A review of recent literature and suggestions for future research. *Personnel Psychology, 42*, 691–726.

Herriot, P. (1993). Commentary: A pardigm bursting at the seams. *Journal of Organizational Behavior, 14*, 371–375.

Hollingworth, H. L. (1923). *Judging human character*. New York: Appleton.

Hough, L. M. (1984). Development and evaluation of the "accomplishment record" method of selecting and promoting professionals. *Journal of Applied Psychology, 69*, 135–146.

Hough, L. M., & Paullin, C. (1994). Construct-oriented scale construction: The rational approach. In G. S. Stokes, M. D. Mumford, & W. A. Owens (Eds.), *Biodata handbook: Theory, research, and use of biographical information and performance prediction* (pp. 109–145). Palo Alto, CA: CPP Books.

Hough, L., & Tippins, N. (1994, April). New designs for selection and placement systems: The *Universal Test Battery*. In N. Schmitt (Chair), *Cutting edge developments in selection;* symposium at meeting of the Society for Industrial and Organizational Psychology, Nashville, TN.

Hovland, C. I., & Wonderlic, E. F. (1939). Prediction of success from a standardized interview. *Journal of Applied Psychology, 23*, 537–546.

Huffcutt, A. I., & Arthur, W., Jr. (1994). Hunter and Hunter (1984) revisited: Interview validity for entry-level jobs. *Journal of Applied Psychology, 79*, 184–190.

Hughes, J. L., & Dodd, W. E. (1961). Validity versus stereotype: Predicting sales performance by ipsative scoring of a personality test. *Personnel Psychology, 14*, 343–355.

Hunter, J. E., & Hunter, R. F. (1984). Validity and utility of alternative predictors of job performance. *Psychological Bulletin, 96*, 72–98.

Jackson, D. N., & Messick, S. (1958). Content and style in personality assessment. *Psychological Bulletin, 55*, 243–252.

Janz, T. (1989). The patterned behavior description interview: The best prophet of the future is the past. In R. W. Eder & G. R. Ferris (Eds.), *The employment interview: Theory, research, and practice* (pp. 158–168). Newbury Park, CA: Sage.

Janz, T., Hellervik, L., & Gilmore, D. C. (1986). *Behavior description interviewing*. Boston: Allyn and Bacon.

Kenny, D. A., & La Voie, L. (1985). Separating individual and group effects. *Journal of Personality and Social Psychology, 48*, 339–348.

Kinicki, A. J., Lockwood, C. A., Hom, P. W., & Griffeth, R. W. (1990). Interviewer predictions of applicant qualifications and interviewer validity: Aggregate and individual analyses. *Journal of Applied Psychology, 75*, 477–486.

Kriedt, P. H., & Dawson, R. I. (1961). Response set and the prediction of clerical job performance. *Journal of Applied Psychology, 45*, 175–178.

Landy, F. J. (1976). The validity of the interview in police officer selection. *Journal of Applied Psychology, 61*, 193–198.

Latham, G. P. (1989). The reliability, validity, and practicality of the situational interview. In R. W. Eder & G. R. Ferris (Eds.), *The employment interview: Theory, research, and practice* (pp. 169–182). Newbury Park, CA: Sage.

Latham, G. P., & Wexley, K. N. (1977). Behavioral observation scales for performance appraisal. *Personnel Psychology, 30,* 255–268.

Latham, G. P., & Wexley, K. N. (1981). *Increasing productivity through performance appraisal.* Reading, MA: Addison-Wesley.

Lawshe, C. H. (1975). A quantitative approach to content validity. *Personnel Psychology, 28,* 563–575.

Lin, T. R., Dobbins, G. H., & Farh, J. (1992). A field study of race and age similarity effects on interview ratings in conventional and situational interviews. *Journal of Applied Psychology, 77,* 367–371.

Maas, J. B. (1965). Pattern scaled expectation interview: Reliability studies on a new technique. *Journal of Applied Psychology, 49,* 431–433.

Mael, F. A. (1991). A conceptual rationale for the domain and attribute of biodata items. *Personnel Psychology, 44,* 763–792.

Mael, F. A., & Hirsch, A. C. (1993). Rainforest empiricism and quasi-rationality: Two approaches to objective biodata. *Personnel Psychology, 46,* 719–738.

Marchese, M. C., & Muchinsky, P. M. (1993). The validity of the employment interview: A meta-analysis. *International Journal of Selection and Assessment, 1,* 18–26.

Mayfield, E. C. (1964). The selection interview—A re-evaluation of published research. *Personnel Psychology, 17,* 239–260.

McDaniel, M. A., Whetzel, D. L., Schmidt, F. L., & Maurer, S. D. (1994). The validity of employment interviews: A comprehensive review and meta-analysis. *Journal of Applied Psychology, 79,* 599–616.

McHenry, J. J., Lough, L. M., Toquam, J. L., Hanson, M. A., & Ashworth, S. (1990). Project A validity results: The relationship between predictor and criterion domains. *Personnel Psychology, 43,* 335–354.

McMurry, R. N. (1947). Validating the patterned interview. *Personnel, 23,* 263–272.

Messick, S. (1960). Dimensions of social desirability. *Journal of Consulting Psychology, 24,* 279–287.

Messick, S. (1993, August). *The matter of style: Manifestations of personality in cognition, learning, and teaching.* Presented as the 1993 E. L. Thorndike Award Address at the annual meeting of the American Psychological Association, Toronto.

Owens, W. A. (1976). Background data. In M. D. Dunnette (Ed.), *Handbook of industrial and organizational psychology* (1st ed., pp. 609–644). Chicago: Rand-McNally.

Parkinson, C. N. (1962). Genius by the yard. *Saturday Review, 45*(41), 32–33.

Pearson, R. W., Ross, M., & Dawes, R. M. (1992). Personal recall and the limits of retrospective questions in surveys. In J. M. Tanur (Ed.), *Questions about questions: Inquiries into the cognitive bases of surveys* (pp. 65–94). New York: Russell Sage Foundation.

Prewett-Livingston, A. J., Feild, H. S., Veres, J. G., III, & Lewis, P. M. (1996). Effects of race on interview ratings in a situational panel interview. *Journal of Applied Psychology, 81,* 178–186.

Reilly, R. R., & Chao, G. T. (1982). Validity and fairness of some alternative employee selection procedures. *Personnel Psychology, 35,* 1–62.

Roth, P. L., & Campion, J. E. (1992). An analysis of the predictive power of the panel interview and pre-employment tests. *Journal of Occupational and Organizational Psychology, 65,* 51–60.

Rothe, H. F. (1950). Use of an objectivity key on a short industrial personality questionnaire. *Journal of Applied Psychology, 34,* 98–101.

Ruch, F. L., & Ruch, W. W. (1967). The K factor as a (validity) suppressor variable in predicting success in selling. *Journal of Applied Psychology, 51,* 201–204.

Russell, C. J. (1994). Generation procedures for biodata items: A point of departure. In G. S. Stokes, M. D. Mumford, & W. A. Owens (Eds.), *Biodata handbook: Theory, research, and use of biographical information in selection and performance prediction* (pp. 17–38). Palo Alto, CA: CPP Books.

Ryan, A. M., & Sackett, P. R. (1987). Pre-employment honesty testing: Fakability, reactions of test takers, and company image. *Journal of Business and Psychology, 1,* 248–256.

Rynes, S., & Gerhart, B. (1990). Interviewer assessments of applicant "fit": An exploratory investigation. *Personnel Psychology, 43,* 13–35.

Schmitt, N. (1976). Social and situational determinants of interview decisions: Implications for the employment interview. *Personnel Psychology, 29,* 79–101.

Schneider, B., & Schmitt, N. (1986). *Staffing organizations* (2nd ed.). Glenview, IL: Scott, Foresman.

Schoenfeldt, L. F., & Mendoza, J. L. (1994). Developing and using factorially derived biographical scales. In G. S. Stokes, M. D. Mumford, & W. A. Owens (Eds.), *Biodata handbook: Theory, research and use of biographical information in selection and performance prediction* (pp. 147–169). Palo Alto, CA: CPP Books.

Shahani, C., Dipboye, R. L., & Gehrlein, T. M. (1991). The incremental contribution of an interview to college admissions. *Educational and Psychological Measurement, 51,* 1049–1061.

Sisson, E. D. (1948). Forced choice: The new Army rating. *Personnel Psychology, 1,* 365–381.

Stokes, G. S. (1994). Introduction and history. In G. S. Stokes, M. D. Mumford, & W. A. Owens (Eds.), *Biodata handbook: Theory, research, and use of biographical information in selection and performance prediction* (pp. xv–xix). Palo Alto, CA: CPP Books.

Stone, D. L., & Jones, G. E. (1994, April). Perceived fairness of biodata as a function of the purpose of the request for information and gender of the applicant. Presented at the Conference of the Society for Industrial and Organizational Psychology, Nashville, TN.

Stone, E. F., & Stone, D. L. (1990). Privacy in organizations: Theoretical issues, research findings, and protection strategies. In G. Ferris & K. Rowland (Eds.), *Research in personnel and human resources management* (Vol. 8, pp. 349–411). Greenwich, CT: JAI Press.

Super, D. E. (1960). The biographical inventory as a method for describing adjustment and predicting success. *Bulletin of the International Association of Applied Psychology, 9,* 18–39.

Ulrich, L., & Trumbo, D. (1965). The selection interview since 1949. *Psychological Bulletin, 63,* 100–116.

Van Vianen, A. E., & Willemsen, T. M. (1992). The employment interview: The role of sex stereotypes in the evaluation of male and female job applicants in the Netherlands. *Journal of Applied Social Psychology, 22,* 471–491.

Wagner, R. (1949). The employment interview: A critical summary. *Personnel Psychology, 2,* 17–46.

Walters, L. C., Miller, M. R., & Ree, M. J. (1993). Structured interviews for pilot selection: No incremental validity. *The International Journal of Aviation Psychology, 3,* 25–38.

Webster, E. C. (1964). *Decision making in the employment interview.* Montreal: McGill University.

Wiesner, W. H., & Cronshaw, S. F. (1988). A meta-analytic investigation of the impact of interview format and degree of structure on the validity of the employment interview. *Journal of Occupational Psychology, 61,* 275–290.

Wright, O. R., Jr. (1969). Summary of research on the selection interview since 1964. *Personnel Psychology, 22,* 391–413.

Zedeck, S., Tziner, A., & Middlestadt, S. E. (1983). Interviewer validity and reliability: An individual analysis approach. *Personnel Psychology, 36,* 355–370.

14

Multiple Assessment Procedures

Just one predictor of performance is rarely as useful as several. Most personnel decisions are based on multiple assessments. For simple jobs, formal assessment of one truly critical trait may be enough, but even that assessment is likely to be augmented by other information; more complex jobs call for more complex assessment programs. This chapter describes two systematic approaches to multiple assessment, that is, individual assessment and group assessment center programs that usually include assessments of performance on specially developed exercises.

USE OF TEST BATTERIES

To introduce these topics, I start with a condensed, partial reprise of chapter 8 and some principles of multivariate prediction. These principles form a background for individual and group multiple assessment procedures.

The usual prototype of multiple assessment is a battery of tests combined to predict a single criterion. Scores on the several tests are added (with or without weights) to form a composite score which, by itself, has no particular meaning beyond a predicted criterion level. Prediction, based on linear multiple regression, is enhanced when scores on each test in the battery predict the criterion and have low correlations with each other, that is, are not redundant.

The use of additive, compensatory models is well-established and not to be abandoned capriciously. However, we need a new concept of compensatory batteries. Essentially, the additive model is described with the word *and*: the decision is based on a composite consisting of test A *and* test B *and* test C, and so on. What is often needed is compensation by alternatives where the operative word is *or*. This is implied in the Dunnette selection model depicted in Fig. 2.14. It seems especially necessary under the accomodation provisions of ADA. Moreover, it seems feasible in algorithms for judgmental policies.

Individual and group assessment programs combine multiple assessments judgmentally, not statistically. One advantage of them may be that they facilitate compensation by alternatives—*or* rather than *and*. Of course, what we know of judgmental versus statistical prediction suggests that such efforts can have the serious disadvantage of being less valid.

Statistical models for prediction are usually multivariate only on the predictor side of the equation; typically, a single criterion is predicted, although it may be quite global and complex. Consider, however, a circumstance in which different criteria are predicted, and perhaps even one in which the different predictions suggest different decisions. Such a situation might arise if the predicted criteria are actual job production (in some dollar amount per unit of cost) and a contextual criterion such as dependability or integrity. These may be predicted by different tests. If both criteria are placed on a standard scale ($M = 50$; $SD = 10$), what should a manager do with a candidate whose predicted level on one of these criteria is 70 (calling for a favorable decision) and 30 (calling for rejection) on the other?

This is a common enough problem, evaded rather than solved by the common practice of insisting that all validation research use a single, global criterion. Different predictions cannot be expected to have universally consistent implications for decisions unless the different criteria are correlated highly enough to justify combining them. There seem to be three possible nonevasive solutions to the problem. One is to average predictions, perhaps weighting them by the judged importance of the different criteria. Another is to set minimum acceptable criterion levels on each one (a multiple cut-score approach for predictions). The other is to use managerial judgment, comparing the relative importance of the different criteria to current organizational needs. Long ago I argued that the different predictions should be made and that decisions should be based on the criteria most important when the decision must be made (Guion, 1961). I still consider such judgment the best practice.

The opportunity to exercise such judgment can be useful in organizational diagnostics. I once found that the same scores predicted good performance ratings and early quitting. Top-down selection would create a highly capable but unstable work force. Good management judgment would ask why the best people were most likely to leave; the problem of selection decisions should be secondary to the organizational question.

INDIVIDUAL ASSESSMENT PROGRAMS

Some years ago, I experienced a memorable example of a need for individual assessment. A small electrical supply firm wanted to select an employee for training in interior decorating to develop ways to decorate with light. The training would be expensive but a potentially good investment. Who should be chosen? We had no prior research to guide such a decision. How can the candidates be assessed so that the choice is well-informed? Situations like these call for assessing people one at a time, that is, for individual assessments.

General Practice in Individual Assessment

Little research on individual assessment has been reported, and most published reports are old. Nevertheless, individual assessment is alive and well as an area of professional practice, if not as an area of research.

A General Pattern of Practice. The distinguishing feature of individual assessment, of course, is that it assesses one person at a time. Ryan and Sackett (1987) said that an equally important and defining feature is that one psychologist conducts a final, integrating interview and one psychologist (maybe the same one) writes the assessment report.[1] Interviewing and report writing could be the work of panels of assessors, but that is uncommon. The assessor may call on various resource people for parts of the assessment process, but one assessor is finally responsible for integrating all information and reporting to the client (typically the decision maker rather than the person being assessed).

Ryan and Sackett (1987) surveyed members of the Society for Industrial and Organizational Psychology (SIOP) and found that those doing individual assessments are likely to be full-time, licensed consultants, and to be one of several in the organization who do such assessments.

Respondents reported many purposes; selection and promotion (including planning for succession) and outplacement were the major ones. They also reported that assessment typically required at least a half day; some were shorter, and some required 2 full days. Assessment tools

---

[1] I recognize that individual assessment for personnel decisions is done all the time by people who are not psychologists. Trainers, managers, former school teachers, and others who are "nice people who get along well with others" assess candidates for various opportunities. For all I know, they may do it as well as or even better than psychologists, but the lack of systematic procedure is even more pronounced if we extend the field so widely. Ryan and Sackett (1987) restricted their definition to psychologists as the assessors, and I do likewise rather than try to unravel the additional tangle of idiosyncratic procedures introduced by expanding it.

included personal history data, ability tests, personality and interest inventories, and interviews. The general pattern for arriving at conclusions about assessees was strictly judgmental; mechanistic techniques for setting specific composite scores as cutoffs for recommendations were unpopular. A few respondents reported using the same assessment procedures regardless of the position to be filled (a practice not inconsistent with seeking global appraisals), but most assessors varied the content of their assessments to fit the position. Information about organizations and positions was typically gathered through conversations and interviews, not from more systematic organizational and job analyses. Information sought included the usual emphasis on tasks and responsibilities, KSAs, and critical incidents involving prior successes and failures. Individual assessments were thought to need a wider variety of information than is common in job analysis: interpersonal relationships, supervisory expectations, and broad statements of functions were common, and some respondents mentioned such considerations as organizational climate, opportunities for advancement, subordinate characteristics, and the criteria used in evaluating performance in the position.

Written reports were usually followed by telephone or face-to-face discussions with the client. Reports rarely included actual test scores—and should not[2]—but strengths and weaknesses and suggestions for personal development were usually included. Reports did not necessarily include recommendations; about a third of the respondents reported making

---

[2]The "should not" comment needs to be considered with reference to the age of the person who made it—me. In my professional formative years, in the 1940s and 1950s, telling a person his or her test score was considered absolutely unethical, especially if that person had not been appropriately trained in tests and measurements. By the time the 1974 *Standards* was published (American Psychological Association, American Educational Research Association, & National Council on Measurement in Education, 1974), some ambivalence was evident, brought on largely by the emphasis on personal and civil rights during the 1960s. For example, Standard J2 said that scores should "ordinarily be reported only to people who are qualified to interpret them," but it went on to say that if they are reported to people not so qualified, the report should be accompanied by a lot of explanation. The very next Standard, J2.1, said that a person tested (or that person's agent) "has the right to know his score and the interpretations made"—even to the extent of knowing "scores" on individual items. Standard J2.1 was identified as an ethical rather than a technical standard, and the conflicts between it and standards of test security were recognized; the comment went on to say that it was preferable to have a qualified intermediary sympathetic to the interests of the person tested get and interpret the score. By the 1985 version (American Educational Research Association, American Psychological Association, & National Council on Measurement in Education, 1985), no fewer than 13 standards referred to reporting actual scores, all based on the "right to know" rather than on technical arguments. From a technical point of view, I still adhere to the view that reporting actual test scores, especially to clients who are representatives of organizations rather than the individual tested, should not be done in individual assessment; interpretations are far more important and far less likely to lead to bizarre and idiosyncratic misinterpretations.

ratings on specific traits or expected performance dimensions. (In my own work, I explicitly refused to make recommendations, preferring to end appraisal reports with a series of questions suggested by my conclusions about the candidate. These questions were intended to force the person ultimately responsible for a hiring decision to get independent information (e.g., through telephone calls to earlier employers) and to form his or her own conclusions without abdicating responsibility to an outsider.)

Special Emphases in Position and Situation Analysis. Most assessees are in management or sales, occasionally in relatively high-level technical positions. At these levels, positions are often defined by the incumbents. The specific tasks, responsibilities, and ways of doing things defining the position as it was handled by the previous incumbent may not be precisely the specific tasks, responsibilities, and procedures defining it for the new person; typical task analysis is therefore less appropriate than a broad understanding of the situation. Understanding may require answers to questions like these: (a) Is the person to fill essentially the same functions filled by a predecessor, or will functions be shifted around? (b) Is the vacancy created or influenced by new technology or by division of existing duties? (c) How is the position defined relative to others? (d) What must be done right away, and what can wait for some training or learning on the job? (e) What specific qualifications are essential; what qualifications would be nice to have? (f) How much freedom (or constraint) does the position offer? What will be permitted, encouraged, or frowned upon by superiors and coworkers? The questions arise not only from concern about future performance but about how the assessee will "fit" into the organization. That latter topic will be discussed later.

According to Ryan and Sackett (1987), the answers typically come from interviews or conversations with people in the organization, although job or position information come from written or oral job descriptions or from job or organizational analyses, more likely to be casual than systematic.

Varieties of Individual Assessment Programs

Individual assessment programs differ. Programs described and evaluated in the literature are old ones, generally dating to the 1950s and 1960s. Legal uncertainties of the EEO era may have inhibited publication of such programs. Legal uncertainty remains; Ryan and Sackett (1987) reported that nearly 30% of their respondents were not sure that their practices were consistent with the *Uniform Guidelines*. Their survey also supported the notion that newer programs have introduced few innovations.

A Psychometric Emphasis. In the 1950s, a research and consulting group at Western Reserve University[3] developed an assessment program for "higher level" sales and managerial personnel. The program description is still the most complete in easily accessible literature (e.g., Campbell, 1962; Campbell, Otis, Liske, & Prien, 1962; Huse, 1962; Otis, Campbell, & Prien, 1962). The seven-article series is a prototype for assessment and assessment research, and I highly recommend careful study of it beyond this brief synopsis. The basic program included:

1. A staff member visited clients to learn about the job to be filled, the organization, and the social environment; information gained was used to tailor the assessment program.
2. Two psychologists together interviewed candidates, independently rating them on several scales. They did not have access to test data.
3. Projective test responses were analyzed by a clinical psychologist who rated the candidate on the same scales without seeing the candidate personally and without knowledge of other test results.
4. A test battery was developed specifically for the job in question; the battery minimally included two personality inventories, an interest inventory, and tests of abilities considered important to the job.
5. One psychologist–interviewer wrote a report describing social skills, intellectual functioning, drive and ambition, personal adjustment, and a judgment of probable effectiveness.

The program emphasized the battery of psychometric tests which were generally the most valid components of the program.

A Clinically Oriented Program. An assessment procedure developed for district marketing managers of a national firm featured an intensive 2-hour interview by a clinically oriented consulting psychologist, and included a personal history form, two traditional mental ability tests, a sentence completion test, and a human relations problems test (Albrecht, Glaser, & Marks, 1964). The interviewer prepared the report with final ratings.

Criterion ratings were obtained on four scales by the consultants, by high level managers, and by peers. Multitrait–multimethod convergent validities provided rather good evidence of construct validity.

The report may best be described as a demonstration project. The promotion decisions had already been made, but the project was done

---

[3]After a merger, the University became Case-Western Reserve.

to evaluate the assessment program. There were only 31 districts, and therefore $n = 31$. In 1964 (but not now), this was considered a sufficient sample; the sample size would have been still lower if this had not been a trial conducted on managers of all districts. The number of cases available for evaluating such a program is usually much smaller; sometimes $n = 1$ for a given client. In such cases, the issue of whether clinical or statistical prediction is better is moot; clinical prediction is all that is realistically available.

A Content-Oriented Approach. Robinson (1981) reported an approach beginning with detailed job analysis, identifying important job objectives or dimensions, the behaviors required to meet them, and critical tasks. Critical tasks were seen as content samples from a broader job universe. Major assessment procedures were work sample tests specifically sampling job content, but a structured interview was also part of the procedure. Candidates recruited through advertising were assessed, and one of them was hired. The evaluation consisted of a report that he was considered to be doing well a year later.

Some Assessor Habits. Ryan and Sackett (1989) asked three volunteers, experienced assessors trained in experimental or clinical psychology but members of SIOP, to assess three "candidates," providing a total of nine assessments for a study of assessor reliability. These assessors were chosen in part because they used different methods and were all well-regarded in the business community. The ostensible job opening was for a director of training and development; the three volunteer "candidates" were people involved in sales training. The study provided a "client contact" person. My focus here is on comparing the approaches of these assessors.

They did some things alike. All obtained job requirements from the client contact, included cognitive and personality measures (although not the same ones), and used semi-structured interviews. None asked for detailed job specifications or used work samples or simulations. All provided written, narrative reports. But they did some things differently.

Assessor 1 gathered organizational information from the client contact; the others did not; she also gathered more job information than the others. She used a long personal history form, and her average interview time was relatively long. She focused on job experience and secondarily on personal background. Her written reports, alone among the three, included actual test scores or percentiles for cognitive tests.

Assessor 2, using tests and an interview focused on critical incidents, was most interested in ability requirements for supervision, including administrative skills and decision making.

Assessor 3 was more clinical in orientation, including more emphasis on personal background and the only one to use projective techniques. The latter formed the basis for many interview questions, but the average interview time was the lowest of the three.

Common and Uncommon Features. These examples do not describe the full variety of individual assessment programs, but they identify some features, both common and unique. Common to all of them was that they could be used for employers with a single position to fill. In all cases, the kinds of positions to be filled were those where the cost of a poor choice among candidates could be high, economically and in terms of organizational relationships. In all, the choice of assessment instruments was based on position and organizational characteristics. All included interviews as part of the assessment process, although the nature of the interviews and their ground rules differed.

Personality assessment was included by most of these assessors. Projective methods were used by some of them, but not as major components of most of them. Probably the most important of the unique characteristics was Robinson's use of work sample tests, assessing directly relevant job skills instead of abstract constructs. Another uncommon feature was in the Western Reserve interviews which, according to their ground rules, were conducted without knowledge of other assessment information.

Criticisms of Individual Assessment

Individual assessment programs are open to some major criticisms:

1. Individual assessment is rarely subjected to serious validation efforts, except for the Western Reserve program. Traditional validation is often not possible, but job-related constructs could be identified and evidence could be acquired to evaluate the validity of inferences drawn. Program evaluation methods could also be used, at least in firms doing a lot of assessment.

2. Assessment conclusions are often unreliable. Different assessors evaluate candidates differently, perhaps because they rely on different information and perhaps because they have no standard basis for consistency. An intractable reliability problem exists insofar as different readers of a report draw different inferences from it (Ryan, 1992; Ryan & Sackett, 1989). The three assessors described by Ryan and Sackett (1989) agreed on the rank order of the nine candidates and on some candidate characteristics, but not on ratings of suitability for the position. For example, the assessors said, respectively, that the first candidate was "marginally qualified," "not likely to be successful," and "appears to have considerable potential." Data

from these assessments were used in a later study to see if students or active managers could group together the three reports for each candidate. The answer was no (Ryan, Barbera, & Sackett, 1990). Putting it bluntly, reports differed across assessors so much that report readers could not recognize a person encountered previously in an earlier report.

3. Assessment summaries are too often influenced by one or two parts of the assessment program that could have been used by themselves. This is not surprising; assessment summaries are judgments of the report writer, and judgment research shows that judgments are typically based on only a few of the available cues.

4. Great emphasis is placed on personality assessment without matching evidence of the relevance of the traits assessed. Where assessments are statistically validated against job performance criteria, scores on one or two traditional cognitive tests are usually more valid than scores or clinical judgments based on personality tests (e.g., Dunnette & Kirchner, 1958). Relevance, however, may go beyond traditional performance criteria to relevance to criteria like organizational defense (e.g., against theft) or selection for adaptability to change. Personality traits may be more important for such criteria.

5. Individual assessments, limited to one person, cannot assess interpersonal skills from actual interpersonal behavior. Most individual assessment is done with candidates for managerial or sales work, work that requires interaction with others; assessment without such interaction may be deficient; this may be one reason why group assessment center approaches have dominated the assessment literature in recent years.

6. It may be ethically and legally questionable to seek information not explicitly relevant to the work to be done, yet individual assessments typically include intellectual and personality exploration, gathering general and diverse data about a person. Many people think collecting information without direct job relevance is an unwarranted invasion of privacy. Other people consider it unfair or unethical or incompetent to base decisions on one or two traits without a complete picture of the individual.

All of these points can be answered by appropriate design. Validation efforts combining evidence of relevance of traits assessed with evidence of the construct validities of the assessments may be better validity evidence than a single validity coefficient; that is, well-developed predictive hypotheses should dictate and justify assessment content. Greater use of work samples (or of exercises based on them) could provide easy justifications of content. Where a lot of individual assessment is done over time, program evaluation or lens model analyses may be a way to get empirical evaluations—and to identify instances of possible overemphasis on certain variables (so can careful attention to forming predictive hypotheses). The absence of interpersonal behavior in the assessment process itself is not so serious if personal records of interpersonal achievements can be assessed by achievement records and other biodata, or where interview structure focuses on such history.

AN OVERVIEW OF ASSESSMENT CENTERS

Instead of assessing characteristics of one person at a time, assessment centers assess small groups of people at more or less the same time. Instead of one person being responsible for the final assessments, a group of observers may work together to form a consensus about assessees.

A center is usually a place where something happens; assessment centers, however, are not places but processes. Like individual assessments, assessment center programs use multiple methods of assessment to make multiple assessments. The methods may not include literal work samples or simulations, but they nearly always include exercises chosen to reflect a major aspect of job performance.

Assessment center history, as a formal procedure for psychological assessment, is generally reckoned from the work of the World War II Office of Strategic Services (OSS), a wartime intelligence agency in the United States. The OSS assessment center was, in fact, a place: a farm near Washington, DC, where candidates for intelligence positions were sent for a secret week of interviews, tests, and exercises intended to show whether they had the necessary personal qualities: mental ability, motivation to serve, physical stamina, emotional stability, stress resistance, and others. "To this end they were sent over obstacle courses, attacked in stress interviews, and observed when they were falsely told they had flunked out—the week was calculated to reveal every asset and weakness they might have" (Bray, Campbell, & Grant, 1974, p. 17).

Personality variables are obviously critical for such work, and the director of the OSS assessment center was the leading personality theorist, Henry A. Murray; subsequent assessment centers have followed the pattern and have been heavily laden with the sort of global, general personality assessment used by the OSS, with perhaps less dramatically threatening exercises. Dr. Douglas W. Bray, of the American Telephone & Telegraph Company, was involved in that assessment center and is generally credited with initiating the widespread use of assessment center procedures in assessing people for management work.

Assessment Center Purposes

Most assessment centers are organization-specific. Consulting firms may provide generic assessment center services, primarily for smaller organizations, but they are more likely to assist organizations in developing their own programs. Most assessment centers, especially for managerial purposes, are built around organizationally specific values and practices, perhaps because most of them are developmental more than decision tools. They are not always designed for managers; many are for sales people or public safety jobs.

Purposes differ within occupational categories. Thornton and Byham (1982) divided managerial assessments into those for early identification of potential managers, for promotions, or for management development. The different purposes call for differences in program design. Different purposes may call for assessments of different constructs. Some diagnostic purposes may require psychologists or educators as assessors, but other developmental purposes may be better accomplished with managers as assessors—managers not unlike those to whom assessees will later report. An overall assessment rating (OAR) may have no importance for diagnostic purposes but may be crucial for personnel decisions like hiring or promotion. The discussion here focuses on selection or promotion.

Assessment Center Components

An organizing principle of assessment center development is that the program should be a *multiattribute assessment*, assessment on several dimensions relevant to the decision to be made. A further principle is that the assessments should not depend on specific methods of assessment—they should be *multimethod* assessments. Any attribute is to be assessed by more than one method. The multimethod aspect of assessment center programs is not a merely a matter of numbers for increasing reliability, although it may serve that purpose. The reason is "rather that the process of seeking confirmation from several exercises leads to more validity of measurement of complex dimensions" (Thornton & Byham, 1982, p. 227). It leads to greater validity through more comprehensive domain sampling and through the convergent evidence of validity of dimensional assessments.

Assessment centers have many components. Job or task analysis provides background; special exercises are based on task analyses (Thornton & Byham, 1982; Zedeck, 1986). Standardized tests are often chosen for important KSAs. Any component should be clearly relevant to the job, provide reliable and valid assessments, and contribute meaningfully to an OAR, if one is used. Some varieties of assessment procedures are briefly discussed here, but the list is not at all exhaustive.

Tests and Inventories. Traditional tests and inventories are included in most assessment centers. Their role in an OAR raises some questions. How should they be combined with various ratings? Statistically? In an additive model with nominal weights? If given to the assessors as information to consider with exercise ratings in arriving at the OAR, should they be given as raw scores, z-scores, percentiles, or other interpretive scores?

Tests and inventories, by themselves, often have validities as high as any overall composite of assessment center components. This may be due to superior reliabilities but, whatever the reason, should they be given credence beyond that of the exercises? This is in part a reprise of the performance test versus traditional test issues of chapter 11, but it is more than that. When considering the importance of interpersonal skills in many kinds of jobs, do the group exercises provide more important assessments than those obtained with traditional tests and inventories?

Exercises. Most assessment center exercises are performance tests; they are samples or abstractions of aspects of the jobs for which people are assessed. Many are low in fidelity to the job, but high fidelity simulations would be inappropriate for assessees who do not yet know the job. It is content sampling of sorts, but it is content suggested by (highly abstracted from) the job, not literal job content.

The most frequently used assessment center simulation is an In-Basket exercise (Frederiksen, Saunders, & Wand, 1957). In-Basket tests simulate administrative work, usually with a set of reasonably typical memos, clippings, letters, reports, messages, and even junk mail that can accumulate on a person's desk (Zedeck, 1986). Instructions generally tell the assessee to play the role of a person new to the job, working when no one else is around, trying to clear the desk; In-Baskets are not group exercises. Materials range from simple to complex, from trivial to urgent, and are often interrelated. Additional documents may or may not be provided as reference material (e.g., a file cabinet containing both relevant and unrelated items of information). The assessee may be interviewed after the exercise to explain reasons for actions taken, with ratings based on the interview. Some In-Basket tests, however, have scoring protocols and require no further information from the assessee.

A equally common exercise, not clearly a simulation, is the Leaderless Group Discussion (Bass, 1954; Thornton & Byham, 1982). The group is given a problem to solve, a time limit in which to do so, and perhaps a requirement for a written solution. No one is assigned the role of chair; leadership functions must emerge during the discussion. Specific roles might be assigned to the various group members, often with the competitive requirement of trying to convince others to adopt a particular position. Many variants on the theme have been used.

Interviews. Assessment centers usually use interviews, but they are not like employment interviews. Various examples include stress interviews, interviews as role-playing simulations, and panel interviews.

Ordinary problems of interviews occur in these, but assessment center interviews can be more standardized, without being test-like, than other interviews.

Assessors

Functions of Assessors. Zedeck (1986) identified three assessor functions. A major function is simply to observe and record behavior in the exercises. Behavior is commonly recorded in descriptive (and perhaps evaluative) reports written about the observations. Fulfillment of this function requires careful, standard training. Ratings for a given dimension may be made by different assessors in different exercises. Differences in the behavior observed and the dimensional inferences drawn from it are necessarily attributable in part to the differences in exercises, but they should not be attributable to different assessors having different understandings of the nature of the dimension. A related problem is that the observers may also be part of the stimulus, and different observers may stimulate different reactions. Videotaped exercise performance may help with this; the assessors can observe tapes, even with "instant replay" if needed (Ryan et al., 1995).

A second function is as a role player, an active partipant in an assessment exercise. In many exercises, assessors are interviewers, usually with another assessor in a purely observer role. In such exercises, an assessor serves as a stimulus to which the assessee responds. One problem for this function is lack of standardization. Role players may change their own behavior during the sequence of interviews. In a stress interview, for example, some may get harsher over a sequence of interviews whereas others may say, in effect, to heck with it—and cause less stress. If different assessors play the same role, standardization is still more unlikely. I think assessors should not be role players. First, trying to be an actor and an observer simultaneously is cognitively difficult. Second, assessors are unlikely to be good actors; standardization would be easier if roles were played by professional actors, especially those experienced in improvisation. Third, assessors (in my judgment) should be as unobtrusive as possible.

Zedeck's third function is as a predictor. Assessors may make explicit predictions, or prediction may be based on the ratings, whether dimensional ratings or OARs.

Assessor Qualifications. Assessors may be psychologists, HR staff, or job experts (e.g., managers in managerial assessment centers). Staff psychologists may be assessors with managers, they might chair assessor panel discussions, or they might simply be resource people. Assessors from whatever source should receive intensive training with frequent refreshers; they should be fully familiar with the exercises and the kinds of behavior they might observe, and they should fully understand the language and concepts related to the ratings they are asked to make.

Managers are organizationally well-informed assessors, and their practical knowledge of the organization and its policies and climate make them useful decision makers. Such benefit must be weighed against the cost of taking them from their jobs for periods of training and for the actual assessment center activity. If assessors receive 2 weeks of training, if assessment centers take 1 week at a time (many do, although others are substantially shorter), and if the assessors are to work six times during a year, then the assessment center may require 8 weeks of high level management time. Many organizations consider the cost acceptable for the benefits accrued, but many others may find it excessive.

In any case, assessors should be good observers, objective in temperament, intelligent, and articulate in conference.

Numbers of Assessors Needed. Typically, the ratio of assessees to assessors is 2:1. Thornton and Byham (1982) considered this a desirable ratio. It may depend on the design of the program—for example, what ratings are made and when, or other assignments to observers. Cognitive demands on observers are heavy and can be reduced by adding more assessors, but that can be daunting for the assessees. It may be better to use fewer assessors over a longer time period viewing videotapes (Ryan et al., 1995).

Other questions emerge. Should assessors become specialists? Should one assessor be a specialist in the leaderless group discussion and another a specialist in personal history interviews? Perhaps a specialist for certain dimensions? In group exercises, should each assessor try to observe and rate all candidates in the group or be assigned to observe and rate no more than two at a time? These are questions about ways to use assessors as observers and raters to maximize reliability and validity of the assessments provided. I do not know the answers and call again for more research.

Dimensions to be Assessed

There is disagreement about the dimensions to be rated. The dimensions (constructs) might be personal traits, job-defined competencies, or performance levels on aspects of jobs reflected in simulations. Assessors might be asked to rate only overall performance in an exercise, or perhaps component aspects of exercise performance. Traits rated might be generalized, habitual behaviors. Task performance may be rated in terms of outcomes or processes. A dimension can be defined by behavior exhibited only in particular kinds of situations. All of these constructs, except the last one, should generalize across situations, therefore across exercises. The last one is an idea of a dimension that has not been traditionally espoused in the assessment center literature. The choice of dimension is partly a matter of purpose, as shown in Table 14.1.

In early assessment centers, personal traits, largely personality traits that were thoroughly defined and discussed by psychologists like Henry Murray (1938), were rated; more recent ones favor behavioral categories that, unfortunately, are often poorly defined. The literature on assessment center dimensions is not exemplary. More bluntly, much of it is silly. Trait constructs are often denied because traits are (mistakenly) defined simply as personality variables that "cause" behavior, apparently irrespective of circumstances. Task competencies are often rejected because they are seen as being concerned only with outcomes, another unwarranted restriction in definition. Thornton and Byham (1982, p. 118) preferred to refer to "behavioral dimensions"—dimensions inferred from job analysis, defined behaviorally in terms of directly observable behaviors, and free of any inferences about underlying personality traits.

In my judgment, the real issue is not whether the dimensions should be called traits, competencies, or behavioral dimensions; after all, they can all

TABLE 14.1
Illustrative Assessment Center Dimensions for Different Purposes

Early identification	Promotion	Developmental planning
Communication skills	Oral communication	Oral communication
		Oral presentation
	Written communication	Written communication
Energy	Energy	
Job motivation	Job motivation	
Career ambition	Career ambition	
Initiative	Initiative	Initiative
	Creativity	
Sensitivity	Sensitivity	Sensitivity
Leadership	Leadership	Individual leadership
		Group leadership
		Behavioral flexibility
		Negotiation
	Tolerance for stress	
Planning and organizing	Planning and organizing	Planning and organizing
	Delegation	Delegation
	Management control	Management control
Decision making	Decision making	Analysis
		Judgment
		Decisiveness

Note. From Thornton, G. C., III., & Byham, W. C. (1982). Assessment centers and managerial performance. New York: Academic Press. Reprinted with permission.

be defined in behavioral terms. The real problem is in the operations defining the dimensions. For most assessment center exercises, ratings are the assessments, so the issue is the typical problem with ratings.

Dimension Definition. Dimensions to be rated differ for different purposes (Thornton & Byham, 1982). If the purpose is early identification of those with strong management potential, the dimensions can be broad, few in number, and independent of particular backgrounds. For promotional purposes, more detailed and more complete descriptions may be needed. For diagnostic or developmental purposes, personal characteristics (which are harder to develop) may be omitted, and some characteristics important for promotional assessments may be further refined into finer, trainable categories. Illustrative examples are shown in Table 14.1.

My understanding of Table 14.1 (maybe not theirs) is that the early identification dimensions, which might also be the dimensions for initial selection, are indeed traits, relatively permanent by adulthood, hard to develop if not developed by adulthood, and likely to generalize across a variety of situations. The list for promotional purposes is similar but more detailed. Many of the dimensions in these lists can be defined as traits, effectiveness or quality of outcomes, or behavioral categories. Whichever, the meanings of their definitions should be the same across exercises and clearly relevant to the job under consideration.

Rating scales should fit the definitions of the attributes (constructs) they operationally define. A summated rating scale for oral communication skill might include an item like, "uses words that convey precise shades of meaning." Such an item would fit a construct that is meaningful for a TV eyewitness reporter, but it probably does not fit an oral communication construct for an air traffic controller, where oral communication skill implies communication that can be heard easily and clearly. Lack of clarity in the conceptual definition of an attribute is the first obstacle to valid assessment of it. Dimension definition begins with job analysis. When the important job behaviors are clearly identified, dimension definition should be comprehensive. Definitions are too often perfunctory statements—short phrases or single sentences. Working definitions should be more complete, in two ways.

First, they should be definitions with explicit relevance to job demands. Thornton and Byham (1982) illustrated the point well. They gave a list of common dimensions, defined with single phrases, used in management assessment centers. Judgment is one such dimension, defined as "developing alternative courses of action and making decisions based on logical assumptions that reflect factual information" (p. 139). That is better than usual, but later they expanded on it for more than a printed page, including examples of judgments made on the job.

Second, the dimension should be defined as constructs are defined, with likely correlates of the dimension, things that tend to invoke it causally or to result from its activation, and the things that it does *not* mean made explicit. The convergent and discriminant logic showing how the dimension relates to other dimensions and is distinguished from still others further clarifies the meaning of the dimension intended by the assessment center developers. Only if raters have such a common understanding of the meaning to be attributed to their ratings can multiple assessments of the same dimensions realize their validity-enhancing potential.

Ratings. Exercises stimulate behavior, the behavior is observed by assessors, and the observations are the foundation for the ratings—which, like scores on tests, must have a meaning to be validated. If ratings of an attribute are valid, and if the same attribute is rated in two or more different exercises, then permissable inferences from ratings of the attribute should be at least somewhat consistent across those exercises; if not, they are not assessing a common construct.

Dimensions may be rated either immediately at the conclusion of the exercise or later in staff conferences. In principle, I would expect immediate ratings to be more closely tied to actually observed behavior than those made later. However, Silverman, Dalessio, Woods, and Johnson (1986) found better construct validity evidence by rating dimensions on the basis of data from all of the relevant exercises.

Behavior in an assessment center exercise should generalize to behavior on a job. This is generally expected of predictors, but it seems especially central to assessment center logic. The logic of multiple assessment is that prediction is better, because assessment is more reliable when assessments are replicated. In assessment centers, replication implies measuring a predictor in more than one way. If the predictors are the rated dimensions, then assessments (ratings) of an attribute in one exercise should generalize to (be correlated with) assessments in another. This is not a psychometric statement of parallel or equivalent forms; it is a statement that, if two exercises are designed so that they reveal (for example) skill in oral communication, then the communication effectiveness in one should be similar to the communication effectiveness in the other. As we see later, it rarely works out that way; I think the problem lies in failure to be clear enough and explicit enough in defining the attributes to be assessed.

Overall Assessments. Most assessment centers call for an overall summary rating, the OAR. Different programs use different procedures for developing the OAR. Is the OAR an operational definition of a definable attribute? It might be, but often it is not; it is likely to be analogous to the composite score computed implicitly in multiple regression, when the composite is simply a complex predictor variable composed of a set of essentially unrelated but valid predictors. The similarity is evident in cases where policy-capturing research creates a set of weights to be used in arriving at a composite rating. Other procedures might call for a mechanical averaging of overall ratings given to individual candidates by the various assessors. More commonly, however, there is a consensus meeting at which candidates are discussed, ratings on attributes are agreed on, independent OARs are made and shared, differences are discussed and resolved, and a consensus achieved. Many people consider the consensus meeting a key feature of the assessment center concept.

THE AT&T MANAGEMENT PROGRESS STUDY

The general characteristics of assessment centers, and the differences among them, may be more clearly seen with a couple of diverse examples. The first is the original managerial assessment center developed when the American Telephone and Telegraph Company (AT&T) began a longitudinal study of the development of managers, the Management Progress Study. The AT&T of the 1950s was a different organization from that of the 1990s; it was the giant, ever-present Bell System. The Management Progress Study, along with the famous Hawthorne studies (Roethlisberger & Dickson, 1939) is another reason for AT&T's reputation for major personnel research.

I do not discuss the developmental processes uncovered by the research; I only describe the methods used and a few results. Even that is further restricted to the assessment of college recruits as reported in Bray et al. (1974). The procedures described are those of the 1950s, so an appropriate disclaimer is that they surely differ from those that Bray and his associates, or others, would choose 40 years later, after much assessment center experience and research.

Overview

The first groups were assessed in groups of 12 for a 3½ day period. Assessors–observers were psychologists or other behavioral scientists from various universities. Assessees knew they were in a research program and that all information collected would be held confidential, even from company management.

Assessors. Assessors observed and rated assigned assessees and then wrote detailed reports of assessee performance. The staff of assessors met in conference for the last day and a half of each assessment week to discuss, rate, and make predictions about individual assessees. A clinical psychologist subsequently examined all materials in detail for each assessee and wrote a highly detailed, and rather lengthy, report for the record.

The Management Progress Study Variables. Variables named as important to managerial success in the scientific literature and by personnel executives were reviewed; 25 attributes chosen for assessment (Bray et al., 1974) are listed in Table 14.2. Factor analysis showed seven factors: (a) administrative skills, (b) interpersonal skills, (c) intellectual ability, (d) performance stability, (e) work motivation, (f) career orientation, and (g) dependence on others.

Assessment Procedures. Component assessments included cognitive tests of general mental ability, critical thinking, and general knowledge; two personality inventories and two projective tests; and an In-Basket, two group exercises, and extensive interviewing. One exercise was a business game for groups of six assessees. Another was a group discussion with assigned roles.

Ratings. During the week, tests were scored and reports were written for each assessee about his performance in the interview, the two group exercises, the In-Basket test, and the projective tests. At the staff conference in the final day and a half of the week, the assessors considered and rated each of the 12 assessees. Each one was considered the responsibility of one

TABLE 14.2
Attributes Assessed in the Early Management
Progress Study Assessment Centers

Variables and Definitions

---

1. *Scholastic Aptitude* (later, General Mental Ability)
   General mental ability as measured by tests of intelligence, scholastic aptitude, or learning ability.
2. *Oral Communication Skill*
   Skill in presenting an oral report to a small conference group on a subject known well.
   Written Communication Skill
   Skill in composing a communicative and formally correct memorandum on a subject known well.
3. *Human Relations Skills*
   Effectiveness in leading a group to accomplish a task without arousing hostility.
4. *Personal Impact*
   Forcefulness and likability in making an early impression.
5. *Perception of Threshold Social Cues*
   Readiness to perceive minimal cues in the behavior of others.
6. *Creativity*
   Likelihood of solving a management problem in a novel way.

(Continued)

TABLE 14.2

(Continued)

Variables and Definitions

7. *Self-Objectivity*
   Realism in viewing assets and liabilities; insight into motives.
8. *Social Objectivity*
   Freedom from prejudices against racial, ethnic, socioeconomic, educational, and other kinds of groups.
9. *Behavior Flexibility*
   Readiness, when motivated, to modify behavior to reach a goal.
10. *Need for Approval of Superiors*
    Extent of emotional dependence on authority figures.
11. *Need for Approval of Peers*
    Extent of emotional dependence on equal and lower status associates.
12. *Inner Work Standards*
    Strength of desire to do a good job even if a less good one is acceptable to the boss and others.
13. *Need for Advancement*
    Strength of desire to be promoted significantly earlier than peers.
14. *Need for Security*
    Extent of valuing a secure job.
15. *Goal Flexibility*
    Readiness to change life goals in accordance with reality opportunities.
16. *Primacy of Work*
    Extent to which satisfactions from work are more important than those from other areas of life.
17. *Bell System Value Orientation*
    Likelihood of incorporating Bell System values, such as service, friendliness, and justice of company positions on earnings, rates, and wages.
18. *Realism of Expectations*
    Extent to which expectations about work life with the company conform to what is likely to be true.
19. *Tolerance of Uncertainty*
    Extent to which performance will stand up under uncertain or unstructured conditions.
20. *Ability to Delay Gratification*
    Extent of ability to work over long periods without great rewards in order to reach later rewards.
21. *Resistance to Stress*
    Extent to which performance will stand up in times of personal stress.
22. *Range of Interests*
    Interest in a variety of fields of activity, such as science, politics, sports, music, and art.
23. *Energy*
    Ability to continuously sustain a high level of work activity.
24. *Organization and Planning*
    Effectiveness in organizing work and planning ahead.
25. *Decision Making*
    Readiness to make decisions, and the quality of the decision made.

Note. Adapted from Bray, D. W., Campbell, R. J., & Grant, D. L. (1974). *Formative years in business: A long-term AT&T study of managerial lives.* New York: Wiley. Reprinted by permission of John Wiley & Sons, Inc.

staff person who read aloud all reports about the assessee and all of his test scores; others took notes. Discussion of an individual assessee required 60–90 minutes, after which each staff member independently rated the assessee on all 25 variables, using 5-point scales. When differences among the ratings were substantial on a variable, they were discussed in detail to arrive at a common interpretation; discussion usually led to consensus. At the end, each staff member made an overall assessment of management potential, saying yes or no to the question, "will this person reach the third level of management within 10 years?"

Validity

Table 14.3, in the right-hand column, gives empirical validity evidence where the dichotomous criterion is whether the person had or had not reached middle management 8 years later. Ratings on 17 individual variables are significant at the 5% level. The uncorrected correlation coefficients, spuriously low because of dichotomization, were as high as .33 with an 8-year interval; of those expected to reach middle management within 10 years, 64% had done so; 32% of those predicted *not* to reach middle management in that time had in fact done so.

An important moderator proved to be perceived level of job stimulation and challenge, as rated from annual follow-up interviews during the 8-year interval. Of those predicted to reach middle management and who reported high levels of job challenge, 76% had made it to level 3 by the 8-year reassessment; only 33% of those with low challenge did so. For those predicted not to make it in 10 years, 61% of those with challenging jobs had done so, compared to only 5% of those with little challenge.

In Retrospect

The AT&T asessment centers have been widely copied and often modified. Similar programs have been used, not only for managerial jobs, but for many others where the cost of poor decisions is high and the rate of hiring or promotion is low. However, some aspects of the AT&T program remain unusual and merit special comment.

1. Despite a whole-person emphasis and an overall rating, the thrust of the staff conference seems directed to predicting rate of promotions. In theory, this was a global prediction based on all 25 variables, but different raters seem to have emphasized different variables—and only a few variables—in arriving at their ratings. No holistic psychological construct seems implied by the prediction, and achieving consensus on the ratings seems to have had low priority. In theory, at least, such

TABLE 14.3
Correlations Between Assessment Variable Ratings and Overall
Ratings and Management Level Attained Eight Years Later

Variable	Overall Assessment Rating (n = 207)	Level at Reassessment (n = 123)
Human relations skills	.66	.32
Behavior flexibility	.63	.21
Organizing and planning	.61	.28
Need for advancement	.60	.31
Decision making	.59	.18
Perception of threshold social cues	.59	.17
Personal impact	.57	.15
Creativity	.57	.25
Oral communications skills	.53	.33
Resistance to stress	.51	.31
Energy	.51	.28
Primacy of work	.48	.18
Inner work standards	.46	.21
Scholastic aptitude	.46	.19
Range of interests	.45	.23
Realism of expectations	.42	.08
Tolerance of uncertainty	.39	.30
Self-objectivity	.38	.04
Need for security	−.32	−.20
Ability to delay gratification	−.30	−.19
Need for approval of superiors	−.18	−.14
Need for approval of peers	−.16	−.17
Bell System value orientation	.15	−.02
Goal flexibility	−.13	−.18
Social objectivity	.04	.13

Note. For overall assessment rating, correlations of .14 or higher are significant at the 5% level; for management level, correlations of .18 or higher are significant at that level. From Bray, Campbell, and Grant (1974). Reprinted with permission.

heterogeneity of reasoning should have reduced the chances for valid predictions; apparently it did not.

2. In most such programs, assessors are organizational members, not outsiders; half to more than half of the assessors used are likely to be working managers. Was use of college professors an advantage or problem? I suspect it was an advantage; outsiders would be less affected by the culture of the organization and the stereotypes of success it might have.

3. The AT&T program made more use of standardized tests than most later programs have. Testing has always had critics, but no special antitest movement was evident when this assessment center was being planned. Leaderless group discussion had been advocated earlier (Bass, 1950); work samples were old hat. Only the simulation exercises (e.g., the In-Basket)

were developed specifically for the Management Progress Study. Recent assessment centers rely less on traditional tests and more on group exercises. Is this an advance or a retreat? I think it is a retreat. However, the AT&T program used a lengthy, unstructured interview. Without a formal survey, my impression is that most recent assessment centers have rather well-structured interviews. That is an advance.

4. Projective tests were considered an essential part of the program; there is evidence that they contributed importantly to assessment staff ratings and to the validity of the predictions (Grant, Katkovsky, & Bray, 1967). Now they are rarely included. Were they superfluous for AT&T, or are contemporary program designers missing a boat?

5. Of the 25 assessee attributes considered, some seemed more critical than others for specific tests and exercises. Nevertheless, unlike many later assessment centers, ratings of these salient variables were not tied to specific tests or exercises; they were were rated only after all assessment exercises were completed. We know from judgment research that this is too many to be considered in making a single overall judgment. It can also be asked whether ratings of dimensions should wait so long after recording observations.

AN ASSESSMENT CENTER FOR POLICE OFFICERS

A second example, also old, was an assessment center for police in one of America's large cities; it was to solve some problems associated with EEO litigation.[4] Along with cognitive abilities, job analysis indicated that personality traits were important to police performance. Assessment centers seemed preferable to personality inventories because they permit inferences from direct observation of behavior in structured situations.

Several thousand candidates were given a battery of written tests in a massive 1-day testing program. More than half were subsequently interviewed, and an eligibility list was based on interview ratings. On the day of the interview, further written tests were administered. With this already extensive background of assessments, recruits chosen for academy training went through the assessment center the week before beginning training.

---

[4]The research for developing and evaluating this assessment center was done primarily by us—Kenneth M. Alvares and I and our associates—at Bowling Green State University. It was not published while it was still new because of continuing litigation; by the time the case died, those of us involved had become too widely scattered, and had become involved in too many other projects, to prepare a scientific report. The report here omits many details; its purpose is less to describe the program and its results than to show why we have some questions about assessment centers.

Overview

The assessment center, after pilot studies, lasted 1½ days. Tests were given to all recruits at once in each of five recruit classes. Exercises were done in groups of six recruits, seven groups in a class.

Some special procedures were used because of the litigation. Because race and sex might bias some observers, it was decided that each recruit would be rated by different observers in different exercises and OARs would be made by people who had not seen the recruits they assessed, based on paper records purged of references to a recruit's sex or race.

Assessor–Observers. Assessor–observers were police command officers and civilians in various city offices; each recruit was observed in each exercise by both a police officer and a civilian. Instead of outside behavioral scientists, we wanted observers who understood police work. The police command officers obviously did. Most civilian observers were social workers, court personnel, hospital workers, or in other jobs with at least some police contact.

Each group of six recruits was observed by four assessors (two police, two civilian); the assessee to observer ratio was 3:2. At first glance, this seems better than typical. However, to maintain the police–civilian pairing for each recruit, and to equalize observational loads across assessors, each observer was responsible for observing and rating three recruits. In retrospect, this may have been an excessive cognitive load. During exercises, each observer took notes and, after the exercise was over, rated each of the assigned recruits on dimensions specified for the exercise. A behavioral checklist was used, presented as a summated ratings scale, and was followed by a 9-point graphic rating scale.

Before the first class, assessors were given intensive training by the Bowling Green research group. For subsequent classes, assessors who had served earlier were given brief refresher training; the full training was given by academy staff to first time assessors.

Dimensions and Exercises

Different tests and exercises assessed different dimensions, and every dimension was supposed to be assessed in at least two tests or exercises. The pattern of assessments, without details, is shown in Fig. 14.1. The ideal of multiple assessments for each dimension was not realized, as shown in Fig. 14.1. Perceptual skill (as defined for this purpose), written communication skill, team spirit, stress tolerance, and four of the five peer ratings were each assessed in only one exercise.

Dimension	Test or Exercise									
	Sitn	PSkl	MMem	MTrB	GDAR	GDNR	Comp	AInt	StrI	Peer
Reasoning	X							X		
Perceptual Skill		X								
Memory		X	X	X						
Oral Communication Skill					X	X				
Written Communication Skill	X									
Leadership/Assertiveness					X	X	X			X
Persuasiveness					X	X				
Team Spirit							X			
Stress Tolerance									X	
Sensitivity/Consideration										X
Dependability										X
Honesty and Integrity										X
Desire for Police Work										X

Legend

Sitn:	Situations Test
PSkl:	A Test of Perceptual Skill (movie test)
Mmem:	Movie Memory Test (immediate and next day)
MTrB:	Training Bulletin Memory Test
GDAR:	Leaderless Group Discussion, Assigned Roles
GDNR:	Leaderless Group Discussion, No Assigned Roles
Comp:	Competitive Exercise
AInt:	Analysis Interview
StrI:	Stress Interview
Peer:	Peer Ratings

FIG. 14.1. A matrix of assessment procedures and the attributes being assessed in the police assessment center; cells with X are those where the assessment method was hypothesized to reflect the attribute.

Situations Test. A test booklet presented three situations, each followed by statements of two witnesses. Open-ended questions asked for differences between the statements, for additional information needed to get at the truth, or for judgments of the relative credibility of the witnesses.

A Test of Perceptual Skill. This was the movie test described in chapter 11. It measured perceptual alertness when not having anything specific to look for. Immediately after the film, a brief memory test was given covering information presented early in the film. A second memory test based on the movie was given the next day.

Leaderless Group Discussions. Two leaderless discussions were held, one with and one without assigned roles. In each, an observer read instructions and presented a problem. The group was to reach consensus within 30 minutes, by which time there should be a written copy of a decision acceptable to all of them.

Competitive Exercise. Each group of six was further divided into two teams of three. Each worked at a table at which were three sets of 31 colored blocks differing in size and shape. Each recruit "owned" a set of blocks of a particular color. Each block had a number on it representing its point value.[5] The task required each team to build a structure according to a plan provided. Individual scores and team scores were computed. The individual score consisted of the point values of one recruit's blocks in the final structure, bonus points for having the highest or second highest point total on the team, and further bonus points if the team won. The team score was the total number of points on the blocks in the structure; using blocks with high point values increased both one's individual and the team scores. The exercise was designed to create some conflict between competitive and cooperative actions, that is, between maximizing one's own scores versus helping the team win. Leadership and team spirit were assessed.

Training Bulletin Study Period and Interviews. Four assessment center components were interrelated. Two of these were interviews, one calling for an analysis of a problem, the other a stress interview. One was a group memory test, based on the content of a set of police training bulletins. The fourth was a study period to get ready for that test—and to build some degree of stress prior to the stress interview.

The stress tolerance assessment merits more description. One of the most important attributes of police candidates is the ability to function well under stress. Poor tolerance of stress can be manifest in several ways such as anger, defensiveness, nervousness, and visible anxiety. Any such reaction interferes with an officer's effectiveness in dealing with other people; a police officer must be able to "keep his or her cool."

Simply being assessed is somewhat stressful, especially in an employment situation. By the end of a long day of assessment exercises, stress can be cumulative, so the stress interview ended the day. The Training Bulletin study period was the framework within which stress might be felt. All 42 recruits were assembled in a classroom, given a formidable stack of training bulletins, general orders, and special orders—and told to study them for a test to be given the next day. To make the situation more stressful, they could not take notes. They were warned that there would be six times during the study period when a courier would enter

---

[5]I confess that, during the development of this exercise, that I had a recurring dread—a nightmare of sorts—of seeing a newspaper headline reading, "Bowling Green Psychologists Have City Police Officers Playing With Blocks." As a matter of fact, this exercise proved to be the one most popular and the one taken most seriously! Had such a headline materialized, our most ardent supporters would have been assessees.

the room and call out certain recruits for other exercises; they were told that each recruit could expect to be called out twice. By presumption, anticipation of these interruptions, as well as the interruptions themselves, might offer some additional stress.

The first interruption was for an Analysis Interview. In this, an individual recruit met with two observers and was given a crime description. The police observer played the role of a witness to be interviewed by the recruit for further information. Then the recruit wrote up a report on conclusions reached. Performance was rated on reasoning ability, but the unfamiliarity of the task was believed to add another increment of stress.

The second interruption was for the Stress Interview. The recruit met with two observers, but this time an officer in uniform interviewed the recruit. He posed a police problem, one for which the recruit was not yet trained, and asked the recruit how it should be handled. These were situations for which no genuinely satisfactory answer existed; even experienced officers would be hard pressed to know what to do. Any solution offered by the recruit could surely be criticized. The interviewer's first criticism was scripted to be kindly; the difficulty with the answer was pointed out and the recruit was invited to try again. As the interview progressed, the interviewer became more overtly hostile and denigrating. The entire performance, about 5 minutes in all, was observed by the civilian observer. Both observers rated the recruit on stress tolerance.

With the interviews alone, recruits would have had idle time waiting their turns; it might have led to relaxation and conversation about the interviews. The training bulletin study period not only filled time but added a second memory test. This seemed useful, but it meant that the three assessments lacked independence.

Peer Ratings. Peer ratings were to be obtained, so group members needed to become fairly well-acquainted. Opportunities were provided for recruits to be together in their groups without observers, once with an exercise somewhat like a party game, to talk and listen to each other.

Peer nominations were made on five dimensions: assertiveness (leadership), sensitivity and consideration, dependability, honesty and integrity, and desire to be a police officer. For each of these, the recruit was asked to identify a first, second, and third choice from among the five fellow group members.

Further Tests and Inventories. The Missing Cartoons test (a test of social intelligence), the Guilford–Zimmerman Temperament Survey (GZTS), and The Adjective Check List were also part of the assessment record. Use of these tests was exploratory, not hypothesis testing.

Overall Ratings

In most assessment centers, the assessors meet in conference at the end to discuss their ratings and to arrive at consensus on both dimension ratings and an overall assessment. In this case, panels of four people, each of whom had been an assessor and was therefore familiar with the exercises, looked at records of recruits they had *not* observed; these records were purged of information revealing the recruit's sex or race. For each recruit, the final OAR was the mean of individual panelists' OARS.

Reliability and Validity

Interrater reliability coefficients were higher for the first class, for which rater training was intensive, than for later classes when training was more relaxed. Exercise composite ratings were also developed, combining ratings on different dimensions. Coefficient alphas were computed for various exercise composites; most of them were above .70 and many were above .90, suggesting that the composites were internally consistent despite being based on apparently different constructs.

Factor analysis of the ratings on individual dimensions (two methods were used) resulted in exercise factors only. For example, the six ratings for either LGD exercise (three different dimensions rated by two slightly different methods) all had their only substantial loadings on a factor for the exercise. What had been expected—what would have demonstrated construct validity for the dimensional ratings—would have been factors for the different dimensions, irrespective of exercise. Construct validity was therefore questionable for the ratings.

So was criterion-related validity. Four different criterion measures were available: (a) success in academy training, (b) performance in field training, (c) sergeant's ratings 2 years after the assessment center, and (d) activity ratings based on daily police records. These were standardized and summed to form a composite. Ordinary multiple regression for all cases combined, using the Test of Perceptual Skill, three exercise composites, the oral communication composite, and two GZTS scales gave a multiple correlation of .38; for individual subgroups defined by sex and race, correlation coefficients ranged from .38 to .64. What required a cautious interpretation, however, was the set of correlations of various assessment center composites and the supervisory ratings by sergeants 2 years later; these uncorrected coefficients reached well into the .40s for all groups combined, suggesting good validity. However, both the mean supervisory ratings and mean assessment center composites were highest for White, male, English-speaking, big people—apparently a stereotype of the "good cop." There is no way to know the degree to which these differences reflect actual subgroup differences in either assessment center or work perform-ance evaluations, but the presumption of bias was strong enough to recommend some major changes in the assessment center procedures and reliance on test scores independently of the assessment center.

ASSESSMENT CENTER PROBLEMS AND ISSUES

The two examples differ, and each of them differs in salient ways from the general picture presented first. The differences emphasize that there is no orthodox one best way in assessment center design; each program is different, in part to fit its different set of circumstances. The differences also highlight some problems of program design and some issues on which experts may disagree.

Construct Validities of Dimension Assessments

The biggest issue focuses on the dimensions, or constructs, rated by observers. In the AT&T example, ratings were done after all tests and exercises were completed. Ratings in the police example were made immediately at the conclusion of an individual exercise developed to assess the rated construct. In other assessment centers, no cross-exercise constructs are rated at all; rather, global performance on each exercise is rated—which seems to go against the logic of multiple methods of as-sessment (the different exercises) to make multiple assessments (of the different constructs). According to that logic, a dimension (construct) identified as important is assessed in more than one way; it should generalize across methods (exercises) and to actual job performance.

Can internally consistent constructs be validly assessed by substantially different assessment exercises? Converging validity evidence is consis-tency in assessments of the same construct across exercises in which it is rated. Lack of convergence may not indicate invalid ratings; it may indi-cate only confusion about what is being assessed.

Dimensional Consistency. If the attribute (construct or dimension) is defined and the exercises developed so that the attribute rated reflects the same construct in two different exercises, then the correlation between the two ratings on the dimension should be, not high, but substantial. Exercises are not designed as parallel forms, so correlations need not approximate reliability coefficients. The multitrait–multimethod logic should apply, however, where different exercises are intended to tap the same constructs. Correlations between ratings of the same dimensions on different exercises should be larger than the correlations between ratings on different dimensions within the same exercise; factor analysis of such a matrix should yield factors consistent with the dimensional constructs.

Results of Factor Analyses. Factor analysis results for the police assessment center are summarized in Table 14.4.[6] Clearly, the factors are defined, not by the dimensions, but by the exercises. The factor analysis provides no support for the construct validity of the dimension ratings and, in fact, supports the alternative position that dimension ratings are exercise specific rather than generalizable over exercises (and, by extension, to comparable aspects of performance on the job).

This is not an isolated example. Sackett and Dreher (1982) analyzed data from three independent assessment centers and, in all three cases, found factors that were defined by exercises, not attributes. Others have reported similar results (Bycio, Alvares, & Hahn, 1987; Silverman et al., 1986; Turnage & Muchinsky, 1982). Bycio et al. (1987), for eight ability dimensions and five exercises, used confirmatory factor analysis to test three models. Model 1 originally hypothesized eight ability factors (later five) and five exercise factors. Model 2 hypothesized one general factor and five exercise factors. Model 3 hypothesized simply five exercise factors. None of the models could be unambiguously said to fit the data better than either of the others, but exercise variance consistently dominated the ratings in all of them.

Silverman et al. (1986) looked for convergence experimentally in an assessment center with three exercises, each rated on the same six dimensions. In a within-exercise method, candidates were rated on each relevant dimension immediately on the conclusion of the exercise (as in the police example). A within-dimension method, a modification of the AT&T procedure, made dimension ratings after a staff conference. In the within-exercise method, all factors were exercise factors. Results were less clear for the within-dimension method, however. It also gave three factors, somewhat like the three within-exercise factors, but there were strong secondary loadings. Ratings of leadership, for example, had factor loadings of at least .35 on all three exercises. In short, these were not dimension factors supporting the validity of construct inferences from dimensional ratings, but neither did they form the clear alternative factor pattern. Their results suggest that procedural adjustments can improve the construct validity of the ratings.

One such adjustment was suggested by Kleinmann, Kuptsch, and Köller (1996). In an experimental study, they manipulated "transparency," meaning that candidates were or were not informed about the dimensions

---

[6]This was done in an unpublished study by Dennis Sweeney, then at Bowling Green State University.

TABLE 14.4
Rotated Factor Pattern of Police Assessment Center Ratings

Exercise and Dimension	Factor[a]						h^2	r_{xx}[b]
	I	II	III	IV	V	VI		
Leaderless Group Discussion (NR)								
Assertiveness—1[c]	30			88			88	70
Persuasiveness—1				88			87	66
Oral communication skill—1				81			75	58
Assertiveness—2	32			82			80	75
Persuasiveness—2				60			40	64
Oral communication skill—2				82			78	40
Leaderless Group Discussion (AR)								
Assertiveness—1	87						86	79
Persuasiveness—1	88						86	73
Oral communication skill—1	79						70	65
Assertiveness—2	82						78	76
Persuasiveness—2	57						38	68
Oral communication skill—2	75						63	52
Competitive Exercise								
Assertiveness—1			83				77	76
Team spirit—1			83				72	72
Assertiveness—2			83				76	70
Team spirit—2			86				78	67
Analysis Interview								
Reasoning—1						88	83	89
Reasoning—2						89	84	85
Stress Interview								
Stress tolerance—1					87		78	83
Stress tolerance—2					87		77	71
Situations Test								
Reasoning—1		88					79	42
Written communication skill—1		83					69	32
Reasoning—2		63					37	50

[a]Only factor loadings of .30 or higher are listed; decimal points omitted. [b]Interrater reliability coefficients. These are spuriously low; acceptable reliability estimates are necessarily higher then communalities. [c]1 indicates graphic ratings, 2 indicates checklist summated ratings.

to be rated and the nature of the desired or undesired behavior relevant to them. Confirmatory factor analysis showed that both exercise dimensions and clear construct dimensions accounted for variance in transparent conditions, but not in nontransparent conditions.

Reasons for Inconsistency in Dimension Ratings. Dimensions can be viewed from two extreme points of view. Neither makes much sense but, together, they help focus on the problem posed by the factor analysis results. At one extreme the dimensions are viewed as unalterable traits (not necessarily genetic, but well-established by adulthood) exhibited consistently in behavior in virtually all circumstances. From this extreme view, multiple assessments of a dimension would serve no purpose other than increasing reliability, but they *would* converge. At the other extreme, the dimensions are simply aspects of behavior in a given situation, without generalizability to any other situation. Carrying this position to its logical extreme, prediction of future performance is impossible; even generalization from one exercise to another—even where both call for somewhat similar behaviors—is unlikely.

The extremes are patently false; behavior can have both typical and situationally determined components. Low consistency across exercises may reflect inconsistent behavior; typical behavior may not be elicited in atypical situations or in situations having their own intrinsic behavioral imperatives. A person who is typically judgmental and vocal may be judgmental and vocal in a leaderless group discussion but inhibit that typical behavior in a simulation where one is to help two conflicting parties negotiate or reconcile their differences. Ratings on forcefulness of oral communication in these two exercises cannot reasonably be expected to correlate highly. If both of these extremes are ruled out, other reasons for the persistent exercise factors might be considered:

1. Ratings across exercises may be influenced, but not determined, by situational differences. However, ratings failed to converge even across alternate forms of an In-Basket Test (Brannick, Michaels, & Baker, 1989). Despite high interscorer reliability, correlations between scores on the same dimensions of these presumably parallel forms tended to be lower than the within-form correlations between different dimensions. These findings are not consistent with situational explanations.

2. Typical rating procedures (rating immediately after the exercise) focus cognitively on within-exercise consistency. This explanation fits findings by Silverman et al. (1986).

3. Assessees may not behave consistently across exercises. Changes in self-confidence may occur while going through the exercises. Moreover, Kleinman (1993) pointed out that an assessee has two tasks in an exercise. One is dictated by the exercise instructions, but the other is to look as good as possible. An assessee may try to guess what will be rated; inappropriate behaviors may follow bad guesses. If guesses differ for two exercises actually rated on a common dimension, the resulting differences in assessee behavior can be enough to cause differences in ratings. The transparency recommendation may help here (Kleinmann et al., 1996).

4. The many sources of rater error (see chapter 12) may explain some inconsistency. When all ratings for dimensions tapped in a given exercise are made at the conclusion of the exercise; it may exaggerate true

correlation between component behaviors. If a rater's general impression is of poor overall performance, little will be found to praise in any aspect of that performance—the general impression halo (Fisicaro & Lance, 1990).

5. Separately rated dimensions in an assessment center exercise are not independent, being based on overlapping behavioral observations. These within-exercise dependencies spuriously increase within-exercise correlations. The low alpha coefficients reported by Brannick et al. (1989) did not merely indicate low internal consistencies; they suggested that exercise heterogeneity (often sought in exercise development) can actually inhibit the internal consistency of dimensional ratings.

6. Factor analysis may be inappropriate, at least if it lacks data external to the variables defined by exercises and dimensions within an assessment center. Construct validity is best evaluated within a broader network of relationships; a postulated construct is defined by relationships with some variables but not with others. Factor analysis offers one source of evidence, but there are others.

7. Some dimensions may be easier to rate, and therefore rated more consistently, than others. Shore, Thornton, and Shore (1990) classified dimensions as performance-style or interpersonal-style dimensions, and they found ratings of these particularly well-related to cognitive or personality measures, respectively. Perhaps performance or cognitive dimensions are assessed better by tests than by ratings, and interpersonal-personality dimensions may be assessed better by ratings; if so, the consistency (validity) of ratings might well differ in the two categories. I do not attribute this suggestion to Shore et al. (1990); they may disagree.

8. I tend to favor one further explanation. Rating dimensions with the same names may not mean the same constructs were rated. Constructs to be rated are rarely defined thoroughly; the usual case settles at best for a brief definitional phrase.

The research literature has offered me no help in choosing among these or other explanations; until it does, I must accept this:

> It is difficult to interpret the patterns of within- and across-exercise correlations obtained. . . . The findings suggest severe problems for assessment centers: In all three centers, method variance predominates, and [in two of them] there is essentially no convergence among the various measures of a dimension. (Sackett & Dreher, 1982, p. 406)

And this: "broad construct-oriented research strategies will not be successful unless assessment developers depart from the traditional methods of using poorly defined dimensions as starting points" (Reilly, Henry, & Smither, 1990, p. 83).

Solutions? The most common suggestion for solving the problem is the use of behaviorally based ratings or checklists. Reilly et al. (1990) asked assessors to write examples of behavior corresponding to dimensions they had rated previously on 5-point scales. A large pool of items remained after editing, and the Smith–Kendall retranslation procedure was used (Smith & Kendall, 1963). Items that were almost always assigned to the intended dimensions were placed in checklists for the dimensions, and assessors were instructed to use the checklists immediately after an exercise, indicating 0 (*behavior did not occur*), 1 (*behavior occurred once*), or 2 (*behavior occurred more than once*). Ratings on the dimension, for that exercise, were then made on the same 5-point scale previously used. Much better convergent validity was found when the checklist was used.

The use of a different sort of construct might help. Joyce, Thayer, and Pond (1994) classified possible dimensions as either person-oriented ("traditional" dimensions) or task-oriented (their alternative to traditional dimensions). Examples of task-oriented dimensions included "Structuring and staffing tasks: Allocating manpower and resources to tasks, delegating assignments, and organizing the work of subordinates," and "Establishing effective work group relationships: Recognizing, praising, and encouraging employees and co-workers; maintaining a high level of morale" (Joyce et al., 1994, p. 113). A natural experiment was possible because two essentially parallel assessment centers were run by the same organization. One of these assessed managers as they entered a management training program, the other assessed them again 2 years later at the completion of the program. The first used traditional dimensions; the second used task-oriented dimensions. Results were familiar: factor analysis of the dimensions, whether personal attributes or job functions, resulted in factors defined by exercises, not by either of the alternatives.

In short, the solution to the construct validity problem is not yet at hand. The trite expression, more research is needed, is applicable.

Standardization

It bears repeating: If people are to be compared, the basis for comparison should be standardized. This basic psychometric principle is not easily applied to assessment centers. Often, not even a common sequence of exercises is feasible. Some components, such as tests, can be administered to everyone at once, others are given individually, others in small groups. Different groups or individuals may need to be assigned to different rooms, at different times, in different sequences. There should be no lost or idle time, for assessees or for observers. The problem is one of logistics. It is not merely an administrative problem; it has strong psychometric implications, including contextual problems. Suppose, for example, a candidate goes directly from a stress interview into an exercise requiring handling a grievance; suppose further that the grievance simulation is the first exercise after lunch for another candidate who has not yet had the stress experience. Is it reasonable to assume that they both come to the grievance simulation with the same psychological set, that either of them behave the same way in the simulation directly after these different antecedent activities? Probably not, but standardization of sequence is not feasible in many assessment centers.

Another standardization problem occurs when exercises require role playing. Even professional actors in theaters often report that their performances vary in response to different audiences; there are surely differences in the way a role is played when the audience is one assessee (or at most a few). I recall one incident when a generally mild group member played an aggrieved employee with real flair: rapid speech, dialect, a great deal of apparent anger, and an utter lack of reason. The person playing the soothing supervisor became very angry and finally blurted out, "OK, if that's the way you want it, have it your way!" Group laughter, along with that of the aggrieved employee, ended that exercise. Performance of that "supervisor" could hardly be compared to the performance of others playing that role against less talented actors. Standardized tasks are more likely if the same person, preferably a paid professional actor, plays the role to which the assessee is to react, but even this does not guarantee standard role performance. Unless the actor is indeed highly skilled and experienced, performance of the role will change over repetitions.

I need not belabor the problem. Standardization is hard to achieve.

Criterion-Related Validities

Despite many problems, assessment centers have amassed a good record of criterion-related validities. We do not know the underlying constructs, and we have little evidence to say that ratings of these (usually) poorly defined constructs are valid assessments. Nevertheless, dimension ratings and OARs have been valid predictors of future performance. A meta-analysis reported by Gaugler, Rosenthal, Thornton, and Bentson (1987) found a mean corrected validity coefficient of .37, with a lower bound of the 95% confidence interval well above 0, indicating generalized validity.

Situational specificity, however, could not be ruled out; 46% of the variance among validity coefficients could not be explained by the artifacts. This is not surprising; different assessment centers have different exercises, performance is rated on different (and different kinds of) dimensions, rater training varies widely, purposes differ, and different kinds of criteria are predicted. After careful moderator analysis, Gaugler et al. (1987) offered these generalizations:

1. Mean age of participants is unrelated to validity, but other demographic variables have some moderating effects (e.g., validities are higher where the proportion of women is larger and the proportion of minorities is smaller). Meta-anlysis gives results but does not explain them. On the basis of prior research, Gaugler et al. (1987) ruled out group differences in validity as the basis for these findings. An alternative explanation, that differences in demographic composition of assessment groups change the dynamics of the group processes, also lacks prior support.

2. Predictive validity was higher when more kinds of assessment exercises are included. This might seem at first to be function of the length (in days) of the assessment center, but length did not moderate the validities. Simply throwing in more exercises does not achieve a validity advantages. The multiple exercises should be multiple samples of job-related behavior, and multiple assessments of the same constructs, not simply alternative ways to get a larger bundle of scores.

3. Validities were also higher in those assessment centers where peer evaluations were included. This point, and the preceding one, may merely indicate that more thoroughly developed programs are more valid.

4. Assessors' backgrounds moderated validity; they found (contrary to some earlier findings) that OARs in assessment centers using psychologists as assessors were more valid than those where managers were the assessors.

5. Validities were much higher for ratings of potential for management progress than for predictions of future performance (.53, compared to .36).

Other criteria—indeed, purposes of assessment generally—did not moderate validity, nor did several other study characteristics.

Some skepticism is warranted. The police assessment center was never made operational, despite substantial criterion-related validity, because apparent validity was attributed to common stereotypes. A "good cop" stereotype can influence both assessments and criteria, providing no more than an illusion of validity. Similar stereotypes might be invoked to explain the validity of assessment centers in predicting rate of advancement among managers; a stereotype of "who does well in this organization" may influence both the assessments and the rates of promotion (Klimoski & Brickner, 1987). A contaminating source of variance destroys validity—unless it contaminates both assessment and criterion, in which case it gives an illusion of increasing validity by increasing the coefficient.

Group Dynamics

Zedeck (1986) raised some issues about group processes. His principal concern was the dynamics of the assessor group in reaching consensus on an OAR. Achievement of consensus might depend on group size; assessor groups are typically small—perhaps three or four people. Increasing the size of the group increases the breadth of knowledge and ability among assessors and also the variety of schemata related to the job for which assessees are considered. Is that an advantage or a disadvantage? Existing literature on group size can be interpreted either way. Larger groups may create more conflict, making it harder to achieve consensus, but they also increase pressure toward conformity. Specific research in the assessment center context is needed to determine which is the greater likelihood.

Many things known about group processes lead one to wonder how consensus is ever reached. Assessors, especially managerial assessors, are people who have themselves achieved and are likely to form strong opinions. Merely declaring a position in a group tends to solidify that position. Group discussion can lead to polarization of opinion as well as to consensus, and it takes good discussion leadership to move toward consensus. If each member of a group forms a rather strong opinion of a candidate and strengthens that opinion in oral discussion, someone must give way to someone else if consensus is to be reached. So why do consensus judgments sometimes get reached with apparent ease? Zedeck suggested that assessors develop a group management behavior schema during assessment training, experience in prior assessment centers, and in the discussion. This, he said, develops without explicit or deliberate organizational efforts.

Again, is this an advantage or a disadvantage? What Zedeck (1986) called a common schema may be what I called a common stereotype. Just as police gave ratings that reflected a widely held view (among police) of the peripheral characteristics of "a good cop," so also can a common stereotype promote relatively easy arrival at consensus within an assessor group.

Group processes also influence groups of assessees. In a typical assessment center this is a group of 6 to 12 people, all interacting in a common enterprise; they may start out as strangers, but they seem to become more cohesive as time goes on. The effect of group cohesion on the behavior of its members is substantial. The perception of approval or disapproval may be more powerful than the fact. If one is clearly a minority within a group, (e.g., the only White male, or the only Hispanic female), it may be easier (even if somewhat paranoid) to detect or imagine signs of disapproval than if in a group of people "like me." The resulting behavior may be more tentative, less confident, less assertive. An assessor will not be able to distinguish tentative, unconfident, unassertive behavior typical of the person from that due to the group influence. It is part of the problem of standardization, a standardization problem not likely to be solved. I have used the obvious example of sex and ethnic differences, but differences in social influences would remain from one group to another even if all groups have the same mix of sex and ethnic characteristics.

A Point of View

So-called authentic performance assessment, described in chapter 11, shares a background with assessment centers. Both educational and managerial assessment people have been uncomfortable with traditional testing, questioning its appropriateness for their purposes. The discomfort has not been a traditional concern over reliability and validity so much as a concern about whether the right things have been measured. In-basket tests, for example, became widely used assessment center exercises not because of superior reliability or predictive power but because they tap the everyday decision-making skills of managerial work.

Not just the single exercise but the entire assessment center concept is popular and widely used; Gaugler et al. (1987) estimated more than 2,000 organizations using some such program. When we gave our progress report on the police assessment center at a 1977 convention (Guion & Alvares, 1977), an attorney–discussant who was excoriating testing passed up the opportunity to comment on our program because he thought it would be too expensive to be used and it was obviously valid, anyway! Like him, most people have no doubt about assessment center validity.

Moreover, good validities are reported in research and hold up over long periods of time. Most validities decay over time, but Gaugler et al. (1987) found no moderator effect for length of time between the assessment center ratings and the collection of criterion data. Some mean validity coefficients, especially when ratings of potential are correlated with advancement over time, are very high even without correction for statistical artifacts.

Others, however, seem ordinary, even low. The corrected validity coefficient for predicting performance was .36 in the Gaugler et al. study. Corrected validity coefficients in studies reported in chapter 8 were as high as .53. Why would one go to the trouble and expense of developing an assessment center that, on the average, might yield a lower validity than achieved by less expensive, more traditional methods? And how much confidence can one have that even the best validities cannot be explained away as the result of common stereotypes?

I confess that, because of such questions, my earlier enthusiasm for assessment centers has dissipated somewhat. There are other skeptics. Klimoski and Brickner (1987), in asking why assessment centers work, referred to "the puzzle of assessment center validity." They offered several possible answers, including "subtle criterion contamination" (more inclusive than a common stereotype), performance consistency (where assessors are given background information identifying those with notable achievements), and an idea of "managerial intelligence," which influences both exercise performance and subsequent job performance and advancement. Some such solutions either cast doubt on the genuine predictive validity of assessment centers or on their efficacy relative to more traditional assessment methods.

Skepticism implies questioning, not rejection. The questions should lead to research, not to abandonment or undue abbreviation of assessment centers. Some explanatory research has been done, and suggestions for redesign of assessment procedures have been offered. Many researchers explain the problem of construct validity as due to excessive cognitive demands on assessors (Gaugler & Thornton, 1989). Perhaps assessors should be specialists for a few dimensions or a few exercises.

Should the most general kinds of assessments (such as g) be used in describing people and predicting their behavior, or should assessments be as narrowly specific as possible (such as Guilford's 120 factors)? As Smith (1985) made clear, the answer depends on one's purpose, but the argument lingers as an ideological one pitting those who favor a gestalt approach of generality against the analytic preferences of the atomists. To suggest that the argument be settled by data is to open oneself to charges of "raw empiricist" (to which I have no special aversion).

More general dimensions mean fewer ratings; the value of the suggestion may depend on the purpose. Look again at Table 14.1. The number of dimensions increases as one moves from early identification to promotion to development. For individual personnel decisions such as selecting people for development or promotion (the major focus of this book), the dimensions of interest are broader and fewer than for developmental purposes.

Two questions seem to require data. How many dimensions are needed to arrive at a stable OAR? How many are needed to predict the criterion? For either question, assessment center development requires an analog of the item analysis procedures of traditional test development or the indices of the lens model. That is, the developer should determine, for each dimension and for each exercise, what it does in fact contribute both to the judgment and to the prediction. This requires pilot studies and a willingness to discard and perhaps replace dimensions or exercises that do not contribute.

Assessment centers, individual assessment programs, and multiple regression methods of multiple assessments have some common features. First, they must be based on defensible hypotheses derived from clear knowledge of jobs and organizational needs. Second, the several assessments resulting from these programs must be valid assessments of the attributes defined as important to jobs or organizational needs. Finally, where at all feasible, they should be subjected to close, empirical scrutiny.

REFERENCES

Albrecht, P. A., Glaser, E. M., & Marks, J. (1964). Validation of a multiple-assessment procedure for managerial personnel. *Journal of Applied Psychology, 48,* 351–360.

American Educational Research Association, American Psychological Association, & National Council on Measurement in Education. (1985). *Standards for educational and psychological testing.* Washington, DC: American Psychological Association.

American Psychological Association, American Educational Research Association, & National Council on Measurement in Education. (1974). *Standards for educational and psychological tests.* Washington, DC: American Psychological Association.

Bass, B. M. (1950). The leaderless group discussion technique. *Personnel Psychology, 3,* 17–32.

Bass, B. M. (1954). The leaderless group discussion. *Psychological Bulletin, 51,* 465–492.

Brannick, M. T., Michaels, C. E., & Baker, D. P. (1989). Construct validity of in-basket scores. *Journal of Applied Psychology, 74,* 957–963.

Bray, D. W., Campbell, R. J., & Grant, D. L. (1974). *Formative years in business: A long-term AT&T study of managerial lives.* New York: Wiley.

Bycio, P., Alvares, K. M., & Hahn, J. (1987). Situational specificity in assessment center ratings: A confirmatory factor analysis. *Journal of Applied Psychology, 72,* 463–474.

Campbell, J. T. (1962). Assessments of higher level personnel. I. Background and scope of the research. *Personnel Psychology, 15,* 57–62.

Campbell, J. T., Otis, J. L., Liske, R. E., & Prien, E. P. (1962). Assessments of higher level personnel. II. Validity of the overall assessment process. *Personnel Psychology, 15,* 63–74.

Dunnette, M. D., & Kirchner, W. K. (1958). Validation of psychological tests in industry. *Personnel Administration, 21*(May–June), 20–27.

Fisicaro, S. A., & Lance, C. E. (1990). Implications of three causal models for the measurement of halo error. *Applied Psychological Measurement, 14,* 419–429.

Frederiksen, N., Saunders, D. A., & Wand, B. (1957). The in-basket test. *Psychological Monographs, 71.* (Whole No. 438)

Gaugler, B. B., Rosenthal, D. B., Thornton, G. C., III, & Bentson, C. (1987). Meta-analysis of assessment center validity. *Journal of Applied Psychology, 72,* 493–511.

Gaugler, B. B., & Thornton, G. C., III. (1989). Numbr of assessment center dimensions as a determinant of rater accuracy. *Journal of Applied Psychology, 74,* 611–618.

Grant, D. L., Katkovsky, W., & Bray, D. W. (1967). Contributions of projective techniques to assessment of management potential. *Journal of Applied Psychology, 51,* 226–232.

Guion, R. M. (1961). Criterion measurement and personnel judgments. *Personnel Psychology, 14,* 141–149.

Guion, R. M., & Alvares, K. M. (1977, August). *An assessment center for the selection of police officers.* In a symposium at the meeting of the American Psychological Association, San Francisco.

Huse, E. F. (1962). Assessments of higher level personnel. IV. The validity of assessment techniques based on systematically varied information. *Personnel Psychology, 15,* 195–205.

Joyce, L. W., Thayer, P. W., & Pond, S. B., III. (1994). Managerial functions: An alternative to traditional assessment center dimensions? *Personnel Psychology, 47,* 109–121.

Kleinmann, M. (1993). Are rating dimensions in assessment centers transparent for participants? Consequences for criterion and construct validity. *Journal of Applied Psychology, 78,* 988–993.

Kleinmann, M., Kuptsch, C., & Köller, O. (1996). Transparency: A necessary requirement for the construct validity of assessment centres. *Applied Psychology: An International Review, 45,* 67–84.

Klimoski, R., & Brickner, M. (1987). Why do assessment centers work? The puzzle of assessment center validity. *Personnel Psychology, 40,* 243–260.

Murray, H. (1938). *Explorations in personality.* Cambridge, MA: Oxford University Press.

Otis, J. L., Campbell, J. T., & Prien, E. P. (1962). Assessment of higher level personnel. VII. The nature of assessments. *Personnel Psychology, 15,* 441–446.

Reilly, R. R., Henry, S., & Smither, J. W. (1990). An examination of the effects of using behavior checklists on the construct validity of assessment center dimensions. *Personnel Psychology, 43,* 71–84.

Robinson, D. D. (1981). Content-oriented personnel selection in a small business setting. *Personnel Psychology, 34,* 77–87.

Roethlisberger, F. J., & Dickson, W. J. (1939). *Management and the worker: An account of a research program conducted by the Western Electric Company, Hawthorne Works, Chicago.* Cambridge, MA: Harvard University Press.

Ryan, A. M. (1992). Psychologists' evaluations of individual assessments: A comparison on the basis of graduate training and professional affiliation. *Journal of Business and Psychology, 6,* 371–386.

Ryan, A. M., Barbera, K. M., & Sackett, P. R. (1990). Strategic individual assessment: Issues in providing reliable descriptions. *Human Resources Management, 29,* 271–284.

Ryan, A. M., Daum, D., Bauman, T., Grisez, M., Mattimore, K., Nalodka, T., & McCormick, S. (1995). Direct, indirect, and controlled observation and rating accuracy. *Journal of Applied Psychology, 80,* 664–670.

Ryan, A. M., & Sackett, P. R. (1987). A survey of individual assessment practices by I/O psychologists. *Personnel Psychology, 40,* 457–487.

Ryan, A. M., & Sackett, P. R. (1989). Exploratory study of individual assessment practices: Interrater reliability and judgments of assessor effectiveness. *Journal of Applied Psychology, 74,* 568–579.

Sackett, P. R., & Dreher, G. F. (1982). Constructs and assessment center dimensions: Some troubling empirical findings. *Journal of Applied Psychology, 67,* 401–410.

Shore, T. H., Thornton, G. C., III, & Shore, L. M. (1990). Construct validity of two categories of assessment center dimension ratings. *Personnel Psychology, 43,* 101–116.

Silverman, W. H., Dalessio, A., Woods, S. B., & Johnson, R. L., Jr. (1986). Influence of assessment center methods on assessors' ratings. *Personnel Psychology, 39,* 565–578.

Smith, P. C. (1985, August). *Global measures: Do we need them?* Presented at the annual meeting of the American Psychological Association, Los Angeles.

Smith, P. C., & Kendall, L. M. (1963). Retranslation of expectations: An approach to the construction of unambiguous anchors for rating scales. *Journal of Applied Psychology, 47,* 149–155.

Thornton, G. C., III, & Byham, W. C. (1982). *Assessment centers and managerial performance.* New York: Academic Press.

Turnage, J. J., & Muchinsky, P. M. (1982). Transsituational variability in human performance within assessment centers. *Organizational Behavior and Human Performance, 30,* 174–200.

Zedeck, S. (1986). A process analysis of the assessment center method. In B. M. Staw & L. L. Cummings (Eds.), *Research in organizational behavior* (Vol. 8, pp. 259–296). Greenwich, CT: JAI Press.

Author Index

Subject Index